A Handbook of Media and Communication Research

A Handbook … ntitative approaches tc … he social sciences and t … practical concerns witl … w of the field and a sei … inication studies in diff …

The Handboc …

- An histori …
- A systema … ler social and cultu …
- A practica … ncluding illustrativ …

Written by i … eywords, updated refe … work for students and …

The second … he development of th …

- Each cha … s, media discourses …
- The intro … interpersonal, onl …
- Three new … ; multiple methods t …

Klaus Bruhn … inication, University of … *rnational Encyclopedia* … dia.com), for which he serves as Area Editor of Communication Theory and Philosophy, and *Media Convergence: The Three Degrees of Network, Mass, and Interpersonal Communication* (Routledge, 2010).

A Handbook of Media and Communication Research

Qualitative and quantitative methodologies

Edited by

Klaus Bruhn Jensen

2nd edition

LONDON AND NEW YORK

First published 2012
by Routledge
2 Park Square, Milton Park, Abingdon, Oxon OX14 4RN

Simultaneously published in the USA and Canada
by Routledge
711 Third Avenue, New York, NY 10017

Routledge is an imprint of the Taylor & Francis Group, an informa business

British Library Cataloguing in Publication Data
A catalogue record for this book is available from the British Library

Library of Congress Cataloging in Publication Data
The handbook of media and communication research : qualitative and quantitative methodologies / edited by Klaus Bruhn Jensen.
p. cm.
Includes bibliographical references and index.
1. Mass media--Research--Methodology. 2. Humanities--Methodology. 3. Social sciences--Methodology. I. Jensen, Klaus Bruhn.
P91.3.H35 2011
302.23--dc23
2011018290

ISBN: 978-0-415-60965-4 (hbk)
ISBN: 978-0-415-60966-1 (pbk)
ISBN: 978-0-203-35725-5 (ebk)

Typeset in Sabon and Gill
by Saxon Graphics Ltd, Derby

Contents

Communicating research

Illustrations

FIGURES

TABLES

RESOURCE BOXES

ANALYSIS BOXES

Peter Larsen. Professor at the Department of Information Science and Media Studies, University of Bergen, Norway. He is the author of books and articles on semiotics, rhetoric, music in the visual media, textual analysis and text theory in connection with film, television and other forms of visual communication.

Amanda D. Lotz is an Associate Professor of Communication Studies at the University of Michigan. She is the author of *The Television Will Be Revolutionized* (New York University Press, 2007) and *Redesigning Women: Television After the Network Era* (University of Illinois Press, 2006), and editor of *Beyond Prime Time: Television Programming in the Post-Network Era* (Routledge, 2009). She is co-author, with Timothy Havens, of *Understanding Media Industries* (Oxford University Press, 2011) and, with Jonathan Gray, of *Television Studies* (Polity, 2011).

Graham Murdock is Reader in the Sociology of Culture at the University of Loughborough, UK, and has been a visiting professor at the Universities of Bergen, Brussels, California, Mexico City, and Stockholm. His work has been translated into nineteen languages. Recent books include, as co-author, *The GM Debate: Risk, Politics and Public Engagement* (2007), and as co-editor, *Digital Dynamics: Engagements and Disconnections* (2010) and *The Blackwell Handbook of the Political Economy of Communication* (2011).

Horace Newcomb is Professor of Telecommunications and Director of the George Foster Peabody Awards at the University of Georgia. Newcomb is the author of *TV: The Most Popular Art* (Anchor Press, 1974), co-author of *The Producer's Medium*, editor of seven editions of *Television: The Critical View* (Oxford University Press, 1983) and editor of *The Museum of Broadcast Communications Encyclopedia of Television* (www.museum.tv). He has lectured widely in Europe and Asia on the current state of television and culture.

Paddy Scannell. Professor, Communication Studies, University of Michigan, formerly at the University of Westminster, UK. He is a founding editor of *Media, Culture & Society*, co-author (with David Cardiff) of *A Social History of British Broadcasting, 1922–1939* (Wiley-Blackwell, 1991), editor of *Broadcast Talk* (Sage, 1991), author of *Radio, Television and Modern Life* (Blackwell, 1996) and co-editor (with Elihu Katz) of *The End of Television? Its impact on the world—so far* (Sage, 2009). He is currently working on a trilogy, the first volume of which, *Media and Communication,* was published in 2007 (Sage), while *Television and the Meaning of "Live"* is forthcoming, and *Love and Communication* is in preparation.

Kim Christian Schrøder is Professor in Communication Studies at Roskilde University, Denmark. His books in English include *The Language of Advertising* (Blackwell, 1985), *Media Cultures: Reappraising Transnational Media* (Routledge, 1992), *Researching Audiences* (Arnold, 2003), and *Digital Content Creation* (Peter Lang, 2010). His current research deals with news consumption in the media landscape of the digital age, and with methodological issues around the quantitative/qualitative divide.

Preface

One of the chapters in the first edition of this Handbook was entitled, "Contexts, cultures, and computers." The chapter was designed to review research on the embedding of media in diverse social and cultural contexts, emphasizing the growing role of the internet and other digital media in reconfiguring the "contexts" of communication – in space and time, as material as well as virtual relations. Ten years on, this process of reconfiguration has been accelerated to such an extent that an overview of the field calls for a reconsideration of its constituent categories – 'contexts' and 'computers,' even 'media' and 'communication' – not just within, but across chapters.

Throughout this second edition, the Handbook highlights the interplay between 'new' and 'old' media. It devotes a full chapter to the increasingly counterproductive divides of 'mass' versus 'interpersonal' communication research, and of 'online' versus 'offline' interaction. And, it includes additional chapters illustrating the relevance of a wide range of methodologies – old and new – to a media environment in historical transition.

In its second edition, the Handbook provides an updated account of the state of the field of media and communication research – its sources, current debates, and future potential. A resource for students, researchers, and media professionals, it offers an in-depth treatment of both methodological approaches and theoretical frameworks. The development of the domain of study – the media themselves – has accentuated the need to combine quantitative and qualitative approaches to media and communication studies, and to continue the integration, manifest in the field during recent decades, of insights from the humanities as well as the social sciences.

The Handbook grows out of several long-term collaborations. First and foremost, I am grateful, both to the old hands from the first edition and to the new contributors, for joining me in this venture in a spirit of interdisciplinary dialogue. Since the 2002 edition, I have received much inspiration from the research group on Digital Communication and Aesthetics that I direct and, in recent years, from colleagues in and around the Center for IT Innovation, both at the University of Copenhagen. Farther afield, I have been given a great deal of constructive criticism on related papers and other presentations, not least in the context of the Association of Internet Researchers, the International Communication Association, and the biannual Nordic conferences on media and communication research. I also am privileged to serve as Area Editor of Communication Theory and Philosophy for the *International Encyclopedia of Communication*, published in 12 volumes in 2008 (Donsbach, 2008), and subject to continuous updating in its online version, www.communicationencyclopedia.com.

In addition to reworking the first edition, this second edition of the Handbook draws on my own recent title, *Media Convergence* (Jensen, 2010). The present volume incorporates some portions of text from that other volume; specifically, Chapters 1 and 10 in this Handbook rework parts of the monograph for present purposes.

Klaus Bruhn Jensen
Copenhagen, April 2011

Note on the text

Key concepts and terms are indicated by a marginal note when they are first mentioned in the text. The symbol ◀ in the text indicates a cross reference to the preceding text which can be found below. The symbol ▶ at the foot of a column indicates the cross reference linked to its mention in the above column.

1 Introduction

The state of convergence in media and communication research

Klaus Bruhn Jensen

- a characterization of the field as an *interdisciplinary crossroads* of different academic faculties
- a typology of *media of three degrees*: humans as embodied media, mass media, and network media
- a comparative review of definitions and models of the key concepts of *information, communication, and action*
- an account of media as a distinctive set of *institutions-to-think-with*
- an *outline* of the handbook, its purposes and premises.

FIELDS AND FACULTIES

The field of media and communication research has emerged over the last half-century at the crossroads of several disciplines and faculties, which themselves had taken shape over a period of 200 years. In 1798, around the time of the formation of the university as a modern research institution (Fallon, 1980; Rudy, 1984), Immanuel Kant had identified a conflict among its different faculties, arguing that the humanities (the philosophical faculty), not the theological faculty, should provide the foundations for inquiry into natural as well as cultural aspects of reality within the other faculties (Kant, 1992[1798]). Around 100 years ago, the social sciences gradually detached themselves from the humanities to produce new forms of knowledge about, and more professionals to administer, increasingly complex modern societies. About 50 years ago, an interdisciplinary field of research began to take shape in response to the greatly increased role, not least, of print and broadcast *mass communication* in society, drawing on concepts and methods from both the humanities and the social sciences and, to a degree, natural sciences. With the rise of 'new,' digital media in recent decades – the internet and mobile media – and the ongoing digitalization of the 'old' media, the field is more central to political, economic, and cultural developments than ever before, while still struggling to understand what comes *after* mass communication.

Throughout its brief history, media and communication research has remained a site of divides and, occasionally, conflicts among the faculties.◄ Most research traditions will subscribe to summary descriptions of key ideas such as information, communication, and action. Media are vehicles of information – they make representations of and insights into reality available, as articulated in text, image, and sound. Media are channels of communication – they make information accessible to communicators, and communicators to each other. And, media are means of action – communication is performative, as it unfolds, and as it ends. Most researchers will agree in principle that *apartheid* is counterproductive to the production of new knowledge about each

► history of media and communication research – Chapter 19, p. 355

of these aspects of media and communication – the difficulty is how, in practice, to avoid *imperialism* (Jensen, 1995: 141–145). In a future perspective, one test of the maturity and viability of the field is whether it will be able to close, or bridge, persistent divides – between different research traditions, and between 'mass' and 'interpersonal' communication as examined in previous theory, methodology, and empirical work (Rogers, 1999).

neither apartheid nor imperialism

In its second edition, the Handbook takes the ongoing reconfiguration of mass, interpersonal, and networked communication, and of the media environment at large, as an occasion to review and assess the state of convergence in the field of research – specifically between and across social sciences and humanities – which has been recognized and debated at least since the self-consciously titled "Ferment in the Field" issue of the *Journal of Communication* (1983). Media convergence is no sweeping process of merging previously distinct technologies, institutions, and discourses seamlessly into shared platforms and similar formats. Theoretical and methodological convergence, equally, is a complex and often conflicted process. The aim of the Handbook is to provide an updated, diverse, and in-depth resource in order to advance academic convergence, so that readers, researchers, and practitioners may contribute to a more robust and relevant understanding of 'media convergence' (K. B. Jensen, 2010). It is a practical resource in so far as, "in a practical discipline of communication, theory is designed to provide conceptual resources for reflecting on communication problems" (Craig, 1999: 130).

This introductory chapter presents a framework for the rest of the Handbook, with three main elements. First, I distinguish between media of three different degrees: the human body enabling communication face-to-face; the technically reproduced means of mass communication; and the digital technologies facilitating networked interaction one-to-one, one-to-many, as well as many-to-many. Like the mass-interpersonal divide, the online-offline dichotomy has become increasingly unhelpful in the attempt to conceptualize and study contemporary communications.

media of three degrees

Second, I review the main variants of those communication models which, explicitly or implicitly, continue to inform undergraduate textbooks as well as cutting-edge theory development. The review is structured around distinctive conceptions of the key ideas of information, communication, and action in various humanistic, social-scientific, and natural-scientific contributions to the field.

Information, communication, action

Third, I characterize media as a special kind of institutions – institutions-to-think-with – that enable societies to reflect on and negotiate their common existence. Communication solidifies as culture; it lends meaning to human actions and social structures over time. To place the present media environment in historical perspective, I return to Jürgen Habermas' model of the public sphere,◄ and note how new forms of political, economic, and cultural action, facilitated by shifting media forms, can be seen to push at the boundaries of the classic public-sphere model.

institutions-to-think-with

MEDIA OF THREE DEGREES

Determination in the first instance

The media of communication occupy a middle ground between material and immaterial reality. Printed pages, celluloid strips, electromagnetic signals, and bit streams are all material phenomena. At the same time, different material media provide access to a wide variety of actual, possible, and barely imaginable worlds. Being programmable in distinctive ways, digital media have invited more or less radical claims that the boundaries between material and immaterial reality might be shifting in fundamental ways. Research addressing such boundaries ranges from the largely failed attempts since the 1950s to program a general sort of artificial intelligence (for an overview, see Boden, 1996; Partridge, 1991), via an early mainstream of new-media studies embracing cyberspaces, cybercultures, and cybersocieties (Bell and Kennedy, 2000; Benedikt, 1991; Jones, 1998), to cultural criticism projecting a cyborg future and a posthuman era of life (Haraway, 1991; Hayles, 1999).

► the public sphere, p. 17

RESOURCE BOX 1.1 GENERAL REFERENCE WORKS AND JOURNALS

ENCYCLOPEDIA

- International Encyclopedia of Communication – the largest available resource on media and communication research, including theoretical, historical, methodological, and culturally comparative perspectives. A twelve-volume publication (Donsbach, 2008), and an online reference work subject to continuous updating, www.communicationencyclopedia.com

ABSTRACTS

- Communication Abstracts – abstracts and keywords of current research in media and communication studies
- Web of Science – a broader and interdisciplinary resource covering diverse journals and conference proceedings

HISTORIES

- Briggs and Burke, 2010 – an overview of media from the printing press to the internet
- Winston, 1998 – an account of electronic media since the telegraph, emphasizing differences between their technological potentials and their actual social uses
- Peters, 1999 – a history of the very idea of communication, with important implications both for the general history of ideas and for current media studies

HANDBOOKS AND TEXTBOOKS

- McQuail, 2010 – a standard introduction to positions in the field, with a relative emphasis on social-scientific traditions
- Lindlof and Taylor, 2011 – an overview of qualitative research methods, including some of their theoretical and philosophical sources
- Berger, *et al.*, 2009 – a handbook summarizing work that approaches communication studies as a 'science'

JOURNALS

- *Journal of Communication* – since the mid-1970s a flagship journal in the field, accommodating both quantitative and qualitative, administrative and critical work
- *Communication Theory* – another key journal contributing to theory development about technologically mediated as well as face-to-face communication
- *Critical Studies in Media and Communication* and *Media, Culture & Society* – two representatives of critical and interpretive strands of media and communication research
- *Journal of Broadcasting and Electronic Media* and *Journalism and Mass Communication Quarterly* – two representatives of mainstream and quantitative research traditions
- *Cinema Journal* and *Screen* – two journals focusing on film (and television) as art forms and cultural practices, with implications for the wider field
- *New Media and Society* – a central journal addressing 'new,' digital media.

matter matters

Matter matters. Despite the extraordinary flexibility of digital technologies, they lend themselves, like any tool or technology, to certain social uses, and not others. It seems necessary to reemphasize this premise, because some media and communication research, in recent decades, has shied away from issues of determination, perhaps partly to distance itself from early and still popular notions of strong and direct effects, partly under the influence of

RESOURCE BOX 1.2 SELECTED STUDIES AND REFERENCE WORKS FOR INDIVIDUAL MEDIA

Books

- Vincent, 2000 – an overview of the development of literacy in modern Europe, with reference to books and other media of communication
- Radway, 1984 – an exemplary study of romance novels as institutions, texts, and everyday resources

Newspapers

- Habermas, 1989[1962] – still an essential resource regarding the historical development and contemporary functions of the press
- Schudson, 1978 – a social history of the US press, complementing the European focus of Habermas
- Hallin and Mancini, 2004 – a comparative approach to the press and media systems in the western hemisphere (for other culturally comparative perspectives, see Chapter 11, this volume)

Film

- Andrew, 1976 – an introduction to classic film theories
- Braudy and Cohen, 2004 – an anthology of key texts in film studies

Radio

- Crisell, 2008 – a three-volume collection of classic and contemporary writings
- Scannell and Cardiff, 1991 – an exemplary social history of radio, with implications for other media

Television

- Williams, 1974 – the seminal study that defined television (and radio) in terms of their characteristics of 'flow'
- Newcomb, 2004 – a four-volume encyclopedia and reference work on television as an institution and a cultural form

Digital and mobile media

- Lievrouw and Livingstone, 2009 – a four-volume collection of key texts addressing 'new' media as technologies, institutions, and discourses
- Perron and Wolf, 2008; Salen and Zimmerman, 2004 – two volumes covering games as technologies and cultural practices
- Ling and Donner, 2009 – an overview of mobile communication in everyday life
- Castells, *et al.*, 2007 – a comprehensive review of mobile media in a global and cross-cultural perspective

an underspecified constructionism◄ across the social and human sciences (for a critical discussion, see Hacking, 1999).

A reformulation of the question of determination was suggested by one of the founders of cultural studies,◄ Stuart Hall (1983), who introduced a distinction between determination in the final instance and determination in the first instance. In a reappraisal of Marxism, he questioned a tendency for a great deal of critical theory to take for granted that, ultimately, it is the economic bases of society that determine how humans live their lives and make their history. When all is said and done, money talks. Reversing this analytical perspective, Hall recognized how prevailing

► constructionism – Chapter 3, p. 51
► cultural studies – Chapter 2, p. 46

economic and other material conditions establish outer limits to human agency and social interaction, but underscored the relative indetermination and variability of how, for example, technological inventions are put to particular social uses. Technologies have unforeseen, even unforeseeable consequences.

(A comparable conception of determination as a layered process with multiple causal agents was termed overdetermination by Sigmund Freud in *The Interpretation of Dreams* (Freud, 1911[1899]). He noted how the events of an ordinary day will mix with long gone and perhaps repressed experiences in the content as well as in the form of one's dreams. Transferring Freud's terminology to critical social theory, Louis Althusser (1977[1965]) questioned the economic determinism of traditional Marxism, and underscored the relative autonomy of political and cultural practices in shaping social developments.)

over-determination

affordances

text messaging (sms)

Technologies have affordances (Gibson, 1979; Hutchby, 2001), or potentials that must be actualized. To illustrate, text messages (sms) have been a key factor in the diffusion of mobile telephony around the world over the past decade (Castells, *et al.*, 2007). This is in spite of the fact that such messages were initially thought of as a way for service providers to contact customers, or to offer specialized services, not as communication between subscribers. Neither the technical potential (which had to be realized and refined) nor the general profit motive (which is a given in market economies) will explain the current prominence of text messaging – the first killer application of mobile communication. The social practice of texting was technologically (and economically) determined, but only in the first instance.

The material conditions of communication are, evidently, outside the control of any individual human being. The perceptual, cognitive, and interactive capacities of my body, while cultivated through socialization and education, are the limits of my communications. Although we commonly say that we *have* a body, we also *are* a body; my body is my "general medium for having a world" (Merleau-Ponty, 1962[1945]: 146). The extensions of human capacities into diverse technologies (McLuhan, 1964) are collective accomplishments that circumscribe and embed the individual as second nature, as elaborated by the tradition of medium theory.◄

Bodies and tools – the first degree

In the perspective of the history and theory of communication, human beings can be understood as media. The human body is a versatile material platform, hosting speech, song, dance, drama, painting, and creative arts generally – capacities that are cultivated into competences by children as well as professional artists. In itself, the human body is a necessary and sufficient material condition of communication; our bodies become productive and receptive media of communication through socialization and acculturation. In comparison, tools – writing utensils or musical instruments – are neither necessary nor sufficient, but extend the human body and its communicative capacities in significant ways. Media of the first degree – human bodies and their extensions in tools – externalize accounts of actual as well as possible worlds,◄ and enable each of us to communicate with others about such worlds for both reflective and instrumental purposes.

human body as necessary and sufficient condition of communi-cation

Embodied communication is perhaps most commonly associated with speech and oral interaction. The everyday conversations that join family and friends, neighbors and coworkers, into groups and communities are key to all social life. Face-to-face interaction, however, comprises diverse modalities of expression. We encounter other people as audiovisual media and in multimodal communication. And, our tools and artifacts create more or less durable mediascapes (Appadurai, 1996). One historical example is so-called rough music, as studied by the historian E. P. Thompson (1991: 467–538) in eighteenth- and nineteenth-century England, which had parallels in other European countries and in the US. If an individual or a family had offended the rest of a community, it was a common practice to name and shame them by chanting, shouting obscenities, and banging pots and pans. And,

humans as audiovisual media

► medium theory – Chapter 2, p. 24
► possible worlds, p. 14

rough music is not entirely a thing of the past: On March 11, 2005, BBC World News reported that authorities in Andhra Pradesh, India, had sent groups of drummers to tax evaders' houses to make them pay up (BBC, 2005).

language as privileged modality

Verbal language, nevertheless, constitutes a privileged modality – in evolutionary, psychological, and social terms. Language relays categorical information that can be recategorized – restated, responded to, reprogrammed – in ways that no other modality can. As noted by the linguist, Émile Benveniste (1985[1969]: 236), "the signs of society can be interpreted integrally by those of language, but the reverse is not so." Speech interprets images, but images rarely interpret speech, except in the occasional aesthetic experiment.

For most of human history, of course, bards or singers of tales were the only media around – singular and localized archives of information and means of communicating a cultural heritage. The literature on non-literate, prehistoric societies describes oral cultures as context-bound and present-oriented (Goody and Watt, 1963; Ong, 1982; Scribner and Cole, 1981). Far from labeling these as inferior, medium theory does suggest that primary orality – a state of culture that is "totally untouched by any knowledge of writing or print" (Ong, 1982: 11) – is incompatible with a sense of a historical past, and of a different future. (This is in contrast to a secondary orality, which Ong (1982: 11) associated with the spoken word of broadcasting, and a tertiary orality that may be emerging with digital media.) In a primary oral culture, communication is an expression and an event in context, rather than a representation and a resource across contexts.

orality – primary, secondary, tertiary

writing

In a comparative perspective, I include writing with media of the first degree. To be sure, manuscripts supported vast and complex economic, social, and scientific systems for millennia, by fixating information as knowledge and facilitating the reflective production of ever more knowledge. As constituents of communicative practices, however, manuscripts depend on multi-step flows of social interaction. Because copies are precious and few, they will be distributed in an extremely selective fashion to central individuals within established institutions. Such individuals – priests, generals, literate servants, etc. – will pass on even more selective and contextually adapted information with oral commentary within dedicated organizational hierarchies. The point is not only that social hierarchies may restrict public access to information (and to the literacy required) – which has notoriously been the case throughout history. Nor is it merely that the copying of manuscripts is laborious and subject to error, which limits access to precise and applicable information. Rather, in a scribal culture, communication remains an expression and an event that is primarily enacted in local contexts by embodied individuals. Even a utopian state that would encourage and financially support the literacy of its people, and their copying of as many manuscripts as possible for as wide a group of other readers as possible, would require sheer human labor on a scale that makes anything approaching equal access to the culturally available information inconceivable. Mass communication is not a potential of the medium of writing.

In unsentimental terms, Joshua Meyrowitz (1994: 54) noted that the comparatively inefficient forms of reproducing and distributing writing made it "a transitional cultural form." Writing by hand, of course, remains as a major cultural practice. Writing is integral to upbringing and education; to much drafting of texts in political life, business administration, and scholarship; and to communication with one's intimates and, importantly, oneself through notes. In news studies, reference is sometimes made to source media (Ericson *et al.*, 1987: 41) – oral interviews, scribbled notes, printed press releases, etc. – all of which feed into what is reported as news in media of the second and now third degrees. As media of record, however, and of interaction within and between the main institutions of society, however, embodied individuals and written texts were superseded by a second degree of media.

Technologies – the second degree

Until quite recently, it was still common to refer to 'the mass media' – media that distribute the same, or similar, messages from a few central

'the mass media'

senders to many distributed receivers. The philosopher, Walter Benjamin (1977[1936]), famously defined mass media in terms of their technical reproduction and dissemination, specifically of artworks, but with implications for other communicative practices, as well. Whereas Benjamin focused on photography, film, and radio, I take media of the second degree to include the various analog technologies – from printed books and newspapers to film, radio, and television – all of which took shape as one-to-many media institutions and practices of communication. Their common features were, first, one-to-one reproduction, storage, and presentation of a particular content; and second, media of the second degree radically extended the potential for dissemination of and access to information across space and time, irrespective of the presence and number of participants.

technical reproduction of communication

Benjamin noted a specific ambiguity that arises from reproduction. On the one hand, it results in the loss of what he termed aura: the sense of uniqueness and, perhaps, transcendence that has traditionally been associated with fine arts – paintings or sculptures, for instance – and with actors or musical performers appearing on stage. Present artifacts and singular actors mediate an absent reality, and thus appear larger than life. (Also other human beings – anyone – could be said to carry an aura, as informed by their biographies and shared histories, and as appreciated by intimates, friends, and strangers in a chance meeting. This, however, was not Benjamin's original point.)

aura

On the other hand, technical reproduction represented a major civilizational advance. When artworks and other cultural products are divorced from their unique, but local origins, they afford many more uses by many more people. Reproduction entails a shift of emphasis in the understanding of art, from singular expression to social communication. Accordingly, Benjamin (1977[1936]: 390) concluded, art need no longer be subordinated to religious and other ritual uses:

> [...] for the first time in world history, mechanical reproduction emancipates the work of art from its parasitical dependence on ritual. To an ever greater degree the work of art reproduced becomes the work of art designed for reproducibility. [...] the total function of art is reversed. Instead of being based on ritual, it begins to be based on another practice – politics.

"Designed for reproducibility": reproduction is not an incidental, but a planned activity with social implications. Two classic examples – books and newspapers – suggest the point. Books, pamphlets, and other printed formats could be considered a necessary (though far from sufficient) condition of Renaissance and Reformation (Eisenstein, 1979). Newspapers, in turn, served as material vehicles in political revolutions and in the formation of nation-states (Anderson, 1991; Habermas, 1989[1962]). Print media were at once impersonal and public, potentially outside the reach of the auratic leaders of religious and political establishments. The printing press, thus, facilitated the modern understanding of religion as a personal matter, and of politics as a public matter.

religion as personal matter, politics as public matter

Compared to the printing press, technologies for recording and disseminating sound came late to media history, from the 1870s onwards (for overview, see Millard, 1995). For the first time in human history, sound events – from song and other musical performances, to political speeches, to natural environments – could be preserved as part of the cultural heritage. Sound became constitutive of the central mass media of the twentieth century: radio, film (from 1929), and television. Moreover, analog sound technologies contributed to new kinds of soundscapes (Schafer, 1977), in private and in public. In shops as well as in workplaces, an important and underresearched ingredient of urban life has been muzak (see, e.g., Barnes, 1988; Lanza, 1994). In the home, radio broadcasts and recorded music came to compete, in different social groups, with piano recitals and community singing. With several radio, television, and stereo sets per household, private listening increasingly equaled personal listening. From the 1960s, the transistor radio made music, news, and other genres accessible on the move.

sound recording

soundscapes

INFORMATION, COMMUNICATION, AND ACTION

> Common linguistic habits render information as an attribute of messages or data, or as the purpose of human communication – as if information were an objective entity that could be carried from one place to another, purchased, or owned. This conception is seriously misleading.
>
> (Krippendorff, 2008b: 2213)

And yet, it is a commonsensical conception of the 'content' of communication that underlies the most diverse kinds of research. Also research traditions that prefer to speak of content in terms of its 'meaning' have tended to approach the object of study in essentialist terms, asking: 'Where is meaning?' In which material units, discursive structures, mental states, or behavioral events does meaning reside? By considering a different question – 'When is meaning?' (K. B. Jensen, 1991) – studies may recognize the categorically different forms in which information and communication manifest themselves in multiple stages and contexts of human cognition and social interaction.

The authors of communication models have mostly agreed on the constituents, but have disagreed, often fundamentally, about their status and interrelations (McQuail and Windahl, 1993). Figure 1.1 lays out the basic constituents of communication, as presented in a humanistic perspective (adapted from Jakobson, 1960),◄ italicizing two elements that have tended to be conceived differently in humanistic, social-scientific, and natural-scientific or engineering models. First, models differ regarding the role and importance of *codes* of communication, i.e., registers of signs and symbols, beyond physical contacts and signals. Second, the *context* of communication has been approached variously as a con-text, in a literal sense, that is always already discursive, or as the social circumstances of communication, broadly speaking, its material as well as institutional conditions.

► Jakobson's communication model – Chapter 10, p. 197

	Context	
Addresser	Message	Addressee
	Contact	
	Code	

Figure 1.1 Constituents of communication (adapted from Jakobson, 1960)

Not surprisingly, different faculties have defined communication in terms of their specific domain of reality – physical signals (Shannon and Weaver, 1949), discursive codes (Jakobson, 1960), or social practices (Lasswell, 1948). Realizing the complexity of human communication, analysts have introduced metaphors or analogies to link reality domains and academic faculties. One illustration is Warren Weaver's classic commentary on Claude E. Shannon's (1948) information theory. In it, Weaver cautioned that "information must not be confused with meaning" (Shannon and Weaver, 1949: 8), and that technical, semantic, and effectiveness problems of communication should be treated as separate issues. Toward the end of the commentary, nevertheless, he envisioned a general theory of communication that "will surely have to take into account not only the capacity of the channel, but also (even the words are right!) the capacity of the audience" (p. 27). Whether or not these are the right words, is precisely the question.

Information into meaning

Since Warren Weaver's admonition to communication researchers not to confuse information and meaning, the field has been at work to spell out the relationship between the two concepts. In a sense, the whole of meaning is more than the sum of information. The more analytical question has been how to define and parse the elements of communication. What are the degrees of freedom that apply to the selection and combination of these elements in remarkably flexible, yet distinctively patterned ways?

the whole of meaning is more than the sum of information

Predefined inventory of units/events

Predefined structure configuring units/events	+	-
+	Deterministic	Generative
-	Stochastic	Indeterministic

Figure 1.2 Four models of meaning

In Figure 1.2 (K. B. Jensen, 1995: 50), I identify four ideal-typical conceptions of meaning. The figure compares different ways of operationalizing what most research traditions consider as the messages, contents, or texts of communication. On the one hand, the constituents of meaning may, or may not, be understood as a predefined or fixed inventory. (I refer to the constituents as units *and/or* events in order to allow for different emphases on either the *products* or the *processes* of communication.) On the other hand, the combinatorial structures may, or may not, be assumed to make up a predefined or fixed range of message types – narratives, arguments, and other generic formats.

products and processes of communication

At one end of the spectrum, a *deterministic* model assumes that the outcome of predefined inventories and structures is a law-like configuration of what can be thought and said by humans. Few researchers will advocate a strong version of this position; communication represents a measure of indetermination in human experience and social interaction. Nevertheless, research traditions, to varying degrees, have noted how biological and technological circumstances precondition communication. At a biological level, physical and mental capacities make up enabling as well as constraining conditions of human cognition and communication (Cappella, 1996). At a technological level, different media extend human capacities, but in biased◀ ways (Innis, 1951), facilitating some forms of expression and experience above others.

At the other end of the spectrum that is suggested by Figure 1.2, an *indeterministic* model implies that there are, in effect, no boundaries to what might be thought or said. A strong version of the position is found in poststructuralism,◀ which holds that the differential structures of information will forever undermine any closure around particular meanings. Some accounts of interpretive communities◀ (Fish, 1979), similarly, have suggested that texts are essentially empty and open to individual and situated projections of meanings. More moderately, institutional senders (artists, film directors, popular composers, etc.) can be seen to selectively realize cultural tradition, as inflected through their own biography and historical context, just as individual receivers actualize more or less unique meanings in their personal encounters with media.

The other two ideal-types of meaning are representative of the two mainstreams of the current field of media and communication research, namely, quantitative variants of social science and qualitative forms of humanistic scholarship. The *stochastic* type, prominent in social-scientific methodologies, is typified by quantitative content analysis:◀ "the objective, systematic, and quantitative description of the manifest content of communication" (Berelson, 1952: 18). The analytical procedure serves to establish the probability distributions of certain communicative vehicles or content units – words, propositions, images, evaluative statements, etc. – within a sample of messages. Given, first, a predefined range of content units and, second, a set of analytical categories for coding them, the immediate research question is how this multitude of elements enters into differential and relational structures. The more interesting implication is that such configurations within radio newscasts, television series, or chat sequences carry worldviews: their constituents

► biases of communication – Chapter 12, p. 224
► poststructuralism – Chapter 2, p. 42
► interpretive communities, Chapter 9, p. 183
► content analysis – Chapter 13, p. 248

modifying social relations. This performative conception of language has influenced current human and social sciences profoundly. They stand on the shoulders of the philosopher, Ludwig Wittgenstein (1953), who came to understand language, not as a mirror image of reality, but as a set of language games or discourses that, in Carey's (1989b[1975]: 23) terminology, produce, maintain, repair, and transform reality. Language games are played for real and incessantly, and they are inseparable from the life forms, or social practices, that they serve to constitute. In the classic pragmatist formulation, "if men define situations as real, they are real in their consequences" (Thomas and Thomas, 1928: 572).

communication anticipates action

Third, communication anticipates action. Communication is a self-reflective, recursive form of action: it addresses actions that communicate and communications that enact. Communication explores the relations between what is, and what could be – what has been referred to, in several fields of study, as possible worlds. Many different realities are conceivable, as exemplified by science fiction and so-called counterfactual historiography describing what might have happened if key historical events had taken a different turn (Hawthorn, 1991). Only some of these realities, however, are possible in either a material or a logical sense, as examined by philosophical logic (Divers, 2002; Kripke, 1980) and literary theory (Ryan, 1991). For communication theory, one particularly interesting account of such multiple realities came from the philosopher and theorist of science, Karl Popper, who counted three worlds. World 1 refers to the domain of physical objects or states; World 2 is the world of consciousness, mental states, or behavioral dispositions to act. Linking such "external"' and "internal"' worlds, World 3 covers "the world of the objective contents of thought," whether scientific or poetic (Popper, 1972b: 106). As a communicative coin of exchange, World 3 includes fictional, normative, and other contestable accounts of reality in the full range of media.

possible worlds

Worlds 1, 2, and 3

At the juncture of traditional philosophical logic and modern technologies, the digital computer refocused attention on time as a conditioning factor of what comes to be known in the first place. "Propositional logic can describe only states of being. Adding time to it created algorithms – procedural steps – that could describe processes of becoming," which means that "anything that can be stated logically can be converted into an algorithm and becomes, hence, computable" (Krippendorff, 2008a: 1156). By adding time to logic, computing has served to produce not just new quantities of information, but qualitatively different ways of rendering and engaging reality, for example, within atomic physics and genetics. Current knowledge of subatomic reality and the human genome – and actions on both – would be inconceivable without digital computers.

logic + time = computing

Like an algorithm, human communication is executed over time. Unlike algorithms, communicative interactions are not generally subject to a central perspective or procedure, or a common logic. All the computers on the grid of the internet cannot compute the pros and cons of a possible design for the future of the internet into a conclusion. The possible worlds of communication emerge across space, as well, and through the intervention of distributed social actors – through interactivity. While often used as a buzzword, which some researchers would prefer to discard altogether (Aarseth, 2003), the concept of interactivity helps to clarify the relationship between communication and action, not just in the case of digital media.

Interactivities

As currently associated with computing, the idea of interactivity derives from the sociological concept of interaction between subjects – face-to-face, but also indirectly at various levels of the social structure. Parliaments and stock exchanges interact. Most basically, an analogy is suggested between human-human and human-machine exchanges. Originating in the era of batch processing, when technical staff could check the preliminary results of a run on a mainframe computer and then modify it in so-called interactive mode (J. F. Jensen, 1999: 168), interactivity has come to refer to the way in which ordinary users operate computers in a sequentially structured manner (for overview, see Kiousis, 2002; McMillan, 2002). As imported into media and communication research, the

interactivity and/vs. interaction

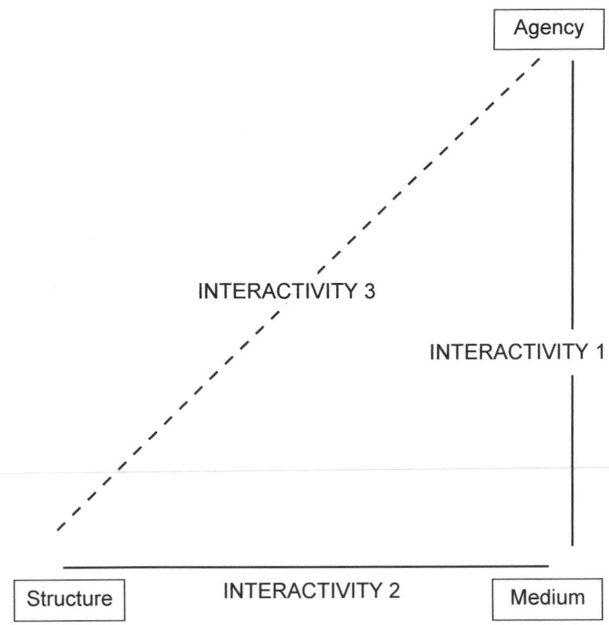

Figure 1.3 Three types of interactivity

terminology has been ambiguous: the field has aimed to account both for people's interactivity with media and for their interaction with each other through media. Communication is that unique form of interaction by which human actors negotiate their common social structure, depending on the media at their disposal.

It is helpful to contextualize interactivity and interaction with two other key concepts of social theory: agency and structure (Giddens, 1984). Figure 1.3 suggests the interdependence of medium, agency, and structure:◀ I treat the category of medium as equal to agency and structure, a constituent of all social interaction, including face-to-face as well as technologically mediated contact, in a three-way configuration. The terminology of Interactivity 1, 2, and 3 reemphasizes the interdependence of three constitutive dimensions of social interaction and the communicative aspect of each:

- *Interactivity 1* is what computer scientists (and ordinary computer users) typically refer to as interactivity: clicking on a web link, entering a message into a chat service, or 'shooting at the enemy' in a computer game. Here, interactivity amounts to sustained selectivity from a preprogrammmed range of options. It corresponds, in important structural respects, to the turn-taking◀ of an ordinary conversation (Sacks, *et al.*, 1974). Mass media, as traditionally understood, offer more limited interactivity in this regard: selecting a radio station, turning to the sports section of a newspaper, and checking in advance whodunit on the last page of a crime novel. All media, however, require measures of navigation, attention, and interpretation by users in order to access the available information.
- *Interactivity 2*, next, refers to the relationship between media and other institutions within the social structure. Depending on theoretical perspective, and on the communicative genre in question, media can be said to perform the role of a watchdog or Fourth Estate (Cater, 1959) vis-à-vis the powers that be. In a wider sense, media constitute a cultural forum (Newcomb and Hirsch, 1983) in which alternative social systems and entirely other possible worlds may be articulated. In a historical and cross-cultural perspective, a central question is whether and how basic technologies have been shaped into media with such potentials.
- *Interactivity 3*, finally, addresses the relationship between the social structure and its constituent actors and interests, from the individual citizen to national political establishments and global corporations. The myriad actors that make up society interact at a distance and over time; communication lends orientation and meaning to the process, providing a sense of where single actions might fit into a larger whole. The classic example is citizens' involvement in political democracy, parties, and popular movements through the media of the public sphere.◀ A recent example is telemedicine: doctors interacting with, diagnosing, and treating their patients in private, virtual

▶ agency, structure, and medium – Chapter 10, p. 200
▶ turn-taking, Chapter 7, p. 119
▶ the public sphere, p. 17

consultations. The human body and the body politic both depend on communication to reproduce and modify themselves.

INSTITUTIONS-TO-THINK-WITH

As part of an anthropological perspective on how the members of a culture communicate, Claude Lévi-Strauss referred to objects-to-think-with. Especially, animals that are part of the cultural diet can become means of classifying and, thus, coming to terms with reality. It is not so much that they are "good to eat," but that they are "good to think (with)" (Lévi-Strauss, 1991[1962]: 89). In a different culture, the same animal or natural object may mean something else, it may be prepared in a different manner, or it may not be considered good to either eat or think with. Also artifacts – from stone tools to oil paintings – serve as more or less programmable tokens of meaningful interchange. In comparison, contemporary media constitute institutions-to-think-with (Douglas, 1987) – highly differentiated and widely distributed material and modal infrastructures that enable reflection and interaction across space and time. Cultures and societies program their media, which, in turn, program them.

objects-to-think-with

Media are a distinctive kind of institution-to-think-with. Compared to other institutions of analysis and reflection – sciences, arts, or religions – media are, in a positive sense, the lowest common denominators of culture and society. They do not require specialized skills or talents of a scientific or artistic nature for interaction and deliberation to occur. Nor do they presuppose the existence of transcendent possible worlds to which only certain privileged texts, individuals, or procedures provide access. Media address and involve anyone as someone (Scannell, 2000) in communication about the ends and means of society, increasingly across time and space.

anyone as someone

the public-sphere model

Habermas' public-sphere model (Figure 1.4) continues to offer a valuable framework in which to examine the relationship between media and other social institutions – as part of a system of interconnected, yet relatively autonomous spheres (for review and discussion, see Calhoun, 1992; Mortensen, 1977; Negt and Kluge, 1993[1972]). The figure notes, to the right, the state agencies that establish and enforce the material, legal, and other infrastructural conditions of social interaction, ultimately with recourse to their monopoly on the use of physical force. To the left, private economic enterprise unfolds in the social sphere, while the intimate sphere represents the domain of personal and family life. The mediating element of the entire system is the public sphere, comprising the main political and cultural institutions-to-think-with, including the press as a Fourth Estate. Although this is frequently neglected in the Anglo-American literature on Habermas, the public sphere has two components, one political, the other cultural. Habermas showed how the cultural public sphere of literary journals and *salons* served, in part, as a precursor and a training ground for political deliberation and debate in a contemporary sense. In its consolidated form, the public sphere came to address two relatively separate agendas through different genres: crudely, the 'individual' issues of culture and arts through fiction, and the 'collective' issues of politics and economy through factual genres.

political and cultural public spheres

Historically, the public sphere had a proactive function in asserting the economic and political rights of individuals in their confrontation with a feudal order. Once in place, the public sphere also acquired a reactive function, negotiating the terms of cooperation among citizens, and between private citizens and the state. The model, thus, represents a dual construct – an actual as well as an imagined reality of structure and agency. On the one hand, the public-sphere model locates media on a structural map of society with other institutions: markets, parliaments, and state agencies are all real and effective. The issue, both theoretically and normatively, has been the exact nature of the interrelations between these institutions. On the other hand, the public-sphere model represents a plan of action – it is neither a neutral organizational chart nor a simple instance of false consciousness. Because the public-sphere model informs the interactions of everyday life, it is reproduced, for better or worse, as common sense or hegemony (Gramsci, 1971) – "a sense of absolute because experienced reality beyond which it is very difficult for most members of the society to move, in most areas of their lives" (R. Williams, 1977: 110).

	Society		State
	Private sphere	Public sphere	
	Intimate sphere	*Cultural public sphere*	The (agencies of the) state ensure(s) the material infrastructure, overall economic stability, law enforcement, and regulation of conflicts by economic, coercive, legal, and ideological means
Object	Religion, sexuality, emotion, friendship, etc.	Preaching, art, literature, music, etc.	
Institution	Family	Organizations, clubs	
	Social sphere	*Political public sphere*	
Object	Private economic activity, production and sale/purchase of commodities, including labor	'Politics' and 'the economy,' including social issues	
Institution	Private enterprises and stores	Parliamentary organs, representing political parties, and the press	

Figure 1.4 The public-sphere model

The last two centuries have witnessed a tug of war, first, along the horizontal dimension of the private, public, and state spheres of social activity and, more recently, along its vertical dimension, as well. Along the horizontal dimension, the classic issue, in different national and cultural contexts, has been the balance between market-driven and publicly administered means of communication: a private press; public-service broadcasting;◄ and an internet variously anchored in military, scientific, and commercial organizations (Abbate, 1999).

Along the vertical dimension of the public-sphere model, networked forms of communicative agency challenge three different boundaries. First, at the juncture of the social sphere (business) and the intimate sphere (personal and family life), new forms of material and immaterial production have been emerging. Benkler (2006: 3), for one, has suggested that the core of predominant modes of production is being affected by the combination of a global information economy, the wide availability of cheap communication technologies with excess capacity, and proliferating networks of non-market, non-state collaboration (see also Von Hippel, 2005). In earlier critiques of Habermas' model, feminist scholars rightly noted a tendency, not just to overlook the *de facto* exclusion of women from the public sphere from the outset, but also to bracket labor being conducted in the home, overwhelmingly by women (Fraser, 1992). Digital media reopen debates on the definition, organization, and control of human labor.

new forms of material and immaterial production

► private and public-service media – Chapter 19, p. 354

Second, the boundary between the political and cultural public spheres was in question from the outset, and has appeared increasingly porous. As an illustration, users may approach comedy shows such as *The Daily Show with Jon Stewart*, available on television and online (1995–2011), on a par with other sources of news (Feldman, 2007). A comparative content analysis of *The Daily Show* and US network television news, in fact, found the "substantive information" of the two program types concerning the 2004 presidential election campaign to be the same (Fox, *et al.*, 2007). In a networked public sphere, such interlinking is accelerated and articulated as part of comparable agendas and modes of address. Business corporations seek to strengthen their legitimacy by addressing the general public not merely as customers or clients, but as citizens, through corporate social responsibility, ethical accounting, and ecological initiatives. State agencies justify themselves to the public in the vocabulary of customer service. Political parties and non-governmental organizations (NGOs) alike must build and maintain constituencies whose members conceive of themselves in a hybrid of economic, cultural, and ethnic identities. And, at least some audiences, some of the time, come to act as senders as well as receivers of information about the definition of 'political' and 'cultural' agendas and issues.

The third column of the public-sphere model – the (nation-)state – mostly remains firmly in place. The system of nation-states had been inaugurated by the Westphalian peace of 1648, and was variously implemented in the following centuries. A world economic system had begun to take shape already from the sixteenth century, at first centered in Western Europe. However, unlike other such historical systems – for example, in the Middle East and China – this economic infrastructure did not develop into an empire or political entity (Wallerstein, 1974: 348). Nations took shape as delimited geographical units and cultural formations – imagined communities (Anderson, 1991) – as supported by newspapers and novels as well as by maps, museums, and the census. With an intensified globalization of economy and politics in recent decades, nation-states enter into transnational alliances, such as the European Union (EU) and the North American Free Trade Agreement (NAFTA), and they negotiate their coexistence in assemblies, courts, and agencies inside and outside the United Nations. During the same period, civil society organizations have reasserted themselves as a third sector of political, economic, and cultural activity beyond states and markets (for an overview, see Edwards, 2004). A transnational public sphere, however, has yet to emerge (Fraser, 2007).

transnational alliances

civil society

OUTLINE OF THE HANDBOOK

The Handbook is divided into three parts, covering the *history* of media and communication research in different disciplines and theoretical traditions; a *systematics* of theoretical and empirical studies addressing the various stages, contexts, and consequences of communication; and the *practice* of planning, conducting, and applying research and its findings and insights in (other) social action. Figure 1.5 lays out these elements with reference to the scope and focus of each part, noting, as well, a key premise of each section. Throughout the volume, methodologies are given special attention, because they encapsulate, at once, the theoretical justifications and the analytical procedures of various ways of 'doing' media and communication research.

- *Part I – History* traces the main sources of science and scholarship that have informed and shaped media and communication research. While noting the roots of the field, from classical rhetoric to early sociology, the two chapters – examining the humanities and the social sciences, respectively – focus on contemporary conceptions of key ideas such as culture and communication, interpretation and interaction. A convergence particularly of social-scientific and humanistic perspectives has been ongoing since the 1980s. While this development, arguably, has strengthened both the academic quality and the social relevance of the field, the contributors to Part I also note some of the challenges and problems of practicing convergence.
- *Part II – Systematics* turns from a diachronic to a synchronic view of different traditions or 'schools' of research. In a systematic perspective, they represent distinctive conceptualizations of the various stages, levels, and contexts of communication. Whereas some traditions are clearly incompatible – in their methodologies, epistemologies, or policies – they can be examined, in a meta-perspective, as complementary perspectives on similar issues, sometimes overlapping in unrecognized ways. One divisive issue has been the degree to which

convergence of social-scientific and humanistic perspectives

	History	Systematics	Practice
Scope	Theoretical concepts and analytical procedures from: - Humanities - Social sciences	Empirical approaches to the stages and contexts of communication, as defined by different research traditions	Practices of conducting, justifying, and applying research
Focus	Past sources of ideas on media, culture, and communication	Present operationalizations and findings	Future uses of research in scientific and social institutions
Premise	Interdisciplinary convergence	Determination in the first instance	Unification in the final instance

Figure 1.5 An anatomy of media and communication research

technological, economic, and other social factors could be said to determine the structure of media and the process of communication. Following Hall (1983) on determination in the first instance,◄ the chapters, in various ways, review how technological, institutional, and discursive conditions both enable and constrain communication: they negatively determine what *cannot* be the case, but they cannot positively predict what *will* be the case.

- *Part III – Practice* presents and illustrates qualitative, quantitative, as well as multi-method research designs. In addition to separate chapters on the qualitative and the quantitative research process, one chapter specifically explores the relationship between different methodologies – the nature and limits of complementarity. Addressing various media forms and communicative practices, three chapters detail the steps of a research process – from the articulation and conceptualization of research questions, via data collection and analysis, to interpretations and inferences. As a group, the chapters begin to suggest how a unification of the field might work, not in the first instance, through a standardization of elementary research procedures, but in the final instance, through an open-ended application and comparison of multiple methodologies. The final chapter discusses research as a social and communicative practice in its own right, returning to the intellectual backgrounds and policy motivations of the field: the classic normative theories of the press, contemporary policy issues, and the instrumental uses of research in processes of social planning – and constant change.

unification in the final instance

► determination in the first instance, p. 2

2 The humanistic sources of media and communication research

Klaus Bruhn Jensen

- *a classical agenda*: the heritage of philosophy for communication theory
- *medium theory*: the implications of modern media technologies for traditional issues of communication and culture
- four theoretical traditions in the history of ideas: *rhetoric, hermeneutics, phenomenology, semiotics*
- humanistic disciplines feeding into the interdisciplinary field of media studies: *art history, literary criticism, linguistics, film studies*
- current challenges to the humanities as well as to media and communication research: *postmodernism, feminism, cognitivism*

A CLASSICAL AGENDA

Contrary to a common notion, the humanities are not direct descendants of classical Greek philosophy (Kristeller, 1961: 3–23). In their recognizably modern form, the humanities date from the early nineteenth century, when universities were taking shape as institutions of research, as associated with the German tradition of Wilhelm von Humboldt (Fallon, 1980; Rudy, 1984). The understanding of knowledge as a product of *research* had been preceded by at least two alternative conceptions of knowledge, either as *self-awareness* (summed up in the Delphi oracle's admonition to "Know thyself!") or as traditional *learning*, administered and passed on by a class of learned people (Kjørup, 2001: 20–22). While the latter two concepts are still encountered as subtexts, it is the development of analytical procedures and conceptual frameworks for research which has occupied humanistic scholars during the immediate 'prehistory' of media and communication research.

knowledge as a product of research

Much of the agenda for this development, to be sure, was inherited from the classics. They continue to be suggestive, less about what to think, than which issues to think *about*.◄ Theories of human communication and theories of human knowledge share similar conceptual problems: what we know is, in one aspect, what we can communicate about. This chapter, accordingly, first retraces part of the classical legacy of communication studies, before outlining the main traditions from the history of ideas that entered into the modern humanities – rhetoric, hermeneutics, phenomenology, and semiotics. These traditions, in turn, informed the disciplines – from linguistics and literary studies to art history and film studies – which ultimately fed into the contemporary field of media and communication. The chapter concludes with an assessment of how recent interdisciplinary challenges – postmodernism,

► agenda-setting research, Chapter 8, p. 161

- c. 35,000	cave paintings by prehistoric humans
- c. 3100	hieroglyphics and cuneiform writing
- c. 1800	Linear A writing
- c. 1450	Linear B writing
- c. 1200	Chinese ideographic writing
- c. 1000	Phoenician alphabet
- c. 730	phonetic alphabet (Greece)
1041	printing from movable type (China)
1241	metal type for printing (Korea)
1455	Gutenberg prints from movable metal type and hand press (Germany)
1605	regularly published newspaper (Germany)
1814	flatbed cylinder press
1839	photography
1844	telegraph
1846	double-cylinder rotary press
1867	typewriter
1876	telephone
1888	phonograph for public sale
1895	films shown to public
1895	radio transmission
1911	television transmission
1920	scheduled radio broadcasting
1936	scheduled television broadcasting
1945	programmable electronic computer
1947	transistor
1948	long-playing gramophone record
1956	videotape
1957	satellite (Sputnik)
1962	television transmission via satellite
1963	compact cassette audiotape
1969	ARPANET
1971	microprocessor
1976	VHS video cassette recorder
1976	teletext
1978	telefax (with international standard)
1979	Walkman
1980	Cable News Network (CNN)
1981	Music Television (MTV)
1981	IBM personal computer
1982	audio compact disc
1984	Apple Macintosh computer
1991	World Wide Web
1991	GSM digital mobile phone network
1993	graphic web browser
1994	(we)blogs
1998	Google search engine
2001	commercial 3G mobile network
2002	social network sites

Figure 2.1 A brief chronology of human communication (adapted from Rogers, 1986: 25–26)

Medium theory offers a fertile framework for studying the historical and cultural variations of media and communication; it also represents a middle ground between the textual focus of the humanities and the institutional focus of the social sciences. Admittedly, it lends itself to hyperbolic formulations of the kind that made McLuhan a personality also *in* the media, as if each new media technology would determine a new type of culture and society. Applied carefully, however, medium theory supports media studies in a middle range (Merton 1968: 39),◄ steering empirical research between the Scylla of myopic methodologies and the Charybdis of grand theories. In the humanities, the main currents of ideas have themselves been shaped, in part, by their orientation toward specific media and their social uses. The primary example, both historically and as a continued influence on the study of human communication, is the art, science, and practice of rhetoric, which revolves around spoken language and humans as embodied media.◄

FOUR TRADITIONS IN THE HISTORY OF IDEAS

Rhetoric

The rhetorical tradition is by far the oldest set of ideas informing humanistic research, and it remained centrally influential from antiquity into the nineteenth century, not just in scholarship, but also within education under shifting cultural and institutional circumstances (for an overview, see Kennedy, 1980). Its legacy for contemporary research on communication and culture can be summarized with reference to three sets of concepts. First, the rhetorical tradition refers to five stages in preparing a speech:

- *inventio* (the collection and conception of the subject matter)
- *dispositio* (structuring the speech)
- *elocutio* (its linguistic articulation)
- *memoria* (memorizing the resulting configuration of form and content)
- *actio* (performing the speech).

▶ middle range theories – Chapter 3, p. 64
▶ media of the first degree – Chapter 1, p. 5

Of the five stages, *inventio*, particularly, recognizes an intimate relationship between knowing something and knowing how to communicate about it. Certain ways of speaking are appropriate in a political arena, others in a courtroom, others again on a festive occasion; each context has its own purpose and subject matter, both of which are given material shape in the speech. *Dispositio* and especially *elocutio*, next, supply the concrete procedures shaping the speech. Rhetorical figures of speech and symbolic forms have entered into both the study and practice of much literature and other arts.

Second, in addressing the audience through *actio*, a speaker draws on three means of persuasion:

- *ethos*
- *logos*
- *pathos*.

These focus, respectively, on the (ethical) character of the speaker, the (logical) quality of his/her arguments, and the (more or less pathetic) emotions which the speech is designed to evoke in the listeners. Importantly, the three means are all present in any act of communication, but in different measures and combinations, depending on the purpose and, hence, the genre of communication. Whereas the three aspects of addressing an audience have their most obvious relevance for such explicitly 'persuasive' genres as advertising and political communication, they lend themselves to the study of most types of technologically mediated communication.

Third, the concept of *topos*, which classical rhetoric considered as one part of *inventio*, is of special interest, because it suggests a figure of thought that suffuses modern humanities, as well. *Topos* means 'place,' and implies that commonplaces are, literally, common places in a known or imagined terrain which speakers share with their audience. This understanding of reality as a text and, conversely, of the text as a spatial and temporal universe that can be searched for traces and clues, has been a persistent metaphor in the humanities up until, and including, theories of the internet and

topos

mobile media. A 'topical' form of argument can rely on one or a few concrete examples, rather than a great deal of formal evidence, as long as the examples fit into the commonplaces which make up the working assumptions of the individuals communicating. Accordingly, Aristotle noted, rhetoric is the source of a kind of knowledge which is probable and reasonable. In this regard, rhetoric is complementary to logic,◀ which addresses other aspects of reality about which necessary or certain knowledge can be achieved (Clarke, 1990: 13).

The close link in classical rhetoric between communication and knowledge was gradually relaxed, as manifested in the development of so many practical manuals of speaking well in public. This shift helps to account for the common pejorative reference to 'only rhetoric' – communication as a superficial form and as misrepresentation and manipulation. Furthermore, rhetorical concepts were redeveloped from their oral sources and applied to literate forms of communication, for example, literary fiction and, later, to 'texts' in general. Nevertheless, the rhetorical tradition has remained an important source of ideas regarding the nature of both face-to-face and technologically mediated communication. During the twentieth century, rhetoric enjoyed a renaissance, sometimes under the heading of a 'new rhetoric' (Perelman, 1979), which, among other things, gave more specific attention to the concrete interaction of communicators with their audiences. A second inspiration came from analytic philosophy and its examination of the structure of informal argument (Toulmin, 2003[1958]).

the 'new rhetoric'

Although European scholarship may have been especially instrumental in feeding the rhetorical tradition into contemporary research, a vigorous American substream also has cultivated rhetorical and other humanistic approaches to communication studies (Kennedy, 1980). Among the most important influences has been the work of Kenneth Burke, who developed a view of language as action (Burke, 1950), and of literature as both a social and an aesthetic phenomenon (Burke, 1957). His perspective was subsequently applied to the mass media, for example, in the case of political communication (Duncan, 1968; Edelman, 1971). In media studies, James Carey (1989a) was a central figure advocating a broadly rhetorical as well as historical perspective on the interrelations between modern media and earlier cultural forms. As expressed in his ritual model,◀ also technologically mediated *communication* serves to create and maintain *community* – the common root of the two words suggests as much.

Saying something amounts to doing something – from everyday promises, excuses, and jokes, to formal ceremonies joining people into partnerships and nations into alliances. Whereas the understanding of communication as a form of action has been particularly pronounced in recent decades, in the longer history of ideas it is one of the lessons of classical rhetoric for contemporary humanistic disciplines. Like rhetoric, media studies have sought to strike a balance between a focus on the textual structures of messages as *products* and on messages as resources of action within social *processes*.◀ This balancing act was witnessed also in the wider humanities over the course of twentieth century in linguistic, communicative, and pragmatic turns.◀ At the same time, a rhetorical conception of communication as action has provided one of the conceptual and methodological bridges between humanistic research on media texts and social-scientific research on communicative practices.

Hermeneutics

While the point of departure for rhetoric was speech, particularly concerning matters of fact and how to argue about them, hermeneutics developed out of the practice of reading and understanding written texts, not least narratives, including fiction. Its general purpose has been to clarify the nature and preconditions of interpretation, with reference simultaneously

▶ logic – Chapter 15, p. 289

▶ ritual model of communication, see Chapter 1, p. 12

▶ meaning as product and process – Chapter 1, p. 11

▶ linguistic, communicative, and pragmatic turns, p. 34

to the structure of the text and to the activity of the reader.

The texts at issue originally belonged to religion and law. The preferred interpretation of both biblical and legal scriptures could make or break individuals; dissenters were, literally, ex-communicated from the communities in question. Equally, interpretive disputes would pit communities and nations against each other in religious struggles, warfare, or both. Over time, the principles and procedures of hermeneutics came to be applied to the arts and additional kinds of texts, even to human experience as such. Indeed, a common humanistic conception of consciousness, shared across the four traditions that are reviewed here, is as a text that calls for constant interpretation. In a historical overview, Paul Ricoeur (1981: Ch. 1), himself a central contributor to modern hermeneutic philosophy, identified a transition in the early nineteenth century from a 'regional' to a 'general' hermeneutics, which now covered both secular and religious texts. The transition was advanced particularly in the work of the German theologian and philosopher, Friedrich Schleiermacher.

religious and legal texts

consciousness as a text

Hermeneutics, thus, participated in a long movement within the history of ideas, from a religious cosmology toward a historical and secular understanding of human existence.◀ The medieval analogy between The Book of Nature and other books, above all, The Good Book, as means of insight into the Great Chain of Being (Lovejoy, 1936), in which everything had its divinely sanctioned place, was finally breaking down. Texts became a new focus of attention in their own right, as sources of scientific evidence and of aesthetic contemplation, rather than being primarily interfaces with the hereafter. At the inception of the modern humanities, then, the Text was taking center stage, together with the individual human being. Hermeneutics appeared to offer means of resolving interpretive conflicts, beyond matters of faith and aesthetics, and in some social affairs, as well.

the Great Chain of Being

The practical implications of hermeneutics for doing communication research are suggested by the key concept of a hermeneutic circle (Figure 2.2). The most basic, ancient insight of hermeneutics is that the meaning of one part of a text can only be understood in relation to the whole of the text. While perhaps commonsensical, this insight contradicts the equally common assumption that the meaning of a message is the sum of its parts, so that communication might be studied by breaking messages down into their constituent elements. Hermeneutics suggests that the very process of reading and analyzing a text is both creative and incremental – readers gradually work out their categories of understanding in order to arrive at a coherent interpretation.

the hermeneutic circle

This dialectic at the level of the individual text, however, is only the first step in working out its meanings and implications. Next, the full text must itself be interpreted as a part of larger wholes. For example, a novel may express the mindset of its author, who might be said to articulate the entire worldview of his/her epoch or culture. Such an understanding of the wider nexus of texts and contexts, as an extension of the basic part-whole dialectic, dates from the period when a general hermeneutics, applying to all types of texts, was conceived. It also anticipated the more recent concept of intertextuality.◀

One further development of the hermeneutic circle, during the twentieth century, specifically took into account the role of the reader. The point is suggested by another set of twin concepts – preunderstanding and understanding – which was developed especially in the work of Hans-Georg Gadamer (1975[1960]). On the one hand, any understanding requires a preunderstanding – a 'prejudice' in the neutral sense. On the other hand, understanding can serve to either reproduce or contest the reader's preunderstanding. Throughout the activity of reading, people perform minimal or subinterpretations, which may realign their frames of interpretation. In doing so, they enter into a 'dialogue' with the text and, by extension, with other minds, past as well as present. Most grandly, they partake of culture – the cultivation and renewal of tradition.

prejudice and pre-understanding

▶ secularization – Chapter 11, p. 206

▶ intertextuality – Chapter 10, p. 192

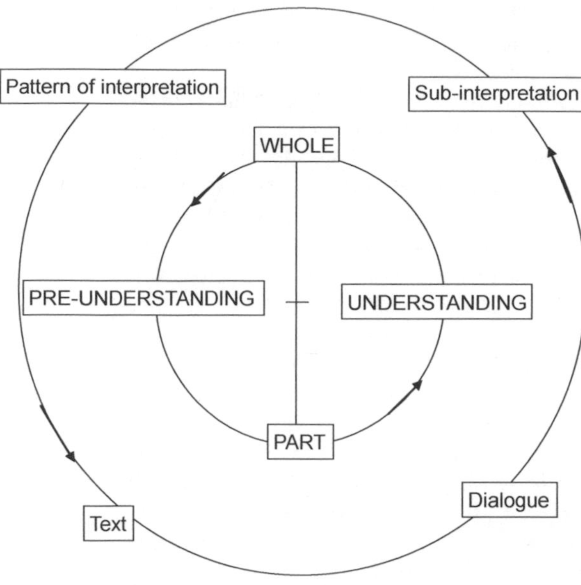

Figure 2.2 The hermeneutic circle (source: Alvesson and Sköldberg, 2009: 104)

The hermeneutic circle can be understood as a model of communication, as it unfolds not just in the here and now between a text and a reader, but down through history, between cultures, and across media. In hermeneutic (and phenomenological) terminology, communicative processes involve a fusion of horizons – a meeting and merging of the expectations that all communicators bring with them into an exchange with others. Recent contributors to the hermeneutic tradition, especially, have pointed to the dangers of such fusion and of an immediate empathy with tradition. Referring to the works of Marx, Nietzsche, and Freud, Ricoeur (1981: 46) identified and redeveloped a hermeneutics of suspicion. Its particular purpose is to discover hidden principles behind what other people as well as social institutions say and do, thus enabling a distinction between surface and 'reality.' People do not always say what they mean, or mean what they say. Since these principles may equally be hidden to those persons and institutions, working behind their backs, the general social charge of hermeneutics can be seen as that of reading between the lines and feeding its interpretations back to society. Particularly the critical tradition in communication research has taken on this task in studies of media texts as well as of institutions and audiences.◄

fusion of horizons

hermeneutics of suspicion

Hermeneutics has had a lasting influence on media and communication studies in three different respects. First, it brings home the general point that human communication is a complex process which always calls for interpretation, and sometimes for suspicion. Second, hermeneutics has been a specific source of inspiration, for instance, in theoretical frameworks regarding the reception of media,◄ and in methodological approaches to historical sources.◄ Third, and finally, the hermeneutic tradition serves as a constant reminder that also research is a hermeneutic, and doubly hermeneutic◄ (Giddens, 1979) activity, interpreting the interpretations of others as to how and why they communicate.

Phenomenology

Interrelated with hermeneutics in the history of ideas and as a methodological orientation to collecting and interpreting evidence, phenomenology emerged as a distinctive school of philosophy around 1900 (for an overview, see Smith, 2009). The date is significant, because phenomenology can be understood as a defensive reaction against the reductionism which was then seen to threaten a traditional humanistic understanding of consciousness as a lived and interpreted whole – whether in the form of positivism◄ or in the psychological and social-scientific disciplines then taking shape. In response, the phenomenological tradition insisted on the unique qualities and insights of ordinary human experience. In the social sciences, its influence has, arguably, been at least as strong as in the humanities, providing a philosophical legitimation for interpretive

► critical media and communication research – Chapter 19, p. 359
► reception studies – Chapter 9
► historiography – Chapter 12, p. 219
► double hermeneutics – Chapter 19, p. 351
► positivism – Chapter 15, p. 291

studies of social life, a minority position in the social sciences.◄ In the humanities, phenomenology entered into the mainstream, but proposed to redevelop certain key concepts of the humanistic heritage, such as interpretation and subjectivity.

Edmund Husserl, the originator of modern phenomenology, was also the author of its ambiguous motto, *Zu den Sachen selbst* (to the things themselves). These 'things' were not material objects, but those elements which constitute the core of human experience and existence, what

lifeworld

Husserl referred to as the lifeworld. In order to gain a better understanding of one's lifeworld, one should perform 'reductions' of various types in order to capture its qualitative essence. Far from breaking up experience into minimal units corresponding to, for instance, sense

epoché

data, a phenomenological reduction involves a 'bracketing' (*epoché*) of experience as a whole from its incidental circumstances. Husserl's ambition was to reinvent philosophy as a science in the strict sense. Central to this ambition was an attempt to close the subject-object divide, which had been haunting Western philosophy at least since René Descartes' formulation of *cogito, ergo sum* (*je pense, donc je suis*, in *Discourse on the Method*, 1637) – I think, therefore I am – as the only human certainty. Husserl argued that human consciousness, or intentionality, is always intentionality *of something*, not a mental state or entity that is forever separated from external entities.

In order to explain more concretely how human subjects relate to objects in reality,

horizon

Husserl introduced the concept of a horizon (as present also in hermeneutics). The concept refers to the configuration of a person's lifeworld at a given moment, pointing both backward and forward in time. A horizon comprises a set of interpretive categories which any person has available from having been socialized and acculturated. This horizon will change or be modified over time, as the person enters into new contexts, undertakes new projects, and interacts with other people. From this general philosophical and mental category, literary and other humanistic research derived a discursive conception of horizons, defined as historically and culturally specific frameworks of expectations that guide the interpretation of particular texts.◄ A 'misunderstanding' of a text can result from an incompatibility between the horizon implicit in the text and the reader's horizon of expectations; a 'disagreement' about the meaning of a text can be the product of conflicting interpretive horizons.

Phenomenology has had less of a direct influence on media studies than either rhetoric or hermeneutics. This may be, in part, because its abstract conceptual analyses have seemed less applicable to the concrete textual vehicles and social practices of communication – phenomenology has no evident 'medium.' Nevertheless, some film studies, particularly, have taken their lead from the phenomenological bracketing of experience, and have gone on to bracket film texts in order to get at their essential experiential qualities that resemble the multimodal lifeworld (Deleuze, 1986, 1989). With reference to broadcasting, Paddy Scannell (1996b) has suggested that the phenomenology and radical hermeneutics (Ricoeur, 1981: 45) of Martin Heidegger may serve to capture the distinctive features of an increasingly mediatized modern existence.

Semiotics

Of the four humanistic traditions, semiotics exercised the most direct influence in the formation of media studies as a field – compared to the other traditions, it addresses all types of media and communicative practices. Defined most famously as a science that studies "the life of signs within society" (Saussure, 1959[1916]: 16), semiotics became one of the most influential interdisciplinary approaches to the study of culture and communication generally from the 1960s onwards. The tradition offers analytical procedures, theoretical models, as well as constituents of a theory of science. In its most ambitious formulations, semiotics proposed to examine languages, images, psyches, societies, even biology and cosmology as sign processes (Posner, *et al.*, 1997–98; Sebeok, 1986).

► phenomenological social science – see Chapter 3, p. 51

► horizon of expectations – Chapter 9, p. 183

More commonly, the semiotic tradition has contributed methodological frameworks that lent a new form of systematicity to humanistic research on texts.

Semiotics had two founding fathers in the late nineteenth and early twentieth centuries – the American philosopher Charles Sanders Peirce and the Swiss linguist Ferdinand de Saussure (the two thinkers were unaware of each other's work). Their disciplinary backgrounds are key to their different conceptions of the study of signs. Recovering an undercurrent in the history of ideas going back to Aristotle, Peirce developed a comprehensive philosophy of signs which he understood as a form of logic that would support inquiry into the nature of both knowledge and being (for key texts, see Peirce, 1992–98). In his definition, any sign has three aspects:

sign, object, interpretant

> A sign, or *representamen*, is something which stands to somebody for something in some respect or capacity. It addresses somebody, that is, creates in the mind of that person an equivalent sign, or perhaps a more developed sign. That sign which it creates I call the *interpretant* of the first sign. The sign stands for something, its *object*.
>
> (Peirce, 1931–58: 2.228)

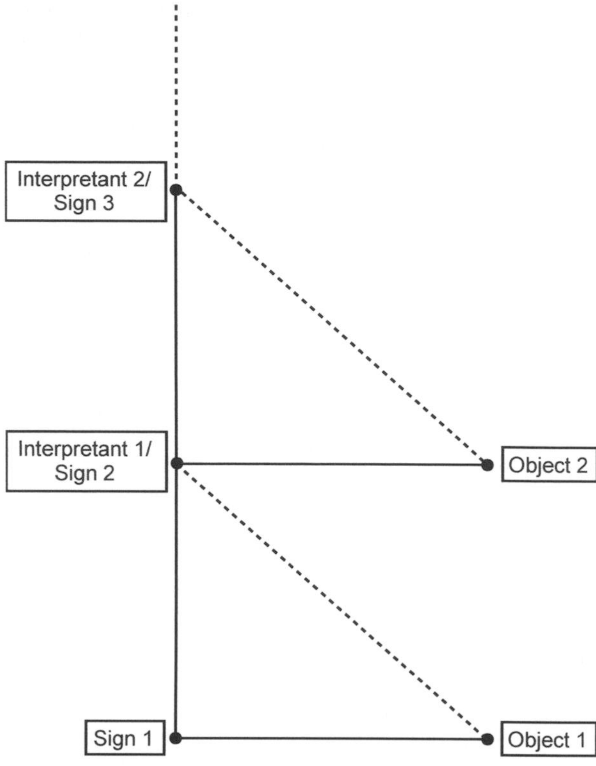

Figure 2.3 The process of semiosis

Although signs are here said to mediate between objects (material and non-material) in reality and concepts in the mind, Peirce rejected any idealist, nominalist, or skepticist position. Peirce instead attempted to marry a classical, Aristotelian realism with the modern, Kantian insight that humans necessarily construct their understanding of reality in particular cognitive categories. Signs, then, are not *what* we know, but *how* we come to know what we can justify saying that we know, in science as well as in everyday life.

semiosis

Peirce further suggested that human understanding is a continuous process of interpretation – semiosis – not a singular act that internalizes external reality once and for all. In this perspective, semiosis occurs in a sequence of interconnected perceptual, cognitive, and behavioral sign types that support the mundane coordination of everyday life, as well as extraordinary scientific and aesthetic accomplishments. Figure 2.3 displays the process of semiosis, noting how any given interpretation (interpretant) itself serves as a sign in the next stage of interpretation. Even though Peirce's outlook was that of a logician and a natural scientist, the model can be taken to refer to the diverse communicative processes by which societies are reproduced and cultures maintained.

Saussure (1959[1916]), in comparison, focused almost entirely on verbal language. Even though it was he who coined the phrase anticipating a general science of signs (of which linguistics would be a subdivision), in practice Saussure and his followers took language as their model for the study of other sign types, as well. Saussure's main achievement was to develop a framework for modern linguistics which, to a degree, proved applicable to other social and cultural phenomena.

In contrast to the long tradition of studying language change in a diachronic perspective – philology (Cerquiglini, 1999) – Saussure wanted to examine language as a system in a synchronic perspective. Language as an abstract system (*langue*) could be distinguished, at least for analytical purposes, from its actual uses (*parole*), and this system could further be analyzed in two dimensions. Along the syntagmatic axis, letters, words, phrases, and so forth, are the units that combine to make up meaningful wholes; each of these units has been chosen as one of several possibilities along a paradigmatic axis, for example, the verb 'choose' instead of 'select.' The resulting combinatory system accounts for the remarkable flexibility of language as a medium of social interaction.

philology

langue and *parole*

syntagms and paradigms

In addition, the interrelation between the paradigmatic and syntagmatic axes gives rise to two specific forms of expression and representation – metaphor and metonymy – which have been especially important in the analysis of media as textual messages. Metaphor can be understood as the outcome of an unexpected paradigmatic choice that affects the message as a whole (the syntagm) and, thus, activates additional frames of interpretation. For example, in the 1980s, the American politician and civil rights activist, Jesse Jackson, became the spokesperson for a 'rainbow coalition' that sought to join various ethnic and disempowered groups into a new political force. This term is significantly different from the traditional reference to the US population as entering into a 'melting pot.' Whereas the melting pot eliminates variety, the rainbow derives its essential quality and beauty from difference and contrast. Speeches and other communications would activate this sense for a particular political purpose, in contrast to the implications of the melting pot. Metonymy, in turn, is the process by which a single sign evokes the full syntagm to which it belongs. When 'the White House' was said to comment on the 'rainbow coalition,' the reference to the building would evoke both the American presidency and the vested interests associated with it (Drotner, *et al.*, 1996: 195).

metaphor and metonymy

arbitrariness of sign relations

One further contribution of Saussure was his account of the arbitrariness of the linguistic sign. The sign is said to have two sides, a signified (conceptual content) and a signifier (the acoustic image or physical token associated with it). The relation between the two is arbitrary, as suggested by the wealth of terms in different languages for the same phenomenon. Saussure has sometimes been taken to imply that also speakers of the same language are paradoxically free to choose their own meanings, so that they might be destined to remain divorced from any consensual reality; or they might be in a position, individually or as subcultures, to reject prevailing conceptions of social reality. The point is rather that the linguistic system as a whole is arbitrary in principle, but fixed by social practices into conventions.

signified (*signifié*) and signifier (*signifiant*)

A great deal of later research has extended the principle of arbitrariness to other social and cultural forms, for example, artworks, myths, and subcultures, all of which may be understood as 'languages' in the broadest sense. The structural anthropology of Claude Lévi-Strauss (1963[1958]) was highly influential of such studies of culture as more or less arbitrary systems of signification. A related perspective was developed within critical theories of social power (Althusser, 1977[1965]; Foucault, 1972[1969]) and of the unconscious as a 'language' (Lacan, 1977). Housed in the broad tradition of structuralism,◄ a common argument in these works has been that the current organization of society, and of the human psyche, is historically contingent, and hence open to challenge and change.

To be precise, Saussure referred to the science of signs, not as semiotics, but as *semiology*. The two terminologies point to the fact that Peirce and Saussure, while contemporary, had no knowledge of each other's work. During its consolidation from the 1960s onwards, *semiotics* became the agreed term, as symbolized by the formation in 1969 of the International Association for Semiotic Studies. It was also during this period that the program for studying the life of signs in society, unfulfilled in Saussure's own work, began to be implemented in systemic, Saussurean approaches to culture and society. In recent decades, the Peircean

semiology

► structuralism – p. 38

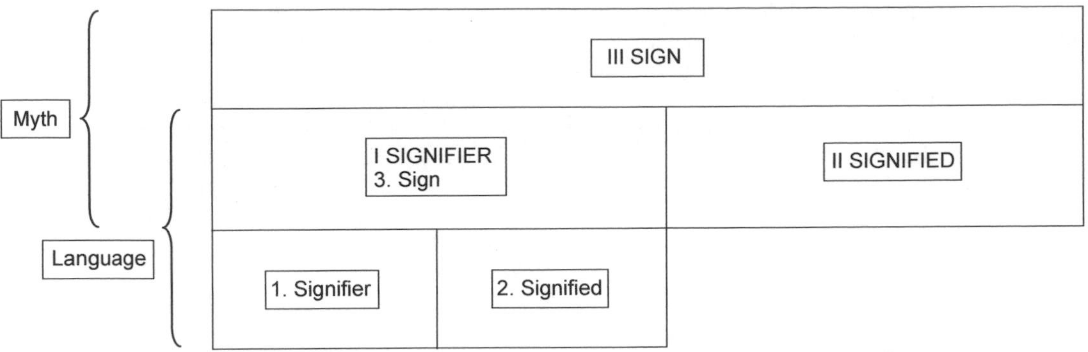

Figure 2.4 Two levels of signification (adapted from Barthes, 1973[1957]: 115)

framework has been gaining ground in a more processual approach to social semiotics, combining semiotic methodology with other social and communication theory (Hodge and Kress, 1988; Jensen, 1995, 2010).

Roland Barthes' widely influential model of two levels of signification (Figure 2.4) suggested one interface between Saussurean and Peircean semiotics, and a common agenda of the semiotic tradition: the analysis of concrete sign vehicles – texts and images – as carriers of culture, ideology, or myth. Barthes (1973[1957]) showed how the combination of a signifier and a signified (expressive form and conceptual content) into one sign (e.g., a magazine cover with a picture of a black man in a French uniform saluting the flag) can become the expressive form of a further ideological content (e.g., that French imperialism was not a discriminatory system). The two levels of meaning are normally referred to as denotation and connotation, building on the linguistics of Louis Hjelmslev (1963[1943]). Barthes' critical point was that this two-layered semiotic mechanism serves to naturalize particular worldviews, while silencing others, and should be deconstructed analytically. (Despite the predominantly critical orientation of semiotics, it has also been recruited for commercial purposes, for example, in 'marketing semiotics' (Umiker-Sebeok, 1987).)

denotation and connotation

It is only a relatively short step to the model of semiosis (Figure 2.3). The Peircean model refers to a potentially infinite process, but recognizes that the process is always, in practice, arrested. Sooner or later, individual sign users must arrive at interpretations, and act in their social contexts. These questions, concerning meaning as process and as product, and concerning the relationship between communication and action, continued to occupy the humanities throughout the twentieth century, and became one of the key issues for the media field.

LINGUISTIC AND COMMUNICATIVE TURNS

In one sense, the humanities have always been preoccupied with language – as a means of persuasion, as testimony of the past, and as a model for other kinds of communication. Heim (1987: 42) referred to the "Logos tradition," arising from classical Greek philosophy, as a long-lived worldview that has given priority to verbal language by assuming a "transcendental intimacy of thought, words, and reality." Whether directly or indirectly, rhetoric, hermeneutics, phenomenology, and semiotics all recognize language as a precondition of human knowledge and social interaction.

The twentieth century, however, witnessed an explicit turn to the study of language and other signs and symbols in a number of disciplines, first and most programmatically in philosophy. The common ambition was to make the procedures for analyzing texts, artifacts, and reality as such more systematic and transparent. In philosophy, the linguistic turn (Rorty, 1967) denotes the effort, particularly among Anglo-

the linguistic turn

American analytic philosophers since the early 1900s, to examine the structures and functions of language as a primary way of knowing the fundamental structures of reality – as well as the conditions and limitations of such knowledge. Much ancient and premodern philosophy had been ontological (asking "What does the world consist of?"); from the eighteenth century, philosophy came to address the same issues in epistemological terms ("What can we know about the world?"). It was these same issues which the twentieth century examined as a linguistic matter ("What do we mean by 'know' and 'world'?"). The linguistic turn, in effect, signaled a somewhat technical and reductionist conception of language as a modularized interface with reality.

The turn to the concrete and formal vehicles of knowledge presented potentials as well as problems. On the one hand, the close analysis of language promised a new degree of precision and intersubjectivity, and in other humanistic disciplines, too. On the other hand, language might end up being treated as a formalist universe unto itself, akin to mathematics. Such an approach would be alien to the traditional cultural, historical, and aesthetic explorations of the humanities. On top of this, an overemphasis on verbal language would not do justice to the specific qualities of either nonverbal fine arts or popular audiovisual media. (Also within semiotics, the analytical distinction between text and image was hotly debated.)◀ This dilemma continues to affect media and communication studies today. It has been addressed and, in part, resolved through additional communicative and pragmatic turns in philosophy and various interdisciplinary fields, and through specific analytical developments within different humanistic disciplines.

The pivot of twentieth-century philosophy was Ludwig Wittgenstein, who emphatically changed his mind and initiated not one, but two separate turns. In *Tractatus Logico-Philosophicus* (1972[1921]), the early Wittgenstein held that all knowledge must be founded on elementary propositions about minimal features of reality. Laws of nature as well as other types of inference and generalization should ultimately be reducible to direct observations of rudimentary phenomena. The ideal of both philosophy and science, accordingly, would be to establish a correspondence between the structures of reality and the linguistic, logical, and other discursive structures expressing our understanding of it. In this way, Wittgenstein prepared the arguments that informed the linguistic turn, and which were extended and applied to the study of both nature and culture by logical positivism◀ of the 1920s and 1930s.

The later Wittgenstein himself rejected this formalist and reductionist view of language. Instead, he came to define language as a complex set of discursive activities – language games – that are inseparable from the life forms or practices which they serve to constitute. His dictum, that "meaning is use" (Wittgenstein, 1953: 20e), summed up the beginning of a wider shift within a range of disciplines and interdisciplinary fields. Meaning inheres neither in the form of language, nor in its correspondence with reality, but in the ordinary as well as extraordinary uses to which language (and other signs and symbols) are put by people in communication. Wittgenstein, thus, can be seen to have inspired an additional communicative turn in the understanding of human knowledge: what we know is what we can communicate about. A shift of focus has been noticeable from language as a medium for representing objects (material and immaterial), to language as a medium of interaction between subjects in the context of culture and society.

language games

meaning is use

a communicative turn

The communicative turn may be said to entail or anticipate a pragmatic turn.◀ Linguistic and communicative turns have made the humanities 'harder' in methodological terms; the understanding of communication as a form of social action in its own right as well as a constituent of other action, has drawn the humanities closer to the social sciences. In certain respects, the social sciences, for their part, have grown 'softer' in what is sometimes referred to as a 'cultural turn' (Ray and Sayer, 1999), reemphasizing the communicative dimensions of both everyday

▶ semiotics of images and texts – Chapter 7, p. 149
▶ logical positivism – Chapter 15, p. 291
▶ a pragmatic turn – p. 46

repertoire of genres and themes. While authors might, thus, be expected to serve as special keepers of the cultural heritage, a distinctive ambition of modern high culture has been to constantly transcend and reinvent tradition. From the Romantic era, a new degree of autonomy was assigned to the individual author. The genius that found expression in literature could be understood, in the words of the British poet William Wordsworth, as the "spontaneous overflow of powerful feelings" (Abrams, 1962: 103). With modernism, authors were expected, more specifically, to provide their readers with striking new insights, not least by linguistic and other formal means. As a social institution, modern literature was called upon to 'make it new' by presenting reality to the reading public in new formats (Berman, 1982; Huyssen, 1986).

Literature only emerged gradually as a field of research in its own right, having been examined as one component of historical and philological research. Moreover, literary research was, for a long time, founded on biographical studies of major authors and on the place of their works in a genealogy of forms and styles (for an overview, see Eagleton, 1983; Wimsatt and Brooks, 1957). The term, 'literary criticism,' further suggests that a central purpose was the appreciation of a particular canon and a continuous evaluation of new artworks by this standard. It was the rise of various formalist approaches during the twentieth century that promoted a more descriptive study of literature and, subsequently, a sustained comparison with popular media and genres.

historical-biographical approaches

The first internationally influential formalist 'school' was the New Criticism. From the 1940s, a group of scholars in the US and the UK advocated studying literature as an objective, self-contained structure of textual paradoxes and ambivalences. Any interest in authorial intention or affective impact was rejected as intentional and affective fallacies (Wimsatt, 1954). Although this position tended to isolate literature from its social circumstances, it helped to professionalize the analysis of literature and to gain academic legitimacy for the discipline. By performing close readings of 'the texts themselves,' while bracketing readers, writers, as well as the literary institution, the New Criticism participated in a linguistic turn toward an immanent analysis of texts.

the New Criticism

Russian formalism, as developed from World War I and into the 1930s (for an overview, see Erlich, 1955), prepared the main ingredients of structuralism, which gradually became the dominant position in literary theory from the 1960s. Compared to the modernists who wanted to make reality new, the formalists noted that literature and other arts already have a distinctive capacity to defamiliarize reality, or to make it 'strange.' An important ambition of structuralism was to account for such general features of literature and, indeed, of all texts, genres, and media.

Russian formalism

de-familiarization

Behind structuralism lies a 'generative' conception of language and meaning.◀ The key idea is that any message amounts to a variation on a structural matrix of the same constants. The term 'generative' is frequently associated with the transformational-generative grammar of Noam Chomsky (1965), who described a 'deep' structure that produces the many variable 'surface' structures of concrete sentences. However, the scope of the idea is much wider. A generative model is implicit, for example, in the sociological concept of social roles, which can be filled, at least in principle, by anyone (e.g., Merton, 1968). In textual studies, particular narratives amount to variations on a relatively few elements. The most famous account of the modular structure of narratives was the analysis by Vladimir Propp (1958[1928]) of the constituents of Russian folktales and their recombination in any given tale. The model has been widely applied, for example, by Umberto Eco (1987a[1965]) in an analysis of the James Bond stories.

structuralism

The concept of intertextuality is another central contribution of structuralism to media and communication research.◀ The many interconnections across individual texts, series, and genres in the media suggest the special importance of examining texts or contents not as singular works, but as instances of 'textuality.' The idea was coined, again, by Russian linguists and literary scholars during the interwar years

▶ generative model of meaning – Chapter 1, p. 11
▶ intertextuality – Chapter 10, p. 192

(Bakhtin, 1981; Volosinov, 1973[1929]), and has been extended and reworked to apply to technologically mediated communication. The concept has prepared the ground for more focused analyses both of such classic issues as the relationship between 'text' and 'context,' and of hypertextuality◄ in computer-mediated communication.

Linguistics

If literary criticism and art history have emphasized the 'content' of culture and communication, linguistics has focused on 'form.' As such, it is a particular variety of language study that differs markedly from philology, which over the centuries had studied languages diachronically – over time and in the context of history and culture. In contrast, linguistics examines language synchronically – as a system of expression and communication. This focus bears witness, on the one hand, to the origin of linguistics in the semiotic tradition and, on the other hand, to its application in the linguistic turn of philosophy and other disciplines.

from diachronic philology to synchronic linguistics

For a long period, then, linguistics, following Saussure,◄ gave priority to the formal study of three main dimensions of language – grammar, semantics, and phonetics – typically with reference to single, abstracted sentences. This approach also made linguistics useful in language teaching: students would learn a language as both form and norm. From the 1970s, however, there was a clear shift, first, toward more descriptive research on the actual uses of language in social settings and, second, toward a critical interest in language as a constituent of interaction and conflict. In linguistic terminology, the shift involved a fourth dimension of language study – pragmatics. In an interdisciplinary perspective, linguistics thus came to provide the basic ingredients for discourse analysis in social and cultural research.◄ It was in this shape that linguistic concepts and procedures exercised most of their influence on media and communication research (for an overview, see Phillips and Winther Jørgensen, 2002; Wetherell, *et al.*, 2001).

pragmatics

It should be noted that, compared to linguistics, literary criticism (and film studies) were relatively more influential in the formation of humanistic media studies. This is likely explained, in part, by an understanding of media as sources of *mass* communication: one-way vehicles of narratives and other representations, rather than resources in interaction. In the last few decades, linguistics has been approaching an equal standing, as explained by developments both in research and in the media themselves. Classic mass media increasingly feature ordinary people and their informal conversations in talk shows (e.g., Livingstone and Lunt, 1994) and various reality genres.◄ Computer-mediated genres – from chat and blogs to social network sites – have further become mainstream forms of interaction, both in their own right as personal media◄ and as elements of established media organizations. In research, scholars have been seeking to conceptualize and examine this reconfiguration of the media environment, to some degree rediscovering the importance of interpersonal communication both in and around mass media (Gumpert and Cathcart, 1986; Scannell, 1991).

One final relevance of linguistics is as a research instrument in collecting and examining evidence *about* media and communication – language is both an object and a tool of analysis. This is especially the case for qualitative methodologies – interviewing, observation, and document studies – which produce large amounts of linguistic data that require systematic documentation and analysis. In addition, language is integral to the qualitative research process – from interaction with informants to theory development.◄ In the widest sense, qualitative and quantitative research projects alike rely extensively on language for conceptualization, operationalization, data collection,

► hypertextuality – Chapter 10, p. 193
► Saussure's semiology, p. 33
► discourse analysis – Chapter 7, p. 113
► reality genres – Chapter 16, p. 304
► personal media – Chapter 18, p. 335
► linguistic analysis of research discourses – Chapter 14, p. 279

and environments around people's lives (Venturi, *et al.*, 1972). Precisely the questioning of high-low distinctions has been central to much postmodernist thinking.

Second, postmodernist forms of expression in arts and media have been taken by some theorists as symptoms of a new historical epoch of postmodernity. In more or less radical versions, commentators have claimed that modernity – specifically the Enlightenment project of achieving general social progress through rationalist science and representative democracy – has ended, or is ending. Such projects have been labeled 'grand' narratives, which could and should be replaced, according to Jean- Francois Lyotard (1984[1979]), by 'little' narratives. These latter narratives amount to open-ended language games which would, ideally, enable an unending dialogue between equal participants in communication, but without guarantees of mutual understanding. Fredric Jameson (1991) has gone on to argue that postmodern culture has a concrete emancipatory potential and, indeed, that postmodernism represents "the cultural logic of late capitalism." One of the most extreme views of postmodernity was advanced by Jean Baudrillard (1988), who suggested that the distinction between signs and reality has broken down, and that this calls for celebration of a resulting culture of 'hyperreality.'

postmodernity as a historical epoch

Third, poststructuralism is a theoretical articulation of postmodernism. (Another term, deconstructionism, is associated especially with US variants of the position, is perhaps becoming the preferred term, but derives from the same seminal texts, such as Derrida (1976[1967]). Their common analytical strategy is to expose internal contradictions in texts and to undermine their stated or apparent intentions. The theoretical premise is that no textual meaning is stable, and that insight into either oneself or others is out of the question.

poststructuralism as a theoretical position

deconstructionism

Compared to most earlier philosophical and theoretical positions, the poststructuralist agenda is one of radical skepticism and relativism. The aim is not merely to show that knowledge is uncertain, or to argue in positive terms that it should be obtained by different means – human knowledge as traditionally understood is said to be literally impossible. And yet, poststructuralism had tended to conceive of itself as a progressive position, taking inspiration from critical social theory (Foucault, 1972[1969]) and psychoanalysis (Lacan, 1977). A key argument is that any fixation of meaning or knowledge can be seen as a way of exercising definitional power, even committing violence against the worldviews of others. In many ways, then, poststructuralism reiterates the ideology critique of the 1960s and 1970s, which sought to unmask texts as the carriers of bourgeois ideology (e.g., Barthes, 1973[1957]; Negt, 1973; Williamson, 1978). By 'deconstructing' dominant discourses, studies might hope to produce resistance and alternatives. As an analytical practice, however, poststructuralism has remained centrally focused on the interpretation of texts.

ideology critique

In media and communication research, poststructuralist studies have examined especially film, television, and other visual texts (for an overview, see Bignell, 2000). A widespread assumption is that images are relatively open to deconstruction and reinterpretation, even though they may tend to fixate audiences in particular subject positions, as also held by the psychosemiotic tradition. In addition, poststructuralism has lent itself, for example, to the study of emerging and experimental genres such as the music video (e.g., Kinder, 1984) and of media formats which are under commercial pressures to innovate, such as advertising and contemporary television series (e.g., Caldwell, 1995). More recently, digital media have given rise to debates on whether 'cyberspace'◀ might house the kind of decentered discourses and identities that poststructuralism has sought to identify and promote.

It should be added that references to postmodernism in cultural theory and media studies have been subject to criticism, especially as a general and underdefined sense of living in contingent, 'postmodern times.' Particularly with reference to the assumption that we have entered a historical epoch of postmodernity, David Harvey (1989), among others, has argued that 'postmodern' culture is

▶ cyberspace – Chapter 1, p. 2

more appropriately examined as a specific set of styles and practices which typify a period or stage of *modernity*. These styles and practices – for example, an aestheticization of politics and a growing mediatization of everyday life – are perhaps best understood as the outcome of an intensifying, but continuous process of modernization.

Feminism

References to 'man' as the object of humanistic scholarship became untenable during the same period as media and communication research was taking shape. Humans are distinguished by gender, in addition to ethnicity, class, and diverse cultural characteristics. Recognizing that biological sex has variable and contestable meanings, anthropology and other social sciences have examined gender as a social and cultural category over the last century (Reinharz, 1992). Since the 1960s, gender studies have been given an explicitly critical inflection, fueled by the women's liberation movement. It was during these decades that feminism became integral to the humanities (for key texts, see Marks and de Courtivron, 1981; Nicholson, 1997).

Feminist media studies emerged as part of this 'second wave' of research and activism. (The 'first wave' covered the securing of formal gender equality in terms of voting and other human rights.) For second-wave studies, an influential notion of 'difference feminism' (Nicholson, 1997: 3) suggested that gender is not simply a characteristic of individuals (a 'variable'), but a constitutive factor in all social interactions and institutions, including the research institution itself. Feminism has served as one reminder that research is shaped, in part, by its historical and ideological circumstances, and by the lives that scholars live outside the academy. Indeed, recent work has referred to a third-wave feminism (Gillis, *et al.*, 2005) that seeks to counter a potential conservatism and essentialism of the second wave, which was pioneered by a generation of white, affluent women in the West, by variously including the voices of younger women (the 'daughters' of second-wavers), emphasizing the ethnic, national, and cultural diversity of 'women,' recognizing popular cultural pleasures, and celebrating sexuality as an essential quality of human existence.

first-wave and second-wave feminism

gender: variable or constituent?

Three varieties of feminist media studies can be identified (for overview, see Carter and Steiner, 2004; Kearney, 2010; van Zoonen, 1992). The earliest studies focused on images of women, particularly stereotypical representations and their likely effect in socializing both female and male audiences (e.g., Tuchman, *et al.*, 1978). Such studies tended to take equality between men and women as a neutral norm, and as an ideal that might be enforced by legal and professional standards. As such, early studies built on first-wave and liberal feminism emphasizing equal political and economic rights, and extended these formal criteria to the domain of media and communication. At issue was the *representation* of women, not only in the political, but in the cultural sense of maintaining a proportional and legitimate presence of women in media and the public sphere as such.

images of women

Also other humanistic disciplines pursued such a politics of representation (Clifford and Marcus, 1986). In literary studies, one feminist concern was to make visible, or recover, female authors from the past, on the assumption that they would provide alternative images of women, and for the future (Moi, 2002: 41–48). In media studies, the industrial organization of image production appeared to largely cancel gender and other differences between media professionals, so that more women employees do not necessarily result in a more balanced representation of women and gender issues (van Zoonen, 1992: 43–65).

politics of representation

The second type of studies sought to broaden the perspective on why, in the end, images of women and men in the media turn out as they do. According to difference feminism, as noted, gender is a pervasive condition of all individual and social being, affecting the thinking and actions of both women and men. Feminism joins cultural studies◄ in assuming that culture is a site of struggle in its own right and across social contexts: gender resides in media production, media texts, as well as media

difference feminism

► cultural studies, p. 46

uses. Certain conceptions of gender, while contestable and contested, are likely to exercise hegemony◄ (Gramsci, 1971), because they are ingrained in predominant media representations and communicative practices. It is this hegemony, accordingly, which has been targeted for critical analysis by much feminist media research. Studies range from examinations of the gendered gaze in visual communication (Mulvey, 1992[1975]), to ideology critiques of popular fiction (McRobbie, 1991), to empirical studies of the secret or ambivalent pleasures of women enjoying popular culture (Ang, 1985; Radway, 1984).

The third variety of feminism, in comparison, has tended to posit a fundamental difference between women, men, and their characteristic ways of communicating and, indeed, of knowing things in the first place. Drawing on poststructuralism and psychoanalysis, the position has suggested that certain kinds of knowledge are available to women only – a kind of gendered 'private language' (Wittgenstein, 1953). Additional arguments have been made to the effect that such unique capacities originate from the specific psychology and/or physiology of the female sex. In an influential work with a deliberately ambiguous title, "This Sex Which Is Not One," Luce Irigaray (1997[1977]) suggested several points – that biological sex and cultural gender have no necessary interrelation; that no woman (or man) has a unified gender; and that the dual shape of the female genitals can be retraced in feminine forms of culture and communication. Women's modes of interaction, accordingly, might be said to privilege process and dialogue, inclusion and care. Whereas the latter argument is familiar from other psychological work (e.g., Gilligan, 1982), and empirically supported in studies of, for instance, internet communication (e.g., Herring, 1999[1996]), the grander position is undermined by its metaphorical line of argument. While otherwise claiming to be staunchly constructivist,◄ poststructuralist feminism, in its analytical practice, commonly engages in equivocation, sliding into a double essentialism that mixes claims about biology and epistemology.

► hegemony, p. 47
► constructivism – Chapter 3, p. 51

essentialism: biological and epistemological

Essentialist feminism has been influential in other humanistic work that proposes to produce new insights by blurring the lines between scholarly and poetic forms of expression; philosophical support has been forthcoming in this regard from, among others, Richard Rorty (1991), who aimed to redefine philosophy as storytelling. In the wider field of media and communication studies, the influence of essentialist feminism has been more limited, even if some research on digital media has envisioned new liberating potentials in the form of 'cyborgs' (Haraway, 1991) and a 'posthuman' condition (Hayles, 1999). In debates over methodology and theory of science, the field has witnessed so-called standpoint epistemology, which holds that it is possible, even necessary, to conduct research from gendered and other 'interested' standpoints.◄ Feminist theorists, such as Gayatri Spivak, thus, have advocated "strategic essentialism" (Nicholson, 1997: 318) as a historically justified position from which to counter male forms of oppression that, arguably, follow from masculine epistemologies.

Cognitivism

The last challenge to the humanities has come from cognitivism and, more broadly, from natural-scientific conceptions of human communication. Compared to the discursive and historical focus of both feminism and postmodernism, cognitivism draws its theoretical inspiration from 'hard' sciences – neurophysiology, cognitive psychology, medicine, and computer science. From the 1950s onwards, these disciplines joined forces in the interdisciplinary field of cognitive science, in part around hopes of developing artificial intelligence (for an overview, see Gardner, 1985). It was particularly from the 1980s that this influence was felt, in both media studies and the wider humanities, in part via the unlikely intervention of film studies.

cognitive science

Natural-scientific, biological, and evolutionary perspectives on human communication, including its continuities with (other) animal

► standpoint epistemology – Chapter 19, p. 364

natural evolution

communication, have long been a niche interest in media studies (for overview, see Cappella, 1996). Also studies of visual arts have been influenced by cognitive science (Solso, 1994). During the 1980 and 1990s, however, film scholars played a special role in reintroducing cognitive theory to the study of visual media, partly overlapping with experimental studies of the psychology of media entertainment (for an overview, see Zillmann and Vorderer, 2000). A particularly influential volume was David Bordwell's *Narration in the Fiction Film* (Bordwell, 1985a), which integrated an information-processing perspective with a structuralist approach to texts and their interpretation. Redeveloping aspects of literary theory, specifically Russian formalism,◄ Bordwell sought to account in detail for the relationship between the discursive structures of film and the viewer's cognitive activity.

In relation to earlier film theory, the cognitivist position was summed up in the title of a stock-taking volume, coedited by Bordwell with Noël Carroll: *Post-Theory* (Bordwell and Carroll, 1996). The introduction noted that the title was not intended to signal "the end of film theory" as such, but to question Theory, defined as "that aggregate of doctrines derived from Lacanian psychoanalysis, Structuralist semiotics, Post-Structuralist literary theory, and variants of Althusserian Marxism" (p. xiii) which had hardened into an orthodoxy of 'grand' film theory.◄ The stated aim of the editors was to promote pluralism in the choice of both theoretical frameworks and analytical procedures. Moreover, the contributors advocated a return to middle-range and empirical work informed by concrete research questions, including economic and historical studies. In effect, the volume denounced the contemporary psychoanalytic mainstream and sought to advance cognitivism, which was said to allow for several articulations – by polemical contrast to a monolithic psychoanalysis (p. xvi).

Complementing early cognitivist approaches to feature film viewing as a form of puzzle-solving, later studies have gone on to examine other genres, such as documentary (Plantinga, 1997), and to develop typologies of the basic human emotions associated with visual communication (Grodal, 1997, 2009). Given its origins in film studies, however, this work has mostly remained divorced from thematically related forms of audience research, for example, on readers' and viewers' recall of information as presented in both print and audiovisual media.◄ More important, the analytical focus has remained squarely on the film text and its appeals to the spectator. It is perhaps ironic that an approach which derives legitimacy from an emphatically experimental tradition of science, should still be practiced mostly by solitary scholars scrutinizing texts. Their 'findings' – or rather readings – are mostly the outcome of a methodological business-as-usual, relying on narratological and hermeneutic procedures resembling those of semiotics before the advent of empirical reception studies.◄

The far-reaching inferences that some cognitivist scholars make regarding the nature and impact of media experience are explained, in part, by the claim of cognitive science to account for universal aspects of human consciousness across individuals, cultures, and historical periods. Within the history of film studies, cognitivist theory can be understood as a case of the pendulum swinging from a subjectivist to an objectivist pole. In a future perspective, one challenge is how to integrate insights concerning the evolutionary and biological preconditions of human communication into the broader field of media and communication research. To one side, cognitivism interfaces with semiotics (e.g., Buckland, 2000) – the understanding of human cognition and social interaction as necessarily mediated in signs. To the other side, cognitivist film studies overlap, as indicated, with a growing body of experimental work on media uses and effects from psychological and social-scientific perspectives (e.g., Bryant and Oliver, 2009; Messaris, 1994; Reeves and Nass, 1996).

Digital media invite further consideration of such integration. Computers – originally of the non-networked variety – provided the key

► Russian formalism, p. 38
► film studies – p. 40
► studies of media recall – Chapter 8, p. 160
► empirical reception studies – Chapter 10

metaphor for a general cognitive science about humans as well as other communicating entities. Fifty years on, the dream of artificial intelligence has, mostly, ended (Boden, 1996; Partridge, 1991). Humans are unique media, even as they extend themselves in other degrees of media.◀ At the same time, computer-mediated communication evidently calls for different analytical strategies than the matching of single films with general cognitive frames or schemata in either textual or experimental studies.◀ The interfaces of communication have become more distributed and differentiated; so must research methodologies.

Cognitivism has reminded research that human consciousness and communication are embodied – they occur in the flesh (Lakoff and Johnson, 1999). As suggested by one of the sources of cognitive science – phenomenology – bodies are not only something that humans have, but something we are (Merleau-Ponty, 1962[1945]: 174). Natural conditions, like technological infrastructures, circumscribe culture and society – they determine communication in the first instance.◀ So far, however, cognitivism has given priority to the way in which humans carry "the body in the mind" (Johnson, 1987) – metaphors and concepts arising from our bodily orientation in time and space – above the ways in which we, simultaneously, carry society and history in the mind.

In media and communication research, cognitivism represents a third academic culture of natural science (Brockman, 1995), in addition to the two main sources of humanities and social sciences. In a longer historical perspective, C. P. Snow (1964) had identified an intellectual divide between 'hard' sciences and 'soft' arts within the academy.◀ This divide reproduced itself in media studies in debates between hard social sciences and soft humanities. Cognitivism, while reiterating issues from those debates, has helped to reintroduce research questions concerning the material conditions of human communication – bodies, technologies, and their interrelations. Humans communicate for a meaningful existence, and for their lives. Communication is constitutive of humanity and society.

▶ media of the first degree – Chapter 1, p. 5
▶ frames – Chapter 8, p. 164
▶ determination in the first instance – Chapter 1, p. 2
▶ two cultures of research – Chapter 15, p. 285

A PRAGMATIC TURN

Following on previous linguistic and communicative turns, the humanities can be seen to have undertaken a pragmatic turn in recent decades, in response to a variety of challenges from interdisciplinary fields and social sciences – and from other social institutions: commercial collaborators as well as public-sector funders. The infrastructural position of the humanities in both society and academy has been changing – over the course of two centuries, and in the post-1945 period. Beyond debates over basic versus applied research,◀ the humanities are increasingly expected to address practical and policy issues with implications for social action. During the formation of the field of media and communication research, the humanities, to a degree, have been reworking themselves – from the preservation and dissemination of cultural tradition, and the training of its keepers for employment in schools, museums, and archives, to remediating◀ tradition and educating practitioners for an expanded range of cultural and communicative professions.

While the larger institutional shift is still ongoing, it is appropriate, in conclusion, to identify some of its theoretical and methodological implications. I do so, first, with reference to the cultural-studies tradition and, second, in terms of a few key premises that are widely shared across contemporary humanities.

A hybrid of humanistic and social-scientific perspectives, cultural studies has contributed, not least, to a humanistic inflection of research questions and analytical approaches in media and communication research (for an overview, see During, 2007; Grossberg, *et al.*, 1992; Hartley and Pearson, 2000). Although researchers in various cultural contexts, predictably, have had different focal points, the British variety of cultural studies, as asso-

cultural studies

▶ basic and applied research – Chapter 19, p. 355
▶ remediation – Chapter 10, p. 188

ciated with the Birmingham Centre for Contemporary Cultural Studies (closed 2002), has been particularly influential (e.g., Hall, *et al.*, 1980). From the 1970s, it established itself as an identifiable 'school,' consolidating itself in the US, Australia, Europe, and elsewhere, and may even be considered *the* current humanistic substream within international media studies.

The distinctive profile of cultural studies as a tradition that draws, at once, on critical theories and interpretive methodologies was captured in a theoretical overview by Stuart Hall (1980), himself a seminal figure in the school (Morley and Chen, 1996). Hall noted that two paradigms came together in cultural studies (suggesting that paradigms, as introduced by Kuhn (1970), may not be as incommensurable as some commentators have assumed). On the one hand, structuralism◀ emphasizes the relative determination of consciousness and communication by economic, political, and other social frameworks. Hall traced this emphasis particularly to Althusser (1977[1965]) and Lévi-Strauss (1963[1958]), in addition to the legacy of Karl Marx.

culturalism

On the other hand, culturalism insists that culture is a practice with a considerable degree of autonomy, and a site of important social struggles in both public and personal settings. In this regard, the inspiration for cultural studies came, not least, from UK historians and literary scholars (Hoggart, 1957; Thompson, 1963; Williams, 1975[1958]), who help to account for the special British connection in international cultural studies. For Hall and others, the two paradigms were joined in the work of Antonio Gramsci (1971), whose concept of hegemony – a dominant range of worldviews that serve to legitimate and reinforce the status quo – could accommodate both structure and agency: social determination and cultural autonomy.

hegemony

One critique of cultural studies has addressed its methodologies, specifically the overwhelming majority of qualitative studies. While drawing its primary inspiration from semiotics and hermeneutics, the tradition would seem to invite further use of quantitative methodologies, especially if it is to live up to its critical aims of facilitating social change (Lewis, 1997). A second, related debate has to do with the outcome of empirical research: what are the actual findings and their practical relevance? Meaghan Morris (1990), for one, worried about the banality of cultural studies – that study after exploratory study may reaffirm the insight that cultural practices are complex and diverse, to such an extent that their consequences for issues of power, pleasure, or pain cannot be predicted or explained in any concrete fashion.

Compared to central conceptual and normative tenets of the humanistic tradition, however, cultural studies signaled a significant reorientation – from fine arts to multiple cultures, and from texts and other artifacts to practices and processes through which media make a difference in the lives of individuals and societies. The reorientation suggests an understanding that media are not merely, or even primarily, means of *representation* and sources of evidence about the past; media are *resources*, at once material and discursive, that enter into the shaping of both the present and the future. The communicative turn entailed a shift from an understanding of language (and other media) as formal structures, to a focus on their uses in social interaction; a pragmatic turn, further, implies that communication is itself a form of action, and one that anticipates other forms of action, from the micro to the macro level of society. This position was given a name in speech-act theory◀ (Austin, 1962; Searle, 1969): by speaking we act and, by extension, we act through each new medium that we invent.

Also other current humanistic scholarship, to varying degrees, can be seen to subscribe to three pragmatic premises concerning media, communication, and culture:

- *A general category of texts.* Beyond artworks and historical sources, the humanities have come to address, on the one hand, popular and audiovisual media and, on the other hand, individual consciousness as well as social institutions and practices as texts.
- *A secular notion of culture.* Culture is now commonly said to refer to both products

▶ structuralism – p. 38

▶ speech-act theory – Chapter 1, p. 13

and processes of meaning: any vehicle or practice of meaningful expression and interaction, as recognized by participants themselves. As such, culture has become doubly secular, having no divine origin or purpose, and abiding by no absolute or timeless standard.◄

- *A performative concept of communication*. As testified by humanistic traditions since classical rhetoric, communication is a form of action, albeit a special kind of action that allows humans to engage in doubt and delay concerning what to do next. Modern information and communication technologies have enhanced the capacity of individuals as well as collectives to interact, and to act at a distance.

These premises have brought the humanities closer, in recent decades, to anthropology, sociology, and other social sciences. The ongoing convergence of humanities and social sciences in media and communication research is one outcome of larger interdisciplinary realignments. The contribution of the social sciences to this development, and to media and communication research, is the subject of Chapter 3.

► definitions of culture – Chapter 11, p. 204

3 Media, culture, and modern times

Social science investigations

Graham Murdock

- a description of media as central constituents of the *modern period*, and of the *social sciences* studying it
- a *recovery* of the different types of *research, analysis, and activism* which characterized early social science, and which fed into later media studies
- a review of work examining the relations between media and *democracy, social space*, and *public culture*
- a reassessment of *precursors of current social science*, e.g. regarding media effects and reception
- a summary of the transition *from structural functionalism to political economy and cultural studies* in contemporary media studies

LINEAGES OF THE PRESENT

Many of the social institutions and patterns of everyday life with which we are now so familiar assumed their present forms in the four decades between 1880 and 1920. Their development was inextricably tied up with the growth of modern media. The arrival of wireless telegraphy in 1895, and of automatic switchboards in telephone exchanges in 1892, allowed greater and greater volumes of information and conversation to be transmitted, conveniently and instantly over greater and greater distances. The ability to reproduce photographs in newspapers and magazines for the first time (1880) transformed the popular press. And the launch of the gramophone, in 1887, and the arrival of cinema in 1895, laid the basis for novel kinds of entertainment and experience.◄

This complex of new communications media played a central role in constructing the contemporary social order in four main ways. First, they allowed both the large business enterprises that were coming to dominate the economy, and the new forms of state and government which were emerging in the political arena, to manage their proliferating activities more effectively. Modern business worked with ever-more complex chains of supply, production and distribution. Modern nation-states were assuming greater responsibility for social welfare, in areas like pensions and education. With the age of total war, ushered in by the First World War I, they faced the problem of managing military operations spread over a huge geographical area. Even in peacetime, the operations of many large corporations and Western nation-states were global in scope. Empires, whether territorial or economic, posed formidable problems of command, coordination and control.

the control society

Second, modern communications were central to the ways in which governments and business corporations secured public support. Mature industrial capitalism was based on

► timeline of communication technologies – Chapter 2, p. 26

the mass production of standardised goods, typified by Henry Ford's Model T motor car (first introduced in 1909). To maximise profits in this new system, mass production had to be matched by mass consumption. Consequently, the development of modern assembly line manufacture and of mass offices using the new typewriters (introduced in 1873) was accompanied by the rise of department stores and mail order catalogues that were designed to engineering consumer desire and to translate wishes and wants into purchases.

mass consumption

At the centre of this selling system stood the new advertising agencies and public relations firms dedicated to promoting their clients' brands, massaging their company images, and combating criticisms and attacks. Modern governments too were in the business of selling. With the development of representative democracy and the extension of the vote, political parties who wished to form a government had to compete aggressively for public support and try to ensure that 'public opinion' reflected their priorities and constructions of events. The public media, particularly the popular press and later commercial broadcasting, rapidly became the main arenas where these competitions for sales and votes were played out. As we shall see, many commentators saw the private ownership of key news media, and the ever-present possibility of self-interested interventions by owners and advertisers, as a fundamental problem for democracies based on the ideal of open debate in the pursuit of the public interest.

advertising and public relations

Third, these concerns were part of a wider debate about the state of public culture. More and more of the language and imagery through which people understood and interpreted the world was manufactured by professionals working in media industries that were dedicated mainly to making a profit. This situation generated fierce debates over whether art and thought which challenged dominant assumptions could survive in the factory-like conditions of the modern newspaper office, film studio, or popular song-writing system. Another question was whether manufactured meanings could ever be an 'authentic' expression of popular feelings and opinions.

Fourth, questions about the central tendencies of mediated public culture led easily on to concerns about their impact on 'ordinary' people.◄ How did popular media influence beliefs and behaviour? How were they changing everyday patterns of activity and sociability? How did people manage the relations between mediated meanings and meanings grounded in everyday experience?

When these issues first emerged, they attracted the attention of a variety of analysts and commentators – from cultural critics to investigative journalists and social activists. But a number of the most important contributions came from people who thought of themselves in one way or another as social scientists. There are good reasons why we should re-read their pioneering interventions. For one thing, the issues they grappled with remain central to contemporary debates, and many of their definitions of core problems remain highly pertinent to present-day debate. For another thing, their attempts to develop systematic techniques of investigation have essential lessons to teach us about the potentials and limits of different methods and how they might be productively combined. To ignore this legacy is to condemn media research to perpetually rediscovering old methods, having forgotten their previous history. We develop intellectually by climbing on other people's shoulders so that we can see further and more clearly. We have no choice but, as a field of research, we should at least acknowledge our debt to them and call them by name.

RESEARCHERS, REPORTERS, ANALYSTS AND ACTIVISTS

The social sciences were relatively late additions to the intellectual field. Their emergence as the university-based disciplines we now know coincided exactly with the development of contemporary social and media systems. Up until then, thinking about individual consciousness, social action and the good society had been overwhelmingly concentrated in departments of philosophy, with history and law making minor

► history of effects research – Chapter 8, p. 154

contributions. Consequently, as John Watson, one of the founders of modern psychology put it, establishing the social sciences meant breaking philosophy's "stranglehold" over social inquiry (1924: xi).

This assault on intellectual monopoly began in earnest in the late 1880s. In 1887, Émile Durkheim was appointed to the first named professorial chair of sociology in France, at Bordeaux. In 1890, Alfred Marshall published his *Principles of Economics*, deliberately rejecting the established tradition of political economy with its strong links to moral philosophy and its concern with the relations between economic activity and 'the good society'. Instead, he argued for a new discipline that would analyse 'the economy' as a bounded sphere of action. In 1892, William James (brother of the novelist, Henry James) invited the German scholar, Hugo Münsterberg, to Harvard to take charge of the pioneering psychology laboratory he had established there. And in 1898, two English anthropologists, Haddon and Rivers, set off for the Torres Straits, intent on replacing the impressions of missionaries and adventurers with a study of tribal life based on first-hand observation.

Underpinning many of these initiatives was the idea that the social sciences were continuous with the natural sciences and should adopt the same basic aims and techniques of inquiry.◀ That conception privileged systematic experimentation and testing, objective observation purged of all personal values, and the translation of 'results' into statistics wherever possible. The aim was to identify the stable patterns governing social life and to formulate the connections binding them together as relations of cause and effect. The result was knowledge that could be used to manage existing institutions more effectively.

This positivist◀ conception of 'science' was strongly opposed from the outset by those who insisted that the study of social life remained an interpretive activity dedicated to understanding what life looks like and feels like to other people. One of the founding texts for this approach was Alfred Schütz's 1932 book, *The Phenomenology of the Social World*, in which he argued that social-scientific inquiry must always begin with "the already constituted meanings of active participants in the social world" (Schütz 1956[1932]: 10).◀ This argument – that social 'reality' is being continually built and rebuilt by 'ordinary' people as they struggle to make sense of their situation and devise strategies for action – has proved massively influential. It underpins the broad tradition of work that is now often called 'constructionism' (a term deliberately chosen for its strong associations with building work) as well as much recent work on 'active audiences'.◀ By highlighting the range of skills required by everyday social practices and exploring the logics underpinning unfamiliar beliefs, early contributors to this tradition hoped to deconstruct prevailing stereotypes and demonstrate the creativity with which 'ordinary' people negotiated the circumstances in which they found themselves.

constructionism

The impetus to illuminate the connections between biography and history was shared by critical researchers aiming to expose the gaps between official promises and everyday realities, ideals and performance. They rejected what they saw as the phenomenologists' "radically individualistic and subjective" approach to the social (Outhwaite 1975: 92), insisting that people's lives and worldviews were shaped in fundamental ways by structural forces that they may misunderstand, or not even be aware of. This argument laid the basis for what has come to be called the critical realist tradition of social analysis (see Sayer 2000).◀ Its supporters saw themselves less as celebrants of the complexities of lived reality and more as critics of the processes that had produced these experiences and meanings and of the prevailing patterns of power that blocked alternatives.

biography and history

These three positions entailed different roles for the professional social analyst:

- management
- interpretation
- critique◀

▶ natural and social sciences – Chapter 15, p. 285
▶ positivism – Chapter 15, p. 291
▶ phenomenology – Chapter 2, p. 30
▶ active audiences – Chapter 9
▶ critical realism – Chapter 15, p. 297
▶ three knowledge interests – Chapter 19, p. 358

All these found a niche within the emerging social science disciplines, but their practice was not monopolised by university departments. Important contributions were made by writers working outside the academy, and the lines separating the academy from the wider worlds of letters and political action were fluid rather than fixed.

Upton Sinclair, who produced one of the best early critiques of press performance (Sinclair 1920), had already achieved early fame with his novel, *The Jungle* (1906), an exposé of conditions in the Chicago slaughterhouses and meat-packing plants, and later went on to run (unsuccessfully) for the governorship of California on a radical ticket. Robert Park had been a journalist as well as the secretary to a well-known black activist before taking a position in the sociology department at the University of Chicago. Here, he played a central role in developing the tradition of urban ethnography, including studies of the media in everyday life, for which the department is best known. The influential cultural analyst, Siegfried Kracauer, moved from the department of sociology at Berlin to become a journalist, and later a cultural critic, for the leading German daily newspaper, the *Frankfurter Zeitung*.

the Chicago School

There was traffic, too, across the border between universities and business. When John Watson was dismissed from his chair of psychology at Johns Hopkins University for moral impropriety, he went to work for the country's biggest advertising agency, J. Walter Thompson, where he eventually rose to become vice president. Similarly, when Ernest Dichter, who had worked with Paul Lazarsfeld, one of the leading academic figures in early communications research, in Vienna, moved to the United States, he set up his own commercial research consultancy where he developed his ideas on the motivations behind consumer choices and became one of central figures in post-war market research (e.g. Dichter 1947).

The traffic across institutional borders had several important consequences. First, it meant that research agendas were often shaped by issues originally raised in political debate, and that leading academics frequently wrote for major magazines and newspapers as well as for professional journals. Many thought of themselves primarily as public intellectuals◄ contributing to national and international debate, and only secondarily as researchers pursuing academic careers.

Second, because media and communications were new areas of inquiry without an established tradition of methodology, researchers were more open to improvisation. Sometimes the choice of methods was the result of pure chance, as in the case of the pioneering Chicago sociologist, W.I. Thomas (see Janowitz 1966: xxiv). One morning, while walking down a back alley in the Polish community on the West Side, he had to sidestep quickly to avoid some garbage just thrown out of an upstairs window. It contained several packets of letters arranged in chronological order. Since he read Polish, he started to read one of the bundles and decided to use letters as the basic data for his monumental study of migrant experience, later published as *The Polish Peasant in Europe and America* (Thomas and Znaniecki 1927).

Early analysts were also more willing to work with a range of methods. True, some favoured rigorous experimentation, sample surveys and structured questionnaires, while others preferred to work with depth interviewing, personal documents and ethnographic observation. However, the separation between quantitative and qualitative methods was often less rigid than it later became. Paul Lazarsfeld, for example, is remembered now as one of the pioneers of statistical methods, and often dismissed as a crude empiricist. In fact, he was a pioneer of multi-method research. His choices were always dictated by the issue to be addressed, and there was no question of one method being suitable for all questions (Morrison 1998: 140).

A third consequence of this movement across intellectual check-points is that the story of the social-scientific contribution to media and communication research is as much a history of commercial research and critical inquiry as of academic projects.◄ Lazarsfeld, whose early work was often funded from commercial

► intelligentsia – Chapter 19, p. 362

► administrative and critical research – Chapter 19, p. 359

sources, argued that because of the way he formulated problems he always "got results which were interesting for the theoretical psychologists and worth the money to the business man" (1934: 71). His critics disagreed, insisting that intellectual inquiry must remain independent of pressure from both government and business, and must define its own terms of inquiry.

In reply, Lazarsfeld could point to *Personal Influence* (1955), which identified the ways people drew on the opinions and recommendations of friends and people they admired when making everyday choices. The research was funded by two commercial sponsors, the magazine publisher Mcfadden and the Roper polling organisation, and examined people's choice of consumer goods and fashions as well as their political choices. However, Lazarsfeld and his co-author, Elihu Katz, used the opportunity to refine the 'two-step flow' model of communications which had emerged (serendipitously) in Lazarsfeld *et al.*'s (1944) earlier work on an election campaign. The model immediately attracted enormous interest and was widely used in later academic studies of media audiences.◀ Ironically, however, new ideas and methods that were pioneered within the academy were often more enthusiastically adopted by commercial researchers than by academics. As we shall see, focus groups are a case in point.

Retrieving the history of the social-scientific work on media and re-assessing the contemporary relevance of key studies is a mammoth task, and will have to wait for another occasion. Here, I simply want to indicate how some of the most interesting early contributors set about tackling central issues which we still face, and I will suggest how their pioneering work illuminates contemporary debates. Important contributions have come from across the range of social science disciplines – from sociology, anthropology, and psychology, to economics, political economy, and political science (for overviews and references, see Alexander *et al.* 1997; Boudon *et al.* 1997). It was primarily political scientists and other concerned observers who raised the central question of the role of media in modern democracies.

social science disciplines

political science

▶ two-step flow model – Chapter 8, p. 174

MEDIA AND DEMOCRACY

Liberal democratic models of mass democracy presupposed universal access to certain basic informational and cultural resources:

- citizens required comprehensive and disinterested *information* on developments that affected their personal and political choices, particularly where changes were being promoted by agencies – whether governmental or business – with significant power over their lives;
- citizens were entitled to see their own experiences, opinions, and aspirations given a fair *representation* in the major media of public culture; and
- citizens had a right to *participation* in open debates over the relative merits of competing explanations of prevailing conditions and rival proposals for change.

Surveying the state of public media at the turn of the twentieth century, particularly the popular press, which was the main forum for information and debate, many commentators detected a substantial gap between democratic ideals and press performance. As America's leading political philosopher of the time, John Dewey, noted in his influential book of 1926, *The Public and its Problems,* the popular media had signally failed to convert a people into a public fully involved in the political process. Their failure to provide adequate communicative resources for citizenship had, he lamented, left "the public [...] formless [...] seizing and holding its shadow rather than its substance", a phantom, glimpsed occasionally only to disappear again (Dewey 1926: 141). Dewey's criticism focused on the eclipse of political news and debate by coverage of "crime, accident, family rows, personal clashes and conflicts" (p. 180). As we shall see below, his alarm at this 'sensationalist' turn was widely shared.

More radical critics, however, offered another explanation of the press's democratic failure, focusing on journalism's role in providing what Upton Sinclair in his savagely critical book, *The Brass Check* (1920), called the "day-to-day, between-elections propaganda" which allows the "Empire of Business" to maintain its effective "control over political democracy" and to ensure that its agendas and priorities prevail (p. 222). In Sinclair's view, this eclipse of the public interest by private interests had two origins. First, newspapers were privately owned and therefore open to abuses of power by proprietors pursuing their opinions or those of their allies and associates. Second, they were funded primarily by advertising, leaving them open to pressure from companies wanting to promote their corporate interests.

"What," asked another prominent critic, Will Irwin, "does the advertiser ask as a bonus in return for his business favour ? […] suppression of […] disasters injurious to his business" (Irwin 1969[1911]: 15). He supports his argument by pointing to the substantial publicity given to the relatively trivial sums which some train conductors had 'fiddled' from their employer, compared with the lack of coverage given to a case of wrongful arrest for shoplifting brought against a department store by a woman who had almost died of shock when apprehended. He gleefully notes that in both cases the companies involved were major advertisers. The argument that money talks and also buys silence had been made even more forcefully by Edward Ross, a sociology professor at the University of Chicago. In one of America's leading journals of opinion, *The Atlantic Monthly*, a year before, he wrote a piece provocatively entitled, "The Suppression of Important News" (1910). His major concrete examples concerned the press coverage of labour relations and strikes, which could be considered the touchstone of a corporation's treatment of its employees.

Other commentators at the time analysed the news management activities of government, focusing particularly on the mismanagement of information flows in times of national crisis. This second major 'filter' of news (alongside the filters operating within the media themselves) was starkly illuminated by the prominent political scientist, Walter Lippmann, and his associate Charles Merz, in their case study of the *New York Times*' coverage of the Russian Revolution, entitled "A Test of the News" and published in 1920. Their detailed textual analysis revealed that, at every stage of the Revolution and the ensuing civil war (in which the United States had intervened to support the Communists' main opponents), some of America's leading journalists had been seriously misled by "the official purveyors of information" offering opinions dictated by vested political interests rather than 'trustworthy news' (p. 41). As a result, "a great people in a supreme crisis could not secure the minimum necessary information on a supremely important event" (p. 3).

Still other critics of press performance focused on ways in which the press amplified incidents of social deviance and helped provoke a public and, subsequently, an official reaction which was out of proportion to the scale of the original threat and may well have added to the problem rather than alleviating it. In 1922, for example, Roscoe Pound and his colleagues undertook a detailed study quantitative study of crime reporting in Cleveland newspapers for the month of January 1919, using column inch counts.◀ They found that whereas, in the first half of month, the total amount of space given over to crime was 925 inches, in the second half of the month it leapt to 6,642 inches. This was in spite of the fact that the number of crimes reported to the police had only increased from 345 to 363. They concluded that although the city's much publicised 'crime wave' was largely fictitious and manufactured by the press, the coverage had very real consequences for the administration of criminal justice. Because the public believed that they were in the middle of a crime epidemic, they demanded an immediate response from the police and the city authorities. These agencies, wishing to retain public support, complied, caring "more to satisfy popular demands than to be observant of the tried processes of law" (Pound and Frankfurter 1922: 546). The result was a greatly increased likelihood of miscarriages of justice and sentences more severe than the offences warranted.

▶ quantitative content analysis – Chapter 13, p. 248

This vigorous tradition of news critique in the context of political democracy, although largely unacknowledged now, paved the way for four major currents of work that have been very influential in media research:

- work within the *political economy* of communications explores the corporate control of public communications. It is typified by Robert McChesney's volume, *Rich Media, Poor Democracy* (1999);
- an account of the various filters blocking and directing news flows on behalf of the powerful has been outlined in the influential '*propaganda model*' of news production which was developed by Edward Herman and Noam Chomsky in their book *Manufacturing Consent* (1988). The model is pursued in detail in their successive case studies of reporting in the American press in times of war and crisis;
- a substantial body of work has analysed *systematic biases* in news reporting of social conflict, including labour disputes. The Glasgow University Media Group's *Bad News* study (1976) has played a particularly prominent role; and
- analyses of *moral panics* and media amplification generally have played a major role in studies of public responses to youth subcultures (see Thompson 1998) and to environmental and other risks (see Douglas 1997; Renn 1991).

MEDIA, NETWORKS AND EMPIRES

As commentators recognised at the time, the rapid growth of the telegraph in the 1830s and 1840s was a truly revolutionary development in human communications. By separating communication from transportation for the first time in history and translating messages of all kinds into patterned electrical pulses – travelling over wires, through undersea cables and, later, through the atmosphere – it dismantled the material barriers that are presented by washed-out roads and storms at sea. The effect was to create new communicative spaces released from the confines of geographical place. These spaces inhabited a no-man's land between the point of transmission and the point of arrival.

The importance of this development was forcefully put by Charles Cooley in a long essay on "The Theory of Transportation", published in the official journal of the American Economic Association in 1894. He had been a senior civil servant in the transport division, and he went on to become a significant figure in early American sociology. At the time of writing, however, he was working as a political economy teacher at the University of Michigan. He argued that any "study of communication from the point of view of place relations [...] cannot penetrate more than skin-deep into the social meaning of communication" because "in communication, place relations, as such, are of diminishing importance, and since the introduction of the telegraph it may almost be said that there are no place relations" (Cooley 1894: 293). Or, as a poem of 1872, written in honour of Samuel Morse, whose code of dots and dashes had become the global language of telegraphy, put it: "And science proclaimed, from shore to shore,/That Time and Space ruled man no more" (quoted in Standage 1998: 23).

At the time, this vivid perception that communicative spaces were displacing geographical places as the key organising nodes of social activity was not pursued particularly vigorously by social analysts. Most saw 'society' as more or less synonymous with the nation state.◀ The Canadian political economist, Harold Innis, was a notable exception. His early work, *The Fur Trade in Canada* (1930), had explained the choices facing Canada with reference to its place within the centre-periphery systems which characterised relations between empires and their colonies more generally. His later work, *Empire and Communications* (1950) and *The Bias of Communication* (1951), focused more concertedly on the relations between communications and empire, arguing that all communication systems exhibited a 'bias' that favoured either control over time or control over space. By facilitating coordination over greater and greater distances, the development of portable and mobile media had facilitated both the extension of modern imperial systems

▶ the nation-state – Chapter 11, p. 205

and the corporate concentration of control over key communications facilities.◀ Innis's dense writing style and the fact that much of his empirical material was historical discouraged many social scientists from pursuing his ideas. But the perception that communication was central to contemporary forms of imperialism was gathering momentum elsewhere.

By the mid-1920s, it was clear that American popular culture was rapidly becoming a global lingua franca, led by Hollywood's ascendancy in the international film market. As one observer put it, "Language varies, manners vary, money varies, even railway gauges vary. The one universal unit in the world to-day is that slender ribbon [of film] which can carry hocus-pocus, growing pains and dreams" (Merz 1926: 165). Countries at the other end of this cultural chain were rapidly coming to see America's cultural ascendancy as a new form of imperialism, based on the annexation not of territory but of imagination. Commentators in Britain were particularly alarmed, viewing the language that they shared with America as a Trojan horse. In 1937, the radical art historian, F.D. Klingender, collaborated with the activist, Stuart Legg, to produce *Money Behind the Screen,* detailing the parlous state of Britain's national film industry and the extent of American dominance. It was one of the first studies of its kind and set an important precedent for future work on the organisation of the media industries. However, because it focused mainly on the economic and financial aspects of film-making and distribution, it had little to say about the social and cultural impact of imported movies. It was left to an American, Charles Merz (Lippmann's collaborator on the "Test of the News" study), to put these issues on the table.

Merz saw the sale of movies in overseas markets as the heavy artillery in a trade war which was designed to make the American way of life the model for popular aspirations across the globe. This assault was organised consumerism around the ideology of consumerism – the promise that consumer goods can deliver both happiness and freedom – as dramatised in the lives of the stars and the lush settings of popular films. It was exactly this incorporation of film into the culture of selling that had so angered Hugo Münsterberg when he set out to defend American movies from their critics and to demonstrate their potential to become a new art form in his influential book, *The Photoplay,* published in 1916 and reprinted as *The Film* (1970).◀ In his view, whenever spectators were encouraged to think of themselves as consumers, any possibility of true art was annihilated. "The interior decoration of the rooms is not exhibited as a display for a department store [...] A good [film] is not an advertisement for the newest fashions" (Münsterberg 1970[1916]: 81). Writing less than a decade later, Merz was in no doubt that the battering ram of seductive consumer style was breaking down resistance to 'the American way' around the world. He observed that:

> Automobiles manufactured here are ordered abroad after screen shadows have been observed to ride in them [...] rich Peruvians buy piano-players; orders come to Grand Rapids from Japanese who have admired mission armchairs in the films [...] Yorkshire manufacturers of boots and clothing have been obliged to alter their plants because the near east now wishes to dress like Rudolph Valentino.
>
> (Merz 1926: 162)

Later writers have returned to these economic and imaginative flows by way of the notion of 'cultural imperialism',◀ as outlined in it most forceful form in Herbert Schiller's book, *Mass Communications and American Empire* (1969).

The tangled connections between modernisation◀ and Americanisation was also a major theme in studies of the waves of economic and political migrants who had moved from Europe to the United States in the two decades on either side of 1900. The shifting relations between place and space were at the heart of the immigrant experience. They were simultaneously living in the United States and being members

▶ medium theory – Chapter 2, p. 24

▶ film studies – Chapter 2, p. 40

▶ cultural imperialism – Chapter 11, p. 214

▶ modernisation – Chapter 11, p. 206

of global diasporic cultures◀ which linked their new homes to their original homelands through multiple ties of kinship, memory, travel and economic remittance.

As one of the major destinations for inward migration to the United States, Chicago offered a rich locale for investigating these issues, and a number of sociologists took up the challenge. In these studies, the role of mediated communications in sustaining old allegiances and identities, as well as in building new ones, emerges as a major theme. The letters collected in Thomas and Znaniecki's (1927) study of the Polish migrants contain multiple references, for example, to the importance of family photographs in cementing memories and marking change. Robert Park, with his background in journalism, undertook a major study of *The Immigrant Press and its Control* (1922). One of the Chicago department's graduate student, Paul Cressey, went on to make young people's movement through the imaginative landscapes of American consumerism, as offered in the movies, one of the major themes in his unpublished (1936) ethnography of juvenile delinquency in the Italian quarter of New York (see Jowett *et al.* 1996).

In a situation where migration and diaspora are increasingly characteristic of people's everyday experience around the world (the major focus, then and now, of anthropological research), and where American brands and cultural productions have achieved global currency, these pioneering attempts to explore how place and space intersect to organise memories, identities and desires are more pertinent than ever. Similarly, as Manuel Castells has argued in his influential analysis of transnational networks (1996), the role of electronic communications in shifting the relations between space and place is central to understanding the structural organisation of social and economic life in the era of globalization.◀ Other commentators, like John Urry, go further, arguing that, faced with these challenges, sociology needs to focus not on 'societies', but on global mobilities and flows

anthropology

▶ diaspora – Chapter 11, p. 217
▶ globalization – Chapter 11, p. 217

– of images, information, peoples and goods (Urry 2000: 2–3)

This new agenda places issues of communications at the heart of social inquiry. The point can be oversold, however. People still have to live somewhere, and many aspects of their lives are still structured in fundamental ways by institutions and processes operating at local and national levels. As a consequence, national and local media remain crucial resources for people's understanding of themselves and their situation.

TRAVELS CLOSER TO HOME

Although the impact of the shifting relations between physical locations and communicative spaces was felt most acutely by migrants, it was also an integral feature of the way everyday life was being restructured everywhere, even in the most conservative-looking towns. In 1921, Robert Lynd and his wife, Helen, set off for the modest sized city of Muncie in Indiana to assess the effects of social and cultural change on everyday life. Muncie was the archetypal small town, middle-of-the-road politically and in the Midwest geographically, qualities the Lynds captured perfectly in their fictitious name, Middletown. The study was funded by a religious foundation which was particularly interested in shifts in religious behaviour, but from the outset, the Lynds decided to look at life in Muncie in the round.◀

The researchers were immediately struck by how comprehensively and rapidly a town sixty miles away from the nearest sizeable city and a half a day's train ride from the nearest large city, was being transformed by change. They were particularly impressed by the way that "increasingly frequent and strong culture waves sweep over us from without, drenching us with the material and non-material habits of other centres" (Lynd and Lynd 1929: 5) They saw this process as centrally driven by the increasing diffusion of two technologies – cars and radios – the first offering physical release from the confines of the town, the second imaginative mobility. They pictured the radio

▶ researching in the round – Chapter 16, p. 303

"rolling back the horizons of Middletown for the bank clerk or the mechanic sitting at home and listening to a Philharmonic concert [...] or to President Coolidge bidding his father good night on the eve of election" (p. 269). And they were adamant that it was impossible to study "Middletown as a self-contained, self-starting community [...] when one watches these space-binding leisure-time inventions imported from without [...] reshaping the city" (p. 271).

The fact that Muncie had a population of only 35,000 made it possible for the Lynds to study it relatively intensively, using a range of methods from documentary research to personal observations and interviews. Larger towns and cities, however, posed formidable logistical problems for this intensive style of 'community study' (as it came to be called). Consequently, urban ethnographies of everyday media activity have tended to focus on particular neighbourhoods or locales within a city.◀

The Lynds' central focus on the role of communication technologies in restructuring everyday life gave added impetus to long-standing concerns about the range of cultural and informational resources which the popular media offered for meaning-making.

MEDIA AND PUBLIC CULTURE

Looking at the popular press – the major forum for information and debate before the launch of radio broadcasting in the 1920s – earlier commentators had seen the discussion of political affairs and public policy being steadily edged out by crime, scandal and human-interest stories. They lamented this movement towards the appeals and styles of entertainment and theatre because it seemed a move away from the rational public debate which democracy required, and mark to an eclipse of active citizenship by spectatorship.

sensationalism

In the ensuing debate on 'sensationalism' (as this new journalistic style came to be called), many contributors were content to rely on illustrative examples selected for their rhetorical effect. Within the emerging social sciences, however, there was a desire to calibrate this shift more precisely. Addressing the first meeting of the German Sociological Association in 1910, the country's leading sociologist, Max Weber, urged his audience to pick up "scissors and compass to measure the quantitative changes of newspaper contents during the last generation." Interestingly, however, he was careful to emphasise that these initial counts should be seen as the first stage of a wider research programme that "will proceed to qualitative [analyses]" (quoted in Hardt 1979: 181–182).

In the United States, however, Weber's programme was already well underway. In 1900, for example, Delos Wilcox had published an extensive study of the differences between 'serious' and 'yellow' (or 'tabloid') newspapers in one of America's most prestigious scholarly publications, the *Annals of the Academy of Political and Social Science*. His painstaking 'column by column' count of the space occupied by various categories of content, demonstrated that critics of the popular press were right (Wilcox 1900: 65). 'Yellow' newspapers carried more news of crime and vice, whereas 'serious' (or 'conservative' papers as he called them) carried more of the political and business news as well as letters and exchanges, as required by classical democratic models of the press as a public sphere (Habermas 1989[1962]). This argument is also encountered today in discussions over the 'tabloidization' of contemporary news and accusations of 'dumbing down' (see, e.g. Sparks and Tulloch 2000). Quantitative content analysis continues to play a central role in furnishing empirical evidence for these debates.

By no means all commentators saw the popular press as the enemy of democratic ideals, however. In a seminal paper on the human interest story, the Chicago sociologist, Helen Hughes, argued strongly that by incorporating the stories of ordinary people into the news, the popular press was rebuilding the empathy for strangers which modern life had eroded, and which a democracy that is based on equal respect and attention to plural voices required. In her view, "moral speculations are not evoked by news of court procedure; they take form on the reading of an intimate story that shows what the impact of law and convention

▶ ethnography – Chapter 9, p. 180

means as a private experience" (Hughes 1937: 81). Again, analysts have recently returned to these relations between personal testimony and democratic sensibilities in detailed studies of both tabloid news (e.g. Langer 1998) and a new wave of confessional television talk shows (e.g. Murdock 2000).◀

While some early social scientists were mapping popular representations using content analysis, others were addressing the second part of Weber's programme, namely, the development of detailed case studies◀ of particular texts. Critical analysts were particularly interested in how the themes and styles of popular media constructed the world in ways that supported prevailing relations of power. Siegfried Kracauer's 1927 essay, "The Little Shopgirls Go to the Movies", is a particularly good example of this tradition of ideology critique◀ in action. Movies, he argues "are babbling a rude secret, without really wanting to. In the endless sequence of films, a limited number of typical themes recur again and again [revealing] the sum of the society's ideologies, whose spell is broken by [...] interpretation" (Kracauer 1995[1963]: 295). This characterisation of the critic as a guerrilla fighter in the war of signs, revealing the power behind the pleasures, has been central to much subsequent work in textual analysis. However, proponents of this model of strong media have too often assumed that audiences are vulnerable or, at the very least, not properly equipped to see through the disguises of power without the help of a professional analyst.◀

Kracauer emphatically sees the 'little shop-girls' watching the films that he deconstructs as open to suggestion. After sitting absorbed in a film that reveals the soft heart concealed within the iron chest of a Berlin business man, for example, he imagines them learning to forget their exploitative and unequal working conditions and coming "to understand that their brilliant boss is made of gold on the inside as well" (p. 300). Interestingly, Roland Barthes employed almost exactly the same metaphor thirty years later in his 1957 book, *Mythologies*. He argued that it is only once "a typist earning twenty pound a month *recognizes herself* in the big wedding of the bourgeoisie" that ideology can be said to be fully effective (Barthes 1973[1957]: 154).

Barthes' semiotic approach to critiquing popular media went on to exert an enormous influence on later work in media and cultural studies. However, it was also subjected to fierce criticism from commentators who argued that it did scant justice to the complexities of women's relations to the media they consumed. This argument was later pursued in a range of detailed empirical work which fed into a more general celebration of the 'active audience'. Once again, however, far from marking a decisive break with the past, as some commentators have claimed, this general perspective has long roots in social science inquiry.

In 1913, Emilie Altenloh, a graduate student at the University of Heidelberg, published the doctoral thesis in sociology which she had conducted under the supervision of Alfred Weber (Max Weber's brother). Entitled *The Sociology of Cinema*, it was based on replies to over a thousand questionnaires given out to cinema-goers, supplemented by personal observations and interviews. In contrast to Kracauer, she sees the women at the centre of her study not as dupes of prevailing ideology, but as self-reflexive actors in the new social and imaginative spaces opened up by the cinema and the modern city. Their choices are crucially determined by the dynamics and pressures of a mature capitalist economy (see Hansen 1990). However, this sociological approach to audiences as actively negotiating mediated meanings and experiences, but embedded in wider social contexts that structured their responses in complex ways, had an uphill struggle. It was faced with the growing enthusiasm for the stimulus-response models being developed within individual psychology.

psychology

▶ reality television – Chapter 16

▶ case study – Chapter 14, p. 270

▶ ideology critique – Chapter 2, p. 42

▶ audiences as semiotic guerrilla fighters – Chapter 9, p. 183

QUESTIONS OF INFLUENCE AND EFFECTS

One of the leading proponents of this psychological model was John Watson. His 'behaviourist' approach saw all human action, from "jumping at a sound" to "writing books" as responses to environmental stimuli (1930: 6). He further insisted that only records of behaviour that was observed directly in the laboratory counted as relevant data in social inquiries wishing to claim the mantle of 'science'.

behaviourism: stimulus and response

As he conceded, however, "the social problems which psychology sometimes has to study" could "probably never be brought under laboratory control" (Watson 1924: 28). He had discovered this for himself when he set out in the summer of 1919 to evaluate the impact of a government-sponsored film on the sexual behaviour of young people, which warned that promiscuity could lead to venereal disease. After a monumental research effort involving over a thousand questionnaires, nearly a hundred personal interviews, and a number of observations of film screenings, he reluctantly concluded that his evidence suggested that "there is no indication that behaviour is modified significantly" (Lashley and Watson 1922: 216). A powerful stimulus, expressly designed to persuade, appeared to have had no discernible effect that could be detected by his measuring instruments. Unfortunately, this cautionary tale did not dissuade subsequent psychological researchers from pursuing the Holy Grail of direct media 'effects', both in and out of the laboratory.◄

Had later researchers looked closely at Watson's own description of his research, they would have come across a brief account of an incident that pointed to an alternative strategy of inquiry. Watson was disturbed to find that far from instilling the fear and disgust that the producers had hoped for, the film frequently provoked ribald and risqué comments. After one screening, members of the research team decided to talk "with a number of young men, loafers about the hotel lobby, and the like". They told the researchers that when "boys and girls who had seen the picture talked about it afterward [... flippancy and innuendo prevailed in their talk" (p. 204). Watson saw this 'talk' simply as an interesting supplement to his main data. For other researchers, however, listening attentively to casual talk and loafing around hotel lobbies and other places where people socialised spontaneously, provided the basis for an entirely different approach to investigating the role of media in everyday life.

LIVING WITH MEDIA: ACTIVE AUDIENCES

When Paul Cressey set out to study the place of movies in the lives of young men living in the predominantly Italian area of East Harlem in New York in the early 1930s, he declared his wish to "avoid the 'social vacuum fallacy' so prevalent in much [...] psychological research" and to "see the motion picture" in "relationship to all the other forces and influences which bear in upon the delinquent boy in these areas" and in the motion picture theatre (quoted in Jowett *et al.* 1996: 160). Cressey had already undertaken an acclaimed ethnography of a dance hall (later published as *Taxi Hall Dance)* for his master's degree in sociology at Chicago. He decided to approach this new study as an ethnography of an urban neighbourhood, drawing on systematic observation and open-ended interviews to construct a thick description◄ of cinema's role in the social and imaginative lives of the boys he was asked to study.

Cressey produced a path-breaking manuscript which suggested fertile links between the movies' equation of success and happiness with money and consumption, his subjects' sense of themselves, and the careers actually open to them. Crime, he argued, was not a simple 'effect' of crime films, but was produced in the cracks between consumer aspirations and blocked social opportunities. "For boys who have been restricted on all sides by poverty, the appeal of [the] expensive apartments, costly automobiles, and 'flashy' clothes" enjoyed by the gangsters in the films they watched is "in itself an invitation towards that type of activity and aspiration" (Jowett *et al.* 1996: 209).

► effects research – Chapter 8

► thick description – Chapter 14, p. 273

Unfortunately, the study was never published, and the unfinished draft lay unread in the archives and was rediscovered only recently. However, if we look at other ethnographies of young people undertaken in the same period, such as Frederick Thrasher's *The Gang* (1927), we see the same drive to anchor accounts of deviance in everyday experiences and to present young people as actively creating their own meanings. Some of these meanings (as Thrasher argued) might form the basis for a distinctive subculture with its own rituals and emblems of identity.

Again, these early studies of youth subcultures,◄ together with the preference for ethnographic modes of inquiry and the insistence on placing everyday media activity in its wider contexts, have all been enormously influential within academic studies of audiences and consumption over recent decades. This has particularly been the case within cultural studies.◄ Prompted by the early ethnographic work of the Birmingham Centre, researchers have returned to the tradition of inquiry pioneered by Cressey, Thrasher and others. Now as then, however, there have been relatively few full ethnographies based on contact and observation sustained over several years. For practical reasons, most researchers have had to settle for qualitative studies compressed into much shorter time periods, using open-ended interviews, focus groups or personal documents to access grounded interpretations and everyday experiences. Given Lazarsfeld's reputation as an arch number-cruncher, it is ironic that three of the most important efforts to develop qualitative methods and apply them to the study of audience activity should have come either from researchers working on projects he helped to set up, or from his close collaborators.

The value of conducting detailed interviews with respondents had been amply demonstrated in a study of public reaction to Orson Welles' 1938 radio dramatisation of H.G. Wells' *The War of the Worlds*. Welles, who already had a reputation for breaking established generic rules, decided to present this story of a Martian invasion of Earth in a form that was as close as possible to the conventions of radio news reporting. Some listeners believed it was a newscast and panicked. Although the leader of the research project, Hadley Cantril, was a psychologist, he saw very clearly that personal differences could not explain the complex variations in responses to the programme, as described by the 138 people his research team interviewed. Instead, he sought to account for differences in terms of inequalities in the amounts and types of social and cultural capital◄ people possessed, such as how familiar they were with contemporary artistic conventions, and whether they had someone they trusted they could ask for advice.

Read in this way, Cantril's explanatory framework is closer to the account that the French sociologist, Pierre Bourdieu, gives of the social basis of cultural taste in his highly influential book *Distinction* (published in English in 1984). To characterise it as simply another exercise in 'selective influence', as one widely read American textbook on media research does (Lowery and DeFleur 1983: 83), is to ignore how thoroughly the study emphasises the 'social' in social psychology.

Cantril's *Invasion From Mars*, published in 1940, was the first book produced by the Radio Research Project, directed by Paul Lazarsfeld. The following year, Herta Herzog, one of Cantril's co-authors and a member of Lazarsfeld's project team, published a path-breaking study of women's relations with daytime radio soap operas. The study was based primarily on personal interviews with one hundred women living in the Greater New York area, initially open-ended, but later using a prepared questionnaire. This work is often presented as an early example of 'uses and gratifications' research.◄ Herzog certainly uses these words, but again, to see it simply in these terms is to miss its more radical implications. Like Emilie Altenloh, almost thirty years before, what emerges if we read the data carefully is an account of women's strategies for coming to terms with the expectations, inequalities and

► subcultures – Chapter 11, p. 210
► cultural studies – p. 65
► social and cultural capital – Chapter 8, p. 169
► uses and gratifications research – Chapter 8, p. 157

buried resentments of domesticity, and of how the imaginary worlds of the soaps intersect with the mundane realities of everyday life. As such, it stands as an early precursor of the very influential qualitative work on women as audiences for romantic fictions and television soaps that followed the emergence of feminist scholarship in the 1970s.◀

Another of Lazarsfeld's intellectual colleagues, Robert Merton, also used personal interviews to good effect in a study of news magazine readership in a small town (Merton 1949). After preliminary work, he was intrigued to find that influential people in the community approached the magazine with very different purposes. 'Local' influentials, who had grown up in the town and owed their position to their local social connections, showed very little interest in stories dealing with national or international affairs. In comparison, 'cosmopolitan' influentials, who had come from elsewhere and owed their reputation to nationally recognised qualifications, tended to gravitate to these items first.

local and cosmopolitan social types

Interestingly, it was exactly this last group that Edward Ross had had in mind when he called in 1910 for the establishment of a newspaper endowed by public subscription to promote serious news and debate. He admitted that it was unlikely to attract a general readership. But he hoped that "it would inform the teachers, preachers, lecturers and public men, who speak to the people eye to eye"(Ross 1910: 311) This describes exactly the 'two-step flow' model of communications that Merton and Lazarsfeld developed in their work. However, to see Merton's work on 'locals' and 'cosmopolitans' simply in these terms is once again to miss its full implications. Merton's emphasis on variations in cultural and social capital, and on differences in the strategies of distinction and advantage pursued by different social segments, prefigures Bourdieu's work. In this regard, Merton can be seen as one of pioneers in establishing a distinctively sociological approach to differences in media consumption and cultural tastes.

Merton also played a major role in developing a method that has been central to recent work on active audiences – focus group research.◀ He developed the technique which he called 'the focussed interview' during his involvement in wartime studies of military motivation and morale. Just after the Second World War, he published a paper outlining its uses and rationales in one of the major professional journals of sociology (Merton and Kendall 1946). At the time, however, the growing ascendancy of quantitative methods tended to discourage academic researchers from pursuing its possibilities. It was taken up within market research (see Morrison 1998), but it is only recently that it has re-emerged as a major technique in social-scientific studies of audiences.

Sometimes, however, direct interviewing proved impossible because of shortage of time, limited resources or difficulties of access. In these instances, researchers wishing to work with qualitative materials fell back on the 'frozen speech' embodied in personal documents. We have already noted how W.I. Thomas built his study of Polish migrants to America around collections of existing family letters. Where there were no existing documents, researchers set out to create them.◀ Herbert Blumer, another leading figure in the Chicago sociology department, collected "a number of autobiographical accounts dealing with motion-picture experiences" (Blumer and Hauser 1933: 20). He then used these as the basis for a study eventually published as *Motion Pictures and Youth*. As with Cressey's study (which formed part of the same Payne Fund research programme),◀ Blumer's materials, with their strong emphasis on situated experience, led him to emphasize the importance of "social milieu" and "social background" in forming film preferences and organising responses (p. 202).

At the same time, the scope of Blumer's study was limited by the project's focus on the possible links between the cinema and juvenile crime. A

▶ qualitative studies of women audiences – Chapter 9, p. 178

▶ focus group research – Chapter 14, p. 271

▶ autobiographies and other documents – Chapter 14, p. 274

▶ Payne Fund studies – Chapter 9, p. 173

more open account of the relations between cinema-going, everyday life, and aspirations was offered by J.P. Mayer in his 1948 study, *British Cinemas and Their Audiences*. He had hit on the bright idea of collecting cinema autobiographies by placing an advertisement in one of the major magazines for film fans, *Picturegoer*, asking people to write to him. Ien Ang was later to use the same technique to collect Dutch women's accounts of their experiences of watching the American television soap, *Dallas*, for her very influential study, *Watching Dallas* (Ang 1985).

Mayer freely acknowledges his debt to Blumer's pioneering efforts, but uses his own material to explore a range of themes not tackled in Blumer's work. These include the central role of films, particularly American films and their stars, in offering models for personal style and consumption. As one of the women who wrote to Mayer explained,

> When I was 17 I saw a star (I forget her name) about whom the boy I was with said: 'She has the most lovely feet and her shoes are always beautiful.' I had nice feet and made a vow that the same should be said of me. I don't know whether it ever was, but I always bought the nicest shoes and stockings I could afford and shoes are still my pet luxury.
>
> (quoted in Mayer 1948: 25)

Mayer claimed in the introduction to the study that despite the self-selecting nature of his sample, his "anonymous contributors speak for twenty million or more" addressing us, the readers, directly in their own words, rather than "through the mouth of the 'superior' intellectual who by chance or choice went to a better school, to university" (p. 11). This celebration of the authenticity of everyday talk and its ability to offer the analyst direct, unmediated access to 'real' experiences and feelings is a blind spot comparable to the wholesale rejection of such evidence by some quantitative researchers. This inclination to romanticise 'ordinary' lives runs through much later work on everyday life and media consumption within cultural studies and qualitative sociology like a goodwill message embedded in a stick of seaside rock. Its impetus is generous and democratic in spirit, but by playing down the researcher's responsibility to reinterpret people's own accounts and to tease out the hidden threads that bind biographies to histories, strategies to structures, it blunts the critical edge of social investigation.

REACTIONS, RUPTURES AND REDISCOVERIES

The account offered here has deliberately concentrated on work conducted in the first half of the twentieth century in order to show that current research in media and communications continually draws on traditions of social science inquiry which are longer, richer and more varied than many contemporary writers imagine. However, there is no doubt that the majority of research in the field has been conducted since 1950.◀

Along with other specialisms, media and communication research benefitted enormously from the rapid growth in social-scientific research both inside and outside the universities in the post-war years. But it was also profoundly shaped by the political climate created by the onset of the Cold War between the United States and the Soviet Union. This ideological conflict dominated the intellectual landscape. In the US, the obsessive hunt for communist 'subversives' in cultural and intellectual life, spearheaded by Senator McCarthy's investigations into 'un-American' activities, had a profoundly chilling effect on scholarship, and it comprehensively discouraged the pursuit of critical inquiry.

The dominant model of the social order during that period, structural functionalism, fitted this climate of caution perfectly. The principal architect of the position was the American sociologist, Talcott Parsons, whose key book, *The Social System*, published in 1951 (in the early years of the Cold War), saw every social institution as having a particular role or 'function' in maintaining social stability and cementing consensus. Media and communications systems were assigned a central role in this gluing-together process.

structural functionalism

▶ history of media and communication research – Chapter 19, p. 355

This model of society as a smoothly functioning, self-correcting organism was itself highly functional politically. It presented post-war America as a society that had successfully transcended the class conflicts that the Soviets (following Marx) saw as the major driving force of historical change. It was also a useful intellectual weapon in the fierce global-wide struggle for the hearts and minds of citizens in the former colonial territories that had achieved political independence after the war. It allowed the United States to present the 'American way' of doing things as a self-evidently superior path to 'modernisation', both materially and morally, one that would deliver social integration as well as economic improvement. In line with this view, degrees of 'modernisation' came to be measured in terms of how closely a country approximated to the United States in terms of the relative distribution of selected consumer goods, including communications goods.

Although the long shadow cast by the ideological and military struggle between the world's two great superpowers silenced or deflected many sceptical voices within the American academy, there were exceptions, most notably C. Wright Mills. Mills had studied sociology at the University of Wisconsin under Edward Ross (whose blistering attack on the press we looked at earlier). He shared his mentor's radical populist perception that the democratic rights of 'ordinary' people were continually blocked by entrenched centres of power intent on retaining their privileges and extending their influence. This led him to argue that, far from being agents of organic unity and voluntary consensus, as Parsons supposed, mediated communications were central to the play of power. We cannot, he argued, "merely assume that some set of values, or legitimations, *must* prevail lest a social structure come apart" (Mills 1970[1959]: 46). On the contrary, if there is

> a unified symbol sphere, one monopolised by certain master symbols, [it] is more likely to be the result of a monopoly of channels of communications, and of forceful tabooing of certain countersymbols, than the result of any harmonious institutional basis. It is more likely to be imposed than to grow.
>
> (Gerth and Mills 1954: 297).

Mills went on to develop this point five years later, in his most influential book, *The Power Elite* (1959b[1956]). In it, he presented America, not as the ideal democracy of official Cold War rhetoric, but as "a naked and arbitrary power", controlled by the interlocking interests of industry, the military, and government, in which "the second-rate mind is in command of the ponderously spoken platitude" and "its men of decision enforce their often crackpot ideas on world reality" (Mills 1959b[1956]: 360–361). Measured against the scale of this perceived threat to democratic ideals, it is not surprising that Mills found that most work by his colleagues in the social sciences fell some way short of the challenge.

In his manifesto for engaged inquiry, *The Sociological Imagination* (1959a), he argued that the social sciences are distinguished from other forms of commentary precisely by their "capacity to range from the most impersonal and remote transformations to the most intimate features of the human self – and to see the relations between the two" (Mills 1970[1959]: 14). This required all aspects of social life to be placed squarely in their full historical and structural context. Their failure to do this was his principal complaint against Merton and Lazarsfeld, his colleagues at Columbia, where he was then working.

the sociological imagination

If Parsons' bland, empty categories represented the betrayal of 'grand theory', Mills saw Lazarsfeld and Merton's concentration on 'theories of the middle range' (working concepts and models like the 'two-step' flow model of communications) as prime examples of the derelictions of what he called 'abstracted empiricism'. How, he asked, could Lazarsfeld, in his well-known study of the 1940 election campaign in Erie County Ohio, *The People's Choice* (Lazarsfeld *et al.* 1944), focus so enthusiastically on voting behaviour and still make "no reference to the party machinery for 'getting out the vote,' or indeed to any political institutions" (Mills 1970[1959]: 63).

theories of the middle range

abstracted empiricism

As noted earlier, though, this characterisation of Lazarsfeld as an essentially conservative figure does him less than justice. In a speech he made soon after arriving in America from Vienna (where he had been active in the socialist movement), Lazarsfeld described himself as 'a Marxist on leave'. Mills clearly felt that this leave had become permanent. However, a careful reading of Lazarsfeld's writings reveals strong continuities with his radical youth. In an essay written jointly with Merton, he had presented a strong critique of corporate control over communications, arguing that "increasingly, the chief power groups, among which organised business occupies the most spectacular place [seem] to have reduced direct exploitation, achieved largely by disseminating propaganda through the mass media of communication" (Lazarsfeld and Merton 1960[1948]: 493).

Mills died in 1962, before one of the other major challenges to structural functionalism, the revival of phenomenology, had got fully into its stride. Had he lived to comment, his observations would have been highly critical, since the leaders of this movement signally failed to take account of "the historical structures in which the milieux of everyday life are organised", or to relate biographies to histories as he had advocated (Mills 1970[1959]: 175). The attempt to build on the phenomenological approach to everyday life, as pioneered by Alfred Schütz, was led by Harold Garfinkel. He called his work ethnomethodology because it was based on closely observed accounts of the 'methods' that people ('ethnos') use in everyday encounters. In many ways, the research collected in his best-known book, *Studies in Ethnomethodology* (1967), can be read as an attempt to radicalise Parsons by interrogating the tacit agreements that his model of social consensus depends on, but which he had taken for granted (see Sharrock and Anderson 1986: Ch. 3). By exposing the provisionality of the rules and schemas governing personal interaction, and detailing how they were continually recreated and reaffirmed in everyday social encounters, Garfinkel presents 'ordinary' people as the true architects of social order and social change. In this conception, "social structure cannot refer to anything more than members' everyday sense [of it] since it has no identity which is independent of that sense" (Filmer *et al.* 1972: 54).

ethnomethodology

This radically reductionist account of social structure, with its exclusive focus on the micro-politics of everyday life, could not offer a concerted challenge to structural functionalism, because it refused to examine the structural sedimentation of institutional power. Such challenges were beginning to gather momentum elsewhere, however. When the political consensus was finally broken open in the 1960s – by the Civil Rights Movement, the opposition to the American war in Vietnam, and the international student movements – critical traditions of inquiry began to gain increasing currency and support. Two intellectual movements, in particular, have had a major impact on contemporary work in media and communications – the revival of critical political economy and the development of cultural studies.

Although some of the key figures in the return to political economy, like Dallas Smythe and Herbert Schiller, had trained as economists, their political allegiances were always to the older tradition of inquiry with its deep roots in long-standing debates about the relations between economic organisation, cultural and social life, and the common good. From the mid-1960s onwards, writers like Herbert Schiller returned to this central focus on the relations between the production and circulation of material goods and the constitution of the good life and the good society. Borrowing from Marx and from earlier radical commentators like Upton Sinclair, they developed a powerful critique of the role of the American media and communications industries in supporting prevailing inequalities of power and benefit, both at home and overseas.

critical political economy

At the same time, the emerging field of cultural studies◀ was exploring how the general dynamics of capitalist cultural production worked themselves out in styles and representations which were carried by everyday artefacts and in the strategies devised by audiences and consumers in constructing their own meanings and uses. From the outset, cultural studies was

▶ cultural studies – also Chapter 2, p. 46

a point of intersection between two intellectual traditions – ideology critique and ethnographies of everyday cultural practice. Consequently, within the corpus of literature it has produced, accounts of powerful media have continually rubbed up against celebrations of audience refusal and resistance. Analyses of the unequal distribution of vernacular and radical discourses and meaning systems (as in David Morley's influential work on *The 'Nationwide' Audience* (1980)) further attempted to mediate between the two traditions.

ON NOT REINVENTING THE WHEEL

For many analysts, including myself, illuminating the exercise of power and structural constraints and exploring the possibilities for change, remain the central aims of a critical social-scientific approach to media and communication. As I have tried to indicate, in pursuing this task, we have a rich stock of concepts and methods to draw upon. Their originators are not distant figures to be consigned to dusty back rooms in the museum of ideas. They remain our contemporaries. We still confront the central questions they grappled with, and their search for answers still has much to teach us. We are part of a continuing conversation about the structure and meaning of modern times and the ways they are changing. They stand at our shoulder, advising, carping, urging us on. To refuse their invitation to debate is to condemn ourselves to regularly reinventing the wheel.

PART

II Systematics

PROCESSES OF COMMUNICATION

An implicit model of communication

The bulk of media studies have been premised on a commonsensical and often implicit model of communication that centers attention on senders, messages, and recipients. That is in spite of the fact that most current research recognizes problems of segregating the various stages of the process of communication, and of divorcing media and communicative practices from their social and cultural contexts.

Part II employs this sequential model of communication as a structuring device that facilitates a review of earlier empirical as well as theoretical contributions. The chapters, however, also consider how various conceptions of, and evidence about, one stage of communication reflect on the process as a whole. In particular, Chapter 10 explores the interrelated stages and levels of mass and interpersonal, and online as well as offline communication, whereas Chapters 11 and 12 cover research on the relationship between media and their cultural and historical contexts, respectively.

Media organizations

The two chapters on media organizations examine the complex process of producing media content – on the one hand, news; on the other hand, fiction and other entertainments. Reviewing classic studies and illustrating concrete field research of production practices, the presentations draw attention, among other things, to differences between media types – print, broadcast, and networked – and between national and international levels of media organization. Finally, each chapter considers the changing role of users in processes of media production and coproduction, 'prosumption,' or 'produsage.'

- *Entertainment production* (Chapter 4). The first chapter reviews the several interrelated levels of production and organization that shape entertainment media products, including the international economy, national media systems, technological developments, and professional work routines. The importance of these levels is exemplified with reference to cable television production and the process of buying advertising on US television networks.
- *News production* (Chapter 5). The second chapter revisits the distinction in previous research between news production as either a selection or a construction of social reality, elaborating on the relevance and some of the limitations of classic concepts such as gatekeeping and news values. Also addressed is the variety of news genres, sometimes overlooked in an emphasis on the study of 'hard' news. And, the chapter considers the state of online journalism, including its ingredients of user-generated content.

Media texts

The messages of communication have been studied as both 'texts' to be interpreted and 'content' to be counted by different theoretical and methodological traditions. Fiction has primarily lent itself to qualitative approaches, as derived from the study of literature and other arts. Factual genres, in their turn, have more commonly been examined through a mixture of quantitative and qualitative approaches. In addition, digital media have posed new research questions concerning the languages and narratives that are the concrete vehicles of computer games, blogs, and other genres, and which enter into 'intertextual' networks.

- *Media fact* (Chapter 6). This chapter addresses both quantitative content analysis and qualitative discourse analysis of media texts. The chapter reviews developments within content analysis in recent decades, and compares different varieties of discourse studies, including approaches to visual media content. One of the example analyses explores still images and their interrelations with verbal texts.
- *Media fiction* (Chapter 7). Following a brief account of quantitative studies of fiction, the next chapter gives special attention to semiotic, structuralist, and narratological approaches to media texts. Referring to classic feature movies – *The Big Sleep* and *Die Hard* – the chapter shows how various models of analysis can be applied to different media, genres, and modalities, including computer games and sound media.

Media audiences

From the beginnings of the field, audiences have been a central concern and object of analysis, and have been studied most often by quantitative social science through survey and experimental methodologies. In recent decades, more research with a textual or qualitative orientation has come to examine audiences empirically. The resulting convergence of approaches to 'reception' and 'effects,' respectively, holds additional potentials for studies of user-driven genres and networked communication generally.

- *Media effects* (Chapter 8). After a brief history of the notion of 'effects,' this chapter summarizes the multiple traditions of inquiry that have developed since the 1930s. The various contributions are presented in a systematic that integrates multiple stages of communication and influence, and short-term as well as long-term effects.
- *Media reception* (Chapter 9). The following chapter begins by conferring recognized 'milestones' of the effects tradition with important contributions to qualitative reception studies. Next, the chapter reviews different varieties of reception analysis, and considers the potentials and problems of 'ethnography' as practiced in media studies.

Media contexts

Three chapters address the relationship between media and their social, cultural, and historical contexts, emphasizing the communication component of media and communication studies. Whereas this aspect has been recognized, to varying degrees, in earlier research, processes of digitalization as well as globalization have reconfigured key constituents and conditions of communication: media, texts, and contexts; senders and receivers; and the social organization of space and time.

- *Social contexts* (Chapter 10). The first of the three chapters on contexts confronts some of the fundamental issues that digital and mobile media pose for research, revisiting the mass-interpersonal and online-offline divides of the field. Beyond their *contribution* within contexts of social interaction, media also serve to *constitute* contexts of both communication and action across space and time.

- *Cultural contexts* (Chapter 11). The next chapter takes up the specific embedding of media in cultural practices at various levels of social organization – from the local to the global level. Raising issues of both identity and power, this area of research has witnessed a number of theoretically as well as politically motivated controversies.
- *Historical contexts* (Chapter 12). The last chapter on contexts traces the place of media technologies in the long history of human communication. Perhaps surprisingly, 'the media' is a recent notion, dating from the 1960s. The chapter considers the history of both 'communication' and particular 'media', and reflects on concepts and methodologies for studying contemporary media in historical perspective.

Determination in the first instance

Each chapter in this part of the Handbook identifies a number of factors that shape and affect processes of communication, within media organizations, through media discourses, and in diverse contexts of communication. A central premise is that each individual factor – whether technological, economic, political, or cultural – may exercise a determination in the first instance◄ (Hall, 1983), but not a determination in the final instance. Neither the products nor the practices of communication are the outcome of any simple causality. Different traditions of research have identified, and have tried to interpret and explain, empirical variations of how media operate and communicative practices unfold. Here, the traditions are brought together and compared as part of a systematics of media and communication studies.

► determination in the first instance – Chapter 1, p. 2

4 The production of entertainment media

Amanda D. Lotz and Horace Newcomb

- an outline of the main *levels of analysis* in production research – from *political economy* to *professional routines*
- a *review* with examples of previous studies at each level of analysis
- a description of the diverse *sources of evidence* and of relevant *methods of analysis*
- two *illustrations*: the production of a cable television series, and the process of buying advertising on US television networks

INTRODUCTION

Throughout the last decade, an earlier bias of media studies toward textual or audience analysis has been righted somewhat by rapid expansion in research focused on the structures that affect, and the institutions that create, media and their content. Such studies are commonly classified as 'production studies' or 'media industry studies.' This chapter focuses on methods for examining the production of entertainment media in particular. Whether addressing a particular show, the negotiations between a studio and a distributor, an industrial practice such as dubbing, or a sector of a national media industry, studies of entertainment industries and production practices explore the ways in which various creative personnel work within determined and structured systems that, nevertheless, allow for variations within routines. The points of tension between standardization and differentiation are of equal significance and equally instructive in exploring the significance of media entertainment. It is necessary, then, to provide a more thorough and detailed analysis of production practices than the usual generalizations about 'media factories' that are presumed to churn out endless reiterations of mindless fare.

One approach is outlined in Bordwell's concept of 'historical poetics' (Bordwell, 1989). Under that category, he suggests that it is important to explore options open to media makers at given points in time and in specific social contexts, attending to industrial, economic, and regulatory factors. While Bordwell tends to focus on those options generating the standardized elements found in much mass-mediated material, we believe it is possible to discover important manipulations of production processes that indicate the relative autonomy or circumscribed agency of individuals, groups, even organizations within media industries. What this suggests, most importantly, is that any study of the production of media entertainment must recognize multiple types of influence. Factors ranging from policy formation to the application of new technologies may affect the production of any particular instance of media entertainment. While research taking account of multiple causal elements usually provides stronger explanations, it often remains the case that

relative autonomy

circumscribed agency

specific instances of production studies privilege particular aspects over others. In some cases, this results in reductive assertions about causation or influence, although in most instances it means simply that one factor is taken as dominant, overdetermining◀ all others. These factors and the relations among them can be described as 'levels of analysis.' We emphasize that this term should not imply a universally effective hierarchy of influence or determination. But it is the case that such a categorization of influence works from more general to more specific sites and applications. The most effective production research will indicate an awareness of the multiple levels and seek to identify the interdependence of the influences, even if focusing upon particular cases, settings, and systems.

LEVELS OF ANALYSIS

National and international political economy and policy

The production of particular media artefacts within specific industrial systems obviously takes place within more general contexts. Among the most influential works at this level are those exploring differences between commercial broadcasting or film industries and media reliant on various forms of state support (e.g., Blumler, 1992; Katz and Wedell, 1977; Schiller, 1969). Although analyses of production practices generally acknowledge such differences, broad assumptions rather than detailed analysis commonly guide the study of the relations between policy and production. This is so, in part, because descriptive and source material related to media policy often focuses on generalizations rather than cases, while detailed case studies take the constraints of political economy for granted. Overlooked in both models is the fact that individual productions are enabled as well as constrained by general conditions. Varied responses to those conditions illuminate the complexity of the larger structures, reminding us that while media production is indeed a modern, factory

commercial and state-supported media

product, the differences among the products are as telling as their similarities. Nevertheless, a number of policy works provide useful contextual information for production research. Among them, Alexander, *et al.* (2003), Hoskins, *et al.* (1998), and Moran (1996) offer extensive overviews of contemporary media industry policies that can be applied analytically.

Some studies do, in fact, bring together the macro-levels of policy and economic structure with analyses of cases. They include explorations of the ways in which media products are affected by social problems, such as 'censorship' or 'violence.' Doherty (1999) and Gardner (1987) provide examples of the first topic, showing how particular American films were produced before and during periods of heavy social control. Cowan (1979) focuses on engagements with policy by individuals (e.g., Norman Lear) and institutions (e.g., The Writers Guild of America) with regard to sex and violence on television, and shows how production strategies were affected by congressional actions mandating a 'family hour' for commercial television.

As these publications suggest, a major approach to studying the relationship between policy and production has been historical.◀ Boddy (1990), for example, explores relations among television executives, the US Congress, and television critics in the 1950s. He carefully establishes how, in the struggle among these groups, industry executives managed to secure their economic interests through legislative and judicial decision-making. The outcome of these battles led to major industry developments, such as the shift from 'live' television production in New York to filmed programming from Hollywood, resulting in fundamental changes in aesthetics, altered production practices, and ultimately the distinctive place of television fiction in US culture.

Or, consider more recent work that connects changes in the norms of media production with macro-level industrial adjustments. McMurria's (2003) study of shifts in long-form television production showed how changing competitive norms, globalization, and international trade

► overdetermination – Chapter 1, p. 5

► historical studies of media – Chapter 12

policy have affected the content and reduced the quantity of long-form television. Focusing more on the policy side, Holt (2003) examined the consequences of US deregulation, specifically the phase-out of the Financial Interest and Syndication rules. The elimination of these rules, which prevented networks from owning much of the content that they distributed, led to self-dealing and other questionable production and distribution practices within media conglomerates.

Methodologically, all these works have depended on the analysis of archival data.◀ While public policy records are usually freely available, corporate papers have sometimes been deposited in reference archives, making access for researchers relatively simple. In other cases, such materials may be proprietary and access severely restricted. These records are essential for production research, because the documents contain evidence both of conflicting points of view and of concrete decision-making related to particular media artefacts.

Specific industrial contexts and practices

Historical approaches have also been prominent in research examining the institutional configuration of media industries, but here analysis is focused more precisely on specific industrial practices. Among the strongest examples is *The Classical Hollywood Cinema* (Bordwell, *et al.*, 1985), which examined the development of the Hollywood film industry and the resulting reliance on a particular narrative style, as indicated in the title.◀ The study tracks the establishment of regularized industrial strategies, consequent divisions of labor, instrumental applications of new technologies, and other features of the Hollywood film factories. It suggests that, after a period of experimentation, the US film industry narrowed into certain industrial operations that were developed in the service of particular narrative conventions. The analysis also demonstrates how this general pattern of regularization was realized in particular films. The central argument points to the reduction of preferred narrative strategies and, ultimately, of the styles, genres, and meanings within an industry that was increasingly successful on its own terms. The ideological result was the establishment of a particular cultural meaning of 'cinema' to the exclusion or marginalization of alternative forms.

Here again, researchers rely heavily on primary historical records – contracts, inter-office memoranda, extant interviews, handbooks, production manuals, instructional pamphlets, variously revised scripts, and story conference memoranda recording decision-making processes. These are explored in order to describe, analyze, and contextualize the actual production practices involved in film, television, and other media-making. Because sustained archival research is needed to uncover more evidence, and because the study of media entertainment, in particular, is of relatively recent development, new histories continue to refine our knowledge of much needed background and circumstances. Hilmes (1990), for example, provided new information regarding the shifting arrangements among media industries, including the radio industry, which have altered the cultural definition of 'film' and 'television' in the US.

Such work need not be historical, however, and in recent years many scholars have turned to studying contemporary media industries and their practices. Gitlin's (1994[1983]) *Inside Prime Time* provides a classic example. Gitlin researched television network practices in the early 1980s to offer a detailed account of the multitude of negotiations that are part of the creative process. The narrower focus of industry-level studies begins to allow somewhat different sources than feasible at the level of national or international political economyand policy. Researchers of contemporary conditions generally have much less access to the types of archival documentation that historical researchers might secure, but interviews and observation may be available.◀ The content and slant of the interviews can also be checked

▶ archival data – Chapter 12, p. 231

▶ Hollywood cinema – see also Chapter 7, p. 133

▶ qualitative interviewing and participating observation – Chapter 14, p. 270

and compared by reference to contemporary trade press accounts◄ and attendance at meetings of industry professionals.◄

Gitlin's study captures the operation of an entire industry sector – the US broadcast television industry – at a particular moment in time. In a different case, still at the industry level, Havens (2008) addresses international television distribution. His research seeks to understand the complexities of distribution and its implications for what media industries produce by examining how and why concrete television entertainment texts circulate around the globe as they do. Havens combines interviews with distributors and buyers with fieldwork at major distribution markets such as NATPE and MIPCOM to inform his study.

Caldwell's (2006) research on below-the-line (craft and technical) production workers offers another case of research at the industry level. Caldwell endeavored to explain how the introduction of new production tools has affected traditional models of work and relations among crew members. In addition to interviews with production workers and observations of the process of production, Caldwell analyzed demo tapes to explore how they teach others in the industry about new videographic techniques and, thus, function in the establishment of new aesthetic norms.

A final example illustrates how industry-level analysis can take research beyond more generalized descriptions. Montgomery (1989) focused on the different ways in which interest groups engage television networks in order to gain a more favorable representation. Using interview and ethnographic methods, as well as analysis of records and contracts, she also examined individual television texts to show how these groups variously succeeded or failed in their attempts to alter detailed television production practices. Interest groups have used strategies, such as boycotts or threats of boycotts, which recognize the role played by political economy and government policies in media production.

interest groups

► trade press, p. 79
► professional meetings, p. 80

Particular organizations: Studios, production companies, networks

Studies of institutional relations often rely on the next more specific level of analysis, exploring the connection between a media organization and the industrial configuration in which it operates. Textual analysis◄ of individual works or collections of films and television programs is much more prominent at this level, frequently with an emphasis on genre and format as indicative of an organizational 'style.' An outstanding example of this type of analysis is Schatz (1988), who focused on regularized and systemic aspects of the film industry, using sources and approaches similar to other histories of cinema. In using archival sources, however, his primary method was the case study,◄ and by focusing on several studio organizations, the production of particular films, and the roles of powerful individual studio heads, he placed greater emphasis on human agency and documented important variations. The findings, again, indicate greater diversity within 'the studio system' than is sometimes assumed in studies of the general institutional arrangements.

the studio system of film

For television, a primary example is Feuer, *et al.* (1984), a study of the MTM production company, which argues for the existence of a 'signature style' associated with a number of its productions. The identification of that style enabled the authors to describe variations within the general structures of both genre (the situation/domestic/workplace comedy) and the US television industry as such. Cunningham (1988) provides a similar example of house style from Australian television. Such studies must rely heavily on company histories and production case studies in order to support the textual analyses that identify particular elements as a distinctive 'style.' In addition, they may make use of interviews and observations when access to individuals and ongoing productions can be arranged.

house style in television – see also Ellis (1982)

Studies at this level might not attend so much to questions about texts and style, however, and instead address how the culture of a

► textual analysis – Chapters 6 and 7
► case study – Chapter 14, p. 270

media organization can lead to certain textual qualities in its output. For example, Perren (2001–2) examined how the independent film studio Miramax developed niche marketing and low-budget production strategies that revised Hollywood aesthetics, economics, and structure during the 1990s. In a public-service context, Born (2005) used sociological and anthropological methods to examine the operation of the vast broadcast institution of the British Broadcasting Corporation. She relied on access to meetings and as many as 220 interviews with those working in and contracting for the BBC over eight years to develop a richly informed examination of the internal workings of the BBC and the organizational politics that contributed to various programming strategies and initiatives.

Individual productions

A yet more specific level of analysis focuses on the creation of individual artefacts – films, television programs or series, computer games, etc. Here, for example, we would include works exploring 'the making of' particular films and other media products such as Carringer's *The Making of Citizen Kane* (1996). Often, such works are designed to be more popular in appeal, providing behind-the-scenes information for fans or interested observers. Their popularity, however, does not necessarily diminish their usefulness for more complex research, and they may be cited as evidence in any of the other types of analysis described above. And, when such cases are examined within a more generalized theoretical framework, they can result in production studies of great analytical power. Indeed, scholarly works often offer similar information, making them informative for general readers as well as for researchers. Part of the strength of Gitlin's work, addressed above, was his comparisons of specific productions in order to show both variation and similarity within the production process and in the resulting product. Relying on interview and observation methods, combined with close analysis of both production techniques and narrative strategies, Gitlin used his cases to support more far-reaching inferences regarding the role of television in American culture.

'the making of'

One of the most significant examples of work focused on an individual television production is D'Acci's *Defining Women: The Case of Cagney and Lacey* (1994). In this book, D'Acci traces the development of the program, explaining the roles of individual writer-producers, actors, studio executives, network heads, programmers, publicity teams, and other participants. She also examines the responses of critics, viewers, and organized interest groups, showing how their commentary contributed to keeping the series on the air, in addition to continuing the debate on television portrayals of women. By combining this wealth of background material with her own detailed textual analysis, D'Acci presents one of the most complete pictures of the production of a fictional television program to date.

social roles in production units

Levine (2001) offers another useful set of categories of analysis to aid researchers studying a particular production. In some ways, her categories mirror the levels of analysis offered here, although her focus is clearly the individual production. She recommends five 'categories of analysis' (production constraints, production environment, production routines and practices, production of characters and stories, and the audience in production). Her article illustrates how to examine these categories through a case study of the US daytime soap opera *General Hospital*. Her rubric reminds us of the need to acknowledge factors that we place at the level of national/international political economy and industry levels when analyzing an individual production.

The scope of individual production studies has been expanded in recent years as transmedia storytelling◄ – narratives spread across various media – has become increasingly popular both for fans and as an industrial strategy. Jenkins (2007) argues that "transmedia storytelling represents a process where integral elements of a fiction get dispersed systematically across multiple delivery channels for the purpose of creating a unified and coordinated entertainment

► transmedia storytelling and intertextuality – Chapter 10, p. 192

experience." Indeed, just as internet distribution has made boundaries among media increasingly porous – as it enables us to experience much media content outside of the platform for which it was initially created – so too has it necessitated that the study of a particular production attend to all of its storytelling extensions. Thus, *Lost* is not only a television series, but also a novel, a variety of websites, and an alternate reality game, to name just a few of the other media that extend its storytelling.

Little scholarship has yet considered transmedia storytelling through an industrial lens. Meehan's (1991) examination of the political economy of *Batman* provides one illustration of how this has been considered in the past, while recent work from Johnson (2011) focuses broadly on the transmedia storytelling of media franchises with considerable insight into many of the levels of analysis suggested here. Nevertheless, we can imagine the contours of other studies. Perhaps the key question is how media industries create transmedia possibilities and how such industrial norms, next, affect storytelling properties. Clearly, decision-making at the corporate level, where executives recognize or are persuaded of the potential of these kinds of extensions, would be central to the analysis. Existing corporate practices, such as transforming a particular narrative into a theme park ride, offer examples of how financial interests lie at the heart of such large-scale decision-making. Given the breadth of transmedia entities, a case study approach is likely appropriate. Studies of transmedia storytelling, more than some other, more conventional studies would involve comparisons and connections among the levels of analysis. How might policies regulating several different media come into play? Already, for example, contractual negotiations between distributors and the various professional organizations of writers, actors, and technicians have faced thorny discussions of how the new media versions of their work are to affect pay scales. How might industrial organization be altered in light of the need to transfer a text across platforms? What conceptions of audiences would drive decision-making at the corporate, studio, or distribution levels? Certainly, such a study would also require examination of the next level of analysis to be discussed below: the effort of creative individuals or teams whose work, from concept to completion, can be altered in the new digital environment.

Individual agents

Closely related to case studies of individual productions are projects focusing on the 'makers' of entertainment content, on their enactment as well as manipulation of all these structural factors. Many works at this level, among them most studies dependent on 'auteurist' theories of creative control, grant extraordinary freedom to individuals and their 'genius' (e.g., Bogdanovich, 1967; Sarris, 1968). Equally as significant, however, are contributions critiquing such notions. One of the most influential studies of the television industry, for example, is Cantor (1988[1971]). Using surveys and interviews in which producers remain anonymous, her work highlights the systemic constraints on 'true' notions of creativity as it might have been exercised by producers. In Cantor's analysis, the fundamental structure of American media industries – rooted in capitalism, supported by advertising, organized as oligopoly, and structured as factory labor – prevents its creative potential from being realized.

auteur theory

Other approaches have worked from a different assumption: that personnel involved in creating media fiction are in fact aware, to varying degrees, of the constraints and opportunities implied in the levels of influence, as reviewed here, which affect their work. The final emergence of any media product is seen as the result of intensely collaborative processes – something frequently acknowledged within the industries as well as in theory. Thus, the work of individuals is viewed as tightly woven into such collaboration, which, further, is embedded in the more general levels of influence. In another study of American television producers, for example, Newcomb and Alley (1983) emphasized the potential for awareness and creative manipulation of the very same systemic constraints cited by Cantor. Their analysis also depended on interviews with producers self-reporting their decision-making processes, and

individual creativity and systemic constraints

was amplified with textual analyses designed to check those reports.

Primary data for studying the work of individuals need not always be gathered by interview or survey, however. For example, the University of Texas at Austin library lists 85 works related to Alfred Hitchcock, and while many, perhaps most, of these are textual analyses of aspects of Hitchcock's films, a number provide original commentary on the production process. Gottlieb (1995) collected, in the director's own words, explanations, theories, and accounts regarding the production of 'his' works. In a related cross-reference, Behlmer (1981), by gathering David O. Selznick's memos relating to numerous productions, offered another, the producer's, perspective on some of Hitchcock the director's projects. A complete analysis of the specific projects on which they collaborated, and of their respective individual contributions, can be developed only in the production contexts where their sometimes conflicted relationship is fully evidenced.

directors and/ vs. producers

It is worth noting, however, that few studies of individual agents in media production have been able to provide generalized findings useful beyond the case at hand. Too often, research at this level succumbs to simplistic 'great man' or 'creative genius' assertions, which our attention to the multiple levels of analysis is meant to deconstruct. Media production requires hundreds of hands and minds, and although a single voice may be featured on a DVD commentary or highlighted as auteur, it would be a mistake to discount the collaborative nature of media-making.

Prosumers and produsage

Public as well as professional debates over individual agency have been intensified by the increased affordability of 'professional' quality production technologies and the ease of distribution proffered by the internet. Thus, it is increasingly common to find arguments forecasting a future of media production by individual 'prosumers.' Originally coined by Alvin Toffler (1980), this neologism meant to indicate a wider blending of production and consumption in industry and society; media audiences, for one, might no longer be relegated to simply consuming commercially produced goods.◀ 'Produsage' (Bruns, 2008a), more specifically, addresses communal or participatory forms of production in digital media environments. Perhaps most helpful for analyzing these developments in relation to entertainment production is the approach grounded in a concept of participatory culture, which Jenkins (2006) defines as occurring when "fans and other consumers are invited to actively participate in the creation and circulation of new content" (p. 290). The contemporary mediascape does indeed include a sector of amateur production that might be examined at the level of the individual producer, or perhaps as an aggregation of such content, as in the case of Burgess and Green's (2009) study of YouTube.

Studying 'prosumers' or 'produsers' is made difficult by the lack of an industrial infrastructure through which researchers might observe production processes. In many cases, this emerging type of media production is done by an isolated individual who creates content and then distributes it outside of what have been the mainstream media industries, for example, through outlets such as YouTube. As a result, research design likely requires some creativity on the part of the researcher. Researchers might first interview the amateur creator to learn about the particular production and distribution 'infrastructure' – if that is the right term – including informal participatory networks, in order to gauge what additional methods, such as observation online or offline, might be warranted.

Although there has been considerable speculation suggesting an amateur revolution through which the increased distribution possibilities for amateur production will harm media industries, there is little yet to suggest this is the case. Indeed, the great majority of amateur media creators toil in relative obscurity. Their art may be personally important or significant to small clusters of fans, but this context of production is unlikely to be applicable to the central questions of media and culture that inform the other studies reviewed here. For research on media industries, the relevant pattern seems to be a

amateur production

▶ produsage – Chapter 5, p. 102

few amateurs who break through to a wide audience – a breakthrough that leads them to forego their status as amateurs, as representatives of the industry subsequently offer deals that then incorporate them into conventional industry operations. For example, a 16-year-old from Nebraska, Lucas Cruikshank, created a series of short videos about a child character, Fred Figglehorn. By March 2010, his videos had been viewed, in aggregate, over 400 million times. The popularity of the Fred videos online led the children's cable channel Nickelodeon to offer Cruikshank a deal for a film, *Fred: The Movie*, with a budget in the low seven figures. Thus, amateur production at this point appears to have created a new venue for entrance into media industries, rather than developing as a meaningful competitor to established industries.

At the same time, more and broader surveys are needed of the conditions of production that are common to amateur productions. Examining how the mechanics of production and storytelling change as amateurs move within the established media infrastructure might yield new understandings of the norms of both amateur and industrial production. Such studies might also provide empirical evidence that could demystify much of the utopian rhetoric that has surrounded the development of amateur spaces. Even in these new arenas, however, it is possible to consider how questions of policy (e.g., 'net neutrality'), of organization (is the home considered a 'studio?'), or of high-level controlling structures (whose 'show' is selected for further development, and why?), all come into play, expanding, but not challenging the levels of analysis outlined in this chapter.

To sum up, the review of previous research supports our central recommendation: to fully account for the production of entertainment media, it is necessary, at some point and in some measure, to acknowledge the extraordinary range of levels of influence, from the broadest structural arrangements to the most particular creative or administrative decisions made. It is the interdependence of these factors that, above all, defines media production practices. In outlining these levels, we do not mean to create a hierarchy of importance of study, but to offer a way of organizing the expanse of possible studies and topics. Deliberate attention to the level(s) of analysis chosen – as well as those not chosen – also reaffirms the need for purposeful selection of methods. In designing a production study, it is crucial to identify methodologies and refine research questions that correspond to the level of analysis.

SOURCES AND METHODS

In order to develop an accordingly complex study of media production, it is necessary to apply a wide range of analytical approaches to an equal range of sources. Research on current entertainment production may usefully begin by describing the historical development of the contemporary situation. As already indicated, newer histories continue to provide substantial additional detail, hence elaborating a more precise understanding of how media industries came to their current status. A project may next require a description of the general regulatory and economic context at the level of the media system (commercial, public service, mixed, etc.). In addition to legislative sources concerning such industrial formations, macro-level information is usually available in national statistical abstracts. These latter sources provide details of import and export, viewer ratings and other statistics for television, gross numbers of completed productions for various media industries, distribution and attendance figures for films, the contribution of specific industries to the Gross Domestic Product, and so on. The significance of this information is often best recognized in comparative studies, as in Sinclair, *et al.* (1996), where shifts in national policies and support systems are linked to changes in production practices. Comparative data can also be found in publications of organizations such as the European Audiovisual Observatory or the European Broadcasting Union.

legislative sources

national statistics

For the study of individual corporations or production companies, some limited information can often be found in public corporate records, annual reports, and similar documents. More general information such as the size of companies, principal officers, location

corporate records

and address, and recent projects is provided in sources such as the annually published *International Television and Video Almanac* and the *International Motion Picture Almanac.* It is far more difficult to obtain access to current corporate records concerning specific projects or corporate strategies. As alternatives, or complements, both original interviews and trade press reportage are valuable on this topic, but researchers must be aware that much of the information may be designed for public relations purposes.

Even more difficult to obtain is information related to the costs and other financial arrangements of particular productions. Still, generalized budgets are widely acknowledged. It is well known, for example, that the cost of a one-hour episode of a US fictional broadcast television series was typically in the range of $4 million by the late 2000s, although cable series might be closer to $2.5 million, and unscripted, 'reality' shows might cost much less. Similarly, high film budgets, such as those reported for *Avatar*, or low expenditures, such as those for *The Blair Witch Project*, are discussed in the trade and general press as directly related to aesthetic choices, creative decision-making, and resulting works.

production budgets

Although much of the detailed economic information that would often be most helpful to production studies remains proprietary and next to impossible to obtain, one of the rare opportunities to see the true accounting of a media production occurs when lawsuits or legal filings are made, as often occurs in disputes over royalty payments and compensation. Such occasions may be unusual, but the depth and precision of legal filings that become part of the public record can reveal hidden practices and arrangements that undergird the economic practices of media production.

legal filings

But financial matters are only part of the complex negotiations leading to media production. It is more difficult still to account for the exercise of power that is involved in bringing a film to the screen or a television program to distribution, because the process involves complicated interactions involving many complex organizations. It is perhaps for this reason that historical production studies, with some benefit of hindsight, have been among the most informative. Works such as Schatz (1988) are based on archival records which, to some surprise, maintain detailed accounts of some of the most complicated, acrimonious, and revealing exchanges in the production of particular films. The accounts of struggles within the creative process are extremely instructive, so long as one remembers that each case is likely to work variations on standard industry practices.

Comparable contemporary 'behind the scenes' information, while often among the most important sources in these matters, may be the least available. Most of it must be gathered from the trade press, newspaper and magazine publications, now often primarily distributed online, focused on the media industries that provide extensive coverage of the financial arrangements within the film, television, cable, new media, music, and legitimate (stage) theater industries. Moreover, the trade press presents detailed information about individual productions, publish running records of box office receipts, provide extensive coverage of countries other than the US, and frequently offer interpretive analysis of industry changes. Trade sources including *Variety*, *Broadcasting & Cable*, *Advertising Age*, and *TV Week*, for instance, are all helpful for examining the television industry. Other media industries feature publications that attend to their particularity. What might be classified as trade literature is also helpful in developing an understanding of the operation of media industries. These include books by industry journalists about the industry and even biographies of significant figures. Although such works are often more descriptive than expected of academic media research, their detail and authors' access to decision-makers can provide valuable secondary source material.

trade press

trade literature

Ultimately, in order to develop a broad understanding of any media production, it is necessary to augment such background information with field research. This entails observation of production practices and interviewing of the personnel involved, supplemented by published interviews and other library sources. Perhaps surprisingly, it is often rather easy for academic researchers

field research

to gain access to media production sites, where creative personnel working on a project are likely to be open regarding the choices they make, though less likely to provide details related to individual power struggles. In other cases, it can be quite difficult, especially when examining the levels of analysis at which creative enterprises operate much more as conventional 'businesses.' When access to the day-to-day functioning of media institutions is impossible, researchers can look for events and opportunities where they conduct their business in more public locations. For example, Havens' (2008) research on distribution, already noted, takes advantage of the fact that distribution markets are open to almost anyone able to pay the admittance fees. Similarly, Lotz's research on US broadcast networks' 'Upfront Presentations' to advertisers (2007) and the television critics' tour (2005) took advantage of the more liminal spaces of these events. Although she still needed to gain permission for admittance, the semi-public nature of these marketing events made access easier. Additionally, many industries hold regular conferences and meetings, typically organized by trade associations, which similarly provide opportunities to observe aspects of industrial practices or hear key industry practitioners speaking to each other. Some organizations even feature specific programs for and outreach to researchers.

professional meetings

Preparations addressing the various contextual levels should precede the analysis of a specific set of creative practices. Even if the research question at hand specifies a study at the level of the individual production, a researcher must first develop an appreciation for where that production fits within larger organizational, industrial, and political-economic contexts before entering the field. The more thorough the preparation, the more precise and efficient the observations and interviews conducted in the case study. Demonstrating full preparation also makes it more likely that access to the production site will be granted by self-conscious professionals. To illustrate these points, and to elaborate the various levels of analysis in production research, Analysis Box 4.1 identifies key procedures for embarking on fieldwork.

ANALYSIS BOX 4.1: STUDYING MEDIA INDUSTRIES IN THE FIELD

Here we reflect on two examples:

- the processes used in field visits to a particular production – the original cable television series *Any Day Now* – produced for the Lifetime cable channel (Lotz, 2004);
- research investigating the process of buying advertising on US television networks that was carried out at a media buying/planning firm (Lotz, 2007).

Although the information is often quite specific, the tips should easily transfer into other contexts.

Preparing the field visit

Securing access is a crucial first step – and must be achieved even before making extensive plans for the research project. Often this can be done by first contacting the site by letter or email and then following up with a telephone call. A first challenge is frequently figuring out who has the power to grant access. Some sort of personal contact can be quite helpful – consider whether alumni of your university can help make an introduction, or contact a professional organization. In Lotz's research on media buying, she identified the media buying agency she wanted to study, based on seeing one of its executives make presentations at a number of industry conferences. She learned he was involved in the trade organization, and asked the trade organization to help facilitate the field visit and introduce her to the executive.

cont.

personal contact as gatekeeper

It is helpful to the researcher to plan visits far in advance, even if the day-to-day schedules of media workers may shift at the last minute. It is normally best to secure access months in advance and then fine-tune the specifics of the trip a week or two before the planned visit. A key component of the first visit and any early correspondence is establishing a personal relationship with whomever will facilitate the visit.

permission of access

To obtain permission for the visit, the researcher should provide information regarding the purpose of the research, the general topics of study, lists of individuals who might be involved in interviews, and details of an official university affiliation. Such requests are common and natural, and researchers should be prepared to respond in detail. The information is best provided in a succinct (two-page) letter that describes the research in general terms, and explains the significance of the fieldwork for the larger project. The researcher should also explain how the information will be used and where it might be published.

The letter further should outline what the researcher seeks to observe. In the case of the research on the production of *Any Day Now*, this included being present at writers' meetings, observing production in progress, and interviewing writers, producers, and actors. At this stage, no interviews may be firmly scheduled, especially if there is a component of general observation involved. It is often difficult to pre-plan which aspects of the process will be most beneficial for the larger project, or which appointments might have to be canceled later. Because the production of media is affected by anything from an actor's illness to bad weather, researchers must be prepared to respond quickly to changes in schedules and to seize occasions for gathering information in unexpected and unplanned ways. Frequently having a few days of observation in advance of interviews helps the researcher to ask more informed and specific questions.

Logistics

Once the agreements are confirmed and the visit scheduled, the practical arrangements can be completed through several telephone calls over the next few months. The last call before the visit should secure logistical information such as what is needed to get past the security reception common at many production sites and executive buildings.

In production research, the daily schedule is often quite unpredictable. In the US television industry, writers tend to work fairly stable eight-hour days from about 10:00 AM to 6:00 PM, but individual writers are also variously involved in general production meetings, depending on whether their script is currently in production, or if they are writing an upcoming episode. A production crew works twelve-hour days, with each morning's call-time dependent on when work was finished the previous night. Typically, shooting concludes between nine and ten in the evening, and production resumes the next day around noon, although many members of the crew are on hand and preparing earlier. Securing this information early on makes some aspects of production at least partially predictable, but hardly controllable.

Upon first entry to the site, whoever arranged for the visit will often provide a basic tour of the site, and introduce the researcher and the general purpose of the visit. There is no standard length for an observation. In the case of the *Any Day Now* research, Lotz spent three and a half days visiting the series, a duration largely dictated by the time available to Lotz for this portion of her project. In the case of the media buying study, she spent two work weeks that largely coincided with the yearly 'upfront' buying process. The 'upfronts' are a brief period of time in early summer during which 70 to 90 percent of annual advertising budgets are committed to the full year of programming. Despite the relatively brief length of the visits, it was sufficient for the purpose of the inquiries, and because such visits are granted out of professional courtesy, it is unlikely that a longer stay could be arranged except under exceptional circumstances. A few researchers, such as Born (2005), have been able to conduct research on an ongoing basis over a period of years.

cont.

During a visit it is frequently the case that many events and meetings are scheduled, canceled, and rescheduled in just a few days, which makes it difficult to plan ahead for every event. What actually takes place during a short visit often must be left to chance. However, even if the visit is thus completed without securing some important interviews, researchers are commonly able to establish a relationship in that time which assures that additional or follow-up interviews can easily be arranged at a later date or that questions can be answered by phone or email.

follow-up interviews

On the set

the production set

the actors

the production crew

the director

On the set of *Any Day Now* (and in the media buying office), Lotz was largely free to do as she wished. If the writers were meeting, she generally sat with them, and when they were out, or working independently, she visited the set. Here, the observations were, in part, determined by the concrete production process in film and television, which is very slow going, indeed quite tedious. Production of *Any Day Now* followed standard television industry practices and protocols. For each scene, the actors come on the set first, rehearse their lines and the 'blocking,' the process in which they learn their 'marks,' their positions and movements during the scene. Next, the actors move out, and the 'second team' comes on: Doubles for the actors take their places while the production crew sets the lighting, camera, and audio equipment. The full process may take as much as an hour for a scene of less than five minutes. Once the stage is set, the actors return and perform the scene, which is repeated until the director is satisfied with the 'take.' Being present on the set afforded particular opportunities to observe the dynamics among the writer, director, and actors, but ultimately far less insight than one might expect.

the executive producer

the writers

the writing process

For this particular project, however, observing the writing process and the roles of the Executive Producers was more important. In their meetings, the central decisions regarding the series concept, the contribution of individual episodes to that concept, and the general social agenda of the Executive Producers became increasingly clear. During the visit, the writers were working on scripts for the final episodes of the season, planned to air about six episodes after the one in production. The writers used one of the Executive Producers, Nancy Miller's office, a comfortable space lined with overstuffed couches and chairs and decorated with memorabilia from *Any Day Now* and Miller's other series. Here, it was possible to observe meetings on each step of the writing process, which followed a well-known and relatively routine procedure.

network executives

The process began with outlining script ideas, and proceeded to the presentation of ideas to Miller, followed by Miller's discussion of the ideas with the Lifetime executives assigned to work with the show. After securing approval from Miller and Lifetime, the writers would continue to develop the story, and the individual writer assigned to an episode would spend a few days writing alone. In the meetings, Lotz was able to watch the group dynamic of developing and polishing scripts that were in the later draft stages. In other meetings, writers brainstormed ideas for many other possible episodes and discussed the future trajectory of the series with Miller.

pilot season

assistants to executive producers

One fortunate aspect of this visit was that it occurred during 'pilot season,' when the company was in the process of presenting ('pitching') ideas for new series to various networks. The environment was constantly chaotic, and it was actually being present within this activity that allowed the best understanding of the overall production process. A significant amount of research time was spent merely sitting in the production company office observing the assistants to each of the Executive Producers. Lotz developed a relationship with the assistants, and gained a great deal of information about the series through talking with them. Their tasks provided additional insight into the ways in which the series was being developed. They also agreed to maintain contact after the visit, making themselves available for inquiries about developments, ratings information, and for addressing questions that would inevitably arise during the analysis and writing related to the series.

cont.

During the visit, it also became clear that there was much to be learned by looking around, listening, and asking simple questions. For example, on the wall in the writers' office was a list of criteria – a reminder to the writers – of the vision the Executive Producers were aiming for in each episode. Similarly, by being present in the office during the daily telephone calls between the studio and Lifetime, it was possible to develop an understanding of the intricate relationship between the producers and the network airing the series.

Because of developments in production, interviews with the Executive Producers were repeatedly postponed. In some ways, this was beneficial, for as the week progressed, other personnel answered some questions, while new questions arose. It was necessary to be flexible, but also persistent in order to get some of the important interviews, for example, finally being granted 'a few minutes' during a smoke break – that ended almost an hour later.

Although only some interviews were taped, the recorder was also valuable for reviewing each day's events during the hour-long commute back to the city. While it would probably have been possible to tape the entire writers' meetings, these were often long, rambling discussions about characters and current events which went on for hours, and which might have been inhibited by recording.◄ Instead, it was possible to create notes about specific discussions and to gather information important to the larger study.

Staying close to Miller during the week led to attendance at some meetings discussing topics not previously defined in the production research literature. For example, a 'tone meeting' was held as part of planning the production of the next episode. Here, the writer, director, and first assistant director met with Miller, and went through the script to make sure all the participants agreed on how the episode should be acted and shot in terms of tone and attitude. While the term 'tone meeting,' may be specific to this production company, it is likely that others engage in similar activities, but may not have been observed in the process. In another instance, by sheer chance, a promotions meeting was held during the visit, and proved an excellent opportunity for gaining information on competing visions of the show held by various participants in the production process. The meeting included representatives from two promotions companies, one hired by Lifetime Television, one hired by Miller and Randall (two of the three Executive Producers), co-star Annie Potts' publicist (by telephone), and (also by telephone) a representative from Spelling Entertainment, the parent production company.

Much of the information gathered during this field visit confirmed earlier conceptions and ideas related to the program and to the topics of feminism and racism embedded within it (Lifetime is a network that targets women and the series was about a life-long cross-racial friendship). But other information amplified and refined those ideas, and provided details that would not otherwise have been available. The observations and interviews further enabled later stages of the analysis to draw on the multiple perspectives of those involved in the creative and production process.

In the office

In the case of observing the upfront buying process at a company that purchases television advertising for major national advertisers, meetings again provided some of the most insightful observations. Media buyers often work around the clock during the upfront period, as different firms compete to secure the best deal with each network. Being present during this important time aided Lotz because she could ask about particular situations and issues within the client and network negotiations she was observing to build an understanding of this relatively unknown process.

cont.

► note-taking and/vs. tape-recording – Chapter 14, p. 274

Gaining access to these 'business' practices is often quite difficult. In the case of the media buyer, the firm had to get the approval of all of its clients to have an observer present. Lotz credits the approval of her project from the top – from the executive who worked with the trade organization, as mentioned – with making this research opportunity feasible. In another similar research opportunity, Lotz needed to sign various non-disclosure agreements. Often researchers are only seeking access to general practices and care little about specific clients, so that such legal documents do little to curtail the research project. Researchers should review non-disclosure agreements carefully to make sure they understand what they can and cannot report in their publications before beginning their research. In most cases, the long delay to publication and the circulation of ideas among the small academic community aids the researcher in gaining access to sensitive business environments. In an age of blogging◀ and other informal information economies, however, it is increasingly crucial and often more specified in agreements that researchers be sensitive to the privacy requests of those they study and maintain confidences appropriately. Researchers should also follow protocols regarding working with human subjects as required at their specific home institutions or intended publishers that safeguard proper and ethical research behavior.◀

non-disclosure agreements

CONCLUSION

Far more examples of media research examining various aspects of industrial organizations, productions, and practices can now be found, so much so as to suggest a burgeoning sub-discipline (Holt and Perren, 2009). Accordingly, a rich array of conversations about the theories and methods that support this type of study has also begun to emerge (Mayer, *et al.*, 2009; Havens, *et al.*, 2009; Hesmondhalgh, 2010). Even in this environment of considerable scholarly dynamism, a basic taxonomy such as the levels of analysis we offer remains useful as a preliminary rubric for sketching the relevant range of analytical sites and methods as researchers begin to delimit their studies.

This may especially be the case as the growing depth of media industry studies leaves researchers facing new challenges. As a result of the relative paucity of entertainment production studies, many among the first generations of studies necessarily provided heavily detailed descriptions of the very processes they analyzed. Few academic scholars had detailed knowledge of industrial production practices and found it necessary to describe basic features prior to attempting more theoretically informed analysis. Future scholarship should build on these sources and focus on analysis rather than repeated description. As Hesmondhalgh (2010) recently commented, although the field has been enriched by newer studies considering "culture, codes, rituals, representation and discourse" of media production, these analyses have not been "integrated into an explanatory and normative framework of the kind associated with critical social science" (p. 10).

It is also crucial that case studies, especially those dealing with individual productions, be carefully considered and assessed for their broader relevance and application. In all but the most novel of cases, it is important to connect specific studies with a more expansive range of practices to draw out information or perspectives that transcend the single case. In this way, discussions of the roles of individuals and particular productions also serve as a reminder that the analytical process should move back 'up' the levels of analysis. For instance, in the film industry, creative control is primarily assumed by directors, while writers are relegated to a lower status and involvement, but in the television industry, writers often move into the producer role and assume creative control of a series. Film directors are not under contract,

film production vs. television production

▶ blogging – Chapter 5, p. 103
▶ research ethics – Chapter 19, p. 366

but make professional arrangements, through agents and lawyers, to work on individual projects. And, unlike television producers, who are most often directly involved in the creative process, the role of the film producer is generally focused on arranging financing for specific productions. In the context of the more general economic arrangements for entertainment production, still other differences emerge. Film financing is based on income from the box office and home rentals, both nationally and internationally. Television financing comes from either advertising or nationally regulated license fees and other support, or a combination of the two. These differences in political-economic contexts, which will tend to shape institutional structures, organizational practices, and the consequent roles of individuals, demonstrate how levels of analysis vary from context to context, and should be taken into account in concrete production studies.

Partly for these reasons, many of the most significant current questions within production research involve corporate mergers, technological interconnections, and the cultural and other social implications of new industrial configurations. As we suggest above, when a book may become a movie that becomes a television series that becomes a theme park ride that becomes a video game that becomes a line of toys, production researchers find themselves involved with new sets of issues.◀ The research process may start with any one of these media products, studying the distinctive work processes at a given production site. But it should ultimately address not only the goals of creative individuals, but also the configuration of media organizations with particular industrial strategies which are embedded in, and responding to, large-scale political-economic conditions.

The current state of entertainment in the US, and increasingly elsewhere, as defined in part by technological developments leading to more, and more differentiated, distribution outlets, may favor those who work to place their visions on screens, even if viewed by comparatively smaller numbers. Within the commercial political economy, the creative process of producing media entertainment remains complex, dense, and variously inflected by those involved. Particularly at a time when media systems throughout the world are in a process of vital change, resulting from economic, regulatory, and technological developments, it is important that comparative studies of production processes be undertaken, including different national and regional contexts.◀ Analyzing these processes in more detail, will complement studies of audiences in relation to media products, and will help explain the equally complicated responses recorded in reception studies.◀ In this way, our understanding of the social and cultural roles of mediated entertainment will be enriched and more precisely understood.

Academic researchers must also remember how their task differs from that of researchers employed by media organizations that operate in the expressed interests of media industries.◀ Although media practitioners can learn from critical scholarship, the task of the critical scholar is to draw connections among the practices and entities they study and broader social and cultural concerns.

The general area of media industry studies has grown considerably, but much remains unknown and needs study. The field needs research, for example, that employs empirical methods to test existing theories about conglomerate operation. Similarly, many significant roles in industry operation – such as that of agents and public relations – lack meaningful analysis, especially analysis based in careful fieldwork.

Finally, it is clear that many media industries and the production of entertainment within those industries have faced substantial challenges to long-held operational norms in the last two decades. Such periods of change provide profound opportunities for the realignment of interests and structural power. Thus, the disruption caused by digitization,

▶ cross-media production and intertextuality – Chapter 10, p. 192

▶ culturally comparative research – Chapter 11

▶ reception studies – Chapter 9

▶ administrative and critical research – Chapter 19, p. 359

and the modifications in established practices required by the necessity of competing in increasingly global media systems, may make it beneficial to revisit earlier studies of industry operation. Historical comparisons◀ would sharpen our knowledge of specific cases, of processes of change in entertainment media production, and of the broader theories which we construct and on which we rely. Once again, it is context, ever more important in the fluid or unstable state of media industries, that we most strongly emphasize.

RESOURCE BOX 4.1: ONLINE RESOURCES ABOUT ENTERTAINMENT MEDIA AND PRODUCTION

Media industries generally

- Media Industries – "a range of links and resources for those researching and writing about the media industries": www.themediaindustries.net
- Valuation Resources – a guide to "industry information, research, and analysis for over 400 industries": www.valuationresources.com/IndustryReport.htm

Books

- Book Business: www.bookbusinessmag.com
- Book Industry Study Group: www.bisg.org

Film

- Box Office Data, News: www.the-numbers.com
- Screen International: www.screendaily.com
- Motion Picture Association of America (MPAA): www.mpaa.org

Magazines

- Publishing Executive: www.pubexec.com
- Magazine Publishers of America: www.magazine.org

Radio

- Inside Radio: www.insideradio.com
- Radio Industry News Blog: www.radiostreamingnews.com

Television

- Broadcasting & Cable: www.broadcastingcable.com

Video games

- Gamasutra – "The Art & Business of Making Games": www.gamasutra.com
- Game Industry News: www.gameindustry.com

▶ historically comparative research – Chapter 12

5 The study of news production

Stig Hjarvard

- a review of research on news production as either a *selection* or a *construction* of social reality
- a critical discussion of classic concepts, including *gatekeeping* and *news values*
- a characterization of news as a product of contextualized *exchanges* between *sources* and *journalists* that caters variously to local, national, and transnational *markets*
- an overview of different types of *news genres* and their distinctive social functions
- an account of the development of *online journalism*, including the role of *user-generated content, gatewatching*, and *blogging*

INTRODUCTION

At the beginning of their classic study of news production, *Making the News* (1979), Peter Golding and Philip Elliott quote an exchange from Neil Simon's comedy, *The Odd Couple* (1966), involving the journalist Felix and two women:

> Cecily: What field of endeavour are you engaged in?
> Felix: I write the news for CBS.
> Cecily: Oh! Fascinating!
> Gwendolyn: Where do you get your ideas from?
> Felix: (He looks at her as though she's a Martian) From the news.
> Gwendolyn: Oh, yes, of course. Silly me...
> (in Golding and Elliott, 1979: 5)

Golding and Elliott (1979) use this dialogue to highlight the widespread belief among journalists that their work is simply to report what is already there. For journalists, news is not made, but found. The production of news is a self-evident practice: everyone knows what news is, although journalists, through years of practice, may have developed a particularly good 'nose for news.'

Golding and Elliot's 1979 book was part of a wider sociological turn in research on news that challenged this professional naivety in the late 1970s. Within a very few years, a whole series of studies – Herbert Gans' *Deciding What's News* (1979), Philip Schlesinger's *Putting "Reality" Together* (1978), Michael Schudson's *Discovering the News* (1978), and Gaye Tuchman's *Making News: A Study in the Construction of Reality* (1978) – established a new and critical research agenda on news production. Despite other differences, these contributions all focused on news as a social artifact: news is the result of particular work practices, and is socially patterned. This sociological turn highlighted the following general characteristics of news:

- The production of news takes place in institutional and organizational settings in which the type of ownership, managerial hierarchies, allocation of resources, available technology, and market considerations influence how news reporters work and, therefore, the kinds of stories they produce.

- News is not value free, but constructs a social reality.◀ In spite of journalism's adherence to norms of objectivity, journalists as a profession share certain ideas and standards – news values – that make certain social conflicts and other occurrences into news while neglecting others. Furthermore, the corporate ideologies of news organizations may enter into the news judgment of the journalists they employ.
- The practices and norms of journalism have been formed through historical processes. The ideal of impartial news reporting and of journalism's role as a fourth estate◀ was the product of a wider social transformation during the nineteenth and twentieth centuries through which the press gradually became detached from political parties. In this process, a new category of media workers – journalists – acquired special legitimacy through their adherence to emerging cultural norms concerning facticity and democracy.
- News is a product of interaction between news organizations and journalists, on the one hand, and actors from other social institutions, on the other. Through the routinized coverage of certain news beats, certain kinds of sources get privileged access to the news media. Journalists are dependent on sources for the production of news, and the differential authority and legitimacy of various sources likely is reflected in the treatment they get in the news.

Since the late 1970s, these sociological insights have continued to inform the study of news production; the original studies have become standard references in this area of research. Also the methodological approaches of these studies – a strong emphasis on observation in the newsroom combined with qualitative interviews, document study, and content analysis – set an example for later research. In this chapter, I present contributions to research that built upon as well as expanded and revised these studies in view of contemporary changes, including the rise of digital and interactive news media. To begin, I consider some of the contributions that preceded the sociological turn, but which continue to hold relevance for the study of news production.

▶ constructionism – Chapter 3, p. 51
▶ the press as a fourth estate – Chapter 19, p. 353

CONSTRUCTION OR SELECTION

Two different perspectives on the news production process have dominated research: *construction* and *selection*. The sociological turn was clearly informed by the construction perspective. The social institution of journalism, and society at large, could be considered independent variables that influenced a dependent variable, the news.◀ In this perspective, news is a social construction of reality that, in turn, influences the ways in which society comes to understand its own public life. This perspective challenged the previously dominant perspective of news as *selection*. The selection perspective comes closer to the commonsense understanding held by journalists, in the sense that news is understood in relation to the 'news event.' Events in the world, thus, represent independent variables, and journalists play a secondary, intermediate role as 'selectors' or gatekeeper of the news: the journalists perform such functions as selecting, rejecting, and re-editing news on the basis of preexisting characteristics of the event. Compared to journalistic common sense, however, studies from the selection perspective have tried to discern systematic patterns and structures in the ways in which journalists and news organizations rework the news in various steps.

'the news event'

The oldest example of a selection perspective in news studies is the gatekeeper paradigm. The metaphor of gatekeeping was originally developed by Lewin (1947) to describe the decisions in a family household that determine what kinds of food end up on the dinner table.

gatekeeping

▶ dependent and independent variables – Chapter 13, p. 239

Through the seminal study by White (1950), this metaphor was introduced to the field of journalism in analyses of the news production process as a sequence of gates through which the news must pass in order to make it from the original news event to the published newspaper page. It was further elaborated in research on international news (e.g., McNelly, 1959) that included the full sequence of gatekeepers – from the first reporting of an event in a foreign location, through the gates of foreign and national news agencies, to the gatekeepers at local news media in another part of the world. The later tradition of international news flow studies◄ (e.g., Stevenson and Shaw, 1984; UNESCO, 1985) was, to some extent, informed by the gatekeeping paradigm. The study of the unequal flows of news between the so-called third and first worlds often rested on either implicit or explicit assumptions that Western news media, and Western news agencies in particular, performed a crucial role as gatekeepers controlling the flow of news to and from various corners of the world.

The gatekeeper model has received criticism for suggesting an overly simplistic model of the news production process. The original model focused on the decisions made by individual journalists, and did not pay much attention to the larger social context of news production. It implied a rather passive role of journalists primarily reacting to what enters the 'gate.' Consequently, the model appeared less applicable to the proactive role of journalists seeking out information or stories before they become 'events' (McQuail, 2010: 309). One handbook of key concepts in communication and cultural studies concluded that "the gatekeeper concept is now generally regarded as oversimplified and of little utility" (O'Sullivan, *et al.*, 1993: 126–127). However, later contributions have tried to develop more complex gatekeeper models (Shoemaker, 1991). Shoemaker and Reese (1996) proposed five levels of analysis in order to examine influences on media content: individual, media routines, organizational, extra-media, and ideological levels. Shoemaker, *et al.* (2009), further, suggested that gatekeeping procedures have also become embedded in computerized algorithms and metadata that manage the continuous selection and distribution of news on the internet,◄ for instance, news.google.com.

NEWS VALUES

Closely related to the concept of gatekeeping is the notion of a *news value*. News values are commonly understood as a "system of criteria which are used to make decisions about the inclusion and exclusion of material" (Palmer, 2000: 45). Furthermore, news values may influence the prominence that a particular news story is given within the overall composition of the selected news. There is no agreement, however, about the exact number or definition of news values. Bell (1991: 156–160) lists eighteen news values, whereas McQuail (2000: 342) lists ten "primary news values in Western media." Despite such differences, frequently cited news values concern:

- *Significance*: News should report on events or issues with significance for many people or society at large.
- *Intensity*: News should report on conflicts and unexpected occurrences, giving priority to actions and the responses of the actors involved.
- *Topicality*: News should report on current events, i.e., what has just happened and what is likely to occur in the immediate future.
- *Closeness*: News should report on issues or events that are close to the audience. This proximity may be geographical, cultural, or psychological.

Galtung and Ruge's (1965) work represents the most ambitious and frequently cited attempt to develop a framework for examining the factors influencing the selection and composition of news. They suggested twelve factors: eight of these (e.g., unambiguity and unexpectedness) can be considered stable across cultural contexts, whereas four (e.g., reference to elite people and elite nations) are important specifically "in the

► international news flow studies – Chapter 11, p. 215

► metadata – Chapter 10, p. 194

north-western corner of the world" (Galtung and Ruge, 1965: 68). When news passes through a sequence of gates, the twelve factors have a cumulative effect on the selection of news. As such, they constitute a three-step cycle of selection-distortion-replication:

1 The more events satisfy the criteria mentioned, the more likely that they will be registered as news (selection).
2 Once a news item has been selected, what makes it newsworthy according to these factors will be accentuated (distortion).
3 Both the process of selection and the process of distortion will take place at all steps in the chain from the event to the reader (replication).

(Galtung and Ruge, 1965: 71)

Despite their detailed emphasis on the factors underlying selection, Galtung and Ruge's social critique of news was not radically different from the critical construction perspective of the late 1970s. Inherent in Galtung and Ruge's conception of news factors is that these generate a particular outlook on the world (Hartley, 1982). As a result, news as genre or institution produces a biased or even distorted view of the world. Galtung and Ruge themselves found only partial empirical confirmation of their factors and hypotheses, and also later attempts to verify them have produced mixed results. A major review of research about the area in English concluded that "the generality of the proposed hypotheses remains questionable because one hypothesis has been supported in some studies and rejected in others" (Hur, 1984: 367). Large-scale German research projects using Galtung and Ruge's news factors reached similarly inconclusive results (Schulz, 1976; Wilke, 1984).

The lack of empirical validation may also reflect an inherent theoretical weakness in the notion of news values. News values are used by journalists and editors, who apply these values to possible news stories on the basis of inherent features of the news event. Thus, the very notion of news values entails a journalism-centered explanation of news production. This does not take into account the fact that news may be influenced by other social actors, such as powerful economic or political sources that bring other values to bear on the news production process. Similarly, values arising from particular organizational constraints (type of ownership, level of resources) as well as audience demands are considered less often in research as origins of news values. In empirical studies, news values are mostly identified through content analysis,◀ which leaves open the question of whether news values are features of the text or of the operating principles of news production. Hartley (1982) contends that news values may say more about *how* news stories are reported whereas they "give little clue as to why the story was deemed newsworthy in the first place" (p. 79). Bell (1991), however, makes a useful distinction between three classes of news values relating to the content of the news (the nature of the events and their actors), the news process (production), and the text (presentational features). Eilders (2006), further, distinguishes between news values as event characteristics and news values as characteristics of the reality construction carried out by journalists. Both of these last two kinds of news values may be understood as relevance indicators, but in the second case relevance is understood as an active social construction on the part of journalists, rather than as a reaction to the characteristics of the event itself.

news values as event characteristics, textual features, or production principles

The idea that news production is strongly influenced by a limited number of news values also tends to neglect the diverse types of news media and their national contexts. It is unlikely that very different news media such as the German *Bild-Zeitung* (tabloid newspaper), British *The Times* (elitist newspaper), American Fox News (opinionated television news), or South Korean OhmyNews (citizen-generated internet news site) would operate according to a shared set of news values. Moreover, the ongoing differentiation of news according to themes and audiences (health news, business news, consumer news, etc.) further questions the explanatory force of common news values. While news values appear less productive for capturing *commonalities* of news, they may be more suited for investigations of *differences*

▶ content analysis – Chapter 13, p. 248

between news media. As Harcup and O'Neill (2001) and Zelizer (2004) have pointed out, the various lists and typologies of news values should "remain open to inquiry rather than be seen as a closed set of values for journalism in all times and places" (Zelizer, 2004: 55).

If, in fact, very different news media share some characteristics, this may have less to do with a common set of news values, and more to do with certain intrinsic features of news as a social form (Barnhurst and Nerone, 2001; Park, 1940). These empirical as well as theoretical reservations about the importance of news values in news production, however, do not deny the fact that they may play a central role in journalists' self-understanding. Since many journalistic textbooks teach journalism students the importance of news values, they are integrated into the journalistic profession as common sense. Despite theoretical criticism and mixed empirical results, then, the concepts of gatekeeping and news values have remained part of the framework of media studies. Intuitively, they correspond to basic empirical observations in the newsroom: news stories are selected, rejected, and re-edited on the basis of various criteria that are shared, at least in part, by professional journalists within and across specific contexts of country, medium, and market.

news as a social form

NEWS AND MARKETS

The sociological turn of the late 1970s focused, in particular, on news organizations and on the internal constraints and policies influencing news production. Other studies have supplemented this perspective by examining external conditions, not least market considerations, and their interplay with internal factors. The question of market influences on the news is as old as journalism itself. In many Western countries, a commercial press either coexisted with a political press or succeeded it during the nineteenth and twentieth centuries. The more popular this press became, the more it gave rise to public criticism of sensationalist news, entertainment, and populist politics. Thus, there is a considerable continuity between the various public discourses on late nineteenth-century newspapers' 'yellow journalism' (Campbell, 2001), twentieth-century tabloid television news (Langer, 1998), and twenty-first-century market-driven news in a converging media market (McChesney and Nichols, 2010).

internal and external conditions of news production

Several research traditions have tried to substantiate, qualify, or reconsider this criticism. From a political-economy approach,◀ Herman and Chomsky (1988) have developed a 'propaganda model' identifying five filters through which editorial processes are influenced by commercial and political pressures. The general profit motive of private media organizations, and the specific pressure for advertising to gain higher circulation among commercially attractive audience segments, arguably, become more important in the editorial process than a consideration of the public interest. According to this model, the commercial incentive also makes news organizations vulnerable to pressure from powerful sources (governments, corporations, etc.) because, as routine sources, they supply the news media with cheap, but important information. Such powerful sources may deny critical news media access to information, thereby threatening their commercial viability. Due to an increased globalization of media during recent decades, the predominantly American commercial model of media has been exported to many other countries. According to Thussu, there has been a particularly harmful influence on television news: "In a market-driven, 24/7 broadcasting ecology, television news is veering towards infotainment – soft news, lifestyle and consumer journalism are preeminent, a conduit for the corporate colonization of consciousness, while public journalism and the public sphere have been undermined" (Thussu, 2007a: 11).

propaganda model of news

In contrast, cultural studies approaches◀ do not consider the commercialization of news as a decline of the public sphere. Instead, this tradition generally looks at journalism as inseparable from popular culture, which has always been at least partially dependent on the market. Hartley (2009: 310) identifies "popular

▶ political economy – Chapter 3, p. 65
▶ cultural studies – Chapter 2, p. 46

culture as the true origin of modern journalism" and considers the historical development both of a general reading public and of the expansion of popular democracy as intertwined with the expansion of modern markets and a consumer culture. From Hartley's (2009) point of view, it is a misleading dichotomy to think of popular culture as the domain of leisure, entertainment, and fictional narratives, while journalism is associated with the democratic process and with rational deliberation. Historically, market-driven news media have facilitated popular engagement in public affairs. Similarly, Hermes (2005) and Dahlgren (2006) emphasize the connection between popular culture, everyday life, and civic engagement. From a somewhat different perspective, Schudson (2008), too, contends that the US model of market-driven news media, despite its many flaws, serves valuable democratic functions.

commercialization

In spite of these divergent interpretations and normative evaluations of the possible consequences of market-driven media, there is general agreement that the overall global trend of news and journalism has been towards increased commercialization. Comparing European and Anglo-American media systems, Hallin and Mancini (2004) state that commercialization is pushing European media systems towards the Anglo-American commercial model: this "changes the social function of journalism, as the journalist's main objective is no longer to disseminate ideas and create social consensus around them, but to produce entertainment and information that can be sold to individual consumers" (Hallin and Mancini: 2004: 277). The commercialization of news has also been studied through the lens of Bourdieu's field theory (Benson and Neveu, 2005). From this perspective, the field of journalism has a high degree of 'heteronomy,' i.e., it is influenced by other fields, such as politics and the market. Historically, journalism has been influenced – in some countries even dominated – by the field of politics (e.g., the party-political press). Today, it has regained some autonomy in relation to the political field, even while paying the price of a growing dependency on the market. From an institutional perspective, then, commercialization has not necessarily limited the political role of news media. News media have gained a degree of autonomy vis-à-vis political institutions, becoming a new kind of institution that is deeply involved in the daily construction of the political agenda (T. E. Cook, 1998).

NEWS AS A PRODUCT OF EXCHANGES

McManus (1994) has developed a helpful model of news production in a market-driven media system. Analytically, he distinguishes between four different markets that the media engage with in order to produce the news. Markets are considered as exchange relationships, and the final product – news – is influenced by all these exchanges. Figure 5.1 presents an adapted version of McManus' model.

four markets: advertising, audiences, sources, and owners

The four markets consist of advertisers, audiences, sources, and owners. In the advertising market, news media trade the attention of the news audience for money from the advertisers. In the audience market, news media deliver information and entertainment to audiences who, in return, deliver both money (subscription and single-copy sale) and attention. In the market of news sources, news media deliver attention to sources who, again, provide the raw material of news: information. In the fourth and final market, owners invest money in the news business in order to gain a profit. Some of this profit may be reinvested in the news media operations. That, however, will depend on the overall policy of the news medium in question, for instance, the extent to which it is driven by a profit motive, and/or by political or broadly publicist objectives. Thus, news media do not only produce economic profit, but also create public value.

These various markets, moreover, are interdependent both in quantitative and qualitative terms. From a quantitative point of view, the audience size will influence the income from advertisers as well as the willingness of news sources to talk to journalists. Other things being equal, powerful news sources will spend more time on news media with large audiences than with news media that have a small circulation. Equally, the level of investment from owners will influence the staffing of both

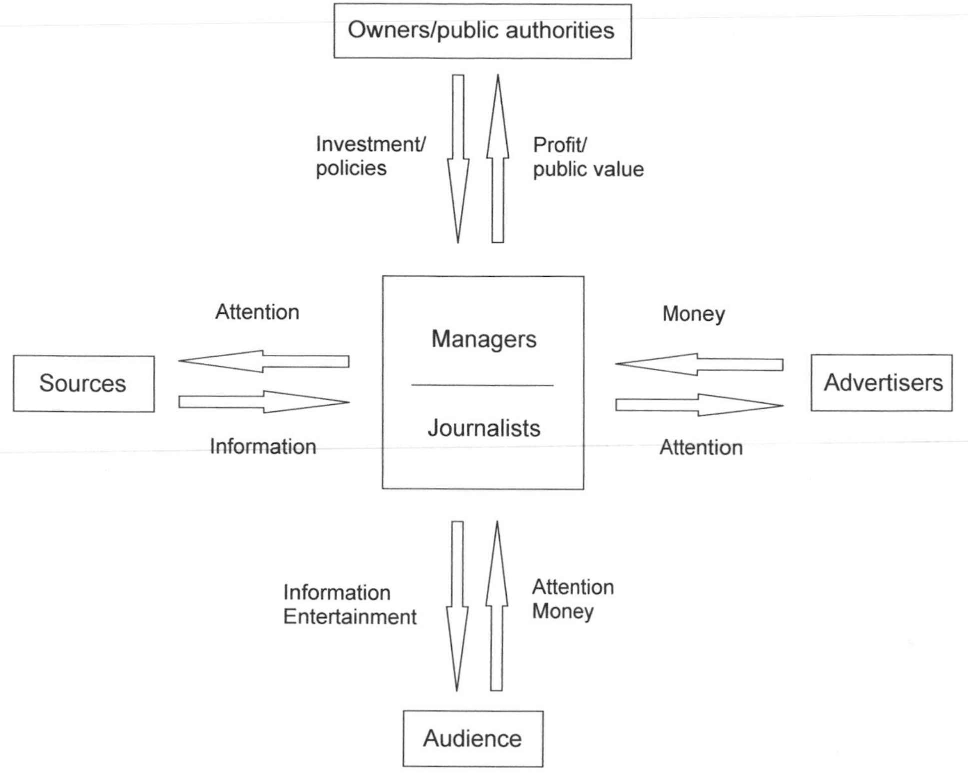

Figure 5.1 Exchange relationships in the production of news (adapted from McManus, 1994: 60)

the newsroom and the marketing division and, hence, the potential journalistic value of the final product and the possible sales of the marketing division. From a qualitative point of view, the type and quality of news will influence the social and cultural composition of the audience. So-called serious or quality papers like German *Die Welt* or American *New York Times* have well-educated readers with a high income, whereas free newspapers like the international newspaper chain *Metro* or tabloids like Britain's *The Sun* have readers with a more average education and income. These qualitative exchange dependencies, in turn, influence the level and type of advertising that a news medium can attract.

quality newspapers

free newspapers

tabloids

Journalists do not engage directly with actors in all these markets. Their relationships with owners, advertisers and, to some extent, audiences are mediated through the managerial level of the news media. Accordingly, the commercial demands of those markets manifest themselves indirectly to journalists, who mainly work in two markets: researching stories among news sources and producing news stories for audiences. Whereas journalists' choices of stories and the ways in which they report on them, thus, are influenced by all four markets, the levels and types of influence on journalism are, of course, variable. Analytically, McManus (1994) distinguishes between the (cognitive) orientation and the (emotional) entertainment value of news in order to demonstrate how economic considerations come to influence journalists' production of actual stories. By orientation value, he means the ability of news to inform audiences about important issues in their social environment. Since a news story may be high or low in either orientation or entertainment value, McManus

orientation value and entertainment value

(1994: 122) distinguishes between four types of news:

I. Low entertainment value and high orientation value: Here we find the type of news that is "important but dull" (McManus, 1994: 122). Such stories draw a rather limited audience, despite the fact that they may have been costly to produce. News media with large resources sometimes invest more work in the presentation of these stories in order to move them to type II news, thereby increasing audience size.
II. High entertainment value and high orientation value: This is the type of news where market demands and professional journalistic values converge. The uncovering of big political scandals such as Watergate demands a lot of resources and, in return, produces stories of considerable public importance as well as high social drama. Due to its high cost, this type of journalism is more the exception than the rule.
III. High entertainment value and low orientation value: This is the realm of celebrity news and oddities like 'man bites dog.' Such stories have considerable market value, but may be rather costly to produce if they are to sustain attention beyond average gossip or VIP coverage.
IV. Low entertainment value and low orientation value: This might appear an almost empty category, only to be filled with a few stories originating from mistaken journalistic judgment. Nevertheless, news media end up with very many stories in this category, since their production costs usually are very low. Routine stories about small accidents and minor political occurrences are taken from news agencies and used as 'fillers.'

Studies by McManus and others confirm that market-driven news organizations tend to produce more news of entertainment value and less news with orientation value. For example, a comparative study of two public service television news services in Denmark and Finland and two commercial television news services in United States concluded that "the public service model of broadcasting gives greater attention to public affairs and international news, and thereby fosters greater knowledge in these areas, than the market model" (Curran, *et al.*, 2009: 22).

Allern (2002: 142) has pointed out that "market-orientation in journalism is much more than commercial news media's indulging popular tastes and interests." In addition to the different economic costs of various types of news production, referred to by McManus (1994), Allern suggests two important factors: the geographical area of coverage and its types of audiences; and the competition between news media. News media have their primary markets within local, national, or transnational areas, and among certain segments of the population within such areas. This basic market condition informs the production of news: what is considered newsworthy depends, to some extent, on whether or not it takes place within the area in question and is of interest to particular segments of its population. The competition between news media, further, makes the question of exclusivity important. Whereas shared news stories are considered less competitive, the possibility of securing a big exclusive story – a scoop – may encourage news media and journalists to invest many resources in that story.

SOURCES AND JOURNALISTS

Sources deliver the raw material of news: without sources, no news. The fundamental dependency on sources has made the problem of access to and control over sources a key issue in the study of news production. Two different questions concerning sources are key: how do journalists manage to secure continuous interaction with relevant sources in order to produce news of adequate quantity and quality? And, what is the power relationship between journalists and sources regarding the framing of news stories?

access to and control over sources

Tuchman (1978) used the metaphor of the news net to describe how news organizations develop work routines and a division of labor in order to secure a daily 'catch' of usable sources. The news net is designed according to geographical territories and to organizational and topical specialization. Metaphorically speaking, the meshes of the news net are not

the news net

of equal size, but are specifically designed to catch certain sources and leave others untouched. Journalists seek out specific places, organizations, and types of people (parliament, police, experts, etc.) that they know will provide information of the right kind on a continuous basis. As such, the news net "is a hierarchical system of information gatherers" (Tuchman, 1978: 24) that reflects the priorities of the news medium in question and its internal division of labor. Senior journalists are assigned key topics and powerful institutions, while less important topics and places are left to freelancers and stringers. Other news media and news agencies are also part of the news net, and often serve a backup function in the supply of information.

The news net brings journalists in contact with relevant types of sources, but not all of these are of equal value to journalists. Gans (1979) identified six different considerations that influence their choice of sources. If a source has proven *suitable in the past*, delivering 'good' stories, the journalist is more likely to use him or her again. Source *productivity* allows a journalist to gather much information with minimal effort, and a *reliable* source is favored because it requires less work in terms of checking facts. If it proves difficult to check the reliability of a particular piece of information, the general *trustworthiness* of the source becomes an important additional consideration. Sources with an *authoritative* or official status are also preferred because their opinions, and the information they offer, are more persuasive. Finally, *articulateness* is an important feature, if sources are to be interviewees: they must be able to deliver their argument in a concise and eloquent manner.

Many studies have documented that the choice of sources by news media does not reflect the composition of society in general, but favors elite sources such as official spokespersons and powerful interests (Glasgow University Media Research Group, 1976; Gans, 1979; Reese, *et al.*, 1994). This predominance of elite sources is particularly pronounced in foreign news coverage (Cohen, 1963); during times of war, news media may depend on controlled access to military and governmental sources (Bennett and Paletz, 1994; Kristensen and Ørsten, 2007).

elite sources

The prominence of elite sources has led many researchers to question the extent to which journalists actually control their interaction with sources, and whether they allow sources (undue) influence on the content of the news. Sources may not only control the kinds of issues that enter the news (agenda setting),◄ but they may also influence the ways in which news is presented (framing).◄ A news agenda is understood as a selection of issues that is organized in a hierarchical order of importance (McCombs, 2004). To frame is "to select some aspects of a perceived reality and make them more salient in a communicating text, in such a way as to promote a particular problem definition, causal interpretation, moral evaluation, and/or treatment recommendation" (Entman, 1993: 52).

While journalists and sources may struggle to control how a story is to be reported, there are several ways of conceptualizing their relationship and interaction. Blumler and Gurevitch (1981) distinguished two different models: the adversary model and the exchange model. The adversary model, which has been very influential in news studies, considers the source-journalist relationship as a power struggle between actors with different or even antagonistic interests. The source will try to persuade, or manipulate, the journalist to report the story in a way that is favorable to his or her interests. The journalist, being a representative of the fourth estate, will try to reveal information that may discredit the source, but which is important for society at large. Hall, *et al.* (1978) considered the source-journalist interaction as an ideological struggle in which elite sources usually have the power to act as 'primary definers' of social events. Due to their ideological hegemony, these sources are able to project their definition of social reality onto the news. Journalists, accordingly, act as 'secondary definers' of social occurrences, in the sense that they play a secondary role in reproducing the definitions given by accredited sources. Even though news media and their sources may be adversaries, the news media

the adversary model and the exchange model

primary and secondary definers of news

► agenda setting – Chapter 8, p. 161
► framing – Chapter 8, p. 164

"stand in a position of structured subordination to the primary definers" (Hall, *et al.*, 1978: 59). Altheide and Snow (1991) present another version of the adversary model which attributes more power to the news media by emphasizing that, for instance, political sources, must adjust to the 'logic' of the media.

TANGO AND SPIN

Blumler and Gurevitch (1981) criticized the adversary model for having too narrow a focus on the conflicting interests of journalists and their sources, which makes it impossible to explain why sources and journalists continue to engage with each other on a daily basis. Instead, the metaphor of exchange, which has also been used in relation to the various markets of journalism,◀ may prove more useful in understanding the interdependence of source and journalist and their mutual interest in the co-production of news. The exchange model rests on the assumption that both parties benefit from the exchange. This cooperative model of news-making was apparent already in Gans' (1979: 116) observation that "the relationship between sources and journalists resembles a dance." Precisely because of their common interest in influencing the news agenda and framing the news, they are attracted to one another, which does not preclude an uneven relationship: "Although it takes two to tango, either sources or journalists can lead, but more often than not, sources do the leading" (Gans, 1979: 116).

Ericson, *et al.* (1989) were skeptical regarding the general proposition that sources have the upper hand in their transactions with journalists. In their study, the sources generally perceived the media as the stronger part who would leave little room for strategies of non-cooperation. Instead, sources tried to police the flow of information to journalists through a combination of enclosure and disclosure: in some areas they would be restrictive, even secretive, whereas in other areas they would perform an open or promotional information strategy. Strömbäck and Nord (2006) concluded on the basis of Swedish data that "it is the journalists and not their political sources that lead the tango most of the time" (p. 147). On a more general note, Schlesinger (1990) has criticized research on journalist-source relationships for a high degree of media-centrism, so that sources are studied primarily from the point of view of the media. As Schlesinger (1990) argues, sources compete internally and are in conflict both with each other and with the media "*prior to or contemporaneous with the appearance of definitions in the media*" (Schlesinger, 1990: 68, emphasis in the original). Consequently, the question of who is the primary definer of the news – sources or media – cannot be answered in general, but must refer to practice, because "*primary definition becomes an achievement rather than a wholly structurally determined outcome*" (Schlesinger, 1990: 79, emphasis in the original).

The proliferation of various forms of media management and spin (Palmer, 2000), especially by political sources since the 1980s, is clear evidence of a growing awareness among sources of their need to tip the balance of power between the news media and themselves. A well-documented way of 'leading the dance' is the ability of sources to instigate news stories themselves through proactive encounters and information subsidies (Lewis, *et al.*, 2008). Political communication has become professionalized (Negrine, 2008) through the employment of 'spin doctors,' media training of politicians, and the usage of marketing research techniques such as focus groups. Davis (2003) concluded, on the basis of data from Great Britain, that the state and political parties have successfully used public relations instruments to "increase their long-term media access advantage and to manage difficult media relations" (p. 42). In some cases, however, less resourceful campaigning groups such as Greenpeace have also had some success in influencing the media's agenda through the deployment of spectacular media strategies. Still, sources' reliance on media management and spin can prove a two-edged sword. When political parties internalize media strategies in their policy development,

spin

▶ markets as exchange mechanisms of journalism, p. 92

they may win individual battles with journalists but, in the long run, they may lose the war with the media, because politics as an institution is becoming mediatized, and thus increasingly dependent on the logic of the news media (Hjarvard, 2008b; Strömbäck, 2008).

mediatization

Even with due attention to the diverse strategies of various social actors trying to lead the dance around the news, the exchange model has its shortcomings. Blumler and Gurevitch (1981) themselves suggested an expanded framework which, among other things, would take into account the role-regulated nature of their relationship and the emergence of a shared culture in which both parties recognize the values and practices of the other. Davis (2010) has taken the idea of a shared culture of news one step further in his study of the interaction between journalists and political sources. Political journalists are not only engaged in a co-production of news with political sources; they are implicated in the 'social construction of politics.' As far as politicians are concerned, news media and journalists are an indispensable part of their political work, and they use journalists to gain information and interpretations about ongoing political affairs. Even communication between parties and among party members is often mediated by journalists. As a result, journalists "come to act, often inadvertently, as political sources, intermediaries and political actors" (Davis, 2010: 81).

GENRES AND ROLES

Studies of journalism have focused overwhelmingly on news in general and political news in particular. It is, however, important to recognize that journalists produce a variety of other genres, from feature stories and portraits of interesting people, to diverse forms of review, analysis, and commentary about ongoing events.◄ News media report on high and low art forms like music (Jensen and Larsen, 2010) as well as broader cultural affairs and lifestyle phenomena (Kristensen, 2010). Generally speaking, journalism addresses more than public issues of relevance for citizens – they provide general guidance for living to consumers and private individuals (Eide and Knight, 1999). In dealing with these wider issues, journalists do not always adhere to the classic norms of factual and neutral reporting associated with the news genre. Often they are not only allowed, but expected to provide interpretations, evaluations, and opinions. Although journalists are trained to separate news from views, in practice they combine news and views in a variety of ways (Hjarvard, 2010b).

The different journalistic genres serve to guide both journalists and audiences regarding the purpose and structure of the textual content and the level of subjective opinion that is appropriate. Each genre can be placed on a scale from low to high degrees of opinion that are allowed and expected of the journalist (Figure 5.2). The traditional news genre, along with service announcements, is at the informational end of the scale, while editorials and commentary are at the opinionated end of the scale. Feature articles constitute a broad genre that often balances between interpretation and evaluation, whereas reviews are expected to provide explicit evaluations, perhaps even recommendations in the form of quantitative ratings ('stars'). Evidently, the position of each genre on this scale of opinion will vary according to the specific news media in question, the topic of coverage, as well as the cultural context. On the whole, the system of genres informs journalistic production through general guidelines of how to address various issues with different levels of subjective involvement.

objectivity

The question of objectivity or subjectivity in journalism is not only a question of generic conventions, nor only of how to report 'non-political' issues. On the contrary, studies of news media have, for a long time, highlighted the social construction of "objectivity as a strategic ritual" in news production (Tuchman, 1972), simultaneously criticizing the news media for an ideologically biased reporting of political events, disguised as journalistic impartiality (Hall, *et al.*, 1978). Instead of employing a simple dichotomy of partisan and nonpartisan journalism in political news reporting, it is useful to develop a typology of a wider spectrum of journalistic roles as they relate to

► genres – Chapter 10, p. 196

Low		Degree of opinion		High
Information	**Interpretation**		**Evaluation**	**Opinion**
News	Interview	Analysis	Portrait	Editorial
Services	Reportage	Feature	Review	Commentary

Note: The figure locates journalistic genres and their relative position on a scale from information to opinion. Positions may vary according to type of news medium, topic of coverage, and cultural context.

Figure 5.2 Journalistic genres on a scale of opinion

political issues. Blumler and Gurevitch (1977) suggested a typology of four roles for media personnel's involvement in political communication: editorial guide, moderator, watchdog, and entertainer. Part of the value of their typology is that it relates journalistic roles to the corresponding roles of audiences and politicians. Weaver and Wilhoit (1986) proposed a distinction between an information dissemination role and an adversary role, with an interpretative/investigative role in between the two. Neither of these typologies, however, engaged directly with the question of subjectivity or partisanship in journalism.

Patterson (1998) put forward a helpful distinction between active and passive journalistic roles, which apply to both neutral and partisan news reporting. Although he used it to map a field of journalistic roles in five different countries, the distinction supports a more general framework covering various forms of partisan roles in journalism. The passive and neutral role occurs when the journalist acts as a *disseminator* of information, trying to give the audience the bare facts of the event. The neutral, yet active role is held by the *watchdog* who exercises investigative reporting in order to criticize any misuses of power in society. The active and partisan role is performed by the journalist as an *advocate* who uses the media as a platform for explicit criticism and advocacy. The partisan role, finally, has a passive counterpart in the role of the *supporter*, i.e., a journalist who does not explicitly act as an advocate, but rather stays loyal to a normative or political cause, and provides selectively partisan reporting of facts and events.

Patterson's (1998) distinction between active and passive forms of journalism did not take into account the fact that some journalism has developed an interpretative stance that may entail subjective involvement, but which is not partisan in the sense of consistently favoring a particular ideology or political movement outside journalism. Gulati, *et al.* (2004) demonstrated the growing importance of such interpretative genres as news analysis and commentary in both print and electronic media, and McNair (2000) called attention to "'the columnary explosion' (and its broadcast equivalent – the proliferation of pundits and specialist correspondents)" (p. 82). Also in the case of interpretative journalism, it is possible to distinguish between passive and active roles. If the journalist, as an interpreter, takes the position of an *observer*, his role is predominantly passive. The observer tries to keep a distance from the subject matter, and aims primarily at explaining why certain political actions or events take place. In contrast, the *commentator* takes on the more active role of interpreting and evaluating the motives behind politicians' actions, as well as suggesting likely outcomes. The observer remains detached, while the commentator – willingly or unwillingly – may become part of the political game (Hjarvard, 2010b). Figure 5.3 provides an overview of these different journalistic roles and generic practices.

	Neutral	Interpretative	Partisan
Passive	*Disseminator:* Reporting of facts and events	*Observer:* Explaining actions and events	*Supporter:* Selective reporting of facts and events
Active	*Watchdog:* Critical and investigative reporting	*Commentator:* Evaluation and prediction of actions and events	*Advocate:* Criticism and advocacy

Figure 5.3 Journalistic roles and types of discursive practice (source: Hjarvard, 2010b: 32). The typology is partially based on Patterson (1998).

ONLINE JOURNALISM

As a practice and a profession, journalism flourished throughout the twentieth century, in close conjunction with the proliferation of the major mass media – printed newspapers and broadcast news. From the end of the twentieth century, the spread of digital and online news media, first on the internet and later on mobile platforms, has radically changed the conditions of journalistic work. As Deuze (2007: 140) has proclaimed,

> journalism as it is, is coming to an end. The boundaries between journalism and other forms of public communication – ranging from public relations or advertorials to weblogs and podcasts – are vanishing, the internet makes all other types of news media rather obsolete

Even if one takes this prophecy with a grain of salt, there is little doubt that both news media and journalism have been in a peculiar state of permanent transition during the last two decades (Hjarvard, 2010a). There is a high degree of uncertainty – from utopian visions to worst-case scenarios – about democracy, business models, and the relationship of news media to their audiences.

While the readership of paid newspapers – and thereby their income – has been declining for decades in most Western countries, no viable business model for news in digital media has been found. The users of the internet and mobile platforms generally are not willing to pay for news, and other traditional sources of income such as classified advertisements have been taken over by other players on the internet. This puts a double pressure on existing news media: they must reduce the costs associated with old news media while simultaneously investing in new media platforms, with no guarantee of earning new money. Consequently many traditional newspapers have folded, and journalists are facing growing unemployment.

declining newspaper readership

unemployment among journalists

In the newsroom, the arrival of new media has changed work routines and the required skills, as well as journalists' understanding of the news format as such. New media have placed an added premium on the immediacy of news. In one sense, news has always been preoccupied

immediacy

with the present tense because of the news format and the constant pressure to meet an upcoming deadline. This became even more pronounced in the production of broadcast news – what Schlesinger (1978) described as a "stop-watch culture." The arrival of satellite news gathering and 24-hour television news channels like CNN further accentuated the ideal of immediacy and live news reporting (Hjarvard, 1992; Cushion and Lewis, 2010). And, as Domingo (2008) has demonstrated in his study of online internet newsrooms, the "ability to permanently update the website was seen as the defining feature of online news when compared to traditional media" (p. 115). Interestingly, the primacy of immediacy was "overwhelming" in online news media affiliated with traditional media, whereas online-only media represented an alternative news agenda, and did not experience the same need to compete on immediacy with their colleagues in off-line media.

The convergence◀ between old and new media has transformed news organizations, so that they may be able to produce news for a whole range of media platforms: printed newspapers, radio, television, internet, and mobile media. Earlier, the practice of journalism had been tied to specific media, but since the 1990s bi- or multimedia newsrooms have gradually become the standard. In his study of BBC News, Cottle (1999) demonstrated how the introduction of new technologies along with the simultaneous production of news for two or more media demanded multi-skilled personnel who mastered both general journalistic methods and specific technological skills relating to, for instance, radio as well as television. Many journalists have experienced this process as a threat to professional standards, as their work may be spread out too thinly across many tasks: multi-skilling may result in de-skilling (Cottle, 1999). Other studies report that, in fact, journalists may find working together with former competitors rewarding, so that the expected 'cultural clashes' between online and offline news have turned out less significant than expected (Singer, 2004). A comparative study of digital newsrooms in Britain and Spain found that

multimedia newsrooms

multi-skilling or de-skilling

> digitization seems to have an ambivalent impact on journalism. Multi-skilling leaves journalists less time to fulfill traditional journalistic practices such as double-checking of sources [...] On the other hand, digital archives make it easier to use file material, which can allow journalists to contextualize their stories more fully.
>
> (Avilés, *et al.*, 2004: 99)

With the growing number of media platforms, there is a growing demand for a larger output of news. This, in turn, may shift the balance between journalists producing original stories and rewriting these stories for another medium. The online availability of news has also pushed journalism towards a continuous updating of news stories at the expense of researching new stories. Observational studies of online journalism in five different German news organizations demonstrated a high dependency on 'external' news stories from news agencies and from other online news media (Quandt, 2008). Digital content management systems have become very important for the organization of work, and many online journalists rarely leave their newsrooms. As such, these may – paradoxically – become 'closed' social networks in which journalists "are producing news about 'the outside world', but most of the time, they do not make contact with the outside world" (Quandt, 2008: 93–95). In principle, new digital technologies make it easier for journalists to produce and distribute multi-media reports from remote locations. Whether or not this potential is realized depends not only on the technology, but on the resources and policies of the news organization in question.

demand for larger news output

digital content management systems

THE ACTIVE AUDIENCE

Perhaps the biggest challenge to journalism comes not from the new media themselves, but

▶ convergence – Chapter 1, p. 8

from the fact that they enable audiences to play a much more active role in news production. Concurrently with the proliferation of new media, new notions of citizen journalism, 'news you can use,' and user-generated content have gained momentum as ways of conceptualizing – and putting into practice – an altered relationship between journalism and its audience. New media allow audiences to bypass journalists and to research some news stories for themselves. At the same time, the transition from traditional 'push' media such as newspapers and television to digital 'pull' media means that audiences can compose their own news diet from the menu of various media.

In the past, journalism had demonstrated a professional ignorance of sorts about audiences. Even in a commercial media system like American network television, in which audience research provided news departments with a continuous flow of data about their actual audiences, Gans (1970) observed little interest among journalists in news consumers. The journalists "are presenting the news, not trying to satisfy an audience, and the less they know of the audience, the more attention they can pay to the news" (Gans, 1970: 9; quoted from Schlesinger, 1987: 115).

Today, an increased orientation in journalism towards the audience has not simply been prompted by the possibilities of new media, but is – to borrow a phrase from Sigmund Freud – an overdetermined process.◀ Encouraged by several factors at the same time, news media and journalists can no longer afford to ignore the audience. As mentioned, news media have been subject to strong commercial pressures during recent decades, and the former separation between newsrooms and marketing divisions has, in many cases, been replaced by cooperation. Also the coming of new audience research techniques has influenced editors and journalist, for instance, by assisting newsrooms in developing comprehensive reader profiles based on social, economic, and life-style demographics◀ (Willig, 2010). Since the 1990s, moreover, ideas that have been labeled variously as public journalism, citizen journalism, or civic journalism have gained momentum in the United States, and have spread to other parts of the world. While drawing on several different philosophical and political roots (Eksterowicz and Roberts, 2000; Glasser, 1999), these ideas articulate a common ambition of reconnecting journalism with ideals of civic participation in democratic life. In journalistic discussions and practices, they have often been intertwined specifically with the participatory ideals and potentials associated with new media, particularly the internet including its bloggers and social network sites. In this way, new ideals within the journalistic profession have resonated with, and have been legitimated by, a variety of factors that jointly push journalism towards the audience.

public, citizen, or civic journalism

user-generated content

This orientation towards the audience is witnessed in the growing importance of user-generated content (UGC) in many news organizations. UGC encompasses many types of content – from amateur news footage to brief user comments on blogs – that reflect very different kinds and levels of user involvement. Generally, the attitude among journalists has been a cautious one of not relinquishing control over content to users (Newman, 2009; Örnebring, 2008), emphasizing their own role as the providers of reliable information. User influence represents a real challenge to the professional journalistic values of autonomy and credibility (Singer and Ashman, 2009). While finding user input and responses interesting, journalists typically have opposed influences on their independent news judgment and their 'authorship' of the news. There are signs, however, that editors are perhaps gradually becoming accustomed to the interactive nature of the internet, seeing "information less as an end product than as a basis for user engagement, participation and personalization" (Singer, 2006: 265).

User-generated content, further, is valued differently for different journalistic genres. A study of tabloid news content in the UK and Sweden reported that "users are mostly empowered to create popular culture-oriented content and personal/everyday life-oriented content rather than news/informational content" (Örnebring, 2008: 783). The users

▶ overdetermination – Chapter 1, p. 5
▶ lifestyle research – Chapter 8, p. 168

themselves, likewise, are not equally interested in other users' contributions about all aspects of news. Wahl-Jorgensen, *et al.* (2010) found that users value UGC when it is seen as "immediate and fresh, authentic, emotionally engaging and democratizing. By contrast, audience comment is viewed as suspect because it is considered to be of questionable quality" (Wahl-Jorgensen, *et al.*, 2010: 190). In the specific case of breaking news, UGC and services like Facebook, YouTube, and Twitter have become both important new sources of information and influences on when and how established news media report events. For breaking news, journalists may no longer be the first to report what is happening, and must instead focus on acquiring, verifying, and evaluating information from users and other sources (Newman, 2009).

GATEWATCHING AND BLOGGING

Some researchers have taken a more radical stance on the future of journalism in a digital and converging media environment. They see the rise of citizen-produced news media such as Global Reporter and OhmyNews, the general spread of social network sites, and the influence of citizen bloggers as evidence of a profound change in the role of news media and journalism. From this point of view, new digital media represent a paradigmatic change in the social production and distribution of information, including news, which may – at least in the long run – render traditional journalism obsolete. Bruns (2005b, 2008b) has argued that the authority of journalists to act as gatekeepers is rapidly eroding, and is being supplemented or even replaced by a new paradigm of "gatewatching." On the internet, it is possible for anybody to watch

gatewatching

> the many gates through which a steady stream of information passes from these sources, and [to highlight] from this stream that information which is of most relevance to one's own personal interest or to the interests of one's wider community.
>
> (Bruns, 2008b: 177)

In gatekeeping, journalists remain in control of every step of the process, from source encounters to the final editing of the news. By contrast, gatewatching allows users, individually and collaboratively, to watch, comment, and edit at every stage of the communication process. The idea of gatewatching is closely related to Bruns' (2008a) concepts of 'produsage' and 'produsers,' which refer to the conflation of production and usage into user-led forms of collaborative content creation.

produsage

From Bruns' perspective, every user may, at least potentially, be engaged in some form of gatewatching and, hence, in news production and content sharing. Some users, however, demonstrate a much more active and organized interest in production. Schaffer (2007: 13) distinguishes different categories of citizens' media outlets, including:

- *community cooperatives* that are typically run by voluntary labor in a local area, and which may have no or only limited professional experience;
- *blog aggregator sites* or portals that facilitate citizens scanning multiple blogs, and where bloggers may interact with each other; and
- *legacy media sites* that are set up by established media, but which allow users to dominate content, in contrast to their professional sites.

Citizen journalism may represent both advantages and disadvantages, compared to professional journalism. Reich's (2008) study suggests that citizen journalists may be more prone to pursue and report stories on their own initiative when they have firsthand knowledge of events. They find it more difficult to deal with stories that involve potentially conflicted encounters with organized interests from politics or industry, or which require a juxtaposition and interpretation of several different sources. Most citizens have neither the resources nor the authority to conduct interviews with elite sources, and they cannot sustain long-lasting relationships with such sources. Instead, they must rely on information from technologies such as the internet and from personal experience (Reich, 2008).

As Schaffer (2007) has observed, citizen journalists do not report in the same objective news format that professional journalists are trained to use. They do not "contribute fully reported articles with leads, middles, and ends" (Schaffer, 2007: 10), but may prefer different and more opinionated formats. Citizen blogging rarely involves any kind of independent research into news stories, but mostly relies on existing news and information (Lowrey and Latta, 2008). The most successful citizen bloggers may come to resemble the pundits and commentators of professional news media: they produce opinionated columns on contemporary issues, often delivered in a personal style, and in order to sustain a daily output with a certain quality in terms of substance, writing, and audience appeal, blogging also become highly routinized. Like their commercial counterparts, they may be highly sensitive to audience figures, often basing themselves on material from traditional news media. As a result, the production routines of high-profile bloggers may in some cases come to resemble those of professional journalists (Lowrey and Latta, 2008).

blogging

Blogging has no doubt increased the diversity of available information and opinion. In a comparison between the news agendas of blogs, other user-driven media, and traditional news media, Pew (2010) reported that the stories and issues that get the most attention in user-driven media differ considerably from the priorities of traditional news outlets, with significant additional differences between the news agendas of blogs, Twitter, and YouTube. Nevertheless, Pew (2010) also found that "despite the unconventional agenda of bloggers, traditional media still provides the vast majority of their information. More than 99% of the stories linked to came from legacy outlets like newspapers and broadcast networks."

The general importance of user-driven and citizen news media perhaps derives from their ability to distribute stories, to provide interpretations, and to engage users – more so than from any substantial production of independent news stories on a continuous basis. The evidence so far contradicts the idea that new media and citizen journalism will render professional journalism superfluous. The more interesting question may be how old and new media will complement and interact with each other in the field of journalism, and how the borders between journalism and other forms of technologically mediated communication and social interaction will be reconfigured in the future. As Schaffer observed, "citizen journalism is emerging as a form of 'bridge' media, linking traditional forms of journalism with classic civic participation" (Schaffer, 2007: 7).

complementarity of blogging and journalism

A WIDER CONTEXT FOR NEWSROOM STUDIES

The sociological turn in journalism studies from the late 1970s onwards established a new, critical research agenda that challenged previous assumptions in research and self-conceptions among journalists. Cottle (2000) has argued that this sociological legacy may itself have become a kind of orthodoxy that needs to be challenged in order to account for the rapidly changing conditions of journalism in contemporary society. One key insight from the sociological turn has been the importance of *routines* for the production of news. As argued by, for instance, Tuchman (1978: 45), "a news medium cannot process idiosyncratic phenomena. It must reduce all phenomena to known classifications." Only by "routinizing the unexpected" (Tuchman, 1973) is a news organization able to produce a continuous output on the basis of the chaos of events in the world. From Cottle's (2000) point of view, the strong focus on routines may suggest an organizational functionalism that loses sight of the competences and reflexivity of journalists acting adequately in relation to highly diverse situations and different news media. In today's differentiated news ecology, a generalized idea of 'journalism' is no longer plausible, Cottle suggests, which leads him to advocate a conceptual shift from routine to practice. By focusing on practices in their institutional contexts, the prevailing journalistic procedures

routines or practices

may be seen as enabling and facilitating as well as repressive and limiting. Similarly, the dominance of a shared ideology of objectivity may have been overstated. Various forms of journalism – public journalism, advocacy journalism, and emotionally charged tabloid journalism – are not produced according to professional ideals of objectivity, but may rather be informed by a "subjectivist" news epistemology, Cottle (2000) notes, calling for a "second wave of news ethnography."

Still, there may have been valid reasons for the focus on general organizational routines and shared professional ideals in many of the sociological contributions during the 1970 and 1980s. Scientific paradigms◄ are usually established through a set of key studies that emphasize some general findings and assumptions, while it is up to later contributions to introduce nuances, variations, and exceptions into the paradigm. Furthermore, the sociological turn in news studies coincided with a phase in the history of journalism during which the journalistic profession and news organizations had acquired a level of organizational maturity, professionalism, and social recognition. It may be hypothesized that both the news media and journalism displayed rather more common features during that phase than in the present diversified news ecology. Since then, news organizations have become part of larger media corporations (Bagdikian, 2004) that often try to impose their agenda on news divisions while, at the same time, new digital media have blurred the boundaries between news and other genres (Deuze, 2007). As a result, news media today may no longer enjoy the same degree of distinctiveness and autonomy.

In addition, the relative autonomy of the journalistic profession is generally considered to be under pressure, once again from new media as well as commercial interests. Preston (2009) has argued that the Keynesian◄ regulatory regime of the mid-twentieth century allowed for new social spaces in which professional norms and vocational values had a greater say. During this period, also, journalists acquired greater control over their particular field of knowledge production; during recent decades "spaces for non-marketised knowledge production shaped by specialist professional norms, values and criteria have been eroded by the neo-liberal regime of regulation" (Preston, 2009: 173). Journalism as a profession clearly is in need of 'maintenance work,' and must renegotiate its contract with society (Eide, 2010), since it is no longer evident what separates journalism from other kinds of media practices.

Örnebring (2009) sheds light on this development by using Evetts' (2006) distinction between two kinds of professionalism. *Occupational professionalism* is the traditional kind in which a group develops a shared identity, a work practice, and a code of ethics, mainly controlled by the group itself through professional associations and by education and training. The group exerts an occupational control over their own work that is based on trust among practitioners, employer, and clients. In contrast, *organizational professionalism* is both a discourse and a practice regarding the management of organizations that focus on the standardization of work practices, targets, performance assessments, and certification. This type of professionalism does not emerge from within, but is typically promoted from the outside by managerial interests. Historically, journalism has aspired to occupational professionalism, on a par with archetypal professions such as medicine and law, but it has never achieved the same status, because, among other things, anyone may practice journalism. Örnebring (2009) demonstrates how journalism increasingly is informed by the norms and practices of organizational professionalism. The deregulation of labor markets, the proliferation of short-term contracts, and other forms of flexible work (Sennett, 1998) make it more difficult for journalists to retain occupational control over their work. At the same time, the increasing centrality of technologies in the workplace, including demands on journalists to acquire multi-media skills, may tip the balance in favor of organizational professionalism. Other professional groups – doctors, teachers, researchers, and civil servants – experience a similar kind of managerial push towards a regime of organizational

professsionalism – occupational or organizational

► paradigms – Chapter 15, p. 285
► Keynesian economics – Chapter 19, p. 355

professionalism. Thus, journalistic work may be said to increasingly resemble other types of knowledge-intensive work.

While the outcomes of these processes are still unresolved, they suggest that future studies of news production must take into account both a more diverse news ecology and its interplay with other media and with society at large. News production and journalism are subject to many of the same developments that affect other cultural industries (Hesmondhalgh, 2007). It therefore becomes urgent to look beyond the specificities of news production and to consider how news and journalism resemble and are intertwined with other forms of media production. Furthermore, journalists increasingly share the working conditions of other members of the so-called creative class (Florida, 2002) in late-modern societies, which means that newsroom studies may find inspiration in the wider sociology of work.

The study of news production has already created a wealth of findings to inform this area of research. A future research agenda will benefit from a broader perspective that contextualizes news production both to the wider domain of cultural industries and to culture and society as such. In *The Odd Couple*, Gwendolyn asked a seemingly naïve question of the journalist, Felix: "where do you get your ideas from?" Metaphorically speaking, this is still an important question for news production research. But the answer to her question would benefit from a research agenda that does not take Felix's response for an answer and looks beyond the news.

RESOURCE BOX 5.1: ONLINE RESOURCES ABOUT NEWS MEDIA AND NEWS PRODUCTION

- Portal to the *world's online newspapers*: www.onlinenewspapers.com
- *MediaChannel* – a US website with critical information and arguments about the media's influence on politics, culture, and society: www.mediachannel.org
- Website and blog about the concept produsage: www.produsage.org/about
- Blog and website with a focus on *free newspapers*: www.newspaperinnovation.com/index.php/resources
- *The Knight Citizen News Network* – a "self-help portal that guides both ordinary citizens and traditional journalists in launching and responsibly operating community news and information sites": www.kcnn.org/site
- Jan Schaffer: "Citizen Media: Fad or the Future of News? The rise and prospects of hyperlocal journalism," 2007. Online book about *local community media* and their possibilities: www.j-lab.org/publications/citizen-media-fad-or-the-future-of-news

6 Discursive realities

Kim Christian Schrøder

- an overview of the *development of quantitative content analysis*
- an *example* of content analysis in practice
- a comparison of six forms of *qualitative discourse analysis*
- a review of approaches to the study of *visual media content*
- an example of the analysis of *images and texts* in advertising

> What's in a name? That which we call a rose
> By any other name would smell as sweet.
>
> *Romeo and Juliet*, II, ii, 1–2

WHAT'S IN A NAME?

What we call things matters, in spite of the fact that – as Juliet says – a name for a thing is in principle arbitrary. Naming is framing. Most people probably remember the global flu pandemic that broke out in April 2009 as 'the swine flu.' But during the early stages of the pandemic it was by no means certain that this label would be the one to prevail. Other equally accurate and sensible names for the disease (among them Mexican flu, new flu, and H1N1) were brought forward by various actors on the global scene, and several of these labels gained widespread currency until the label 'swine flu' succeeded in outmaneuvering the other candidates, after a discursive struggle of global proportions in which the economic, religious, cultural, and scientific stakes were high (Vigsø 2010).

In the early stages of the epidemic,

> there was a large amount of uncertainty regarding the spreading of the flu, the number of victims, the degree of fatality, and the effects of treatment and inoculation. The result of this combination of alleged seriousness and uncertainty paved the way for intensive media coverage.
>
> (Vigsø 2010: 229)

Since the consequences of contracting the disease could be lethal, the outbreak of the flu was clearly a health issue. But when it was first named 'the Mexican flu,' because the first cases were discovered in Mexico, the Mexican government immediately responded to this label as a tourism issue, fearing that it would stigmatize Mexico in the eyes of potential tourists to the country. Mexico therefore contested this label in the relevant international health fora.

The 'swine flu' label, which was derived from the fact that the virus had a family resemblance to types of flu found in pigs, was not precise because unlike previous swine flus, this variety attacked humans. Moreover, because pigs are religiously impure for Jews and Muslims, it was argued that merely to pronounce this name would be degrading to these groups. For pork-producing and -exporting countries the consequences of the swine flu label could be economically devastating, and the repercussions would also implicate countries depending on corn and soy beans, which are staples in pig breeding.

To call the pandemic 'the new flu' would be more accurate, because the virus was actually a new, hybrid form that combined swine, avian, and human flu – but in case the epidemic became long-lasting, this name would not be appropriate. 'H1N1' would be the objective, scientific label for the flu, but clearly lacked dramatic appeal.

In a discourse-analytical perspective, the reason why the naming of the pandemic became an issue of nation-branding and strategic reputation management (Vigsø 2010: 231) has to do with the power of a word to bring with it a whole semantic field, i.e., an ensemble of meanings that invites associations to do with the character of the pandemic, its medical and national origins, its dissemination across borders, the appropriate counter-measures, and a host of popular narratives. For the health authority of the global community, WHO, the most expedient term was the most scientific one (H1N1), which would be most likely to prevent irrational reactions to the pandemic. However, as Vigsø (2010: 237) observes,

semantic fields

> which of the frames will become the successful one depends to a large extent on the logic of the media, [...] it is quite clear that the Mexican and the Swine Flu have the largest potentials for fitting into the media agendas,

because they lend themselves to vivid dramatization.

The struggles over the naming of the H1N1 pandemic encapsulate and exemplify a pervasive discursive phenomenon, which occurs across all types of human encounters and verbal exchanges, mediated as well as non-mediated by technologies: the power of words, and of signs generally, irrespective of mode of signification (such as visual and audio signs), to frame and define social reality. The world as we know it is constructed through words (as well as other types of signs), and the particular choices and combinations of words, images, and sounds that social agents (such as the media) use to make sense of events, processes, and institutions produce 'versions' of reality that are negotiated in public and private space on their way to becoming accepted as legitimate and 'true.' or as inadequate and 'biased.'◀ To the extent that modern societies are 'mediatized' societies (Lundby 2009; Hjarvard 2008a; Livingstone 2009b), the power to define our shared reality is increasingly negotiated through the mechanisms of media logics.

This chapter deals with the ways in which the media present events in the real world in verbal and visual form, thus constructing versions of reality which shape the meanings and values that inform our attitudes and behaviors as, for instance, citizens and consumers. The public's dependency on media representations to keep track of events in order to make decisions in civic and everyday life has often led media researchers to focus attention on the precise manner in which pictures of social reality are constructed for us by the media through framing mechanisms, topical structures, and expressive forms.

THE CRITICAL ANALYSIS OF MEDIA CONSTRUCTIONS OF SOCIAL REALITY

While complaints about 'bias' in the media are legion across the spectrum of public debate, academic research has most often been driven by a 'critical' interest◀ in exposing the differential *news* treatment of social groups in conformity with entrenched hierarchies of power and privilege, for example, in the strategic area of industrial conflict (e.g., Glasgow University Media Group 1976; Hall, *et al.* 1976). Similarly, studies of *advertising* have taken on stereotypical gender roles (e.g., Andrén, *et al.* 1978; Goffman 1976; Millum 1975) and the promotion of consumption as a solution to complex social or personal problems (e.g., Williamson 1978; Vestergaard and Schrøder 1985; Leiss, *et al.* 1986). A third

▶ constructionism – Chapter 3, p. 51
▶ critical research traditions – Chapter 19, p. 359

body of research has examined the realities implied in media fiction, particularly *television series* – from the 1960s (e.g., DeFleur 1964), via US commission reports on television as a social issue (Surgeon General 1972), to cultivation research.◄ Over several decades, cultivation studies have identified a discrepancy between real-life crime statistics and the amounts and kinds of violence depicted on television, as well as the possible impact of TV violence especially on heavy viewers and its potential political support for conservative law-and-order policies (Gerbner and Gross 1976; for critiques, see Newcomb 1978; Hirsch 1980).

A critical orientation is commonly found on both sides of the quantitative-qualitative divide, even though this is sometimes overlooked in overviews aligning critical theory with qualitative methodology, and more mainstream theories with quantitative approaches. At the same time, scholars' readiness to accept a conception of discursive representations as a 'construction' has varied in the development of textual and content studies. In a first phase, a number of studies tended to assume that the media could be studied as a phenomenon separate from the rest of society, asking how 'faithfully' media represented social reality (Fowler, *et al.* 1979). This has been the rationale of many quantitative content studies (Glasgow University Media Group 1976), but also of some varieties of critical discourse studies, reviewed below (Fowler, *et al.* 1979). A second phase has emphasized the mutual constitution of media and modern societies, so that it may not be feasible, methodologically or epistemologically, to compare 'media realities' with any independent indicators. The various forms of discourse analysis dealt with below, but also certain approaches to content measurement, increasingly take as their premise that media content is not so much a secondary reflection as an artefact and a practice in which society is both reproduced and contested. This premise makes it all the more important to critically examine the discursive frames through which the media construct authoritative versions of vital aspects of contemporary human existence, such as climate change (Carvalho 2005) or the discursive interfaces of Western and Islamic cultures (Barkho 2010).

► cultivation research – Chapter 8, p. 166

QUANTITATIVE CONTENT ANALYSIS

Questions that audiences – and researchers – ask

The analysis of the struggles over the discursive framing of the H1N1 pandemic above was mainly carried out with qualitative tools of analysis. Having formed an intuitive impression of the relative dominance of the different names of the pandemic, Vigsø (2010) suggested that media logics would favor the more vivid labels (Mexican flu, swine flu) over the more neutral and scientific ones (new flu, H1N1), which seemed to be preferred by health authorities. The way to verify such assumptions is to do a quantitative content analysis of the issue, in which one counts systematically the occurrence of the set of pandemic names in a well-defined corpus of media discourse.

Such an analysis need not always be large-scale in order to satisfy one's curiosity with respect to the frequency of the occurrence of different labels. Vigsø (2010) opted for a small-scale content analysis in which he simply counted the occurrence of pandemic names on the Twitter sites of two institutional actors in Sweden: the official institution of crisis communication and the Swedish public service broadcaster (Table 6.1). The content analysis confirmed Vigsø's assumption that the official crisis authority would follow the WHO's recommendation of the more scientific names, while the media site opted for the more evocative popular label.

I next look at a more developed example of content analysis, but still one which is feasible and meaningful without having to devote a huge amount of time and statistical expertise to the task. Analysis Box 6.1 takes as its example a TV program belonging to the annual *Review of the Year* genre, in which around New Year a national TV channel (the BBC in 1998) offers a selective, collective memory of what happened in that year. This particular year included events like the Bill Clinton-Monica Lewinsky

Table 6.1 Use of names for the flu in Swedish Twitter

	H1N1	*New flu*	*Swine flu*	*Others*	*No name*	*Total*
Official crisis authority	38%	18%	8%	20%	16%	100%
Public service broadcaster	–	6%	90%	4%	–	100%

Source: Vigsø 2010

case, the Football World Cup in France, South African President Nelson Mandela's eightieth birthday, pop singer George Michael being arrested for lewd conduct at a public lavatory, *Titanic* – the most expensive movie ever made (by 1998), and many other events from the domestic and international scene grouped under themes like sports, medical breakthroughs, women in the public eye, highlights of the world of entertainment, spectacular crimes, obituaries of the year, etc. In just over one hour, this retrospective program provided one particular answer to the question, "What happened in 1998?", at the same time implicitly labeling numerous other events as not worth remembering.

Having watched a program like *Review of the Year 1998*, the audience, being instinctively analytical, or semiotic, creatures, is left with certain general impressions of what the program was 'about,' and how this 'content' is likely to affect both viewers like themselves and the larger society represented. Predictably, there will be critical comments about women being depicted as secondary in political and economic matters, about a supposedly serious news review spending too much time on the trifles of the entertainment world, or about Third World events being all but ignored in an increasingly global society. In interpersonal everyday discussions, people will next try to substantiate their claims by referring to specific program elements, but because lay discussion rarely is sustained beyond impressions or speculations, it is difficult to determine who is right and who is wrong. One task of media and communication research, in the garb of 'content analysis,' is to address such issues, supposedly on behalf of a democratic society as an input to, and influence on, political and public debates about how its citizens and their concerns should collectively be portrayed by the media.

In order to interpret the implications of findings regarding both gender and other categories, content analysts need a standard of comparison. If one subscribes to the first-phase focus on media as separate from other social structuration, one may refer to 'reality itself,' as documented typically with official statistics regarding, for instance, the proportion of women and men in parliaments or occupational roles. If, instead, one relies on the second-phase premise regarding the mutual constitution of societies and mediated symbolic forms, an internal standard suggests itself, such as previous 'review of the year' programs going back five, ten, or twenty years, perhaps comparing, as well, with other genres. Additional sources of potential comparison arise from the distinction between public-service and commercial channels, and between print media, broadcast media, and network media.

It remains to emphasize that the analysis in Analysis Box 6.1 provides an illustration of, andreflection on, basic principles and applications of content analysis, not a full-fledged methodology of representative sampling, dual coding, and hypothesis testing.◄ A main advantage of quantitative content studies is that they can serve to confirm or disconfirm intuitive impressions by performing a systematic description of a large set of media discourses through numbers that express the frequency and prominence of particular textual properties (see also Mautner 2009). A drawback, or tradeoff, is the inevitable reduction of complexity that follows from the decontextualization of meaningful elements.

► quantitative content analysis: sampling, coding, and statistical procedures – Chapter 13, p. 248

ANALYSIS BOX 6.1: CONTENT ANALYSIS OF REVIEW OF THE YEAR 1998, BBC1 1998

Table 6.2: Representation of protagonists on *Review of the Year* 1998, BBC1 1998

	Men	%	Women	%	Total	%
Geographical belonging						
British	39	56%	15	65%	54	58%
American	8	11%	4	17%	12	13%
European	8	11%	2	9%	10	11%
Rest of the world	14	20%	1	4%	15	16%
Unidentifiable	1	1%	1	4%	2	2%
Total characters	**70**	**100%**	**23**	**100%**	**93**	**100%**
Social arena						
Politics	38	54%	7	30%	45	48%
Showbiz	22	31%	12	52%	34	37%
Sports	*16*	*23%*	*4*	*17%*	*20*	*22%*
Entertainment	*6*	*9%*	*8*	*35%*	*14*	*15%*
Science	2	3%	0	0%	2	2%
Everyday life	8	11%	4	17%	12	13%
Total characters	**70**	**100%**	**23**	**100%**	**93**	**100%**
GENDER	70	75%	23	25%	93	100%

Note: Some percentage columns add to 99% rather than 100% because of rounding.

Table 6.2 displays a basic quantitative content analysis of the BBC's 1998 *Review of the Year*. Among several potential categories, the analysis singled out the human individual, specifically characteristics of the program's personalities. It was decided to consider only the protagonists, defined as individuals at the center of attention by virtue of their being both mentioned verbally by name (in spoken or written form) and appearing visually on screen. Thus, media tycoon Rupert Murdoch, mentioned in the voice-over but not shown, and actor Leonardo DiCaprio, shown but not named, were excluded from the counts. This criterion is controversial, and led to the inclusion of perhaps less prominent individuals like few-month Russian Premier Primakov. The point is that such criteria must be justified theoretically through the operationalization of 'protagonist,' and then applied consistently across all cases. A particular theoretical motivation for analyzing individual protagonists is that they are the vehicles of particular social and cultural characteristics which together delineate a particular possible world.◀ Three types of characteristics were studied for present purposes:

▶ possible worlds – Chapter 1, p. 14

- *geographical origin* (perhaps suggesting a view of the world from a particular perspective);
- *gender* (considering claims about male dominance in the world of television); and
- *social arenas of activity* (exploring the prominence of four different sectors with which protagonists may commonly be associated: Politics, Showbiz (subdivided into Sports and Entertainment/Media), Science, and Everyday life).

It should be noted that categorization and subsequent quantification (lasting approximately four hours for this 75-minute program, including calculation of percentages with a pocket calculator) is by no means an automatic process. Almost every instance requires the discriminating ability of the analyst before assigning, for example, Princess Diana to the Entertainment category, Bill Clinton's mistress Monica Lewinsky to Politics, former astronaut and US senator John Glenn as a contributor to Science (rather than a Politician or Media Celebrity), Russian president Boris Yeltsin (and Russia) to Europe. In one interesting case, the Israeli singer Dana International was categorized as female (before a sex change, 'she' was a man) and European (appearing because she won the *European* Eurovision Song Contest). Any discussion about findings and their validity must begin by thus explicitly noting the criteria, procedures, and decisions of the analysis as conditions of intersubjectivity, disagreement, and research dialogue.

The findings regarding *geographical origin*, indicating three British out of every five protagonists, are hardly surprising in a British national program, whereas the minor role of European protagonists might raise eyebrows among EU observers at an insular British outlook. (A further breakdown would reveal that four of the ten Europeans are sport stars, four are Russian presidents or premiers, leaving then German Chancellor Helmuth Kohl and Serbian President Slobodan Milosevic as the sole representatives of non-Russian Europe.) In comparison, the Rest-of-the-world figures might seem high, but includes protagonists from Africa (3), Asia (6), the Middle East (3), and Latin America (3). Moreover, a preliminary, qualitative assessment suggests that most of the events dealt with in this rag-bag category are economic or political crises and natural disasters.

Regarding *social arenas,* citizens might welcome the fact that almost half the protagonists belong to the realm of politics, and might worry about the fact that Showbiz accounts for no less than a third (mainly Sports personalities) of the program's main characters, while Science, site of both revolutionary discoveries and ethical concerns, reaches a low of 2 percent. Again, a qualitative look behind the numbers suggests that 'Politics' is seen repeatedly through a lens of ridicule, in the case of the American presidency, parliamentary struggles in the Russian Duma, and the sexual politics of male British Members of Parliament. And, the apparently astonishing fact that people from Everyday Life are almost as prominent as Entertainment personalities is placed in perspective when it turns out that no less than 11 of the 12 instances represent either victims or perpetrators of sensational crime.

Finally, regarding *gender*, across the board three-fourths of the protagonists in this particular program are men, one-fourth women. The variations, however, suggest that women are relatively more prominent in the British than in the Rest-of-the-world category, less so in Politics and Science, more so in Showbiz, and even outnumbering men in Entertainment.

While qualitative researchers have sometimes been blunt in their critique of what appeared a scientistic attempt "to eliminate, as far as possible, any human element or bias" from the research process (Fiske 1990: 135), content analysts also have engaged in a critical redevelopment of their premises and procedures.

Revising categories

So far, this chapter has used the cumbersome term 'quantitative content analysis,' but the literature normally refers simply to 'content analysis,' while the qualitative study of media texts is variously called 'textual analysis' or, more recently, 'discourse analysis.' In a sense, quantitative social science has monopolized the generic term, as suggested by classic titles like *Content Analysis in Communication Research* (Berelson 1952), *Content Analysis. An Introduction to its Methodology* (Krippendorff 1980), or *Content Analysis for the Social Sciences and Humanities* (Holsti 1969). In the early decades of the twentieth century, quantitative newspaper analysis measured the column inches devoted by newspapers to particular subject matters, seeking to reveal "the truth about newspapers" and possibly criticize journalistic practice (Street 1909, quoted in Krippendorff 1980: 14). Other studies used content-analytical procedures not just to learn about media, but to monitor topics in press content in continuous surveys so as "to establish a system of bookkeeping of the 'social weather' comparable in principle to the statistics of the U.S. Weather Bureau" (Krippendorff 1980:14), and comparable, in certain respects, to agenda-setting research◀ half a century later. A third ancestor of modern content analysis were the propaganda studies◀ of enemy media during World War II, when American researchers monitored "domestic enemy broadcasts to understand and predict events within Nazi Germany and its allies and to estimate the effects of military actions on war mood" (Krippendorff 1980: 16).

► agenda-setting research – Chapter 8, p. 161
► propaganda studies – Chapter 9, p. 174

Around 1950, following developments in survey and other analytical techniques since the 1930s, content analysis was coming into maturity. In his famous and henceforth authoritative definition, Bernard Berelson (1952) synthesized earlier methodological reflections on the approach: "Content analysis is a research technique for the objective, systematic, and quantitative description of the manifest content of communication" (p. 18). The fundamental distinction in the analytical process, according to Berelson, is between 'knowledge' and 'interpretation' of media content ('inferences' to Berelson). While he recognized that the end goal of research is to make interpretations of the media, and of their relationship with either the intentions of senders or the consequences for the attitudes and behaviors of recipients, Berelson stipulated that such interpretation must not be mixed into the analytical process proper. The distinction appears from the statement that "knowledge of the content can legitimately support inferences about non-content events" (p. 18), and is clarified in a discussion of the difference between qualitative and quantitative approaches:

> In 'qualitative' analysis the interpretations (i.e., inferences about intent or effect) are more often made as *part* of the analytical process whereas in quantitative analysis the interpretations are more often likely to *follow* the analytic procedure. [...] The tendency of the qualitative analyst is to make his interpretations as he goes through the material – whenever a piece of material cues him in some way. The tendency of the 'quantitative' analyst is to base his interpretation upon the total completed analysis in order to see particular pieces of content in perspective.
>
> (Berelson 1952: 122–123, emphasis in the original)

The quantitative analyst, then, can hope to avoid 'interpreting' his data only if he concerns himself entirely with 'manifest,' or denotative, meanings and excludes latent, or connotative, meanings,◄ since manifest meanings are defined as those which everybody (both senders and recipients of messages) will spontaneously agree on. Berelson does acknowledge that, in a strict sense, 'manifest content' is merely that end of a continuum of meaning where meanings are *more* likely to be shared than at the other, radically polysemic◄ extreme. In hermeneutic terminology,◄ Berelson still assumed that one can, after all, examine understanding without a preunderstanding or horizon of expectations.

What amounted to a suppression in research practice of the role of interpretation in any human activity, has been at the heart of controversies in the theory of science since Berelson (see the early critique of Berelson by Kracauer (1953)). More recent definitions, also within content analysis, have involved a marked departure from Berelson's model. Thirty years on, Krippendorff (1980) advanced an alternative and influential definition: "Content analysis is a research technique for making replicable and valid inferences from data to their context" (p. 21). In developing his definition, Krippendorff was explicitly critical of Berelson's position, which he found unnecessarily restrictive. Krippendorff did agree that content analysis must be replicable, and therefore systematic, but he saw no reason why content analysis must be quantitative, and also dismissed the exclusion of latent meanings from the researcher's legitimate horizon of interests. Although his book remained focused on the mechanics and accreditation of content quantification, his conceptualization of interpretation differed fundamentally from Berelson's, despite relatively subtle differences of wording. Crucially, Krippendorff identified inferential processes in all stages of the research process, "from data to their context." In the establishment of analytical categories, the ascription of textual units to these categories, as well as the correlation of findings with theoretical conceptions of society and culture, the content analyst is inevitably an interpreter. This point was amply demonstrated in the discussion of the content categories to be counted in the analysis of the *Review of the* Year TV program above. In Krippendorff's (1980) words, the analyst is a reader of the meanings of a text, someone who is not merely engaged in "'extracting' content from the data as if it was objectively 'contained' in them. [...] meanings are always relative to a communicator" (p. 22).

With a cautious interpretation, one might suggest that this definition of 'content analysis' implies a constructionist reconceptualization of quantitative measurement. As such, Krippendorff's (1980) intervention represents one specification of the sometimes rather abstract acknowledgment that quantitative and qualitative approaches, also to media texts, are complementary in that they produce different analytical versions of reality, as an input to public debate about social reality and its mediation. In the qualitative literature on media texts, both the constructionist and critical points of departure have been in evidence from the beginning.

QUALITATIVE DISCOURSE ANALYSIS

The landscape of discourse studies

Discourse constructs social reality, including discourse studies itself as a scholarly field. This means that different scholars in this field draw maps of the world of discourse studies that are to some extent different. It is a fact that thousands of scholars around the world engage in discourse studies and label their work 'discourse analysis,' but they do so from a variety of different ontological, epistemological, theoretical, methodological, and analytical perspectives, and they see themselves as metaphorically inhabiting different scientific continents, nations, and sub-national regions.

► denotation and connotation – Chapter 2, p. 34
► polysemy – Chapter 9, p. 183
► hermeneutics – Chapter 2, p. 29

From their observation tower, Glynos, *et al.* (2009) see the field as consisting of six scholarly territories, which they label Political Discourse Theory, Rhetorical Political Analysis, Discourse Historical Approaches in Critical Discourse Analysis, Interpretive Policy Analysis, Discursive Psychology, and Q-Methodology. In spite of their differences, Glynos, *et al.* do not deem these approaches to be incompatible. This is, first, primarily, due to the fact that compared with other paradigms of social science research they share common concerns, notably a "centrality attributed to subjects in the construction and apprehension of meaning," and they "all conceive of themselves as responses to positivist and essentialist approaches that privilege causality over understanding and laws over contingency" (pp. 6–7).

Another comprehensive overview of discourse studies, Jørgensen and Phillips's *Discourse Analysis as Theory and Method* (2002), designates three types of discourse analysis: Laclau and Mouffe's Discourse Theory, Critical Discourse Analysis, and Discursive Psychology, which they see as different but compatible approaches. Thus, in spite of inevitable and necessary struggles between the different approaches, each in search of greater insight and explanatory power, the field of discourse studies is characterized by a moderate and respectful eclecticism (shared by this author), which allows the analyst to combine theoretical conceptualizations and methodological toolboxes from different approaches (see for instance the joint implementation of the toolboxes of Critical Discourse Analysis and Discursive Psychology for the analysis of political discourse in Schrøder and Phillips 2007). As Glynos, *et al.* (2009) put it, if we focus on the actual analytical problems, we can "treat the boundaries between different approaches as a lot more porous […]. In practice […] ontological presuppositions do not always act as the rigid barriers to inter-approach conversations that they are often made out to be" (pp. 6–7).

In this chapter, the focus is on two 'continents' in the world of discourse studies: First, *Critical Discourse Analysis* (CDA) and some of its derivations that are most applicable to doing media and communication studies: the Discourse-Historical Approach, Discourse Ethnography, Mediated Discourse Analysis, and Multimodal Analysis (taking these varieties as representatives of what Wodak and Meyer (2009: 3) call "the CDA group"), and second, the interrelated traditions of *Discursive Psychology* and *Conversation Analysis*, which are closely aligned in their theoretical and methodological principles (Hammersley 2003).

Critical discourse analysis

Intellectually rooted in 'critical linguistics'◀ (Fowler, *et al.* 1979), but since supplemented and extended with a range of social and cultural theories, CDA represents a significant theoretical as well as methodological contribution to the interdisciplinary study of media discourse. This scholarly paradigm's origins can be traced back to a symposium of its founding parents in Amsterdam in 1991 (Wodak and Meyer 2009: 3), whose participants (Teun van Dijk, Norman Fairclough, Gunther Kress, Theo van Leeuwen, and Ruth Wodak) have all since made significant contributions to the development of CDA's common core, as well as to a number of important spin-off approaches.

Its theoretical framework, relating textual features, first, to the concrete social situations in which texts are produced and consumed, and, second, to social processes at large, is usually displayed as a model of three embedded boxes developed by Norman Fairclough (1992, 1995) (Figure 6.1). 'Texts' stand at the core of the model, and are explored largely through linguistic categories. The second dimension of analysis concerns 'discourse practices,' for instance, the processes through which specific media texts are produced in media organizations and consumed, or 'decoded,' by audiences in the context of their everyday lives. These discourse practices are understood as mediators between institutionally produced texts and much wider 'sociocultural practices,'

▶ critical linguistics, p. 115

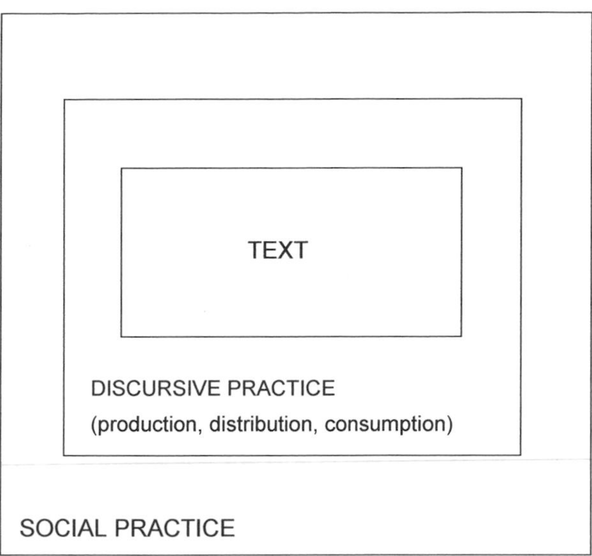

Figure 6.1 Dimensions of critical discourse analysis (source: Fairclough 1995: 59)

which constitute the third dimension of analysis. At this third, macrosocial level, the discursive phenomena brought to light at the first two levels are adduced in claims about, and interpretations of, the prevailing 'order of discourse' at a given historical time, relating discourses, for example, to processes of globalization, commercialization, neoliberalization, etc. Thus, CDA has sought to join a linguistic, analytical approach to concrete discourses, in the plural, with a critical, theoretical conception of one dominant discourse, in the singular, following Foucault (1972[1969]).

orders of discourse

two definitions of discourse

CDA, as noted, has its roots in the 'critical linguistics' tradition in the 1970s, which was able to document a close relationship between the linguistic details of media texts and the production of ideology and, by implication, to substantiate that media ideology contributes to the reproduction of a social order founded on inequality and oppression. Building on Halliday's functional grammar and social semiotic (Halliday 1973, 1978), numerous publications from the late 1970s and into the 1980s (e.g., Fowler, *et al.* 1979; Hodge and Kress 1988) identified linguistic features (including lexical processes, syntactic transformations, modality, and presuppositions and implicature) that "will probably repay close examination"(Fowler 1985: 68).

critical linguistics

While critical linguistics remained closely focused on linguistic indicators, which were equated with ideological effects, CDA went on to place such indicators in their communicative and social contexts, by inscribing discourse analysis in critical social theory. Inspiration was found in theoretical debates about 'structure' and 'agency' (e.g., Beck 1994; Giddens 1984, 1994),◄ which were coupled with CDA's constructivist position, specifically the dual role of media as constituted by, as well as constituting, the social formation. The following 'authorized' definition of CDA synthesizes its theoretical components:

> CDA sees discourse – language as used in speech and writing – as a form of 'social practice'. Describing discourse as a social practice implies a dialectical relationship between a particular discursive event and the situation(s), institution(s) and social structure(s) which frame it. The discursive event is shaped by them, but it also shapes them. That is, discourse is socially constitutive as well as socially conditioned [...]. It is constitutive both in the sense that it helps to sustain and reproduce the social status quo, and in the sense that it contributes to transforming it. [...]. Discursive practices may have major ideological effects – that is, they can help produce and reproduce unequal power relations between (for instance) social classes, women and men, and ethnic/cultural majorities and minorities through the ways in which they represent things and position people.
>
> (Fairclough and Wodak 1997: 258)

In order to account for such social and discursive processes, 'intertextuality' and 'interdiscursivity' have been imported as key analytical concepts into CDA. Concretely, 'intertextuality'◄ means that any text is

► structure and agency – Chapter 10, p. 200
► intertextuality – Chapter 10, p. 192

indebted to innumerable source texts, and may itself become the source of an infinite number of future texts. Any text is therefore intrinsically a recontextualization of multiple previous texts.

inter-discursivity

'Interdiscursivity' is a term denoting the blending of discourses with origins in different sociocultural realms. For example, a political event, such as the parliamentary process leading to legislation in the area of climate change, is likely to blend political, economic, and scientific discourses, because this discursive ensemble is required in order to properly illuminate the substance of the proposed, and possibly contested, new legislation. Often the occurrence of interdiscursivity is a harbinger of social change (positive or negative, depending on one's point of view), because the discursive blending may herald and promote an innovative destabilization of the traditional, 'tidy' sense-making in a specific socio-institutional realm. Fairclough (1993) thus demonstrated how the arena of higher education was being transformed in the early 1990s through the blending of academic, managerial, and market discourses.

The intertextual and interdiscursive perspective also attains relevance at the macrosocial level of the 'orders of discourse,' where, ultimately, the social consequences of discourses and practices can be evaluated. One example is what Fairclough terms the 'conversationalization' of public discourse in the media – the spread of informal speech and colloquial expressions. On the one hand, this might trivialize complex social issues and relations; on the other hand, by making key problems more accessible, it might be a source of cultural democratization (Fairclough 1995: 149). Similarly, Fairclough has referred to a colonization of public speech by commercial discourses as 'marketization,' while he has been less aware of the complementary process of the 'politicization' of market discourses, as ecological and ethical considerations gain attention in the business world (Smith 1990; Schrøder 1997).

conversation-alization

As the name indicates, CDA is committed to social critique, and thus "constantly sits on the fence between social research and political argumentation" (Wodak and Meyer 2009: 32). Van Dijk explicitly defines CDA as a combat unit aiming "to expose and help to combat [...] injustice" and sets up a strongly normative framework based on his conviction that "discourse as social interaction may be *illegitimate* according to some fundamental *norms*, for instance those of international human and social rights" (Van Dijk 2009: 63). Fairclough (2009: 167) expresses the critical intent by requiring the analytical process to start the task with a "focus upon a social wrong, in its semiotic aspects." The analytical process then consists in demonstrating how this social wrong is clothed discursively, and to unclothe it in order to face it politically.

Theoretically, CDA's notion of critique is derived from the critical theory of the Frankfurt School◄ (Adorno and Horkheimer 1977[1944]), and consists of a desire and an obligation to intervene in social processes characterized by unequal power relations and mystifying ideologies, which are reproduced by discursive means. The critical intervention takes place at three different levels (Reisigl and Wodak 2009: 88). First, the analyst performs a *discourse-immanent critique*, where the aim is to discover inconsistencies and self-contradictions in the media text. Second, relying on social theories and contextual knowledge, the analyst engages in *socio-diagnostic critique* in order to demystify the ideological and manipulative character of discursive practices not least in the public sphere. Third, seeking practical relevance for their findings, analysts may develop a *prospective critique*, in which, if possible, the insights harvested through the analysis are applied towards the change of oppressive discursive practices, such as "elaborating guidelines against sexist language use or [...] reducing 'language barriers' in hospitals, schools and so forth" (Reisigl and Wodak 2009: 88), or playing "an advocatory role for socially discriminated groups" (Wodak and Meyer 2009: 19).

This political agenda could mean that many potential users of CDA will find it difficult to feel at home in the scholarly universe defined by its adherents, who appear to presuppose a certain

► the Frankfurt School – Chapter 19, p. 359

left-of-center agreement about what constitutes a 'social wrong.' Nevertheless, while it is clear that people who find 'excessive taxation' or 'immigration from the Arab world' to be social wrongs would not feel welcome in the CDA community, they may nevertheless be able to follow CDA's theoretical and analytical recipes by reversing the political continuum to the advantage of right-of-center ideological positions.

The main scientific (as opposed to political) limitation of critical discourse analysis has been that no empirical attention is given to the middle range of the discourse practices. Fairclough, for instance, has deliberately excluded this aspect from his own analyses, stating that "my emphasis will be upon linguistic analysis of texts [...] I am not concerned [...] with direct analysis of production or consumption of texts" (Fairclough 1995: 62). As a research program, the neglect of empirically studying audiences and other social agents involved in media discourses, which is still widely adhered to among members of the CDA congregation (Van Dijk 2009; Fairclough 2009; Vestergaard 2008), tends to limit the applicability and explanatory value of the approach (Philo 2007; Barkho 2010: Ch. 5).

discourse practices neglected by CDA

However, from modest beginnings, a few discourse analysts have empirically addressed the issue of how media texts are processed by language users at the production and/or reception stages of the media circuit. Bell (1994) compares media and citizen discourses about climate change, emphasizing how news audiences' imprecise and inadequate understandings of global warming and ozone depletion may cause those in political office to give these issues a lower priority than they deserve. While not blaming the media, whose climate change coverage was on the whole accurate, Bell uses his findings to advise the media how to "present information in a manner that minimizes exaggeration and confusion" (p. 62). In similar vein, Deacon, *et al.* (1999) trace "the natural history of a news item" from inception to reception, analyzing the transformative intertextual processes through which social scientific research findings are negotiated by scientific sources, news producing journalists, and lay audiences.

While classic CDA, thus, has all but ignored the empirical challenge of investigating discourse practices, some prominent discourse scholars, notably Ruth Wodak and Ron Scollon, taking their point of departure in the common roots of CDA, have extended the theoretical, methodological, and empirical scope of this tradition by launching research programs which have become recognized under the labels of the Discourse-Historical Approach, Discourse Ethnography, and Mediated Discourse Analysis. Other scholars, notably Gunther Kress and Theo van Leeuwen, have addressed those analytical shortcomings of CDA that stem from the privileged role accorded to linguistic methods, and have devoted their efforts towards the development of an inclusive multimodal approach equipped to do analytical justice to semiotically complex media products.

The discourse-historical approach

The essence of the Discourse-Historical Approach (DHA) consists in recognizing, in an empirically committed diachronic perspective, the interdiscursivity and intertextuality of any instance of discourse. Studies within this tradition thus explore the historical embeddedness of any contemporary, synchronic discursive intervention in a given social area, in order to "explain the implications of previous discursive positions on subsequent ones" (Carvalho 2008). As a brief, striking example of the possible insights provided by looking at the temporal evolution of mediated discourses, Viehöfer (2003) in a study of the media coverage of climate change from 1974 to 1995 was able to set up a historical typology of the shifting emphases of media discourses. The study distinguished a historical succession of six 'problem narratives' over the twenty year span: stories of global cooling, the climatic paradise, cyclical sunspots, climate change as scientific and media fiction, the nuclear winter, and global warming (cited in Reisigl and Wodak 2009: 119). As was the case with the naming of the swine flu pandemic, above, each narrative comes with its own set of definitions, possible consequences, and possible reactions to the problem.

problem narratives

The historical scope of DHA as "a time-sensitive discourse analysis" (Carvalho 2008: 164) means that it is empirically more ambitious than mainstream CDA (which tends to sample a few 'typical texts' for analysis), both with respect to the reliance on large textual corpora, which require ample resources in terms of funding and human labor, and in terms of applying a plurality of analytical methods. DHA thus performs linguistic analysis of texts such as institutional documents (texts from the legislative process, memoranda from interparty negotiations, white papers, etc.) and media coverage of the relevant discursive events (news reports across media, for instance, from successive climate summits (seen as "critical discourse moments", Carvalho 2008:166)), TV debates, climate campaign ads, car ads, popular science media, etc. In addition, DHA often engages in fieldwork in the form of interviews with key actors (Abell and Myers 2008; Krzyzanowski 2008), as well as ethnographic 'inside' studies conducted in the institutional environments which form the social habitats of these actors (Oberhuber and Krzyzanowski 2008) (see further below). DHA is also open to the joint application of qualitative and quantitative methods, usually assigning primacy to the former (Reisigl and Wodak 2009: 96).

critical discourse moments

The specific research undertaken under the label of DHA conforms to the 'critical' objectives pursued by CDA. Scholars have studied the historical constitution of anti-Semitic stereotypes in public discourse, as manifested in the presidential campaign of Kurt Waldheim in Austria (Wodak, *et al.* 1990). Transnational perspectives have been pursued in a large-scale study on European identities (Muntigl, *et al.* 2000), while the topic of climate change and global warming has been a favorite among discourse-historical scholars (Carvalho 2005; Reisigl and Wodak 2009). Carvalho carried out a thorough 'biography' of the greenhouse effect as a public issue by systematically comparing the climate change coverage of three British quality newspapers with different ideological profiles in the period 1985–2000 (diachronically). She focused on the different journalistic interventions of the three papers at a number of critical discourse moments (synchronically), defined by significant political interventions of key politicians (Margaret Thatcher, Tony Blair) attempting to control public perceptions of the climate change issue according to their political and ideological agendas (Carvalho 2005: 5).

Discourse ethnography and mediated discourse analysis

Drawing on the distinction between 'data found' and 'data made,'◀ the interest in developing a discourse-ethnographic approach originates in the realization among discourse analysts that existing discourse data do not suffice, and that therefore it is necessary to apply fieldwork strategies which can enhance insights by analyzing the text-producing discursive interactions of "particular socio-cultural locales" (Oberhuber and Kzryzanowski 2008: 182). Discourse ethnography differs from full-fledged ethnography by relying on limited encounters with the field of study, and in some cases also stipulating the centrality of textual data, while the fieldwork methods serve to provide a rich context and background knowledge for understanding the texts.

discourse ethnography

Discourse ethnography originates in organizational analysis, from the realization that the sense-making universe of an organization cannot be understood simply by analyzing the *textual* manifestations of organizational life. It is necessary also to include organizational *talk* in the analysis. Such talk can be of two kinds: naturally occurring verbal interaction (business meetings, informal interaction) (Drew and Heritage 1992; Boden 1994), and verbal accounts elicited by the researcher in the form of interviews and focus groups (Abell and Myers 2008; Krzyzanowski 2008). Wodak (2000) used a combination of observational studies of EU committee meetings and interviews with officials to study "from the inside" (Oberhuber and Kzryzanowska 2008: 191) the transformative discursive process of co-constructing a policy paper.

An ethnographic agency-oriented and situated approach to discourse analysis has also been developed by Ron Scollon under the terms

▶ data found and made – Chapter 15, p. 288

mediated discourse analysis

'mediated discourse analysis' (MDA) and 'nexus of practice' (Scollon 2002; Scollon and Scollon 2004). On a moderately constructionist foundation, MDA pieces together an analytical recipe for understanding social issues at the macro level. The analytical practice consists of dissolving the macro phenomenon into concrete situational events in which social actors materially and discursively enact these phenomena at the micro level (Scollon 2002).

Like CDA, MDA is concerned with social critique and the illumination of hegemonic power relations at a time characterized by globalization and neoliberalization in many areas of the world. Due to its bottom-up procedures, however, the analytical project appears less dogmatic and self-righteous than CDA:

> We can begin to shed light on the dialectic between the broad contemporary neo-liberal, neo-capitalist discourses [...] and day-to-day social action in the study of something as mundane and apparently irrelevant as having a cup of coffee in a coffee shop.
>
> (Scollon 2002: 143)

In this analytical field, CDA would typically analyze a handful of texts produced by a major global corporate player like the Starbucks company, exploring how its corporate communication addressed to customers and critical citizens produces a version of reality which serves to consolidate its corporate power as well as the neoliberal global order. MDA instead goes to a Starbucks coffee shop and explores the social practices of people engaged in having coffee in this particular context, considering how the practice of being a regular Starbucks customer is made sense of. This happens in a universe of meaning that is also influenced by the company's textual materials (such as green claims made on their cardboard insulating sleeve and more extensive corporate social responsibility (CSR) materials) as well as by relevant media coverage of the issue. MDA looks at the way in which these situated practices may or may not legitimate corporate interests and a whole social order.

In the field of media studies, adoption of the discourse ethnographic approach and MDA has been based on the conviction that the texts produced by the media "must be interpreted in the context of their creation and reception" (Bird 2010:10; see also Deacon, *et al.* 1999). In a case study of corporate advertising, which seeks to win consent for the corporate social responsibility of a large oil company, Schrøder (2007) found that what appears *in the text* as an altruistically motivated oil company (see the analysis in Box 6.2 at the end of this chapter) turns out *in the production* environment to be a more pragmatically and strategically motivated oil company. *In the reception* context, when faced with this ad, sixteen ordinary people tend generally speaking to be quite cynically or at least skeptically oriented (Schrøder 2007: 95). Such findings show that the use of a plurality of methods, applied to a plurality of discursive texts and practices, is, on the one hand, a safeguard against the habit, often found in CDA, of fitting the data to illustrate the critical purpose underlying the research. On the other hand, the more inductive, or abductive,◀ multi-method approach brings with it the challenge of how to integrate the findings gained with different methods, and to clarify what the often-heard slogan of 'complementarity of methods' means in practice (see Chapter 15, this volume).

Conversation analysis and discursive psychology

Among the heterogeneous ancestry of discursive psychology, the most formative influence has come from the traditions of ethnomethodology◀ and conversation analysis, particularly when it comes to its analytical procedures. Since its early beginnings five decades ago, the aim of conversation analysis, defined as "the study of how participants in interaction organize their talk moment to moment and turn to turn" (Myers 2008: 122), has been to explore the situational micro-mechanics of verbal interaction. Many studies have probed, for example, speakers' turn-taking through so-called adjacency pairs, the role of silences and interruptions in the flow of interaction, the management of topic

conversation analysis

▶ induction and abduction – Chapter 15, p. 289
▶ ethnomethodology – Chapter 3, p. 65

development and topic change, and several other structuring features (for overviews, see Nofsinger 1991; Have 1999).

discursive psychology

Like conversation analysis, discursive psychology takes its point of departure in the situational contexts of language use. Its purpose, however, is to go on to account for the ways in which the communicative micro-mechanics enter into everyday as well as institutional processes of social life, for instance, in the case of nationalism or racism (Billig 1995; Wetherell and Potter 1992).

Among other things, discursive psychology is concerned with speakers' fact construction and their own positioning in co-constructing social reality, that is, their attempts to establish their own 'versions' or accounts of social events as true and factual, and to undermine the factuality and truth of their interlocutors' versions. When staking a claim for their own version, communicators will draw on 'interpretive repertoires,'◀ a concept which sees discourse as a practical, situational resource:

> By interpretative repertoires we mean broadly discernible clusters of terms, descriptions and figures of speech often assembled around metaphors or vivid images. In more structuralist language we can talk of these things as systems of signification and as the building blocks used for manufacturing versions of actions, self and social structures in talk.
>
> (Potter and Wetherell 1996: 89)

In an interview-based study of discourse and racism in New Zealand, Potter and Wetherell (1996) found that white New Zealanders would draw on two different interpretive repertoires regarding the position of Maori culture in contemporary society, which they called Culture-as-Heritage and Culture-as-Therapy. The former repertoire verbally frames culture, almost in biological terms, as an endangered species, something to be preserved and treasured; the latter conceives culture in psychological terms as a need, particularly for young Maoris, who "need to rediscover their cultural 'roots' to become 'whole' again" (p. 90). An important analytical point is that the repertoires are not mutually exclusive, but may coexist also in a given individual's discourse about race, serving different rhetorical purposes in different situational circumstances. Most important, interpretive repertoires are neither personal nor socially specific 'attitudes,' as in much social psychology and survey research, but the concrete linguistic manifestation and exercise of social practices of discrimination, and thus of social power (for a comparative analysis of the interpretive repertoires used by media and citizens to make sense of politics, see Schrøder and Phillips (2007)).

Although the mass media have not been central to discursive psychology – some introductions do not even mention its applicability to media studies (Potter and Wetherell 1996) – it seems clear that the approach has much to offer, theoretically as well as analytically, especially as the electronic media have become increasingly dominated by formats that borrow from or replicate everyday verbal interaction◀ (as also suggested by Fairclough's 'conversationalization'), and as verbal exchange through digital/mobile media serves to establish new forms of 'virtual' community.◀ Researchers in the tradition suggest as much in their choice of empirical materials. For example, J. Potter's (1996) analyses of the situational construction of facticity are full of single examples from media discourses, as he demonstrates how hosts in news programs take great pains verbally to demonstrate that they do not 'have an axe to grind' – how interviewees may voluntarily confess to having a stake in some matter in order to create an impression of honesty and trustworthiness, or they claim that 'the facts show' something to be the case. Discourse psychological insights about discursive positioning strategies may also be applied to the planning and analysis of research interviews with focus groups◀ (Puchta and Potter 2004).

So far perhaps the most systematic and directly applicable work on spoken media

▶ interpretive repertoires – Chapter 9, p. 183
▶ reality television formats – Chapter 16
▶ mobile media use – Chapter 18
▶ focus groups – Chapter 14, p. 271

discourses has come from scholars who see themselves as conversation analysts, rather than discursive psychologists (or critical discourse analysts) (e.g., Drew and Heritage 1992; Greatbatch 1998; Heritage and Greatbatch 1991; Scannell 1991; Hutchby 2006; Tolson 2001, 2006). One growing body of work has analyzed the inherently interactive genre of the news interview (Ekström, *et al.* 2006). In such studies, attention is focused not on the possible ideological meanings of a sequence of utterances, but on the social as well as discursive dynamics of the exchange – on communication as a form of action that is embedded in several contexts at once. These contexts of interaction can be specified, in part, by comparing turn-taking patterns in media genres with those of ordinary conversation, but also by comparing the political and professional conditions of journalistic discourse production in, for example, public-service and other professional news organizations. Noting that news interviews deviate systematically from ordinary conversation in replacing the latter's question-answer-receipt pattern with a question-answer-question sequence, Heritage (1985) explained this difference with reference to 'the overhearing audience' of the interview: By avoiding the evaluation inherent in the 'receipt' turn of normal conversational sequences, the interviewer declines the role of being the (only) recipient of the answer, while maintaining his/her role as the elicitor of ever more answers, in both cases on behalf of the overhearing audience.

the news interview

the overhearing audience

Recent conversation-analytical work on media discourses has attempted to diversify our understanding of news interviews, as a genre consisting of a number of subgenres all worthy of interpretive attention. Montgomery (2008), for instance, argues that attention has disproportionately been focused on the subgenre of 'accountability interviews' in which interviewers for institutional reasons must negotiate a platform of neutrality for themselves when calling a public figure (such as a politician) to account for their responsibility for a controversial issue. He goes on to demonstrate some of the affordances and constraints operating on the participants in other kinds of news interview, such as 'the experiential interview,' often with an ordinary eye-witness member of the public, 'the expert interview' with people holding technical or medical expertise on a topic of public concern, and 'the affiliated interview' where the interviewee is an employee of the same news institution as the anchor/interviewer. Montgomery also calls for increased scrutiny of what he terms 'the interview fragment,' where a quotation from either of the four types of interview mentioned above is inserted seamlessly into a report orchestrated by a reporter.

Analyzing formalized TV presidential debates in the US, and placing them in a typological framework of other kinds of campaign talk, Myers (2008) similarly demonstrates how conversational analysis of broadcast debates is able to meticulously map the micro-mechanics of the turn-taking processes, as they are played out as interactions between political candidates, the moderator-hosts, and the two overhearing audiences: in the studio and at home.

Outside the area of news talk, scholars have directed analytical attention towards the conversational processes of talk shows along a continuum from political enlightenment (Livingstone and Lunt 1994) to therapeutic empowerment (Abt and Seesholtz 1994). Macaulay (in press) compares how talk show hosts Oprah Winfrey and Dr. Phil, through a variety of insinuating indirect questions, use the off-screen pre-interview narrative information provided by their guests to construct their own meta-narrative with themselves in the role as problem-solving heroes of the dramas of everyday life.

talk shows

There is a burgeoning research literature directed towards understanding the communicative forms enacted on and mediated by the internet, the World Wide Web, and mobile technologies. Often, due to the hybrid reliance of these communicative forms on diverse textual and interactive genres, this research has taken inspiration from discourse analytical as well as conversation analytical approaches. Gruber's study (2008) focuses on the ways in which postings on scholarly email discussion lists can be seen in the light of traditional written academic discussions, considering how they are molded by the medium's technological affordances into a hybrid of written and oral forms. He suggests, more generally, that by researching new networked forms of communication such as hypertexts (websites), email, chat, and text messages (sms), we may get an insight into "the emergence of new genres as combinations of existing generic conventions, new technological means of communication and new communicative goals of users" (Gruber 2008: 72).

Gruber further suggests that before embarking on the analysis of one of these communicative forms, it is helpful to set up a typology that creates a systematic overview of prototypical forms (see also Herring 2007). As shown in Figure 6.2, Gruber distinguishes six dimensions along which four communicative forms or genres that are characteristic of network media can be conceptualized as vehicles of communication:

1 The new genres can be seen as primarily written or spoken, or as a mixture of the two;
2 they may apply one or several semiotic modes;
3 they can be monological or dialogical;
4 they can be one-to-one, one-to-many, or many-to-many (see also Jensen 2010: 71f.);
5 in terms of durability, they may be intended to last for a long time or to be ephemeral; and
6 with respect to use, they may be asynchronous or synchronous.

Gruber's subsequent analysis of postings on scholarly email discussion lists enables him to create a generic profile of this particular form of communication, concluding that "scholarly email postings show characteristics of traditional academic prose, but also display features of oral genres of everyday conversation. [...] technological features (software affordances) are used to realize 'traditional' characteristics of academic prose in a new form of communication" (Gruber 2008: 71). (Readers interested in exploring the discursive and conversational aspects of network media, from text-messaging through chat rooms and social network sites to online games, are invited consult relevant journals such as *Language@Internet*. For empirical explorations of computer-mediated communication in other languages than English, see Danet and Herring (2007).)

Dimensions	***Hypertext/website***	***Email***	***Chat***	***Text message***
Mode of communication	Written	Written, spoken	Spoken, written	Spoken, written
Semiotic modality	Multimodal	Primarily textual	Textual	Textual
Primary communicative function	Monological	Dialogical	Dialogical	Dialogical
Number of communicators	One-to-many	One-to-one	Many-to-many One-to-one possible	One-to-one (one-to-many possible)
Degree of intended persistence	High	Medium	Low	Low
Time mode	Asynchronous	Asynchronous	Synchronous	Asynchronous

Figure 6.2 Characteristics of new media as communicative forms (based on Gruber 2008)

	Critical linguistics	Critical Discourse Analysis	Discourse-Historical Approach	Discourse Ethnography	Discursive Psychology and Conversation Analysis	Multimodal Analysis
Socio-cultural practices	(+)	+	+	+	(+)	+
Discourse practices	–	(+)	+	++	++	+
Textual/ verbal analysis	++	++	++	+	+	++
Non-verbal modalities	–	–	–	–	–	++

Figure 6.3 Different approaches to qualitative discourse analysis

Figure 6.3 summarizes the relative emphases of the six main qualitative approaches to media texts, as reviewed here. (The parentheses in the figure indicate that a dimension is recognized, in principle, but not developed in analytical practice. Multimodal discourse analysis is dealt with in the next section.) The integration and redevelopment of these dimensions remain a general challenge for future research, both theoretically and analytically, in interdisciplinary studies of the media-society nexus. In that process, theories and analyses of visual media represent a special challenge.

VISUAL MEDIA DISCOURSES

In all of the above approaches, including quantitative content analysis, the visual aspect of news and other factual genres in newspapers, magazines, television, and computer media is at best given secondary attention, in spite of the conventional wisdom of research that the media environment is increasingly dominated by still and moving pictures. Content analysis may be relatively ill-suited for the analysis of visual communication beyond the identification of, for instance, types of protagonists or formal features, given its categorical conception of meaning, as discussed above, vis-à-vis the typically context-dependent and continuous features of visuals (see Rose (2007: Ch. 4) for a recent account of the insights to be gained from "counting what you (think you) see" in visual media (Rose 2007: 59)).

Qualitative discourse analysis has greater promise in this regard, and has been given several different formulations, most often with recourse to one of two theoretical sources – Roland Barthes and Charles Sanders Peirce. Deacon, *et al.* (2007) carry the analysis from still photographs to moving images, while Rose (2007) offers a comprehensive introduction to the analysis of visual media.

Barthes (1977[1964]) suggested that the denotative and connotative◀ 'levels of meaning' apply also to the analysis of visual signs. In a photograph, for instance, we may distinguish between the denotative level, which carries the 'innocent,' factual meanings available to any observer irrespective of cultural background,

▶ denotation and connotation – Chapter 2, p. 34

and the connotative level, which carries the visual meanings that a specific culture assigns to the denotative message.

In the 1964 article, moreover, Barthes theorizes the possible relationships between different sign systems within the same message, specifically "the linking of text and image," asking "what are the functions of the linguistic message with regard to the (twofold) iconic message?" (Barthes 1977[1964]: 38). Barthes discusses two such functions: anchorage and relay, which may coexist in a message, and which share the function of "fix[ing] the floating chain of signifieds" of the inherently polysemic image (p. 39).

anchorage and relay

Anchorage, which may appear in the form of a title, a caption, or an accompanying press article, can be subdivided into *identifying anchorage*, where "the text helps to identify purely and simply the elements of the scene" as a "denoted description of the image" (p. 39), and *interpreting anchorage*, which guides the interpretation of the connoted meaning away from too personal associations or ideologically undesirable meanings.

Relay, which may appear via comic strip balloons or film dialogue, is established through snatches of text that may be perceived as an utterance spoken by a character in the image. Here, text and image stand in a "complementary relationship" to each other, the text "setting out [...] meanings that are not to be found in the image itself," and the joint meaning of image and text being "realized at a higher level, that of the story, the anecdote, the diegesis" (p. 41).

While analytically useful, this conceptualization of the text-image relationship can nevertheless be criticized, echoing a famous chiasmus from the history of communication research (Katz 1959), for being mainly interested in what the text does to the picture, to the relative neglect of what the picture does to the text – an issue taken up again below.

From Peircean semiotics,◄ it is particularly one set of analytical concepts which has been applied selectively to arrive at a typology of three possible relations between (visual) signs and objects in reality (Peirce 1985). First, a 'symbol' is a sign whose relation with its object is arbitrary and a matter of convention. The 'symbol' can be exemplified, in verbal language, with words such as 'swine flu' or 'Mexican flu' in the media discourses considered at the beginning of this chapter. In the visuals of web design, a text accentuated by color saturation conventionally signifies the function of a clickable link.

symbol, icon, index

Second, an 'icon' is related to its referent through similarity. Visually, a photograph in a news article is an iconic sign resembling certain real-world phenomena. A widely published 2007 health ad from the Danish National Health Board warned against the hazards of the excessive consumption of alcohol by showing an X-ray of the human chest in which a champagne cork inside one of the veins iconically signified thrombosis. A verbal example of an iconic sign is the words imitating animal sounds such as 'oink.'

Third, an 'index' signifies its object through some existential or physical connection with it. While classic visual examples include smoke as an index of fire, in media and other cultural forms an index may operate at a more inferential level, so that a diverse group of people appearing in a corporate ad can be understood as indices of the age group, gender, or ethnicity, or the personnel profile of the company, which they appear to represent. A verbal index occurs when a British news report announces that 'Downing Street' has issued a political statement, where the street address of the British prime minister's home stands for the prime minister himself. In this specific respect, indexicality is comparable to metonymy◄ in the Saussurean tradition.

The typology is immediately complicated by the fact that, for example, an (iconic) photograph is also an index of a segment of reality imprinting itself on film. The complication arises, in part, from Peirce's epistemology, which emphasized that signs are not entities, but relations or functions mediating knowledge of objects in reality. One interpretation is to understand the three sign relations as properties of any sign, whose combination helps to account for the cognitive status and experiential qualities of a

► Peircean semiotics – Chapter 2, p. 32

► metonymy – Chapter 2, p. 33

given sign (Johansen 1993: 95). To exemplify, a news photo of the White House can be, at one and the same time, an iconic representation of a particular building located in Washington, D.C.; an indexical representation of the government of the United States, housing and standing for its chief executive officer; and a symbolic representation, depending on the context, of values conventionally associated with the US or its president, from global capitalism to liberal democracy.

The two sources of semiotic concepts – Barthes and Peirce – have been drawn on, liberally and in combination, by numerous analysts, and have had considerable heuristic value for illustrative analyses of how media images communicate (Deacon, *et al.* 2007). However, it has also been complained that the findings of analyses often seem commonsensical.

Other, more specific, complaints have targeted key theoretical premises of visual analysis so far. Despite Barthes' (1970) redevelopment of the distinction between denotation and connotation, as well as other critiques of the implicit threshold between 'natural' and culturally invested meaning (Eco 1976), studies have often in practice performed a heavy-handed operationalization of the dyad, just as icon, index, and symbol have been approached as separate sign types, rather than complementary functions of one sign complex. Equally, anchorage and relay would seem far from exhaustive as categorizations of image-text relations in different genres and media.

Addressing some of these criticisms, but also leaving many of them unsolved, Rose (2007) updates the available methods for doing analysis of visual materials, in a culture whose overwhelming visuality has materialized in global events such as the attacks on the World Trade Center, the torture perpetrated in the Abu Ghraib prison in Iraq, and the devastation produced by the 2004 tsunami in countries around the Indian Ocean. In all these cases, global audiences were able to witness events firsthand through the mediations of shifting mixtures of visual sources, including live TV news, print media images, amateur videos and photos published on social network sites as well as appropriated by institutional news media, photos used in appeals for aid to tsunami victims, etc.

Rose adds to the dominant semiotic and discourse-oriented approaches a range of tools from more fieldwork-oriented approaches such as reception analysis◀ and anthropology.◀ Thus, her analytical recipe recommends that visual analysis, as part of analyzing the media context into which the visual signs are incorporated, should systematically consider three sites of meaning: production, the image itself, and audiences.

The specific challenges of analyzing visuals in the age of the internet are only given peripheral attention by Rose. One bid for how to address some of these challenges is offered by Thorlacius (2010), who re-theorizes and re-operationalizes the functional communication model of Roman Jakobson (1960)◀ in order to understand website signifying practices. The re-theorizing consists mainly in adding the intersemiotic, navigational, and interactive aspects of website interfaces to Jakobson's framework, and in arguing (like Rose) that analysts need to move beyond the visual text and to incorporate fieldwork methods, in order to not just deduce, but to analytically document the intentionalities of website designers and the sense-making of website users.

While authoritative overviews of visual studies such as Rose (2007) can be said to represent the mainstream of the field, another development stands out from the approaches inspired by linguistic discourse analysis and semiotics. Cognitive media theory takes as its premise that visual stimuli from the media activate the same mental processes as other perception and cognition. Contrary to much semiotics, cognitivism finds that images have no explicit syntax of minimal elements, communicating instead through iconicity and indexicality. Whereas most cognitive media studies have examined film and other moving images, in one cognitivist analysis of still media images, Messaris (1997: 182–203) suggested

cognitive image analysis

▶ reception analysis – Chapter 9

▶ anthropology – Chapter 3, p. 57

▶ Jakobson's communication model – Chapter 10, p. 197

a more general typology of 'propositions' or principles in visual communication, involving causality, contrast, analogy, and generalization. In this regard, cognitive image analysis joins attempts in other communication theory at integrating the analysis of 'texts' with an understanding of its place in human cognition and action.◄

MULTIMODAL ANALYSIS

With a background in critical linguistics and in Halliday's theory of social semiotics (Halliday 1978; Hodge and Kress 1988), Gunther Kress and Theo van Leeuwen (1996) have proposed to go beyond a mere extension of discourse analysis from linguistic to visual signs. They emphasize that the modern media, from school textbooks and newspapers through television formats to the World Wide Web, increasingly feature texts which are 'multimodal,' comprising a range of representational and communicative forms (modes) within the limits of one text, such as, in addition to verbal language, sound, graphics, and images (including gestures and proxemics). To these may be added the tactile, olfactory, and gustatory modes of communicating which may seem rather peripheral, but which may become more widespread through multi-sensory, digital simulation technologies.

O'Halloran (2011) encapsulates the theoretical and analytical foci of multimodal analysis (see also Jewitt 2009) in an agenda that identifies the need to model and analyze multimodal phenomena on three different dimensions:

1 the *semiotic resources* provided both by language and by semiotic modes which are fundamentally different from language;
2 the *inter-semiotic aspects* of meaning as semiotic choices are integrated into multimodal phenomena; and
3 the *resemioticization of multimodal phenomena* as part of the performance of social, contextualized practices.

► cognitivism – Chapter 2, p. 44

In an illustrative analysis of a televised political debate program, O'Halloran demonstrates in tabular form, on the first and second dimensions, how the integration of a range of semiotic modes and sub-modes is required in order to understand the ways in which political agenda-setting and positioning processes are negotiated by the studio host and the invited politicians: *spoken language* (grammar, lexicon, prosodic features such as intonation and rhythm, turn-taking, etc.), *kinetic* resources (gaze, body posture, gesture, etc.), *cinematography* (camera angle and movement, frame size, etc.), as well as other semiotic resources (studio lighting, clothing, proxemics, seating arrangements, etc.). On the third dimension, it is demonstrated how the debate program is resemioticized on the TV station's website, with a discursive framing of political debate as sport that is different from the original broadcast program, and with an opportunity for audience-citizens to take on the role of participant by posting comments on the interactive blog, as the genre of 'expert debate' is transformed to 'public debate.'

In the classic conceptualization of the founding fathers, multimodal analysis was seen not primarily as a theoretical framework for analysis of mediated products, but rather as a model of intersemiotic meaning-making, conceptualizing the practice of human signifying processes, from everyday conversation through mass-media to shopping malls or city planning. Kress and van Leeuwen (2001) thus proposed a theory of four domains of practice, or 'multimodal *strata*' (Discourse, Design, Production, Distribution), to explain the creative stages of all human communication, mediated as well as non-mediated. It follows from the ambition of multimodal analysis to register and interpret the interweaving of multiple semiotic meaning systems that a major challenge consists in keeping track of and managing the detail and complexity involved in analyzing multimodal objects. Lemke (2002) has taken up the particular challenges of analyzing websites, in which the hypermedia aspects of links and other navigational resources must be combined with the traditional verbal and visual aspects.

CONCLUSION

This chapter has outlined the main approaches to the analysis of factual media texts, recognizing the division into quantitative and qualitative studies, as well as identifying variations within each tradition, some of which suggest shared concerns across the traditions regarding both the definition of discursive or content 'entities' and the development of context-sensitive analytical procedures.

Since neither the intentions of communicators nor the meanings created by audiences can be 'read off' media by means of discourse or content analysis, a more complete understanding of the production and circulation of meaning in society requires a differentiated analytical attention to media texts as vehicles which are necessary but not sufficient conditions of communication; to their specific moment in the communicative process; and to their interrelations with other moments. This requirement has been underscored by the development of 'interactive' media, in which ordinary, increasingly digitally literate users (Buckingham 2003) navigate an enhanced intertextual and intermedial supply of meaning – selecting, combining, and interpreting what is, to a degree, their customized text and one which, in both work and leisure, blends into the context of use.

We are hastily entering an age of digital content creation (Drotner and Schrøder 2010) in which the previously separate moments of production and reception of the mass media culture are blending into processes of verbal and visual cut-and-paste 'produsage' (Bruns 2005a), carried out by the 'prosumers' (Toffler 1980) of digital landscapes,◀ informed by 'collective intelligence' (Jenkins 2006). The challenge for discourse and content studies under changing technological and historical circumstances remains one of clarifying its particular domain of analysis and explanatory value, particularly to distinguish the *descriptive discovery* of a text's verbal and visual characteristics from the *hypothetical interpretation* of its potential meanings for different audience-users, and from studies of its actualized meanings in social processes of production and reception. Both in analytical descriptions and in the generation of hypothetical interpretations, the relative relevance of the available, qualitative as well as quantitative approaches must be assessed with reference to the purpose of analysis and the particular object of analysis. Irrespective of their theoretical and methodological origins, all of these approaches are faced with socially constructed textual objects, and are themselves socially constructing whatever insights they provide.

descriptive discovery

hypothetical interpretation

▶ produsage and prosumption – Chapter 4, p. 77; Chapter 5, p. 102

ANALYSIS BOX 6.2: DISCOURSE ANALYSIS OF ADVERTISEMENT FOR BP (*THE GREEN MAGAZINE*, DECEMBER 1991, INSIDE FRONT COVER)

Figure 6.4 BP advertisement

cont.

The BP advertisement, "Oil companies tend to invite criticism. At BP, we actively encourage it," appeared in *The Green Magazine*, a publication whose readership have a greater-than-average interest in the environment.

In the reading situation, as the readers turn the front page of the magazine, they encounter a page which presents itself at first glance as a multimodal visual and verbal puzzle. The graphic layout of the page with its distribution of iconic and symbolic signs, and the BP logo in the bottom right corner, identifies it as an advertisement. The headline functions as a caption of the picture, and as an attention-catching device – many readers read no further! It provides no 'identifying anchorage' for the composite picture, merely an aid to interpretation ('interpreting anchorage'), assisting the readers' inferential processes about who the people in the picture are and what they are doing.

As the caption-headline associates "oil companies" with "BP" and a pronominal "we" who "encourage criticism," the inferential process of interpretation may perceive the iconic representation of the eleven individuals around the periphery as also an indexical representation of BP employees. They further indexically represent several social backgrounds: men and women, age groups between their 20s and 50s, and different ethnic groups (one black man, one Asian woman, the remainder white). Their common gesture of placing an open palm behind an ear is an iconic-symbolic sign conventionally used to indicate a listening attitude. The headline may, therefore, also be seen as a collective utterance by the eleven employees on behalf of the company, i.e., text as 'relay.'

The headline's choice of the nominalization "criticism" begs the question of the agency behind the criticizing activity, which may, however, be inferred, from the situational context now established, to be environmental activists, thus filling in the identity of the central picture element. The speaker depicted in the middle wears a suit but no tie, which may connote that he belongs neither to the Establishment, nor to a counterculture – he is a decent person, someone to be taken seriously, his visible teeth perhaps an index of a certain insistence. A first reading thus suggests that not only are the diverse employees of BP responsive to criticism, so that there might be no need to shout, but the company is responsive precisely because it is made up of a cross-section of the society it serves.

In addition to the paradigmatic choices already mentioned, the syntagmatic ensemble◀ of the ad also springs from the choice to use black and white only, as opposed to color. The absence of color is just one of a number of 'absences' in the semiotic composition of this ad as opposed to consumer advertising, which distances this ad from any glamorous impression or visual 'hype,' instead suggesting soberness.

The language of the copy is straightforward, fairly colloquial, with no difficult or specialist terminology. It uses declarative sentence structures only, apart from a few cases of independent sentence fragments, one example being the adverb "loudly," punctuating the rhetorical authority of the critics and establishing an intratextual link of recognition to the pictorial representation of the megaphone. The absence of imperatives and interrogatives, compared with consumer ads, comes to represent the absence of any direct attempt to actively involve the reader (Myers 1994: Ch. 4). Again this adds to the impression of soberness, of the company simply putting its case forward, leaving it up to the reader to pass the verdict of relevance or irrelevance, acceptance or rejection.

This feature of the sentence structure is supplemented by a complete absence of the second-person pronoun 'you.' The ad thus, without any sense of intrusion, merely invites the reader to witness an account of a relationship between the company ('we') and different representatives of third parties, i.e., community and environmental groups ('they'). The 'we' used is an 'exclusive

cont.

▶ paradigms and syntagms – Chapter 2, p. 33

we' throughout most of the text; however, it slides imperceptibly into an 'inclusive we' in the last sentence of the copy, which is repeated in the slogan "For all our tomorrows." This may be seen as an attempt to subtly involve the reader in BP's objectives by instilling a logic which may run something like this: 'If BP is doing all of this for our (shared) tomorrows, BP is worthy of my respect.'

The text has two instances of wordplay. The headline plays on two meanings of the phrase "invite criticism," one to attract *unwanted* criticism, the other to welcome criticism, to even help create it. The effect may be one of surprise at the fact that BP faces myths about ruthless oil companies head-on, and appreciation of the copy-writer's ingenuity. The other instance of wordplay concerns BP's "patronizing" the environmental groups, so that they may all the better supply advice to BP. Again BP faces a common myth about multinational companies, i.e., that they 'show inappropriate superiority,' then turns the myth around by exploiting the other meaning of 'patronize': 'to enable someone to develop their full potential.'

These instances of wordplay may also be seen as a kind of absence vis-à-vis consumer ads. What is absent in the BP ad's wordplays is the frivolousness of the typical advertising pun, the cheap-joke impression. In the BP ad, wordplay is used as an intelligent, even sober, way of anticipating the reader's objection to the claims of harmony between the oil company and environmental activists.

This unflawed impression of cooperation and dialogue is made possible, in part, by the absence of the past in the ad's universe. There is no mention of a 'yesterday' before the publication of the ad, possibly a time when oil companies *did* ruthlessly exploit the environment and when there *was* antagonism between oil companies and environmentalists. The absence of a lexicalized 'yesterday' is supported by the absence of past tense verbs.

The verbal and visual signs of the BP ad, thus, appear to create a universe of meaning in which all conflicts between oil companies and environmental activists have been harmonized away, in a spirit of sympathy and mutuality. Whether this universe, as mapped here through a mixture of descriptive discovery and hypothetical interpretation, corresponds to the respective meaning universes of the corporate communicators and the magazine readers, is for the empirical study of encoding and decoding processes to discover (for a discourse ethnographic approach to corporate advertising, see Schrøder 2007).

7 Mediated fictions

Peter Larsen

- a description of *quantitative studies of representation* in media fiction
- *formal* studies in the semiotic tradition, including *shot-to-shot* analyses of film
- *narrative* studies and models, applied *across media* types
- a presentation of *genre* analysis as a middle range, connecting text and context
- a discussion of *sound* as an under-researched aspect of media 'texts'
- *The Big Sleep* (1946) and *Die Hard* (1988ff.) as analytical examples

INTRODUCTION

The word 'text' is derived from the Latin verb *texo*, meaning to weave or twine together, and to construct or build something. The Latin noun *textum* means woven cloth or fabric, but was also used about speech and writing. A written or spoken text, then, is like a woven cloth – a construction of meaning made out of words.

Since the 1960s, 'text'◄ has been used as a general term covering diverse phenomena such as music, still images, films, etc., in addition to written and spoken language. The underlying argument is that all these means of expression are semantic constructions – 'fabrics' of signs – and most of them are meant to be 'read' in linear, temporal sequences. Such constructions can be described and analyzed by analogy to a verbal text, drawing on concepts, models, and procedures that were developed within disciplines and fields like linguistics, semiotics, and literary studies. Analyses of 'texts' in this broad sense form a central part of media studies. Whether such analyses are carried out as studies of single texts or important textual genres, or as part of projects studying media reception and media institutions, the central concern is with questions of meaning and interpretation. The point of departure is the texts themselves – their structure and their content.

Like any other form of analysis, textual analysis examines a given object – a text or a group of texts – as closely and as systematically as possible in order to answer specific research questions. These questions can lead to two basic types of textual analysis: one focused on *generalities*, the other on *particulars*.◄ The first one describes recurrent, typical features in order to establish textual models or prototypes. The second one examines the texts in question as isolated occurrences with reference to their specificities. Obviously, there are both transitional variants and logical connections between the two types. In practice, generalities are always established through the study of particulars, and the analysis of particulars presupposes some knowledge about generalities.

► texts as a general category – Chapter 2, p. 36

► generalities and particulars – Chapter 15, p. 385

Importantly, qualitative and quantitative methodologies both lend themselves, in specific ways, to the study of generalities as well as particulars.

This chapter presents a number of content-analytical and text-analytical traditions in media studies. Many of the relevant procedures and principles are not specific to particular media or genres. However, the chapter mainly focuses on fiction in film and television, which accounts for the bulk of mediated fiction, and which has also been the point of departure for the most significant developments in research.

QUANTITATIVE CONTENT ANALYSIS

Content studies of media representations

Some questions about *generalities* can be answered in relatively precise terms by measuring or counting certain textual features. Since the 1940s, such quantitative analyses have played an important role in several forms of media research. In the first general account of this type of analysis, Bernard Berelson (1952) used the term 'content analysis,' defining it as a research technique "for the objective, systematic, and quantitative description of the manifest content of communication" (p. 18).◀

As this definition suggests, content analysis is basically descriptive. Certain well-defined textual elements or characteristics are measured in various ways – for example, the amount of newspaper coverage of certain issues, the topics of television news programs, the occurrence of particular symbols in fictional genres, and so on. Such quantitative descriptions of the features of a group of texts are then typically used as a basis for more general inferences about the meaning of these texts and their implications regarding various social phenomena.

One early example of this approach was Leo Lowenthal's study of 'mass idols' from 1941. In a quantitative analysis of biographical articles in popular US magazines, he showed that while political leaders, businessmen, and scientists were portrayed in 46 percent of the cases at the beginning of the twentieth century, this percentage had dropped to 25 by 1940, and the interest was now focused, instead, on film actors, entertainers, and athletes. This shift had begun in the 1920s, and was accompanied by an additional shift of focus from the public life and achievements of the people in question, to their love life, their ways of dressing, and other private matters. Lowenthal interpreted this change of emphasis from 'idols of production' to 'idols of consumption,' and from the public to the private sphere, as a textual expression of general changes in social values during the period.

'mass idols'

Leiss', *et al.*'s (2005) study of changes in Canadian advertising is a comparable, more recent, example of how quantitative methodology has been used to trace historical trends in media representations.◀ Leiss and his collaborators chose two general-interest, mass-circulation magazines that spanned a period of more than seventy years of history, one directed at a female audience, the other with a predominantly male readership. In order to minimize the effect of variations and changes in the types of products advertised in the magazines, they constructed profiles of *types* of products and counted the frequency of advertisements for each product type in both magazines by randomly sampling two copies of each magazine for each year, examining a total of fifteen thousand advertisements. The study, further, limited the final sample to a selection of product types concerning smoking, automobiles, clothing, food, personal care, alcohol, and corporate image advertisements, but still covered more than 50 percent of products advertised in the two magazines at any time. The sample was coded with reference to four aspects of representation – people, products, setting, and text – and, importantly, the display area devoted to each aspect in each ad.

The study, first, found a major shift from textual to visual representation during the period under study. In the early period, the text would provide an overall interpretation of the relationship between product and consumer,

▶ content analysis – Chapter 13, p. 248.
Example analysis, Chapter 6, p. 110

▶ advertising studies – Chapter 6, p. 129

while contemporary ads often contain nothing more than a brand name, a slogan, and a few words of explanation. Second, the growing quantity of visual features entailed a qualitative change in the advertisements' mode of address to readers.◄ Early on, all textual and visual elements were aimed at explaining the product and its use value, where contemporary ads typically establish symbolic relations between products, consumers, and the wider cultural setting, thus addressing the given product to a specific social segment of users and their lifestyle.◄

Since the early days of content analysis, quantitative methodology has been used in a variety of research contexts, often in combination with other methodologies. The main varieties have included (for a detailed overview, see Wimmer and Dominick, 2011):

- studies of patterns and trends in media *representations as such* (illustrated by Lowenthal and Leiss, *et al.*);
- studies of the relationship between textual representations and '*the real world*'; and
- studies concerning media *effects*.

In some studies, the overall content of a specific media genre, for example, television news, has been analyzed by the Glasgow University Media Group (1976, 1980). Other studies have undertaken analyses of how the media handle specific events, such as political demonstrations (e.g., Halloran, *et al.*, 1970) and wars (e.g., Morrison and Tumber (1988) on the Falklands conflict, and Morrison (1992) on the first Gulf War).

Violent media content

The depiction of violence, particularly in television fiction, has been a favorite topic. In such studies, researchers commonly start by defining how 'violence' should be understood, and in which specific discursive contexts it should be measured. Next, coders watch samples of television programs and count the incidents which match the definition. The longest-running and most well-known of these studies was started in the late 1960s by George Gerbner. In the initial research design, he defined violence as "the overt expression of physical force (with or without a weapon) against self or other, compelling action against one's will on pain of being hurt or killed, or actually hurting or killing" (Gerbner, 1972: 31). From this definition, Gerbner further established a series of guidelines regarding the types of events to be included in studies with reference to their place in the fictional universe and their relation to the overall plot (see Gerbner and Gross, 1976; Gerbner, *et al.*, 1977).

Continued by Gerbner and his team, this series of studies is an example of research projects in which content analysis is used to compare media representations with actual occurrences in society. These studies have repeatedly shown that the world of US prime-time television fiction is a far more violent place than the real world, and that the portrayal of certain social groups as frequent victims of crime is inconsistent with social statistics. The same set of studies have also addressed media effects: Comparing content analyses with survey data, Gerbner and his team have argued that television fiction 'cultivates' or shapes people's perceptions of social reality, so that heavy viewers tend to have misconceptions of the role of violence in everyday life.◄

A quantitative analysis of classical Hollywood cinema

Many content analyses, thus, form part of larger projects concerning media effects or the relationship between media representations and real life. Other quantitative analyses, however, have focused on research questions regarding media texts in their own right. A well-known example of the use of content analysis for describing and interpreting particular textual genres is a study by David Bordwell (1985b) of the style of classical Hollywood cinema.

The point of departure for that study was a list of the approximately fifteen thousand

► mode of address – p. 147
► lifestyle studies – Chapter 8, p. 168
► cultivation research – Chapter 8, p. 166

feature films produced in the US in the period 1915–1960. Bordwell and his co-authors (1985) used a table of random numbers to select 841 films from this list. Of these, one hundred could be located in various collections and archives. As the authors emphasize, this was not, strictly speaking, a random sample,◂ since each film did not have an equal chance of being selected, because not every film on the original list had survived. The point, however, is that the actual choices of films "were not biased by personal preferences or conceptions of influential or masterful films" (Bordwell, 1985b: 388). In fact, four-fifths of the resulting sample were fairly obscure productions.

The authors studied each film in the sample on a viewing machine, recording stylistic details of each shot and summarizing actions scene by scene. On the basis of these descriptions, they constructed a model of the 'typical film' of the period, with special attention to style and narration, and went on to test this generalization by analyzing almost two hundred other Hollywood films from the same period. Although many of the films in this second sample were chosen precisely for their quality or historical influence, the analyses confirmed the general model (Bordwell, 1985b: 10). The study stands as an impressive account of typical aspects of the classical Hollywood film in terms of features such as story construction, narrational strategies, the construction of time and space, etc. Moreover, this description of invariables and stabilities provides an important framework for further research on the equally obvious stylistic changes during the classical Hollywood period.

QUALITATIVE TEXTUAL ANALYSIS AND SEMIOTICS

While quantitative content analyses are descriptive in nature, aiming at "the manifest content of communication" (Berelson, 1952: 18), textual analyses in the tradition of literary criticism and art history are usually interpretive, aiming at what is sometimes termed latent meaning. The basic questions, consequently, are 'qualitative': What does the text *really* mean and how are its meanings organized? Still, analyses may be concerned with either particulars or generalities. Even while focusing on features that are characteristic of a single work or a small group of works, studies may also examine how the given works differ from all other works in structural and thematic terms.

manifest and latent meanings

The sources of this analytical practice include the attentive 'close reading' practiced by the Anglo-American school of New Criticism◂ and its French counterpart, the *explication du texte*. In both of these traditions, it is the singular or *particular* analytical object, its parts and its whole, which is at the center of interest. The underlying assumption, and the very reason for giving particular attention to the works in question, is that they are thought to be significant carriers of cultural values and insights, or that they provide important and valuable aesthetic experiences. This type of textual analysis has been transferred successfully to film studies – an area of media studies that deals with textual objects which are, in some ways, comparable to the unique works analyzed by literary critics and art historians (see, for example, Robin Wood on Hitchcock (1965) and on Hawks (1968)). However, the basic aim of most other media research has been to study prototypes, regularities, repeated patterns, and features which are shared by masses of texts. Accordingly, textual analyses of media have most often taken their inspiration from humanistic traditions which are oriented toward the study of *generalities*, particularly structural linguistics and general semiotics.◂

Applied to media studies, Ferdinand de Saussure's (1959[1916]) linguistic dichotomy of *langue* and *parole*◂ has proven to be an effective conceptual tool. Concrete media texts may be regarded as instances of *parole*, as generated from one or more *langues*. Even though the various instances of *parole* are carried by different types of signifiers (images, written or spoken language, combinations of these, etc.); are transmitted through different

▸ random sampling – Chapter 13, p. 245

▸ New Criticism – Chapter 2, p. 38

▸ linguistics and semiotics – Chapter 2

▸ langue and parole – Chapter 2, p. 33

media; and are produced according to specific rules, it can be argued that all sign production is based on certain general principles. Whether the analytical intention is to reconstruct the *langue* behind a group of texts, or to study a single text as *parole*, knowledge of such general textual principles is useful. The underlying *langue* is usually understood as a 'code' that consists of signs, on the one hand, and of syntactic rules, on the other. Meaning production, thus, is thought of as a process by which signs are selected from groups of possibilities (paradigms) and combined according to relevant syntactic rules into strings of text (syntagms).◀

Saussure (1959[1916]) defined the sign as a material object – a *signifier* – evoking a certain mental representation – a *signified*.◀ Corresponding to these two aspects, there are two main types of semiotic media analysis: a formal and material study of signs in the media, and an analysis of media contents as representations with inherent meanings. However, since the two aspects of the sign are interdependent, there can be no absolute distinction between the two types of textual analysis.

FORMAL ANALYSIS

Formal analyses (of signifiers) highlight the material specificity of the medium in question. What are its particular properties, and how do these properties translate into communicative possibilities? In the case of visual media, key theoretical questions have been: What is an image? Are images signs? (Barthes, 1977[1964]; Eco, 1968, 1975; Sonesson, 1989). How do photographic images differ from other types of signs? (Barthes, 1980; Messaris, 1997). Concrete analyses in the area have dealt with questions concerning pictorial representation, composition, and style, in some cases relying on concepts and analytical procedures from the study of traditional arts (for a brief overview, see Bryson, 1991).◀

▶ paradigms and syntagms – Chapter 2, p. 33
▶ signifier and signified – Chapter 2, p. 33
▶ art history – Chapter 2, p. 36

Moving images: Syntagm analyses

The ways in which moving images are produced and structured raises special theoretical and analytical problems.◀ One of the first researchers to address these problems from a semiotic perspective was the French linguist, Christian Metz. In an influential study of how cinematic signifiers are organized, he showed that the majority of films are based on seven types of 'syntagm,' or seven basic series of shots (Metz, 1968).

seven types of syntagms

Four *narrative* syntagms indicate temporal relations between narrative events:

- The *scene* is the most widely used of these – a series of shots presenting an event in continuous time and space;
- In the *alternating syntagm*, there is cross-cutting between several narrative spaces (for example, in a 'chase') as well as indications of temporal simultaneity between the shots;
- In *sequences*, the shots indicate discontinuous time: the *ordinary* sequence is an elliptical construction in which unimportant events and other details are left out; and
- The *episodic* sequence, in comparison, organizes the shots so that the omissions suggest a compressed chronological development.

In addition to the four narrative syntagms, there are three *a-chronological* ones:

- The *descriptive* syntagm is a series of shots suggesting spatial co-presence of people or objects;
- The *bracket* syntagm depicts typical aspects of a phenomenon or a concept ("poverty," "morning in the city," etc.); and
- The *parallel* syntagm organizes two series of contrasting motifs ("rich and poor," "town and country," etc.).

Metz's intention was to describe cinema as a general *langue*, or at least one of its main component structures. His framework has also proven useful, however, for the analysis of

▶ analysis of still images – Chapter 6, p. 123

individual films. Knowledge of the basic syntagm system can serve as an "attention-focusing device" for the analyst (Stam, *et al.*, 1992: 48), and is also helpful when one aims at defining fundamental formal characteristics of specific genres or films (see, for example, Ellis (1975) on Ealing comedies; Flitterman-Lewis (1983) on soap operas; Heath (1975) on Orson Welles' *Touch of Evil*).

The Big Sleep A brief example from a classical Hollywood movie, Howard Hawks' *The Big Sleep* (1946), illustrates this point. The story concerns old General Sternwood, who hires the private detective Marlowe to solve a mystery. The case involves the general's youngest daughter, Carmen, who is being blackmailed. As Marlowe is working on the case, additional mysteries are introduced: A former employee with the general has disappeared; the blackmailer is found murdered; a powerful gangster plays an obscure role in all of these events. Along the way, Marlowe also falls in love with the general's oldest daughter, Vivian. At the end of the film Marlowe solves the mysteries, and the gangster, who is the main culprit, is shot by his own men.

During the first few minutes of the film, we see Marlowe visiting the Sternwood mansion. First he meets Carmen, one of the general's daughters, in the hall; then he meets the general himself in a winter garden; and finally he meets Vivian, another daughter, in her room. A butler leads him from room to room and finally back to the entrance. From these encounters, Marlowe – and we, the audience – learn a lot about the Sternwoods and the case. Next follows a shot of a sign saying "Hollywood Public Library," a close-up of books and documents, and a series of shots of Marlowe sitting in the library, reading and taking notes.

On the level of signifieds or content, the introduction provides Marlowe (and the audience) with necessary background information. On the level of signifiers or form, this information is organized in three distinct 'scenes' (Marlowe's three encounters in Sternwood mansion, each

Figure 7.1 The introduction to *The Big Sleep*

of them presented in spatio-temporal continuity). When he starts working on the case, a summarizing 'ordinary sequence' follows (Marlowe is seen in the library studying, but unimportant details are skipped). (See Figure 7.1.)

Most of the rest of the film is constructed along these lines. The narrative is presented mainly in the form of scenes and ordinary sequences, in addition to the occasional alternating syntagm. This is a familiar pattern, the pattern of classical Hollywood cinema. Most films from this period use a similar, very limited part of the general syntagm system, as described by Metz. Indeed, Bordwell (1985a: 158), analyzing classical Hollywood films from a cognitivist perspective,◀ arrived at a similar conclusion: The majority of films in this period are based on only two syntagms or 'segments' as he calls them – the 'scene' and the 'montage sequence' – corresponding roughly to Metz's 'scene' and 'sequence.'

The correspondence between a semiotic and a cognitivist description of the classical Hollywood film is no coincidence. When Metz worked out his system, he followed the general semiotic and linguistic principle of describing his materials according to the distinctions that a 'native speaker' – in his case, an experienced film spectator – would make. Each of his syntagms is defined with reference to the characteristic spatio-temporal effect that any member of a cinema audience would immediately recognize. There is an evident connection between this approach and cognitivist studies of the various 'schemata' (organized clusters of knowledge) which people apply in their everyday lives. In both cases, the intention is to describe and systematize what 'everybody' intuitively 'knows' about the world (for a discussion of the relation between semiotics and cognitive science in film studies, see Buckland, 2000).

Compared to other types of films, classical Hollywood films constitute a class of their own in terms of both formal and narrative strategy. The so-called montage films that were produced in the USSR during the 1920s are obvious counterexamples to this norm. They are overtly 'rhetorical,' constantly presenting political arguments by visual means. While, for instance, the 'parallel syntagm' is very rare in classical Hollywood cinema, it is a central device in these Soviet films, where it was used to suggest all kinds of rhetorical analogies or contrasts (Bordwell, 1985a: 239).

montage films

▶ cognitivist film theory – Chapter 2, p. 44

Shot-to-shot analyses

Whereas Metz's concerns were theoretical, his account of the basic syntagm system provides a useful, if rather broad, framework for the analysis of particular films. Raymond Bellour is an example of a film semiotician whose work is not theoretical in a strict sense, but primarily concerned with practical, analytical questions and, as such, more closely related to traditional literary analysis. During the 1970s, Bellour presented a series of 'close readings' of well-known Hollywood films (see the collection in Bellour, 1979). By means of meticulous shot-to-shot analyses, primarily of formal features and often of very short fragments, he described the films in question, established their individual cinematic systems, as it were, and used these characterizations as a basis for conclusions about formal aspects of the classical Hollywood system in general.

shot: continuous visual sequence, filmed by one camera, without cuts, wipes, dissolves, or other editing

One example of this procedure is his analysis of a short segment from *The Big Sleep* (Bellour, 1973). Consisting of twelve shots, the segment, inconspicuous, almost trivial, marks a transition between two action-packed, narrative climaxes. After a shoot-out at a gas station in the country the two main characters, Marlowe and Vivian Sternwood, drive away in a car; on the road toward the final shoot-out, they declare their love for each other.

Bellour describes the twelve shots with regard to framing, camera movement, camera angles, absence or presence of characters in shots, absence or presence of speech during shots, and relative length of shots. His results can be summarized as follows. Although nothing much happens, the number of shots is relatively high – a fact which Bellour explains as a strategy of discontinuity, of introducing variations into the filmic space within the given time frame.

At the same time, these variations appear against a background of similarities. After an establishing shot of the car driving along, as seen from the outside, there follows a series of almost identical medium-close shots and close-ups of the two characters inside the car. This repetition of formal qualities produces a sense of constraint around the actual variation in the actors' dialogue and comportment, making the variations stand out as differences which ensure the forward movement and continuity of the narrative. Bellour finds this formal arrangement to be characteristic not only of *The Big Sleep*, but of the classical Hollywood cinema as such.

NARRATIVE ANALYSIS

narratology

Narrative semiotics or narratology – the study of basic narrative patterns and procedures – has been one of the most fertile interdisciplinary fields of study during recent decades, and has proven particularly effective and valuable for analytical purposes. By way of introduction, it should be noted that narrative is both a mental structure and a specific type of text. As a mental 'tool,' it functions as a fundamental interpretive frame: humans make narratives in order to organize their experiences and to make their world intelligible (on the relations between narrative thought and narrative discourse, see Branigan, 1992; Bruner, 1986, 1994; Labov and Waletzky, 1967).

narrative: textual and mental structure

Narrative texts appear in all kinds of discursive forms and in all kinds of media (Barthes, 1966). As a textual type, however, the narrative is defined solely by its *content:* a narrative is a representation of *events* in time and space. These events are organized in series of *causes and effects*, and viewed in relation to *human projects* which they either further or impede (for detailed definitions of narrative, see Bal, 1977; Branigan, 1992; Bremond, 1966; Rimmon-Kenan, 1983; Todorov, 1971).

Narratives as sequences of events

The causal organization of events leads to characteristic narrative patterns. In 1928, the Russian formalist Vladimir Propp showed that virtually all narratives within a large selection of folk-tales were based on identical events and, further, that these events were presented in identical order (Propp, 1958[1928]). Some of these recurrences could be explained as the result of genre conventions, but later studies have confirmed that there is a more general and systematic regularity at work in the ordering of narrative events. Not only these Russian folk tales, but all narratives are, at a basic level, series of variations on a simple pattern, consisting of an initial state which is transformed by a dynamic event into a new state (Bremond, 1966; Todorov, 1971; Branigan, 1992).

No matter what a narrative is about, it will always be constructed from such modules or 'elementary sequences.' The same characteristic pattern can also be observed at the narrative macro level. A narrative will usually start with the presentation of a situation, a setting, the principal characters, the general state of affairs, etc. This initial situation is then gradually transformed by a series of events and actions, until a new situation has been established and the story ends. According to story-comprehension psychologists, this macro pattern is also the mental schema that people mobilize when they recognize and try to structure unfamiliar narratives (see Bower and Cirilo, 1985; van Dijk and Kintsch, 1983; Gulich and Quasthoff, 1985; also Branigan, 1992).

elementary sequences

At the macro level, the narrative sequence from beginning to end usually involves a movement between central thematic positions or 'values' – from an initial, problematic, and unstable situation, through successive actions, to a final, stable, and acceptable situation. In analyses of concrete narratives, it is therefore helpful to begin by describing how the string of elementary sequences is organized at the macro level. This procedure provides not only a rough outline, but a way of gaining important insights into the underlying value system.

The what and how of narratives

Any narrative may be viewed from two different points of view. On the one hand, there is the series of events; on the other hand, there is the actual text by means of which these events

story and discourse

are represented. These two aspects can be defined in terms of the general sign model: the *what* of the narrative (the series of events) is the narrative signified, while the *how* (the actual text) is the signifier. This distinction is usually referred to in narratology by the terms story and discourse (Genette, 1972; see also Chatman, 1989) or as story and plot (Bordwell and Thompson, 2009).

syuzhet and fabula

The Russian formalists◄ employed a similar distinction, but emphasized the audience's active participation in the construction of narrative coherence. David Bordwell has reintroduced the formalists' term *syuzhet* to cover the series of events which is presented explicitly in the narrative text, while *fabula* refers to the spectator's construction of connections between these events. No narrative discourse presents the full story – there will always be indeterminacies and vaguenesses. To understand a narrative is precisely to interpret the available information (syuzhet), and to construct textual coherence (fabula) (Bordwell, 1985a).

The construction of the fabula by the audience, then, is dependent on the syuzhet, but the specific syuzhet, in its turn, also is only one among many possible implementations of the fabula. Moreover, the particular way in which crucial narrative information from the fabula is organized and presented in the syuzhet has important consequences for the audience's expectations and comprehension. The fabula-syuzhet relationship may even be a decisive element in the definition of a particular narrative genre. Mystery and other suspense stories are well-known examples of this. Their narrative strategy is to generate suspense by breaking the chronological order of events, so that crucial fabula information about the original cause of the mystery is presented very late in the syuzhet.

adaptations across media

Macbeth

Just as one fabula may give rise to a multitude of syuzhets, it can also be implemented in many discursive forms and media types. Consequently, the fabula-syuzhet distinction is very useful for analyzing adaptations of narratives across different media. Take, for example, Shakespeare's tragedy *Macbeth*, written in 1605, and performed since then all over the world. All these performances are interpretations of a text that was published in 1623, seven years after Shakespeare's death. The play that we see on stage, then, is actually an interpretation of a written text that can be read either in the original English or in translation. Giuseppe Verdi turned the text into an opera in 1847; Orson Welles made it into a film in 1948. Shakespeare's original play is set in a long past era; the director Ken Hughes transferred the action to a contemporary American gangster setting in his film *Joe MacBeth* (1956), whereas Roman Polanski returned the story to a vague European past in his version from 1971. Shakespeare's play has also been performed as television drama and as ballet, and the text has been summarized in popularized prose versions and as cartoons.

Many aesthetic qualities, evidently, are lost when the original text is transferred to other media. However, in spite of any and all variations, these different versions do have something essential in common with Shakespeare's *Macbeth*. First, they are manifestations of the same fabula. If this were not the case, it would be quite simple to show which elements were missing or had been inappropriately changed. For example, in Akiri Kurosawa's film *Kumonosu-jô* (*Throne of Blood*, 1957), the action takes place among Japanese samurais. But while Shakespeare's text ends with Macbeth being killed by a rival, he is killed by his own men in Kurosawa's film, so that, strictly speaking, *Throne of Blood* is not a version of Macbeth. Second, most of the versions use the same organization of the syuzhet as Shakespeare's play, presenting the necessary narrative information in more or less the same order as the original text.

Characters and actants

Narrative series of events, then, are structured according to certain basic patterns. Similar regularities apply to the individual characters or agents who are involved in and affected by the events. On the face of it, there is a multitude of characters, each of them endowed with specific, individual traits and qualities. However, these characters have rather limited spheres of action.

► Russian formalism – Chapter 2, p. 38

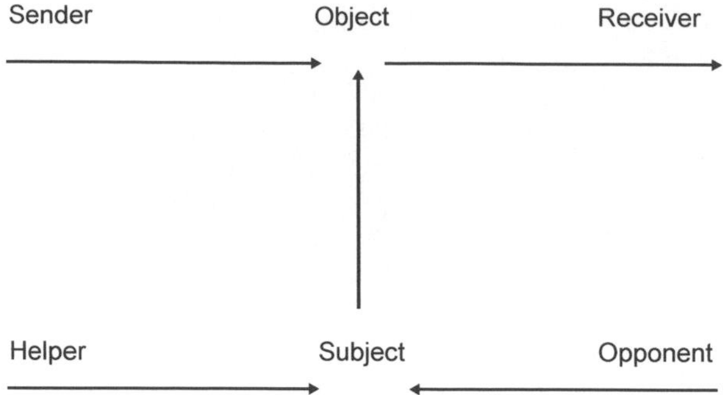

Figure 7.2 The actant model

As demonstrated by A. J. Greimas, there are six 'basic positions' that characters can assume in relation to the central project of the narrative. The multitude of narrative characters or agents can, thus, be viewed as surface manifestations of six underlying narrative roles, the so-called 'actants' (Greimas, 1966). The actant model is presented in Figure 7.2.

agents and actants

The moment a narrative *project* is stated, two actants are established: a *Subject* who desires an *Object*. In addition, all narrative projects have to do with *communication* in the sense of 'transport': the Object has to be 'moved' between two positions. Therefore, the statement of a project also establishes two further actants, the potential *Sender* who 'has' the Object, and the potential *Receiver* who 'lacks' it. The transport of the object is usually complicated by a *conflict* between competing projects within the narrative universe. In such cases, the Subject is faced with an *Opponent* who will try to prevent the transport. Furthermore, there will often be a *Helper*, i.e., an actant who supports the project and works to facilitate the transport of the Object.

The actant model is a simple and effective analytical tool. Its strength is that it accounts for all actions and characters from the same point of view. Focusing on how characters are positioned in relation to the core project, the model makes it possible to provide a description of the most basic relations and conflicts in a narrative.

Die Hard

Consider the *Die Hard* series of US blockbuster films. The central characters in the first *Die Hard* film (John McTiernan, 1988) are the New York cop, John McClane, and his estranged wife, Holly Gennaro, who works for a multinational Japanese corporation. He travels to Los Angeles on Christmas Eve to make up with her, but moments after meeting her, they are separated as the ultra-modern high-rise housing corporation is taken over by a group of international gangsters, led by the German Hans Gruber. The rest of the film chronicles McClane's action-packed attempts at getting help from the outside, killing the villains, and saving his wife.

The basic project for McClane (*Subject*) is to save Holly (*Object*), who is being held hostage by the gangsters (*Sender*). McClane, who wants to be reunited with his wife, is also the *Receiver* of the *Object*. As he tries to rescue Holly and the other hostages, McClane is constantly fighting the gangsters (*Opponent*), killing them off one by one. At some point, he comes into radio contact with a local cop, who then becomes his *Helper*. In addition to the gangsters, even the LA police chief and some FBI agents fill the *Opponent* position. Although they repeatedly try to sabotage McClane's strategy, he succeeds in killing the gangsters and getting the hostages out. He and Holly – Subject and Object – are reunited.

As this summary analysis shows, there is no one-to-one relation between characters and actants. For one thing, one actant position may be filled by many different characters. In this case, both the Sender and the Opponent positions are filled by groups of characters. For another thing, the same character can have several functions in the narrative, thus taking up several actant positions. Some of the characters occupying the Opponent position in *Die Hard* are also found in the Sender position – quite a common constellation. McClane's being both Subject and Receiver is another common constellation: in many narratives, the 'hero' undertakes the narrative project for his or her own sake. In other cases, however, narrative Subjects work selflessly for others.

The actant model offers a description of the narrative as seen, as it were, from the point of view of the core project. Who is the Subject wanting the Object? Who is helping the Subject? Who is opposing the transport? But most narratives could be described from other perspectives, as well. It is, for example, quite easy to see the *Die Hard* narrative from the point of view of the leading gangster, Hans Gruber. He (Subject) wants to steal $600 million worth of bearer bonds (Object) from the Japanese corporation (Sender). He is surrounded by efficient collaborators (Helper), and everything is going according to plan until McClane (Opponent) interferes. The definition of the core project in itself entails a choice of an analytical point of view.

The actant pattern of the first *Die Hard* film, further, provides a basis for analyzing the following three films in the series. *Die Hard 2* (Renny Harlin, 1990) has an almost identical pattern; this time McClane (Subject) has to save Holly (Object) from a plane crash as a group of right-wing terrorists (Sender, Opponent) is holding an airport hostage, whereas the Helper position is filled by a series of minor characters. In the two last films (so far), this pattern has been changed. Here, the McClane-Holly relation is no longer central to the narrative. Instead, McClane more or less accidentally is involved in spectacular terrorist attacks, and becomes the Subject in various action-packed projects of saving New York (*Die Hard: With a Vengeance*, John McTiernan, 1995) and the USA (*Live Free or Die Hard*, Len Wiseman, 2007).

A final observation is that the actant model may be used in two different ways. It is most commonly applied to the fabula as a whole – as in these brief analyses of the *Die Hard* series. However, characters can – and often do – change actant position in the course of a narrative, such as an Opponent suddenly becoming a Helper. Thus, the model may also usefully be applied to shorter narrative sequences as a means of getting an overview of 'local' or individual projects and their configuration within the unfolding presentation of the 'global' narrative.

local and global narrative projects

The canonical story

A textual presentation of a coherent series of events around a human project – this is a broad definition aimed at covering all narratives. Some narratives, however, are obviously more suited for a given purpose than others. Story-comprehension researchers have argued that the main narrative forms of Western culture represent a special variant of the basic pattern.◄ This 'canonical story' is the foundation, for example, of the classical Hollywood film, which, according to David Bordwell,

> presents psychologically defined individuals who struggle to solve a clear-cut problem or to attain specific goals. In the course of this struggle, the characters enter into conflict with others or with external circumstances. The story ends with a decisive victory or defeat, a resolution of the problem and a clear achievement or nonachievement of the goals. The principal causal agency is thus the character, a discriminated individual endowed with a consistent batch of evident traits, qualities, and behaviors.
>
> (Bordwell, 1985a:157)

Compared to the general definition of narrative, this description of the canonical story is far more detailed. All narratives involve human projects, but in the canonical story, the series of events appears totally controlled by individuals. The resulting clarity is the most general feature of this mode of narration. The central characters are clearly defined in terms of their psychological make-up; their problems and goals are clear; the story ends with a resolution, etc.

The canonical story is even predefined at the level of actants. The main narrative project and the Object are clearly stated from the outset, and the other actant positions are filled with individuals. There is always a conflict in this narrative universe, i.e., conflicting projects and hence a clearly defined Opponent. In addition, there are also parallel projects. The canonical story commonly presents two storylines with the same Subject. One part of the story is 'private' and deals with the (usually male) Subject's project of getting the Object woman he loves; the other part is more 'public,' in that it deals with "another sphere - work, war, a mission or quest, other personal relationships"

parallel projects: private and public

► intercultural communication – Chapter 11, p. 212

- A *nondiegetic narrator* is present inside the text as well as inside the fiction, but is outside the 'diegesis,' or the *story world*. This type of narrator observes the story world, but does not act in it. Well-known cinematic examples are the titles that help spectators orient themselves in the story world, ranging from simple statements of time or place ("Los Angeles") to more elaborate presentations of narrative information, such as the text at the end of George Lucas' *American Graffiti* (1973) from which the spectator learns what later happened to the main characters ("John Milner was killed by a drunk driver in December 1964. Terry Fields was reported missing in action near An Loc in December 1965 ..."). Such a narrator obviously 'believes' in the fiction and refers to the characters as if they were real persons.
- The *diegetic narrator* is inside the story world and can address *events* in which he or she has participated. Narrators of this type manifest themselves whenever characters in the story world tell each other about their experiences. In addition, entire narratives may be told by diegetic narrators. A novel like Joseph Conrad's *Heart of Darkness* (1899, revised 1902) is an example. Here, the complex story of a fateful journey to Africa is told in retrospect in the first person by one of the characters. When Francis Ford Coppola made *Apocalypse Now* (1979), a film adaptation of Conrad's novel, he chose the cinematic counterpart to diegetic narration by letting the main character report and comment on narrative events on the sound-track in voice-over (see Lothe, 2000; for a discussion of voice-over narration, see Kozloff, 1988).

diegesis

voice-over narration

The term narrator suggests the presence of a 'voice.' Beyond this, characters within the story world may provide us with information about that world in other ways than simply by 'telling' it:

- *Characters* enable us to learn about them as we observe their *actions*, what is also known as 'character narration.'
- *External focalization* is one way of learning about the story world by sharing a character's experiences. Here, the character is presented from the outside, but we understand that we are in his or her world – that it is this particular character who is the source of our knowledge.
- *Internal focalizations* allow us to see the story world more literally from a character's perspective. In the first type, *surface focalization*, we share a character's subjective experience, for example, by seeing what the character sees by means of a point-of-view-shot.
- In a *deep focalization*, finally, we – the audience – share a character's thoughts, dreams, hallucinations, etc.

character narration

point-of-view-shot

Narrative analysis is always centrally concerned with how a given narrative applies these several modes of narration. A narrative gets its distinctive character not only from its presentation of various events and characters to the audience, but also from the specific ways in which information about these events and characters is organized, and how the audience is addressed. Some narratives belong to genres which adhere to relatively fixed narrational systems. A brief account of how Western television news is presented illustrates this point. The example also serves to emphasize that, as textual forms, narratives cut across traditional boundaries between fact and fiction.

factual and fictional narratives

A typical news program is made up of various stories from real life. These stories are told primarily by anchorpersons and journalists in the studio, and by journalists reporting from the field. In Branigan's (1992) terminology, the anchorpersons and journalists in the studio are nondiegetic narrators who observe the story world and talk about it from the outside. Journalists in the field, on the scene where the events are taking or have taken place, are diegetic narrators. Reporting from inside the story world, these journalists may interview people who are directly involved in events. When talking about their experiences, these people equally become diegetic narrators, as do people who are interviewed by journalists in the studio.

The relations between these narrators are usually indicated by a simple visual code (Larsen, 1974). The most important elements of this code are, first, the presence or absence of eye contact with the viewers, and, second, the

	Studio	Field
Eye contact	Anchorpersons, journalists	Journalists
No eye contact	Interviewees	Interviewees

Figure 7.5 The visual code of television news

distinction between being present in the studio or in the field (Figure 7.5).

The anchorpersons and journalists in the studio as well as the journalists in the field are allowed to address the audience directly, thus simulating face-to-face communication, In contrast, the interviewees both in the studio and in the field have to address the interviewer. These distinctions – direct/non-direct address; studio/field – thus form a simple system which helps the audience to distinguish between the various types of narrators, and to understand their relative authority within the narrative hierarchy. The most important feature of each narrative sequence is decided by the eye contact, which shows, in a very concrete and visually explicit way, who has the right to address the viewers, and to interpret the world for them. However, this system varies historically. With the increasing use of satellite transmission and digital technology in news production during recent decades, it has become common to allow expert witnesses and commentators sitting in far-away studios to have eye contact with viewers.

narrative hierarchy

In a mainstream feature film, the relations between the various levels of narration are considerably more complex, and not marked as clearly as in a news program. The characters in a film address each other – they talk and act 'inwards' into the story world, seemingly unaware of the audience outside the text. In certain cases, the narration becomes rather conspicuous – for example, when the audience is allowed to share a character's perceptions and thoughts by means of internal focalization – but mostly the story seems to tell itself in an almost imperceptible manner. This general impression of 'invisible narration' in the mainstream film is the result of a subtle narrational system that is based primarily on non-diegetic narration via the camera and various forms of external focalization (see, for example, on editing, Bordwell and Thompson, 2009).

invisible narration

camera narration

GAME WORLDS AND NARRATIVES

Interactive digital games – as played on computers and consoles, in arcades or on handheld devices – challenge the traditional view of what a narrative is, posing several analytical issues. Even if one chooses to deal only with games in virtual environments, i.e., games that take place in some form of simulated world, the field is vast, complex, and heterogeneous. Aarseth, *et al.* (2003) have suggested that such games can be classified according to a whole range of criteria: the number and status of players, the nature of the simulated world, the players' view of this world, the rules and aims of the game, the range of possible player-actions, the representation of time and space, etc.

games in virtual environments

Take the *Die Hard* games as an example. *Die Hard*, released for the Nintendo Entertainment System in 1991, is a *single-player game* based on the first *Die Hard* film (1988). It is, further, a *third-person shooter game* in which the player controls an *avatar*, a character in the simulated world, and where the game consists primarily of shooting. The avatar is the figure of John McClane who, like the character in the film, must try to rescue hostages and kill terrorists. The simulated world is presented on the screen from a top-down perspective. Five years after the Nintendo version of *Die Hard*, the *Die Hard Trilogy* for PC or PlayStation was released, with three games based on the first three *Die Hard* films. While also these are single-player games, they each feature a different type of play. The first is a third-person shooter game; *Die Hard 2: Die Harder* is a *first-person shooter*, i.e., a weapons-based combat game in which the player experiences the action through the eyes of the avatar, from a 'first-person perspective'; and the third, *Die Hard: With a Vengeance*, is a first-person *racing game* in which the player drives a sequence of cars through New York trying to find and defuse explosives.

avatars

Almost all blockbuster films since the 1980s have provided the basis for games, often – as with the *Die Hard* series – in several versions. At the time of writing, there are even more *Indiana Jones* games than there are *Indiana Jones* movies. Popular games have also been used as the basis of films – from *Super Mario Bros* (1993), *Street Fighter* (1994), and *Mortal Kombat* (1995) to *Lara Croft: Tomb Raider* (2001) and *Doom* (2005).

Games like *Die Hard* or *Indiana Jones* use the settings, the characters, and a few central plot devices from the films, but they do not present the full story lines. The *Super Mario Bros* film employs characters and a few other elements from the game, but expands the setting and places the characters within a broader, traditional narrative framework. These and other examples of games based on films, or films based on games, then, are not narrative *adaptations*◀ in the strict sense of the word.

The absence of adaptation proper has been taken by a number of researchers – sometimes referred to as ludologists – to indicate that not only the games in question, but also games in general are not narratives and should not be subjected to narrative analysis (Juul (2001); for similar arguments, see Frasca (1999), Eskelinen (2001), Aarseth (2004)). The debate over narratology and ludology has been central to the area of game studies.

narratology and/vs. ludology

It can, however, be argued that games do have quite a few features in common with conventional narratives, and that traditional narratological methods offer helpful tools for game analyses (Simons, 2007). Most games establish a diegesis – a simulated world – and present the player with a narrative project: enemies must be killed, mysteries solved, quests completed, etc. In the course of the game, the player engages with representations of events in a simulated time and space. Events are organized in classic cause-effect sequences, and their functions within the game world are closely related to the overall project of the game. Both game segments at a micro level and the game as a whole follow a familiar narrative pattern: an initial state is transformed by actions until a new orderly state is established, and eventually the game ends with the player's successful or unsuccessful completion of the project in question. Also, the characters that are represented within the simulated world may be described with reference to the actant model.◀ In the attempt to complete the game-project, the player-Subject fights Opponents, meets magical Helpers, and so on.

During the game, the player follows, but also helps to create the narrative syuzhet. When the game is over, s/he is in a position to construct the 'real' story, or the game fabula. In many cases, narrative elements are presented out of chronological order in the syuzhet by various diegetic narrators, i.e., characters who act in the story world and speak about it. In other cases, additional fabula materials are presented by narrators who consider events from a more distant position. By means of written texts, or through sounds or voices, non-diegetic narrators tell players who they are supposed to be, what they ought to do, or what has happened before the game started. Extra-fictional narrators, further, allow players to shift perspective, to get an overview, and to see the story world as a game system that is governed by a set of rules or mechanisms.

A narrative analysis of a game may identify its main project, segment the total game sequence into elementary sequences, compare syuzhet and fabula structures, etc. However, game analyses must, in addition, account for those features that distinguish games from traditional narratives, first and foremost the experiential differences of *playing a game*, as opposed to watching a film or reading a novel. Film spectators and book readers observe the story world, the characters, and the narrative events 'from the outside.' They may identify with one or more characters, but they have no control over actions within the narrative universe. Game players, on the other hand, are immersed in their story world. They usually control an avatar with certain more or less predefined features and possibilities for action, and they engage in an interactive co-construction of the story world and the syuzhet.

immersion

interactive co-construction

For a more fine-meshed analysis, building on work by game theorists Fuller and Jenkins (1995) and Friedman (1995), Rune Klevjer

▶ adaptations – p. 139

▶ the actant model – p. 140

(2008) has suggested that analyses (of single-player games) should account for two aspects of gaming: the game system and the player's mode of participation. The game system is the system of elements and rules that decide how the game must be played. A vital part of this system is the core 'game mechanics,' or the set of standard actions that the game in question allows, for example, loading and shooting in first-person shooter games, or the jumping and travelling forward in games of the *Super Mario* variety. The mode of participation, next, determines how players may immerse themselves in the simulated world. It is defined by (i) physical interface elements like screen, speakers, game controllers, etc.; (ii) how information is supplied to the player – via written texts, speech, music, sounds, images, etc.; and (iii) simulated corporeality. In this last respect, in shooter games, the player is immersed in the game world through the avatar that acts as a kind of substitute for the player's body; in many strategy games, the player acts from a bird's eye position above the game world.

game system

mode of participation

GENRE ANALYSIS

Genre is the French translation of the Latin *genus*, a word originally referring to phenomena which resemble each other due to their common source or other close, mutual relations. *Genus* means *origin*, but also *family*, biological *genus*, grammatical *gender*, and, more generally, *kind*, *sort*, or *class*. Its French counterpart similarly is used in reference to groups of texts or works of art that are connected by a number of common features. The underlying assumption is that a unique text is quite a rare phenomenon. Most texts belong to larger classes of texts, and these classes, in turn, are defined by the features shared by the individual texts.

Classical writings on textual genres dealt with a relatively manageable field. The classes were few and defined by a limited number of textual features, as witnessed by the traditional partitioning of the field into drama, epic, and poetry. Contemporary theorists of genre who deal with media texts face a more complex situation. Throughout the media system, and particularly in the area of film and television fiction, there is a multitude of genre categories, and a constant proliferation of new genres and sub-genres (on film genres, see Altman, 1999; Grant, 1986, 1995; Neale, 1980, 2000; on television genres, see Newcomb, 1974; Kaminsky and Mahan, 1985; Rose, 1985).

drama, epic, poetry

The media industry itself uses genres as convenient labels in production planning and in the marketing of new products. From the audience's point of view, references to genre function as appetizers that suggest the type of interpretive frame which should be applied to a particular text. Genre references, then, create certain expectations which are based on the audience's prior experience with similar media products. As such, a genre can be regarded as a kind of 'contract' between the media industry and its audience. More specifically, it amounts to an agreement between sender and receiver about some basic features of a certain type of textual product which is designed to perform a particular cultural task.

genre as contract between sender and receiver

In sum, a genre is a system of textual conventions, or – to use semiotic terminology – a kind of latent *langue* governing the production of individual instances of *parole*. Because of the contractual nature of the relation between sender and receiver, it can also be regarded as a kind of mental tool, provided by the media and feeding into cultural processes. Media audiences use such tools to interpret the world and to address certain recurring sociocultural issues within familiar formats.

Practical and theoretical genres

In some cases, a 'genre' refers to a group of texts which is classified differently by the media industry and by portions of the audience. The prime example is the term *film noir*, which was introduced by French film critics after World War II to refer to a group of Hollywood films that the industry was marketing as crime stories or melodramas (Borde and Chaumeton, 1955). By using the term *film noir*, the film critics suggested that the films in question were somehow united across the established industrial genre categories (the history of the *film noir* concept is discussed in Cook, 1999).

film noir

Film noir has been called a 'theoretical' genre as opposed to the 'practical' genres employed by the producers and consumers of media texts. The distinction calls attention to the fact that any given genre term usually covers two different phenomena. On the one hand, a genre is part of the practical, almost unconscious knowledge about textual features and classes which members of the audience draw upon in their everyday lives. On the other hand, it is also a theoretical and analytical object, or rather it becomes such an object the moment people start discussing which textual features define a particular group of texts, or how this group differs from other groups (see Todorov, 1978). *Film noir* is one of the relatively rare examples of a classification which started out as a theoretical genre, was accepted by the industry and the audience, and ended up being a practical genre.◀

The theoretical definition of genres is no easy task. The history of genre theory shows that it is, in fact, quite impossible to classify texts on the basis of simple, well-defined features, or to make genres form a clear-cut, unambiguous system. One solution is to rely on the concept of 'family resemblances,' as defined by Wittgenstein (1953): While it is quite rare for a few common features to constitute an entire genre, a group of texts may nevertheless be closely related because of the partial and incremental overlaps between its various sub-groups – just as individual children within a family may have features in common with both their father and their mother without resembling each other. Genres are, indeed, defined with reference to a common pool of textual features, but these features may not all be shared by all members of the group. In this view, a genre amounts to a series of transitions or displacements between texts, an aspect which makes the concept particularly useful for the description and analysis of the historical development of textual forms. The individual genre can be regarded as a mobile textual field in which new sub-categories or branches are constantly being developed.

family resemblances

▶ practical and other 'theory' – Chapter 19, p. 352

When texts are used recurrently to perform more or less similar cultural and social functions, prototypical forms develop almost automatically. And, as these recurrent discursive features are institutionalized and codified, individual texts will eventually be produced and received in accordance with the codified norms. According to Todorov (1978), a genre is precisely such a codification of discursive characteristics, i.e., a group of texts that serve a common purpose, and which therefore have certain discursive qualities in common. Still, as implied by the concept of family resemblances, these characteristics may be associated with many different textual levels and aspects.

Textual characteristics of genres

The genre label suggests an interpretive frame to the audience as well as to the analyst. To analyze a particular film *as* a western or *as* a *film noir* is to regard it as an example of a general type. It is also to identify a series of textual features or aspects which this particular film has in common with other films, and which may be relevant for the analysis. There are several basic textual aspects at work in genre definitions (on these aspects, see further Todorov, 1978).

Some genre definitions focus on signifieds or 'content,' or what linguists might call 'semantic' aspects of the texts in question (What is the text about? What kind of 'themes' or 'motifs' does it deal with?). If, for instance, a film is labeled a *mystery movie,* we expect a mystery, a crime to be solved, usually, but not always, by a private investigator or a police officer. In addition, semantic definitions may raise questions of referentiality (Is the textual universe presented as fictional or factual? What kind of sociohistorical context does the text refer to?). An example is the *western* label, which leads us to expect narratives about conflicts at the American frontier during the nineteenth century.

semantic definition of genre

Other genre definitions refer to what Todorov (1978) calls the 'verbal' aspect of the text, its 'material' form. The material aspect concerns questions of 'style' or 'mise-en-scène' – the way in which events are staged for the camera in terms of setting, lighting, costumes,

material definition of genre

mise-en-scène

and character behavior (see Bordwell and Thompson, 2009). The genre label *action movie* is not only a semantic definition, pointing to a certain kind of content; it also suggests a certain stylistic pattern with spectacular, colorful images of collapsing buildings, exploding cars, and crashing helicopters, as well as a fast editing rhythm.

syntactic definition of genre

Finally there is the 'syntactic' aspect – the actual structuration of the text, its sequential organization or composition. In the case of mystery movies, the central characteristics follow from the relation between syuzhet and fabula, as already described: Fabula events are presented in reverse chronological order within the syuzhet; the film presents murders and mysteries, but withholds information about their causes until the very last moment.

The specific configuration of semantic, material, and syntactical aspects is articulated in a number of textual features. Moreover, since genres are established and institutionalized according to the functions of texts in fixed, recurring situations, they also always have a 'pragmatic' aspect. What are the demands of the situation on the discursive characteristics of a given genre? What is the intention governing the production of the texts? What is their purpose? Even though this fourth aspect of a definition of genre primarily concerns the social context, the pragmatic functions which a text has to fulfill within a given context obviously affect the details of its discursive construction. In this regard, one particularly important issue is the way in which the text addresses its audience.◀ As indicated by the brief analysis of television news, this is one textual genre in which a central pragmatic question – the interpretive authority of different narrators – is solved by means of a fixed narrational system.

pragmatic definition of genre

HETEROGENEOUS TEXTS

A film is not only a sequence of moving images, but an organized mixture of images, words, texts, music, and noises. Most media texts are like this – *montages*, or heterogeneous constructions that are characterized by a constant displacement and circulation of meaning. In film and television, in newspapers and magazines, and in websites and other digital media formats, information is doubled or tripled, presented through several channels, discourses, and senses at once.

This complexity raises a series of theoretical and analytical issues which are often neglected in media studies. Like much earlier film theory, Christian Metz' semiotic works in the 1960s were primarily concerned with sequences of shots. The focus of many current film studies is primarily on the fabula – the narrative as constructed by a spectator after the fact. Journalism studies frequently approach newspaper stories and even television or online news as merely verbal phenomena.

Similarities and differences

Although the need for studies of the heterogeneity of the modern media was acknowledged by the semioticians of the 1960s, the problem proved difficult to handle within a theoretical framework which takes the homogeneous verbal text as its model. In his authoritative introduction to semiotics, Barthes (1967[1964]) simply stated that semioticians, like linguists, must work primarily with homogeneous materials. Even if he saw the need for descriptions of, for example, films or fashion magazines as complex structural totalities, he wanted to postpone the analysis of such heterogeneous materials and to concentrate on studies of individual, homogeneous substances.

Nevertheless, in his influential essay on "The rhetoric of the image," Barthes (1977[1964]) did suggest some basic relations between two such substances, namely, image and text.◀ According to Barthes, a text can function as an 'anchorage' of visual signifieds, either by identifying the objects represented by the image (e.g., a caption for a news photo), or by suggesting and authorizing how the image should be interpreted (e.g., the title of a painting). The anchorage relation is based on redundancy: the text repeats or explains the information given by the image. In contrast, the other basic relation,

▶ mode of address – Chapter 10, p. 196

▶ anchorage and relay – Chapter 6, p. 124

'relay,' operates on differences. In this relation, text and image are complementary, and the unity of the message is realized at a higher level. Barthes' own example was the relation between dialogue and images in a film. Here, text and image carry different signifieds; the text adds meanings to the narrative which are not found in the sequence of images.

With this simple sketch, particularly the concept of relay, Barthes hinted at ways of analyzing not only text-image relationships, but the total mix of substances which are characteristic of films, television programs, and the internet. In various versions, this notion of complementarity has been a key issue since the 1980s in studies trying to account for the heterogeneity or 'multimodality'◀ of media materials (Kress, 2010; Jewitt, 2009).

Studies of sound

Many discussions of media heterogeneity have been focused on the status of sound and its functions in film. In 1980, in a seminal issue of *Yale French Studies* on cinema and sound, Rick Altman (1980) criticized traditional film theory as well as contemporary film semiotics for their focus on the cinematic image and their corresponding neglect of sound. Here and in later writings, he argued that sound is just as important as – and in certain respects perhaps even more important than – images for the total cinematic experience (e.g., Altman, 1992). From a similar position, French sound theorist Michel Chion has argued in a series of books that most film theory is characterized by 'vococentrism.' In so far as film sound is acknowledged at all, it is usually the human voice of the dialogue, or the voice-over, which is privileged analytically in favor of, for instance, music or noise. Chion presents detailed analyses of the importance of sound in film and television with particular emphasis on the 'point-of-hearing,' i.e., the effect which is obtained by the positioning of the sound source in relation to the point-of-view of the camera (see Chion, 1982, 1985, 1988, 1998).

vococentrism

point-of-hearing

▶ multimodality – Chapter 6, p. 126

In their justified criticism of the dominant focus on visuality in previous film and media studies, Altman and Chion sometimes place themselves at the opposite extreme, claiming the superiority of sound in relation to images. Most later works in this area emphasize the complementarity of sound and image. This, for example, is the position of Sarah Kozloff in her studies of the various ways in which voice-over and dialogue are used in film (Kozloff, 1988, 2000). It is also the dominant position at present in studies of music and its functions in film.

The role of music in film

Traditional film studies tended to distinguish between two types of music, one supporting the image, the other working contrapuntal to the image (e.g., Eisler and Adorno, 1947). Arguing that music should be described more directly for its relations with the narrative and its events, Chion (1985, 1990, 1995) suggests three basic categories:

- *empathetic* music, which supports and expresses the emotions of the characters;
- *a-empathetic* music, which is independent of the actions on the screen; and
- *didactic* music, which is employed as a distanciating, often ironical commentary on the action.

In concrete studies of music in film and television, a more differentiated analytical framework is needed. As in narrative studies and genre studies, classical Hollywood cinema has also been the central case in studies of film music. Examples are Claudia Gorbman (1987), Kathryn Kalinak (1992), and Peter Larsen (2007), who take the practice of classical Hollywood cinema as the basis for a general description of narrative film music. A common theme in these studies is that analyses of film music must start by considering how the music relates to the cinematic narrative. Using the terminology of narratology, one can distinguish between *diegetic* and *non-diegetic* music. Diegetic music is part of the story world; it is the music that is played by musicians, or heard on the radio, within the fictional space. This type of music usually serves to characterize the story world and its characters.

The function of non-diegetic music is more complex. This is music that comes 'from without,' adding a kind of running commentary to the narrative events. But how does this commentary work? In my own work (Larsen, 2007), I have suggested that non-diegetic film music can be analyzed from formal, narrative, and emotional perspectives:

- *Formal functions.* Music makes films 'hang together' in many different ways. At the broadest level, music lends wholeness to the individual film, helping to distinguish it from other films. At the level of the narrative, music lends form to a sequence of shots. The structure of the music structures the events on the screen, separates them from each other or links them, points out connections and transitions, closes sections off, and opens new ones. At the level of a scene and a montage sequence, continuous music indicates the connection between the individual shots, while in transitions between scenes, music will normally be used to emphasize narrative discontinuity.
- *Narrative functions.* Film music is used to underscore most of the defining features of the narrative. It marks the time and space of the story world, often with the aid of musical stereotypes. It emphasizes, anticipates, and 'interprets' crucial individual narrative events; it often serves to mark the tempo of events, even to intensify them. It creates its own arcs of tension, which underline those of the visual and spoken narrative. Music, further, is used to characterize the agents in the narrative, for example, with the aid of *leitmotifs* – these may be connected to the characters as formal signals, but can also sometimes be understood as statements about them, their personal qualities, or their role in the plot.

leitmotifs

- *Emotional functions.* The third main function of music is to shape 'emotions' and 'moods' – in the narrative as a whole or within individual sections. The most important emotional function of music in mainstream films is to articulate or intensify moods that have already been indicated with other effects – images, dialogue, camera angle, etc. In certain situations, however, the music can actively shape the mood of the narrative or, more precisely, indicate to the spectator how a particular scene is to be understood and experienced.

Sound and media

The turn towards sound in film studies during the 1980s was, if not prompted, then at least reinforced by the remarkable technological developments of the period. The introduction of the Dolby noise reduction system in 1977, the successive generations of Dolby stereo and surround sound, the new multitrack recording systems – all these inventions greatly improved the quality of cinema sound, and also led to a series of experiments with sound by both avant-garde and mainstream directors. Although television went through almost identical technological developments during the very same period, resulting in a similarly increased emphasis on sound communication in the medium as a whole as well as in individual programs and genres, there has been no corresponding focus on sound in television studies.

The role of music is sometimes discussed in studies of major television genres (see, e.g., on music in soap operas, Gripsrud, 1995: 183f.). The establishment of international promotional channels like MTV during the 1980s prompted some studies of the music-image relationship in music videos (e.g., Kaplan, 1988; Larsen, 1989). Regarding television sound in general, however, the only major work is a short article from the mid-1980s in which Rick Altman discussed the function of sound in relation to the domestic viewing situation (Altman, 1986). More recently, there have been additional studies, for example, by musicologist Nicholas Cook (1998) of the ways in which music, words, moving pictures, and dance work together in television commercials and music videos. On the whole, however, there have been remarkably few contributions so far to the study of sound and media.

Obviously, this is an area of media studies in which further research is greatly needed, not only because of the evident centrality of sound in the media, but because such research may contribute to a better understanding of sound as 'text,' in its own right and in conjunction with other media texts. Recent overviews have suggested elements of a research agenda (Bull and Back, 2003; Jensen, 2006), including the role of voice, music, and complex soundscapes in digital media in general, and mobile media in particular. Some studies have examined how spoken interaction serves to coordinate the gameplay in online gaming (Jørgensen, 2009; Williams, *et al.*, 2007). The field remains wide open for further research on the modality of sound, as it enters into different media, genres, and texts.

8 Media effects

Quantitative traditions

Klaus Bruhn Jensen

- a brief *history of research* on media effects
- a review of the main traditions of audience studies, which have focused on different *stages of the process of communication*
- a presentation of additional work on the steps and contexts in which media serve to *socialize* individuals, and to *institutionalize* society
- an example of studies of broader sociocultural *lifestyles*, as they relate to media and communication

INTRODUCTION

If any one issue can be said to have motivated media studies, it is the question of 'effects.' From the perspective of policy-makers and the general public, the field could be expected to provide evidence of what media do to individuals and, by implication, to society at large. From an academic perspective, the field has gained legitimacy and attracted funding by proposing to explain what specific difference the media make for modern culture, politics, and the economy. Effects have mostly been addressed in the sense of relatively short-term cognitive and behavioral impact of media and their contents on the members of mass audiences, as examined by quantitative methodologies. Especially in this area, it is still appropriate to speak of a dominant paradigm of research (Gitlin, 1978; Webster and Phalen, 1997), even if that mainstream has been critiqued and complemented by a qualitative substream (Chapter 9, this volume).

'effects' – short-term cognitive and behavioral impacts on individuals

the dominant paradigm

The present chapter reviews the main varieties of quantitative audience studies and the stages of the communicative process that they each focus on. Whereas current research commonly distances itself from a conveyor-belt model of communication, each tradition is defined, in part, by its orientation toward a particular moment in the interchange between media and their users. An overview of the various stages in sequence, further, helps to indicate the scope of each tradition, and to specify areas of contact or overlap between them. To anticipate an argument underlying this and the two following chapters, each tradition can be said to examine a social context of interaction between media and users.◄ For example, an 'early' stage or context is examined through measures of media exposure, such as the number of visitors to, and the number of minutes they spend on, a given news website; a 'late' context has been studied in terms of the so-called knowledge gaps that the use of websites and other news media may, in fact, serve to deepen rather than close (Tichenor, *et al.*, 1970). In each case, an interchange occurs that has implications for the user's orientation and action in social contexts.

► contexts of communication – Chapter 10

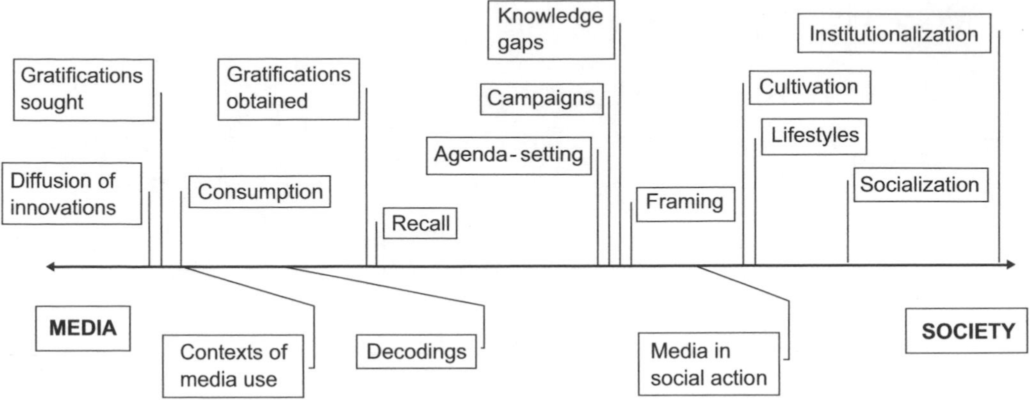

Figure 8.1 The stages of communication, as defined by audience research traditions (Note: The qualitative traditions, indicated below the line, are reviewed in Chapter 9.)

The act of surfing the web is a specific use of time and a choice of one communicative activity over another; having access to certain forms of public knowledge via one's media diet is a necessary condition of political and other social participation.

Figure 8.1 lays out the main stages, as defined by different research traditions. Before examining each tradition in turn, the chapter briefly reviews the history of effects research. This history bears witness to surprisingly shifting assessments of the nature and scope of media effects; it also suggests variable notions of what it means to be an audience, a user, or a member of the public. The following sections describe and illustrate each research tradition, with special reference to its theoretical assumptions and preferred methodologies. A more elaborate account is given of research on lifestyles, which relates media and communication studies to broader issues of cultural identity and social structure, and which has been one interface between quantitative and qualitative studies of media use.

HISTORIES OF EFFECTS RESEARCH

Because media effects have attracted so much public and scholarly interest, it is one of the largest and most differentiated areas of communication research; it is also an area with an identifiable history. As summarized by Denis McQuail (2010: 455–462), four phases of effects research can be singled out:

- *Phase 1: all-powerful media.* From around 1900, when an identifiable specialization in communication research was emerging (Simonson and Peters, 2008), to 1940, mass media – press, film, and radio – were widely thought to be able to shape both opinion and behavior through propaganda (e.g., Lasswell, 1938). However,

  > this view was based not on scientific investigation but on awe at the possibilities for mass persuasion that seemed to open up and on observation of the enormous popularity of these media that intruded into many aspects of everyday life as well as public affairs.
  >
  > (McQuail, 2010: 456)

- *Phase 2: theory of powerful media put to the test.* With a consolidation of academic media studies from the 1930s onwards, research came to suggest that, in most instances, at least no direct link could be established between media stimulus and audience response. Klapper (1960) presented an influential digest of findings supporting this conclusion.
- *Phase 3: powerful media rediscovered.* The 1960s witnessed a return to hypotheses

about the power of media, partly supported by a reassessment of earlier evidence (see Chaffee and Hochheimer, 1985; Delia, 1987). Such hypotheses were also prompted by other developments, both in research and in the media themselves: more studies of cognitive rather than of attitudinal or behavioral effects; a resurgence of critical social theory and political economy;◄ and, last but not least, the arrival of television.

- *Phase 4: negotiated media influence.* Since around 1980, a further differentiation in the understanding of media impact – and of relevant theoretical and methodological approaches – has been in evidence, both with the growth of qualitative reception studies, and with the coming of digital media. The very category of 'effects' may require additional and significant reconceptualization if the field is to account for the implications of networked forms of communication in the case of mobile, ubiquitous, and pervasive media.◄

As these phases suggest, effects and media studies as such have been intimately connected with other social and historical developments – two worlds wars, the rise of television as a centerpiece of popular culture, and the early stages of a digital media environment. The founding of the field in an era of *mass* media – with few centralized senders and many dispersed recipients – helps to explain why the overwhelming emphasis of research has been on individual users: they were the members of what a 1950 volume conceived as *The Lonely Crowd* (Riesman, 1950). A recent volume summarizing effects research made a special point of signaling in its title what may be the beginning of a reorientation from (media) effects to (communicative) processes: *The Sage Handbook of Media Processes and Effects* (Nabi and Oliver, 2009). In their introduction, the editors referred to "the full range of media *effects processes*, which are often complicated, fluid, and interactive" (p. 4 – emphasis added). It is precisely the question of what "effects processes" might mean – whether and how effects can and should be studied as processes rather than products or events – that has continued to challenge the field in both theoretical and empirical terms.

► critical political economy – Chapter 3, p. 65
► ubiquitous and pervasive media – Chapter 1, p. 9

MOMENTS OF IMPACT: FROM DIFFUSION TO CULTIVATION

Diffusion of innovations

In order to serve their communicative purposes, media must be both materially available and discursively accessible to a significant part of the population in question. On the one hand, the availability of a medium presupposes its invention, development, distribution, and relative affordability in a given historical and cultural context. On the other hand, its accessibility depends on whether users will perceive its likely applications as attractive, and whether they have (or are able to acquire) the relevant cognitive and cultural competences. While the diffusion-of-innovations framework, thus, lends itself to various media – from writing and literacy to social network sites – it should be noted that the research tradition has addressed innovations in a far broader sense: information with an instrumental value in agriculture, healthcare, family planning, etc. An important background to this particular research tradition was development communication◄ – post-1945 attempts at modernizing developing countries through innovative practices and institutions of communication.

material availability

discursive accessibility

The general theoretical model of diffusion – of ideas as well as technological innovations – was presented by Everett M. Rogers (1962); his seminal volume has appeared in five editions (Rogers, 2003), and has been widely influential in communication studies and beyond. The basic idea is that new information will be disseminated in a gradual and staggered fashion throughout a social system: users can be divided into innovators, early adopters, early majority, late majority, and laggards (the last term implying that information as well as innovation are, normally, good for people and

innovators, early adopters, early majority, late majority, laggards

► development communication – Chapter 11, p. 212

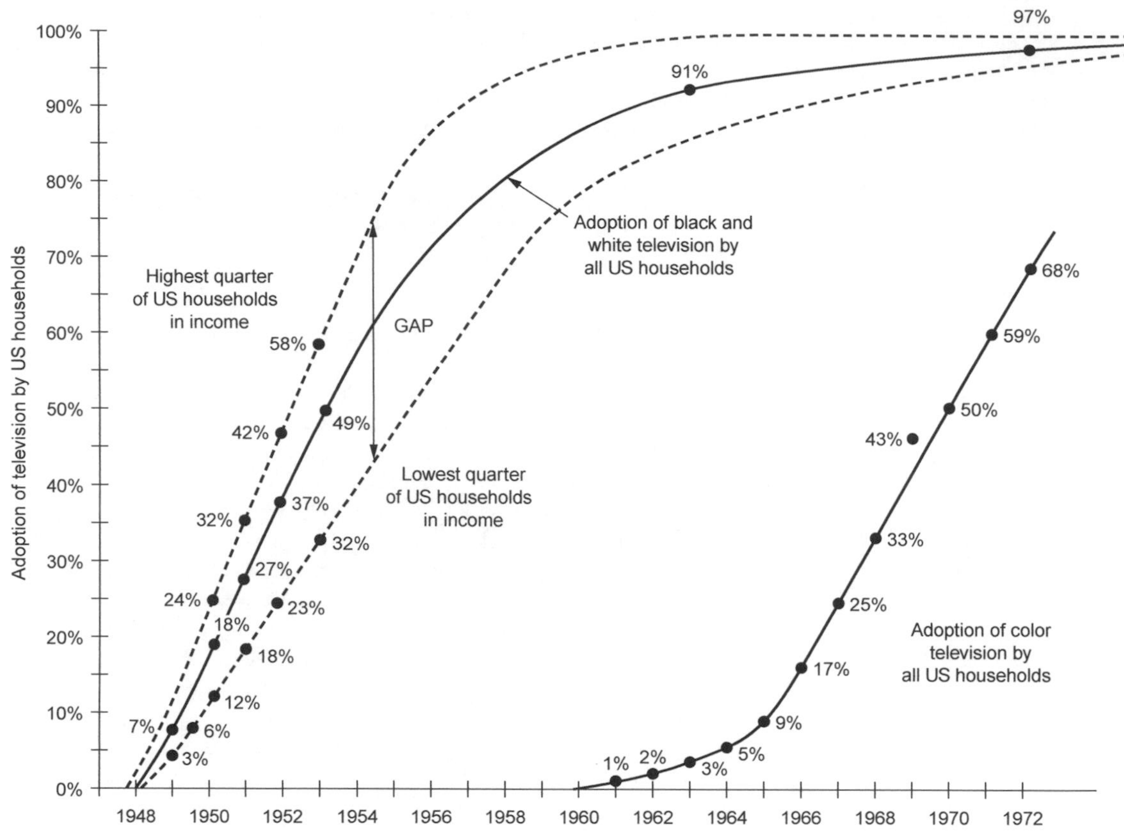

Figure 8.2 Adoption of black-and-white and color television in the US, in percent over time (source: Rogers, 1986: 171, reprinted with permission of The Free Press, a division of Simon & Schuster, Inc., © 1986 The Free Press)

should not be opposed). The adoption process constitutes five stages: knowledge, persuasion, decision, implementation, and confirmation. The 'ideal' S-curve moves from a slow and unequal start, via an accelerated diffusion, to a plateau where the medium is available to practically everybody. Evidently, diffusion will vary, not least, by people's economic means, also in rich societies, as illustrated by Figure 8.2 displaying the adoption of black-and-white and, later, color television in the US.

knowledge, persuasion, decision, implementation, confirmation

Whereas various communication technologies were found to be important in the first stage of diffusion (knowledge), personal contacts and individual experience, importantly, would prevail in later stages.◄ In addition, studies of the diffusion of news suggested that the higher the proportion of a population that knows about an event or issue, the higher the proportion that learnt about these from an interpersonal source (Greenberg, 1964). This presents a useful reminder regarding the role of one-to-one communications in the current media environment. The internet and mobile media simultaneously accelerate and differentiate the diffusion of information by multiple media and communicative practices.◄ (The mobile phone itself has had the fastest rate of adoption historically

► embodied communication – Chapter 1, p. 5

► multistep flows of communication – Chapter 10, p. 187

of any communication technology on a global scale (ITU, 2010).)

The most common approach to studying the diffusion of innovations has been survey methodologies, as accumulated in national and international statistics as well as market research. Such evidence, further, lends itself to secondary analyses◀ that extract additional patterns of diffusion and use from existing data sets. These approaches produce indispensable baseline information by comparing and contrasting the availability and accessibility of media and communication services among different social and cultural groups. In comparison, diffusion research has given less attention to the interpretive processes by which individuals and groups adopt and 'domesticate'◀ an unfamiliar technology – what other research has referred to as symbolic diffusion (Jensen, 1993a).

symbolic diffusion

Gratifications sought

It is the user's approach to media that has been the focus of attention in the second tradition – uses and gratifications research (U&G). The tradition is frequently summarized in Elihu Katz's call for research that asks not only what media do to people, but also what people do with media (Katz, 1959). Following pioneering studies in the 1940s (Berelson, 1949; Herzog, 1944), the tradition was revitalized from the 1960s, partly in response to the contemporary conclusion that media had 'no effects.' The ambition of U&G was to relate the uses and consequences of media to audiences' psychological needs and social conditions, including, importantly, the alternatives to media use. The research program referred to a whole series of steps in a communicative process:

uses and gratifications research

what people do with media

> (1) the social and psychological origins of (2) needs which generate (3) expectations of (4) the mass media or other sources which lead to (5) differential exposure (or engaging in other activities), resulting in (6) need gratification and (7) other consequences.
>
> (Katz, *et al.*, 1974: 20)

U&G became widely influential during the 1970 and 1980s (Blumler and Katz, 1974; Rosengren, *et al.*, 1985). For one thing, studies began to outline various typologies of the media-audience nexus. The relationship between general human needs and specific media offerings was conceptualized as functions, a classic concept in sociology from Émile Durkheim to Talcott Parsons.◀ Studies indicated three main functions of media: information-seeking, diversion, and the maintenance of personal identity (Blumler, 1979; McQuail, *et al.*, 1972). For another thing, U&G addressed the complex question of whether the public perceives particular media and genres as sources of distinctive gratifications (Katz, *et al.*, 1973).

functions of media use

U&G soon came in for theoretical criticism on at least two fronts. On the one hand, critical theorists argued that the entire approach was compromised by its functionalism, specifically the premise that the functions of media might serve a common interest – in a society with fundamental conflicts of interest (Elliott, 1974). When references were made in the U&G literature to dysfunctions (Lazarsfeld and Merton, 1960[1948]; Wright, 1959), these were conceived as deviations from a norm, rather than as indicators of structural antagonisms. On the other hand, work in cultural studies found that communication understood as active participation in cultural processes could not be captured by this framework (Carey and Kreiling, 1974). In addition, empirical studies questioned the explanatory value of the key notion of gratifications. Lichtenstein and Rosenfeld (1983), for example, found that both heavy and light viewers of television, and fans as well as non-fans, tended to agree about their gratifications; they concluded that respondents may reproduce generally accepted views of media and content types, at least when questioned according to U&G methodologies.

dysfunctions

A central point of contention, in fact, has been methodology. Despite occasional

▶ secondary analysis of statistical data – Chapter 13, p. 247

▶ domestication – Chapter 9, p. 184

▶ classic sociology – Chapter 3, p. 51

qualitative or experimental studies, studies have relied primarily on surveys to examine diverse levels and aspects of the audience experience of media. As such, U&G has contributed systematic accounts of the public's perception and expectations of various media and genres. In comparison, the tradition has been less suited to documenting audience interpretations and contextual uses of media; a criticism advanced by qualitative reception studies from the 1980s (Chapter 9). The U&G approach to these aspects is taken up in the section below on gratifications obtained,◄ as distinct from the gratifications sought and expected in advance of media use.

Later work has related the category of gratifications to other aspects of media use, for example, the nature of audience activity before, during, and after media exposure (e.g., Levy and Windahl, 1985) and the relationship between personality and media gratifications (e.g., Conway and Rubin, 1991). U&G research, from the outset, also has sought to integrate its concepts and approaches with other traditions, including 'uses-and-effects' research (Rosengren and Windahl, 1972) (anticipating deliberations concerning 'effects processes,' as noted in the introduction to this chapter).

With digital media, the category of gratifications is, again, open to discussion: the *functions* of digital media may be different in kind, given their interactive *functionalities*. When studies find that the "uses and gratifications of befriending candidates" for political office on the social network site, MySpace, emphasize "social interaction with other like-minded supporters," rather than information-seeking or entertainment (Ancu and Cozma, 2009: 567), that is entirely unsurprising; but it raises the question of how this compares to those more familiar social-interaction gratifications that derive from family television viewing (Lull, 1980), or from para-social interaction◄ (Horton and Wohl, 1956). It is debatable whether a general category of 'social interaction' can still provide valid analytical measures across such different forms of communication.

► gratifications obtained, p. 159

► para-social interaction – Chapter 9, p. 176

Consumption

A staple of media studies has always been measurements of who attends to which media, for how long, and in which combinations and sequences; it is, without question, the kind of audience research to which most resources are devoted overall, even if the majority of studies likely remain proprietary and unpublished because of their commercial value (for an overview, see Napoli, 2003). In systematic terms, such studies document the moment of exposure: the concrete interaction between *a* medium and *a* user, without which there would be no interpretation or effect – no communication. The time and/or money spent, by different socio-demographic groups, on different media and genres, represent necessary baseline information, even while both the categories of measurement and the social uses of findings may be subject to debate. The critical political economist, Dallas W. Smythe (1977), for one, argued that the primary product of media is not content, but audiences. Media deliver audience attention to advertisers – audiences *pay attention* – above and beyond the money that they pay for certain media products and cultural experiences.

media exposure

audience as product

The definition of what constitutes attention is, at once, a highly philosophical and a very concrete issue. Media users will *interrupt* their attention, either because of other events in the immediate use context, or because media products or services fail to hold their attention through a commercial break in a television series or across all top stories of an online news site. Media users will also *divide* their attention, so that viewing, listening, or reading become secondary activities (even if it can be difficult to establish which activity is primary, secondary, tertiary, etc. – eating breakfast, having a conversation, reading a newspaper (on paper or screen), listening to a newscast (broadcast or streamed)). Whereas classic studies found that television viewing is often a secondary activity (Robinson and Converse, 1972) (see also Comstock, *et al.*, 1971; Szalai, 1972), the internet and other digital media that are 'always on' (Baron, 2008) present new challenges when it comes to measuring (and understanding) the

secondary media use

relationship between communication and other social interaction.

To address such methodological difficulties, audience studies have gone through several generations of measurement techniques, in addition to combining quantitative and qualitative approaches (for an overview, see Gunter and Machin, 2009). The general shift has been from in-person techniques, such as face-to-face interviewing and diaries, toward semi-automatic measurements, particularly for broadcasting and the internet. From the mid-1980s, peoplemeters◀ had replaced the original television meters measuring whether a set is turned on, and to which channel it is tuned; peoplemeters rely on respondents to push a button to identify themselves as 'viewers' and, in some systems, to indicate their level of appreciation of programs. On a much smaller scale, studies have videotaped viewers in front of television sets to assess their attention and activity (Bechtel, *et al.*, 1972; Borzekowski and Robinson, 1999; Schmitt, *et al.*, 2003). Overlapping with the field of human-computer interaction (Sears and Jacko, 2008), research has also employed eye-tracking to determine exactly what the users of screen media look at, and how they interact with different elements of content and form. With digital media, which are, in part, self-documenting, large auto-generated data sets lend themselves to detailed analyses of use patterns and user profiles through data mining◀ (Han and Kamber, 2006). Whereas data mining far from replaces data collection, data that are 'found' lend themselves to combination with data that are 'made'◀ (Jensen, in press-a).

viewing the viewers

eye-tracking

Gratifications obtained

Uses-and-gratifications research (U&G) has had little to say, as noted, about the contextual and interpretive aspects of communication. Its preferred survey methodologies are especially suited to capturing conscious and familiar aspects of media use. The contingent and incidental nature of much media use can be more difficult to recall or recognize. Nevertheless, to capture the concrete gratifications of media – pleasurable experiences and relevant information – U&G came to distinguish between expectations of what will be provided (gratifications sought – GS) and the resulting satisfactions (gratifications obtained – GO). GS is, in part, the outcome of a user's past experiences with particular media and communicative practices; GO constitutes feedback to the user on which gratifications to seek in the future, from which media. This processual perspective has been summed up in a formal expectancy value model, which may explain and predict media uses and gratifications (Palmgreen and Rayburn, 1985).

expectancy value

The problem is that the methodologies employed may not provide an adequate description of the processes in question. One study (Palmgreen, *et al.*, 1980), for example, collected responses to two sets of statements, presented in telephone interviews immediately after each other. GS was operationalized as, "I watch television news to keep up with current issues and events." GO, next, was reformulated with reference to the program that the respondent in question would ordinarily watch: "CBS News helps me to keep up with current issues and events" (p. 171). However, whatever correlations obtain between the two sets of statements, the empirical design does not warrant conclusions about the viewer's experience or gratification in any specific sense. Both the GO and the GS statements were presented in one interview session, in equally abstract formulations, and without any concrete point of reference to an actual (set of) broadcast(s) or a context of viewing. Instead, the findings provide insight into the public profile of one news program or organization, compared to others.

An alternative approach is the so-called experience sampling method (ESM), which grew out of Mihaly Csikszentmihalyi's (1975) work on mental states of immersive flow, and which has been applied to television (Kubey and Csikszentmihalyi, 1990). The basic idea is that respondents will be prompted by a portable device at random times; each time, they complete a self-report on what they are doing, and how they feel, through scales as well as open-ended questions. The data can be used to explore

experience sampling method

▶ television- and peoplemeters – Chapter 13, p. 256
▶ data mining – Chapter 13, p. 262
▶ data – found and made – Chapter 15, p. 288

the relationship between media use, other simultaneous activities, and the respondent's state of mind. The approach offers one means of securing immediate feedback from media users in comparatively naturalistic circumstances. With the ubiquity of mobile media, and the availability of open-source software, (www.experience-sampling.org, accessed April 15, 2011), ESM presents itself as a useful complement to more widely applied methodologies (Hektner, *at al.*, 2007).

Memory

One favorite measure of audience research has been memory or recall – media users' ability to reproduce items of information, normally within a relatively short time span after exposure (for overview, see Shapiro, 2008). Regarding both fact and fiction, memory can be taken as an indication of what audiences find important for present or future purposes. It is also a preparatory condition of some later uses and consequences of media, from factual learning, to informed political participation, to aesthetic appreciation. Although the perceived relevance of an item of information, evidently, plays a key role, in addition to repetition and other contextual factors, studies of different *types of users* have concluded that recall is positively correlated with audiences' prior knowledge and, hence, their educational and other social status. The more you already know, the more you will remember, as elaborated in the knowledge-gap hypothesis.◀ Regarding different *types of media*, research has rejected the common saying that 'a picture is worth a thousand words.' Whereas modalities – text, image, sound◀ – have different communicative potentials, audiovisual media, for instance, are not inherently superior to, or more efficient than, print. Instead, narrative, text-image integration, and message structure in general guide comprehension and recall across media types. Memory is not so much the effect of a message, but rather the product of several interrelated communicative and cognitive processes.

▶ knowledge-gap hypothesis, p. 164

▶ modalities of communication – Chapter 6, p. 126; Chapter 7, p. 149

While the question of memory applies to practically any communicative practice, two bodies of research suggest some wider implications for the understanding of media effects. First, research has examined media as resources of learning for the general public. As such, media enter into both formal and informal education, being classroom, workplace, as well as leisure technologies. The development of computer-supported collaborative learning (CSCL) offers additional uses, across the formal-informal education divide (Stahl, *et al.*, 2006). In several European public-service broadcasting organizations, studies of how to promote the comprehension, recall, and active uses of news and other information were conceived, in a sense, as product development in the public interest (Findahl, 1985; Gunter, 1987b). A characteristic feature of such studies has been the close analysis of content in conjunction with audience responses, thus anticipating reception analysis as audience-cum-content studies.◀

A second body of research has been motivated by commercial aims of establishing the extent to which consumers remember and otherwise respond to advertising, public relations, and marketing generally (Dekimpe and Hanssens, 2007). Given the concrete goal of advertising, it lends itself to an exploration of whether or not different stages of communication are, indeed, related. A classic elaboration of the basic stimulus-response model (McGuire, 1973) identified six stages of persuasion: presentation, attention, comprehension, yielding, retention, and overt behavior. In fact, this seemingly logical order is not commonly borne out by empirical research, as recognized by applied communication studies (Windahl, *et al.*, 2009). A consumer may have no explicit recall of a product, and yet may buy it on sight.

stages of persuasion

Studies of memory and recall have relied especially on experiments and surveys (Gunter, 2000: 215–225). Like several other effects research traditions, however, such studies have faced the methodological difficulty that so much media-related behavior is preconscious or

▶ audience-cum-content studies – Chapter 8, p. 178

practical consciousness

practical (Giddens, 1984), in addition to being context-dependent. This may help to explain why, over the last several decades, research has repeatedly hypothesized and examined additional or intervening stages to account for (the absence of) effects. Another strategy has been to reinterpret findings with reference to alternative theoretical frameworks: even if specific items of information about events in the world are not recalled as such, they may contribute to a general sense of ontological security (Giddens, 1991). With reference to several early studies finding that people watch, and hence seem to want, television news, yet recall little or nothing, Kaarle Nordenstreng (1972) concluded that "the main thing retained from the news is that nothing special has happened" (p. 390).

ontological security

Agenda setting

One of the most noted contributions to the understanding of media effects as a multistep and multilevel process has been agenda-setting research. Its insight is summed up in the formulation that, while media may not tell people *what* to think, they can tell people what to think *about*. Agenda-setting research, thus, joined gratifications research in differentiating the question of what media do to people, into what people do with media, and what, as a result, they may think about. (The history of this wording suggests a more general point, namely that research traditions and national literatures can be rather self-contained. In US publications, the formulation is almost always credited to Cohen (1963), but before him, two British researchers, Trenaman and McQuail (1961: 178) concluded, "The evidence strongly suggests that people think *about* what they are told but at no level do they think *what* they are told.")

media tell people what to think *about*

The background to agenda-setting studies is political communication. Accordingly, the unit of analysis has been 'issues,' as compared to 'information' in a broader sense within, for instance, memory studies. Because media are key arenas of public debate, it is of considerable interest to compare their agenda – the events and topics that media give priority in terms of the frequency and quantity of coverage – to other agendas, specifically those of voters and of political organizations and candidates. Which political interests and concerns gain a voice in different media, and what segments of the public come to accept which agendas? Whereas early classics in communication studies, such as *The People's Choice*◄ (Lazarsfeld, *et al.*, 1944), had noted that media, among other things, serve to structure political issues for public debate, the research tradition as such has developed during the last forty years.

The agenda-setting effect was given its name in foundational work by Maxwell E. McCombs and Donald L. Shaw (1972). Their study of a small North Carolina community during the 1968 US presidential campaign found that, although different news media would represent political topics differently, there was a significant correlation between issues that were defined as important by voters and by the media overall: "voters tend to share the media's *composite* definition of what is important" (p. 184). In methodological terms, the study was a prototypical example of hypothetico-deductive research.◄

Subsequent research has extended the approach, both methodologically and theoretically. It is common to distinguish three kinds of agendas – those of the media, the public, and political institutions (Dearing and Rogers, 1996), which raises additional questions of how issues and priorities flow from the public to the media and/or politicians, and vice versa, in a more or less ideal political process. One suggestion has been that more empirical attention should be given to a gradual agenda building in the institutional interplay between media and political interest groups (Lang and Lang, 1981). Moreover, because both the media and the audience sides of the equation have mostly been examined in a delimited setting and as aggregate measures, through surveys and content analysis, there has been comparatively less attention to changes over time. One long-term study, 1946–2004, examined the three-way interaction involving the media, the public,

media, public, and policy agendas

agenda building

► *The People's Choice* – Chapter 9, p. 173

► hypothetico-deductive methodology – Chapter 15, p. 291

and the US Congress (Tan and Weaver, 2007). Another ambitious program of parallel content analysis has been outlined, which would examine the 'content' of both media and public opinion over longer time periods (Neuman, 1989).

parallel content analysis

Studies have continued to indicate an agenda-setting function of media; at the same time, findings suggest that there may be little difference in this regard between media types, such as print or electronic, and public service or commercial, perhaps because of a general similarity and/or a current convergence of news content (Strömbäck and Kiousis, 2010). The tradition shares family resemblances with several other approaches, including experimental studies of how the media may perform a priming of the audiences as to which issues are decisive in assessing political candidates (Iyengar and Kinder, 1987). Research has also gone on to identify a second-level agenda-setting (Kim and Scheufele, 2002; McCombs, *et al.*, 2000), which concerns the perception of detailed attributes of political issues or candidates, and which compares to studies of framing.◀ Finally, even though agenda-setting research has focused on news and political communication, it lends itself to the study of other genres (Dearing and Rogers, 1996: 98), including fiction and entertainment. Users may approach comedy shows as *The Daily Show with Jon Stewart* as equal to other sources of political information (Feldman, 2007). In this regard, the agenda-setting tradition has affinities with Newcomb and Hirsch's (1983) proposal that media be studied not as a distribution system, but as a cultural forum◀ to which matters of public interest can be brought, articulated, and debated.

priming

Campaigns

A significant proportion of contemporary communications is made up campaigns – the use of media as means of social coordination through strategic or planned communication (for an overview, see Holtzhausen, 2008). While campaigns may be associated especially with business and politics, they are also key to the dissemination of public information (Rice and Atkin, 2001), for instance, in an area such as health. State agencies, corporations, and civil-society organizations all seek to inform, persuade, and engage their various stakeholders – as citizens, customers, members, volunteers, collaborators, etc. Following early work on media as means of propaganda◀ during wartime (e.g., Hovland, *et al.*, 1953), studies have diversified to address political, economic, as well as cultural campaign activities. In digital media, campaigns more easily rely on several steps of communication, including so-called viral campaigns. Networked communication extends or delegates communicative agency beyond campaigners as traditionally understood.

strategic communication

viral campaigns

In a classic overview, Rogers and Storey (1987: 821) noted four common features of campaigns – "(1) a campaign intends to generate specific outcomes or effects (2) in a relatively large number of individuals, (3) usually within a specified period of time and (4) through an organized set of communication activities." On this basis, the authors identify variations along three main dimensions of a campaign, as laid out in Figure 8.3.

First, campaigns can have more or less ambitious *objectives*, from informing or persuading, to mobilizing a group of people to act in particular ways. It should be noted that the aim of a campaign may also be to prevent change, in addition to promoting a change of behavior. In both public and private settings, campaign planners need to consider different strategies for introducing, maintaining, and repositioning a product, a brand, or an idea.

promoting or preventing change

Second, the intended effect – the locus of *change* – may lie at the individual, group, organizational, or social level. Although the information will be received and interpreted by individuals, a campaign typically seeks to sway entire segments of a population, such as smokers or car owners, as addressed by tobacco and car manufacturers, health authorities and environmental groups. Also before digital media,

▶ framing, p. 164

▶ media as cultural forum – Chapter 1, p. 13

▶ propaganda studies – Chapter 9, p. 174

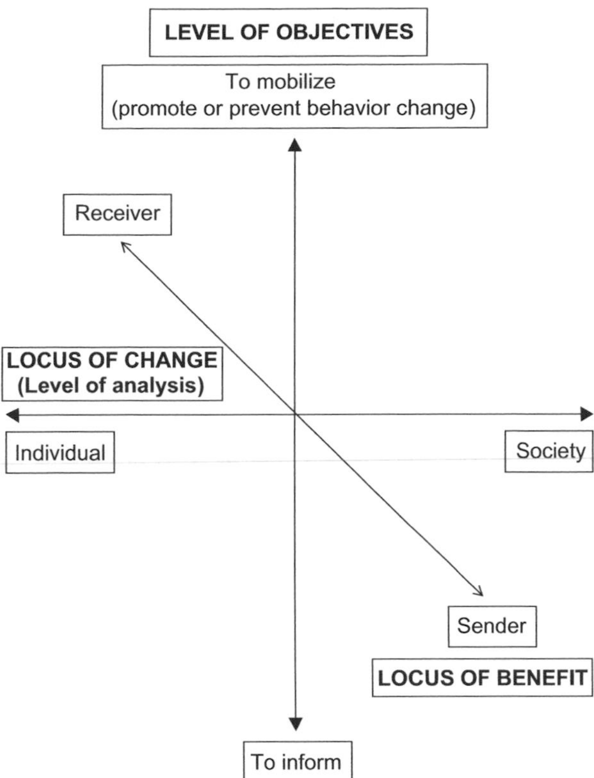

Figure 8.3 Dimensions of campaign objectives and effects (source: Rogers, 1987: 823)

campaigns, like other communications, moved in several steps,◀ including key components of interpersonal communication. It is along this dimension of change that the effects of a campaign are studied empirically.

Third, campaigns differ with regard to their (primary) *beneficiary*. It is important here to note the relative and relational nature of benefits. While commercial advertising occurs on behalf of the company in question, the communication, arguably, also holds informational and economic value for the consumer. And, whereas health campaigns are designed to prevent disease among the general public, or industrial accidents among employees, they likely may save money for corporations, health care systems, and taxpayers.

Given the great diversity of strategic communications and campaigns, they have been studied through a variety of methodologies – surveys, experiments, focus groups, observation, etc. – each of which may tap a moment of impact. A special consideration is what might happen in the *absence* of campaigns and other continuous communication efforts. A saying, attributed to the American industrialist, John Wanamaker, was that "Half the money I spend on advertising is wasted; the trouble is I don't know which half" (Wanamaker, n.d.). Later advertising professionals and researchers have also recognized that it is "almost always impossible to estimate the impact of advertising on sales volume" (cited in Schudson, 1984: 17). Whereas it may, thus, be difficult to document certain specific effects of campaigns, it is testimony to the constitutive role of communication that social actors across sectors and levels find it necessary to maintain a presence in the field of attention that is the media.

Campaign studies share their focus on multiple media and moments of communication with studies of intertextuality◀ – the textual webs that make up the discourses of communication – despite the fundamental theoretical and methodological differences between the two approaches. The marketing strategies of current media can be understood as an instance of strategic intertextuality, for example, the recycling of fictional characters and themes across media, artifacts, and theme parks. In the case of digital media, intertextually inflected communications may promote software as well as hardware. As a brand and a provider of interconnected services, Google has, in certain respects, replaced Microsoft as a central point of access to digital communication for the ordinary user; Apple, in its turn, represents a intertextual configuration of both devices and services, supported by a market-leading design, and extended by imitation among its competitors.

▶ three-step flow of communication – Chapter 10, p. 187

▶ intertextuality – Chapter 10, p. 192

Knowledge gaps

The great differences that, undeniably, exist between those with easy access to information – which is refined in communication and applied as knowledge – and those with little or no access to either, might intuitively suggest that the solution is more communication, whether in a social-structural or an intercultural perspective. This is also a common argument in much public debate and the position of many educators and media practitioners. And, diffusion research◄ has found that new information spreads, sometimes at an accelerated pace, even if it may not reach every last individual. In contrast, research on knowledge gaps has suggested that such inequalities are cumulated over time and reinforced by other forms of social inequality. In short, the knowledge-gap hypothesis asserts that the flow of information in society via media tends to widen, rather than close, existing gaps between the information-rich and the information-poor (Tichenor, *et al.*, 1970).

knowledge-gap hypothesis

Like some other research traditions examining complex or long-term effects, knowledge-gap studies have tended to produce suggestive rather than conclusive evidence. This follows, in part, from the preexisting inequalities in the distribution of informational and other resources among different social segments, of which the media can only be one source – or remedy. Still, by examining knowledge of specific public events and issues that received extensive media coverage during a particular period through survey methodologies, studies concluded that better-educated people were better able to the assimilate the information widely on offer (Donohue, *et al.*, 1987; Tichenor, *et al.*, 1970; for additional experimental findings, see Grabe, *et al.*, 2000).

Elaborating on the implications, the original group of researchers noted that the media may, indeed, serve to close gaps in connection with social conflict, when public information becomes more directly applicable and learnable (Donohue, *et al.*, 1975). Other studies have countered the general hypothesis, finding that the level of interest may be more important than the level of prior knowledge when it comes to gaining information (Genova and Greenberg, 1979). It has also been suggested that different media may work in specific ways, so that television, which reaches a higher proportion of the population than print media, and whose formats do not privilege the well-educated, might help to close knowledge gaps (Neuman, 1976).

interest and/ or knowledge gaps

More recent overviews of the literature conclude that, at the very least, media appear not to be closing or narrowing gaps *between* socioeconomic groups (Gaziano, 1997; Viswanath and Finnegan, 1996), which in itself may be disconcerting in view of the role of media as resources in so many diverse areas of economic, political, and cultural activity. This is in spite of the fact that studies have found it difficult measure developments *over time* within groups and for individuals (Hwang and Jeong, 2009); in line with the original findings by Donohue, *et al.* (1975), Hwang and Jeong (2009) also noted that knowledge gaps appear to be greater for general social and political matters than, for instance, for health issues, and greater for international than for local and personally relevant topics. Additional work has found links between knowledge gaps and other aspects of media users' cognitive dispositions, such as a disaffection with politics (Fredin, *et al.*, 1994). In summary, the evidence indicates that knowledge gaps remain a structural feature of contemporary society, and that media may contribute to reproducing or reinforcing such gaps. The implications of informational and communicative gaps have also attracted renewed attention in research and policy with reference to digital divides◄ – within societies and between different regions of the world.

Framing

The concept of a frame suggests that an item of information – whether arising from one's perception of the environment, from other people, or from media technologies – only makes sense once it is placed in a context of additional information. We select some information from potentially endless masses of information; we

► diffusion of innovations – p. 155

► digital divides – Chapter 19, p. 354

bracket that information in a particular way, which constitutes a frame. Frames are, at once, mental and social categories – the outcome of both interpretation and interaction, a product as well as a process of framing. Compared to studies of memory and knowledge gaps, research on frames shifts the focus from information as entities, and toward the worldviews that orient audiences' actions – in the context of media use and beyond. Compared to agenda setting, which produces a temporary set of priorities, a frame represents a more permanent orientation or disposition. As such, frames are of special interest for the understanding of how media and society are coupled in communication.

frames – mental and social

Research on framing has taken inspiration from quite diverse sources, and represents a meeting place of theoretical positions that have otherwise been treated as alternatives or antagonists. A review of the area (Scheufele, 1999) noted the contributions both of experimental social psychology, particularly Fritz Heider's (1958) attribution theory, and of qualitative microsociology in the form of Erving Goffman's (1974) *Frame Analysis*. In addition, cognitive science has contributed to the area, including the insight that the frames or *Metaphors We Live By* (Lakoff and Johnson, 1980) are so-called basic-level categories◄ (Lakoff and Johnson, 1999), whose yardstick is the human body in everyday space and time.

Also in a methodological respect, work on frames and framing has bridged different positions, combining qualitative and quantitative approaches. In an exemplary study employing in-depth interviewing, surveys, content analysis, as well as experiments, Neuman, *et al.* (1992) showed how news audiences would rely on categories that were derived largely from personal experience in order to make sense of the frequently unfamiliar events and issues of news media – interpretive frames that differed significantly from those relied on by journalists. This is consistent, further, with the lessons of qualitative reception studies, which have found that audiences employ generalized and commonsense super-themes in order to establish meaningful links between the world of news and that of everyday life (Jensen, 1988b, 1998).

super-themes

Framing holds an additional potential for more comparative studies of the relationship between media production and reception. On the one hand, journalists and other professional communicators such as film directors and talk-show hosts are constantly engaged in framing content, and in anticipating how their message may be interpreted by audiences (Ettema and Whitney, 1994; Gans, 1957). On the other hand, media users depend on interpretive frames that are shaped and reshaped over time, partly with reference to media (Gamson, 1992; Graber, 1984). Users, in their turn, have different levels of awareness that both media professionals and their sources have a stake in what is being communicated, and how it is framed. In this last regard, framing studies have theoretical affinities with Stuart Hall's (1973) seminal work on processes of encoding and decoding, including oppositional frames of interpretation.◄

production and reception as framing

In his review, Scheufele (1999) made the additional point that agenda-setting and framing represent different, but interrelated aspects of media effects.

> While the process of issue selection or agenda-setting by mass media [...] needs to be a conscious one, framing is based on subtle nuances in wording and syntax and therefore [...] most likely [has] unintentional effects, or at least effects that are hard to predict and control by journalists.
>
> (Scheufele, 1999: 19)

Regarding the steps and stages of communication, framing has introduced an important differentiation in the understanding of effects: while agenda setting influences *what* issues to think about, "framing influences *how* audiences think about issues" (p. 19). In later work on secondary or attribute agenda-setting, the same author made a similar point, namely, that if basic agenda-setting concerns "what," secondary agenda-setting has to do with "how" people think about issues (Kim and Scheufele,

how to think about issues

► basic-level categories – Chapter 2, p. 46

► oppositional decoding – Chapter 9, p. 178

2002) – even while still treating framing and agenda-setting as the two separate research questions. Despite the need to precisely operationalize one's object of analysis, the phenomena of framing and agenda setting appear so evidently interdependent as to call for more joint theory development, in addition to complementary methodologies. It has also been argued that research has tended to neglect power as an aspect of framing (Carragee and Roefs, 2004): much more than perceptual or descriptive categories, frames are cognitive and, arguably, hegemonic constructs◀ that may serve particular social interests.

Cultivation theory

The further studies move away from the concrete interface between medium and user, the more circumstantial the evidence may seem, and the more debatable the conclusions. One of the most debated types of media effects studies has been cultivation studies, which have examined the extent to which media – with television as the centerpiece – shape their users' worldviews (for an overview, see Morgan, 2008). Part of a wider cultural indicators research program, begun in the late 1960s by George Gerbner, the aim of cultivation studies has been, from a critical position, to document, in quantitative detail, the extent to which the media serve to maintain and reinforce the social status quo. To provide indicators, the research program has also included analyses of program content and of television as an institution – a cultural industry subject to powerful internal as well as external interests.

cultural indicators

cultivation hypothesis

The cultivation hypothesis suggested that television had acquired such a central place in post-1945 American culture that it constituted a symbolic environment in and of itself. As such, it could be seen to shape viewers' conceptions of reality, competing with and, to a degree, substituting other sources, including personal experience, everyday conversation, and other media. To test the hypothesis, cultivation methodology combines surveys and content analysis, comparing the representation of social reality in television content (not least violence, crime, and other risks) with viewers' awareness of and attitudes towards such concerns. (Some studies have also employed experimental methodologies, e.g., Shrum, 1996.) The conclusion of the original group of researchers was that such cultivation of knowledge and attitudes does, indeed, occur (Gerbner and Gross, 1976). 'Heavy' viewers are more likely to give 'the television answer' to survey questions, for example, about risks to them personally, but also about issues such as ethnicity, gender, or poverty.

Criticism has been directed especially at the cultivation hypothesis, more so than the wider research program, and has taken three main forms. First, cultivation researchers have been attacked on their own turf through a reanalysis of the original data sets. In brief, critics have argued that, if sufficiently stringent statistical controls are introduced, the cultivation effect disappears (Hirsch, 1980, 1981). Second, researchers with a background in humanities and cultural studies have questioned the theoretical rationale behind the entire effort (Newcomb, 1978), suggesting that the approach neglects cultivation in the sense of variable interpretations of complex narratives. Third, a number of studies in countries other than the US have not found support for the cultivation hypothesis.◀

Cultivation research has continued to attract interest, and has examined diverse aspects of cultivation, including media other than television (Shanahan and Morgan, 1999). In a positive summary, "television makes a small but significant contribution to viewers' beliefs about the world" (Morgan, 2008: 1094). Less generously, the evidence presents itself as mixed at best, particularly if one considers the original scope and critical ambition of the research program. A central question is the status of 'television' as the key reference point of the cultivation tradition. While it is true that much of the available media content remains the same, despite new technologies of distribution and access, it is not clear that cultivation theory and methodology will be suited to capture

▶ hegemony – Chapter 2, p. 47

▶ cultivation studies outside the US – Chapter 13, p. 257

interactive, multimodal, and mobile media and communicative practices after 'the age of television.' A study of online computer gaming, in addition to extending earlier methodological criticisms, found that cultivation may be a very specific outcome of playing games with certain characteristics, rather than a general effect of the kind hypothesized by Gerbner and his colleagues (Williams, 2006).

SOCIALIZATION BY MEDIA

The interdisciplinary communication theorist, Paul Watzlawick, made the point that humans "cannot *not* communicate"◀ (Watzlawick, *et al.*, 1967: 49): as embodied beings, we cannot *not* see, hear, and interpret each other in local space and time. Given the present pervasiveness of media technologies across space and time, most people cannot *not* be affected to some considerable degree, literally from cradle to grave. Consequently, technologically mediated as well as face-to-face communication cannot *not* play a significant role in the process of socializing individuals as members of particular societies and cultures – even if research has found it difficult to ascertain the specific nature and degree of such long-term effects. Faced with these difficulties, media and communication studies have pursued several strategies. Before describing two central approaches that are in line with the theoretical and methodological conception of 'effects' as presented in the present chapter, some other main strategies should be noted. First, qualitative empirical reception studies, as examined next in Chapter 9, have provided complements to quantitative studies since the beginnings of the field. Second, research has turned to historical approaches in order to contextualize media in relation to other cultural, political, and economic developments; from the 1990s, media history has attracted a markedly increased research interest.◀ Third, partly overlapping with the historical reorientation of research, partly with studies of 'new' digital media, research has sometimes turned to 'grand' theories of communication and society, including medium theory◀ and theories of modernization.◀

Within studies of 'effects,' one recurring issue has been the impact of media on children and youth. First of all, a distinction must be made between primary and secondary socialization – children learning basic knowledge and norms, typically from their parents, as compared with children and youths, as well as adults, maintaining and adjusting their knowledge and norms throughout life, through reference to information and communication technologies – and to schooling, professional training, leisure activities, etc. Historically, such institutions have been gaining importance as socializers, in quantitative terms of the time spent on formal education and technologically mediated leisure, and in qualitative terms of where individuals' conceptions of the society that they belong to come from (Beck, *et al.*, 1994). Also the line between primary and secondary socialization has increasingly been blurred, as examined by a long line of research on media in young people's lives – from the Payne Fund studies on film during the 1930s,◀ via early classics on television such as Himmelweit, *et al.* (1958) and Schramm, *et al.* (1961), and later studies by Rosengren and Windahl (1989) and Livingstone and Bovill (2001), to research about kids online (Livingstone and Haddon, 2009).

primary and secondary socialization

A second approach to the relationship between media and socialization comes from research on lifestyles and, more broadly, the life forms and everyday practices of different socioeconomic groups. Studies in this area have been a rare meeting ground, theoretically and methodologically, between critical social theorists in university settings and marketing professionals. The two sectors have been brought together by an ambition of understanding the complex interrelations between cultural practices and social structures. Academic research has been influenced by a renewed interest, in recent decades, in the role of human agency and reflexivity in the ongoing structuration of society, specifically through

lifestyle and life forms

▶ humans cannot not communicate – Chapter 1, p. 13
▶ history of media and communication – Chapter 12
▶ medium theory – Chapter 2, p. 24
▶ modernization – Chapter 11, p. 206
▶ Payne Fund studies – Chapter 9, p. 173

the work of Pierre Bourdieu (1984[1979]) and Anthony Giddens (1984) – following a stand-off between structural functionalism and Marxism in post-1945 social sciences.◀ During the same period, the marketing sector has been challenged to refine its tools of planning and prediction in competitive markets with highly selective consumers. An important means to this end has been a better understanding of how consumers make sense of products, and of themselves, to a significant extent through media and communication.

Analysis Box 8.1 presents an example of lifestyle research, and relates it to some of the theoretical sources of the area. Figure 8.4 illustrates the methodology and its characteristic way of displaying findings.

ANALYSIS BOX 8.1: CORRESPONDENCE ANALYSIS OF LIVING CONDITIONS, LIFESTYLES, AND MEDIA USE

In order to relate people's material living conditions with their own interpretations of those conditions, a common strategy is, first, to ask them a complex set of survey questions regarding their fundamental values in life, in addition to information about their demographic background – age, gender, education, occupation, cultural activities, etc. Next, both sets of information are analyzed and compared through the multivariate technique of correspondence analysis (Greenacre, 2007).◀ This analysis serves to establish the extent to which different answers are correlated as well as the patterns of the correlations; the outcome is a segmentation of the population in

Figure 8.4 1995 chart of values among Danish media users (source: Schrøder, 1999: 57, reprinted with permission of Sage Publications, Ltd.)

cont.

▶ structural functionalism and Marxism – Chapter 3, p. 63
▶ correspondence analysis and multivariate statistics – Chapter 13, p. 260

question according to social positions and cultural values. The configuration of values for a given segment, thus, may be interpreted as a worldview of sorts that orients the economic, political, and cultural practices of individuals. Because the approach normally relies on large samples, lifestyle research can produce robust findings. And, because it is longitudinal, tracking shifts and trends◄ in the general public's orientations and preferences, it offers an approximation of the zeitgeist of a given historical period and social setting. By entering media into the design, studies suggest how media uses and communicative practices relate to the demographics and values of different audience segments.

In technical terms, the various responses constitute data points in a multidimensional mathematical space; they are normally displayed in a two-dimensional model, as in Figure 8.4. The two dimensions of the model, again technically speaking, are the two axes that best account for the distribution of data; as such, they have no inherent meaning. As they relate to the values and orientations in question, however, they represent two explanatory principles that can be stated in the vocabulary of social theory, and which have become a standard in studies of this kind. Figure 8.4 exemplifies a configuration of values with reference to a study of everyday life and political participation in Denmark, conducted in 1994–95 (Schrøder 1999). The vertical dimension indicates a relative orientation toward a 'modern' (top of the figure) or a 'traditional' (bottom of the figure) life form, respectively, as related, for example, to levels of education and to a global or local outlook on the world. The horizontal dimension distinguishes between a pragmatic and an idealistic worldview, respectively, as associated, in a European context, with the left-right spectrum of national politics (slightly confusing in terms of the model itself, with leftwing views toward the right, and rightwing views toward the left of the figure).

At issue along these dimensions, then, are the 'big' questions of economy, politics, culture, technology, and ethics. One example from the European context arises from different types of broadcasters. While the original public-service monopoly in the Danish study has its stronghold in the upper, 'northern' part of the chart, especially its 'eastern' segment, a preference for the commercial broadcasters that were added during recent decades is associated with the values clustered in the lower, 'southern' part, especially its 'western' segment.

In commercial settings, the approach of the Research Institute on Social Change (RISC) has been broadly influential. "Since 1978, socio-cultural models have been developed by RISC in around 40 countries. [...] It can be compared in some respects with market research tools such as Semiometrie, Kompass and ValueScope" (Hujanen, 2008: 183). Another research program is the World Values Survey, which builds on the work of Ronald Inglehart about long-term social change at the level of generations (Inglehart, 1990, 2008), and which has emphasized a culturally comparative perspective (Inglehart, *et al.*, 1998).

Probably the most sophisticated framework was developed by the sociologist, Pierre Bourdieu (1977; 1984[1979]). Moving beyond classic categories of class and ideology, he emphasized both the many different kinds of social fields, such as art and education, in which specific norms and rules of interaction apply, *and* the role of culture across such fields; he used the term habitus for the embodied and often preconscious dispositions that orient individuals' actions in everyday life. In communication and cultural studies, reference is commonly made to Bourdieu's several concepts of capital – scarce, but accumulated resources – particularly the distinction between economic and cultural capital, sometimes operationalized as income and education. In terms of Figure 8.4, whereas the two upper quadrants generally have more resources at their disposal than the two lower ones, the top left quadrant will command relatively more economic, the top right quadrant more cultural capital.

social fields

habitus

economic and cultural capital

► trend studies – Chapter 13, p. 246

INSTITUTIONALIZATION BY MEDIA

Research on the consequences of media use, as noted, has focused overwhelmingly on individuals as the point of uptake and the site of measurement. As presented in other chapters in this volume, additional research traditions have examined such consequences at the level of social structures, practices, and institutions. In the borderlands of individuals and institutions, media participate in the ongoing process of *institutionalizing* society – the shaping and reshaping of states, markets, families, communities, etc. From various perspectives, at least four bodies of research have examined these 'late stages' of communication.

- *Natural experiments on the introduction of media*. Particularly for television, which coincided with the development of media studies as a field, the first introduction of the medium into a community or culture provided an opportunity to assess structural changes, for example, in the use of time and the role of the new medium as a reference point for conversation or play. Given the before-after situation, such developments have lent themselves to natural experiments.◄
- *Public events*. A key role of modern media is that they present events and issues for public consideration. In doing so, they necessarily contribute to diffusion, presumably to agenda setting and framing, and perhaps to the public's memory of social and cultural markers. While some work has lamented that the media may create 'pseudo-events' (Boorstin, 1961), several classic studies (Dayan and Katz, 1992; Lang and Lang, 1953) have noted how the modern mass media have enabled public participation in events with society-wide implications, from national ceremonies to political scandals and international sports; media are among the primary conditions for, rather than secondary representations of, such media events. The historical and constitutive nature of media events is also suggested by the fact that a follow-up study to Dayan and Katz's (1992) influential volume, which had underlined their integrative role, found that disruptive events that are not preplanned have gained new prominence (Katz and Liebes, 2007).

media events

- *Institutional practices*. Media occupy a special position among other modern institutions because they constitute a common arena – a cultural forum◄ – in which the ends and means, standards and priorities, of other social institutions may be presented and debated. This is especially evident for *politics*, which is subject to a specific public accountability through the news media and their normative functions.◄ In comparison, private *economic* enterprise is exempt from detailed public control; and high forms of *culture* are still commonly conducted and covered in separate arenas and media. The more specific sense in which individuals and social groups are structurally dependent on media has been examined by the tradition of media system dependency theory (Ball-Rokeach and Jung, 2009).

media system dependency

- *Cultural formations*. Most generally, media and communication may contribute to making certain discursive and cultural forms dominant in society, as also suggested by medium theory.◄ Earlier work argued that a 'media logic' (Altheide and Snow, 1979) could be seen to invade other social domains; recent work has suggested that, in a process of 'mediatization,' the media as an institution may be reshaping expressions and interactions in other institutions, such as politics, leisure, and education (Lundby, 2009).

In conclusion, this chapter has reviewed the main traditions of quantitative audience research, each of which can be seen to identify and examine one stage in the longer and wider process of communication. While the theories and methodologies addressing the various stages are complementary, they also call for supplements from qualitative reception studies, which have focused on the everyday contexts of media use and on some of their long-term cultural implications. Qualitative audience research is the topic of the next chapter.

► natural experiments – Chapter 13, p. 254
► cultural forum – Chapter 1, p. 13
► normative media theories – Chapter 19, p. 353
► medium theory – Chapter 2, p. 24

9 Media reception

Qualitative traditions

Klaus Bruhn Jensen

- a presentation of the *established 'milestones'* of quantitative audience research, along with *seminal qualitative contributions*
- *a review* of the main topics of *reception studies*: everyday contexts of media use; decodings of media content; and media as resources in social action
- an assessment of *media ethnography* as a methodological position
- a discussion of the place of *media discourses* and other empirical evidence in reception studies

MILESTONES REVISITED

One way of encapsulating the field of study has been through *systematics*, such as Figure 8.1, which identified the main stages of the process of communication and the audience research traditions associated with each. Another way of taking stock has been to identify *historical* milestones◀ – studies that defined influential ways of conceptualizing and empirically examining various stages of communication. By way of introduction, this chapter revisits some of the milestones of audience studies, as received – and sometimes overlooked – in later research.

Figure 9.1 lays out fourteen milestones, as defined by Lowery and DeFleur (1995) through three editions of their widely used textbook, and adds a number of candidates from outside the dominant paradigm◀ of quantitative social science. In the case of the established US 'Milestones I,' it is apparent how several contributions were shaped by their historical and social contexts◀ – from wars to public or policy demand for evidence about the effects of media, for example, on children. Also 'Milestones II,' which introduce European, critical, and qualitative perspectives, bear witness to the importance of social context for research practice, including the events of '1968.'◀ Those circumstances, far from disqualifying either set of milestones, provide a background for assessing their explanatory value, also in a future perspective.

To further contextualize the milestones, it should be noted, first, that the listing only considers publications after 1900. Before there was a field of media and communication research, most scholarship about communication and its effects was undertaken within the humanities – in rhetorical and aesthetic traditions of inquiry.◀ Second, because the field largely established itself through journals, conferences,

▶ historical and systematic approaches to research – Chapter 1, p. 18
▶ the dominant paradigm – Chapter 8, p. 153
▶ historical origins of media research – Chapter 19
▶ "1968" – Chapter 11, p. 210
▶ rhetorical and aesthetic effects – Chapter 2

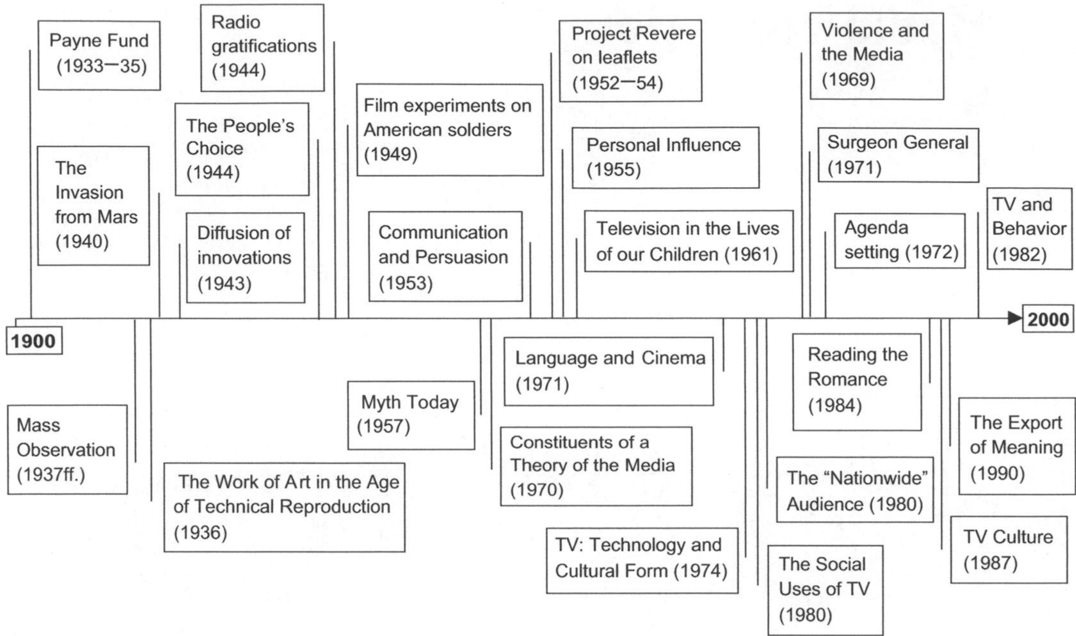

Figure 9.1 Milestones of media and communication research

and other institutions originating in the West, both sets of milestones reflect work originating in either Europe or the US; intercultural perspectives on communication◀ are addressed in Chapter 11. Third, much previous communication research – qualitative as well as quantitative – has examined audiences and messages in comparative isolation from each other. Whereas the treatment of content as discourses has often been rudimentary in quantitative research traditions, humanistic and other qualitative scholars, until quite recently, simply neglected the empirical users of media.

The two groups of 'milestones' are noted here for the record, and as a point of departure for theoretical and methodological interchange across traditions. This is important, both for young and interdisciplinary researchers entering the area and for the field as such; traditions are still handed down in selective fashion in doctoral programs, journals, and reference works.

▶ intercultural communication research – Chapter 11, p. 212

Symbolically, the second edition of Lowery and DeFleur's (1988) 'milestones' volume had made reference to an emerging "meaning paradigm" (p. 455), which presumably would admit some humanistic milestones. Only seven years later, however, in the third edition (Lowery and DeFleur, 1995), this hint at convergence had been replaced by a return to multiple parallel "focused theories," each of which might explain "some set of events or phenomena that has clear boundaries" (p. 397).

The family resemblances are many, for instance, between the early Payne Fund and Mass Observation research programs, and between more recent approaches to the framing◀ and the decoding (Hall, 1973; Morley, 1980) of media representations of reality. Cantril's (1940) milestone, employing a non-sectarian mix of qualitative and quantitative methodologies, still stands as an early messenger about the potential of convergence between traditions. An

▶ framing – Chapter 8, p. 164

MILESTONES I

- *Payne Fund.* This first substantial media research program in the US examined the effects of movies on children and youths through a variety of content, survey, experimental, and other methodologies, arising from and feeding into contemporary concerns and debates (for an overview, see Jowett, et al., 1996).
- *The Invasion from Mars.* Hadley Cantril's (1940) multimethod study of how the American public responded to Orson Welles' radio dramatization of the *War of the Worlds*, suggested, among other things, how to combine qualitative and quantitative methodologies for a concrete research purpose. (For a critical assessment, see Rosengren, *et al.*, 1978.)
- *Diffusion of Innovations.* Following 1940s studies on the adoption of agricultural techniques, diffusion research expanded to address other kinds of innovations and their place in processes of social change, including media and their dissemination of information (Rogers, 1962).
- *The People's Choice.* In certain respects the inaugural work of US communication research, this study examined the place of media in a presidential election process, relying on panels and other state-of-the-art survey methodology (Lazarsfeld, *et al.*, 1944). At least in its reception history, the study has been taken to suggest that media reinforce, rather than change people's opinions, and that, overall, media serve political democracy (for a classic critique, Gitlin, 1978).
- *Radio gratifications.* Among the contributions of the first generation of US communication researchers, were some of the seminal ideas that were later redeveloped in uses-and-gratifications research. Apart from its inherent qualities, the work by Herta Herzog (1944) was unusual in focusing on a genre addressed to women, namely, daytime radio serials.

MILESTONES II

- *Mass Observation.* The mass observation studies in the UK, from the 1930s onward, documented various aspects of ordinary people's lives, including cinema going and other media use (for an overview, see Richards and Sheridan, 1987). Comparable in certain respects to the American Payne Fund program, the studies represent an early approach to the place of media in everyday life, including qualitative insights into the reception and experience of media.
- *The Work of Art in the Age of Technical Reproduction.* This title (sometimes translated 'mechanical' reproduction) refers to Walter Benjamin's (1977[1936]) early attempt to conceptualize what was distinctively new about the cultural forms being disseminated by technological media. Taking 'medium theory' (see Chapter 2) to the level of concrete textual analysis, this work identified, on the one hand, the loss of 'aura'◄ in media, compared to traditional artworks, and, on the other hand, the democratic potential for public participation in politics and culture facilitated by mass media. Like other critical social theory of the 1930 and 1940s (e.g., Adorno and Horkheimer, 1977[1944]), Benjamin's work was, in part, an intellectual response to fascism – a response that was different in kind from US milestones relating to the war effort, but which engaged similar historical circumstances.
- *Myth Today.* Following the rebuilding of post-war Europe, new societies (and research institutions) were taking shape, in which the definition of 'culture' was again at issue, not only in debates over the 'Americanization' of European culture, but with reference to popular culture as such (Webster, 1988). One of the seminal early influences on research in the area was Roland Barthes' (1973[1957]) work on modern 'mythologies,' as disseminated in large part by mass media. Particularly his

cont.

► aura – Chapter 1, p. 7

MILESTONES I

- *Film experiments on American soldiers.* As part of the US involvement in World War II, a series of experimental studies were conducted of Frank Capra's *Why We Fight* films, exploring to what extent they might not only provide information, but also shape attitudes (Hovland, *et al.*, 1949).
- *Communication and Persuasion.* Departing from this and earlier experimental research, and from theories about the selective influence of media on individuals, the Yale Program of Research on Communication and Attitude Change proposed to generalize this perspective; however, studies were only able to document especially short-term changes in attitudes (Hovland, *et al.*, 1953).
- *Personal Influence.* Elaborating, in part, on the (serendipitous) finding of Lazarsfeld, *et al.* (1944), that media take effect, not least, by being mediated further in interpersonal communication involving opinion leaders, Katz and Lazarsfeld's (1955) volume helped to establish the two-step flow of communication as a generally influential model.
- *Project Revere.* At the height of the Cold War, and with the Korean War still being fought, this project (1952–54) was funded by the US military to explore the use of airborne leaflets to replace, or circumvent, other channels of communication (for an overview, see DeFleur and Larsen, 1987).
- *Television in the Lives of Our Children.* This first major study of television's effects on children in the US was characterized partly by the diversity of issues (and methodologies) included, partly by a renewed uses-and-gratifications perspective (Schramm, *et al.*, 1961). A close (and earlier-born) European cousin, not recognized among the 'milestones' of Lowery and DeFleur (1995) (but duly noted in the preface to Schramm, *et al.*, 1961), was Himmelweit, *et al.* (1958).

MILESTONES II

essay, "Myth Today," introducing the distinction between denotation and connotation◀ into analyses of how meanings are offered by media, and taken by audiences, shaped an understanding among the first generation of European critical media researchers of how media take effect and shape both individuals and societies.

- *Constituents of a theory of the media.* Hans Magnus Enzensberger's (1972[1970]) article returned to Bertolt Brecht's (1993[1932]) original point regarding radio during the 1930s, that the equipment for receiving programs could as well be used for sending messages and participating in a society-wide dialogue, thus suggesting the critical potential of media (as well as the constitutive role of media in social systems). In addition to his period-specific ideological message, Enzensberger's theoretical message anticipated later work on 'active' audiences and on the interactivity of digital media.
- *Language and Cinema.* The title of one of the main publications by the film theorist, Christian Metz (1974), suggests the 'milestone' nature of a larger body of theoretical work, during the 1960 and 1970s, in France and other European countries, exploring the distinctive characteristics of verbal and visual vehicles of communication, and their modes of addressing the audience. The central question – whether cinema and other non-alphabetic communication might be studied as 'languages' (and if not, then how) – was given one of its most elaborate treatments by Metz and other European semiotics and structuralism.◀
- *TV: Technology and Cultural Form.* Raymond Williams' (1974) definition of broadcasting (radio and TV) as a historically unique 'flow,'◀ rather than a collection of 'works,' identified a central aspect of much technologically mediated communication, and anticipated

cont.

► denotation and connotation – Chapter 2, p. 34
► film semiotics – Chapter 7, p. 135
► broadcasting as flow, p. 184

MILESTONES I

- *Mass Media and Violence*. Growing out of US government and public concern over social unrest during the 1960s, this report (Lange, *et al.*, 1969) summarized earlier research, and presented new evidence and conclusions, particularly on the effects of violence in entertainment programs, relying on approaches which were extended in cultivation research.◀
- *Surgeon General*. Traditionally referred to as the "Surgeon General's Report on Television and Social Behavior," the relevant work (Comstock, *et al.*, 1971) is, in fact, a multivolume collection of studies that informed this report. Following up on several previous 'milestones,' this time on a grand scale, the publication addressed issues and presented findings that were oriented toward social problems and policy issues.
- *Agenda setting*. Since the 1970s, agenda-setting research◀ has been influential in reorienting the focus of political communication research, from the changing of attitudes to the setting of agendas, reminding research of the multistep and multilevel nature of effects (McCombs and Shaw, 1972).
- *Television and Behavior*. Explicitly following up on the "Surgeon General's Report," this last 'milestone' took stock of research ten years on, but included a wider range of research questions (Pearl, *et al.*, 1982). While no new research was commissioned, the integrative reviews of the massive research output since 1971 provided an authoritative overview, with special reference to television.

MILESTONES II

various aspects of digital media and networked communication. (See also Ellis, 1982.)

- *The "Nationwide" Audience*. Drawing on both discourse analysis and gratifications research, David Morley's (1980) volume was the first major publication to bring together social-scientific and humanistic perspectives on the audience in a qualitative empirical study of television news reception; it is reviewed in detail below, together with other foundational works in reception studies (by, among others, Lull and Radway).
- *The social uses of television*. In the same year as Morley, James Lull (1980) went beyond the individual focus of gratifications research, to study the social uses of television in the family, relying on a qualitative methodology and reemphasizing the explanatory value of microsociological traditions.
- *Reading the Romance*. Janice Radway (1984) presented a comprehensive study of the institutions, texts, and audiences of the print romance genre; the audience fieldwork, especially, provided a model for further reception studies.
- *Television Culture*. As part of a textbook on television studies, John Fiske (1987) offered an operational approach to intertextuality,◀ beyond the immanent analysis of narrative structures and textual modes of address.
- *The Export of Meaning*. This qualitative study of the experience of the *Dallas* television series among different cultural and ethnic groups (Liebes and Katz, 1990) was one of the first internationally comparative reception studies (see also Jensen, 1998).

▶ cultivation research – Chapter 8, p. 166
▶ agenda-setting research – Chapter 8, p. 161
▶ intertextuality – Chapter 10, p. 192

exemplary volume on *Canonic Texts in Media Research* (Katz, *et al.*, 2003), which brought together broader 'schools' of media research within the covers of one book, beginning with the Columbia School of Paul Lazarsfeld and the Frankfurt School of Theodor Adorno and Max Horkheimer, suggested that canons – whether explicit, implicit, forgotten, or repressed – should be articulated and recognized for what they offer: premises and benchmarks that will continue to be challenged by developments both in research and in the media themselves.

Whereas the next chapter turns to some fundamental challenges to canonic conceptions of media and communication that are presented by digital technologies, the rest of the present chapter reviews the contributions of qualitative audience research to the field. While being late starters, these traditions have produced new insight into at least three different moments of the process of communication: the everyday contexts of media use; audience decodings of media content; and the uses of media forms and contents as resources in a variety of social contexts. One section discusses 'ethnography' as an influential methodological position in reception studies. Finally, the chapter returns to the role of texts or discourses in the study of media use. A distinctive feature of qualitative reception analysis is that it has addressed media contents as well as media audiences – audience-cum-content analysis (Jensen, 1988a).◀

MOMENTS OF INTERPRETATION

Everyday contexts of media use

As indicated in Figure 9.1, one focus of qualitative audience research has been the concrete everyday contexts of media use. Although the topic had been taken up early on in the British mass observation studies of cinema (Richards and Sheridan, 1987), and later in video observations of television viewers (Bechtel, *et al.*, 1972), the seminal work by James Lull (1980) examined television viewing in naturalistic settings. The study drew on several undercurrents in the social sciences with a qualitative orientation: symbolic interactionism, ethnomethodology, and other 'microsociology.'◀ In methodological terms, it relied on prolonged observations of television viewing in American households. Parting with the individual focus of other uses-and-gratifications research,◀ the analyses developed a typology of the social uses of television in family settings. (However, the social uses of media in a political, economic, or cultural regard, or in public domains, were not considered.) The typology identified, first, the 'structural' uses of television in generating an environment or atmosphere in the home, and in regulating, for instance, children's bed times. Second, the study documented various 'relational' or interactional uses of television, for example, in facilitating (or avoiding) contact between parents and children, or between spouses.

structural and relational uses of media

During the 1980 and 1990s, a variety of studies examined how media are integrated into everyday activities (for overviews, see, e.g., Alasuutari, 1999; Ross and Nightingale, 2003). The focus remained on households and the dynamics of family life, with some additional reference to other social contexts of television viewing (e.g., Gauntlett and Hill, 1999) – and to media use in public places (Lemish, 1982), in quasi-public settings such as a prison (Lindlof, 1987), and in peer groups (Buckingham, 1993). The special focus on households and families is explained, in part, by the attention given to television during this period, also in other media research; for reception studies, the family represented a naturally occurring social and cultural unit whose interpretive and communicative processes could be examined in context and in detail. Later studies have also considered, for example, audiences' live commentary about, or 'communication with,' broadcasting (Wood, 2007); this is comparable to the classic finding regarding television viewers engaging in para-social interaction with program figures (Horton and Wohl, 1956).

media use in public settings

para-social interaction

Radio, while examined, for instance, in a historical perspective (e.g., Moores, 1988; Scannell, 1988), has generally been underresearched

▶ audience-cum-content analysis, p. 178

▶ microsociology – Chapter 3, p. 65

▶ uses-and-gratifications research – Chapter 8, p. 157

in media studies◀ (it was, in part, eclipsed by television as the field was being founded). Similarly, the reading of print media – from books to magazines to newspapers – has rarely been studied as a contextual activity. In the perspective of literary criticism◀ and other arts, reading has been considered a solitary experience of certain aesthetic representations of reality. In a communicative perspective, however, print media are social and cultural resources, and reading has a range of contextual uses, for seeking or avoiding contact, and for establishing a social space in which one may be 'absent' even while physically present (see the discussion below of Radway, 1984). Film, again, has been studied more as an art form than as a social practice,◀ even though some research has examined, for instance, the inherently social act of going to movies, sharing and later remembering the experience (e.g., Gomery, 1992; Kuhn, 2002). Relatively fewer reception studies have explored how several media simultaneously enter into the everyday lives of individuals and families (e.g., Barnhurst and Wartella, 1998; Jordan, 1992). At the margins of the media field, studies have also considered other cultural institutions and practices, such as museum visits (e.g., Heath and vom Lehn, 2004), as communicative interactions.

museums as contexts of communication

Observation, with variable degrees of participation,◀ has presented itself as the methodology of choice for studies of media use in context. Like the original 1980 article and later work by Lull (1980, 1988b, 1991), studies have relied on participating observation to produce a fine-grained analysis of media and communication in a particular locale (e.g., Gillespie, 1995). In other cases, the main method of data collection has been qualitative interviewing, either individually or in groups (Gray, 1992; Hobson, 1980; Morley, 1986). While relevant for many purposes, interview methodologies depend on the respondents' introspection, retrospection, and verbal recollection of past events and actions, which necessarily reproduces them from a present perspective. In some instances, interviewing may be preferred because observation is considered too intrusive or controversial, in view of either the media users or the content in question. In any event, when planning as well as assessing studies of use contexts, it is particularly important to weigh the strengths and weaknesses of observation and interviewing, so that inferences are made with reference to appropriate evidence.

Observational studies, in their turn, have not commonly included analyses of media users' response to particular genres or narratives. Indeed, Lull (1980) did not explicitly relate the various social uses of television, and their relative prominence, to different genres. One way of summarizing two central decades of qualitative reception studies, 1980–2000, would be to note that, despite multimethod combinations, observational studies have detailed the place of media in the everyday lives of different social groups, whereas interview studies have probed their decodings of a range of media texts and genres.

It is fair to add that reception studies – of use contexts as well as of decodings – appear to have become fewer and, at least, less prominent in the field and its debates since 2000. In a sense, qualitative audience studies may have made their point – vis-à-vis both text-centered and behavior-focused colleagues – and have established themselves among the traditions studying the multiple levels and steps of media impact. Coincidentally, digital media and networked communications have presented a new range of research questions, at least some of which break the bounds of reception (and effects) studies as traditionally conceived. Multiplayer online gaming◀ or the micro-coordination (Ling and Yttri, 2002) of everyday life via mobile telephones are rather different categories of social interaction than conversations around a television set. The dividing line between media and their contexts has come into question; it is taken up in more detail below in the section addressing media use in relation to other social contexts of action, and in Chapter 10.

media in/as contexts

▶ radio studies – Chapter 12, p. 226
▶ literary criticism – Chapter 2, p. 37
▶ film studies – Chapter 2, p. 40
▶ participating observation – Chapter 14, p. 272
▶ games – Chapter 7, p. 145

Decodings

Research on decodings – audience interpretations of media discourses such as television series, radio newscasts, or print fiction – accounts for the majority of qualitative reception studies (for overviews, see, e.g., Livingstone, 1998; Schrøder, *et al.*, 2003). The tradition emerged from literary and cultural studies with a dual motivation: exploring the classic humanistic question of how meaning is produced and shared, and addressing that question in empirical terms with reference to how ordinary users – rather than critics and pundits – interpret media. The approach, in practice, has undertaken comparative analyses of media discourses and audience discourses – audience-cum-content analysis. As such, decoding research has had several sources: classic hermeneutics and phenomenology,◄ as developed also in literary reception aesthetics◄ (Holub, 1984; Wilson, 1993); the ritual model of communication;◄ and, most influentially, cultural studies.◄ Taking inspiration from semiotics (e.g., Eco, 1987b) and critical social theory (e.g., Parkin, 1971), the cultural-studies tradition has given special attention to the relative indeterminacy of meaning. Like wider cultural practices, micro interpretations of media may be considered sites of struggle; decodings can make a social difference.

audience-cum-content analysis

The concept of decoding was derived from Stuart Hall's (1973) theoretical encoding-decoding model, which had suggested the less than perfect correspondence between media practitioners' encoding of texts and the audience's decodings, even if Hall took texts to have ideologically 'preferred' meanings. Questioning both critical work that assumed a more massive ideological effect of media, and the individualist position of uses-and-gratifications research, David Morley (1980) applied Hall's model in a seminal study of the decoding of television news. Employing a focus-group methodology, Morley identified a range of decodings of the 'preferred' meaning, which had been established through discourse analysis (Brunsdon and Morley, 1978) – from an accepting or 'dominant' reading, via a 'negotiated,' to a critical or 'oppositional' reading. Across the different focus groups, these readings were correlated, not just with the socioeconomic status of the participants, but also with their cultural or organizational involvement. For example, the combination of low social status with shop-floor union involvement produced some of the most explicitly oppositional readings (Morley, 1980: 141). Like some researchers, these media users could be seen to perform a hermeneutics of suspicion.◄

encoding-decoding model of communication

dominant, negotiated, and oppositional readings

More than the specific study and its findings, it was the general approach, linking the social-systemic and the discursive-interpretive attributes of media users, which became highly influential. Morley (1981) himself was among the first to criticize the one-dimensional conception of decoding as essentially a question of the (degree of) reproduction of a dominant ideology, pointing to the need to study, as well, basic comprehension and the pleasurable experience of watching news (see further Lewis, 1983, 1985). Later studies noted several varieties of oppositional decodings, and suggested the difficulties that even comparatively sophisticated users may have in unpacking the implicit messages of media texts (Hacker, *et al.*, 1991). Twenty-five years on, a reexamination of Morley's (1980) original findings reemphasized the importance of social class as the key explanatory factor, while also outlining an approach to quantifying decoding studies (Kim, 2004).

Regarding different audience backgrounds, other studies have addressed both gender and class, including the interrelation between the two factors in the concrete experience of media (e.g., Press, 1991; Schlesinger, *et al.*, 1992). Also ethnicity has been examined, both as a source of variable decodings and with reference to different ethnic groups' interpretations of each other, as represented in media (e.g., Duke, 2000; J. Lewis, 1991; Parameswaran, 1999; Park, *et al.*, 2006). Age, perhaps surprisingly,

► hermeneutics and phenomenology – Chapter 2
► reception aesthetics, p. 83
► the ritual model of communication – Chapter 1, p. 12
► cultural studies – Chapter 2, p. 46
► hermeneutics of suspicion – Chapter 2, p. 30

has rarely been given attention as a theoretical category, in either reception or effects studies, except in the case of research on media and youth, despite the different media habits and cultural practices of populations across the life span (but see, e.g., Jensen, 1990b; Press, 1991; Tulloch, 1989).

gender, class, ethnicity, age

Regarding different media and genres, television, again, has been the preferred medium of decoding studies, with news and melodrama as preferred genres. Beyond the general focus of research on this medium, television invited critical reception studies, for example, in the European setting during the 1980 and 1990s when deregulation introduced many more international, especially commercial formats into national media cultures. Overlapping with such concerns were debates on the politics of popular culture.◀ Much work in the area could be seen to rediscover pleasure, both as a source of audience empowerment and as a legitimate topic of research; television provided a good percentage of the pleasurable experiences had by the general public during the decades in question. However, also other media and genres have been taken up in qualitative reception studies, including books (Parameswaran, 1999; Radway, 1984), magazines (Hermes, 1995; Lutz and Collins, 1993), and advertising (Mick and Buhl, 1992; Schrøder, 1997). And while, traditionally, film studies◀ as a field has not taken much of an interest in the empirical audience, reception studies have examined film as a central constituent of, and influence on, the rest of the media environment (Barker and Brooks, 1998; Cooper, 1999; Stacey, 1994; Stokes and Maltby, 1999). Research has also explored the differential decoding of various genres, for instance, satire, finding different ways of getting (or missing) the joke, coupled with different levels of critical engagement (Johnson, *et al.*, 2010).

television, news, melodrama

Regarding methodologies, finally, interviews – either focus groups or in-depth individual interviews – have been, by far, the most widely applied approach to decoding studies. Interviewing has served as the generator of audience discourses to be compared with media discourses, so as to explore their interchange in meaning production. That interchange, mostly, has been examined in retrospect, with reference to media contents that users were recently exposed to; this is in addition to efforts, for instance, in Tamar Liebes and Elihu Katz's (1990) 'milestone' study of the television series, *Dallas*, to engage viewers in dialogue while viewing, and other attempts to elicit user interpretations live through think-aloud techniques (Vettehen, *et al.*, 2004). One analytical issue has been how to examine the reception of television and other audiovisual media through the verbal accounts of audiences; this presents a general difficulty, also for other kinds of communication studies, and has been taken up through various visual methodologies.◀

think-aloud

Media in contexts of social action

Studies of the third stage – the embedding and use of media in other contexts of social action – produced a relatively smaller body of research during the 1980s' and 1990s' heyday of reception studies, but may be gaining ground in the digital media environment. Digital media could be said to refocus research attention, from media as *representations* that call for decoding, and as *conditions* circumscribing local use contexts, to media as *resources*. As interactive and, to a degree, mobile entities, digital media represent a new type of resource across locations or contexts; users 'import' information that may reorient or enhance their local interaction – a purchase, a political discussion, a cultural event. Digital media also enable users to engage – or establish – distant contexts of interaction, as they 'export' information, communicate, and act at a distance in relation to individuals and institutions, from partners and children, to employers, banks, and political interest groups. Whereas Chapter 10 elaborates on these aspects of communication, this section presents some contributions of earlier reception studies to the area.

media as representations, conditions, and resources

▶ the politics of popular culture – Chapter 19, p. 363
▶ film studies – Chapter 2, p. 40
▶ visual methodologies – Chapter 14, p. 275

Three types of studies – on different media and genres – illustrate the implications of research on communication as a constitutive element of contexts of action:

- In her study of *print romances*, Janice Radway (1984) showed how, in addition to producing a variety of interpretations of such texts, readers conceived of romances as resources in daily life. Romances were seen to provide at least indirect advice on married life; they also presented the women in the study with an occasion to insist on 'my time' for reading. Thus, compared to decoding studies, the focus was shifted away from the text and its interpretation, toward the act of reading and its implications for gendered everyday practices.

the act of reading

- In a study of American *television news*, the present author examined news stories from the viewers' perspective, less as accounts than as resources for political and other social participation (Jensen, 1986, 1990a). The findings suggested that viewers may approach the news genre with a divided or ambiguous consciousness: while dutifully arguing for the inherent importance, both of news as a political resource and of the citizen's act of news viewing, the respondents simultaneously suggested the limited practical value of any information in the news for voting in elections, debating concrete issues, or other specific purposes.
- Studies of *fan cultures* (e.g., Jenkins, 1992; L. Lewis, 1991) have shown how texts and other artifacts around which fandom develops – a feature film, the music of a rock band – may become resources for a wide range of cultural practices. Beyond their active engagement with and decoding of texts, fans have long redeveloped such texts in their own writing, music, or audiovisual production, also in analog media. One question specifically regarding digital media, raised by, among others, Henry Jenkins (2006), is whether the practices of fan communities may be generalized into a participatory culture◄ that involves ordinary media users in general as co-creators of culture. While this is, in large part, an empirical question, Nancy Baym's (2000) study of television soap-opera viewers sharing information about and perspectives on their favorite series via the internet, at least, suggested how new media may extend and reconfigure interpersonal communication *about* mass communication.

► participatory culture – Chapter 10, p. 200

The common denominator of these rather heterogeneous studies is their emphasis on media as resources in other social interaction, beyond the moment of either individual or collective attendance and appreciation. Media are resources for managing and, perhaps, challenging gender roles in everyday life; for accumulating real-world knowledge and, perhaps, stimulating political involvement; and for participating in and, possibly, extending the available range of cultural forms. In a more recent terminology, these practices can be understood as instances of user-driven communication and, perhaps, innovation (Von Hippel, 2005) – innovation of cultural products and/or cultural processes. With reference to traditional effects studies, such social uses of media share a number of family resemblances, for example, with processes of framing, socialization, and institutionalization. Research on media as resources in contexts of social action also has anticipated current issues concerning networked communications, as addressed in more detail in Chapter 10.

MEDIA ETHNOGRAPHY?

As part of the development of qualitative reception studies, references to 'ethnography' became widespread from the 1980s and into the 1990s. The terminology could be understood as an attempt to specify the nature of an emerging hybrid of humanistic and social-scientific approaches to media and communication that would avoid both reified texts and decontextualized audiences. Early on, Radway (1988) had pinpointed the difficulty of how, concretely, to examine texts as well as audiences with simultaneous attention to contexts:

ethnography

Audiences [...] are set in relation to a single set of isolated texts which qualify already as categorically distinct objects. No matter how extensive the effort to dissolve the boundaries of the textual object or the audience, most recent studies of reception, including my own, continue to begin with the 'factual' existence of a particular kind of text which is understood to be received by some set of individuals. Such studies perpetuate, then, the notion of a circuit neatly bounded and therefore identifiable, locatable, and open to observation.

(Radway, 1988: 363)

Radway's alternative was classic ethnographic fieldwork, as developed in the discipline of anthropology since the early twentieth century.◄ She envisioned a project covering the cultural and other social practices, work as well as leisure, of an entire community:

[...] a collaborative project that would begin within the already defined boundaries of a politically constituted municipality and attempt to map there the complex, collective production of 'popular culture' across the terrain of everyday life. [...] a project that would take as its object of study the range of practices engaged in by individuals within a single heterogeneous community as they elaborate their own form of popular culture through the realms of leisure and then articulate those practices to others engaged in during their working lives.

(Radway, 1988: 368)

Radicalizing the call for contextualization, Ien Ang (1991) argued that ethnographies rely on an entirely different epistemology than that of either qualitative reception studies or quantitative effects research. Rejecting both these positions, Ang suggested that very category of 'audiences' represented a form of discursive violence against the complexity of users and their cultural practices:

From this [ethnographic] perspective, 'television audience' is a nonsensical category, for there is only the dispersed, indefinitely proliferating chain of situations in which television audiencehood is practised and experienced—together making up the diffuse and fragmentary social world of actual audiences.

(Ang, 1991: 164)

Even though it seems unclear how, then, empirical studies might proceed, this general line of argument became influential in parts of media and cultural studies, resonating with postmodernist ideas.◄ Also the less radical position of Radway (1988) presented problems of what would be the research questions and the concrete domains of data collection and analysis. Unless 'media' and 'users' could be delimited as legitimate objects of analysis, there would be little difference between media studies and other anthropological fieldwork. One dilemma for 'ethnography' in the case of media becomes what *not* to study.

The record shows that media studies have rarely delivered comprehensive ethnographies of the communicative practices of communities. This is in spite of the fact that an early sociological classic such as *Middletown*◄ (Lynd and Lynd, 1929) had presented a model for precisely this kind of fieldwork. Instead, there developed an unfortunate tendency, in some qualitative audience studies, to describe assorted qualitative methodologies, including interview designs, as 'ethnography.' Lacking the required standards of data collection, analysis, and reporting, this practice generated debate and criticism, summed up in James Lull's conclusion that "'ethnography' has become an abused buzz-word in our field" (Lull, 1988a: 242).

In response, other research sought to reclaim and justify the terminology, partly by acknowledging the scholarly requirements of the approach, partly, again, by suggesting that ethnography constitutes not just a specific methodology, but a distinctive epistemology (e.g., Drotner, 1994, 1996; Schrøder, *et al.*, 2003). In media and communication studies, the term

► anthropology – Chapter 3, p. 57

► postmodernism – Chapter 2, p. 41
► Middletown – Chapter 3, p. 57

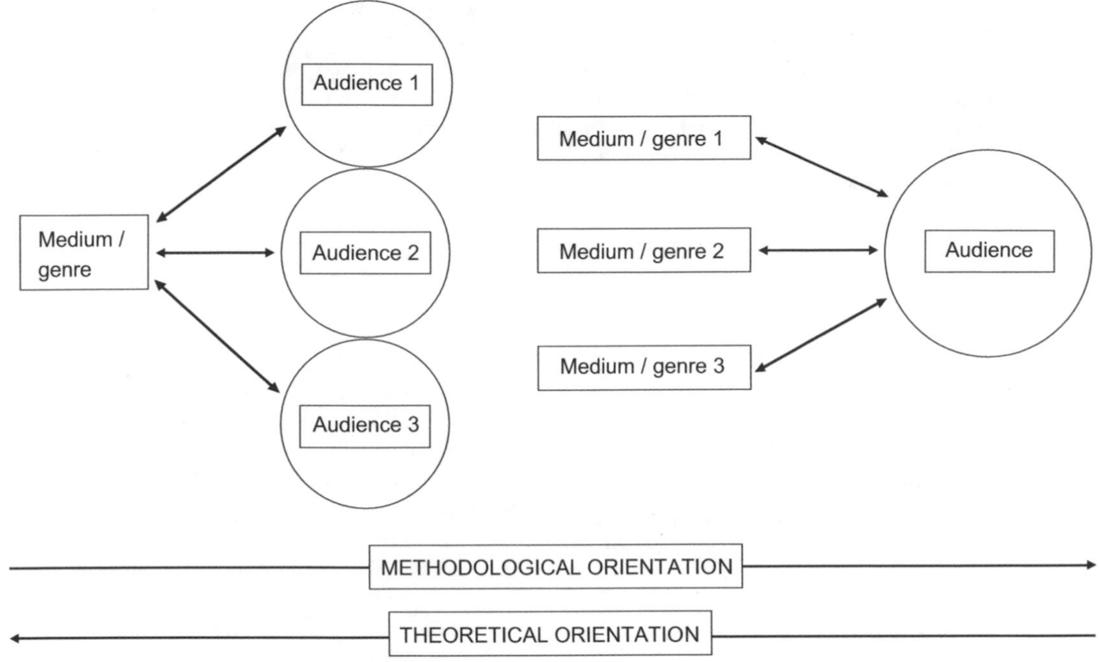

Figure 9.2 Two varieties of reception studies

might imply a focus, not on media, but on the social practices and gendered identities to which media contribute across contexts. However, it has remained unclear how such an approach would differ from the qualitative methodologies and constructivist epistemologies that have characterized most reception studies. In some instances, 'media ethnography' has appeared to imply an extension of the approach to the study of institutions and discourses, as well. The terminology has also been applied to the internet with reference to 'virtual ethnography' (Hine, 2000).

'virtual ethnography'

It is more informative and precise to refer to most self-described ethnographic media research as relying on multimethod and, perhaps, multidisciplinary research designs.◄ Inevitably, studies must limit themselves to empirical microcosms, even as they relate their findings to theoretical macrocosms, and to other evidence. Figure 9.2 indicates two prototypical varieties of audience or user studies. One type of study will emphasize the characteristic uses of a given medium or genre by several different user groups; the other type explores how one particular group uses various media and genres. The methodological orientation, in both cases, is to the media: what difference do the media, rather than other institutions and practices, make for the users' interaction in and with society and culture? The theoretical orientation, in turn, is toward the historical and cultural contexts embedding both media and users. In empirical terms, meaning flows from media to society and into history; in theoretical terms, meaning flows from, and must be interpreted with reference to, society and history.

MEDIA DISCOURSES AS INTERPRETED AND USED

A constant challenge for reception studies – as audience-cum-content analysis – has been how to conduct comparative research on media discourses and audience discourses that does

► multimethod research designs – Chapter 15, p. 300

not privilege either the text or the user. While reception studies, from the outset, had rejected textual analysis as the final arbiter of what a given media content 'really' means, researchers also worried that empirical audience studies might lose sight of the text altogether (e.g., Brunsdon, 1989). Such concerns were motivated, in part, by influential theoretical contributions that painted (media) texts as 'empty,' waiting to be filled with meaning by readers acting as interpretive communities (Fish, 1979). Other contributions seemed to exaggerate the polysemy of media texts – the openness and indeterminacy of the meanings that audiences might ascribe to them (Fiske, 1987). Umberto Eco (1976: 150) even suggested that audiences, both ordinary media users and researchers, might engage in semiotic guerrilla warfare by interpreting the texts of the dominant media against the grain. Before outlining the different kinds of media discourses that enter into empirical reception studies, this section briefly reviews some of the key concepts that have been applied to the text-audience nexus.

interpretive communities

polysemy

semiotic guerrilla warfare

The audience in the text

A classic notion in literary criticism◄ has been that of an implied reader, or an audience anticipated by the text. While reference had traditionally been made to the 'point of view' of a literary work or genre, twentieth-century theories made the more specific argument that texts 'inscribe' or involve readers into narrative and other discursive structures. The notion was given various formulations in different theoretical traditions – by 1960s structuralism and semiotics noting how texts 'enunciate' their messages to readers, and perhaps most influentially by German reception aesthetics. In this last tradition, Hans Robert Jauss (1982) developed the idea of a horizon of expectations◄ within which readers encounter a text, whereas Wolfgang Iser (1978[1976]) identified structural blanks in a text – apparently missing components – as invitations for the reader to complete the text. Umberto Eco (1987b) distinguished between texts that are open and closed, respectively, in terms of their range of likely decodings; Eco, further, referred to *interpreting* a text along the lines suggested by its structure, and *using* it for the reader's more or less idiosyncratic purposes.

reception aesthetics

textual blanks

open and closed texts

interpretations or uses of texts

In empirical reception studies, the idea of interpretive communities became particularly influential. An important redevelopment and operationalization of the concept was that of interpretive repertoires (Potter and Wetherell, 1987). Rather than assuming that individuals somehow belong to certain delimited communities, the latter term suggests that media users may rely on a whole range of repertoires, depending on their socioeconomic background, the text at hand, as well as the specific context of media use. Accordingly, the analysis of, for example, interview discourses can trace the semantic relations, metaphors, and other interpretive procedures that different respondent employ (Jensen, 1990b). In this way, interpretive repertoires avoid the implication, either that interpretive communities are on a par with geographical or political communities, or that they might arise entirely ad hoc for one text or one reading. A wider implication for media and communication studies is that interpretive and socio-demographic categories may be mapped onto each other in different qualitative (and quantitative) research designs.

interpretive repertoires

interpretive and socio-demographic categories

The texts in front of the audience

In contrast to studies of literary and other arts, which traditionally have examined single – and singular – 'works,' media and communication research has typically taken individual texts as instances or representatives of some larger class. Media studies can be said to examine discourses◄ – the social uses of language and other modalities – rather than self-contained texts. For better or worse, mass-mediated texts do not have the aura◄ of unique artifacts. Moreover, the texts that are interpreted and used are often the outcome of some audience activity, notably so for interactive digital media,

► literary criticism – Chapter 2, p. 37
► horizon of expectations – Chapter 2, p. 30
► two definitions of discourse – Chapter 6, p. 115
► aura – Chapter 1, p. 7

but also, for example, in the case of radio and television programs that are selected and combined by listeners and viewers as a flow. Whereas Chapters 6 and 7 present different research traditions within the analysis of media contents, this chapter, in conclusion, notes the range and types of media discourses that lend themselves to audience and user studies.

- *Discursive elements*. Reception analysis has mostly examined entire narratives and full news stories. Some studies, however, have traced the presence of particular themes or images in media, for instance, in a critical perspective to assess the mark they may leave on the users' consciousness (e.g., Philo, 1990). In quantitative audience research, specifically studies of memory and recall, this has been a standard approach.◀
- *Single texts*. In certain instances, media content acquires the status of a singular vehicle of communication – a text. A 'milestone' example was Orson Welles' 1938 radio production of *War of the Worlds*, which attracted attention because of its impact on the general public (Cantril, 1940). Other examples include entertainment programs or formats that become influential, symbolic, and, sometimes, debated in different cultures, from fiction series such as *Dallas* and *Dynasty* (Gripsrud, 1995), to *Big Brother*, *Idol*, and other reality television◀ (Hill, 2005).
- *Genres*. Given the focus of media studies on *types* of discourse, genre represents a key level of analysis, also in reception analysis, as witnessed in studies of decoding and social action contexts: what are the interpretive strategies that audiences apply to the main genres of media fact and fiction, and to what extent do different genres serve as resources of action, in institutional settings and within the flow of everyday life (e.g., Baym, 2000; Jensen, 1986; Radway, 1984)? Genres constitute modes of address◀ that anticipate the social uses of their variable contents.
- *Media*. While mostly understood as (discursive) forms and contents, 'media' are also material artifacts and infrastructures that condition communication and other social interaction. This has been noted, most consistently, by the tradition of medium theory,◀ and has also been explored in user studies under the heading of domestication – the interpretive and interactional processes through which individuals and groups integrate a new and largely unfamiliar technology into family life and other settings (for an overview, see Silverstone, 2006). With digital technologies, media as material, yet malleable structures present new potentials – for use and for research.
- *Flow*. Following Raymond Williams' (1974) definition of broadcasting – radio and television – as a flow, rather than as discrete programs, the flow of different media presents itself as another key level of analysis. Differentiating Williams' concept of flow in the context of reception studies, the present author outlined a three-part model comprising individual channel flows, the total or super flow of a given television system or market, and the actual viewer flows within and across these other flows (Jensen, 1994). The model is laid out in Figure 9.3. More generally, the concept of flow, including transitions between otherwise separate discursive sequences, can be seen to capture important aspects of other media and communicative practices, from turn-taking in a conversation to collaboration or combat in a computer game. Such flows are examined in more detail in Chapter 10 in a discussion of three-step flows of communication.◀
- *Hypertexts*. Though comparable, in certain respects, to the flows of broadcasting, hypertexts afford more interactive options in sending and receiving information, and in producing and accessing content. And, while also anticipated by other kinds of writing and print media (Bolter, 1991), hypertextual

domestication

▶ memory studies – Chapter 8, p. 160
▶ reality television – Chapter 16
▶ mode of address – Chapter 10, p. 196
▶ medium theory – Chapter 2, p. 24
▶ three-step flows of communication – Chapter 10, p. 187

structures enable categorically new forms of media use, which feed into multiple steps of communication.◀

- *Media environments*. Most generally, the entire configuration of media in a historical setting can be understood as a cultural environment, by analogy to the natural environment – a material, institutional, and discursive infrastructure that both enables and constrains the role of communication in social coordination and collaboration. Whereas certain discursive aspects of media environments have long been examined with reference to intertextuality◀ – the many explicit or implicit references between media and genres that generate additional meanings in the course of communication – the question of how, specifically, media serve to constitute social and cultural environments has taken on new salience with digital media. The next chapter examines media environments as 'contexts' of communication and other social interaction. Media communicate *within* contexts; they also serve to establish, maintain, and modify contexts *across* time and space.

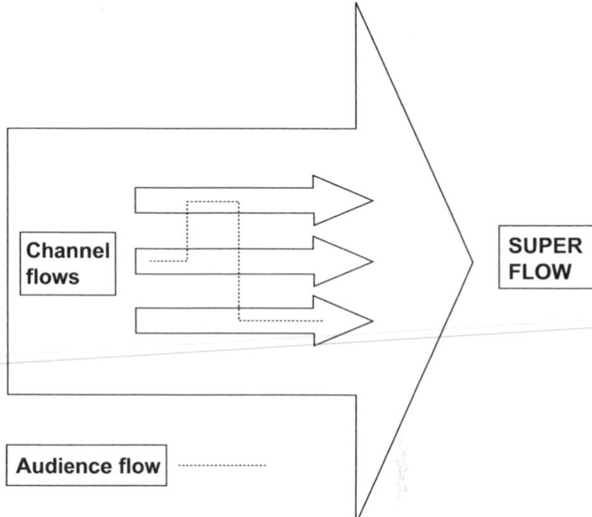

Figure 9.3 Three flows of media use

▶ hypertexts – Chapter 10, p. 193
▶ intertextuality – Chapter 10, p. 192

10 Communication in contexts

Beyond mass-interpersonal and online-offline divides

Klaus Bruhn Jensen

- *a three-step flow model of communication* – across media of the first, second, and third degrees
- *intertextuality* – the multistep flows of information in textual and social networks
- *meta-communication* – communication that serves to establish contexts of communication and other social interaction
- *web search engines* – an illustration of meta-communication in practice
- *media, genres, texts* – a reconsideration of a classic analytical hierarchy for digital media studies
- *time-in culture and time-out culture* – a discussion of communicative practices as constituents of cultural reflexivity and social structuration

THE FLOWS OF COMMUNICATION

The concept of flow has been associated, in media studies, with Raymond Williams' (1974) characterization of radio and television broadcasting. Especially in commercial television formats, viewers are expected and encouraged to go with the flow – to keep watching throughout commercial breaks and transitions between programs. Figure 9.3 laid out an analytical distinction between different types of flow: the *channel flow* of each station enters into the *super flow* of all the contents on offer, whereas *audience flows* move across the various channel flows◄ (Jensen, 1994). In digital media, the flows of communication are comparable, yet different. The super flow of the internet is more composite and complex than any traditional television market. The channel flow of any site or service is more differentiated as well as more integrated with other channels. And, the user flows, on top of selections from and navigation between channels, include interactivity within the various channels in question. Even more important, digital networks, along with mobile terminals, enable distributed contexts of communication and action that were precluded in broadcasting and other mass communication: interactions with other users about the information on offer in and through a range of channels, and coordinated actions on the basis of such information in dispersed physical settings, integrating face-to-face communication, as well.

In order to examine the flows of communication across media of all three degrees◄ – humans, mass media, and network media – and across geographical and social contexts, one may first distinguish three constitutive types of flow:

- *Information flows*. Like a broadcast channel, any internet site can be understood as a flow

► the flows of broadcasting – Chapter 9, p. 184

► media of three degrees – Chapter 1, p. 5

of information, broadly speaking, including fictional narratives and entertainment genres. Like broadcast news and series, internet content draws on both real-life and literary sources, and gives rise to all manner of dialogues, online as well as offline. Unlike previous media, digital networks integrate one-to-one, one-to-many, and many-to-many flows of information – technologically, discursively, and institutionally – into diverse contexts of interaction.

- *User flows*. Users flow across all available and accessible media types; other users serve as embodied media. The internet, at once, enables one-to-one, one-to-many, and many-to-many interactions; it also supports users flowing across all of these in one session, or a later point in time, perhaps with reference to records of earlier sessions. In addition, mobile technologies allow users to flow across several different physical contexts of communication. Digital media use, further, anticipates the use of print and broadcast media, in addition to ordinary conversation.
- *Context flows*. Mobile media studies have drawn attention to the importance of contextual mobility (Kakihara and Sørensen, 2002). What is mobile in mobile communication is not so much the information, the user, or the technology, but the context in which they come together in communication. In mobile communication, entire configurations of social relations – present and absent – move about. One example, commonly cited in the literature (Jenkins, 2006; Rheingold, 2002), has been the use of mobile telephones to organize social protests in various national settings: text messages make real people take to the streets to communicate among themselves and to the powers that be, while continuing the conversation with absent friends via mobile media.

Gone is the relative simplicity of a delimited set of broadcast channels from which individuals or households would pick and choose and, more generally, of a relatively few mass media feeding information into interpersonal interaction. It is this multitude of flows that constitute one of the central challenges for media and communication research in the early twenty-first century, as media proliferate and communicative practices crisscross media of the first, second, and third degrees.

THREE-STEP FLOW

Media and communication research developed as a field of study from the mid-twentieth century in response to an infrastructural demand for more knowledge about the social uses and consequences of print and broadcast media.◄ One early finding was that, contrary to widespread contemporary assumptions, these media had rather limited direct effects on the attitudes and behaviors of the general public – instead, media appeared to work in a two-step flow,◄ affecting a relatively few so-called opinion leaders who, in turn, would influence their immediate social relations through conversation and other interpersonal communication (Katz and Lazarsfeld, 1955; Lazarsfeld, *et al.*, 1944). While debated (Gitlin, 1978), the two-step model contributed significantly to a more nuanced understanding of mass communication as a multistep process with multilevel effects.

Perhaps surprisingly, given the prominence of this model in the literature, research has experienced a clear disconnect between 'mass' and 'interpersonal' communication studies. If communication moves in two steps, the field has taken one step at a time, in two different directions. As evidenced in bibliometric research, in practice it has amounted to "two subdisciplines of communication study" (Rogers, 1999). This is in addition to other theoretical and ideological divisions between social-scientific, interpretive, and critical scholarship (Fink and Gantz, 1996). While these latter divisions may be inevitable and, indeed, a source of dynamism, the former great divide between mass and interpersonal communication has been and remains counterproductive, particularly at the present moment of media history. Many-to-many communication

► media research as a social institution – Chapter 19, p. 355

► two-step flow – Chapter 8, p. 174

	Media types		
Communicative practices	**Media of the first degree**	**Media of the second degree**	**Media of the third degree**
One-to-one	PROTOTYPE Face-to-face conversation, hand-written letter	Telegraph, telephone, fax	Email, text message, instant messaging, IP telephony
One-to-many	Manuscript, theater, painting, sculpture, architecture, musical composition	PROTOTYPE Book, newspaper, magazine, broadcasting, audio and video recording	Web 1.0 / webpage, download, streaming (mass) media
Many-to-many	Cave painting, gaming, graffiti, notice board, agora, marketplace, stadium	Community media, public-access radio and television, telephone chat services	PROTOTYPE Web 2.0 / wiki, file sharing site, online chat, massively multiplayer online gaming, social network site, blog, auction site

Figure 10.1 Communicative practices across media types

in internet communities, social network sites, mobile messaging, and other formats yet to be imagined and invented, have been added to the classic two-step model that coupled one-to-one and one-to-many communication. A third variant of networked communication, and three-step flows, has become constitutive of the contemporary media environment (Jensen, 2009, 2010).

In order to examine the ongoing reconfiguration of media and communication, it is helpful to start from the communication: how are not just earlier media and genres, but also common practices of communication being remediated (Bolter and Grusin, 1999) – in the face of technological, discursive, as well as institutional processes of change? Figure 10.1 lays out and exemplifies key communicative practices in relation to media of the first, second, and third degrees (see further Jensen and Helles, 2011). Along its vertical dimension, the figure distinguishes between communicative practices according to the number of participants. In essence, how many get to say something to how many others? Whereas each kind of communicative practice is instantiated in both network and mass media as well as in face-to-face interaction, each kind also has a prototype, associated with a specific set of material or technological affordances and institutional frameworks. Along the horizontal dimension, the figure distinguishes between media of the first, second, and third degrees. Figure 10.1 summarizes the contemporary media environment in terms of its intermediality (Jensen, 2008a), highlighting the interrelations between different media types and the communicative practices that they variously enable.

remediation

intermediality

Here, it is the framework of communicative prototypes, and the flows of communication across different media forms, which are of particular interest. First of all, it should be emphasized that, in three-step (and two-step) flows of communication, the steps typically are not equivalent. The two-step flow (Lazarsfeld, *et al.*, 1944) comprised not just steps, but *types* of communication. News announcers and political commentators of the 1940s addressing their listeners was one type of communicative event; listeners, whether opinion leaders or not, conversing locally with one or a few other people about their preferred presidential candidate, were quite a different type. Equally, there is a categorical difference between, on the one hand, A telling something to B in the street, who later talks about it with C at home or at work and, on the other hand, A listening to a radio newscast and, next, engaging in a multiparty and multistep online interaction with B and C (and perhaps others) about it. Not all communicative steps are created equal.

It seems especially important to underscore this point, because much research and public debate has held out the potentials of many-to-many communication as a new source of public participation in social life across political, economic, and cultural domains. Before drawing conclusions for or against such potentials and practices, it is important to clarify the nature of the various communicative steps and flows; these, further, lend themselves to empirical studies, in part, according to those theoretical and methodological principles that have been developed so far for 'mass' and 'interpersonal' communication. To illustrate, research has examined the hypothesis that network media and many-to-many communication might promote both more diverse political information and more informed political debate via news and discussion sites. A growing number of studies suggest that, on both counts, new media do not change old communicative practices radically: traditional media still predominate as information providers and agenda-setters (Himelboim, 2010; Meraz, 2009), and blogs may not promote dialogue between citizens (Kenix, 2009). Dialogue "may simply be two people taking turns broadcasting at each other" (Peters, 1999: 264).

At the same time, theory development about new genres and media has begun to address what I conceptualize here as a three-step flow, reconsidering the flows of interpersonal, mass, and networked communication with reference to classic issues of the diffusion of information in society,◄ political agenda-setting,◄ as well as two-step flows (Brosius and Weimann, 1996; Himelboim, *et al.*, 2009; Vu and Gehrau, 2010). Over time, these flows of communication serve to produce and maintain society and culture. Contexts can be understood as the concrete sites – at once material and discursive – in which users and information intersect and interact. If users and information are the nodes of communication, the contexts that they constitute are the nodes of more expansive networks of social interactions and institutions.

FLOWS AND NETWORKS

The network terminology has been widespread in recent theories of communication and society. The most influential formulation has been offered by Manuel Castells (1996, 2009), who diagnosed an epochal network society – a world-historical transition from industrial capitalism to informational capitalism. While subject to debate (Webster and Dimitriou, 2004), Castells' framework helped to foreground a shift *from information as a resource*, not least in material production and administration ('the information society' (Bell, 1973; Porat, 1977)), *to communication as a process* across all sectors of society. Three key notions suggest the implications of the general argument for communication research: spaces of flows, timeless time, and a culture of real virtuality. Dispersed physical spaces of social interaction are linked in real time; local times are subordinated to global flows of exchange; and our sense of reality includes both present and absent individuals and settings. The point is not that we enter 'virtual realities' in exceptional instances of media use, but that a substantial portion of all social interaction is technologically mediated – which does not make it any less real and consequential.

the network society

spaces of flows, timeless time, a culture of real virtuality

Also as a methodological category, networks have been gaining ground, in part, as a response to the coming of digital networks as central objects of study and, simultaneously, as tools of analyzing such networks. Whereas

► diffusion of innovations – Chapter 8, p. 155
► agenda-setting – Chapter 8, p. 161

social network analysis

the tradition of social network analysis (SNA) has predominantly employed quantitative metrics (Wasserman and Faust, 1994), emerging qualitative approaches (Hollstein and Straus, 2006) are providing a necessary complement. Networks comprise both global measurable structures and local nodes and links with contextual meanings. Not surprisingly, network analysis has proven applicable in previous communication studies (Monge and Contractor, 2003). Communication is an inherently relational phenomenon: information represents states of affairs; users access information via diverse media; and users interact with information, and with each other, in contexts – which themselves may be interrelated.

Network analysis is characterized by its focus on relations, rather than entities. The central units of analysis are the relational ties between social actors (or the nodes in other kinds of systems – from ant colonies to financial markets), not their attributes as entities. Parents and children, buyers and sellers, elected officials and electorates – all can be defined by their interrelations. Relational ties can be understood as channels or vehicles for the flow of resources, which may be either material or immaterial (Wasserman and Faust, 1994: 4). Parents provide food and emotional care to their children; buyers and sellers relate via goods as well as contracts; votes generate both symbolic positions and material benefits to the successful candidates for office.

relational ties

Communication is a special, self-reflective type of relational tie: it represents the human capacity to consider how things, including all other types of social ties, might be different. Communication is a source of doubt and delay before individuals, groups, and entire societies do things that might have irreversible consequences. In most cases, communication is a constituent of other social interaction; in some cases, communication is a dedicated activity of deliberating on the ends and means of social coexistence. The nature and import of such deliberation, of course, depends on the historically and culturally available media technologies and institutions, which facilitate different kinds and numbers of communicative steps. Modern societies have developed media as distinctive public institutions-to-think-with.◀

communication: the human capacity to consider how things might be different

The common terminology of 'contexts' suggests that no text is an island – that texts are typically interrelated, but also that social settings can be understood as con-texts: meaningful configurations of human interaction, whether collaboration or conflict. While networked communication has directed renewed attention to the importance of context, research on the relationship between text and context, and between media and their social uses in communication, has a long history.

CONTEXTS AND INTERTEXTUALITY

Is there a text in this network?

In a famous book title, the literary theorist, Stanley Fish (1979), quoting a student, asked, *Is There a Text in This Class?* His provocative and influential suggestion was that texts – meaningful discourses – are not found in classrooms, libraries, media, or any other location. Instead, texts have a virtual existence in the minds of their readers and in readers' dealings with each other as interpretive communities.◀ Moreover, the meanings of texts as well as their boundaries – what is (not) part of a given text – will remain open to interpretation by additional readers and other interpretive communities.

Fish's suggestion was provocative because it sought to deconstruct the traditional conception of texts within the humanities as delimited objects of immanent analysis, interpretation, and introspection, typically regarding unique artworks with an aura◀ transcending historical time (Benjamin, 1977[1936]). His suggestion also proved influential, in part, because it extended and radicalized the redefinition of texts, meaning, and information as relational structures that had been gaining currency in twentieth-century semiotics and cybernetics. Readers and other communicators have a stake in, and could be considered a part of, the text, along with its explicit or implicit

▶ institutions-to-think-with – Chapter 1, p. 16
▶ interpretive communities, Chapter 9, p. 183
▶ aura, Chapter 1, p. 7

cross-references to other texts. All the while, a broader understanding of 'texts' as any vehicle of meaning, including images, conversations, and everyday artifacts, became the norm in twentieth-century scholarship on communication and culture.◀

The term 'text,' whose Latin root means to weave a fabric or an account, highlights the process in which a content of ideas is given form: it is in-formed. To be sure, the classical traditions of rhetoric◀ and hermeneutics◀ had approached texts as composite structures of meaning in layers, webs, and circles. What theories of intertextuality came to insist on was the transience of texts – in contrast to any transcendent content or form. Neither a literary work nor any other message could be considered a site of essential or stable meaning. Texts make sense, not in themselves, but in relation to other texts. The seminal contribution had come from the Russian literary scholar Mikhail Bakhtin and his circle in the early decades of the twentieth century (Bakhtin, 1981). His most basic concept concerning the relationship between different literary works – dialogism – was translated as intertextuality by Julia Kristeva (1984[1974]). Among other things, she reemphasized the structural point of semiotics◀ that signs are defined in relation to other signs. By extension, texts acquire their meaning as part of a network of texts, past as well as present. Texts are momentary manifestations of a general textuality; texts selectively articulate a cultural heritage. A culture could be understood as the most complex instance of intertextuality.

intertextuality

This line of argument, on the one hand, suggests that all texts – all human acts of communication – are created equal, at least as a working hypothesis. The task of research, accordingly, would be to establish how specific texts with particular origins and trajectories feed into cultural patterns and social structures. On the other hand, ironically, the bulk of intertextual studies have looked for interrelations among a small and select category of texts. Through formal and thematic readings of literature, visual arts, film, and television, research has identified a wide variety of explicit and, more commonly, implicit references to other texts, for instance, metatextual relations hinting at the historical origins of key cultural symbols, or paratextual relations between a novel and its cover text (Genette, 1997[1982]). It is particularly striking that intertextual studies mostly have given no empirical attention to readers or audiences. Presumably, they are the interpretive agents who establish the links between the nodes of textual networks.

The shift of analytical focus from delimited texts toward textual or discursive practices – and from media to communication◀ – has been a long time coming. In part, it has been the response of academia to a changing media environment. As long as the legitimate objects of analysis remained a comparatively few canonical or prototypical works summing up and disseminating cultural tradition, it might seem natural to study intertextuality with reference to such texts only. With mass media, certainly on the scale witnessed in the industrialized world over the course of the twentieth century, that approach became increasingly untenable. Mass-mediated texts are the products of a meticulously planned, systemic kind of intertextuality; mass media anticipate their audiences as more or less willing partners in intertextuality across time, media, and genres. By the 1980s, humanistic studies of media as texts had also come to devote more explicit attention to audiences in qualitative reception studies.◀

From primary texts to hypertexts

In an important contribution, John Fiske (1987) distinguished two aspects of intertextuality: horizontal and vertical. The horizontal dimension refers to the traditional understanding of intertextuality in literary studies as a transfer of meanings across historical time – over decades and centuries – as preserved in the

horizontal and vertical intertextuality

▶ 'text' – Chapter 2, p. 36; Chapter 7, p. 131
▶ rhetoric – Chapter 2, p. 27
▶ hermeneutics – Chapter 2, p. 28
▶ semiotics, Chapter 2, p. 31
▶ communication and/vs. media, Chapter 1, p. 8
▶ reception studies – Chapter 9

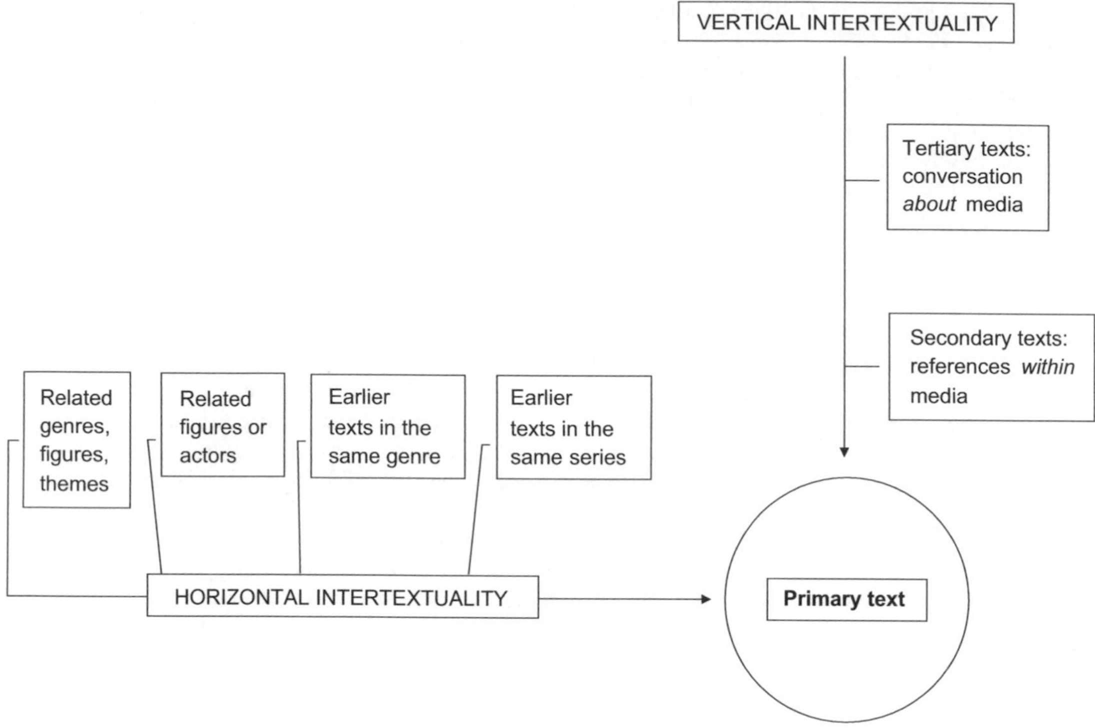

Figure 10.2 Horizontal and vertical intertextuality

metaphors, characters, and styles of both fine arts and popular media. Vertical intertextuality, in comparison, focuses attention on the media system that circulates themes, issues, and agendas in a shorter time frame – from minutes to months. Importantly, the vertical dimension includes audience members as media in their own right, who may respond to or debate both the contents and the forms of mass media texts among themselves.◀

To specify the processes circulating meaning in society, Fiske identified three categories of texts. Primary texts are carriers of significant information or insight in their own right – not necessarily aesthetic masterpieces or trend-setting media products, but privileged texts, nevertheless. To exemplify, if the primary text is a new feature movie, the secondary texts will consist of studio publicity, reviews, and other criticism. The tertiary texts are audiences' conversations and other communications about the movie – before, during, and after a visit to the cinema. Figure 10.2 lays out the two axes of intertextuality.

primary, secondary, and tertiary texts

Research has explored the trajectories of texts across media, audience groups, and time periods. Studies have examined, for instance, James Bond (Bennett and Woollacott, 1987) and the Batman (Pearson and Uricchio, 1990) as cultural icons that have provided sounding boards for political as well as existential reflections. Methodologically, the process of intertextual meaning production has been examined through, for instance, oral history◀ interviews and analyses of the creations of fan cultures (L. Lewis, 1991). In the case of television, as noted, viewers can be seen to shape their own intertextual sequences by selecting and combining (parts of) programs, preannouncements, and commercial breaks from multiple channels in

▶ humans as media, Chapter 1, p. 5

▶ oral history – Chapter 14, p. 272

the flow of any given viewing session (Jensen, 1994). However, as suggested by the terminology of primary, secondary, and tertiary texts (Fiske, 1987), research on mass-mediated intertextuality has tended to still approach the entire process of communication from the perspective of texts, as if meaning flowed from a relatively few mass media, perhaps via other media and texts, and on to audiences.

Digital media, from the outset, invited research on the distributed processes in which users interact both with texts and with each other through texts (Aarseth, 1997; Bolter, 1991). With digital technologies, intertextuality became an explicit and operational set of structures – hypertextuality – typified by the familiar hyperlinks that connect various computer-mediated texts and applications. Links make explicit, retrievable, and modifiable what might have remained a more or less random association in the mind of either sender or receiver. Full-fledged hypertexts can be organized and marked up both for creative purposes of interactive story-telling and for instrumental purposes of indexing, searching, and combining items of information (Nelson, 1965). Like other 'texts,' hypermedia mix visual, auditory, and alphabetic modalities of communication. A click on a news headline activates a video clip; a click on a photograph brings up a text box or a spoken commentary.

hypertextuality

hypermedia

The world wide web is the most massive example, so far, of a multimodal hypertext, appropriately named to suggest the weaving of texts in a worldwide network. While some commentators, returning to avant-gardist positions, have claimed that hypertextual representations of social reality would tend to be aesthetically innovative and socially transgressive (e.g., Landow, 1997), the more pertinent research question is how, in practice, users approach and apply this wealth of texts and their constitutive elements. In addition to their browsers and graphic user interfaces, web users depend on a distinctive kind of intertextual resource – search engines – that identify, relate, and rank texts. Search engines bring home the point that texts are much more than representations of, or items of information about, the world; the web is a point of access to diverse communicative functionalities (Herring, 2004: 30) – a resource for political mobilization, distributed production, and cultural involvement. As far as millions of daily searchers are concerned, there are texts in the network. The question is which texts will be considered primary, in which contexts, and for what purposes. The answer depends not only on users' search terms, but also on the organization of search engines, and on the intertexts, metadata, and algorithms that link service providers with searchers, and searchers with each other.

the world wide web

search engines

ANALYSIS BOX 10.1: SEARCH ENGINES AS COMMUNICATION AND META-COMMUNICATION

To be precise, what is mostly referred to as 'search engines' are web search engines (for overview, see Halavais, 2009; Hargittai, 2007). Search engines include a variety of digital retrieval systems that facilitate access to information also in stand-alone databases and on personal computers; an example of this last type is the Spotlight feature of Apple's MAC OS X operating system, which identifies search terms in different file types, so that I may trace, for instance, my own writings on search engines, the sources that I relied on, and the advice that I received from colleagues by email.

Beyond household names such as Google, Yahoo!, and MSN, there exists a great variety of web search engines. First, they are differentiated by language (including national or regional variants of the 'same' service). In the People's Republic of China, the most popular search engine is Baidu (www.baidu.com, accessed April 15, 2011), which is also a major global player, ranking third in share of searches after Google and Yahoo! in December 2007 (Comscore, 2008). In Europe, the practical as well as symbolic implications of search was suggested by the French-German Quaero initiative to develop a "European" search engine with multilingual (and multimedia) functionalities (Quaero, n.d.; Machill, *et al.*, 2008: 599). Second, there is a wealth of specialized search engines that address different areas of social activity. In the case of Refugees United, search acquires an existential meaning: this particular search engine seeks to "reconnect refugees with their families, no matter where in the world" (www.refunite.org, accessed April 15, 2011).

climate change

Web search engines provide prestructured access to information for living. A few basic searches regarding climate change suggest some general implications of searching as an intertextual process (www.google.com, accessed February 21, 2008). For the text string "climate change," the Top 20 results, which searchers will typically give a certain weight, included, first, official sites of national and international entities, such as United Nations agencies, and, second, 'green' or environmentally concerned voices. In comparison, the Top 20 for the string "global warming" produced a mixture of 'green' and 'skeptical' positions, including organizations arguing against the reality of global warming, or advocating different cost-benefit strategies from, for instance, internationally coordinated limits on carbon dioxide emissions. Also in the case of internet domain names, naming implies at least attempts at framing: www.globalwarming.net represents a 'green' position, featuring an Extreme Event Index, while www.globalwarming.org advances a 'skeptical' position under the motto, "reasoned thinking comes from cooler heads" (accessed February 21, 2008).

Search and ye shall find, depending on your search terms. Results, however, also depend on the structure of search engines and on the skills of searchers. As noted by an early contribution to the still limited research on web search engines, search algorithms normally remain proprietary information, so that the premises of any given search are difficult to assess (Introna and Nissenbaum, 2000). Also the media literacy◄ of users is in question. One study concluded that "users have only the basic skills required to use search engines; this is exacerbated by search engines' lack of transparency" (Machill, *et al.*, 2004: 321). In one respect, search engines open up the web. In another respect, searches close in on and around particular items of information and communicative relations. Like communication, searching ends.◄ Closure is facilitated by metadata – data about data.

metadata

Metadata, briefly, concern the origins, characteristics, and trajectories of any given piece of information, understood as data (see, for instance, the international Dublin Core initiative (Dublin Core, n.d.)). While referring, in principle, to any kind of data, in any medium – for the present book: its title, author, date, publisher (and company webpage), ISBN number, contents, index, etc. – metadata are key to digital communication systems. The data in question document which items of information are available, which ones are accessed, by whom, at what time, in which formats and, perhaps, in which combinations, sequences, and contexts of use. ('Image searches,' incidentally, are still performed on linguistic and other associated metadata, rather than on visual data as such.) Crucially, metadata are documented in and of the operation of search engines (and other digital systems), and they are fed back into the system. The search strings that users enter are stored by search engine providers, and are used to generate one more layer of metadata on online content. Also on the web, you cannot *not* communicate◄ (Watzlawick, *et al.*, 1967: 49); my search anticipates your search, and vice versa.

Whereas metadata are commonly associated with technical and legal aspects of centralized system maintenance, copyright administration, security clearance, etc., the senders or providers of both data and metadata include, in principle, anyone in a networked communication system:

► media literacy, Chapter 19, p. 363
► the end of communication, Chapter 19, p. 369
► humans cannot *not* communicate – Chapter 1, p. 13

search engine optimization

companies that specialize in 'search engine optimization,' tweaking the system to deliver favorable results for their clients, as well as ordinary users who add so-called 'folksonomic' (as opposed to taxonomic or expert) tags to content and share them via dedicated websites such as Delicious (www.delicious.com, accessed April 15, 2011). Clearly, the capacity of different types of users to send, receive, and apply metadata for their own purposes depends on their technological and economic resources. The potentials of search, further, depend on the political and legal frameworks that regulate the coding of communication at the national and international levels. As summed up by Larry Lessig (2006), in a digital communication infrastructure, code is law.

folksonomy

code is law

Also in other media, code – conventionalized and institutionalized uses of discourse – is law in specific ways. Metadata have functional ancestors in media of the first and second degrees that hold important implications for media of the third degree. We constantly communicate about whether and how we would like to communicate with each other. We cannot *not* meta-communicate.

we cannot not meta-communicate

META-COMMUNICATION IN THREE DEGREES

The first degree

meta-communication

The key formulations regarding meta-communication came from Gregory Bateson, who was examining contexts of face-to-face interaction. Departing from work in anthropology, psychiatry, and cybernetics, he suggested that "human verbal communication can operate and always does operate at many contrasting levels of abstraction" (Bateson, 1972[1955]: 150), above and beyond the exchange of literal information. Taking a standard example from logic – 'the cat is on the mat' – Bateson noted that this proposition carries a denotation◀ that refers to an actual state of affairs: the position of a furry four-legged organism in space (on a mat that we can point to) and time (is, not was). Apart from such denotations, people introduce, first, meta-linguistic information into their interactions, for example, to clarify that they may mean the word 'cat' to include tigers. Second, Bateson noted, they also meta-communicate about their relationship as communicators, "e.g., 'My telling you where to find the cat [tiger] was friendly,' or 'This is play.'" Not only does communication thus operate at several levels at once; "the vast majority of both metalinguistic and metacommunicative messages remain implicit" (p. 151) and must be inferred from their 'context' – in a discursive, material, or social sense. In another publication, Bateson added that "a majority of propositions about codification are also implicit or explicit propositions about relationship and vice versa" (Ruesch and Bateson, 1987[1951]: 209). The meaning of what we say to each other implies the meaning of our relationship.

▶ denotation – Chapter 2, p. 34

Because communication operates at several levels at once, it is ripe with potential conflicts regarding what people are actually saying to each other and, not least, why. Bateson (1972[1956]: 173–198) showed how schizophrenic disorders can be understood in communicative terms as the outcome of a 'double binds' in which a person is unable to resolve several conflicting levels of communication. Of course, most people, most of the time, are remarkably good at mastering such communicative complexity. We recognize that 'this is information' (a signal of something else), and that 'this is *this* kind of information' (a message in a specific modality and code, with a particular reference to reality, and a likely relevance for us in context). We establish and adjust our communicative relationships, relying on conventional forms of expression, turn-taking, and role-playing. In doing so, we establish contexts that are both psychologically and socially real, what Bateson described as frames (Bateson, 1972[1955]: 157). The concept was developed further by

double binds

Erving Goffman (1974) to suggest how frames are continuously observed or broken, modified and replaced, in social interaction. Media studies have later used the concept of frames to explain how audiences make sense of texts with reference to other texts and to their contexts of use.◀

Like Goffman, Bateson remained focused on embodied interactions in local contexts. However, his two aspects of meta-communication – codification and communicative relationships – are constitutive of mass and network communication, as well. Technologies and meta-technologies◀ transport texts across contexts, and frames across social settings.

codification and communicative relationships

The second degree

Mass media address their audiences at a distance: hail, fellow, well met! (Hartley, 1982: 87). To establish a communicative relationship among absent partners – a contract of sorts – they depend on genres:◀ discursive conventions of expressing and experiencing a particular subject matter. The concept comes with a long history since Aristotle's *Rhetoric*; it has lent itself to spoken, written, print, and electronic forms of communication; and it has remained a central analytical category within literature, aesthetics, and other humanities. Recent research has witnessed a revived interest in genre across the humanities and social sciences, simultaneously as a discursive and a social phenomenon (Bawarshi, 2000; Miller, 1984, 1994; Yates and Orlikowski, 1992). Genres include not just epic, dramatic, and lyrical formats, but job interviews and online dating, as well. Genres constitute frames of interpretation and interaction, including scripts for social action at a later point in time, beyond the moment of communicative exchange.

One of the founders of British cultural studies, Raymond Williams (1977), usefully identified three aspects of any given genre:

- characteristic subject matter (e.g., the 'public' content of news, the 'private' content of fiction);
- formal composition (e.g., narrative or didactic forms of expression in texts, still or moving images); and
- mode of address (e.g., the anticipated relevance of an advertisement or a public-service announcement for an audience).

Genres are discursive forms with social functions. They signal the nature of what is being communicated and the kinds of social relationships that are being maintained – the two aspects of Bateson's conception of meta-communication. Unlike both the classic transmission and ritual models of communication◀ – but like linguistics and semiotics – Bateson and cybernetics helped to bring the micro-mechanics of communication to the fore. Complementing cybernetics, linguistics and semiotics has contributed additional models that help to describe, in more fine-grained detail, how meta-communication works at the level of discourse and genre.

The classic example of a linguistic-semiotic model of communication was presented by the linguist and literary critic, Roman Jakobson (1960). Compared to the two aspects of meta-communication that Bateson noted – codification and communicative relationships – Jakobson identified an entire set of communicative functions. His model of the constituents of any communicative exchange and the corresponding functions are laid out in Figure 10.3. The implication of the model was that all discourses bear traces of all these constituents of communication – sender, message, and receiver; channel, code, and context – to varying degrees and in shifting configurations. Addressing a classic question in poetics – is there a special poetic language? – Jakobson concluded that there is, instead, a poetic *function* of language, and that this function is manifest in many other genres, for instance, advertising. Poets, while inviting people to ponder what might be the 'message' of their poems (poetic function), also address

▶ frames – Chapter 8, p. 164

▶ technologies and meta-technologies – Chapter 1, p. 6

▶ genres – see also Chapter 7, p. 147

▶ transmission and ritual models of communication, Chapter 1, p. 12

Constituents		
	Context	
Addresser	Message	Addressee
	Contact	
	Code	

Functions		
	Referential	
Emotive	Poetic	Conative
	Phatic	
	Metalingual	

Figure 10.3 Jakobson's (1960) model of communication

their readers (conative function) about some possible world◄ (referential function). Web advertising, in its turn, relies liberally on the poetic function in order to address internet users about the merits of specific commodities that will be sold and consumed in the real world.

In empirical terms, Jakobson (1960) stayed focused on discursive forms. While extrapolating to their communicative functions, his analysis explicitly bracketed the social origins and consequences of forms or functions: "the question of relations between the word and the world" (p. 19). Other humanistic scholars have been more adventurous, seeking to model the common experience that we all listen for tones of voice and choices of words to get the points that others are making – their codes and the communicative relationships that they afford us. Faced with media that communicate at a distance and in additional modalities, audiences read between the lines of texts and the frames of images. This was the insight of Roland Barthes' widely influential two-level model of meaning, departing from Louis Hjelmslev's (1963[1943]) linguistics, and comprising denotations and connotations.◄

► possible worlds, Chapter 1, p. 14

► denotation and connotation – Chapter 2, p. 34

In Bateson's terms, connotations can be understood as codifications – the meta-linguistic aspect of meta-communication. Connotations are codes that accumulate as representations, frames of interpretation, and views of the world. At the same time, codes inscribe communicators into social relations, as recognized by both Bateson and Barthes. Paralleling his model of connotations, Barthes had identified another model which begins to capture some of the distinctive communicative relationships that digital media establish and maintain.

The third degree

Roland Barthes' use of Louis Hjelmslev's original terms and formal concepts was, at best, debatable. Nevertheless, his appropriation of Hjelmslev's basic figure of thought became massively influential in analyses of contemporary culture and communication. Like other twentieth-century linguists, Hjelmslev approached languages as systems – systems of communication, but also second-order systems that either build on or describe such systems. Barthes' accomplishment was to apply this logic to communication as a practice and a process: connotation languages can be examined not only in the analytical rearview mirror, but as they are articulated and take effect. Barthes, further, included other modalities than spoken and written language into his analysis of the several levels of meaning production.

meta-languages

In Hjelmslev's definition, connotation languages and meta-languages have different, but complementary relations to their common reference point, which is first-order language – 'language' as commonly understood. Connotation languages, on the one hand, build on language, and are themselves languages or vehicles of communication, as exemplified by Barthes' myths. Meta-languages, on the other hand, describe language: they are not languages in themselves, but languages about languages, for instance, syntactical or semantic descriptions of the English language. Figure 10.4 lays out the principle of meta-languages. Compared to Barthes' first model (Figure 2.4), the figure inverses the interrelation between signifier and

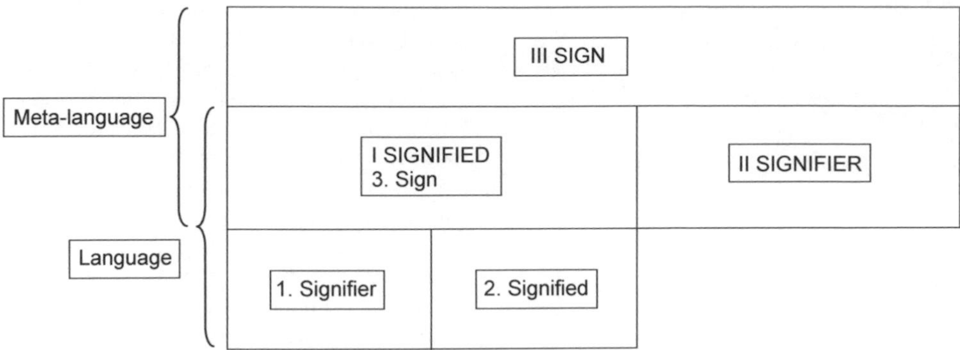

Figure 10.4 Language and meta-language (adapted from Barthes, 1973[1957])

signified at the second level. The connotations add to the codification of the content; the meta-constituents configure the social relationships that people enter into with reference to this content. A linguist, for one, takes the analyst's rather than the user's stance vis-à-vis language.

Hjelmslev had qualified his typology by making an antecedent distinction between scientific and non-scientific languages. Meta-languages would be scientific languages, defined by their formal operations (but presumably accessible, above all, by expert users of language, such as linguists). In some media and modalities, however, meta-languages are accessible to anyone. Here, I treat meta-languages, not merely as analytical systems, but as practices of communication, as well – meta-communication. Ordinary users of digital media effortlessly employ a wide variety of such meta-languages: they customize their own profile at a social network site; they tag the blog entries of others; they forward a news story to a friend from a website via an embedded email service; and they pull a later push of information to themselves through an RSS feed.

Digital media facilitate interactivity,◀ not only with information, or with other communicators about the denotations and connotations of the information at hand, but also with the interfaces and systems of communication. Users customize their own access points to the internet; they may also affect its infrastructure, to a degree, by participating, for instance, in open-source innovation (Benkler, 2006; Von Hippel, 2005). Whereas the potential uses and systemic consequences of meta-communication in the case of digital media are still being discovered, its scope and implications may be suggested by three examples.

First, web search engines◀ present a prototypical example of meta-communication: they codify information and enact communicative relationships. Depending on the coded structure of the available information, I gain access to it (or not) *as* information and as *this* kind of information with some contextual relevance. I further establish a communicative relationship, not necessarily with identifiable individuals or institutions, but with a distributed resource of communication. In and of my search, I both provide input to and reconfigure the search engine, however minimally. My meta-communication prefigures subsequent communications both by myself and by others, whether searching for more information or interacting about, and perhaps acting on, the outcome of our searches.

Second, also in other digital applications, users enter information into the system, more or less willingly and knowingly. Depending on technical and legal frameworks, such information remains available and accessible. The contents and forms of digital media, but also their uses and some of their contexts – the communication as well as the information

▶ interactivity, Chapter 1, p. 14

▶ search engines, p. 193

– lend themselves to data mining◀ (Han and Kamber, 2006). This is in contrast, of course, to most face-to-face interaction, which literally disappears into the air, but also to mass media use, which traditionally has been sampled and documented for dedicated purposes or research, development, and marketing. Most meta-communication in any medium moves below the communicators' radar of awareness. However, meta-communication in digital media is not necessarily or permanently lost. In digital media, a wealth of data and metadata are documented in and of their use. Citizens' and consumers' meta-communication is of obvious interest to big governmental brothers and little commercial sisters, who may treat it as information, communicate about it, and act on it.

Third, digital media transport both texts and contexts across space and time. By responding to the ring tones of mobile telephones and logging onto conference systems, users introduce additional communicative relationships into their current contexts. They do so in several modalities, sometimes as a matter of choice: with mobile phones that are equipped for video calls, users can decide whether or not to look at each other, or they may use the camera to relay images of their immediate surroundings, while conversing at a distance. Television introduced moving images (and sounds) of public events into the private sphere of the home (Meyrowitz, 1985); mobile media have recontextualized private conversations within public spaces (Humphreys, 2005), and have raised additional issues concerning the maintenance of close relationships across geographical distances (Merolla, 2010). A related issue is that of presence – in a physical as well as psychological respect – as examined by a growing body of research (Biocca, *et al.*, 2003). Media of the third degree are particularly rich sources of experienced co-presence and coordinated action at a distance.

presence

TEXTS, GENRES, AND MEDIA REVISITED

Because digital technologies serve to reconfigure the texts and contexts of communication, they present new challenges of how to define and delimit the 'messages' of communication as analytical objects. In studies of mass communication, it has been common to assume a triad of media, genres, and texts: media are technologies and institutions; genres are prototypical discursive formats; and texts are the concrete vehicles of expression and experience. If the digital computer and, by extension, the internet constitute meta-media◀ (Kay and Goldberg, 1999[1977]) – reproducing and recombining all previous media of representation and interaction – the question is how this condition is to affect established conceptual and analytical hierarchies. Where, for example, does the world wide web, or blogs, or social network sites fit into the equation? Whereas meta-communication is a constitutive function of any communicative practice in any medium, meta-media represent an ad hoc conceptualization that is still waiting to be clarified with reference to the full range of media discourses,◀ as outlined in Chapter 9.

It is commonly acknowledged that new media, in part, reproduce old media in a process of remediation.◀ To begin to specify this process, it is helpful to distinguish between media and genres which, respectively, have been 'born' or 'adopted' into new media. On the one hand, the internet has become a new home to most of the traditional mass media, as laid out in Figure 10.1: books, newspapers, broadcasting, etc. Within each of these media, also online, one encounters classic genres: dramatic, epic, lyrical, and didactic, along with the genre systems of fact and fiction inherited from print, cinema, radio, and television. On the other hand, the internet could be considered the parent of a growing variety of new media forms (Bruns, 2008a), including social network sites (Boyd and Ellison, 2007) and blogs (Larsson and Hrastinski, 2011; Rettberg, 2008), each with genre variants, such as, currently, Facebook or LinkedIn and personal, filter, or topic-driven blogs.

media – born and adopted

But, because the conceptual and analytical hierarchies of the field were developed, not least,

▶ data mining – Chapter 13, p. 262
▶ meta-media, Chapter 1, p. 8
▶ media discourses – Chapter 9, p. 184
▶ remediation – p. 188

for the study of analog (mass) media, further theory development is called for. Toward the media end of the media-genre-text hierarchy, the world wide web presents a special challenge. As indicated by Susan Herring (2004: 30), the web can be considered as a portal – it is a point of access to a whole range of communicative functionalities, through browsers, search engines, and graphic user interfaces. If the internet, as a meta-medium, integrates other media, the web incorporates other genres; it is perhaps a meta-genre (Jensen, in press-b). In Bateson's (1972) terms, the web represents a distinctive form of meta-communication, affording users not just one, but several different types of communicative relationships.

meta-genres

Toward the text end of the media-genre-text hierarchy, metadata and, in Hjelmslev's (1963[1943]) vocabulary, meta-languages present additional challenges. While much of this information has an infrastructural function, moving below the radar of human communication, it serves, again, as meta-communication facilitating communication. It establishes communicative relationships; in many instances, such as tagging and searching, it also contributes to the codification of the communication being shared.

'Going meta' may be considered a preliminary approach to reconsidering the constituents of communication in the case of digital media. As shown by John Durham Peters (1999) in his agenda-setting history of the idea, communication was only recognized as a general category of human activity with the rise of electronic communication media from the last half of the nineteenth century; the field of media and communication research only developed within the last fifty years,◀ initially focusing on the processes and effects of mass media. It will be a central task for future research to assess the analytical hierarchies of the field, so that it may continue to account for the place of media and communication in changing practices of cultural reflexivity and social structuration.

▶ the history of media and communication research – Chapter 19, p. 357

THE DUALITY OF COMMUNICATION

The duality of structure

The idea of a duality of structure, while specifically associated with the work of the sociologist Anthony Giddens (1984), sums up a common insight from more than a century of social sciences and cultural studies. Human agency is not the manifestation of an individual free will, nor is social structure a set of external constraints on individuals' actions. Instead, societies are structured by, and they simultaneously structure, the myriad interactions that individuals, groups, and institutions incessantly engage in. Subjects and social systems – agency and structure – are each other's enabling conditions. To exemplify, the press consists of its structural properties – its economic, legal, and technological permanence – *and* of the diverse distributed actions of journalists, advertisers, regulators, and audiences. Like other institutions in society, the press, and the media as such, are reenacted day by day.

agency and structure

Media and communication, surprisingly, have been comparative blind spots of social theory, including Giddens' summative framework (for discussion, see, e.g., Jensen, 1995; Silverstone, 1999; Thompson, 1995). This is in spite of the central distinction that Giddens, also, makes between social interactions that are technologically mediated and those that are not – what he terms system integration and social integration, respectively. Social integration refers to local, embodied, face-to-face interaction; system integration is "reciprocity between actors or collectivities across extended time-space, outside conditions of co-presence" (Giddens, 1984: 377) – which depends on media technologies. Equally, communication has remained a missing link of Giddens' (1979) double hermeneutics:◀ reinterpretations of society – by scholars and (other) social actors – occur and take effect in communication. As indicated in Chapter 1 (Figure 1.3), media are on a par with agency and structure for understanding culture and society. Communication mediates structure and agency.

communication mediates structure and agency

▶ double hermeneutics, Chapter 19, p. 351

Communication accumulates as culture that is remembered, archived, and disseminated, depending on the historically available media. Culture lends meaning both to the social structures emanating from the past and to the human actions shaping the future. Cultural norms and institutions serve to legitimate and prefer certain forms of agency and some social structures above others. Whereas the following Chapter 11 elaborates on the relationship between communication and culture, it is helpful, first, to note a distinctive duality of communication, as it constitutes and structures social life.

communication accumulates as culture

Time-in culture and time-out culture

Communication is both in and out of time – it oscillates between moments of reflection and moments of action. In the case of both expert and lay knowledge, high as well as low culture, communication reflects on structure and anticipates agency. Different media and genres enable different kinds of reflection and action.

As an illustration, consider the world of sports. In basketball and (American) football, coaches can call for a time-out – an interval – to discuss strategy with their teams. While temporarily suspending the game, the time-out occurs within and addresses the total time-in of the game. By analogy, media use and other cultural practices – visits to operas and museums, web surfing and television viewing at home, or music listening en route to either type of activity – establish a time-out. While suspending other activities, in whole or in part, the communication still takes place within the routines of everyday life and with reference to families, markets, parliaments, and other social institutions. As analytical categories, time-in and time-out culture suggests several dimensions along which communicative practices vary. The production of meaning may be more or less integrated into or separate from other activities in context; its form may be relatively innovative or routinized; its function may be experienced as comparatively ordinary or extraordinary; and the meanings being expressed and experienced may present themselves either as resources inviting, even requiring immediate action, or as accounts of past or future events. Time-out culture prefigures, time-in culture configures social interaction; the mediating element is communication.

communication prefigures and configures action

The duality of communication has taken many different shapes, depending on the affordances of the available media technologies and their social organization and regulation as institutions-to-think-with.◀ Historically, time-out and space-out have gone together in dedicated public arenas: theaters, museums, concert halls, Tivolis, and cinemas. Radio and television also began, in many settings, as one-set-per-household media in the dedicated space of a central room in the household. Digital media have shifted the lines of division and transition between time-in and time-out, space-in as well as space-out, by radically extending the accessibility of both information and other communicators, anytime and anywhere. In addition, digital media potentially accelerate the process of communicative turn-taking. This is true of the private coordination of family life, but also of the public negotiation across media and genres of, for example, political scandals (Thompson, 2000). Most important, digital media facilitate the immediate translation of communication into action at a distance, from the coordination of grocery shopping to the closing of million-dollar business deals.

action at a distance

TURNS AND TRANSITIONS

As vehicles of communication and meta-communication, media of the first, second, and third degrees share two basic features: communicators take turns, and they make transitions to action, whether of a consensual or conflictual nature. We navigate the material and modal interfaces of different media – books as well as mobile telephones – in order to gain access to information and to other communicators. To get your point, I listen to your speech sounds and watch your gestures. To update myself on national events, I turn the pages of my morning newspaper, and change the channels on my radio and television sets. To monitor the state of the world, in the public sphere and my own private sphere, I daily surf the web at regular

▶ institutions-to-think-with – Chapter 1, p. 16

intervals and exchange text messages with my partner. In my communication, I take turns with people as well as with (other) media. Navigating different media, we make ourselves accessible for communication, and gain access to other communicators and possible worlds.

The approach to communication as turn-taking◀ was developed by conversation and discourse analysis from the 1970s onwards (Sacks, *et al.*, 1974; Wetherell, *et al.*, 2001). While the focus in linguistics and discourse studies has been on the turns that speakers take in question-answer sequences and other interpersonal interactions, the concept applies more generally to communicative practices in other media. Newspaper articles, feature films, and websites all constitute turns, as do headline glancing, visits to the cinema, and responses to a quickpoll about the news of the day or a new film release. Turns feed more turns, whether in the same or different media. We return for an update of the news the next day, or go to compare a news item with another source on the same day; we look out for the next release by our favorite film director; and we engage in discussions about world events or Academy Award winners in the media at our disposal. One of the main things that people do with media is to communicate about them. They do so in turns, sequences, three- or multistep flows – within and across media.

In computer-mediated communication as in conversation, turn-taking depends on its purpose and context – what the turns are about, and why they are taken. Different genres involve different structures of turn-taking. In a classic stage drama, conversational turns are embedded in the players' action, while the audience, at least today, is expected to take long, silent turns of involvement and immersion. Historical research suggests that, before 1800, the convention was for audiences to give priority to speaking with others in the hall, rather than immersing themselves in an individualized, interior experience of the communication taking place on the stage (Johnson, 1995). Today, readers can decide to read literary classics in brief installments that are sent daily to their computer or mobile device (www.dailylit.com, accessed April 15, 2011). In an online computer game, the distributed players' sustained interactivity with each other, and with non-player characters, is a condition of possibility of the genre – interactivity is the name of the game. The individual players' turns, moreover, decide the completion of levels and, hence, their social identity and standing within the game. In modern urban living, brief mobile phone conversations at the end of a workday coordinate who shops for an evening meal, and who picks up the children from daycare, just as e-banking sessions during a lunch break or the free time of evening serve to pay the family's monthly bills.

In the larger scheme of things, the exchange of minimal items of information and the performance of rudimentary acts of communication produce, maintain, repair, and transform social institutions (Carey, 1989b[1975]: 23): families, banking, theater, popular entertainments, and other components of contemporary society. We cannot *not* take turns communicating; we also incessantly make the transition from communication to other social interaction. Communication both accomplishes and anticipates action. In and through communication, we establish contexts that are meaningful – cultural contexts at different levels of social organization – which are the focus of the next chapter.

we cannot *not* take turns communicating

communication accomplishes and anticipates action

▶ turn-taking – Chapter 6, p. 119

The cultural contexts of media and communication

Klaus Bruhn Jensen

- a presentation of the *concept of culture* as it relates to media and communication
- an overview of research concerning the cultural contexts of communication at various levels of social organization: *local, national, intercultural,* and *global*
- a review of studies addressing *subcultures, cultural imperialism,* and *postcolonialism*
- a discussion of different *research traditions* as being themselves *products of cultural contexts*

COMMUNICATION AS CULTURE

Communication as Culture (Carey, 1989a[1975]) is the title of an influential collection of articles by James W. Carey, who elaborated the ritual model of communication.◄ The title suggests that communication and culture are mutually constitutive: culture is articulated in communication, and communication invariably shapes and reshapes culture over time. If communication is the short-term activity, culture is the long-term outcome, both of which have depended on historically shifting media. Modern media have extended communication radically across space, time, and social collectives, enabling both global and local forms of culture.

This chapter reviews research on the three-way relationship of culture, communication, and media. Because this relationship raises questions that are, at once, theoretically fundamental and politically controversial, it has generated a wide variety of research approaches, frequently with opposite agendas. At stake are classic issues pertaining to identity and ideology: who am I, who are you, and how may we negotiate the terms of our coexistence? The answers to such questions have practical consequences: what we jointly imagine and, perhaps, agree on in communication is translated into political and economic ends and means, institutions and infrastructures.

The first section lays out some working definitions of culture, which is an example of so-called essentially contested concepts (Gallie, 1956). The implications of 'culture,' 'freedom,' or 'art' have remained intensely debated, even if most people will agree about their core meaning. Many of these debates relate to similarly controversial conceptions of communication and media. The rest of the chapter is structured according to different types and scales of cultural formations – from the local to the global level. At each level, it is generally helpful to approach culture as one layer or structure of reality that intersects with other material as well as immaterial layers and structures. Being humans, we observe and engage both nature and society from within culture.

essentially contested concepts

► the ritual model of communication – Chapter 1, p. 12

First of all, national cultures, while contested as analytical categories, remain a key reference point for the contents as well as the infrastructures of media around the world. Below the national level, subcultures variously constitute components of national cultures, transnational formations, and explicit challenges to both national and transnational conceptions of culture. Beyond the nation-state, research has advanced diverse notions of 'international,' 'transnational,' and 'intercultural' communication, seeking to specify what 'inter' and 'trans' might imply. Given the role of culture, frequently in the shape of religion, throughout centuries of conquest and warfare, it is not surprising that research traditions in the area have given special and critical attention to the influence of media on 'other' cultures, for good or ill, and to communication as an exercise of power. To paraphrase the military historian, Carl von Clausewitz (2006[1832]), who described war as the continuation of politics by different means, communication could be seen, in some instances, as the continuation of either politics or war by cultural means.

CULTURE AND CULTURES

The contested status of culture is reflected, in part, in the number of definitions that have been offered by scholars. In 1952, around the time when the field of media and communication research was taking shape, an interdisciplinary review already noted 164 definitions (Kroeber and Kluckhohn, 1952). (Similar issues arose in communication studies; Anderson (1996) identified 249 definitions or theories of communication.) For media and communication studies, however, three main themes can be identified: the difference between culture in the singular and cultures in the plural; the distinction between fine arts and popular entertainments; and the relationship between the production of culture as a process and the resulting cultural products.

164 definitions of culture

249 definitions of communication

First up is the question of having it or not having it: could any individual or group be said *not* to have (a) culture? Historically, the response has been an emphatic yes, as far as diverse peoples and regions of the world have been concerned, including classical Greece, where non-Greeks were labeled barbarians with reference to the *bar-bar* or babble that foreigners were heard speaking. A modern conception of culture dates from the Enlightenment and the Romantic Age, as elaborated in the work of Johann Gottfried von Herder (*Ideas for the Philosophy of History of Humanity*, 1784–91) (Forster, 2008). Culture is that which simultaneously unites and differentiates humans. On the one hand, all human beings share culture – the ability to experience, reproduce, reformulate, and communicate meaning. On the other hand, humans are distinguished by the specific meanings with which they align themselves – the cultural formations or communities to which they find that they belong or feel that they owe at least part of their identity and solidarity. It is this understanding that was formally codified in The Universal Declaration of Human Rights (1948), including the idea that everyone has "cultural rights indispensable for his dignity and the free development of his personality" (United Nations, 1948: Art. 22). Whereas cultures have frequently been equated with social groupings in geographical locations, information and communication technologies increasingly have unhinged culture and place. Alongside communities of place have developed communities of interest.◄

culture unites and differentiates all humans

A second question centers on the relationship between high and low culture – fine arts and popular entertainments. Also in this sense, some people have been, and still are, said by some others to have no culture, that is, being unable to access or appreciate especially fine arts. In a book entitled *After the Great Divide*, Andreas Huyssen (1986) noted that, with mass media, high and low cultural forms increasingly came to appear side by side, influencing and, to a degree, merging with one another. With digital media, this process has been intensified, as both authors and audiences may engage diverse cultural expressions on the same media platforms.

high and low culture

Nevertheless, it must be recognized that notions of 'high' and 'low' remain key to much research as well as public debate; they are grounded in two different conceptions of

► communities of place and/or interest – p. 209

culture – one aesthetic, the other anthropological. On the one hand, culture constitutes a world apart, typically in the shape of representations of reality in the works of high art. Despite the modern questioning of art as disinterested contemplation,◀ certain select ideas and representations might still be said to qualify, in the words of the cultural critic, Matthew Arnold, as "the best which has been thought and said in the world" (Arnold, 2003[1869]: n.p.). On the other hand, culture is part and parcel of the lowly world of practice. Pervading human consciousness and social interaction, it amounts to what a later cultural critic and theorist, Raymond Williams (1975[1958]: 18), called "a whole way of life." Culture is constitutive of all the ordinary things that humans say to and do with each other, our habits as well as our artifacts. It is this great divide that the field of media and communication research has inherited, struggled with, and variously sought to integrate.

culture as extraordinary realm

culture as ordinary practice

A third and final complication relates to the duality of culture.◀ Like communication, culture comprises finished products as well as open-ended processes.◀ Culture has been studied both as concrete 'containers' of meaning and as fleeting processes of mental and social life – in the latter sense, literally, the cultivation of the human spirit in either a secular or a religious sense (Williams, 1983). Overlapping, in part, with the aesthetic-anthropological distinction, and familiar from analog mass media, the product-process juncture has gained new prominence with digital media. For one thing, digital technologies facilitate the reproduction and reembedding of cultural products within one another – texts, sounds, and images – in distinctive ways. For another thing, digital technologies redraw the very boundary between product and process by facilitating the ripping, mixing, and burning of culture (Bowrey and Rimmer, 2002) – whether high or low – in acts of production, reception, and combinations thereof.

▶ modern fine arts – Chapter 2, p. 36

▶ time-in and time-out culture – Chapter 10, p. 201

▶ communication as process and product – Chapter 1, p. 11

To sum up, culture can be understood as communication, as enabled and accumulated by more or less durable media. Culture, in the singular, constitutes frames of interpretation that continuously orient social interaction between individuals and within communities. Cultures, in the plural, are formations with extension in physical space and across social systems. In a horizontal-geographical perspective, media serve to consolidate and maintain certain worldviews far beyond the here and now. In a vertical-institutional perspective, media provide resources for enforcing as well as challenging the social structures that be – instruments of both repression and rebellion. It is, not least, the relationship between moments of production and moments of reception that have generated theoretical interest and empirical studies: What is the relative importance of, for example, transnational economic conglomerates, regional aesthetic conventions, and national political regulation for the local uses and experiences of different media? And, if media remain the centers of communication, how broad and deep are their peripheries – the contexts in which the communications that they carry may form and transform culture?

NATIONS AS MODERN CULTURES

If asked, most individuals will agree that they belong together with many others in some larger entity, variously called a country, state, or nation. Whereas 'country' may be the most commonly used term, 'state' and 'nation' together suggest the ambiguous status of the entities in question. On the one hand, states are political entities with sovereign authority over a particular territory. On the other hand, nations are cultural entities with a common language and history. It is the interrelation or integration of the two in nation-states that have generated some of the most bloody conflicts and heated theoretical arguments in history. Geographical territories have political boundaries as well as cultural meanings, both of which can and will be contested. Regional and independence movements typically understand themselves as nations that have a right to become states. One contemporary symbol of the ambiguity is

nation-states

the United Nations

the United *Nations*, which only admits states, not nations, according to its charter (United Nations, 1945: Ch. 2).

Like the media that helped to shape them, nation-states must be understood with reference to the centuries-long process of modernization◄ that affected most areas of human activity (for an overview, see Thompson, 1995):

- *Economy: industrialization and capitalization* of the material economy, along with a growing division and rationalization of labor, leading into variable phases of market competition, incorporation, imperialism, and conglomeration;
- *Politics: democratization and bureaucratization* of the institutions and practices of political representation and government, including mass parties and electoral systems;
- *Culture: secularization* of the contents and forms of expression, including the securing of niches for non- or anti-religious communication, and the recognition of popular alternatives or complements to the fine arts.

Stretching from the eighteenth century into the twentieth, these interrelated developments depended, to a significant extent, on media as communicative infrastructures with national nodes and variable international links.

the economic world system

First, in the economic domain, a world system of capitalist production and trade had begun to take shape from the sixteenth century, centered in Western Europe and its conquests in other regions of the world. Whereas printed books, along with written accounting systems, contributed to the dissemination and application of available knowledge in material production, a key function of the early press was to provide both general economic news from other territories and local advertising for goods, for example, newly arrived cargoes. In contrast to previous such economic systems in the Middle East or China, this modern world-system did not grow into an empire in the classic sense (Wallerstein, 1974: 348). Instead, it promoted a global division of labor; it also allowed for the development of relatively separate political institutions at national as well as regional and local levels (see further Wallerstein, 1980, 1989).

► modernization – Chapter 3, p. 56

the Westphalian peace

Second, also as political units, nation-states were a long time coming. The starting point is commonly considered to be the Westphalian peace accords in 1648, which ended both a Thirty Years' War and an Eighty Years' War in Europe, and which established the principle of sovereign states with delimited territories. It was, however, during the nineteenth century that the spread of nationalism of various stripes contributed to a consolidation of nation-states as currently understood. In a particularly influential formulation, Benedict Anderson (1991) described nations as imagined communities: they constitute a community – an 'us' in a political and cultural sense – but they are imagined (though not imaginary or fictional) because each individual will never have face-to-face or other direct contact with the vast majority of other community members. It is through media and other public institutions – from newspapers and novels, to museums, maps, and the census – that communities are imagined, represented, and maintained over time.

imagined communities

culture as commodities

literacy

In this regard, a central feature of print media was that they promoted national languages, rather than the sacred languages of scripture or the administrative language of any current ruler. In addition to advancing national languages as the norm and stabilizing their form, print technologies served as means of nation-building and collective self-definition. Increasing numbers of people became audiences for arguments and narratives about the nation that they arguably shared. This society-wide communicative process was accelerated by concurrent economic and political changes: the coming of a mass market in which culture was one of the commodities. More people moved above the level of subsistence, and became able and willing to pay for technologically mediated experiences. At least in this regard, commercialization served democratization. At the same time, educational systems in different national settings contributed to the literacy required to take advantage of the cultural commodities on offer.

dual process of secularization

Third, national cultures developed in conjunction with a dual process of secularization.

Whereas religious culture is premised on an *eternal* order, national cultures understand themselves as *historical*, even as they seek long-lost origins and unbroken bonds with the past, as evidenced in Romantic and nationalist sentiments. (In practice, notions of the divine rights of a particular people, or of monarchs over their subjects, also persisted.) An additional process of secularization can be traced in the diffusion of popular culture through mass media. Compared to fine arts, which commonly have invoked *universal* standards, sometimes with reference to an international canon, popular-cultural practices rather constitute *contingent* approaches to insight and pleasure. Compared to the 'folk' culture that nationalist movements came to celebrate, not as fine or pure, but as authentic, popular culture embraced authentic and synthetic, national as well as international formats. In effect, national cultures, from the outset, were hybrids of folk, fine, and popular constituents, bearing witness to ongoing struggles over the definition of 'the nation' and its 'culture.' Media and communication studies have also rehearsed conflicting normative conceptions of culture, time and time again, from the 'mass culture' debates of the 1950s◄ (Rosenberg and White, 1957, 1971) – whether the newly central mass media would be the source of either enlightenment and education or escape and entertainment – to the 'culture wars' of the 1980s and 1990s (Hunter, 1991).◄

What modern cultures and their variants seemed to share, nevertheless, was an orientation to the future. In a secular and historical perspective on human endeavors, the future presented itself as an open field of action for individuals as well as social groups. It was not just that a different future could be envisioned; in the absence of an inherently meaningful cosmos, the future had to be made. This openness has been identified by much social theory as the distinctive experience of modernity (Berman, 1982; Giddens, 1991; Huyssen, 1986). That experience, in turn, has been described as the origin of much existential uncertainty and of an ambivalence concerning the appropriate ends and means of living one's life. In these circumstances, media became key institutions that would offer frames of interpretation and cultural resources for engaging the political and economic conditions of an uncertain existence, with the nation-state as its comparatively stable center.

Nation-states and their media systems, inevitably, have varied widely. A key reference point for research and debate has been Jürgen Habermas' (1989[1962]) account of the development, in the European setting, of a public sphere,◄ which was instrumental in defining and advancing ideas of both citizenship and nationhood from the eighteenth century. Debates have centered on the extent to which media and civil-society organizations have been able to secure a forum for deliberation despite pressures, to one side, from state agencies and, to the other side, from the market. In an influential analysis of the relationship between national media systems and political systems, Hallin and Mancini (2004) distinguished between three models that, though based on Europe and North America, have proven more broadly applicable: a 'liberal' market-based model (grounded in the US and the UK); a 'Democratic corporatist' or social democratic welfare model (prevalent in Northern Europe); and a 'polarized pluralist' model with a more antagonistic political system and a stronger state influence on media (characteristic of Southern Europe).

national media systems

One limitation of the three-model framework is that it tends to observe the world from a northwestern position. Several of the research traditions that are covered later in this chapter have advanced this criticism; it has also been a central issue in policy-oriented and normative theories of media.◄ Nevertheless, the polarized-pluralist, Southern-European model may be said, after the fall of communism, to capture some main characteristics of the 'new democracies' in Eastern Europe and the former Soviet Union (Jakubowicz, 2007). One consequence of this epochal transition may be a heightened awareness of submerged national and other cultural sentiments – which social science had largely failed to predict as forces behind 1989 and its aftermath (K. B. Jensen, 1999: 427).

Eastern Europe

► mass culture debates – Chapter 12, p. 222
► culture wars – Chapter 19, p. 369
► the public sphere – Chapter 1, p. 17
► normative theories – Chapter 19, p. 353

Another consequence has been studies seeking to document and recuperate, for example, the Baltic nations as cultural formations predating Soviet state and media supremacy (Høyer, *et al.*, 1993; Vihalemm, 2002).

The model in Hallin and Mancini (2004), further, has been extended to account for the rest of the world in terms of six different media systems (Blum, 2005). One current challenge is, indeed, how to model media systems in other regions of the world, notably the People's Republic of China (for an overview, see Zhao, 2008): what can appear, in a Western optic, as a puzzling blend of Party-state control and market forces may require significant rethinking of traditional categories of politics, economy, and culture in the context of Chinese history.

China

One way of summarizing the place of nation-states in relation to media is to refer to the ways in which communication flows to, from, and within a given nation-state.◄ With broadcasting (and, previously, the telegraph (Carey, 1989a[1975])), communication and transportation were decoupled: communication no longer required the physical movement or either people or printed materials, but could flow across and between territories. Still, radio and television developed in the framework of the nation-state and contributed centrally to the construction and maintenance of national cultures during the twentieth century. Here, the official life of the nation was represented in public. Broadcast schedules also support the rhythms of social life, from the twenty-four hour cycle of the family to the seasonal ceremonies of the nation, sometimes understood as a 'family' (Scannell, 1988). A case in point is sports (Boyle, 2006; Coakley, 2000) – a ritualized form of international combat that has remained anchored in the nation-state and an essential component of national schedules and seasons. International sports lend themselves both to local, on-site participation and to vicarious, technologically mediated forms of experience.

sports

With satellite and cable distribution from the 1980s, and the internet from the 1990s, the flows became more flexible. As far as media users are concerned, however, they have remained predominantly national receivers of the content of national senders in their own language. Figure 11.1 lays out three types of flows through which communication reaches audiences in their national contexts:

- *National flow*. The reference is to foreign or imported (over and above home-produced) content that is adapted by distributors to the tastes and cultural backgrounds of a national market. Importantly, such adaptation includes not merely translation, but the 'domestication' of news items through national angles (Cohen, *et al.*, 1996) and the redevelopment of formats for fiction series and other entertainments (e.g., O'Donnell, 1999; Silj, 1988). In this respect, national media, from early newspapers and popular literature onwards, have always been transnational;
- *Bilateral flow*. The classic example of communication flow between two national territories is the direct, regular, and 'accidental' transmission by television (and radio) stations to audiences in a neighboring country. In a wider sense, print media are exported and imported between culturally affiliated countries, and accessed by migrants and tourists;
- *Multilateral flow*. With satellite and cable distribution, there developed major regional television services, for example, Globo in Latin America and STAR in Asia, as well as explicitly transnational formats, such as CNN and MTV. With the internet came the possibility of many more, and more differentiated, flows between countries. The web, however, still bears witness to national borders and to the continued centrality of the US in international communications (Halavais, 2000): studies of network structures indicate that "political and economic forces that have historically led to a hierarchical world system seem to continue to determine the flow of information via the most egalitarian technology," resulting in "the reproduction of the old social structure via the new technology" (Himelboim, 2010: 383, 385).

► flows of communication – Chapter 10, p. 186

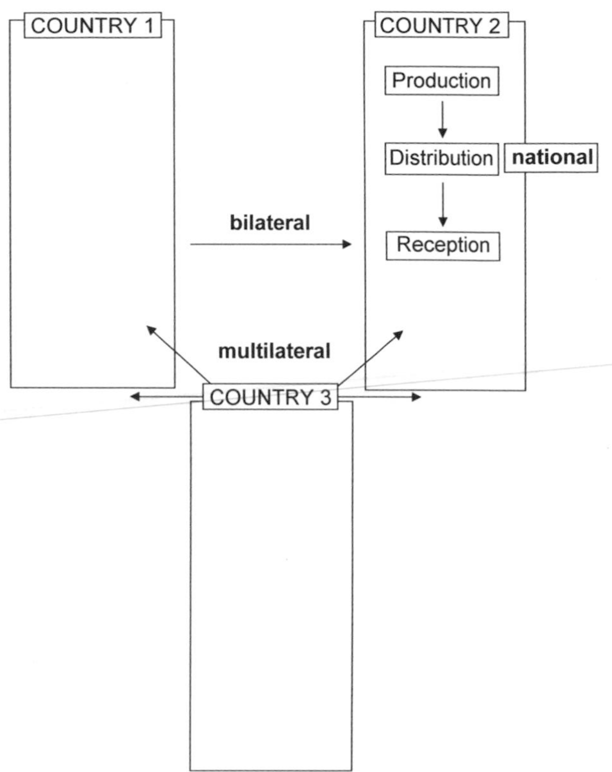

Figure 11.1 Three communication flows within and between countries (adapted from Sepstrup, 1989; see also McQuail and Windahl, 1993)

COMMUNITIES AND SUBCULTURES

References to the contexts as well as the outcomes of communication as 'communities' have been widespread, long before the more recent notion of internet, online, or virtual communities (Rheingold, 1994). As suggested by Anderson's (1991) terminology of 'imagined communities' with reference to nations, communities exist on different scales. Traditionally, however, the reference has been to local entities, either predating the national level of social organization or representing its component parts, for example, a subsection of a city or a rural area on the periphery of an urban center. This first type, then, are communities of place, grounded in a particular location, its history, and its self-conceived identity. Second, communities of interest refer to cultural formations that are united across space by some perceived purpose or identity (Licklider and Taylor, 1999[1968]: 108). In both cases, the nation-state has been an implicit point of reference. Horizontally-geographically, the nation could be seen as a symbolic center, represented by a capital or metropolitan area, with an underrecognized periphery of self-reliant cultural formations. Vertically-structurally, the nation could be understood as a center of power that may have grown out of touch with its constituencies in terms of age, class, gender, or ethnicity.

communities of place

communities of interest

center and periphery

Research interest in communities and subcultures dates, at least, from the beginning of modern social sciences. Ferdinand Tönnies (1974[1887]) outlined a distinction between two forms of social organization which has remained influential:

- *Gemeinschaft* – homogeneous, communitarian, and non-contractually governed social formations; and
- *Gesellschaft* – heterogeneous, individualist, and contractually governed social formations.

It should be underscored that the two types do not map neatly onto different historical epochs, even if *Gesellschaft* principles have been on the rise over the last two centuries. Instead, the two terms refer to different forms of social organization which, to varying degrees, intersect in particular historical and cultural settings. This was documented, from the outset, by, for instance, the Chicago School tradition◀ in key studies of the importance of local communities in American social life during from the early twentieth century.

Like nation-states, the two prototypes – *Gemeinschaft* and *Gesellschaft* – represent both infrastructural and imagined categories, raising questions of what kind of community different social groups seek to promote. Since the Romantic age, around 1800, modern societies and cultures have, from time to time, entertained notions of returning to, or reintroducing elements of, *Gemeinschaft*. And, the potentials and implications of local agency have continued to occupy both social and media theory. The events of '1968' in the West, and the underlying anti-authoritarian movements in various social domains – from politics to education to the family – articulated a critique of certain *Gesellschaft* principles that could be seen to stand in the way of *Gemeinschaft* qualities of life, such as participatory culture and direct democracy. In media studies, classic positions regarding communication as a source of community, and as a resource in struggles for liberation and equality, were rediscovered (Brecht, 1993[1932]) and extended (Enzensberger, 1972[1970]) to apply to press, radio, and television.

'1968'

One important development was the rise of a range of community media, especially local radio and television (for an overview, see Rennie, 2006). While facilitated by new technologies of production and distribution, these media also were shaped by, and helped to shape, social movements seeking to empower the members of local communities in communication and beyond. In some cases, media practitioners and researchers came together to develop this potential through action research.◀ In different national settings, moreover, public access channels were established, for instance, as part of the mandate of cable service providers, so that citizen groups and other non-professionals might gain a voice. In the digital media environment, such initiatives have become more standard fare, and have been part of renewed debates concerning civil society as a third force in society, beyond states and markets, from the local to the global level, that might advance alternative types of both communication and community (for an overview, see Edwards, 2004).

local community media

public access channels

global civil society

Being communities of interest, rather than of place, subcultures depend on media that transcend space and time, commonly involving substantial publics on a regional or global scale. As a specific field of research, subcultural studies developed particularly from the 1970s. The immediate point of reference was those groups of young people who had come to stand out, from the 1950s, through their more or less remarkable cultural practices: clothing, musical tastes, interpersonal interaction, etc. (for an overview, see Gelder, 2005). In one sense, these cultural formations could be considered a part of, and subordinate to, a national culture of sorts. Subcultures, accordingly, might articulate and cater to specialized cultural preferences and lifestyles, as associated also with different commercial market segments.◀ In another sense, subcultures could be understood and studied as full-fledged sociocultural universes – neither part of nor subordinated to, but separate from and in broad opposition to a mainstream or parent culture.

subcultures

It is this last, oppositional conception that subcultural studies have emphasized and, to a degree, promoted (Hebdige, 1979). A particularly influential approach to subcultures has been associated with 'the Birmingham school'

▶ Chicago School sociology – Chapter 3, p. 52

▶ action research – Chapter 19, p. 365

▶ lifestyle and market segments – Chapter 8, p. 168

of cultural studies (Hall, *et al.*, 1980).◀ Building on Raymond Williams' (1975[1958]: 18) definition of culture as "a whole way of life," Birmingham and other critical cultural studies have emphasized the specific role of culture in processes of social conflict and change. Rather than being, in classic Marxist terms, part of a superstructure reflecting an economic (and political-institutional) base, cultural practices are here considered sites of social struggle in their own right. Imaginative expressions can articulate imagined alternatives. To cite the title of an early influential volume, the members of subcultures could be said to exercise "resistance through rituals" (Hall and Jefferson, 1975).

Certainly, cultural practices can be more or less concretely and proactively social. Membership of a subculture need not be different, in practice, from fandom and the cultivation of a personal or age-specific identity. Some critics have characterized cultural studies researchers as disappointed revolutionaries who may find it "reassuring to detect 'resistance' saturating the pores of everyday life" (Gitlin, 1997: 30). Subcultural studies have had their romantic and self-righteous streaks, celebrating the authenticity and legitimacy of certain preferred subcultures. More generally, there has been a comparative neglect of the position of subcultures within the wider social structure. As noted by Middleton (1990: 161) with reference to music-oriented youth subcultures, studies have given less attention to "the subcultures' relationships with their parent cultures, with the dominant culture and with other youth cultures." In fairness, though, subcultural studies have been successful in conceptualizing and interpreting culture, not just as *one* whole way of life, but as a remarkably varied range of *multiple* ways of life with practical implications for different socioeconomic groups and their interrelations.

A special focus of research on subcultures, not surprisingly, has been popular music. Post-1945 subcultures emerged as part of the anti-authoritarian turn of '1968' across social institutions. This generalized revolt was symbolized and expressed in innovative rhythms and lyrics. One issue has been how to integrate music into the analytical repertoire of cultural studies as, precisely, music. Some subcultural studies have relied excessively on identifying abstract homologies – structural similarities between the organization of, for instance, musical materials and the social interactions around the music, as in references to rock'n'roll as "screw and smash music" (Middleton, 1990: 158). Part of the difficulty has been that, also in the wider field of media and communication, music remains one of the most underresearched topics (for overview, see Jensen, 2006). For one thing, until quite recently, popular music had been largely neglected by the discipline of musicology. Compared to departments of literature or art history, popular culture only very slowly seems to be making inroads into departments of music. For another thing, media and communication studies have had noticeable difficulties in accounting for music and other sound as communication. Given the massive presence of music and composite soundscapes (Schafer, 1977) in the contemporary media environment, one current challenge is to develop theoretical and analytical frameworks that may accommodate the several modalities of communication – verbal, visual, and auditive.◀

analysis through homology

Popular music is testimony to the place of cultural practices in processes of social conflict and change, feeding a sense of community, and sometimes solidarity. Rock'n'roll, in its different incarnations, has been a centerpiece of national and international social movements, from Vietnam War protests to Live Aid concerts to YouTube and Facebook support actions for disaster victims. Somewhat paradoxically, both popular music and other cultural artifacts feeding diverse subcultures have, to a great extent, been the product of American and other transnational media industries. In historical perspective, US popular culture, especially, has held an ambivalent fascination around the world after World War II (Webster, 1988); simultaneously, it has served as a resource that could be reappropriated for alternative purposes in local and subcultural contexts.

Beyond communities and nations as cultures in their own right, a central issue for media studies

▶ Birmingham cultural studies – Chapter 2, p. 47

▶ research on music and media – Chapter 7, p. 150

has been communication between and among cultures. Unlike most individuals and groups, both state agencies and commercial media organizations have historically been in a position to address large numbers of people, to a degree, across national borders. Whereas research and debate, from the outset, had primarily addressed interaction 'between' two (or a few) cultures, or between a center of power and its periphery, from the 1990s the interrelation 'among' cultures in a global perspective, along with the potential for individuals and small groups to engage in communication via the internet, moved to the top of the agenda. The next two sections examine theoretical and analytical approaches from each of these perspectives.

BETWEEN CULTURES

Intercultural communication

Cultures, in one sense, do not – cannot – communicate, but their constituent parts can and do communicate constantly, in the shape of heads of states (or of nations), businesspeople, tourists, and media imports/exports. Whereas much work in the area has departed from the codes and practices of face-to-face communication, current research increasingly addresses technologically mediated communication, as well. It is helpful, by way of introduction, to indicate four different conceptions of the general relationship between communication and culture. The four varieties come together under a commonly accepted heading of intergroup communication – interactions between groups of people with different age, gender, ethnic, socioeconomic, and cultural backgrounds (for overviews, see Giles, *et al.*, 2010; Gudykunst and Mody, 2002):

intergroup communication

- *Intercultural communication*: studies of communication between people belonging to different cultures (the focus of the present section);
- *Cross-cultural communication*: comparative studies of communication in two or more cultures (examined in the next section, "Among cultures");
- *International communication*: studies of communication beyond the national level, in practice an integral part of much media and communication research;
- *Development communication*: a specific research tradition exploring the potential of communication in facilitating social progress in developing countries (noted in the present section).

One common premise of work on 'intercultural communication' is that the culturally variable codes of communication will get in the way of people understanding and coexisting with others of different national or ethnic origins. As such, the research tradition has taken an instrumental approach to communication as a means of avoiding or managing conflict. Specifically, foundational work was undertaken by Edward T. Hall (1959) after World War II in the context of the American Foreign Service Institute, which "concentrated on training diplomats to communicate with the different cultures they met outside of the USA" (Giles and Watson, 2008: 2340). Nonverbal behavior, which commonly registers below the level of explicit discursive interaction, has been an important topic of analysis; if understood and tackled appropriately, both verbal and nonverbal behavior offer aids in uncertainty reduction when strangers interact in economic, political, or other practical matters. The tradition, further, has invoked sympathetic, but occasionally naïve ideals such as "the intercultural person as a model for human development" (Gudykunst and Kim, 1992: 253), as if good communication among sincere individuals might remove conflicts of interest regarding a common good.

uncertainty reduction

The classic example of such communicative strategies in social planning was the study and practice of development communication. A variety of initiatives sought to employ information and communication technologies in order to advance general social progress in the developing world – economic growth, family planning, political institutions, schooling, etc. (Lerner, 1958; Schramm, 1964). In fact, the effort largely failed. For one thing, a number of projects could be considered patronizing or, at least, less than culturally sensitive, transplanting Western forms of organization to entirely different social systems. For another thing, the

development communication

faith in communication as a general problem solver, in retrospect, seems exaggerated. As discussed in the sections below on cultural imperialism and postcolonial theory, it was perhaps no wonder that, in an era of decolonization coupled with a global East-West conflict, development communication could be perceived as communication in the interest of the developed, rather than the developing world.

In fairness, several of the originators of development communication research recognized some of its limitations and failures (Schramm and Lerner, 1976). The title of a key volume, *The Passing of Traditional Society* (Lerner, 1958), was recycled in the subtitle of one self-critical article as, "The passing of the dominant paradigm" (Rogers, 1976). The transition from traditional to modern forms of social organization was proving more complex than expected, and might require (one or more) alternative research paradigms.◂ Everett M. Rogers, the author of that self-critical article, for one, continued his involvement in development through communication, for example, entertainment-education, which promotes education and general information for living through entertainment formats (Singhal, *et al.*, 2004).

entertainment-education

Western scholars and politicians have not been alone in having high hopes for communication; nation building, both material and symbolic, has been a key concern for both policy-makers and media practitioners in developing countries. One example was the 1975–76 SITE experiment in India in which community television sets were introduced in as many as 2,330 largely rural villages. While, again, the results were, at best, mixed, the purpose was to transmit especially educational and informational programs – on agriculture, health, and family planning – in addition to promoting particular notions of nationhood and citizenship (for an overview, see *Journal of Communication*, 29(4), 1979: 89–144).

With the internet and mobile media, a new round of policy deliberations and research projects concerning their development potential has begun – with non-profit initiatives such as One Laptop Per Child (www.laptop.org, accessed April 15, 2011), a World Summit on the Information Society (www.itu.int/wsis/index.html) followed by an Internet Governance Forum (www.intgovforum.org/cms, both accessed April 15, 2011), as well as studies finding new communicative divides arising, for example, in China (Qiu, 2009), even as the country was becoming a global economic and technological leader, in addition to being the largest mobile-media market in the world.

Perhaps surprisingly, the discipline of anthropology◂ has not been central to research on culture and (technologically mediated) communication. As noted by an overview of 'media anthropology,' anthropologists have commonly shied away from media as conditions and symbols of modernity, still giving priority to culture as a traditionally and locally conceived phenomenon in non-Western settings (Rothenbuhler and Coman, 2005: 13–15). Instead, anthropological perspectives have been imported into the media field as part of interdisciplinary developments. Regarding cultural differences in the situated experience of media, one classic work was Tamar Liebes and Elihu Katz's (1990) *The Export of Meaning*◂ on the reception of the television series *Dallas*; other studies have examined, for instance, Indian television as a source of middle-class female identities (Mankekar, 1999); Mexican-American girls' interpretations of transnational telenovelas (Mayer, 2003); and the localized reception of Hollywood movies around the world (Stokes and Maltby, 2004). Most specifically, the key anthropological methodology of ethnography◂ has been an important, if debated inspiration in studies of both media reception and media production. In addition, anthropological theories have informed media theories, for instance, regarding media events◂ as integrative social rituals (Dayan and Katz, 1992). This understanding, in turn, has sparked critiques of media rituals as communicative practices through which a repressive social (and international) order may be naturalized and

► paradigms – Chapter 15, p. 285

► anthropology – Chapter 3, p. 57
► *The Export of Meaning* – Chapter 9, p. 175
► ethnography – Chapter 9, p. 180
► media events – Chapter 8, p. 170

reinforced (Couldry, 2003). Such conflicting conceptions of ritual begin to suggest rather different notions of intercultural communication, examined in the following sections.

It should be added that, for historical and structural reasons, both critical and other conceptions of culture and communication have grown out of Western models of research. Whereas a number of publications have explored potential meta-theoretical links between classic scientific worldviews and other ontologies, including world religions (e.g., Christians and Traber, 1997; Dissanayake, 1988b; Kincaid, 1987), it is fair to conclude that no viable synthesis has been offered to date. In some cases, analyses have been premised on stark dichotomies regarding an individualist West versus a collectivist East (e.g., Kim, 2002). In other cases, interventions have been thinly veiled attempts at applying religious axioms to contemporary policy issues (e.g., Mowlana, 1993). It is easy to agree that "a preoccupation with metatheory is a clear sign that a given discipline has attained a certain level of maturity" (Dissanayake, 1988a: 1), and that more meta-theoretical efforts might promote a better understanding of the communicative practices of different cultures.◀ For now, however, the field is heir to two main positions in twentieth-century Western social theory, one seeking consensus, as in the case of intercultural communication research, the other oriented toward conflict, as exemplified most clearly by work on cultural imperialism.

non-Western ontologies

Cultural imperialism

A great deal of research on communication across national borders has performed a critique of 'cultural imperialism' – the extension of physical or economic force by cultural means. Specifically, the predominantly Western mass media of the post-1945 period might be said to subordinate non-Western cultures in an extension of colonialism,◀ which was officially being dismantled particularly from the 1960s. The main thesis can be stated briefly: Western media have served as more or less willing agents of a continued de facto imperialism, as exercised most manifestly by the US over developing nations, and made possible by an international free-market economy. The technologies and the professional competences that are required for indigenous media production to flourish simply have not been available in many regions of the world. Instead, comparatively cheap news and fiction products, which had already made a profit in their primary Western markets, could be marketed massively and cheaply to secondary markets in the developing world – cultural dumping. The thesis was summed up in an early book title: *The Media are American* (Tunstall, 1977). It has remained debated, however, on both theoretical and empirical grounds. With reference to emerging communications infrastructures in other parts of the world, the same author later concluded that *The Media were American* (Tunstall, 2007).

cultural dumping

The historical context of cultural-imperialism work helps to explain both the thesis and the vehemence of the debates it generated. First, research was faced with a divided world in which the post-1945 conflict between two super-powers, the United States and the Soviet Union, had global consequences. The hot World War II had been followed by their Cold War, and the dismantling of colonies was opening an additional front in the struggle for local hearts and minds. The 'Third World' represented a residual to be enlisted, by cultural and any other means, against the other side. Different normative theories, particularly of the press,◀ were invoked by representatives of all three worlds in order to advance their respective causes. The positions were sharpened in policy-oriented research feeding into deliberations in the context of the United Nations, specifically debates under the auspices of UNESCO concerning a possible New World Information and Communication Order (NWICO) that would accommodate more voices in world communications (for key documents, see MacBride, 1980).

the 'Third World'

A second background to cultural-imperialism research and debate was a widespread perception that the culture of global mass media was invading,

▶ meta-theory – Chapter 15, p. 288
▶ colonialism, p. 216
▶ normative theories of media – Chapter 19, p.353

even displacing, local cultures, which might be considered more authentic, more refined, or merely worth protecting and preserving. As in the case of subcultural studies, such reactions displayed a somewhat ambivalent attitude toward American and other popular media formats (Webster, 1988). Notably in the European setting, national cultural establishments seemed to resent the challenge to time-honored traditions, arguably balking at modernization as such, as symbolized by an anti-authoritarian popular culture. However, studies in the area witnessed a more specific concern with the economic logic of cultural dumping, which might make significant minority interests or entire forms of expression unavailable in local and regional contexts. In Europe, a central point of reference of research and debate during the 1980 and 1990s became public service broadcasting, particularly the diversity, or lack thereof, in television programming (e.g., Richardson and Meinhof, 1999; Wieten, *et al.*, 2000).

public service broadcasting

Being part of the revitalization of critical social theory from the 1960s, cultural-imperialism research derived much of its theoretical impetus from the political economy◄ tradition which was then taking shape in media studies (e.g., Murdock and Golding, 1977). Whereas the work of Herbert I. Schiller (1969) became an inspiration to a generation of critical US researchers, a characteristic feature of studies in the area was the alliances that it fostered among researchers on several continents, including Latin America as well as Europe (Roach, 1997). Among the central research topics were the various gaps – technological, educational, and professional – between the media of countries in the North and the South, respectively (Nordenstreng and Schiller, 1979), and specific imbalances in the international flow of news (Sreberny, *et al.*, 1985), which informed the NWICO debates. A different, if related critical approach, focusing on the content rather than the infrastructures of global communications, performed ideology critiques◄ of media texts. One classic study identified diverse ideological implications of Donald Duck comics for non-US readers (Dorfman and Mattelart, 1975[1971]).

international news flows

The general label of cultural imperialism is apparently used less frequently in recent work, and has itself been subject to critique (Golding and Harris, 1997). On empirical grounds, research has emphasized that the global media system has more than one center – in both wholesale and retail. Specifically, studies have long identified the substantial role of regional news organizations (Boyd-Barrett and Thussu, 1992) as well as of the 'domestication' of international news stories for local audiences (Cohen, *et al.*, 1996). Similarly, fictional and entertainment genres bear witness to a great variety of influences and confluences across national, regional, and global media (Straubhaar, 2007; Thussu, 2007b)). 'Local' content, albeit sometimes in 'Americanized' formats, may have the greatest audience appeal (O'Donnell, 1999; Silj, 1988). Also on theoretical grounds, reception studies◄ have explored the various ways in which local audiences may accommodate or resist the worldviews on offer in transnational media contents (e.g., Biltereyst, 1991; Liebes and Katz, 1990). This is in spite of countervailing arguments suggesting that cultural imperialism may be extended, for example, in China, ironically through digital piracy, as young Chinese viewers are exposed to American television programs with a significant element of product placement (Shi, 2010).

One explanation for the apparent demise of the cultural-imperialism position may be that the research tradition had given more attention to global infrastructures than to local cultures, in practice reproducing the center-periphery model of communication being criticized. Faced with more granular evidence, and with a digital media environment in which, despite the persistence of digital and other divides,◄ bandwidth is nowhere near as scarce as in an age of broadcasting, the cultural-imperialism argument may be defeated by its generality. A second likely explanation has to do, again, with infrastructure, this time of communication *research*. Given the institutional resources of North America and Europe, it is not surprising that these cultures have exercised a de facto 'academic imperialism' in the field.

► political economy research – Chapter 3, p. 65
► ideology critique – Chapter 2, p. 42
► cross-cultural reception studies – Chapter 9, p. 178
► digital divide – Chapter 19, p. 354

Recent book titles, however, bear witness to ambitions of *dewesternizing* (Wang, 2011) and *internationalizing* (Thussu, 2009) media and communication research – beyond an abstract East-West synthesis – at the level of middle-range theories,◄ multiple methodologies, and comparative themes of empirical research. Yet another book title suggests the long-term effort required: there is a call for internationalizing also one of the latest subspecialties of communication research, namely, *internet* studies (Goggin and McLelland, 2009).

Postcolonial theory

If cultural-imperialism research constitutes a modernist enterprise, emphasizing the structural preconditions of communication, postcolonial theory represents a postmodernist endeavor, focusing on the discourses in which power may be either exercised or subverted. Conducted from a variety of perspectives by intellectuals in former colonies as well as by literary, historical, and other scholars around the world, postcolonial studies have reemphasized the implications of the colonial past for present cultural forms and social interaction (for an overview, see Ashcroft, *et al.*, 2006).

The most distinctive position has its sources in poststructuralist theories of discourse.◄ Compared to historical or sociological conceptions of postcolonialism, which would focus on the various economic and political mechanisms of exploitation, a discursive conception shifts attention toward the narratives and worldviews that serve as cultural vehicles of (self-) oppression. In particular, postcolonial studies have been informed by Michel Foucault's notion of discursive formations that privilege certain worldviews, while delegitimizing or silencing others (Foucault, 1972[1969]). In addition, work in the area has been influenced by the psychoanalytic theory of Jacques Lacan (1977), who contributed the notion that language (and other cultural forms) create a speaking position from which a dominant group can differentiate itself from – excommunicate – 'others.' Not just individuals and groups, but entire cultural formations can be labeled as an other – not us.

discursive formations

the 'other'

► middle-range theories – Chapter 3, p. 64

► poststructuralism – Chapter 2, p. 42

The classic statement on cultural 'othering' was Edward Said's (1978) work on orientalism. From a wide variety of sources and genres, his volume identified a deep-seated tension in how Western authors – explorers, colonial administrators, artists, etc. – have expressed their understanding of non-Western cultures. These others are, on the one hand, appealing, and, on the other hand, repelling: symbols of deep and dark desires. The ambivalent experience, next, suggests that 'others' must, and can legitimately, be mastered and controlled for 'our' purposes and, perhaps, protected against themselves. (Other research, rooted in traditional orientalist studies, has raised serious doubts about Said's (1978) original argument, both its generality and its supporting evidence (Irwin, 2006).)

orientalism

More recent and equally influential contributions to postcolonial studies have shifted the emphasis even further toward discursive conceptions of oppression and of power generally (Bhabha, 1994; Spivak, 1988). While holding somewhat different perspectives on the degrees of freedom that individuals and groups might have for generating alternative viewpoints, resistance, or liberation for themselves, both Homi Bhabha and Gayatri Spivak have developed remarkably abstract analyses and rather stipulative theories of discourse. A central question has been how – in what discursive forms – an autonomous and genuinely postcolonial subject might finally articulate itself. In comparison, both these authors and the mainstream of postcolonial studies have paid little attention, either to the material and institutional conditions of discourse, or to the variable interpretations that actual people will make of any discourse according to their concrete cultural contexts. Presumably these factors must figure prominently in any explanation of how colonialism works, and in any strategy of ending the suffering and humiliation it engenders. At least some researchers in the area have complained that the preoccupation with discourse may render postcolonial theory an inward looking, irrelevant "academic glass-bead game" (Slemon, 2006: 56).

Within media and communication research as a whole, postcolonial theory has been a marginal influence, although the cultural studies tradition has incorporated some key concepts, for instance, diaspora – the disembedding and reembedding of ethnic and cultural groups across locales – in order to account for distinctive categories and experiences of 'home' (e.g., Morley, 2000). One general lesson of postcolonial studies for the field may be historical, as suggested by different definitions of the very term 'postcolonial': does it refer to the relatively short period since the post-1945 independence of many developing nations, to the longer period since the original colonization, or broadly to social and cultural practices in a world affected by only partially recognized forms of colonialism, in a literal as well as a metaphorical sense (Ashcroft, *et al.*, 2006: xix)? Cultures amount to long-term memories – of themselves and of their others; communication serves to articulate and reflect on such memories, depending on the media available to different cultures. With economic as well as cultural globalization, as stimulated by digital media, research has increasingly come to ask how multiple cultures with intersecting histories both imagine and interact with one other.

diaspora

AMONG CULTURES

The lines of division between intercultural, transnational, and global communications can be difficult to draw, both conceptually and empirically. The 1990s and 2000s, however, witnessed a renewed and marked research interest in globalization, relating, to a significant extent, to media and communication (for overviews, see Robertson, 1992; Tomlinson, 1999). This occurred, in part, in response to the growing diffusion of digital technologies, which contributed to far-reaching changes in the production, distribution, and uses of media products and services. At the same time, it should be underlined that globalization did not follow from digitalization. For one thing, media technologies are never singular or simple causes of social developments, even if each new technology has had specific social affordances.◄ For another thing, digital technologies are much more than media technologies (Braman, 2006: 56–57): they are general resources of material production and social organization and, thus, constituents of other economic and political transformations that are still ongoing, and which perhaps are best assessed with hindsight – in a decade or a century. The transformative potential of the printing press was not, and could not be, anticipated in 1500.

globalization

► affordances of technologies – Chapter 1, p. 5

To begin, it is important to recognize that globalization is not a unique development of the decades around 2000. As already discussed, one aspect of the longer and wider process of modernization◄ was the emergence of an economic world system from the sixteenth century. Moreover, the various aspects of modernization and globalization do not necessarily proceed at the same pace, or according to one central logic. In summary, one can distinguish three aspects of globalization:

- *economic* – which has been ongoing for centuries, including phases of market competition, incorporation, imperialism, and conglomeration;
- *political* – which remains limited in institutional terms, despite the formation of the United Nations, the growth of international treaty systems, and regional entities such as the European Union; and
- *cultural* – which has depended on shifting technological infrastructures – print, cinema, broadcasting, internet – and which has been intensifying in recent decades.

It is in the cultural domain that various other aspects of globalization can be articulated and debated. Media themselves are, at once, commodities in a global economy and local political institutions – products as well as agents of globalization.

Given the potential scope of the transformations, research on globalization has outlined several 'grand' theories, focusing variously on economy and society (e.g., Harvey, 1989; Held, *et al.*, 2000) or culture (e.g., Appadurai, 1996; Hannerz, 1996). Probably the most widely influential framework has been presented by Manuel Castells (1996, 2004), who described the coming of a network society.◄

► modernization, p. 206
► the network society – Chapter 10, p. 189

In order to specify the relationship between communication and other social interaction on a global scale, it is helpful to distinguish between the world as a context of action and as a frame of reference (Tomlinson, 1999: 11). As a *context of action* – including business investments, political negotiations, tourism, and cultural exchanges – the world has undoubtedly become more interconnected in recent decades. In the media field, this is evidenced, for example, by tendencies toward concentration and conglomeration in production and distribution infrastructures, despite countervailing forces in the form of regional and local media organizations.◀ It should be noted that the internet, as an infrastructure, also constitutes a relatively concentrated structure of service providers and other access points, again despite its significant potential for user participation and distributed innovation (e.g., Benkler, 2006; Von Hippel, 2005).

the world as a context of action

It is primarily as a *frame of reference*, however, that globalization affects individuals and communities. For most people most of the time, the rest of the world is an imagined entity, sometimes an imagined community (Anderson, 1991), that they encounter through media and communication. What I know about, and do together with, other individuals and institutions elsewhere – in either a material or an immaterial sense – affects me in all manner of indirect and cumulative ways. This is the technologically mediated condition of modernity, as accentuated by globalization. The media enable a global social system that is complex as well as opaque; they simultaneously provide means of making that system more transparent and actionable.

the world as frame of reference

Also media organizations need to consider the globe as an imagined entity. In order to attract localized audiences and users, producers and distributors of media products and services must take into account the several frames of reference – national, regional, transnational – which enter into 'local' cultures. One lesson from transnational television channels, such as MTV and CNN, was that, when faced with national competition, they may be forced to regionalize their product (Roe and De Meyer, 2000; see also Volkmer, 1999). In theories of globalization, this dialectic has been referred to as glocalization (Robertson, 1995). Web search engines (Halavais, 2009) include both customized versions of, for instance, Google in many languages, and nationally specific market leaders.◀

glocalization

In conclusion, the field of media and communication is a prime candidate for culturally comparative research. And yet, studies of media and their uses in cultural contexts have been relatively few (Blumler, *et al.*, 1992). In one sense, all human and social sciences are comparative:

> After we designate researchers who compare across time (historians) and across space (geographers), researchers who compare communications content (content analysts), organizations (organizational sociologists), institutions (macrosociologists), countries (international relations specialists), cultures (ethnologists), and languages (linguists), and researchers who compare individuals in terms of gender, race, social class, age, education, and religion, what remains?
>
> (Beniger, 1992: 35)

What remains, in media studies, may be, first, a shift of focus from 'mass media' toward the diverse communicative practices that various media types enable in different cultural contexts◀ and, second, a renewed attention to the cultural origins also of any theoretical lens through which empirical studies compare cultures. The ongoing globalization of both media and research infrastructures invites many more culturally comparative studies; it also represents an opportunity for researchers to become more reflective of their own cultural origins and knowledge interests.◀ History – the topic of the next chapter – offers one more lens for reflecting on current conceptions of and approaches to communication.

▶ regional and local media organizations, p. 215

▶ web search engines – Chapter 10, p. 193

▶ from media toward communication studies – Chapter 1, p. 8

▶ knowledge interests – Chapter 19, p. 358

12 History, media, and communication

Paddy Scannell

- an overview of the *history of history* as a field of research
- a discussion of '*media history*' as an inclusive phenomenon
- a presentation of histories of *oral and written communication*
- a review of histories of different technological media, including the *press and broadcasting*
- an example of *archival research* on historical data

INTRODUCTION

In this chapter, I review developments in historical studies of communication and media. In order to contextualize these developments, it is necessary to consider, historically, the formation of history as an academic discipline. Throughout the chapter, I attend to theoretical and methodological issues concerning historiography (the practice of writing history) in order to illuminate some of the more specific problems in writing histories of media and communication. Historiography must come *after* events taking place in the present wherein history is 'made' and is thus, by definition, a retrospective process. The present has to enter into the past in order to become visible, intelligible and writable – in this process 'history' begins to appear. It is an important question as to how much time must go by for the present (in which history is made) to enter into the past, thereby becoming historical. The transition from present to past is the time of generations; the process of change and renewal as older generations (of people, things, technologies) begin to age and die while, in the very same moment, new generations of people, things and technologies are born and enter into maturity. Roughly speaking, the span of generational time is between twenty and thirty years: so that if 2011 is taken as the immediate and present 'now', then at this moment the 1970s and 1980s are moving out of the noisy present and entering into the silent past. They are becoming historical, while the decades that precede them (the 1960s and 1970s) now belong to history.

historiography

I have written accounts of the first two generations of academic work on media and communication (Scannell 2007) in the last century. The first (G1) was the American sociology of mass communication◄ that began at Columbia University, New York, in the 1930s; the second (G2) was British media studies that began at the University of Birmingham in the 1970s.◄ Each of these two moments was concerned with the impact and effect of then new media. In the

► American sociology of mass communication – Chapter 19, p. 357

► British cultural studies – Chapter 2, p. 46

1930s it was radio; in the 1970s, television. Today the field of media and communication studies is preoccupied with the third generation of 'new media'; the internet and the cell phone and the transition from analogue to digital methods of encoding information. But how can we evaluate the impact and effect of the new? The social sciences are on the whole concerned with the measurement of immediate short-run effects in the here and now. Long-term effects (and how long is long term?) do not begin to show up until time has passed and the lasting significance of what was once new starts to become apparent.

Today the general social applications and uses of mobile (cell) phones and the internet are still very much in their infancy. The lasting significance of, say, Facebook and Twitter can only be, at this point, a matter of conjecture. Thirty years from now, another generation of scholars will doubtless look back from where they are to where we are now in order to begin to assess the long-term impact and significance of today's new technologies. We, however, are simply not in a position to say because we cannot tell. What we *can* do, though, is to begin the evaluation of the lasting significance of once new, now 'old' media: the printing press, radio and television. None of these has been displaced by newer media. All have certainly been affected by them. Radio and cinema were profoundly impacted by television in the 1950s as television, in turn, has been profoundly impacted in the last decade or so by the worldwide social uptake and applications of the internet.

The entry into the past of what in the present is new is always the beginning of history. In this chapter I explore this transformational process in relation to modern media and communication technologies and the issues at stake in their historical study. But first it is necessary to reflect, for a moment, on the history of history—the formation of the modern academic discipline of History in which the history of media has recently begun to emerge as a distinctive subfield.

THE HISTORY OF HISTORY

The professionalization of history began in the nineteenth century. A chair in history at the University of Oxford was first established in 1848. In his inaugural lecture, the first Regius Professor of History, H.H. Vaughan, defined the job of the historian as the "disclosure of the critical changes in the conditions of a society" (Stone 1987: 4). From the late nineteenth century, history developed into an independent academic discipline. Separate history departments were established with Ph.D. programmes for the training of future historians. Professional associations were created, taught programmes at the undergraduate and graduate levels were established, and a curriculum (an 'agenda') for the study of History as a distinctive academic subject was put in place within the emerging fields of the humanities and social sciences (Stone 1987: 5).

history as an academic discipline

There were two aspects to this development: first, a definition of the right way of 'doing' history (the professionalization of methods), and, second, a specification of the subject matter of historical enquiry (what history is properly 'about'). Both aspects came to the fore in Germany, where there was pioneering concern with the establishment of history as an academic discipline on a 'scientific' basis. What this meant, above all, was a renewed concern about the 'objectivity' of historical research whose scientific truth claims were underpinned by rigorous research methods linked to temporal distance on the part of the historian from the field of enquiry and careful scholarly interpretation and evaluation of the evidence. The doyen of German 'historicism' (see Bambach 1995) was Leopold von Ranke, whose name is particularly associated with a revolution in sources and methods – a shift away from earlier histories or 'chronicles' to the use of the official records of governments. Historians now began to work regularly in archives, and they elaborated an increasingly sophisticated set of techniques for assessing the reliability of documents. They claimed that their own histories were therefore more objective and more 'scientific' than those of their predecessors (Burke 1992: 7).

scientific objectivity

German historicism

The primary subject matter of these enquiries was the nation-state◄ and, in particular, its administrative and constitutional development,

► the nation-state – Chapter 11, p. 205

as linked to its diplomatic and military relations with other nation-states. National record offices were opened up to academic historians, and the basic political documents relating to these matters were indexed and made publicly available for research free of charge. Thus, by the beginning of the twentieth century the academic profession of history was in place. Its agenda consisted of narrative histories – firmly supported by archival research into primary documentary source material – whose subject matter was the activities of those political and military elites who created, defined and maintained the modern nation-state. Historians no longer wrote for an educated general public (Stone 1987: 3–7). They wrote for each other or for their students, and talked amongst themselves as a self-legitimating subset of a new historical genus – *Homo academicus* (Bourdieu 1988).

narrative history

Not unnaturally, these foundational developments, set in place between the 1870s and the 1930s, were subject to critique in the course of the twentieth century. On the one hand, a set of methodological objections was raised against the privileging of 'narrative' as the definitive mode of historiography (history writing). On the other hand, the narrowly elitist base of the subject matter of history as the actions of 'great men' came under increasing critical scrutiny. The issue of history as narrative is fundamental to it as an academic discipline, since it raises crucial questions concerning the nature and status of historical *events* and of historical *agents*. In short, the problems are: what is history about, who are historical agents, and what is historiography (the writing of history)?

historical events and agents

Political history, history of events and narrative history – these are almost interchangeable terms, as Paul Ricoeur points out in his review of 'the eclipse of narrative' (Ricoeur 1983: 95–120). They were treated as such by the French historian Fernand Braudel, a leading member of the *Annales* School, so called after the journal of that name founded in 1929 by Marcel Bloch and Lucien Febvre, who, along with Braudel, were the leading critics of traditional history and vigorous opponents of what they called *histoire evenementielle* (Burke 1991: 7–8). They argued that it was naïve to think of historical events as being 'made' by historical actors, because what determines or structures events has no level of explanation, in traditional historical narratives, beyond the deeds of significant individuals themselves. Their structuralist◀ critique of history-as-events (or the 'great man' view of history) draws attention to all those shaping factors, ignored in narrative histories, that determine the character and behaviour of historical actors and the scope of their actions. The objectivity claimed by political histories is at the expense of underlying economic, social, political, cultural and religious factors which all, in different ways, combine to predetermine the form and content of historical events. Moreover, and this was the crucial point of Braudel and others, the nature of historical time remains undertheorized in narrative histories, since they presuppose, without any critical reflection on the matter, first, that the time of events is somehow self-evident, and second, that it is essentially the same as the time(s) of history.

the *Annales* School

If history is the sum of all that has ever happened in the past, then a basic methodological and theoretical issue for historians is how they establish manageable time spans for their activities. As Braudel points out, "All historical work is concerned with the breaking down of time past, choosing among its chronological realities according to more or less conscious preferences and exclusions." He is highly critical of 'traditional' history's concern with the short time span and "the headlong, dramatic, breathless rush of its narratives" which are tied to "the individual and the event" (Braudel 1980: 27–28). He points to new kinds of economic and social history whose concern is not with particular individuals, moments or events, but with the larger economic and social forces that structure their terrain, that shape the ground upon which events are enacted. Such macro (large scale) histories necessarily take a more long-term view of the processes of historical change. They are concerned with, for instance, the mapping of the cyclical rise and fall of prices, which calls for complex, large-scale data gathering of quantitative information◀ about prices, wages, money, rent, output *per capita*, capital investment, overseas trade and

macro and long-term history

▶ structuralism – Chapter 2, p. 38
▶ quantitative methodologies – Chapter 13

other key economic variables (Stone 1987:13–14), compared to the qualitative methodologies most prevalent in historical research. The focus of macro histories is not on individuals and their actions, but on underlying factors that mould the processes of social change through time. These 'conjunctural' histories attempt to analyse the ways in which a range of economic variables combine in a particular historical conjuncture to precipitate crises that play themselves out at the level of events and actions. The intermediate time span of such histories is measured in decades; ten, twenty, fifty years. But beyond this lies the long term – the *longue durée* – which stretches over centuries. It is a kind of 'motionless history' which tries to establish the most fundamental constraints upon the shape and scope of human actions: the impact of climate and geography, for example, upon the historical life of a region such as the Mediterranean, the subject of Braudel's most famous work (Braudel 1972–4).

the longue durée

The critique of narrative history as privileging elites came to the fore in the 1950s and 1960s. New kinds of social history were developed which insisted, as the historical novel had done (Lukacs 1989[1916]), on the significance of the apparently insignificant – ordinary men and women, and the character of everyday life (Burke 1991). These 'histories from below'◀ (Sharpe 1991) – as opposed to history from above; political history – rediscovered such 'hidden' or 'invisible' histories as those of the English working class (Thompson 1963), or of women (Rowbottom 1974; Scott, 1991), of the family (Stone 1979), or the body (Porter 1991). Thus, academic history, in the second half of the twentieth century, began to broaden out and diversify. It was in this context of expanding areas of research and enquiry that historical attention began to focus on, amongst other things, the media.

MEDIA HISTORY?

What would a history of the media be about? We must first determine what the word refers to. Note that it is a plural noun: a 'medium', *the* media. This plurality is usually taken to include the press and broadcasting (radio and television), and cinema too, perhaps. One useful way of reconstructing how terms gather certain meanings to them is to look at their historical usage. When did they begin to be used in a particular way, and why? What we can say of 'the media', is that the sense in which it is commonly used today – and by now it is a common-sense term and part of everyone's ordinary usage – is no older than the early 1960s. Earlier usage of the word 'medium' was associated with the late nineteenth-century vogue for spiritualism which, as John D. Peters (1999) has cogently shown, was linked with the impact of new communication technologies: the telegraph and telephone. The idea of a 'media society' shows up for the first time in the 1960s, and coincides with the rapid rise of television as the dominant 'medium' of daily life in Europe. In everyday usage, the term now recognizes that, in our kind of society, the press and broadcasting are central social institutions and a taken-for-granted part of everyone's ordinary, everyday life, but the 'media society' as we know it came into being only in the second half of the twentieth century.

'the media' from the 1960s

To put it like this invites the question, 'What was there before that?' The Norwegian historian, Hans Fredrik Dahl (1994), has pointed out that before the 'media society', there was 'mass society', and terms such as 'mass culture' and 'mass communication' referred to the impact and effect of new technologies of communication on early twentieth century society. So, in the 1930s, we find a whole series of debates (in Britain, Europe and the United States) about the effect on social values, the beliefs and tastes of new kinds of 'mass' journalism, Hollywood cinema, commercial radio and an emerging 'popular' music industry. The issue that Dahl raises is as follows: first, do we try and study historically the development of 'the media', or do we go back and try and trace the development of particular 'mediums'? Second and relatedly, what is the difference between studying 'the media' and studying 'communication'?

mass culture debates

In this chapter, I will treat this difference as essentially one of historical scale. Communication is as old as mankind, insofar as language is constitutive of human being. Modern media

▶ histories from below and oral history – Chapter 14, p. 272

of communication – daily newspapers, radio and television services, and the internet – stand in a long temporal continuum that reaches back through written systems of communication (often taken as the point of entry into History) to spoken language and the beginnings of human social life. Thus, histories of communication are anterior to, and distinct from, media histories. Moreover, 'the media' is a synthetic descriptor and as such misleading when used in respect of something called 'media history', for the different mediums that make up 'the media' have thus far only been studied historically as discrete phenomena, and not as the relational totality which the term itself implies. Accordingly, I begin with histories of communication and proceed thence to more recent histories of different mediums which make up the known and understood 'media society', familiar as such to all of us today. I will then briefly review some issues that arise when trying to 'do' historical work on aspects of 'the media'.

writing as the beginning of History

THE HISTORY OF COMMUNICATION

The fundamental, universal form of communication in all human societies is language, more exactly, spoken language, or speech.◀ We know that systems of writing, as devices for representing spoken language, developed much, much later – on current evidence around 7,000 years ago. There are, of course, different systems of writing, but today two systems prevail: alphabetic systems – the Roman alphabet is massively dominant, but there are others (Greek, Cyrillic) – and ideographic systems (Chinese, Japanese). We can take these two modes of communication – speech and writing – as intimately connected, but there is no doubt that spoken language is ontologically (as well as historically) prior. That is, speech is constitutive of our (human) way of being: some would say it is *the* species-defining characteristic. It is the very essence of our human, social life. All human societies have a spoken language. Far fewer have developed systems of writing. So, a primary question is, if both are systems of communication, what are the differences between them? What is it that we can and cannot do with speech as our only available means of communication? What does writing do for us (and what do we do with it)? And what is it that later means of communication (print, radio, television, internet, mobile media) do for us, and what do we do with them? Such questions have a positive and negative side to them: what does any particular means (medium) of communication enable us to do, and what are the limits to what we can do with it?

alphabetic and ideographic systems of writing

▶ speech – Chapter 1, p. 6

To put this slightly differently, a fundamental constraint on the scope of human actions is imposed by the temporal and spatial characteristics of our available resources, including our resources for communicating with each other. The question, first clearly put by the Canadian economic historian, Harold Innis, is: what are the implications of the available means of communication for the character of a particular human society? (Innis 1972[1950]) What is a society like that only has speech as its available means of communication? Innis's answer was that such societies are necessarily spatially (geographically) small in scale. They may be nomadic or pastoral (they may move about or remain in one place) but, since their shared spoken language is what makes them what they are and holds them together, the size of their community is restricted by its face-to-face character. The group's social memory – its knowledge in the present of 'how and what and when' to do things, as derived from past practices – is orally transmitted in a spoken tradition that is passed on from one generation to the next.

time and space as aspects of communication systems

Systems of writing, Innis argued, developed as means of coordinating and controlling human activities across extended time and space. Writing is a system of record: a way of putting things down, so that information can be transmitted through space over great distances and be preserved through time as a record of what was said and done. Innis drew special attention to the different materials used for writing, and the ways they affect the scope, character and purposes of the messages they record. Messages carved with a chisel on heavy, durable materials – such as slate, granite or marble – have a monumental character that endures through deep, or slow time. Messages written on light-weight materials such as papyrus or paper (invented in

writing materials

China and available in Europe, via the Moors, from the thirteenth century) are portable and easily carried over great distances.

Most generally, Innis argued that different media, using different materials, had different consequences for the human, social control of time and space: he called this 'the bias of communication' (Innis 1951). He noted the importance of written technologies for the establishment and maintenance of empires – the creation of power blocs spread over great distances and preserved through many generations. He observed that the complex task of administering, coordinating and policing a vast imperium, such as the Roman Empire, required written systems both as means of recording decisions, laws, etc., *and* of communicating them throughout the empire. Writing was one essential underpinning of the whole colossal enterprise. Innis's analysis of written systems of communication shows clearly that writing, in its primary functions, has always been linked to political and economic power. Wherever writing has established itself, it has immediately produced a fundamental distinction between the lettered and the unlettered, the educated and uneducated. To have the skills of reading and writing is a passport to individual self-advancement. Literacy gives rise to educated elites (in the past they were called priests; today they are called academics) that gravitate to the centres of power.

the 'bias' of communication

writing as record and communication

literacy and social difference

Innis's major work focused on the character of communication in ancient societies. It was Marshall McLuhan who picked up on Innis's ideas and applied them to modern societies. McLuhan, following Innis, made a fundamental distinction between 'oral' and 'written' cultures. He focused particularly on the impact of the new technology of printing in the late fifteenth century on the older 'manuscript culture' of the Middle Ages. McLuhan argued that Europe's take-off into the modern world was powerfully supported by the new culture of the book, which rapidly spread through Europe in the sixteenth century, creating new 'knowledge communities' based on print (McLuhan 1962). He went on, in *Understanding Media* (1964), to compare print cultures with the newer electronic cultures of modern media, especially radio and television, arguing that they had the effect of rescuing oral forms of communication from the dominance of printed and written forms. McLuhan was one of the first real analysts of modern media as communication technologies. It is in his writings that 'the media' are first examined as interrelated technologies that come together to create media societies. It is from McLuhan that we learnt to think of 'the media.'

print technology

Perhaps his most striking and important perception of the impact of electronic media was that it could no longer be thought of as particular to this or that society. What was new about electronic media was their *global* impact: they created, for the first time in history, the possibility of point-to-point, instant, live communication between any two points on the globe – 'the global village', in his famous phrase (McLuhan 1964). Electronic media have powerful transforming effects on the character of social time and space. In effect, they help to create and sustain the 'world-historical' character of modern life (Giddens 1990). It is increasingly difficult *not* to know what is going on elsewhere in the world today. Time and space have drastically shrunk. Each one of us has the world in our living room. Global television is a very real phenomenon when millions and millions of people, scattered all over the world, have access at the same time to an event such as the Olympics (Dayan and Katz 1992).◄ Television today is intimately linked to the character of national and international politics, business and war. Through television as well as the internet, cultural narratives, images, songs and jokes circulate round the world. When a programme like *Dallas* was watched in over a hundred different countries, it is clear that electronic media have contributed to the formation of a global culture – a culture of consumption, many have argued, underpinned by global capitalism – which has serious implications for national and local cultures. A key aspect of the 'gap' between North and South, the so-called developed and developing regions of the world, is a communications divide – the unequal flow of information and entertainment between first and third worlds.◄

the global village

► media events – Chapter 8, p. 170
► cultural imperialism research – Chapter 11, p. 214

Innis and McLuhan provide a fascinating way of identifying the impact and effect of media of communication on human societies by focusing on them as technologies that extend the scope and scale of human, social activity. Their emphasis on the 'bias of communication' implicit in different media technologies draws attention to their effect on the social organization of time and space. Their approach has an intrinsically historical thrust and, indeed, conceives of history in terms of time periods dominated or characterized by different media: from small-scale oral societies, to empires underpinned by writing, to the early modern European culture of the book, to today's electronic global culture. It is valuable to emphasize that the media are not simply 'neutral' carriers of information, but have a determinate effect on the character and scope of what they convey.

We should, however, note some of the limitations of this approach and, in particular, the charge of 'technological determinism'◄ which is often made against it. As Raymond Williams succinctly put it:

> New technologies are discovered, by an essentially internal process of research and development, which then sets the conditions for social change and progress. Progress, in particular, is the history of these inventions, which 'created the modern world'. The effects of these technologies, whether direct or indirect, foreseen or unforeseen, are as it were, the rest of history. The steam engine, the automobile, television, the atom bomb, have *made* modern man and the modern condition.
>
> (Williams 1974: 13)

The kind of argument advanced by Innis and McLuhan has the effect of making technologies of communication into instruments that appear, somehow, outside and beyond the control of their makers. It is another subtle kind of historicism: a 'grand narrative' of progress in which the hero is technology. The media shape human societies in their own likeness. The effect of such an argument is to remove the very stuff of history – the actions of human beings, politics, war, culture, entertainment – from the analysis. Do we use media or do they use us? For McLuhan, as he famously put it, 'the medium *is* the message'. Its content is irrelevant. But what is missing in this kind of approach, is any attention to how media are caught up in the histories of human societies, and are used in various ways and for various purposes.

the medium is the message

Nevertheless, these pioneering historical studies of human communication as determined by media technologies which shape and constrain human action, have become increasingly influential after a period in the 1970s when McLuhan fell out of favour, particularly with the Left, whose theories were then in fashion (Winthrop-Young and Wutz 1999: xi–xvi). Anthropologists took up the basic distinction between 'oral' societies and those with written or print-based cultures (Goody 1968; Ong 1982). McLuhan's thesis about the transition from manuscript to print cultures in Europe was explored by Elizabeth Eisenstein (1979). Friedrich Kittler's historical study, published in 1986, of *Gramophone, Film, Typewriter* took up the basic insights of Innis and McLuhan, and reworked them in a post-modern, anti-humanist reading of the ways in which "media determine our situation" (Kittler 1999: xxxix).

Kittler's work, in turn, has been an important source for John Durham Peters' remarkable historical study of the *idea* of communication (Peters 1999). There is a history not just of technologies of communication, but also of how we *think* about communication (our changing understanding of what it means). The connections between the two are explored by Peters in a highly original way. Kittler's work showed how new communication technologies – the gramophone, for instance – change the ways in which we think of ourselves. Today we are all familiar with the *idea* that human brains are rather like computers. This seems a natural idea to us. A hundred years ago, it seemed natural to think of the brain as rather like Edison's phonograph (Kittler 1999: 38–45), an idea that to us now seems bizarre.

history of the idea of communication

Peters, following Kittler, shows in fascinating detail some of the ways in which new communication technologies have shaped the ways in

► technological determinism – Chapter 1, p. 3

which we think about ourselves and others. He traces the *idea* of communication as occurring not only between human beings, but also with the dead, with angels, with aliens, with animals and with machines. If this sounds odd, then consider the huge investment, since the 1950s, in 'scientific' efforts to communicate with 'the rest of the universe' on the assumption that somewhere – out there in infinite time-space – there are intelligent alien beings to receive the messages that we are beaming out into the Void. Peters' brilliant description and analysis of the SETI project (the Search for Extra-Terrestial Intelligence), an international scientific programme that began in the USA after the Second World War and which still continues, is indicative of a theme that is central to his book, namely, that an increasing awareness of communication generates increasing anxiety about it (Peters, 1999: 246–261).

It is only in the modern era, with the huge proliferation of technologies of communication, that communication has become an issue for us. Today we are highly aware of the fragility of 'successful' communication and of the endless possibilities of communicative failure or breakdown both as technical problems *and* as social problems of our relations and interactions with others. To think about how we think about communication as such in relation to new means of communicating, is the distinctive contribution that Peters makes to the historical study of communication.

MEDIA HISTORIES

The historical study of communication tends, as the brief review above indicates, to exhibit the following characteristics: especially in Innis and McLuhan, a synoptic approach is taken which operates within large, epochal time-spans, which embraces a 'total' or global view of history transcending national boundaries, and which deploys an analysis of the historical process whereby the emphasis is not on human beings as historical agents (i.e. as 'makers' of history), but on external (technological) factors which determine the scale and scope of human agency. In all these ways, the history of communication is part of the 'new history' which reacted against the ways in which the academic discipline and field of study was originally established. Histories of communication mobilize a deterministic (or structuralist) approach to their field of study and are strongly anti-humanist, notably so in Kittler's (1999) work, which throughout writes mockingly of 'so-called Man'.

Histories of media tend, in comparison, to be old-fashioned, humanist narratives which focus on the histories of particular media institutions or of particular historic 'moments'. They eschew synthetic, synoptic accounts. These differences should not, of course, be thought of in terms of the preferences of individual historians. It is rather that these two different historical 'topics' – communication and media – call for different methods and accounts. Written histories are, of necessity, about the past. But how much time must pass before histories can begin to be written? The history of print goes back centuries. The history of television goes back fifty years. The history of the internet goes back not much more than twenty years in terms of its general social uptake. In order for History to appear, there must be some distance between the present time (in which history is written) and the past time (which is to be written about). In other words, it may not yet be possible to write histories of 'the media', since this presupposes a synthesis so recent that its historical lineaments are scarcely visible at this time. What we find, instead, as Dahl (1994) pointed out, are institutional histories of particular media: newspapers, radio, and television.

institutional histories of single media

But even this is problematic. What are the grounds for taking newspapers, radio and television as 'the media'? Different taxonomies show up in media and communication departments in European and North American universities, where radio, film and television are often studied together along with 'journalism'. The common tendency to bracket film and television together because they are thought of as 'visual media', and the tendency to neglect the study of radio (often called 'the Cinderella' of media studies), are the results of another 'hidden history', namely, the history of the development of the academic field of study itself (Scannell 2007).◄

► the history of media research as a social institution – Chapter 19, p. 355

The legitimacy of any academic field of study takes time to be established. At the beginning of the twentieth century, the study of modern literatures did not exist as an academic discipline, and within a university culture that privileged the study of ancient literatures (Greek and Roman), the study of things like the modern novel seemed trivial and irrelevant (Doyle 1989; Mathieson 1975). The first undergraduate degree in media studies in the UK was established at the then Polytechnic of Central London (now University of Westminster) in 1975. Since then, the emergence and definition of the field has been fitful and uneven, and has often been the outcome of internal institutional reorganization and the rationalization of existing resources. Film studies developed earlier than media studies, and usually within modern literature departments, from which they sometimes broke away. Film histories, however, continued to privilege the cinematic texts.◀ As film studies developed, it extended its interests to what it regarded as cognate fields of enquiry, namely, photography and television. There is no necessary correspondence between the structure of the media in 'the real world' and the ways in which 'the media' are studied in universities. Historically and 'as a matter of fact', radio and television are very closely linked in terms of their technological, economic, political and institutional formation. Yet, they are seldom studied or researched by academics as related to each other under the rubric of 'broadcasting'. It is, thus, necessary to argue the case for treating 'the media' – before the internet – as, in essence, the interconnections between newspapers (the press), radio and television (broadcasting). I have made this case elsewhere, arguing that the shared structural characteristic of all three is 'dailiness'; a specific temporality that is articulated and given substance in the contemporary world by the interplay of daily newspaper, radio and television services (Scannell 1988, 1996b, 2000).

dailiness

PRESS HISTORIES

The time spans of the development of newspapers, radio and television are quite different. Newspapers as we now know them in North America and Europe can be traced back to the seventeenth century. The technology of wireless telephony was worked out in the late nineteenth century, and its widespread social application as radio begins after the First World War. The technology of television dates from the early twentieth century, and the history of its social usage properly begins after the Second World War (for an overview, see Winston 1998).◀ Not surprisingly, historical work on these developments has a different time span in each case.

Histories of newspapers, in the UK, go back at least to the mid-nineteenth century, and there is a large body of literature on particular newspapers (a five-volume history of *The Times* being the outstanding example (Anon 1935–1958)), journalists, and newspaper owners, nearly all of which were written by people in the business, rather than by professional historians. As such they are largely anecdotal, concerned with significant individuals (there is a subgenre of journalism biographies about outstanding newspaper editors, and outrageous newspaper proprietors) and the politics of their day. But from them, James Curran has argued in an influential synoptic account of British press history (Curran and Seaton 2009), a distinctive consensus emerges as to the meaning and significance of its historical formation. It is yet another variant of the 'Whig interpretation of British history' (Butterworth 1965), in which the emergence of a 'free' political press is seen as a victory over government censorship and control (Curran and Seaton 2009). The key moment is the mid-nineteenth century, when newspapers were freed from punitive forms of taxation imposed by government to prevent 'unlicensed' radical newspapers from criticizing those in power and fomenting civil unrest. In this account, 'the market' appears as the hero; the guarantor of civil liberties and the protector of the political independence of newspapers which no longer function as the mouthpiece of various political factions. In Curran's view, the most authoritative academic history of the British press (Koss 1981, 1984) simply extends

British press

Whig interpretation of history

▶ film studies – Chapter 2, p. 40

▶ chronological table of media and communication – Chapter 2, p. 26

this 'myth' through to the present (Curran and Seaton 2009). Curran, however, has his own 'alternative' account of this history, in which the hero is the ultimately suppressed radical press of the early nineteenth century, and the villain is the market, which, he argues, has destroyed the possibility of a properly political press. Thus, his account reverses the terms of the Whig teleology, but retains its premises. The terms in which press history is thought in Curran's account, then, remain within the traditional concerns of political historiography. The past is interrogated and criticized in the light of a set of unexamined political concerns in the present.

US press

The most influential history of the American press starts from rather different premises. It is a social, rather than a political history, and began as a Ph.D. dissertation in the Sociology Department of Harvard University. Its author, Michael Schudson, was interested in the history of ideals and the sociology of values. He combined both in a historical study of the American press, which began as "a case study in the history of professions and in the genesis of professional ideology". As such, its main concern was with the relationship between the institutionalization of modern journalism and general currents in economic, political, social and cultural life (Schudson 1978: 10–11). The issue that brings into focus all these concerns is the question of 'objectivity' as an ideology or norm for practising journalists:◀ it is the history of the rise and fall of this idea that is traced in *Discovering the News*. Schudson's account, though a chronological narrative, avoids the pitfalls of a teleology. 'Objectivity' is neither the triumph of value-free journalism, nor the hidden, self-deceiving bias of a dominant, market-driven press. What is shown, rather, is that 'objectivity' as a social value is intrinsically historical. The early American press had no concept of 'objectivity', which arose only as the press was industrialized and journalism became fully professional in the twentieth century. The separation of 'facts' and 'opinion', information and comment, was the complex outcome of the commercial pressures of mass production and the extension of democracy. Objectivity became the lodestone of professional journalism in the early twentieth century, not out of a naïve empiricism and faith in 'facts', but rather the reverse. It was a bulwark, Schudson argues, against scepticism and anxieties about the corrosive relativism, the arbitrariness of values, and the subjectivity of belief in a world where one man's opinion was as good as another's and neither had any special claim to truth. Journalistic objectivity was one response to "the hollow silence of modernity" (Schudson 1978: 158). But even as it was articulated as a professional value in the 1930s, the criticism of 'the myth' of objectivity was enunciated, and this criticism became routine in the adversarial Left culture of the 1960s (from which Curran attacks the dominant interpretation of British press history).

▶ objectivity in journalism – Chapter 5, p. 97

HISTORIES OF BROADCASTING

Radio and television are products of the twentieth century, and their historical significance as well as their histories have only recently begun to emerge. The oldest, and longest running, history of broadcasting is by the British historian, Asa Briggs, who began working on the institutional history of the British Broadcasting Corporation (BBC) in the 1950s. The fifth volume in this massive history was published in 1995 (at which point Briggs laid down his pen (Briggs 1961–1995)). When Briggs began, he was operating, as he noted, in uncharted waters. There were no general histories of broadcasting in any country to serve as models. The three-volume history of American broadcasting by Erik Barnouw (1966–1970) had not yet appeared. Neither communication nor media studies had yet appeared as academic fields of study.

BBC: institutional history

Briggs, therefore, found himself in the position of 'inventing' broadcasting history, and his reflections on the methodological and other problems he faced are thus of particular interest. He wanted to write a 'total history' that covered all aspects of the activities of the BBC. This was a truly monumental undertaking since, by the time he got to the Second World War, the BBC's activities were on a global scale; in 1942 it was broadcasting in the short-wave radio band to all parts of the world. There were real difficulties of narrative organization and coherence as his history moved forward slowly on all fronts: home broadcasting, overseas broadcasting, radio and, later, television. There were difficulties of writing an institutional history, which might result in a 'history from above' (reproducing the management view of the BBC and underplaying the attitudes of insubordinate dissidents in the ranks). There was the danger of not being able to see the wood for the trees: it was hard to find room for an historical account of the history of output – the programmes themselves – and their impact and effect on contemporary society. There was, finally, the issue of perspective. Briggs was anxious to avoid "reading back into the past current fashions of description and explanation". He wanted his history to be, above all else, definitive: "to be as accurate and as well backed up (in footnotes) by *all* available evidence as possible". He elected to quote at length from original sources – even though this was not then fashionable among historians – partly to capture lost modes of expression and mood, but also to enable readers who might draw different conclusions from his own assessments to have the necessary amount of published evidence before them (Briggs 1980: 8).

Briggs's work is, above all, a historian's history, which allows subsequent researchers to pursue in greater detail the study of, say, programme making without having to reconstruct yet again the house that Briggs built. The social history of the beginnings of broadcasting in the UK that I wrote with David Cardiff (Scannell and Cardiff 1991) could not have been written without the prior existence of a definitive 'total' history of the BBC. Historians of public service broadcasting in other European countries have also acknowledged their debt to Briggs's history (e.g., Dahl 1976).

BBC: social history

It is a truism that histories are as good as the archives on which they depend. Historians of British broadcasting are lucky to have such a remarkable resource as the BBC Written Archives at Caversham (near Reading), whose holdings currently cover all aspects of the BBC's activities from the earliest days through to the end of the 1970s. Historians of the beginnings of broadcasting in other countries have had a more difficult task, since radio almost everywhere began on a local, commercial basis, and data about the very first radio stations has all but vanished. The perishable character of the spoken word shows up in stark contrast with the permanent trace of writing. Lesley Johnson, historian of early Australian broadcasting, notes what a difficult and disheartening task it was to gather information about the radio stations of the 1920s and 1930s (Johnson 1988: viii–ix). Susan Smulyan, in the absence of data from the stations themselves, draws heavily on early popular radio magazines for her history of the commercialization of American radio in the 1920s (Smulyan 1994). And, Cecile Meadel faced similar difficulties when writing the history of the beginnings of French radio. When she did find data on some of the many radio stations of the period, it was invariably scanty, poorly kept and unclassified (Meadel 1994: 16–17).

historical archives

In spite of such difficulties, in North America and in many European countries there are in place, by now, histories of the beginnings and development of national broadcasting systems, starting with radio and continuing with television. These institutional histories have been complemented by more detailed 'genre' studies of particular aspects of broadcast output; news, drama and documentary, for instance, having received considerable attention. Alongside these are social histories of audiences and of the place of radio and television in everyday life (e.g., Lacey 1994; Moores 1988; O'Sullivan 1991; van Zoonen and Wieten 1994).

histories of genres

'DOING' HISTORY

The past in its fullness is beyond recall. Only its traces remain in any today, and the task of piecing together the fragments, interpreting and reworking them into coherent narrative accounts and other formats, is, of necessity, a cumulative and collaborative process. There is no one 'correct' way of doing this. Historical work is partly determined by the available data (or lack of it) and partly by the predispositions and attitudes brought to bear upon the past by historians in their present. The literature referenced above is characterized by the diversity of its approaches and attitudes to history. But those attitudes are only partly determined by the concerns and prejudices of the historian.

They are also shaped by the nature of the topic and the extent to which it is, or is not, established as an object of historical enquiry. In this respect, the problems of 'doing' broadcasting history are instructive.

Why should it be that *in the first place* broadcasting histories tend to be accounts of particular institutions? We can note that the first 'period' of broadcasting (a historiographical construct, of course) is the history of radio and its institutionalization within the context of particular nation-states. For although radio began, almost everywhere, on a small-scale local basis, technical, distributional, and economic pressures rapidly led to the consolidation of the production and distribution of programmes into centralized, large-scale, national institutions, funded either by advertising revenues or some form of hypothecated tax (a 'licence fee'). The history of broadcasting thus begins with accounts of that process. When that is in place, other historians can engage with what might be called 'second-generation' history. That is how I think of my own historical work on British broadcasting. The existence of Briggs' history made it possible to go back into the archives and begin a closer, more attentive study of the complex business of making programmes, across the major areas of broadcast output. How were the practices of gathering and broadcasting 'news' developed? How did broadcasters discover how to produce entertaining programmes for radio? How was music (what music? whose music?) developed as a major area of radio output? Such questions can only be addressed in detail if accounts of the institutional framework within which these activities were situated are already in place. It then becomes a complex business of gathering data, interpreting and putting it into a coherent narrative frame.

first- and second-generation histories

It requires patience and persistence to sift through a holding as massive as the BBC Written Archives. Such work should ideally be done in a concentrated, continuous way. It is no use doing it occasionally over an extended period. You have to immerse yourself in an archive as I did, several days a week continuously for over a year, in order to feel your way around the holdings (so you get a sense of where to look for a 'missing link'), but above all in order to begin, in time, to see how the bits and pieces fit together. It is like doing a gigantic jigsaw puzzle. But a lot of the pieces are inevitably missing, and so you will have to fill in the blanks by circumstantial evidence where necessary. Archival work, then, shares several features with other qualitative research, including an extended stay in a locale as well as iterative procedures of sampling and analysis.◀

The most obviously 'lost' pieces in the puzzle, for historians of early radio, are the broadcast programmes themselves. The BBC began broadcasting in 1923, but there are no extant recordings of any programmes until the early 1930s, and only a tiny fraction of output before the Second World War was recorded and preserved. So how do you deal with this? There is, of course, a complete record of what was broadcast, day by day, in the programme schedules of *Radio Times*, which started up only months after the BBC got going in 1923. Before the war, all programmes were scripted, and in many cases the transcripts of the programme as broadcast (with last minute emendations and corrections pencilled in) were kept. For example, a very good picture of developments in radio documentary (or 'features' as they were called at the time in the BBC) can be built up from recordings and transcripts of programmes, and from a number of very useful production files which reveal (in the best cases) the whole process of the making of a particular programme from the initial idea through to transmission (Scannell 1986).

recordings of programmes

schedules and transcripts

However, to take a notorious example, there are no transcripts of pre-war news broadcasts (with the exception of the General Strike 1926, and transmissions at the height of the Munich Crisis in 1938). The practice of keeping all bulletins began only with the outbreak of war. We simply do not know what news bulletins sounded like nor what, in detail, the structure and content of any bulletin was like before the war. Accounts of the beginnings of broadcast news are thus, in this strict sense, circumstantial. There is, nevertheless, a wealth of secondary source material about news from which a

▶ qualitative empirical methodologies – Chapter 14

ANALYSIS BOX 12.1: HISTORICAL RESEARCH ON ARCHIVAL DATA

On top of questions concerning the availability of data, the nature of the topic and its status in previous research, one needs to be alert to connections between bits of data that one comes across in different contexts and on apparently different issues. In one of the many news files I examined (Scannell and Cardiff 1991), I came across an exchange of letters between the Home Office (the British ministry of interior affairs) and the BBC. The Home Office wrote to John Reith (Director General of the BBC) on 31 October 1932, querying the inclusion in the previous night's bulletin of a protest from the Metropolitan Police Federation about proposed cuts in police pay. Where had the BBC got this story, it wanted to know? Reith immediately replied that it came from the usual agency sources (the Press Association) and added that he had given instructions that "no stuff from the agencies re cuts in pay, protest etc. is to be broadcast … only HMG's [His Majesty's Government] official statements in future." He further remarked that the same bulletin had included a message telephoned through to the News section from the Commissioner of Police, asking the public not to go out to watch demonstrations (Scannell and Cardiff, 1991: 46–47).

It was difficult to make much sense of this, at first, in the absence of any records of news bulletins, but I noticed the date and recalled that around this time unemployment had peaked at over three million. I then remembered accounts of the National Unemployed Workers' Movement which I had read as background to the BBC's handling of the issue of unemployment (Hannington 1977; Kingsford 1982). When I checked out Wal Hannington's book, all became clear. A massive protest march had arrived in London a day or so earlier and 'subversive' leaflets had been distributed in advance, addressed to the police force: "Policemen! Defeat your own pay cuts by supporting Tuesday's demonstration against the economies!" (Kingsford 1982: 156). On the day of the demonstration – the day the Home Office queried the news item – there had been a huge gathering in Trafalgar Square and an impassioned speech from Hannington appealing to the police not to use their batons against the marchers and the large supporting crowd. But violence broke out, and two days later Hannington was arrested and charged with attempting to cause disaffection among members of the Metropolitan Police, contrary to the Public Order Act of 1919.

This example well illustrates the delicate hermeneutic◄ task that the historian faces when confronting primary data. As always, the date of the document, if available, is a crucial clue. But the text remains an enigma without detailed knowledge of what was happening in the country at precisely that time. Only when that has been discovered does the task of historical interpretation properly begin. What exactly does this nugget of information tell us? Does it show something of the subservience of the broadcasters (of Reith) to the government of the day? Maybe. But how should that be understood? And here the attitude of the historian comes into the equation. For it would be easy to construct some kind of conspiracy theory of hidden complicity between the broadcasters and their political masters in the management of news in ways that served the interests of those in power, thereby showing the role of the BBC in maintaining 'the dominant ideology' or something like that. Broadcasters themselves, however, were well aware of such dilemmas. I vividly remember the moment I came across a memorandum, written days after the Munich Crisis, by the ex-Head of News, in which he declared that "we [the BBC] have taken part in conspiracy of silence", and went on to say that the BBC had failed the British public by not giving it the necessary information as to the causes of the crisis or its implications – the inevitability of war (Scannell and Cardiff, 1991: 88–89). A simple 'reading' of the developing relations between broadcasting and politics, starting with the General Strike of 1926 and going through to the outbreak of war, could plausibly develop a 'Bad News' thesis (Glasgow University Media Group 1976) about the BBC's suppression and

► hermeneutics – Chapter 2, p. 28

distortion of what was happening at the time. But this could only be achieved by ignoring all the evidence of attempts by the broadcasters to resist the manipulations of government, most notably over two of the most sensitive political issues of the 1930s – unemployment and foreign affairs. We have documented in detail the resistances of programme and policymakers in both cases (see Scannell and Cardiff 1991: 64–68 on the 1934 Talks series on unemployment called *Time to Spare*; and pp. 74–78 on a 1935 series, *The Citizen and His Government*, which was suppressed by the Government because it contained communist and fascist speakers).

The past must be understood in its own terms, in the first instance, before rushing to judgement with the wisdom of hindsight. In this regard, distant periods pose some of the same analytical challenges as other cultures.◀ Interpretations of the beginnings of broadcasting should be sensitive to the problems encountered by the broadcasters as they became involved in politics. It should be remembered that the formal conditions of full representative democracy were not established in the UK until 1919 by The Representation of the People Act. The *meaning* of democracy is something that gets worked out and discovered through the actual processes of history. This learning process has been at the heart of the relationship between broadcasting and politics from the beginning through to the present. A hermeneutics sensitive to this unending process would note, as we tried to, how the broadcasters gradually came to understand their own complicity with the political powers in the 'management' of news and information in the inter-war period (Scannell and Cardiff, 1991: 23–133). It would point to the basic problems for broadcasters of discovering how to 'do' informing, news gathering and news-telling. There was no News Department in the BBC until 1934, and the practices of contemporary broadcast journalism with which we are all familiar today go back no further than the 1950s in the UK and the US, and the 1960s and later in most other countries.

reasonably accurate account of its development can be built up. The files of the BBC's various management, policymaking, and departmental committees were invariably useful. The magnificent press cuttings collection was invaluable. Contemporary biographies by politicians and broadcasters were occasionally illuminating. *Hansard*, the verbatim record of the day-to-day proceedings of Parliament, was indispensable whenever there was a political row about news.

organizational documents, press cuttings, and biographies

The study of any aspect of broadcasting, and of other media, is impossible without knowledge of the wider political, social and cultural contexts within which they are situated. Again and again in our study of the production process within the BBC, David Cardiff and I had to reconstruct other histories: of entertainment in the pre-war period, or of the state of musical culture at that time. There were no standard social or cultural histories to guide us on such matters, and so we had to reconstruct them ourselves from contemporary biographies, non-academic accounts and from magazines. It is essential to have a feel for the wider contexts within which broadcasting operates in order to write informed historical accounts of the activities of the broadcasters. I do not wish to be prescriptive as to how this is achieved. History is not a social science, and it tends to resist the impositions of rigid methodologies. The precise method of any particular historical investigation will be shaped and informed by the nature of the topic and the available resources. But a willingness to read widely and to explore supplementary sources is vital. To this, I would add a sense of historical continuities and change over longer time spans than the actual period of study. The historian must look at what came before and after the topic which engages her or him. There is a tendency today still to write of the BBC and the meaning of public service broadcasting◀ as if it was set in place, once and for all, by its first Director General, John Reith.

▶ crosscultural and comparative research – Chapter 11, p. 218

▶ public service broadcasting – Chapter 19, p. 354

But the meaning of public service has undergone significant and important changes in the last eighty years, and necessarily so, since it operates today in conditions very different from the 1920s when it began (see Scannell 1990, 1996a).

CONCLUSION

Histories of communication and of the media converge in the twentieth century, as is apparent in the works by Peters (1999) and Kittler (1999) already cited, and in Kern's (1983) fascinating study of 'the culture of time and space' at the turn of the last century, and Winston's (1998) synoptic history of media technology. The early 'mainframe' institutional histories of the press and broadcasting have been supplemented by all kinds of histories on particular aspects of the press and broadcasting in the last twenty-five years. The establishment of academic journals devoted to historical research◄ – *Media History* and *The Historical Journal of Film, Radio, and Television* – also indicates how well-established this hybrid discipline, split across history and media and communication studies, has become. Also histories of the development of the internet, including its social, cultural and institutional backgrounds, have begun to appear (e.g. Abbate 1999; Turner 2006).

I began work on the history of radio in the late 1970s. Television was then very new. Less than twenty years old in Britain, it had no history while that of its parent medium, radio, was only just becoming apparent. Now both appear to be 'old' media, displaced or overtaken by new technologies of communication that have transformed the world since then. Television today has entered into history, thereby becoming historical. How it appears to us today is very different from how it appeared a generation ago. To conclude this chapter I offer some reflections in the present on recent changes both in the histories of communication and media and in their study.

Television in the 1970s was the dominant medium of communication in everyday life for the societies of North America and Northern Europe. In most of the rest of the world it had not yet arrived. Today television has become an everyday reality almost everywhere except in Africa. In China and India, where it did not then exist, it has (very quickly and very recently) become a central media institution and part of everyday social reality for the vast majority of Indian and Chinese peoples. But nowhere today is it quite the hegemonic medium that it was forty years ago in those countries where it was first widely diffused. Two crucial changes have taken place since then. First, channel scarcity was overcome. In the 1970s television in Britain was defined in terms of the BBC and ITV (its commercial competitor) and in America in terms of the three networks (CBS, NBC and ABC). In the 1980s new systems of distribution (by cable and satellite service providers) created a multi-channel environment with the possibility of household receivers having access to hundreds of different channels rather than two or three. Hard on the heels of these developments came the impact of the internet and the mobile (cell) phone in the 1990s, whose full effects have only been felt in the last ten to fifteen years. The effect of these new 'social media', in themselves and in relation to pre-existing media such as television, is naturally a matter of great interest and concern in the field of media and communication studies today. What can we say about these recent developments that are still very much part of the history-making present, but not yet part of history? I offer a couple of tentative thoughts by way of a conclusion.

cable and satellite television

the internet and the mobile (cell) phone

When I started my work it was natural to think of the study of media within the frame of the nation-state, for at that time it formed the natural horizon of thought and experience for everyone, including academics. In the now 'classic' era of television (from the 1950s to the end of the 1970s) a small number of central broadcasting institutions provided national-popular services on a small number of channels to whole populations. This shaped both the experience of television for viewers and the ways in which it was, at the same time, thought by academics. The power of central media institutions then seemed obvious: they set the information and entertainment agendas for whole societies—as such they surely shaped the worldviews, the tastes, opinions and everyday

► journals and reference works – Chapter 1, p. 3

pleasures of countless millions. The role of national television systems in today's multi-media global communications environment, though still important, is no longer as dominant and defining for the understanding of its impact and effect.

What brought about this change? The answer is surely technological innovation driven by the unceasing restless energy of the global economy and its unrelenting creative search for new things to sell in new markets. In the 1970s it seemed as if powerful centralized institutions like the BBC and CBS controlled and defined the medium of television. They no longer do, and what is meant by 'television' today is something altogether more diverse and plural. Television content is no longer accessible only via the 'box in the living room', and the situations and experiences of viewing have been radically transformed. Immobile large-and-wide-screen, high-definition TV has changed the experience of home viewing. Portable (laptop) and mobile (cell phone) devices now allow TV content to be accessed by anyone wherever they are. On-demand services allow individuals to watch in their own time, and viewing is no longer confined to the times of the daily schedules of central broadcasting services. Huge LCD (liquid crystal display) screens now allow for public collective viewing of media events as they are happening. Increasingly sports venues have such screens, strategically positioned for optimum viewing, in order to allow those present at the event the doubled experience of being there *and* seeing it on TV at one and the same time.

These are but a handful of the transformations of television brought about by continuing technological innovation in the last twenty-five years or so. The internet and the mobile phone have had powerful consequences for national television industries and their audiences around the world. The extraordinary success of YouTube has transformed the meaning of TV content, its production and circulation. The detailed analysis of the impact and effect of these and other changes in the production, circulation and experience of TV content is a task for future generations of research. Meanwhile we can point to one consequence of all this for current academic work on communication and media – namely the absolute centrality of the question of technology for their understanding.

In this chapter I offered a sketch of the pioneering work of the Canadian historian, Harold Innis (and, to a lesser extent, his follower, Marshall McLuhan), in establishing what a history of the world in terms of technologies of communication might look like. It was vulnerable, as I indicated, to the charge of 'technological determinism', an over-simplified view of technologies as agents of social change. In the 1970s and 1980s the 'medium theory' approach of Innis and McLuhan (Meyrowitz 1994) was dismissed for its de-politicized formalism – a charge renewed more recently by the leading British historian of the press, James Curran (2002). I have argued, in reply to Curran, for the historical impact of technological innovation as a central issue for all students of communication and media today (Scannell 2008). The differences between us are one small indication of continuing change in our shared field of academic enquiry and debates about the ways in which it is thought. Both are shaped, as this chapter has tried to show, by the changing character of history itself; that is to say, by changes in the material conditions of life in historical societies and the experience of those changes by its members. The media are quite central to the life conditions and experiences of people around the world today. That this is so is due, in no small part, to the role of technologies of communication as agents of historical change. But *how* they work as such is a task for future generations of historians to investigate, since their long-term effects have not yet begun to appear.

PART

III Practice

SCIENTIFIC APPROACHES AND SOCIAL APPLICATIONS

Doing media research

Media and communication research has developed a whole range of analytical procedures, drawing on the social sciences as well as the humanities. In overview, empirical studies have relied on six different prototypical methods, laid out in Figure III.1. The methods are characterized by their forms of data collection and the resulting types of evidence, in addition to their orientation toward either a qualitative or a quantitative form of inquiry. The following chapters are premised on a distinction between such *methods* and *methodologies* – the concrete instruments of research as compared to the research designs that are motivated by a theoretically grounded purpose of inquiry. In a next step, both methods and methodologies raise additional epistemological and political questions that should be considered part of the practice of doing research.

	Qualitative	**Quantitative**
Speech/verbal language	interviewing (individual and focus group)	survey
Action/behavior	(participating) observation	experiment
Texts/documents	discourse analysis	content analysis

Figure III.1: Six prototypical empirical methods

Empirical research designs

The first group of three chapters presents key concepts, criteria, and procedures of empirical research. Two chapters describe and illustrate the logic of qualitative and quantitative research processes, respectively; one chapter explores and reflects on the complementarity of the two methodological paradigms.

- *Quantitative studies* (Chapter 13) are covered both in terms of their basic categories and operations, and with reference to the relevance of surveys, experiments, and content analyses for different research questions, including data mining of digital media and networked communication.
- *Qualitative studies* (Chapter 14) are presented, in turn, in terms of the explanatory value of interviewing, observation, and textual or document studies, and with reference to some of the specific challenges of analyzing qualitative data, increasingly in computer-supported formats.
- The *complementarity* of qualitative and quantitative research (Chapter 15) is addressed both through concrete examples and in relation to classic problems in the philosophy of science, such as generalization.

Multiple media, multiple methods

The second group of three chapters provides elaborated examples of empirical media and communication studies in which special attention is given to the characteristics and complementarities of different methods and methodologies for particular research purposes. The chapters, further, consider the interplay between media, in everyday communication and in the study of a composite and complex media environment.

- *Reality television* (Chapter 16), its rise and transformation in recent decades, is examined with reference to a large-scale and multimethod study that employed surveys, focus groups, as well as in-depth interviews. The study, further, compared the development of this genre at different historical times and across cultures.
- *Parents' regulation of children's and young people's media use* (Chapter 17) is taken up in a meta-analysis that reassesses the quantitative literature in the area in the light of additional, qualitative evidence. As such, the chapter specifies some of the complementarity – methodological and theoretical – of social-psychological and socio-cultural approaches to communication studies.
- *Personal media* (Chapter 18), specifically cell (mobile) telephones, but also the internet, are addressed in a national baseline study that combined quantitative log data with qualitative interview and diary evidence. Challenging a tendency to study young people as central and prime movers of new media, the study probes the place of personal media in everyday life across the life span.

Unification in the final instance

The premise of the Handbook is that qualitative and quantitative methodologies are different, but equal – they are complementary, can, and should be combined in various multimethod designs for diverse purposes. It is this premise that is summed up in the heading of 'unification in the final instance.' Research traditions may be unified, not in the first instance, through a standardization of the instruments of research, but in the final instance, through a comparison of the kinds of information that different methodologies can yield, and of the inferences that they will support.

Communicating research (Chapter 19)

Like the media themselves, media and communication studies are integral elements of the societies and cultures being examined, feeding back findings and insights into practices of communication. The last chapter returns to the social origins and applications of science, and to the interests guiding different types of media and communication research in different sectors of society. Most students and researchers wish to make a difference through their work. As an institution that is constitutive of contemporary life, media and communication studies necessarily make a difference. Like other social institutions, research cannot *not* communicate. The question is how, in whose interest, and through which empirical methodological and theoretical frameworks the field will make a difference in the future.

13 The quantitative research process

Barrie Gunter

- an overview of *basic concepts* within quantitative research, including *hypothesis testing* and *sampling*
- reviews of *survey* research, quantitative *content analyses*, and *experimental* studies of media, with illustrative examples
- a *comparison of surveys and experiments*, their strengths and weaknesses
- a presentation of quantitative *data analysis*, including *statistical procedures*
- the growing importance of *data mining, webometrics*, and *visualisation* of networked communication

INTRODUCTION

The field of media and communication research is characterised by quite a variety of different research perspectives. That fact stems from the hybrid nature of this field of empirical enquiry, in which investigative approaches have been derived from longer established academic disciplines in the social sciences. Anthropology, economics, geography, history, linguistics, political science, psychology, sociology◄ – have all contributed theories and methodologies for studying the structure, organisation, content, uses and impact of media. While media scholars have, accordingly, debated the merits and shortcomings of different theories and methodologies within limited spheres of inquiry (Neuman 2005; Wimmer and Dominick 2011, perhaps the most significant debate within academic circles (though not the highest profile one in the public sphere) has centred on a dispute between different philosophies of social science about the research perspective that offers the most sensitive and meaningful insights into the role and influence of the media in society.◄ A 'positivist' or hypothetico-deductive school of thought has been lined up against critical and interpretive perspectives. These different social-scientific perspectives vary in terms of the perceived objectives of research, the way social reality and human beings are conceived, the role of theory-driven empirical enquiry and the kind of evidence to which most weight is given (see Neuman 2005). Hypothetico-deductive approaches◄ to media enquiry are concerned with the setting up, proving or disproving of hypotheses, and the eventual establishment of theoretical explanations of events or causal laws which explain relationships between individuals' activities in, and experiences of, media, and their knowledge, beliefs, opinions and behaviour. These phenomena are operationally defined, most often, in quantitative terms to facilitate measurement of the strengths of causal links or degrees of association between them.

► social-scientific sources of media and communication research – Chapter 3

► theory of science – Chapter 15, p. 285

► hypothetico-deductive research – Chapter 15, p. 291

It is not the purpose of this chapter to elaborate upon the distinctions between these philosophies of social science, nor to discuss their relative strengths and weaknesses. This chapter is concerned with the nature of quantitative research, examines the basic concepts of this kind of empirical enquiry and discusses the principal forms it takes. The latter will be divided in terms of whether their main aim is to investigate associative links (surveys) or causal links (experiments) between variables. A further distinction will be made between methodologies concerned with the study of either media audiences or media content – the two foci of quantitative media studies. Since quantitative studies of media content mostly involve a form of surveying of media output, this methodology will be discussed under the heading of survey research. It should perhaps be noted at this point, however, that the systematic analysis of media output may form part of an experimental investigation, too.

The chapter will also examine some of the basic principles of quantitative data analysis and presentation. In quantitative research, measurement is conducted through numbers. The quality of the research is crucially affected by the effectiveness of data processing, analysis and interpretation. The discussion of quantitative research methods inevitably examines not just their inherent strengths and weaknesses, but also when their application is appropriate and inappropriate. To be complete, this review also considers the evolution of quantitative research methodologies in relation to theoretical models of media analysis, and attempts to address any weaknesses of this link.

BASIC CONCEPTS IN QUANTITATIVE RESEARCH

The basic concepts that characterise quantitative research methodologies concern relevant modes of measurement and procedures to analyse the relationships between such measurements. A central notion is the *variable*, which is linked to additional fundamental elements of quantitative research such as concepts and constructs.

concepts

A *concept* represents an abstract idea that embodies the nature of observable phenomena, or an interpretation of why such phenomena occur. For example, individuals can be differentiated in terms of their use of media – heavy users may be distinguished from light users. This media usage, in turn, may be linked to patterns of social behaviour, and may even be used to explain different behavioural patterns. In this context, media usage becomes an explanatory concept. In a different context, the concept of cultivation◀ may be used to describe distinctive patterns of perceptions or beliefs that individuals who are heavy media users hold, and that distinguish them from the perceptions and beliefs held by light media users (Gerbner *et al.* 1986; Wober and Gunter 1988).

constructs

A *construct* comprises a combination of concepts. This term is often used to describe a defining characteristic of individuals that is associated with their personality type. For example, the personality construct of 'sensation seeking' is used to distinguish between people who seek varying levels of optimal stimulation from their environment (Zuckerman 1994). High sensation seekers generally need higher levels of environmental stimulation than low sensation seekers. High sensation seekers, for instance, can be characterised by such concepts as sociability, tolerance for strong stimulation, risk taking and a sense of adventure. Constructs have a dimensional quality, so that individuals can be classified as high or low on the personality dimension of sensation seeking.

variables

A *variable* is an empirical representation of a concept or construct. Whereas concepts and constructs have an abstract quality, variables provide operational measures that can be quantified and manipulated by researchers. For example, gender, age and socio-economic class are variables. Personality characteristics such as aggressiveness, locus of control, extraversion and neuroticism can all be treated as variables. Amount of newspaper reading or television viewing also exemplify variables. Variables can be further defined and differentiated in terms of their constituent *attributes*. Attributes are values or categories into which variables can be divided. In the case of gender, there are two categories – male and female. In the case

attributes

▶ cultivation research – Chapter 8, p. 166

of age, individuals can be differentiated by age group or actual age. Television viewers can be differentiated by amount of viewing into values such as light, medium and heavy viewers on the basis of self-reported or independently observed viewing behaviour.

Types of variables

Variables can be defined further in terms of their relationship with each other. A fundamental distinction is made between *independent* and *dependent* variables. The independent variable is a variable which can be manipulated by the researcher. It is also known as the 'causal' variable, in that it is a concept or construct that is believed to produce some measurable response or outcome. The independent variable is also referred to as the predictor variable in some studies. The dependent variable is the measure of the response or outcome. It is therefore also known as the 'effect' or 'criterion' variable. A principal objective of quantitative research is to establish the closeness of the relationship between independent and dependent variables (Neuman 2005; Wimmer and Dominick 2011). Ultimately, researchers wish to provide evidence that a particular independent variable has a causal relationship with a particular dependent variable (Bryman 2008).

independent and dependent variables

To illustrate this idea, a media researcher may be interested in demonstrating that television news can improve the audience's knowledge of a political event or issue.◄ One theorist might argue that this outcome is dependent upon the way political news is presented in a news bulletin. Another might argue that it depends upon the frequency with which individuals are exposed to such stories (Gunter 1987b). In the first case, a study might be launched in which the position of a political news story in a bulletin is varied. For some viewers, the story is presented at the beginning of the bulletin, while for others it occurs at the end or in the middle. A serial-position hypothesis would lead one to predict that presentation in the middle of the bulletin would result in poorer post-viewing recall of the story by viewers (Gunter 1979; Tannenbaum 1954). In this case, the independent variable is the positioning of the story and the dependent variable is the measurement of story content recall by viewers after the bulletin has been presented.

► recall studies – Chapter 8, p. 160

In the second case, a sample of viewers might be presented with a questionnaire that asks them to report how often they have watched television news over the past week or month (Gunter 1985). Similar questions might be asked about exposure to radio news, newspapers and web news sites. The same respondents would then be asked a series of knowledge questions about a political news story. A separate analysis might be carried out of the frequency with which that story was covered by the news media. The latter measure could be combined with the measure of self-reported news media exposure to define the independent variable of relevant political news exposure. Respondents with heavy and light news exposure could then be compared regarding their scores on the measures of political story knowledge, which would be the dependent variable here.

HYPOTHESIS TESTING

Quantitative research is primarily concerned with demonstrating cause-effect relationships, and any research project begins by setting up a *hypothesis*. A hypothesis is a proposition to be tested, or a tentative statement of a relationship between two variables. While hypothesis testing is not unique to quantitative research, it is one of its fundamental elements, and almost a required aspect of quantitative academic research. (Qualitative research, under a 'positivist' school of social science, may eschew hypothesis testing if its aim is purely exploratory, in which case it is concerned more with the discovery of potential hypotheses for future testing.)

hypotheses

Hypotheses make prognostications about the links between variables (Bryman 2008). They propose that under one set of conditions, if an independent variable is manipulated in certain way (as in experimental studies) or is assumed to have a certain strength (as in survey research), it may be expected to exert a measurable impact on a designated dependent variable. The researcher then sets out to discover if that prediction holds true. The essence of quantitative scientific enquiry is to prove or disprove hypotheses, and the outcome is seen as a contribution to the growth of knowledge. Scientists rarely restrict themselves to testing single hypotheses, however. Through repeated hypothesis testing and the development and verification of new hypotheses, a body of understanding is developed that essentially comprises a series of acceptable and accepted explanations for a range of dependent variables.

research as cumulation of knowledge

Reliability and validity

A core aim of social-scientific enquiry, particularly within the 'positivist' tradition, is the establishment and demonstration of the reliability and validity of research findings. *Reliability* concerns the dependability and consistency of the relationship between two variables or in the score obtained on a single variable at more than one point in time. *Validity* indicates whether a measure properly captures the meaning of the concept or construct it represents. If heavy viewing of violent programmes on television is believed to cause aggressive behaviour in viewers, then for this belief to be accepted as true, two conditions must be met. First, repeated evidence must emerge that exposure to violence on television is followed by increased aggressiveness. Second, the measures of exposure to television violence and of aggressive behaviour must accurately represent those behaviours.

reliability through repeated measurements and tests

Reliability can be established by carrying out repeated tests of phenomena and relationships between phenomena, by repeating such tests among different groups of people with the same results, and by having several researchers run the same test (Siegel and Hodge 1968). Where a particular concept or construct, for example, a personality dimension such as extraversion or sensation seeking, is measured by a series of items, it should be possible to select at random any 50 per cent subset of the total set of items and find that they differentiate between individuals in the same way as any other 50 per cent subset of those items. This is known as split-half reliability testing. Alternatively, a researcher could construct two different questionnaires designed to measure the same concept and administer both to the same group of respondents. This is called multiple forms (Goode and Hatt 1952) or alternate forms (Sellitz *et al.* 1976) reliability.

split-half reliability testing

multiple or alternate forms reliability

Validity can be much more difficult to establish with certainty. Partly because of this complexity, validity is assessed in several ways (Figure 13.1):

- *Face validity* offers a basic level of judgement that a measured variable really measures the phenomenon it represents. A test of proof-reading ability might ask individuals to read and correct errors in a passage of text. The test would provide a clear behavioural representation of the kind of ability being measured.
- *Predictive validity* assesses the ability of a measure to predict a future event that is logically connected to a concept or construct. If a test of extraversion distinguishes between how sociable and outgoing people are, then high scorers should be observed to initiate more conversations and speak to more people at a party full of strangers than do low scorers.
- *Concurrent validity* means that a measure is associated with another indicator that has already been shown to be valid. Thus, a new measure of sociability would be expected to exhibit a high and significant correlation with scores on an established extraversion scale.
- *Construct validity* is a more complex method of establishing a measure's validity. Since a construct usually consists of a collection of concepts and indicators, construct validity requires that a new measurement is shown to be related to a variety of other established and previously verified measures. In the development of a questionnaire measure of aggression, for example, researchers may ask whether it differentiates among individuals who might be expected to exhibit different aggression levels on the basis of other established aggression measures, or whether the new questionnaire measure distinguishes between individuals between whom other judges (e.g. friends, peers, parents or teachers) have distinguished in the same way, or between whom one would expect such differences to occur on theoretical grounds (e.g., gender differences in aggressiveness) (Milavsky *et al.* 1982).

Judgement - based	Criterion - based	Theory - based
Face validity	Predictive validity Concurrent validity	Construct validity

Figure 13.1 Types of validity (source: Wimmer and Dominick 2011: 61)

internal and external validity

A distinction can also be made between *internal validity* and *external validity*. Internal validity means that the design of a research project is free from theoretical or methodological error, and is a term mostly used in experimental studies. An experiment's results could be invalidated if it emerged that its measurements failed to capture the phenomena they purported to measure. External validity is also used primarily in the context of experiments. This concept addresses whether the results can be generalised to other situations or groups of people. Low external validity means that the results are unique to the specific experimental setting in which they were obtained, but are unlikely to occur anywhere else.

Levels of measurement

There are four principal types of measurement in quantitative research. The type of measurement reflects the kind of concept or construct it represents. Some measurements make fairly superficial or crude distinctions between entities, while others operate at a higher or more refined level. An initial distinction can be made between *continuous* and *discrete* variables. Discrete variables can be measured at the *nominal* or *ordinal* levels, while continuous variables can be measured at the *interval* or *ratio* levels. Continuous variables have a number of measurable values which can be located along a mathematical continuum, and measurement is along a scale that rises in increments. Hence, the measurement of time can be made in terms of seconds or minutes; the measurement of distance can be made in terms of various units of length. Discrete variables, instead, make distinctions according to relatively fixed attributes. Objects fall into one category or another. Examples of this form of measurement include gender (male or female), marital status (single, married, divorced, widowed), and religion (Protestant, Catholic, Muslim, Hindu, etc.).

continuous and discrete variables

- The *nominal* level is the weakest form of measurement. Numbers can be used here only to signify categories of objects. For instance, voters can be classified in terms of the specific political party they voted for. Any 'object' which is thus placed within a particular category is deemed to be equivalent to any other, and there is no indication of the degree to which an object belongs to a category.
- At the next level of *ordinal* measurement, objects of analysis are ranked along a dimension, such as smaller to greater, or lower to higher. In the case of socio-economic class, for example, people can be ranked as belonging to different classes, with some classes deemed to be higher than others. Middle class is therefore higher than working class, but there is no indication given of how much distance lies between one class and another.
- At the *interval* level, entities are measured along a dimension that has equal intervals. One commonly used example is temperature. The temperature scale rises in degrees with each degree mathematically equal to any other degree. The weakness of the interval scale is that it lacks a true zero or a condition of nothingness. An intelligence scale is another example of an interval scale. Lacking a true zero, however, it is not possible to say that a person with an IQ of 100 is twice as intelligent as one with an IQ of 50.
- The *ratio* scale is the most powerful form of measurement. This has all the properties of an interval scale and the existence of a true zero. Time, distance, and speed are examples of ratio level scales. An object moving at ten miles an hour is moving exactly twice as fast as one moving at five miles an hour.

These basic concepts are applied in quantitative research, in particular, to measure media audiences, media content and cause-effect relationships between media and audiences. Quantitative methods have demonstrated either associations between media and audiences or direct, causal connections between them, and in the remaining sections of this chapter, these methods are examined in turn. In each case, the principal designs are reviewed first, before attention shifts onto illustrations of how they have been applied by media researchers.

SEARCHING FOR MEDIA-EFFECT ASSOCIATIONS: SURVEY RESEARCH

Surveys are a major form of quantitative research that does not involve any manipulation of participants or their circumstances in advance. Surveys collect data after the fact. Because they obtain information from respondents about their knowledge, beliefs, attitudes, values and behaviours on a post hoc basis, surveys cannot test cause-effect relationships directly. Surveys instead explore relationships or degrees of association between variables. Thus, surveys are entirely dependent upon self-report information supplied by respondents, whereas experiments can complement questionnaire responses with direct observations by researchers. In the media and communication context, surveys have been conducted with both the general public (i.e., media audiences) and specialised groups (e.g., media producers). (For further information about best practice in conducting surveys, see Babbie (1990), Fink (1995a, 1995b), Oppenheim (1992) and Bryman 2008).)

relations of association and after the fact

self-report information

The original form of the modern survey, historically, was the census (Converse 1987; Moser and Kalton 1971). A census compiles information about the characteristics of an entire population. Early censuses were conducted to assess property ownership for taxation purposes, but they also provided a means to establish the availability of young men for military service and, in democratic societies, assisted in the division of populations and territories into constituencies electing their representatives in government. Surveys, in their turn, were developed to document poverty following industrialisation and urbanisation in the nineteenth century.

the census

While censuses attempt to obtain data from everyone in a population, surveys use sampling techniques to select subsets of a population for analysis. With a population numbering many millions of people, it usually is not feasible to question everyone, so that smaller and more manageable numbers must be selected for data collection. The most important objective here is to ensure that the achieved population subset, or 'sample', represents the population as a whole. During the first half of the twentieth century, survey research benefited from advances in scientific sampling procedures and questionnaire design techniques.

population and sample

A classic study illustrating the early adoption of survey research regarding media influences was made by Lazarsfeld *et al.* (1944).◀ This study conducted a survey of American voters to try to understand more about the role of the media (radio and newspapers) in election campaigns. Repeat interviewing of respondents was carried out across the duration of a presidential election campaign in order to assess their exposure to campaign material, as well as their opinions about candidates and awareness of policies. Respondents' social category memberships (sex, age, residence, economic status and education) emerged as important variables that influenced their degree of exposure to mass communication and their political candidate preferences. Further research by Katz and Lazarsfeld (1955) utilised survey methodology to establish the importance of informal social networks for public opinion formation. A specific communication process, labelled the 'two-step flow of communication',◀ posited that the media have an indirect effect upon public opinion, which operates through 'opinion leaders'.

Surveys can be differentiated in terms of their purpose; their administration, including sampling; and their time span.

Purpose of a survey

Surveys can be broadly divided into descriptive and analytical exercises:

- A *descriptive* survey simply attempts to document current conditions or states of affairs. Public opinion polls, for instance, can provide information about people's present attitudes on a specified topic. Historically, descriptive surveys can be traced back

▶ *The People's Choice* – Chapter 9, p. 173

▶ two- and three-step flows of communication – Chapter 10, p. 187

to the censuses, whose purpose was to define general characteristics of entire populations.

- *Analytical* surveys also collect descriptive data, but attempt to go on to examine relationships among variables in order to test research hypotheses. Accordingly, a survey may assess the impact of an advertising campaign on public awareness of a brand and changes in the market share of a product. Such explanatory surveys have also played a prominent part in research into the social effects of the media (e.g., the impact of media violence).

Forms of administration

Surveys collect data through either questionnaires or interview schedules (see Figure 13.2). Respondents may complete questionnaires by themselves, or answer questions that are put to them by an interviewer. Self-completion questionnaires are often posted to respondents who complete this 'instrument' at home in their own time and then mail it back to the researcher. Such questionnaires must be self-explanatory, because respondents are not guided through the data collection procedure by a researcher in person. Questionnaires can also be administered to groups of multiple respondents simultaneously in a theatre or classroom situation. On such occasions, researchers can be on hand to assist respondents with questionnaire completion.

mail questionnaires

In addition, respondents can be interviewed orally, and here they are led through the questions by an interviewer. When this happens, respondents rarely see the complete questionnaire, whether the interviews are conducted by telephone or face-to-face. The latter form of administration can take place in respondents' own homes, in the researcher's office, or in the street. Telephone interviews have the advantage that they can accomplish the data collection very quickly, and that they are relatively cheap. Interviews by telephone can also be conducted with respondents who, for geographical reasons, may be difficult to reach at home. However, such interviews must be kept fairly short, and cannot use questions where respondents need to be shown something visually. Personal, face-to-face interviews represent perhaps the most efficient form of survey administration. This is partly because longer interviews of up to an hour or more are possible in the home, although interviews in streets or shopping centres may be even shorter than telephone interviews. In addition to dealing with any meaning difficulties in questions, interviewers can use visual prompts, and with computer-assisted techniques, they can complete both data collection and analysis rapidly.

telephone interviews

face-to-face interviews

The issue of sampling

It is essential that the individuals in a survey should be representative of the total population from which they are drawn, if researchers wish to generalise their findings to the population as a whole. A key aspect of quantitative research, therefore, is sampling. Samples can be constructed either on a probability or non-probability basis. A probability sample is selected according to mathematical guidelines whereby the chance for the selection of each unit is known; a non-probability sample does not follow such guidelines. The advantage of probability sampling is that it allows researchers to calculate the amount of sampling error in a study. This means that researchers can determine the degree to which a sample is different from the population as a whole in terms of specific characteristics, when the distribution of those characteristics for the general population is already known.

Non-probability sampling

This type of sampling is often used in media research. People are selected for study on the grounds that they are available, convenient to access and prepared to participate. Convenience samples can comprise college students enrolled in a researcher's own courses, or people intercepted in the street. Volunteer samples can be obtained by advertising for participants on notice boards or in newspapers. In each of these cases, the researcher has little control over who comes forward to take part in the study. Consequently, such samples are likely to be biased in their demography and psychological characteristics as compared to the population in general.

convenience and volunteer samples

Mail Questionnaires	
Advantages	**Disadvantages**
Cheap to run Can reach wide geographical area Respondents complete questionnaire at own pace Offer anonymity Avoid interviewer bias	Questionnaires not always returned May suffer delays in responses Responses higher for some social categories than for others No control over how respondents complete questionnaires No one available to clarify questions if parts of questionnaire are not understood
Telephone Interviews	
Advantages	**Disadvantages**
Relatively cheap to run Generates higher response rate than mail questionnaires Researcher can control order in which questions are answered Can provide rapid data collection and processing if computer-assisted techniques are used	Interviews must be kept short Can only reach respondents with telephones No visual prompts possible Open-ended questions are difficult to use
Face-to-Face Interviews	
Advantages	**Disadvantages**
Have the best response rate Permit the longest interviews Visual prompts can be used Interviewers control the way questions are answered Interviewers can probe for more detailed responses	Very expensive to run Interviewers may have problems reaching certain locations (e.g., remote areas, unsafe areas) Interviewer bias can be a problem

Figure 13.2 Advantages and disadvantages of different forms of survey administration

More systematic forms of non-probability sampling are, however, available. While these still do not meet the mathematical requirements of probability sampling, they may nevertheless deliver more robust samples:

- A *purposive* sample – often used in advertising research – is taken when respondents are selected according to a specific criterion, such as their purchase of a particular product.
- A *quota* sample is another selection procedure whereby participants are chosen to match a pre-determined percentage distribution for the general population. If, for example, the distribution of males and females is 49 per cent and 51 per cent in the total population, respondents are selected for a survey until this distribution is matched in the sample.

(A further technique is *haphazard* sampling, whereby participants are selected on the basis of appearance or mere practical convenience. This approach relies on subjective judgements by researchers, rather than any clearly devised system of selection. In some cases, researchers may attempt to recruit large numbers in order to compensate for the lack of a selection system, on the mistaken assumption that bigger means better. In representative sampling, it does not.)

Probability sampling

The techniques of probability sampling include random sampling, systematic random sampling, stratified random sampling, and cluster sampling:

- *Random* sampling is the most basic form of probability sampling. Under this scheme, every individual or unit in a population has an equal chance of being selected. For this purpose, researchers may use a table of random numbers or a computer-based system that taps into electronic databases comprising census data or telephone numbers.
- With *systematic random* sampling, a criterion is fixed to select every *n*th person or unit from a population. To exemplify, a decision might be taken to select one in ten members of a population that totals 1,000. A random starting point is then chosen, and from there, every tenth member is selected for a total sample of 100.
- With *stratified random* sampling, further restrictions are placed upon the selection procedure, although the fundamental element of randomness is retained. If, for example, the aim is to exactly match the sample's demographic distribution with that of the population as a whole in terms of gender, age and socio-economic levels, this aim can be built into the sampling frame. Hence, if 51 per cent of the population is female, random selection of females to the sample will cease once that target has been reached, namely, 510 females of a target sample of 1,000. Sampling may also be stratified, or disproportionate, when studies select certain demographic groups in larger proportions than their population distributions because the end-users of the research have a special interest in particular population subgroups. This is typically the case with advertisers whose products are aimed at particular target markets.
- *Cluster* sampling involves a special case of stratification. A population can be divided in terms of its geographical distribution between different regions, districts and postal codes. The random sampling process is, accordingly, conducted in a progressive and hierarchical fashion. First, regions are randomly selected, next districts are randomly selected from within regions, then postal code districts are selected from within larger districts, and finally individuals are randomly selected from within postal codes. The weakness of this procedure lies in the fact that the postal code districts which are thus selected may represent particular kinds of neighbourhood, as defined by the age or class of their residents. Since other neighbourhoods that were not selected might represent different types of people, the final sample could be demographically distorted.

Time span

Surveys can be distinguished into cross-sectional or one-off studies that obtain, for instance, opinions at one point in time, and longitudinal or repeat studies which can be conducted with the same or different groups of people over time. With attitudes, beliefs and perceptions that are prone to change, repeat surveys are, mostly, more informative than one-off surveys. It should be noted, however, that regardless of the survey schedule that is followed, all surveying involves the collection of self-report data from respondents in which they provide verbal accounts of their opinions or behaviour at specific times.

Cross-sectional surveys

synchronic studies

This first type of survey attempts to establish an aspect of public opinion or behaviour at the time when the study is conducted. A sample of television viewers may be questioned about their current viewing patterns or their opinions about the standards of programmes. During political election campaigns, surveys are conducted to find out who respondents would vote for if the day of interview was polling day. A cross-sectional survey can also be used to investigate correlations between the extent and type of media use that is claimed by different segments of the public and their knowledge or opinions about issues.

Cross-sectional surveys have been used, among other things, to investigate the effects of mass media. In the context of the media violence debate, for example, respondents have been asked to identify or recall details about their television viewing and their aggressive dispositions. They may be given lists of programme titles, asked to report the programmes they like watching best of all, or complete viewing diaries to provide the researcher with some indication of how much they watch and what they watch (e.g., Greenberg 1975; Hartnagel *et al.* 1975; McCarthy *et al.* 1975; McLeod *et al.* 1972; Robinson and Bachman 1972). Within this approach, assumptions are made about the contents of named television programmes, but rarely are these assumptions tested by analysing the programmes themselves. Instead, it is taken as axiomatic that action-adventure or crime-drama programmes contain violence. Hence, if a respondent nominates such a programme among his or her favourites, that is taken as evidence of exposure to televised violence. In addition, respondents' personal aggression tendencies have been assessed through self-report measures and sometimes also through reports from other people (e.g., parents, teachers, friends or peers). However, such correlational surveys do not measure actual behaviour; they merely examine degrees of statistical association between verbally described behaviour.

Cross-sectional surveys have not been restricted to samples of the general public, even if these are by far the most frequent type. Surveys have been conducted among media professionals to obtain data, for instance, on journalists' working practices, job satisfaction among people employed in media industries and their opinions concerning the impact of new communication technologies on the future of their businesses (Bergen and Weaver 1988; Demers and Wackman 1988; Ross 1998; Witschge and Nygren 2009).

Longitudinal research

Longitudinal surveys are an efficient procedure for examining long-term relationships between selected variables because they permit the collection of responses over time. One particular strength of longitudinal methodology is that it enables researchers to examine the plausibility of different types of causal hypotheses. First, researchers can begin to untangle the potential bidirectional causal relationships between media and audience attitudes or behaviour. In other words, exposure to media violence may increase the likelihood of aggressive behaviour, but an aggressive predisposition might also cause individuals to favour watching programmes with violence (Huesmann *et al.* 1984; Lefkowitz *et al.* 1972; Milavsky *et al.* 1982). Second, research using longitudinal methodology can determine whether exposure to media is associated with long-term changes in audiences' attitudes and behaviour.

diachronic studies

Three types of longitudinal research can be differentiated:

1 *Trend studies*. A given population may be sampled and studied at different points in time, so that different respondents are questioned in each survey, but each sample is

drawn from the same population. This type of study is used to survey people about their changing opinions and behaviours over time and can be used to track development across different life stages (e.g., Collingwood *et al.* 2010). Here, samples of respondents are surveyed about their voting intentions before, during, and at the end of a political campaign. Furthermore, trend studies can be conducted using data from secondary sources. For instance, researchers have conducted historical analyses of the relationship over time between the penetration of television sets in a population and its crime rates, using existing statistical data (e.g., Centerwall 1989; Hennigan *et al.* 1982).

secondary analysis of statistical data

2 *Cohort studies.* A cohort study focuses on the same specific subset of a population each time data are collected, although the samples may be different. Normally the individuals participating are linked in some way, perhaps by having the same birth date (a birth cohort), or because they have experienced the same significant life event. For example, a study might survey all children aged five to six years in a community before the introduction of television. Then two years later, after television transmission has begun, another survey may be conducted with those same children at age seven to eight years.

Cohort analysis is a technique that is especially suited to monitor changes in attitudes and behaviour which are associated with maturation. However, because exactly the same people may not be surveyed on each occasion (but different samples from the original cohort), any changes may be attributable to unidentified differences between the actual respondent groups, in addition to age and maturation differences.

To exemplify, Rentz *et al.* (1983) conducted a cohort analysis of consumers born in four time periods: 1931–40, 1941–50, 1951–60, and 1961–70. Soft drink consumption was measured in all the samples that were taken from these cohorts with intervals, and a range of potential predictors of this consumption were assessed. The results indicated a large cohort effect, in the sense that the level of soft drink consumption which had been established early in life in each cohort tended to remain stable later in life, compared with the other cohorts. Rosengren and Windahl (1989) also used cohort analysis as part of their in-depth longitudinal study of television usage by Swedish youngsters. Among other things, they found a slight similar cohort effect, but concluded that age was the prime determinant of habitual television viewing.

3 *Panel studies.* Trend and cohort studies permit the analysis of process and change over time, which is rarely possible in a cross-sectional survey. Yet a limitation of these two types of longitudinal study is that, on each occasion, different people are surveyed. As a result, it is not possible to track changes in attitudes or behaviour over time for specific individuals. In comparison, panel studies involve the collection of data over time from the same sample of respondents – this sample is called a 'panel'. For example, in a study to test for the effects of televised violence on viewers' aggression, repeated surveys were carried out with the same individuals at intervals ranging from one to ten years in order to assess whether an earlier diet of violent programmes was associated not only with aggressiveness at that time, but with aggressive tendencies in later life (Milavsky *et al.* 1982).

Panel studies, however, also have their difficulties and limitations. For one thing, they need to be based on original data collection from the specific panel, whereas trend or cohort studies can be conducted through secondary analysis of previously collected data. For another thing, a special problem is the loss of panel members over time. People interviewed in the first survey wave may be unavailable for, or unwilling to participate in, the second or third waves. In other cases, people move home, die or become untraceable. Consequently, it is quite common that such 'attrition' causes the panel to gradually diminish in size as the study progresses.

Survey studies, whether cross-sectional or longitudinal, can only demonstrate correlational links between variables. Their reliance on self-report or other-report measures is fraught with potential inaccuracies. These may arise from the respondents' memory failure, ill judgement or inadequate knowledge, but as importantly from a form of questioning that provides non-valid verbalised representations of the aspects of everyday reality under study. Through experimental methodologies, quantitative researchers have examined relationships between media and audience variables more directly, as a later section explains in detail.

SURVEYING MEDIA OUTPUT

Survey principles can also be applied to the analysis of media contents. This quantitative assessment of media output – content analysis◀ – can be traced back to the 1940s when wartime intelligence units monitored radio broadcasts for their music and news content as indicators of the morale and movements of the enemy (Wimmer and Dominick 2011). Content analysis was soon taken up by social scientists to monitor more general social and economic trends. As early as 1910, Max Weber had suggested launching a study to monitor press coverage of political and social issues alongside surveys of public opinion, thus anticipating agenda-setting research◀ (see Beniger 1978). In the second half of the twentieth century, the methodology was increasingly applied to a wide range of media issues. Prominent applications have examined patterns of news coverage in order to ascertain the agenda-setting role of media (McCombs and Shaw 1972) and patterns in the representation of social groups and events in order to assess cultivation effects of media on public perceptions of social reality (Gerbner 1972).◀

An early definition of content analysis conceived of it as "a research technique for the objective, systematic, and quantitative description of the manifest content of communication" (Berelson 1952: 18). Krippendorf (2004) defined it as a research technique for making replicable and valid references from data to their context. And Kerlinger (1986) suggested that content analysis is a method of studying and analysing communication in a systematic, objective and quantifiable manner for the purpose of measuring variables. This last definition in particular encapsulates the defining ingredients of any traditional form of quantitative analysis of media output. Content analysis is, first, systematic in that it utilises a principled form of media output sampling and content coding. Next, it is objective in that the researcher's own idiosyncrasies and biases should not affect the analysis. Operational definitions and rules for the classification of variables should be explicit, so that other researchers could repeat the procedure. Finally, content analysis is quantifiable in that its main focus is on counting occurrences of predefined entities in a media text. On this last point, purely quantitative forms of content analysis have been challenged for displaying a lack of sensitivity to hidden meanings that may be conveyed by media texts (see Merten 1996). Thus, counting and quantifying may need to be supplemented by interpretive procedures which can clarify the weight and implications of singular media messages in terms of their potential impact upon the audience (Gunter *et al.* 2003).

Five main *purposes* of content analysis have been identified (Wimmer and Dominick 2011):

1 Describing patterns or trends in media portrayals.
2 Testing hypotheses about the policies or aims of media producers.
3 Comparing media content with real-world indicators.
4 Assessing the representation of certain groups in society.
5 Drawing inferences about media effects.

In each case, studies must return to and depart from the basics. A quantitative content analysis is designed to provide a descriptive account of what a media text (film, TV programme, advertisement, newspaper report, web site, etc.) contains, and to do so in a form that can be repeated by others. In putting together a content analysis, then, the researcher must work through a number of stages of measuring and sampling.

▶ content analysis – example, Chapter 6, p. 110
▶ agenda-setting research – Chapter 8, p. 161
▶ cultivation research – Chapter 8, p. 166

Measuring media content

Having decided upon the general topic of investigation, it is necessary first to define the 'things' to be measured. Here, the basic concept is the 'unit of analysis' – the textual element that is to be counted. In addition to the unit of analysis as a whole, there may be features or attributes of that unit about which data are also collected. The data collection process as such proceeds by relying on a 'coding frame'. This is a form on which the occurrences of the different categories relating to the unit of analysis, its features and attributes, can be numerically catalogued.

units of analysis

coding frame

To illustrate, a content analysis of gender representation in television advertising would focus on appearances by males and females. The unit of analysis in this context would be an appearance by a male or female character, either on screen or as a voice-over. Further analytical categories may then be deployed to describe in more detail the nature of these appearances. For instance, the researcher might be interested in establishing not only how often men and women appear at all in television advertisements, but also whether they appear with differing frequencies in different social roles or in connection with different product types (Furnham *et al.* 1997; Furnham and Skae 1997; Furnham and Schofield 1986).

Some studies have identified theoretically relevant patterns simply by analysing media content in terms of its major themes. In an investigation of the extent to which films released in Britain between 1945 and 1991 were characterised by crime themes, Allen *et al.* (1997) assigned films to one of ten genre categories (western, crime, war, romance, fantasy, sex, farce, adventure, drama, other) on the basis of details in the film synopses. The analysis had two parts. First, the presence of crime content in each synopsis was assessed by examining it for mentions of a crime, criminals or the criminal justice system. Then, the film was classified according to the ten genre categories. In the case of crime films, this classification meant that the "primary focus of the narrative is on the causes or consequences of illegal activities, central characters include criminals, victims and those who work in the criminal justice system (e.g., private eyes, amateurs, police, courts, gangsters)" (Allen *et al.* 1997: 92).

In the US National Television Violence Study, units of analysis were defined at more than one level (*National Television Violence Study* 1997; see also Potter and Smith 1999). Whereas previous television violence content analyses had emphasised counting violent acts as such, this study included more global measures of violence that would better represent the contextual features of violence. Three levels of measurement were devised: the 'PAT'; the scene; and the programme. A PAT represented an interaction between a perpetrator (P), an act (A) and a target (T). A sequence of PATs, either continuous or separated by brief cutaways or scene changes, might together make up a violent scene, and such sequences afforded an opportunity to examine relationships between discrete acts of violence and their meanings within the scene. Finally, the researchers argued that larger meanings seemed to be conveyed by the pattern of violence as a whole within a programme, and that this meaningful pattern could only be effectively interpreted when analysed within the full context of the programme.

In addition to such incidents or actions, other units of analysis that are often coded include the agents in either fictional output or news. In the case of news, it is particularly an analysis of the sources of quotes, comments or other material that can yield insights (Lasorsa and Reese 1990). In fictional media content, an analysis of the attributes of actors or characters can yield evidence about the proportional representation of different social groups. Furthermore, studies of the presence of different types of sources in news or other factual output can provide evidence for assessing the balance, neutrality, thoroughness and impartiality of reporting. This form of analysis may examine the range of sources used; which groups, organisations or institutions they represent; and the context (interview, official meeting, press conference) in which they appear. Such analysis may also examine the kind of information sought and obtained from different sources, and any indications of the status of the source (Ericson *et al.* 1991).

Sampling media content

Once the body of content to be considered has been specified with reference to theoretical purpose, and the units of measurement have been selected, the researcher has to determine how much of that content to analyse. In some instances, the universe may be small enough to be analysed in its entirety. More often, researchers must sample a subset of content from the total universe, since it is too large to be analysed in full. In contrast to mass publics, which will have been surveyed in their entirety in population censuses, thus enabling a construction of sampling frames based on known population parameters, such a point of comparison is not available for surveys of media output.

'population' of contents to be sampled

Partly for this reason, sampling in content analysis often takes place in more than one step. A first step may be to specify which content sources are to be sampled. For example, in a study of newspaper coverage of current events, the first step is to decide which particular national or local newspapers are to be analysed. Then a decision must be taken about how many editions of each newspaper to analyse, and over what period of time. A further step may be to decide how much, or which parts of the newspaper to analyse. At this level, one has to consider how many 'stories' to analyse and how these should be defined and delimited. Finally, the analyst will consider whether there are specific story ingredients that need to be measured.

Previous content studies have established some rough guidelines for sampling. Stempel (1952) drew separate samples of 6, 12, 18, 24 and 48 issues of a newspaper and compared the average content of each sample size in a single subject category against the corresponding total for the entire year. He found that each of the five sample sizes was adequate, and that increasing the sample beyond 12 issues did not significantly improve upon the accuracy of findings. In the long-standing content research into television violence, some studies have restricted programme samples to a single week (e.g., Gerbner *et al.* 1977), while others have opted for samples of up to four weeks. In some cases, chronological weeks are sampled, while others have compiled composite weeks by selecting one day from each of seven different weeks (Gunter *et al.* 1996; Gunter and Harrison 1998).

chronological and composite sample weeks

The issue of content sampling was examined very closely by the *National Television Violence Study* (1997). This study analysed a far larger sample of programme output from a larger number of television channels than any previous American content study, and the total project sample, unusually, covered programming broadcast throughout the day. What distinguished this research most of all, however, was its use of a random sampling frame to select programmes over a period of 20 weeks each year. The programmes were chosen with a modified version of random sampling, as described above. Two half-hour time slots (defined by hour of day and day of week) were randomly selected for each channel during each week that sampling occurred. Once a time slot had been selected, the *TV Guide* was consulted, and the programme corresponding to that time slot was entered into a scheduling grid several days before the actual broadcast in the target week, so that recording and coding could be prepared. This procedure was repeated until a full composite week of programmes for each channel had been compiled for analysis.

Limits to quantitative content analysis

Quantitative content analyses tend to be purely descriptive accounts of the characteristics of media output, and often make few inferences in advance about the potential significance of their findings for what they may reveal about production ideologies or the impact on audiences. In order to support conclusions about media processes and effects, theoretically informed decisions have to be made about which aspects of media content to analyse and classify. The most informative content analyses, therefore, will be produced by analysts who choose their content categories with reference to an explicit theoretical framework. Purely descriptive, atheoretical applications of this technique may yield reliable indicators of the manifest content of the media, but will contribute only in a limited way to a better understanding, either of the forces that lie behind that content, or of its eventual impact upon audiences.

TESTING CAUSALITY DIRECTLY: EXPERIMENTAL RESEARCH

Like surveys, experiments have been used in media research for more than 50 years. Experimental research usually involves a quantification of the effects of media upon their audiences, although experimental methods have also been used to investigate the way people use media. In the 1940s and 1950s, experimental methodologies were employed particularly to investigate the impact of media messages on opinions about the enemy in wartime (Hovland *et al.* 1953), and to study the effects of production techniques on learning from informational media (Belson 1967; Tannenbaum 1954; Tannenbaum and Kernick 1954; Trenaman 1967). In the 1960s, experiments came to be used, not least, to study the effects of media violence (Bandura and Walters 1963; Berkowitz 1964; Feshbach 1961). Useful sources of information about experimental practice and designs are Bailey (1994) and Neuman (2005).

An experiment generally begins with a hypothesis about a likely outcome following an event, or set of events, that can be controlled or manipulated by the researcher. In media research, an experiment will typically create a set of conditions under which an individual, or group of individuals, are exposed to a media stimulus, who are then invited to respond in some way. The conditions are constructed in such a way that the media can be said to have caused a particular kind of audience response. For instance, if one wishes to test a hypothesis that a media depiction of violence may have an effect upon the behaviour of an audience, a minimum of two situations will be created in which different audience groups watch either a violent or a non-violent portrayal. Subsequently, both groups will be placed in another kind of situation in which there is an opportunity to behave aggressively. The research hypothesis might predict that those who have been exposed to media violence will behave more aggressively than those who have been shown non-violent material. Quantitative measurements would be taken to establish whether that prediction is borne out by the actual, observed behaviour of the two groups.

Experiments tend to investigate smaller numbers of respondents than surveys, because they operate on a different logic. Participants in an experiment are allocated to either experimental or control groups. The former are exposed to the manipulated independent variable(s), while the latter are not. However, participant samples may be non-representative. One reason for this is that much experimental research on media derives from psychological research traditions, which have conceived of many of the psychological processes of interest as constants across individuals. Non-representative samples are compensated for, in part, by the 'random assignment' of participants to either experimental treatments or control conditions – a key concept in experimentation. Thus, even if the participants do not represent the wider population, within the confines of the experiment the random assignment of participants to the two sets of conditions controls against biases in the findings. This procedure also aids replication. The conditions and steps of an experimental study are so minutely spelled out that another investigator could readily repeat the study to find out if the original results stand up.

experimental and control groups

random assignment of subjects to groups

The main advantage of experimental research is that it enables research to test for evidence of direct cause-effect relationships between variables. Hence, if one variable is presented at a particular point in time, there will be a measurable impact upon a second variable observed at a later point. In addition, experimental research allows the investigator to exercise control over some or all of these variables. In a study of the impact of media on an audience, the researcher can determine the content to which individuals are exposed, the context in which the exposure occurs, and the ways in which they are asked to respond subsequently.

relations of direct causality

One weakness of experiments is that they tend to be carried out in artificial conditions. A laboratory environment is quite different from the everyday, social environment. In media research, the need to control for the inherent complexities of media content when examining the effect of

artificial conditions

one of its aspects may result both in the respondents' consumption of media content under highly artificial conditions, and in a selection of media content extracts that fail to reproduce their normal media experience. An investigation of the impact of televised violence on viewers in which violent extracts of a few minutes' duration are shown to viewers, thus, removes the violence from its original programme context, which under ordinary viewing conditions might influence how viewers respond to violence.

A second weakness is that participants may 'second-guess' what the study is about, and what the experimenter expects to happen. By responding accordingly, they may give the experimenter what he or she wants. Such 'demand characteristics' can bias the results of an experiment, because participants no longer behave the way they might otherwise have done under the specified conditions. A related source of bias is 'experimenter bias'. In this case, the experimenter may unwittingly give away clues about the hypothesis by giving stronger encouragement to participants to behave in one way than in another. To counteract such problems of bias during the interaction, a double-blind technique can be used, in which neither the person running the experimental session nor the participants know whether a given participant is in an experimental group or a control group.

demand characteristics

double-blind techniques

Experimental designs

Experimental designs differ principally in terms of the number of stages and conditions they comprise. Some experiments employ tests before and after a manipulation of an independent variable, others use tests following the manipulation only. In some experiments, only one group of participants is studied, while in others, two or more groups may be studied.

Classic experimental design

This design is also known as a 'pre-test – post-test with control group' design. Such experiments use at least two groups, of which one is a control group. Participants are randomly allocated to these groups, and then tested prior to, and following, an experimental manipulation.

pre-test – post-test with control group

Pre-experimental designs

A classic experimental design is not always attainable, if too few participants or resources generally are available. Researchers may then settle for lesser designs with fewer controls. A *one group, post-test only* design uses just one group and no pre-test. For example, a group of viewers may be shown a television news programme after which their knowledge of the news stories in question is tested. In this case, without a pre-test, it is impossible to determine how much knowledge they already held about these stories before seeing the programme, even if the findings of such a design may reflect on the processing of information from media or on their forms of presentation.

A slightly more advanced design is the *one-group, pre-test – post-test* design with only one group of participants, but including a pre-test as well as a post-test. Extending the example above, participants would here be tested for their knowledge of relevant issues before the news programme, and then for any changes to that knowledge after viewing the programme. In the absence of a control group, who would be 'pre-tested' and 'post-tested' without seeing the news programme, it is again difficult to infer that any change in the experimental group's knowledge resulted from exposure to the programme. One alternative explanation might be that the pre-test itself encouraged participants to rehearse their knowledge of the news, so that by the second test, they were able to perform better. An additional explanation of any knowledge change over time, if there is a gap of hours or days between the two tests, could be participants' exposure to other news media that also contained information about the stories in question.

A third version of a pre-experimental design is a *static group comparison,* in which a post-test only is employed, but applied to two groups. In this case, one group might be shown a news programme while another group would not. Any differences between the two groups in their post-test knowledge scores, however, might be due to pre-existing knowledge differences between them, and should not simply be explained in terms of exposure to a news programme.

Quasi-experimental designs

While quasi-experimental designs do not reach the control standards of the classical design, because they do not include a pre-test stage, unlike pre-experimental designs they do at least employ a control group. With the *post-test only with control group* design, participants are randomly allocated to experimental and control groups, but are tested only after the experimental manipulation has been implemented. Although random assignment reduces the chances that the groups will differ before treatment, without a pre-test a researcher cannot be sure.

It should be added that, even with a pre-test, as in the classical design, measurement issues can arise. Thus, a pre-test may influence the way participants react during and after the experimental treatment because the initial test stage has given away clues as to the purpose of the experiment, or has given them the opportunity to practice a relevant skill. The 'Solomon four-group design' offers a solution to this problem. Here, for some participants in both the experimental and control groups, pre-tests and post-tests are run, while for others, only post-tests are used. The aim is to control for possible effects of the pre-test as well as of the experimental manipulation on the post-test scores. If the groups who were pre-tested differ in their post-test performance from those who were not pre-tested, the researcher can conclude that the pre-test itself had an effect on post-test results, thus potentially biasing the findings concerning the effect of the central experimental manipulation.

Solomon four-group design

Factorial designs

The experimental designs considered so far are all set up to investigate the effect of a single independent variable per group, regardless of whether control groups and a pre-test were used or not. In many studies, however, experimenters are interested in examining the effects of more than one independent variable upon a designated dependent variable among the same group of individuals. It is possible that two or more independent variables produce joint and distinctive effects upon a dependent variable. It is also possible that their effects are interdependent, so that one independent variable only has an influence upon a dependent variable in the presence of a second independent variable.

In factorial designs, accordingly, two or more independent variables or 'factors' are manipulated. Factors, in addition, may have two or more aspects to be considered in the analysis. For example, in an experimental study of the effects of various attributes of both television programmes and advertising on viewers' recall of the advertising, there may be three types of programming (holiday programme, car programme, and cooking programme) and three types of advertisement (holidays, cars and cookery products). In a factorial design, these attributes, which amount to experimental treatments, would produce nine conditions, as each type of advertisement is embedded, in turn, in each type of programme. A full experimental study would thus require nine groups of participants.

Repeated measures designs

As suggested by the previous example, one of the main disadvantages of a factorial design is a practical one, since it requires different sets of participants for each experimental condition. Each time a new independent variable is introduced, the number of cells or groups that is generated within the design increases, requiring an increase also in numbers of participants. One way of resolving this problem is to obtain measures concerning more than one independent variable from the same group of participants. Such a repeated measures design, if applied to the factorial advertising experiment described above, could examine the same number of variables with just three groups. The groups would be defined by the type of programme they are exposed to, but each programme would be embedded with all three types of advertisement. This solution, of course, raises further questions of whether the presentation of the advertisements together, or their sequence, may affect the audience response.

Experimental contexts: the problem with laboratory research

To sum up, then, experiments may be equipped to test causal hypotheses, but are not without serious limitations. An important shortcoming of experiments testing for media effects on audience attitudes and behaviour stems from the conditions they create for examining such links (Cook *et al.* 1983; Stipp and Milavsky 1988). Laboratory conditions do enable researchers to exert control over the behaviour of their participants as well as over various environmental factors which might influence their behaviour in the real world. However, such research may lack external validity; its findings may not be generalisable beyond the laboratory.

issues of external validity

In research on behavioural effects, for example, researchers have frequently created artificial measures of behaviour, especially when studying the effects of media violence on audience aggression (Berkowitz 1964; Berkowitz and Geen 1966; Donnerstein and Berkowitz 1981). While there are sound ethical reasons for this, the responses measured in experiments often fail to resemble what would be more commonly seen as 'aggressive behaviour'. The laboratory creates a social environment all its own in which the usual sanctions against behaving in particular ways (e.g., aggressively) are suspended (Comstock 1998). At the same time, experimenters artificially constrain the responses that participants might make. In aggression experiments, participants are normally given only one behavioural response option – one of aggression. Yet, in a laboratory experiment that was designed to test the effects of exposure to violent pornography on male's behavioural reactions towards a female target, the men under study showed little inclination to use aggression against this female if a non-aggressive response alternative was made available to them. Even when the female had earlier been insulting to them, they chose the non-aggressive alternative (Fisher and Grenier 1994).

priming effects

Studies that utilise the repeated measures designs within a laboratory setting face special problems which arise from 'priming' or conditioning effects. An earlier exposure to similar stimulus materials may affect respondents' reactions to materials which are presented later by providing points of comparison or a frame of reference for judging those later materials. And, again, participants may receive clues from the earlier materials as to the experimental hypothesis, which may lead them to behave in accordance with that hypothesis.

Research in naturalistic settings

ecological validity

To overcome problems of 'ecological' validity, experiments can be carried out in more naturalistic settings. Here, the participants in experiments are observed in surroundings where they may not be aware of the research going on. Two such categories of real-world experiment can be distinguished: those in which the researcher manipulates a set of conditions in a naturalistic environment, and those in which the researcher takes advantage of some naturally occurring event or change of circumstances, the effects of which can be measured. The first type of study is commonly referred to as a field experiment, and the second type as a natural experiment (see MacBeth 1998):

1 In *field experiments*, researchers often study pre-existing groups, but they assign these groups to different conditions of media exposure. The groups may be observed, first, during a baseline period to establish their similarity, and again after the exposure period. An example would, again, be an experiment to study the effects of television programmes on viewers' aggressiveness. In a cable television environment in which the flow of programmes into people's homes could be controlled by the supplier, it would be possible to create two different groups: one that receives programmes containing violence, and another that receives violence-free entertainment. Over a number of days or weeks before, during, and after this treatment, the viewers could be monitored by someone in their family for any changes of mood or behaviour that occurred as a result of this manipulation of their television diet (see Gorney *et al.* 1977).

2 In *natural experiments*, researchers take advantage of a naturally occurring change in the availability of media in order to assess the impact of this change on the people in that environment. For example, a community with access to television or internet could be compared with another community that has

less or no access to the medium in question. Since the early days of television, research has examined communities in which television was introduced for the first time, relying on pre-TV and post-TV observations and tests to assess the impact of television on the community (see Charlton 1997; Williams 1986).

The problems faced by field experiments are mainly ethical and practical. Some research issues would be unethical and socially irresponsible to investigate in the field.◀ For example, studies of the effects of sexually violent pornography upon men's attitudes toward female sexuality, their propensity to commit rape themselves and their sympathy for rapists must be conducted under controlled conditions. The 'effects' measures cannot take the form of real behaviour (i.e., rape), but must rely on simulations in which changes of attitude or perception can be monitored, and then immediately countered through elaborate debriefing sessions with participants.

On the practical front, field experiments can be difficult to run because they occur in environments over which the experimenter's control is restricted. As a result, it may not be easy to create all the conditions that satisfy the requirements of a classic experimental design or of a sound factorial or repeated measures design. Participants may not always agree to make themselves available for observation in the same way they would in a laboratory experiment. Moreover, researchers may need to gain permission to make clandestine observations of participants, or to secretly manipulate aspects of their social environment in an attempt to instigate some change in their behaviour. This last consideration is especially important in research involving children.

SURVEYS OR EXPERIMENTS: HOW DO THEY COMPARE?

This chapter has focused on the two principal forms of quantitative research – surveys and experiments – which have been predominantly concerned with audiences, either by demonstrating cause-effect relationships or by establishing the possibility, through evidence of association, that such relationships might exist between media and audiences. The two approaches have, however, also been used to examine aspects of media production (see Wimmer and Dominick 2011). As general methodologies, surveys and experiments have their own inherent advantages and limitations, to be weighed in designing concrete empirical studies.

Experiments, in sum, are designed to examine cause-effect relationships between variables in a direct sense. For this purpose, researchers manipulate media and audiences under artificial conditions, or else take systematic measurements of phenomena that occur within natural environments where a specific event has taken place to bring about a radical change. There is nearly always an element of artificiality about experiments, because researchers must be able to relate measurable changes in one variable and measurable changes in another variable in such a way that a causal connection can confidently be inferred. The possibility that the 'criterion' or dependent variable was changed by some other factor other than the independently manipulated causal variable must be reduced to a minimum.

The *weaknesses of experiments* can be listed as:

- their use of non-representative samples
- the degree of artificial control over the environment being studied
- the contrived nature of many of the media and audience measures that are deployed
- the difficulty of controlling totally for extraneous factors that could have affected the criterion variables.

The results of experimental studies may therefore lack any validity, in the predictive or explanatory senses, in the real world beyond the controlled environment of the study.

Surveys, by comparison, enable researchers to study media and audiences in their natural environments. Relationships between media, communications and audiences are not manipulated in any artificial sense, but are observed as

▶ research ethics – Chapter 19, p. 366

they occurred, unencumbered by experimental restrictions. Surveys also tend to involve much larger samples of people and media output than do experiments. Furthermore, whereas experiments tend to be dependent upon convenience or volunteer samples because they are usually more demanding of participants than other research methods, surveys are able to draw far larger samples that are representative of the general populations from which they are drawn in terms of important social and psychological characteristics. This means that their results can be more readily generalised to the wider populations from which samples were drawn.

The *weaknesses of surveys* are:

- their dependence on post hoc, self-reports of phenomena, which may suffer from inaccuracies of detail
- their use of verbal measures of observable events that may similarly fail fully to represent what actually occurred
- their reporting only of degrees of association, or correlation, between variables, which cannot on their own conclusively demonstrate causality.

To exemplify, survey respondents' verbal reports of how much time they normally spend watching television in hours per day may be characterised by a significant degree of error. Another means of surveying television viewing, used widely by broadcasting systems around the world, is the TV meter.◄ A metering system usually has two components: one automatically registers when the TV set is switched on and which channel it is tuned to, and the other requires viewers to report their viewing, either in a paper diary or, more often these days, via a remote control handset. While technologically sophisticated, such measurement methods in fact merely indicate the presence of one or more persons in the room in which a TV set has been switched on (and only if the respondents remember to check in), and not whether they are actually watching the screen. Methodological tests have shown that when compared against direct observations, self-report measures are inaccurate to a degree which may render them useless for anything other than a very broad indication of whether someone is a relatively heavy or light viewer (Anderson and Burns 1991; Bechtel *et al.* 1972; Gunter *et al.* 1995).

In media effects studies, surveys are limited in the degree of detail with which they are able to measure a person's media consumption. Even if measures relying on respondents to recall, for instance, web sites they visited or programmes they watched on television in the past week, or newspapers or magazines they read over the past month, are reasonably accurate per se, it may be necessary to know much more about the nature of the specific content of these media in order to assess its effects on audiences' knowledge, beliefs, attitudes, or behaviours.

studies of children's media use

In one particular realm of research, where both surveys and experiments have been prominent, their appropriateness must be weighed with other considerations than the purity of measurement. Studies of children's fright reactions to films and television programmes have variously measured young viewers' responses to horror and other suspenseful content in laboratory settings; have questioned young respondents about their memories of scary movies; and have interviewed parents about their observations of their children's reactions to frightening films and television (Cantor 1994). Although survey interviews can yield interesting insights, they are, again, dependent upon children's or parents' recollections. Experimental methods can, with greater precision, explore whether specific kinds of portrayal cause children to become scared, and they can shed light on how such reactions change with maturity. Experimental studies have shown, for instance, that children under eight years are frightened by scary monsters seen on screen, whereas older children become more anxious about unseen dangers lurking off-screen (Sparks and Cantor 1986). Whether an on-screen character is attractive or ugly, and whether it behaves cruelly or kindly, can have independent and interdependent effects upon how children react (Hoffner and Cantor 1985). These studies have only been able to demonstrate the significance of these mixtures of characteristics by experimentally manipulating

► TV meter studies – Chapter 8, p. 159

ANALYSIS BOX 13.1: SURVEYS AND EXPERIMENTS COMPARED: THE CASE OF CULTIVATION RESEARCH

A prominent example of the difference between surveys and experiments is research into the cultivation effects of television.◀ Through survey evidence, this research has found correlational links between the amount of viewing that is claimed by respondents and certain patterns in their social beliefs, perceptions and levels of anxiety (Gerbner *et al.* 1977, 1979, 1986). Such global measures of television viewing may lack the necessary sensitivity to the significant variations in the message content of television.

More detailed measures of viewing habits, using diaries, have indicated that certain social perceptions may be sensitive to influences from particular types of programmes, but not from others (Gunter 1987a; Wober and Gunter 1988). An analysis of British viewers found no link between their perception of personal victimisation in their local neighbourhood and any aspect of their television viewing, while a corresponding analysis of viewers in Los Angeles found the same perception to be associated with their reported viewing of US-produced crime drama shows (Gunter 1987a). This suggests, among other things, that if the information of certain programmes is seen by viewers to have a direct relevance to their immediate social context, it may affect their particular perceptions of that context. However, surveys can explore this link only in a very general fashion.

In comparison, the application of experimental methodology to cultivation research has made it possible to explore such links in greater detail. Just as certain general features of a television series, such as its cultural setting, may render its content especially pertinent to how some viewers form judgements about certain aspects of their own or other societies, such effects may also be influenced, at a more detailed level, by how, for instance, conflicts are resolved in the series. Experiments have shown that the same television drama can have different effects upon viewers' perceptions of crime and their associated anxiety reactions if the ending is manipulated so that, in the version shown to one group, criminals are brought to justice, while in another version they are not (Bryant *et al.* 1981). Further, reality programmes that depict crime on television can have a more powerful impact on viewers' perceptions of crime than fictional depictions (Tamborini *et al.* 1984). While surveys may also reveal such differential degrees of association between social perceptions and the exposure to particular types of television content (Gunter and Wober 1982), they are less appropriate for establishing whether viewers were especially attentive to certain messages within programmes. If, instead, an experimental methodology is chosen, programmes can be edited to include or exclude specific ingredients, so that differential audience reactions can be systematically measured in post-viewing tests.

a story to create different versions of the same character.

There are occasions, however, when researchers must temper their enthusiasm for using experiments and limit themselves to survey interviews, not least with children. Even though the evidence will be less powerful in an explanatory sense, the experimental manipulation of fear in children may be deemed unethical. The creation of genuinely adverse reactions among children, in response to a specially designed or selected horror scene, might add to the wealth of scientific knowledge, but could likely cause undue harm that may not easily be undone. Accordingly, where there is a possibility that fright reactions may be detrimental to a child's development, such responses rightly tend to be studied after the fact through survey interviews.

Quantitative methodologies, like other research approaches, have strengths and weaknesses that must be taken into account by researchers, both before deciding upon their use

▶ cultivation research – Chapter 8, p. 166

and during their implementation. While there are those who would question the validity of any quantitative approach on epistemological grounds, such techniques have a useful contribution to make, particularly for the understanding of media output, its consumption and effects, provided that the interpretation of data never loses sight of their characteristic limitations. In this respect, they are no different from the qualitative methodologies preferred by other epistemologies.

HANDLING QUANTITATIVE DATA

Quantitative research methodologies generate numerical data. Surveys (whether of audiences or content) and experiments are the basic 'methods' of the data collection, but they enter into theoretically informed 'methodologies' of analysis and interpretation.◄ Once numerical data have been collected, they need to be analysed through statistical techniques. These mathematical techniques are used to describe, organise as well as explore relationships within the data. In epistemological terms, quantitative research is typically grounded in a hypothetico-deductive approach,◄ in which investigators mount hypotheses (or predictions) about the expected associations or cause-effect relationships between variables. The aim of quantitative data collection and analysis, then, is to produce findings which lead to the acceptance or rejection of a specified hypothesis. Numerical data analysis through statistical procedures, as reviewed in this section, represents a systematic and objective way of determining whether significant patterns of relationships exist among those phenomena that have been measured in data collection.

Describing data

Data collected via either survey questionnaires, content coding frames or experimental instruments are coded numerically, and entered into a computerised database, upon which various forms of statistical tests can then be performed. Both the accuracy with which this data transfer process takes place, and the application of statistical procedures that are appropriate for the particular type of data, are crucial to the entire quantitative research project – errors in these early stages can invalidate the final results.

Often, quantitative data analysis begins by adopting a simple descriptive approach in order to establish some initial patterns in the findings. A survey of public opinion, for instance, about the competence of national political leaders might first present the percentages of respondents who agreed, respectively disagreed, that particular political figures were performing well. A further computation might produce the percentages who agreed with such sentiments, as broken down by the gender, age, social class and political affiliations of respondents. Such results can be visually displayed in a bar chart or summarised in a table.◄

A different type of study might ask a survey sample of 1,000 respondents to state how many hours of television they watch each week. Here, descriptive statistics might be applied to show how many respondents viewed nothing, less than one hour a week, between one and two hours, two to four hours or more than four hours. Next, a *frequency distribution* could be generated, which shows how the respondents were distributed across these different volumes of viewing. Such data can be visually represented in a line graph or bar chart.

frequency distribution

Central tendency and variance

Data can be further analysed in terms of summary statistics, which render large amounts of data more manageable. Summary statistics measure two basic aspects of the distribution of 'scores' or measurements in a data set: central tendency and dispersion, or variability. A *central tendency* measure indicates which out of a range of scores is the typical one. This typical score, in turn, can be defined in three different ways:

- The *mode* is the most frequently occurring score in a range of scores. If, in a set of ten scores, five score '4', three score '2', and two score '1', the mode is '4'.

► methods and/vs. methodologies – Chapter 15, p. 287
► hypothetico-deductive research – Chapter 15, p. 291
► forms of representation for research findings – Chapter 15, p. 284

- The *median* score is the mid-point in a range of scores. In the following set of scores, the median is '8': 2 4 5 6 (8) 10 12 15 16. The score '8' lies at the exact half-way point in this distribution of scores. In other cases, where there is an even number of scores, and therefore no exact mid-point, the median must be calculated by averaging between the two centre scores: 3 3 5 8 (8.5) 9 10 13 14. Here, the median is 8.5, or the average of '8' and '9'.
- The *mean* score is the average of the total range of scores. In the last example, the eight scores totalled 65, which, divided by 8, gives a mean score of 8.125.

Another fundamental descriptive measure is the degree of dispersion or variation in a set of scores. While central tendency measures indicate the typical score of a distribution, *dispersion* measures capture the extent to which the scores vary around that central point.

- *Range*, which is the simplest expression of dispersion, is the difference between the highest and lowest scores in a particular distribution.
- *Variance* provides a mathematical index of the degree to which scores deviate from the mean score, and tends to be expressed not in terms of the original scores, but as squared deviations from the mean. To compute the variance, one subtracts the mean of a distribution from each score, and then squares the result. These squared scores are then summed and divided by the number of original scores minus one. Variance is a powerful and widely applied measure, like the standard deviation, and both are illustrated later.
- The *standard deviation* is a third measure of dispersion that utilises the original units of measurement. The standard deviation is computed as the square root of the variance. If the variance of a distribution of scores is 100, the standard deviation (*SD*) for that distribution equals ten.

The normal distribution

The standard deviation and the mean can be used to further compute *standard scores* (z scores). Standard scores permit comparisons to be made between two or more distributions or groups of scores, because all the scores are standardised to the same metric, whereby the mean is zero and the standard deviation is one. Within a given group, the z score expresses the various scores on a frequency distribution in terms of a number of standard deviations from the mean. The point is that scores can thus be expressed in terms of their relative position within a distribution, and not as absolute values. To exemplify, suppose two groups of children, one of average age ten years and another of average age eight years, are found to display average reading ability scores of 85 and 68 respectively. While the older children clearly have better reading scores than the younger children, the most relevant comparisons are not between the two groups, but internally between members of these groups, and between each group and a national average for that age. If, in fact, the average reading score for the ten-year-olds can be shown, relying on standard scores, to equal the average known reading score for their age group nationally (giving them a z score of zero), and the same is true of the eight-year-olds, then both groups can be considered average for their respective age groups.

Standard scores are also used in conjunction with another fundamental statistical concept – the normal distribution curve (Figure 13.3). If a distribution of scores is normally distributed, its graphical curve should be symmetrical and achieve its maximum height at its mean, which is also its median and its mode. One of the most important features of the normal curve is that a fixed proportion of the area below the

the normal distribution curve

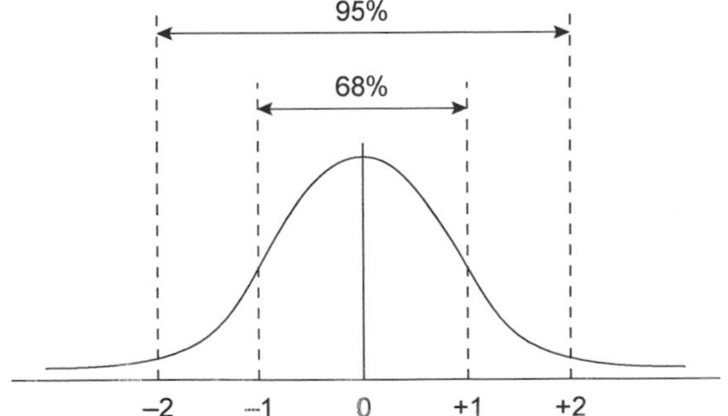

Figure 13.3 The normal distribution curve

curve – representing a known proportion of the population or other phenomena under investigation – lies between the mean and any unit of standard deviation. The normal distribution is an important analytical instrument because a number of natural as well as social phenomena are normally distributed, or nearly so. Not only the scores of mathematical tests, but phenomena such as the heights and weights of individuals, and their IQ scores, all have normal distributions. This means that if the average IQ score is 100 and the standard deviation is 15 points, the proportions of people with scores falling between 85 ($SD = -1.0$) and 100, and between 100 and 115 ($SD = +1.0$) should be the same. Likewise, the proportions of people with IQ scores between 70 ($SD = -2.0$) and 85, and between 130 ($SD = +2.0$) and 115 should also be the same. However, the proportions of people with IQ scores within one standard deviation of the mean will be much greater than the proportions with IQ scores between one and two standard deviations of the mean.

Testing hypotheses

Much quantitative research goes beyond the simple description of data and their distributions. In hypothesis testing, the researcher is interested in establishing whether two or more variables are associated, or whether the scores obtained in two or more groups are different – in both cases in an unambiguous or 'significant' way. When deciding whether to accept or reject a hypothesis, then, the researcher must examine the statistical significance of the results. The starting point is to set up a *null hypothesis*, or a hypothesis which asserts that any statistical differences or relationships that emerge within the data set are due entirely to chance fluctuations or random error. The research hypothesis puts forward the alternative viewpoint – that the statistical relationships or differences are not due to chance, but represent real phenomena that can be explained theoretically in the research.

the null hypothesis

In determining whether a statistical test has upheld the research hypothesis, a probability level must be set, so that the null hypothesis can be tested against it. If the results indicate a probability level lower than this level, the null hypothesis can be rejected in favour of the research hypothesis. Conversely, if the probability level indicated by the statistical test is higher than the pre-set level, the null hypothesis must be accepted. The usual probability threshold is 0.05. This means that there is a 5 per cent chance that a relationship between two variables, or a difference between two groups, occurred randomly. But there is a 95 per cent probability that the result demonstrates a real relationship or difference.

probability levels

In testing hypotheses, it is important to select the appropriate statistical technique for the data type in question. A broad distinction is made between parametric and nonparametric tests. Nonparametric tests are appropriate only for nominal and ordinal data, while parametric tests are appropriate for interval and ratio data. Parametric results can be generalised to the population as a whole, while nonparametric results cannot. Parametric tests assume normally distributed data, while nonparametric statistics do not depend on assumptions about the precise distribution of the sampled population.

Using *nonparametric* statistics, researchers test whether frequencies of the phenomena observed match the frequencies that might be expected to occur by chance. A range of nonparametric tests are available for categorical or nominal (binomial test, Chi-square, McNemar test, Cochran Q test) and rank or ordinal data (Kolmogorov-Smirnov test, Sign test, Wilcoxon matched-pairs, signed-ranks test, Friedman two-way analysis of variance, Kruskal-Wallis one-way analysis of variance) (see Bryman and Cramer 2008; Siegel 1956). Probability tables for these tests can be found in Siegel (1956) and Hays (1973).

nonparametric statistics

Parametric statistics assume that the data are normally distributed, with means, variances and standard deviations readily calculable. As with nonparametric tests, distinctions can be made among different types of parametric statistics, depending on whether the comparisons are being made between groups or samples (t-test for groups in the sense of pairs, analysis of variance for three or more groups, or for samples of individuals). In addition, parametric analyses may explore whether correlations exist among

parametric statistics

ANALYSIS BOX 13.2: TESTING FOR STATISTICAL SIGNIFICANCE: CHI-SQUARE

A popular technique for the analysis of nominal or categorical data, such as results from much content analysis, is Chi-square. In a study of the representation of violence on British television, Gunter and his colleagues examined the distribution of male and female aggressors (Gunter *et al.* 1999). Focusing on aggressors acting on their own (as distinct from in groups, gangs or crowds), a total of 1,282 acts of male-perpetrated violence and 385 acts of female-perpetrated violence were found in drama programming. Together, these two categories comprised a total of 1,667 violent acts. Is this difference in the gender distribution of aggressiveness on television statistically significant?

To find out, a Chi-square analysis was computed. If there is no inherent gender difference, then it would be hypothesised that 50 per cent of acts would be male-perpetrated, and 50 per cent female-perpetrated. Out of the current total, each gender would be responsible for 833.5 violent acts (the expected frequency). To compute a Chi-square, the expected frequency is subtracted from each observed frequency and squared. These squared results are then summed, and the total is divided by the expected frequency (e.g. $[1{,}282 - 833.5]^2 + [385 - 833.5]^2 / 833.5 = 482.7$).

With reference to this value of the coefficient, a goodness-of-fit test can be carried out. It is necessary, first, to determine the probability level (usually 5 per cent or 0.05) and, second, the number of *degrees of freedom*. The latter refers to the number of scores in a test that are free to vary in value. This is calculated as the number of groups of scores being compared, minus one (in the current example, the degrees of freedom would therefore equal one). The researcher next consults a probability table that indicates whether the calculated coefficient is significant. Such a table displays probability levels along the top and numbers of degrees of freedom down the side. If the Chi-square coefficient exceeds the number displayed in the appropriate cell (here, one degree of freedom by 0.05 level of probability), then it is accepted as a significant result. If not, it is rejected as non-significant. A Chi-square with one degree of freedom must exceed 3.84 to be significant at the 0.05 level. The current result is, therefore, highly significant.

degrees of freedom

probability tables

scores on separate variables for one or more groups (using the Pearson correlation coefficient). While simple *correlation* measures a relationship of association between two variables, more complex *regression* analysis can be used to determine the degree to which one variable changes, given a change in another variable. An even more sophisticated form of analysis, *multiple regression*, enables the researcher to find out the extent to which one (criterion or dependent) variable changes as more than one other (predictor or independent) variable changes. In this last case, each independent variable is examined in turn for its impact upon the dependent variable while, in each step of the analysis, statistical controls are introduced for all the other independent variables.

(multiple) regression analysis

Pritchard and Hughes (1997) used multiple regression analysis in a content analysis of how nine characteristics of homicides might determine whether and how they were covered in newspapers. Newspaper stories were classified, and numerically coded, in terms of the presence or absence of specific attributes. There were four dependent variables: the average length of homicide stories; the number of news items about a homicide; the proportion of homicide items on the front page; and whether a homicide story was accompanied by a photograph.

The results are summarised in Table 13.1. It was the average story length and the number of items which were best predicted by the nine independent variables. The scores displayed are so-called Beta weights, which indicate the individual predictive strength of each predictor variable. The scores with asterisks are the significant predictor variables. The R^2 score indicates the percentage of variance in each criterion variable (along the top of the table) which is accounted for by the combination of all the predictor variables (down the side of the table) that entered into that analysis.

Table 13.1: Summary of a regression analysis for variables predicting four measures of homicide newsworthiness

	Average story length	Number of news items published	Proportion of items on front page	Newspaper published photograph
White participants	0.42**	0.38***	0.25*	0.12
Female suspect	0.33**	–0.25*	–0.18	–0.19
Female victim	0.26*	0.30**	0.15	0.23
Victim child/senior	0.33***	0.33***	0.31***	0.31**
Census tract income	–0.02	0.13	0.01	–0.03
Suspect knew victim	–0.11	–0.02	–0.12	–0.10
Risky behaviour	–0.06	–0.02	0.04	0.01
Police information ban	–0.15	–0.16	–0.15	–0.25*
Race/gender interaction	–0.25	–0.25*	–0.22	–0.01
R^2	0.29***	0.31***	0.18*	0.17*

Source: Pritchard and Hughes 1997

Note: N = 100

*p < 0.05, **p < 0.01, ***p < 0.001

In this analysis, the results show that homicides tend to get more newspaper coverage (number of items and average story length) when the event involves white participants, a female suspect, a female victim, or a child or elderly victim. The further likelihood of such a story appearing on the front page increases when the homicide involves whites, and when the victim is a child or old person. And the likelihood of a photograph being published with the story increases when the victim is a child or old person, but decreases when there has been a police information ban on the details that could be released and included in the story.

WEBOMETRICS AND VISUALISATION

With the rapid expansion of the internet and the world wide web, huge volumes of data, images and text are deposited online and are available for analysis by researchers. Significant quantities of content are generated within the context of one-to-one, one-to-many and many-to-many interpersonal communications settings. The emergence of increasingly sophisticated tools for storing, transferring and interfacing with information online has set new challenges for researchers. The rapid rise of online media has created virtual communities◄ that represent new types of population from which samples can be drawn for research purposes.

Such is the vastness of this information universe that traditional analytical methods for sampling and coding of content would be unmanageable. In this context, computer scientists have joined forces with social scientists to create new tools for rapid search and classification of massive quantities of online content and to track the flow of information across the internet. A growing family of toolkits has spawned a new research domain of 'webometrics' or the electronic analysis of web-based content and communications. These tools have been variously referred to as information extraction or retrieval, data or text mining, natural language processing, web mapping, and so on. They comprise computer software that can scan sites on the web and map links between them, or they have linguistic capabilities meaning that 'read' text and extract meanings from it, while varying in their level of linguistic sophistication.

Such tools provide researchers with the ability to search through very large amounts of content

► virtual communities – Chapter 11, p. 209

and to classify it, extract patterns of meanings from it, and to map links between different sites, including directions of the flow of information. Some of these tools can examine communications links between members of online social networks (Thelwall 2008a, 2008b). Other tools have now emerged that can measure sentiment, in effect measuring the nature of 'opinion' articulated online about specific named entities such as brand names, policy issues, political parties and so on (Prabowo and Thelwall 2010).

An example of a web-mapping toolkit is that developed by the VOSON (Virtual Observatory for the Study of Online Networks) project based at the Australian National University (http://voson.anu.edu.au). The software effectively acts as a web crawler, collecting and analysing hyperlinks between web sites. It combines crawling with other methods from computer science (e.g., web and text mining, data visualisation) and social science (e.g., social network analysis, SNA)◄ to provide a rich and multi-dimensional analysis of hyperlinks (see Ackland *et al.* 2006). VOSON software has been used in web mapping exercises to understand the nature of online communications traffic flows between sites that publish a variety of different types of content, including the environment, news, politics and science (Ackland 2005; Ackland and Gibson 2004; O'Neil and Ackland 2006). VOSON can map the structure of the networks and the sites involved, as well as identifying which sites are most prominent within a network and the direction of information flows between sites.

web crawler

Figure 13.4 presents an example of mapping output from a VOSON analysis. In this case, the analysis was conducted over a 24-hour period among a sample of five UK newspapers' web sites. The clusters indicate hyperlink networks between these sites and 3000+ other sites identified by this analysis as linking to those sites. Site clusters around the original seedset of five sites are shown by the large clusters situated around the circumference of the chart. It is clear also that other clusters emerged from this analysis that can be further interpreted through reference to printouts indicating which sites formed those groupings.

► social network analysis – Chapter 10, p. 190

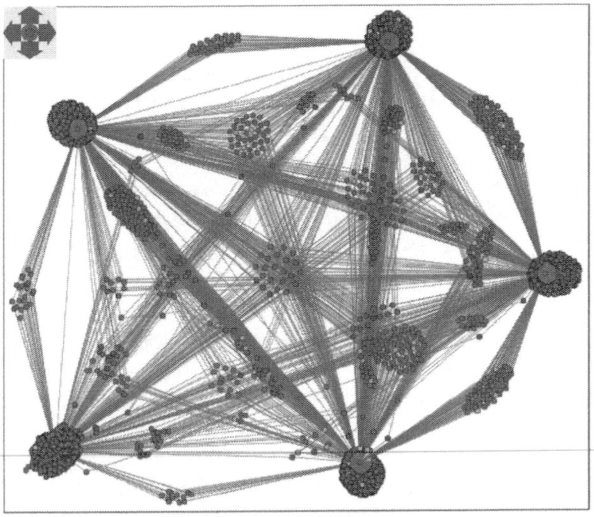

Figure 13.4 A map of information flow links between major news media web sites in the UK (source: Gunter et al. 2008)

This web mapping analysis is a convenient way of examining the web landscape, but then requires other techniques – manual or electronic – to further assess the information content of communications traffic between major sites in the configuration and other more minor sites. To assess the linguistic content of web sites, methods such as sentiment analysis use text mining software with a built-in lexicon that can identify words, their meanings and the evaluative sense in which they are being used. Some tools can derive sentiments not just at the word level, but also in relation to expressions and complete sentences (Prabowo and Thelwall 2010).

CONCLUSION

The present chapter has examined quantitative methodologies as they are applied in media and communication research. These methodologies have been used particularly to study media audiences and media content, and they do so by examining either associations between variables or cause-effect relationships. The guiding principle of quantitative research is the hypothetico-deductive approach – certain hypothetical expectations are proposed, and then accepted or rejected through the collection and analysis of scientific data.

The essential characteristic of quantitative research is that it reduces phenomena to numerical codes. Numerical measurement, however, can occur at more than one level, and an understanding of the different levels of measurement is crucial, both to the correct use of statistical methods of data analysis and to the proper interpretation of data. At the simpler levels, data are used merely to categorise and rank phenomena. At more complex levels of analysis, data can be used to measure relationships among phenomena and to establish causal connections. As more research has focused on internet-related issues, computer software tools have emerged that can scan and classify huge quantities of content and map links between web sites.

As a theoretical enterprise, much quantitative research aims to enhance knowledge by demonstrating both causal links between phenomena and the universality of such relations. In practice, research must frequently make a trade-off between an ideal research design that might effectively demonstrate the nature and causality of social phenomena, and a design that is feasible, given the available resources and the necessary ethical and other considerations. Also for this reason, quantitative studies – like other traditions of research – should be carefully scrutinised for their methodological limitations and the quality of their data before readers and users attach weight and credibility to their findings.

14 The qualitative research process

Klaus Bruhn Jensen

- definitions of *basic concepts* in qualitative media and communication studies: *meaning*, as articulated in *naturalistic settings*, and examined by researchers who are themselves *interpretive subjects*
- a presentation of *systematic design* and *sampling* as key considerations in qualitative research
- an overview, with examples, of the main empirical approaches to qualitative media and communication studies: *interviewing*, *observation*, and analyses of *texts, documents, and artifacts*
- a discussion of *data analysis* as a central challenge for qualitative research
- a review of resources for *computer-supported* qualitative research

INTRODUCTION

Until the 1980s, it was still common for humanistic and other qualitative media and communication researchers to refer to their own contributions as "nonscientific" (Farrell, 1987: 123). For some, this terminology served as a way of securing a (negatively defined) niche for reflections on human communication outside the social 'sciences.' For others, 'critique' represented the preferred alternative to a mainstream 'science' that would limit itself to describing, rather than changing, predominant media and communicative practices. While many methodological, theoretical, as well as political fault lines remain, the last three decades have witnessed two important developments for qualitative research. First, more dialogues – between qualitative and quantitative traditions, between 'critical' and 'administrative' researchers,◀ and across the classic divide between arts and sciences (Snow, 1964) – have been initiated; the chapters in this volume, and many of the works cited, trace this development. Second, journal, textbook, and handbook publications have served to establish standards and procedures for qualitative research. The present chapter reviews the state of qualitative methodologies in media and communication studies, with special reference to the requirements of systematic qualitative research projects.

The chapter, first of all, identifies some of the key concepts of contemporary qualitative research, with sources in anthropology, sociology, and humanities. Next, the planning of empirical studies is described in terms of several strategic, tactical, and technical choices that must be made at different stages of the qualitative research process. These overviews lead into a review, with illustrative examples, of three prototypical methodologies in qualitative media studies, as defined by their means of data collection – in-depth interviewing, participating observation, and various forms of textual,

▶ 'critical' and 'administrative' research – Chapter 19, p. 359

document, or discourse analysis. In each case, data analysis – the coding, categorization, and interpretation of data – presents both a special challenge for qualitative research and an interface with the quantitative research process. The final section, accordingly, outlines and discusses various procedures for the analysis of qualitative data, with specific reference to discourse analysis, thematic coding, and grounded theory, including computer software as a resource for qualitative data analysis.

BASIC CONCEPTS IN QUALITATIVE RESEARCH

The consolidation and institutionalization of qualitative research in recent decades is witnessed in a number of standard reference works, handbooks, and anthologies (e.g., Alvesson and Sköldberg, 2009; Bryman and Burgess, 1999; Denzin and Lincoln, 2005; Huberman and Miles, 2002; Miles and Huberman, 1994) (for practical techniques, see, e.g., Flick, 2007; Silverman, 2010) – in addition to a growing number of journals, monographs, and textbook in different disciplines and fields. While media and communication research has produced its own reference works (e.g., Jensen and Jankowski, 1991; Lindlof and Taylor, 2011), it is characteristic that this field has also taken on board a variety of interdisciplinary influences. Across theoretical and methodological inspirations and traditions, however, qualitative communication studies today have at least three common denominators.

meaning

First, studies focus on *meaning*, both as an object of study and as an explanatory concept. Humans interpret their ordinary lives as well as the extraordinary events that they encounter, increasingly through communication technologies, as inherently meaningful. Researchers, in turn, interpret the interpretations that individuals and groups have of themselves and their communications.◄ People engage in interpretation for a purpose and in a context; they orient themselves in the world and take up positions from which to exercise agency. These interpretations, next, inform actions, for instance, inside media organizations, such as newsrooms (e.g., Tuchman, 1978), and in audiences' engagement with news about the world as part of their personal daily routines (e.g., Scannell, 1988).

Second, qualitative research normally assumes that communication should be examined, as far as possible, in its *naturalistic contexts*. While this might suggest classic anthropological fieldwork, qualitative communication studies have taken several different approaches to grasping "the native's perspective" on his/her reality (Malinowski, 1922: 25). Naturalistic contexts are also selected for particular purposes of research. Like their quantitative counterparts, qualitative projects engage in sampling – of cultures, communities, locales, informants, periods, and practices. As elaborated in the next section, empirical communication studies have various sampling strategies at their disposal – from probability sampling within a well-defined population or universe, to the selection of a single community or case in which diverse instances of a particular communicative practice may be documented. The naturalistic attitude primarily entails an ambition of considering those contexts in which particular communicative phenomena may be encountered and examined; it also recognizes that many aspects of such phenomena cannot be known – or sampled – in advance.

naturalistic contexts

the native's perspective

The third common feature of qualitative studies is the conception of researchers as *interpretive subjects*. In one sense, all scientific research – quantitative and qualitative, natural-scientific and humanistic – is carried out by human subjects as interpretive agents. What distinguishes qualitative studies is the pervasive nature of interpretation throughout the research process. In the prototypical quantitative study, interpretation is carried out in a delimited and sequential fashion. The quantitative research process aims to segregate phases of conceptualization, operationalization, data collection, analysis, and discussion; it also may delegate some phases to coders and other collaborators, and to computerized procedures. In comparison, in the prototypical qualitative study, interpretation is a crisscrossing activity that one scholar undertakes on a continuous basis.

researchers as interpretive subjects

► double hermeneutics – Chapter 19, p. 351

In order to characterize this global interpretive activity, research has referred to two interrelated – *emic* and *etic* – aspects of the study of communication and culture (Pike, 1967). This conceptual pair, while deriving from linguistics, has been widely applied, particularly in anthropology, but also in other social-scientific research. A 'phonetic' approach assumes that language constitutes a continuum of sounds, as measured on acoustic scales. A 'phonemic' approach, in comparison, focuses on a given language as a distinctive and meaningful set of sounds. By analogy, also other cultural expressions can be understood as either an outsider or a native would. Communication, accumulated as culture, can and should be studied from both internal and external perspectives.

emic and etic analysis

The challenge, before and after Kenneth L. Pike's (1967) seminal work, has been how, concretely, to relate the two aspects of understanding and interpretation (Headland, *et al.*, 1990). For one thing, the emic or internal perspective on culture is not simply there; it is identified from some etic, external, comparative perspective. For another thing, the etic perspective is itself, in one sense, emic: it represents a social setting, a historical period, and an academic (sub)culture. Emphasizing this last point, some work has questioned the distinction as such, suggesting, from a postmodernist position,◀ that research findings are not privileged representations, but merely provide one more narrative about the culture in question (Clifford and Marcus, 1986; James, 1995; Marcus and Fischer, 1999; Van Maanen, 1988). Whereas repeated cycles of reflection can be valuable, the distinction remains both conceptually and practically important. In the different stages and levels of any research project, both concepts and conclusions must be constructed before they can be deconstructed.

The three constituents, in combination, begin to suggest how qualitative studies perform their analytical procedures, and how these lead into theory development. Concepts and categories are typically articulated in what Robert K. Merton (1968: 39) described as a middle range.◀ Compared to the description or coding of single statements or images, and to grand theories about culture or society, middle-range theories seek to account for a particular process or context, for instance, the two-step flow of media effects◀ or the socially and culturally variable decodings◀ of media content. In short, middle-range theories mediate between concrete research operations and abstract theoretical frameworks. In qualitative communication studies, they are commonly the outcome of an iterative or repeated process, through which researchers gradually gain a better insight into – learn from – the field of study.

iterative process of research

▶ postmodernism – Chapter 2, p. 41

DESIGNING QUALITATIVE STUDIES

Formatting the field

To design an empirical study is to identify and bracket a portion of reality – 'what' – for further inquiry according to a theoretically informed purpose – 'why' – and through a systematic procedure of data collection and analysis – 'how' (Kvale, 1987). Whereas most researchers will agree that a preliminary delimitation and conceptualization of the object of inquiry is required, even if a central purpose of qualitative research is, precisely, reconceptualization, the additional operationalization of analytical categories and procedures has been subject to debate. After all, qualitative studies claim to learn from the field. Increasingly, however, operationalization has come to be seen as a *sine qua non* also of qualitative studies (S. L. Schensul, *et al.*, 1999: 50). In methodological terms, only an empirical 'microcosm' can be studied in any detail to substantiate 'macrocosmic' inferences (Alexander and Giesen, 1987).◀ In epistemological terms, no knowledge can be produced without some preknowledge or 'prejudice,' as emphasized by hermeneutics.◀ A classic piece of advice came from the anthropologist, Bron-

conceptualization

operationalization

▶ middle-range theories – Chapter 3, p. 64

▶ two-step flow of communication – Chapter 9, p. 174

▶ decodings – Chapter 9, p. 178

▶ empirical microcosm, theoretical macrocosm – Chapter 15, p. 300

▶ hermeneutics – Chapter 2, p. 28

islaw Malinowski (1922: 9), who noted that although preconceived ideas can get in the way of empirical research, the foreshadowing of problems that may arise in the field is a central consideration.

It is helpful to distinguish three aspects of designing empirical research – strategy, tactics, and techniques (Gorden, 1969):

- *Strategy*, first, refers to a general plan for entering a particular social setting, and for establishing points of observation and means of communication, in order to generate relevant evidence. Strategy builds social relations between researchers and their informants in a designated time and space – a temporary structure for communicating about and reflecting on meaningful events and practices.
- *Tactics*, next, refer to the researcher's attempts to anticipate and, to a degree, prestructure social interactions that may yield evidence. A case in point is who to interview. Interviewees can be approached either as well-placed sources (informants, e.g., within a media organization) or as representatives of a position in a sociocultural system (respondents, e.g., from a specific user segment) (Lindlof and Taylor, 2011: 177–180).

informants and respondents

- *Techniques*, finally, are the researcher's concrete means of interacting with and documenting the field – verbal language, but also other sign systems, documents, and artifacts. It is the selection of a set of techniques that most clearly distinguishes qualitative and quantitative research designs. This is in spite of the fact that techniques are prefigured by both strategy and tactics, which, in turn, are anticipated by theoretical purposes and empirical domains. In sum, the 'why' and the 'what' of research come before the 'how' (Kvale, 1987).

Sampling cases

Having operationalized and accessed the field, the next step of an empirical project is to sample elements or constituents of that field. In communication studies, it is most common to think of samples as subgroups of populations that consist of either people or texts, for example, in surveys or content analyses. Qualitative studies, however, frequently sample other units of analysis, for instance, settings, activities, and events relating to communication (Lindlof and Taylor, 2011: 110–112). Also the process of sampling differs from probability sampling◄ in quantitative research: qualitative sampling is driven by a purpose, not by a principle of probability.

units of analysis

Qualitative studies can be characterized, further, with reference to the two or more steps of sampling that they often involve. While a first step identifies a relevant context of communication, the next step will single out certain of its media, users, or communicative interactions for detailed study. In an early classic of qualitative media research in the US, Kurt and Gladys Lang (1953) examined the 1951 MacArthur Day parade by relying, first, on thirty-one observers on-site in Chicago and, second, on two observers monitoring the television coverage at home. From each of these contexts, representations and observations (including recorded observations, overheard remarks, and content elements) were documented and compared. The findings indicated that on-site participants and television viewers had witnessed two distinctively different versions of the same event. (As the two researchers have later emphasized, that important and frequently cited finding was "entirely serendipitous" (Lang and Lang, 1991: 211); they had sampled two separate contexts for breadth and detail, and learnt something new about the field as a whole by data from the two contexts in combination. Also another classic finding, from a quantitative study, was serendipitous, namely, the two-step hypothesis concerning media impact (Lazarsfeld, *et al.*, 1944); in accordance with a quantitative logic, a common assumption regarding direct media effects had been falsified, or questioned, and the new hypothesis could now be examined through additional studies in other contexts (Katz and Lazarsfeld, 1955).)

multistep sampling

Multistep sampling is in keeping with the contextual orientation of qualitative research.

► probability sampling – Chapter 13, p. 245

First, statements and actions are to be interpreted with reference to their context(s). These contexts, importantly, can be extremely varied in nature and scope – from the long discursive sequences of a political campaign or an online game, to media uses in household settings, to nation-states and entire cultures. Second, qualitative studies depend on access to (primary data about) such contexts throughout the process of analysis and interpretation, rather than merely summary measures or second-hand descriptions. In a sense, the qualitative research process amounts to a continuous operationalization of categories and concepts with reference to several stages of analysis and, often, several contexts of evidence. As the Langs (1991) noted, there had been a significant build-up to MacArthur Day in the media, and preliminary suggestions that this had affected the public's expectations and demeanor in the streets could be tested against other evidence, including "badges and behavioral cues" (p. 212).

sampling procedures

Several inventories of sampling procedures have been proposed in qualitative reference works (e.g., Lindlof and Taylor, 2011: 112–116; Miles and Huberman, 1994: 98). Perhaps their main contribution is the fact that, as a group, they are available for considering qualitative sampling, following a long period when this was characterized, *en bloc* and in negative terms, as 'non-random.' Positively speaking, qualitative sampling can be defined as a multistep procedure – *of* contexts and *within* contexts – and with reference to at least three types of criteria:

- *Maximum variation sampling* seeks to capture as wide a range of 'qualities' or phenomena as possible. The concrete range is normally suggested by other characteristics of the relevant phenomena, for instance, the ratings of television programs and the age of their core viewers. In a study of how American viewers evaluated the quality of television, and possible ways of improving it, the present author compared two groups of viewers, one below thirty-five, the other above fifty-five years of age. What distinguished the groups was that they had, respectively had not, grown up with television as a central cultural given (Jensen, 1990b). The study found, among other things, that the two groups relied on different types of metaphors to describe how more, and more diverse, programming might become available. The older group referred to a 'library' of programs to be accessed, whereas the younger group advocated a continuous 'flow' of specialized channels.
- *Theoretical sampling* selects its objects of analysis in order to explore concepts or categories, for instance, 'politics' or 'fandom,' as they relate to communication. Qualitative studies of media organizations◄ have explored the politics of production (what is controversial, for whom, and why) by sampling structures, i.e., interviewees at different levels of the organizational hierarchy or in different stages of the work process generating a particular media product. In fan studies (Jenkins, 1992; L. Lewis, 1991), research may focus on a mainstream, a core group of agenda-setters, or new recruits as either 'prototypical' or 'critical' cases of fandom; they may also refer to contrasting or 'limit' cases, such as a competing fan formation or devotees of atonal music.

prototypical, critical, and limit cases

- *Convenience sampling* is most often encountered as a derogatory term for studying whatever individuals or materials are most easily available. However, a well-documented convenience sample can generate both valid and relevant insights. An early example in communication research was Cantril's (1940) study of the public panic in response to Orson Welles' 1938 radio production of the *War of the Worlds*.◄ That study relied on various qualitative as well as quantitative techniques, including convenience samples of respondents who could be asked to recollect their experience of being frightened. More generally, because of the difficulty of gaining entry into certain (levels of) organizations, communities, or subcultures, convenience in the sense of accessibility – physical and social

► qualitative studies of media organizations – Chapters 4 and 5

► *The Invasion from Mars* – Chapter 9, p. 173

– is a legitimate consideration. (In other instances, concerns about ethics, including the personal safety of informants and/or researchers, may rule out research about an arena.◄) One variant is snowball sampling, where an initial contact generates further informants. For each roll of the snowball, studies should specify how and why certain selections are made, and how more informed choices become possible over time.

snowball sampling

In addition to these three types of qualitative sampling, a characteristic and primarily qualitative design – case study – should be mentioned. Case studies conduct in-depth research on delimited entities, such as communities and organizations, but also singular individuals and events, in order to understand these as interconnected social systems (for overview, see Gomm, *et al.*, 2000; Yin, 2003). In addition to the inherent historical or cultural interest of some cases, a wider purpose, sometimes implicit, is to arrive at descriptions, models, or typologies with implications for other social systems. What case studies share with other qualitative designs is the selection of one, or a few, contexts in which most, or all, of the phenomena of theoretical interest can be explored in empirical detail. Whereas case studies might be considered quintessential instances of qualitative research, comparatively few media and communication studies have been specific or self-described examples of case study, perhaps because 'the media,' rather than the diverse communicative processes that they facilitate in social and cultural contexts, long remained the center of attention.

case study

Having formatted a field of theoretical interest, and having sampled from its empirical constituents, a qualitative project turns to the concrete choice of 'methods' – techniques for interacting with the field. Whereas Chapter 15 returns to the relationship between methods and methodology,◄ the following sections review the three main instruments of data collection in qualitative research: interviewing, observation, and document or discourse analysis.

► ethics of research – Chapter 19, p. 366

► methods and/vs. methodology – Chapter 15, p. 287

INTERVIEWING

Interviewing is one of the most commonly used methods of data collection, in research as in journalism and public administration. Common sense suggests that, "the best way to find out what the people think about something is to ask them" (Bower, 1973: vi). In-depth interviews, especially, with their affinity to ordinary conversation, have been considered choice instruments for tapping the perspectives of users (and other communicators) on media. Speech is a primary and familiar mode of social interaction, constitutive of many media genres and of communication about media, as well. The difficulty is that people do not always say what they think, or mean what they say. As in the case of everyday conversation, researchers, as communicators, must tease out the meanings and implications of what other people – and they themselves – say.

It is essential to recognize, then, that statements from either individual interviews or focus groups (or from survey responses), are not simply representations, more or less valid or reliable, of what people think. All interview statements are actions in a context, arising from the interaction between (or among) interviewer and interviewee(s). Interview discourses are, in a strong sense of the word, 'data.' They become sources of information through analysis, and of meaning through interpretation.◄ For one thing, interview studies ask people to put into discourse certain ideas and notions that otherwise may remain unarticulated, part of practical consciousness.◄ For another thing, interviewers themselves have no perfect insight into either their own performance or the responses that they must process in a split second. The disambiguation of interview discourses (or the conclusion that an ambiguity cannot be resolved) is the outcome of data analysis, and will remain an inference. This is spite of the occasional suggestion in textbooks that a highly competent interview may stand fully interpreted when it ends (Kvale and Brinkmann, 2009: 195).

► data, information, meaning – Chapter 15, p. 285

► practical consciousness – Chapter 8, p. 161

These caveats reiterate a classic insight of rhetoric and hermeneutics: there is no way around language when it comes to studying communication and culture. Language is a condition to be embraced, not an obstacle to be removed through formalization or abstraction. On the one hand, language (and other modalities) are the royal, if winding roads to respondents' self-conceptions, opinions, and worldviews: these must be inferred from narratives, arguments, and other discursive structures. On the other hand, linguistic categories offer means of quality control regarding the 'language work' that researchers engage in, as explained below in relation to data analysis.

Figure 14.1 summarizes the dual role of language in qualitative research, as a tool of data collection and an object of analysis. In sum, interviews 'make' language; document or discourse analyses examine language as 'found,' a distinction that has acquired renewed importance in digital media.◀ Regarding observation, the double notation concerning language as an object of analysis suggests that while language is a source of evidence, it often is not analyzed in systematic detail, as discussed further in the section on observation below.

Qualitative media studies employ three main types of interviewing. The types reflect basic options of interviewing one or more persons, who may or may not have a preexisting social relationship with each other:

- *Respondent interviews*. In comparison to informant interviews (which have tended to be less common in media studies),◀ the interviewee is conceived here as a representative of categories such as gender, age, ethnicity, and social status. The assumption is that these categories are inscribed in, and can be recovered from, the respondents' discourses about themselves and about media. A central example of respondent interviews has been studies of the decoding of media content.◀
- *Naturalistic group interviews*. In order to explore, to the extent possible, what normally goes on in social settings, qualitative studies examine naturally occurring groups within both media production and reception. In production studies, interviews typically enter into observational methodologies, although specific (individual) interview methodologies have been employed (Newcomb and Alley, 1983). For audience studies, household interviews can produce, for example, revealing contradictions in how children and parents describe an average 'media day' in the home (Jensen, *et al.*, 1994). Also interviews with fan groups,◀ (Spigel and Jenkins, 1990) and with children and youth peer groups (Livingstone and Bovill, 2001) can supplement observations of their more distributed activities.
- *Constituted group interviews*. Groups that are constituted specifically for research purposes represent a compromise between the respondent and naturalistic strategies. Group members are the bearers of individual demographics; they also enter into an approximated natural group dynamic. An example is Liebes and Katz's (1990) study of the reception of the *Dallas* television series, for which couples invited acquaintances to their home in order to watch and discuss the program. The classic source on group interviews was the work by Robert K. Merton and his associates, beginning in the early 1940s, on the focused interview (Merton and Kendall, 1955). The general idea became especially influential in the shape of focus groups in marketing research and, later, in media studies (for overview, see Barbour, 2007; Puchta and Potter, 2004). The sometimes crassly instrumental uses of focus groups have been subject to criticism and debate (Morrison, 1998); Merton himself (1987) pointed to some of the discontinuities between the focused interview and focus groups as commonly practiced. In media studies, focus groups have proven useful in articulating socially and culturally distinctive experiences of various media contents and uses (e.g., Schlesinger, *et al.*, 1992).

the focused interview

focus groups

▶ data as found or made – Chapter 15, p. 288
▶ informants and respondents, p. 268
▶ decoding studies – Chapter 9, p. 178
▶ fan studies – Chapter 9, p. 180

Methodology	Language: Tool of data collection	Language: Object of analysis
Interviewing	+	+
Observation	+	+/ -
Documents/artifacts	-	+

Figure 14.1 The role of language in qualitative methodologies

It should be added that a further variety of communicative and other techniques lend themselves to qualitative media studies (see, e.g., Marshall and Rossman, 2006; Punch, 2005). Oral history (Dunaway and Baum, 1996; Perks and Thomson, 1998), relying on lengthy oral testimonies, not least from ordinary individuals who can tell history 'from below,' has made its mark also on media studies (e.g., Pearson and Uricchio, 1990). Beyond the majority of both qualitative and quantitative studies that ask people to respond to media and society as they now exist, certain approaches invite groups of people to consider forms of communication that do not yet exist, thus stimulating the sociological imagination (Mills, 1959a). The study, cited previously, about old and young viewers' conception of television (Jensen, 1990b) relied on such a method, workshops on the future (Jungk and Müllert, 1981). Also other action-oriented varieties of interviewing,◀ such as Delphi and consensus groups, provide alternatives or supplements to focus groups (Barbour and Kitzinger, 1999).

oral history

workshops on the future

Across different interview formats, three issues require consideration and planning:

- *Duration*. Interviews range from brief dialogues to establish the meaning of a technical term at a media production site, to hour-long and repeated sessions with an individual or family about media habits, to comprehensive life-historical interviews (Bertaux, 1981; Chamberlayne, *et al.*, 2000). Duration is suggested by the purpose of a study, but sometimes determined by practical circumstances.
- *Structure*. Probably the main challenge in qualitative interviewing is how, to what extent, to prestructure the interaction. The exchange may cover a predefined set of themes, but in no particular order; or it may follow a particular sequence and structure (see S. L. Schensul *et al.*, 1999: 121–164). In all events, researchers need to justify their choices, and to make explicit the procedures that may support particular inferences and conclusions.
- *Depth*. Regarding relevant and appropriate depth, the qualitative interviewer's responsibility becomes acute. Though one might think, 'the deeper, the better,' in order to elicit respondents' terminologies, or to probe their conceptual structures, the research interview has similarities with the therapeutic interview, and may articulate repressed insights that neither respondent nor researcher are prepared to handle (Kvale and Brinkmann, 2009: 39–46). Depth, the hallmark of qualitative research, poses important issues for research ethics.◀

OBSERVATION

Observation refers broadly to the continuous and often long-term presence, normally of one researcher, in one delimited locale. The observer, in a sense, *is* the method – an instrument of research relying on all sensory modalities and diverse media of information. Apart from the danger of 'going native,' or conflating emic and etic perspectives, a special challenge during one's immersion in the field is continuous

▶ action research – Chapter 19, p. 365

▶ research ethics – Chapter 19, p. 366

documentation, so that various data become available for analysis, and so that the steps from observation to inferences and conclusions become transparent. Without such documentation, fieldwork may become similar to artwork, inspired and inspiring, but inaccessible to intersubjective reflection and discussion. In anthropology, debates on this issue have a long history. In fact, it is only recently that the sharing of field notes with other researchers has become a common practice (S. L. Schensul, *et al.*, 1999: 226).

One of the most influential metaphors for observation, also in media studies, is the anthropologist, Clifford Geertz's (1973) term, 'thick description.' (Geertz derived the concept from the philosopher, Gilbert Ryle (1971: 465–496).) The point is that a very detailed description of social interaction is necessary in order to establish the implications of what people say or do, for example, when they use irony. Rather than spreading one's resources thinly across a larger field, and predefining the phenomena of interest, the efforts should be focused on a small field that can be explored in depth for relevant phenomena as well as appropriate descriptive categories. This is in keeping with a commonly stated qualitative ambition of finding one's analytical categories in the field – even though research questions and other premises inevitably orient the enterprise. Some critics have noted that, because researchers enter the field with only a vague notion of what thick description entails, it may, instead, generate 'thin' descriptions (Murdock, 1997). Nevertheless, in the early phases of a study especially, a wide-angle exploration may be indispensable; it is comparable, in some respects, to pilot studies◄ in other empirical research designs.

thick description

In order to distinguish varieties of observational fieldwork, it is common to refer to their components of observation and participation, respectively. In an influential summary, Hammersley and Atkinson (2007: 82) have proposed a scale from full observation to full participation, suggesting that there is almost always a degree of each element in any fieldwork. Just as any interview question, in a sense, is leading, because it implies a range of relevant answers, so observers participate, and participants observe, as they try to interpret 'what is really going on here.' In studies of media use in households and other private settings (Lull, 1980), it is evidently difficult to maintain the observing role of a fly-on-the-wall. Also the study of media use in public places, however, involves a measure of participation as the observer moves about and communicates (Lemish, 1982). Being humans, researchers "cannot *not* communicate" (Watzlawick, *et al.*, 1967: 49).

participating observation

(In media studies, one advantage of the reference to specified degrees of observation and participation, and to their interfaces with other data-collection methods, is that it avoids the fashionable, but questionable terminology of media or audience 'ethnography.')◄

Regarding field notes, it is still not common to refer to a benchmark of notations and procedures. This is in contrast to various detailed analytical conventions in interview transcripts (considered in the section of data analysis below), and in some qualitative variants of content studies. The presentation and analysis of verbatim notes in publications have remained exceptions, certainly in media studies. While this state of affairs is explained, in part, by the practice, in the parent discipline of anthropology, of keeping research notes private, a wider assumption in other areas appears to have been that field notes serve as extensions of, or complements to, more essential 'head notes.' According to this logic, a valid interpretation of the full set of notes could only be carried out by the researcher who was present at the scene – weeks, months, or years ago. In addition to casting the fieldworker as a singular source, this premise may detract from the legitimacy of a central methodology. When the 'secret' diary of the pioneer anthropologist, Bronislaw Malinowski (1967) emerged, it revealed, among other things, his contempt for the people he studied, undercutting his descriptive monograph and raising doubt about the validity and legitimacy of the fieldwork.

► pilot studies – Chapter 15, p. 300

► ethnography – Chapter 9, p. 180

Over time, increasing attention has been given to the systematic production of field records (e.g., Ellen, 1984: 278–293; Lindlof and Taylor, 2011: 155–167; Spradley, 1979: 69–77). One helpful typology has distinguished three purposes of field notes, each with an associated discursive form (adapted from Burgess, 1982):

- *substantive* notes, which capture representations of the scene under study;
- *logistical* notes, which add information about the circumstances under which the data were gathered; and
- *reflexive* notes, which initiate the process of analysis and theorizing on the basis of observations and other data.

An additional rule of thumb is to focus on substance (what) and logistics (how) in the field, and to reserve the main reflexive activity (why) for later in the research process. Fieldworkers are better able to serve their own purposes through a differentiated and staggered process of analysis, interpretation, and self-reflexivity. A wider lesson for observational studies is to approach notes, not as representations, but as working documents – steps in a process of communication with self and others.

field notes as working documents

A final difficulty for observational studies has been how to document a multimodal reality mainly through writing and photography. Compared to interview studies, which have relied on transportable and affordable audiotape recorders since around 1950 (Fielding and Lee, 1998: 28), it is only recently that video recorders became available to the same extent. More important perhaps, various disciplines and fields have remained remarkably language-centered. In a summary volume on the subfield of visual anthropology, Margaret Mead concluded that anthropology had remained "a discipline of words" (Hockings, 1995: 3). In media and communication research, visual methodologies have, by and large, been applied to film, television, websites, and other media texts, much less to the production and uses of media. To some extent, the multimodal nature of both media and everyday reality has been recognized in a third and more heterogeneous set of qualitative approaches to communication.

visual anthropology

DATA – FOUND AND MADE

What unites the third group of approaches to data collection, compared to observation and interviewing, is that the data are 'found' rather than 'made.' As such, the records that they produce can be considered comparatively naturalistic or 'unobtrusive' (Webb, *et al.*, 2000[1966]). Data such as government reports and executive memos, in addition to feature films or computer games, have long been produced as part of the ongoing business of media. With digital networks, data about the uses of media are, increasingly, also there to be found. Digital media use enables new and distinctive forms of meta-communication◄ which generate metadata – a bit trail – that lends itself to both quantitative and qualitative research. Whereas quantitative studies conduct, for example, data mining◄ of how information and users flow within and across websites and other media, qualitative studies can rely on metadata to explore the contexts in which information and users come together and interact.

metadata

First, the textual, visual, and auditory output of media have been key analytical objects in qualitative media studies, to such an extent that much humanistic scholarship has focused entirely on 'texts' as the site and source of meaning (see the discussions in Chapters 6 and 7). Some of this work has developed the notion of intertextuality◄ to refer to webs of meaningful discourse, including everyday interactions *through* as well as *about* media.

Second, a wide variety of discourses serve as input to and output from media production and reception. As complex organizations, media unceasingly generate documents that prepare and feed into 'content.' At the same time, media and their content have traditionally attracted user responses in the form of audience letters (Collins, 1997) as well as in diaries, autobiographies, and fan fiction. Film studies have relied on such diverse data sources to examine early movie audiences (Stokes and Maltby, 1999). Figure 14.2 categorizes and exemplifies production and reception documents, adding a distinction

► meta-communication – Chapter 10, p. 195
► data mining – Chapter 13, p. 262
► intertextuality – Chapter 10, p. 192

	Production	Reception
Private	autobiographies by film stars, journalists, and other media professionals	clippings and hyperlink collections for a media personality or genre
Public	organizational archives, from policy papers to rewrites and work sheets	letters to the editor, fan magazines, online news groups, meta-tags

Figure 14.2 Production and reception discourses

between evidence that is associated with, and primarily originates from, communication in either private (intimate) or public domains.

Third, artifacts and various physical arrangements around media can become sources of evidence. In addition to being means of representation, media are physical objects and constituents of other social interaction. Reading a newspaper in mass transit provides a means of avoiding social contact; in the home, reading can be a way of insisting on one's personal time and space.◄ Furthermore, both the design of and the advertising for media, such as television sets (Spigel, 1992) or personal computers (Jensen, 1993a), for home or work settings, suggest their anticipated uses. Also cinema architecture establishes an experiential setting, not just for movie viewing, but for the collective activity of 'going to the movies' (Gomery, 1992). In this regard, some publications, overlapping in part with visual anthropology,◄ have suggested the importance of audiovisual methodologies for examining not just non-verbal expressions, but also 'the heard' and 'the seen' (Emmison and Smith, 2000: ix) – the temporal and three-dimensional contexts of communication and other social life (Bauer and Gaskell, 2000; Emmison and Smith, 2000; Prosser, 1998; Rose, 2007; J. J. Schensul, *et al.*, 1999). (For a critical discussion of visual methods in media research, see Buckingham, 2009.)

A fourth and increasingly central consideration in the choice of research methodologies is the wealth of metadata that digital technologies make available. The classic on unobtrusive measures (Webb, *et al.*, 2000), originally published in 1966, had noted infrared recordings of audiences in darkened cinemas (p. 154) and fingerprints used to determine which print advertisements have been read (p. 44). Standard digital communication systems document comparable features – the source of information, its connection with other items, their trajectories across sites and servers, the users of the information, who may add their own meta-information, etc. Qualitative studies are especially suited to exploring the transitions and transformations of communication – an unfolding news story or debate, an online gameplay, a viral marketing campaign – that occur within and across contexts (see further Jensen, in press-a).

To sum up, qualitative communication studies have a variety of resources at their disposal, beyond the most commonly employed interview and observational approaches. In the case of digital media, such resources are becoming preconditions for research in and across diverse media and contexts of communication.

DATA ANALYSIS

Coding and analysis

The understanding of 'analysis' has tended to divide qualitative and quantitative research traditions. In quantitative media studies of, for instance, content, analysis involves coding – rule-governed procedures of segmenting and categorizing the components of content as a basis of interpretation. In comparison, qualitative studies typically perform paraphrases and other redescriptions of long as well as short textual elements – new 'syntheses' that

► media as resources in action contexts – Chapter 9, p. 179

► visual anthropology, p. 275

already imply a (re)interpretation of the object of analysis. While multiple forms of analysis are valid and legitimate, depending on the purpose of inquiry, it should be recognized that qualitative research has traditionally been limited by its low degree of specification and documentation of analytical procedures; data analysis remains the Achilles heel of qualitative media studies. Even if most studies do not depend on, or require, mathematical and other operational models, like any scholarly enterprise qualitative publications must deliver the bases for supporting, or resolving, different and sometimes conflicting interpretations and inferences regarding the evidence presented. References to 'patterns' that 'emerge' through 'spirals of interpretation' will not do.

analysis and synthesis

A distinguishing feature of qualitative research is that key terms and concepts are articulated and defined as part of the research process. So is the delimitation of the context or domain of study. Accordingly, analyses and syntheses are not separate acts, but constituents of an iterative process. In this chapter, the concrete elements and procedures of this process are considered in methodological terms; Chapter 15 returns to its epistemological aspects, including abduction◀ as a feature of qualitative research and a complement to inductive and deductive reasoning.

Qualitative data analysis can be characterized further with reference to two different conceptions of coding – the mapping of mental categories onto phenomena in reality through words, numbers, and other notations. The two conceptions have been referred to, variously, as indexical and representational devices (Fielding and Lee, 1998: 176) and as heuristic and factual codes (Silverman, 2010: 262).

codes as representations or indexes

On the one hand, a code can offer an account or *representation* of a part of the domain of study, capturing certain qualities of a person, event, action, text, or other unit of analysis. One purpose is to arrive at a set of mutually exclusive and exhaustive categories; another purpose is to enable later comparisons across cases as well as categories. A common aim of coding as representation, further, is to work with standard descriptions, so that various qualities, for instance, of the experience of a media text can be established without reference to the full text or its context. Decontextualized codes facilitate comparison as well as quantification.

► abduction – Chapter 15, p. 293

On the other hand, a code can serve as an instrument or *resource* for identifying and retrieving a portion – small or large – of a text or context. In the next analytical steps, this data can be examined in further detail – broken down into additional units of analysis, characterized with reference to immanent structures and specific qualities, compared to other portions of this or related data sets, etc. Here, the aim is to rely on an open-ended set of categories and procedures that may be adapted to different contexts and levels of analysis. Contextualized codes facilitate an iterative process of analysis and synthesis.

The two conceptions of coding are, of course, the legacy of quantitative and qualitative research prototypes, respectively. At the same time, coding offers an interface between the two traditions, since an index may be developed into a representation, and vice versa. Typically, a qualitative study will identify subsets and sequences of data that are related thematically or structurally, and which can be singled out for further systematic and comparative analysis. Like field notes, other data and discourses, such as audiotapes and transcripts with detailed conventions for notations (see Potter, 1996: 233–234), constitute working documents and steps toward final research reports. Importantly, each of these steps – including memoing and modeling, drafting and editing – lends itself to documentation. By analogy to financial audits of companies, the term audit trail (Lincoln and Guba, 1985) has been used to refer to a systematic documentation of the entire process, which may keep it transparent to the researcher in question, and accountable to colleagues and readers.

interview transcripts and other coded texts as working documents

audit trail

Variants of data analysis

The history of qualitative data analysis has been informed by classical rhetoric, hermeneutics, and semiotics. Also much early social science was based on the exploratory study of diverse institutions and practices, rather than the coding of well-defined phenomena, partly in search of theoretical frameworks for emerging disciplines. Case studies were a standard and prevalent approach from the 1920s onwards, notably in the Chicago School studies of urban life, but also of media as in the Payne Fund studies.◄ Another approach – analytic induction – was outlined by Znaniecki (1934), who wanted to replace enumerative induction and probabilistic statements with the intensive and stepwise study of single cases in order to arrive at general, even universal categories of social phenomena. Despite examples of the approach in media studies also (Lang and Lang, 1953), it has not been widely used, partly because of its time-consuming procedures, partly because of epistemological doubts about the status of the resulting categories. Grounded theory, discussed below, derived part of its inspiration from analytic induction.

analytic induction

By the 1950s, a noticeable shift had occurred in the social-scientific mainstream that could be summed up as a "transition from case-based to code-based analysis" (Fielding and Lee, 1998: 27).◄ Still, a social-scientific substream – sometimes a counterstream – continued to use and develop qualitative methodologies. It was during this period that media and communication research began to consolidate itself, inheriting that dual legacy and integrating, from the 1960s, additional humanistic approaches to media and culture. Occasionally, proposals have been made for formalizing qualitative data analysis into matrices or truth tables. For example, Charles C. Ragin's (1987, 1994) comparative method has sought to account for cases (social events, processes, or units) by tabulating the combinations of historical and cultural conditions under which they occur. The common denominator of most qualitative analysis, however, is that it stays close to its original data and their context. While a range of more or less distinctive techniques exist (Lindlof and Taylor, 2011; Silverman, 2006), it is possible to identify three main analytical types, two of which have been widely used in media studies.

► Payne Fund studies – Chapter 9, p. 173

► case-based and code-based research – Chapter 15, p. 286

Thematic and narrative analysis

Building on linguistics, literary studies, and, to a degree, anthropology and sociology, one common type of analysis performs an in-depth and iterative categorization of interviews, observational notes, and other texts with reference to their 'content' (concepts, metaphors, themes, etc.) and/or their 'form' (narratives, arguments, turn-taking, etc.). An early classic identified narrative structures in African-American vernacular speech (Labov and Waletzky, 1967), and much later work has examined narrative as a key aspect of social interaction (Gubrium and Holstein, 2009; Riessman, 2008). By comparing, contrasting, and organizing narrative and other discursive constituents in categories, studies are able to abstract various conceptions of 'the meaning of' particular media content, organizations, or audiences, as far as specific informants are concerned. In a next step, these categorizations support inferences, for instance, concerning journalists' definitions of a 'story' (Tuchman, 1978), or the decodings of news items by different user groups (Morley, 1980).

Some qualitative communication studies have relied on consensual or group coding of themes to validate their conclusions (e.g., Neuman, *et al.*, 1992: 32–33). Research has also relied on models and other nonverbal tools of analysis: Miles and Huberman (1994) emphasized the role of data display in the form of figures and graphics, not just as a presentation of findings, but as an integral part of data analysis. Perhaps surprisingly in a field that works with and through visual representations, such approaches to qualitative communication research have been rare in the published literature. The increasing use of computer software for qualitative analysis may contribute to more multimodal analyses.

consensual coding

data display

The present inclusive understanding of categorical analysis is compatible, for some analytical purposes, with coding as performed in content and survey studies. In an early, but rarely cited contribution to qualitative research methodology, Lazarsfeld and Barton (1951) explored different ways of transforming categorizations of empirical data into typologies, indices, and models. While inclined toward formalization, the authors highlighted the many varieties and stages of empirical data analysis; they also acknowledged the necessary interpretive labor throughout the analytical process.

Grounded theory

The second variant of qualitative data analysis is grounded theory (Glaser and Strauss, 1967), which became influential in the social sciences from the 1960s as an approach that would legitimate an alternative, not least, to survey research. As suggested by the name, it is a methodology which assumes that theory can and should be grounded in the field of study, that is, generated in a constant interplay with the social actors and interactions in question (for an overview, see Charmaz, 2006; Strauss, 1987; Strauss and Corbin, 1990). Whereas media studies have rarely pursued a full-fledged version of the approach, the grounding of research in the field of study is widely referred to as the hallmark also of qualitative media and communication research.

constant comparative method

Relying on a constant comparative method, the grounded-theory tradition has developed a detailed set of procedures for collecting and analyzing empirical data. One characteristic feature is the several, reiterated stages of sampling, analyzing, memoing, and interpreting materials; another feature is a stepwise process of coding data at different levels of abstraction. Most important, the assumption is that these sequences may ultimately produce theoretical saturation – an equilibrium of empirical evidence and explanatory concepts.

theoretical saturation

The approach has remained disputed, however, on several counts (see Alvesson and Sköldberg, 2009: 53–75). The terminology appears more widespread than the practice, and is "sometimes invoked ... to legitimize an inductive approach" (Fielding and Lee, 1998: 178). For one thing, critics have questioned the apparent premise of grounded theory that a researcher may enter the field without theoretical presuppositions. In addition to being epistemologically dubious, the premise may encourage and justify researchers in *not* reflecting on the theoretical or social conditions and implications of their work. Instead, textbooks have suggested highly detailed procedures that are designed to ensure a grounding of categories, but whose origins or motivations are often not clear. For another thing, at least in Strauss and Corbin's (1990) widely cited version, the analytical procedures tend to cut off social events from their context, as each event is analyzed, reanalyzed, and condensed in increasingly abstract categories.

The uncertain status of the concepts and procedures associated with grounded theory was part of the backdrop to an unusual confrontation between the two founders of the tradition. Glaser (1992) attacked his coauthor for an "immoral undermining" (p. 121) of their original joint contribution, demanding the withdrawal of Strauss's coauthored 1990 volume (which has not happened). In the end, it remains unclear what might distinguish grounded theory beyond sampling, comparing, and reflecting on evidence in a reiterated sequence, as conducted by most (qualitative) researchers. As part of a recent constructivist redevelopment of the tradition, Charmaz (2006: 135) recognized that grounded theory, in fact, has generated little theory.

Discourse analysis

The third approach to qualitative data analysis in media and communication research draws its inspiration from linguistic discourse studies.◀ It is given special attention here because it holds a specific potential for redeveloping a 'statistics' or systematics of qualitative communication research. On the one hand, discourse studies offer a multilevel and multistep approach to coding and analysis, including consensual and thematic procedures. On the other hand, it may avoid the abstraction and decontextualization of meaning that typically follows from grounded theory.

"statistics" of qualitative research

One way of combining the strengths of coding and close analysis is to incorporate two main stages of data analysis:

- *Heuristic coding* – a preliminary assignment of verbal and other codes to different segments and levels of a data set. Examples

▶ discourse studies – Chapter 6, p. 113

ANALYSIS BOX 14.1: DISCOURSE ANALYSIS OF QUALITATIVE INTERVIEW DATA

In a study of the reception of television news by American men at different educational levels, the present author employed a combination of heuristic coding and discourse analysis to explore the experiential qualities and social uses of the news genre (Jensen, 1986). The heuristic coding served to identify references to a set of themes that had been operationalized in the interview guide, but which were addressed at various points of each interview. Next, the different textual sequences were examined in further detail through discourse analysis. Referring to categories that are explained in the main text, the following illustration pays special attention to the level of continuous discourse or argument. Of special interest at the discourse level are the following categories:

- *Generalizations* – summary statements, often signaled by adverbials, conjunctions, and verbal or 'do'-emphasis, and by initial or final placement in a speaker's turn;
- *Substantiations* – the supporting reasons, including examples, given for a generalization;
- *Implicit premises* – the unquestioned point of departure for an argument, either a logical presupposition or a natural assumption in context; and
- *Implications* – what follows from a statement with varying degrees of certainty, depending on the speech community, the immediate communicative context, as well as the wider social and cultural setting.

At issue in the following quotation is the theme of flow (Williams, 1974) – whether the respondent carries over from another television program to the news. Asked by the interviewer (I) whether he does that, this respondent, a junior university professor, says:

> "No. (I: No?). I don't think so, because I have a real thing, when I was living at home my sister is one who just always has some appliance on (I: H-hm), and I really, something deep in me, I really dislike that (I: H-hm), so that, no, if I get up and if the first story didn't catch me, or maybe even if I was done with that program I'd turn it off (I: H-hm) and not keep it on just because it had been on the hour before."
>
> (Jensen, 1986: 177)

The generalization – a denial of this possibility – is expressed both in the initial emphatic "no" and in the summarizing "so that, no." However, two quite different substantiations are offered. The first reference is to a situation where the first story does not catch him; the implied premise of the uncompleted sentence is that if that story did catch him, he would, or might, keep watching. The second substantiation, perhaps on second thought, asserts that if the previous program had ended, he would turn off the TV.

The disjuncture between the two substantiations served as one occasion to reconsider other responses by this and other respondents. One conclusion of the study, as suggested also by other research, was that the respondents aimed to offer an implication – to project an image – of themselves as rational and committed citizens, not least in relation to a 'serious' genre such as news. Presumably, they ought to select news specifically as part of their media diet. In the interviews, the theme of watching the news as a way of participating in political democracy tied in with other themes, particularly the feeling of being a legitimate member of an imagined political community (Anderson, 1991). In contrast, respondents found it difficult, or impossible, to account for news as a political resource with a concrete instrumental value.

At the level of *discourse*, the brief quotation also contains the rudiments of a narrative regarding family life, specifically the respondent's sister, with implications for gender-specific media use – and perceptions thereof. The narrative is constituted, both through grammatical choices and at the level of entire *speech acts:*

- *Personal pronouns* – a characteristic feature is the consistent and insistent use of "I," a self-assured and self-aware position, which the respondent associates equally with living at home and with his current living conditions.
- *Impersonal grammar* – in reference to his sister, the respondent seems to suggest that she does not actively use the media, but merely "has on" a semi-autonomous technology, what is derogatorily termed "some appliance." (It is worth adding that, also in his own case, the first news story is something that must "catch him," not vice versa.)
- *Metaphor* – is not a strong feature in the example. Still, metaphors serve to emphasize the respondent's distanciating evaluations ("deep in me," "have a real thing"). Similarly, the reference to media as "appliances" (and to a program "catching" a person) signals a distance between the speaker and certain uses of the medium.

At the level of communicative *interaction*, the respondent reemphasizes his position:

- *Turn-taking* – the research design gave respondents the opportunity to elaborate at length, which this respondent did; this was one of his shorter replies. Here, he responded to the verbatim question, "If you were watching the program right before the news program, would that make you more inclined to watch the news?" It is worth noticing that the relativity of "inclined to watch" is canceled by the respondent who instead frames a clear-cut choice, as signaled initially by a firm "no."
- *Semantic networks* – a longer sequence, preferably the full interview, would be needed to demonstrate further interrelations between the concepts referred to. Still, the lexical choices, including various emphatic formulations ("a real thing," "just always," "really," "something deep in me"), are in line with the respondent's profiling of himself as a self-assured person – and a rational citizen.

range from metaphors, expressed in a single word or image, to complex fictional or factual narratives. Heuristic coding allows researchers to produce a summary, outline, or working document concerning the elements and structures of the empirical materials. In later stages, this overview can support, for instance, an assessment of hypotheses and the identification of counterexamples.

- *Discourse analysis* – a more detailed categorization of various data segments and their constituents. As exemplified in Analysis Box 14.1, aspects of both form and content offer relevant units of analysis, from a respondent's use of pronouns in an interview, to the narratives constructed jointly by a team within a multiplayer online game.

Discourse studies grow out of a reorientation of language studies, since the 1970s, from form and norm, and toward uses and contexts, including the uses of language in research. In his influential functional linguistics,◀ Halliday (1973, 1978) identified three aspects of language use: the ideational aspect of using language to represent, and act on, our surroundings; the interactional aspect of relating to others in communication; and the textual aspect of producing coherent discourse.

Speech acts

Although commonly thought of as representations of the world, all linguistic utterances perform a certain type of speech act, accomplishing purposes in contexts.◀ *Orders* will be negotiated within a media production team; journalistic sources may be offered a *promise* of anonymity in return for a statement. In addition, three lexicogrammatical

▶ functional linguistics – Chapter 6, p. 115
▶ speech acts – Chapter 1, p. 13

or formal elements of utterances lend themselves to analysis as indicators:

- *Personal pronouns* (I, you, one, they, etc.). Especially in reference to themselves, speakers' (and writers') uses of pronouns signal variable degrees of distance from a topic or opinion, and from other people.
- *Impersonal grammar.* Through passive sentences and other linguistic choices, both media organizations and ordinary individuals are often less than precise regarding 'who did what.' In some cases, such agentless structures may imply a view of the world in which things just happen.
- *Metaphors.* Alone, in pairs, and in sequences, metaphors can serve as an organizing principle for a story or argument and, hence, as a key to respondents' conception of particular phenomena.

Interaction

The interaction between two or more individuals, which is the point of departure for most empirical media studies, can be examined for at least two purposes. First, the gradual development of viewpoints, for instance, in a focus group, invites close analysis that traces the articulation and reworking of conceptual distinctions, metaphors, social relations, etc. Second, the researcher's own role as party to the interaction calls for quality control – what is addressed more generally under headings of the reliability or intersubjectivity of research.◀ In qualitative research, such analyses help to assess whether, in fact, studies explore 'the native's perspective.' For both purposes, two categories can provide indicators of the nature of the interaction:

- *Turn-taking* – a description of the structure, order, and length of the turns taken by respondents and researcher(s) (Sacks, *et al.*, 1974). More simply, do researchers listen to what respondents have to say?
- *Semantic networks* – an examination of central terms and concepts, as introduced and redeveloped by both researcher and respondent(s) (e.g., Corley and Kaufer, 1993).

▶ reliability and quality control – Chapter 15, p. 288

Discourses

Defined as meaningful wholes with narrative, argumentative, and other communicative purposes, discourses represent the largest unit of qualitative data analysis. In addition to rhetorical and literary traditions, a source of inspiration for this level of discourse analysis has been the study of informal argument (Toulmin, 2003[1958]) and other everyday interaction. To exemplify, the actant model,◀ which was developed from folk tales, has proven applicable to how people narrate and argue about themselves – the 'Story of Me' (Jensen, 1995: 137).

The analysis in Analysis Box 14.1 illustrates the principles of all three levels. To be clear, the purpose of this presentation of discourse studies as a resource for qualitative data analysis is not to call for exhaustive formal analyses of interviews and other data *as language*. Instead, the analysis of language (and other signs) as discourse is an auxiliary operation to better understand how qualitative research evidence arises *from communication*, with spoken and written language as the primary vehicles. Whereas many discourse analysts examine language as structure, qualitative data analysis emphasizes language and its uses as forms of evidence (Gee, *et al.*, 1992: 229–230).

discourse as structure and evidence

Verbal language and its constituent elements are key in qualitative research. Language enters into a trinity of terms, concepts, and objects of inquiry: in order to relate a conceptual understanding to matters of fact in the world with some degree of intersubjectivity, we must rely on language – in research as in (other) communication. Despite the centrality of visual and other types of data – found or made – language constitutes a privileged modality that can rearticulate other modalities. Speech interprets images, but images rarely interpret speech, except in aesthetic experiments. Language relays categorical information that can be recategorized – restated and responded to – in ways that no other modality can.

terms, concepts, and objects

Language and its uses in qualitative research for producing as well as analyzing data are analogous to the place of mathematical and logical notations and procedures in quantitative

▶ the actant model – Chapter 7, p. 140

research. Numbers have quite a different relevance for media researchers than they do for mathematicians, but are, nevertheless, essential conditions of quantitative media studies. Equally, qualitative researchers need to analyze language, even though they are not linguists. Like many other interdisciplinary fields, media and communication research has transferred and integrated diverse methods; studies also frequently depend on additional interdisciplinary collaboration or the use of consultants from other fields. Quantitative projects routinely consult with statisticians; qualitative projects may increasingly involve discourse analysts in interdisciplinary groups or, indeed, as consultants. This is suggested both by a growing emphasis on systematic and transparent analytical procedures in qualitative research, and by the increasing availability of resources for this purpose, specifically software packages.

Computer interfaces

Since the mid-1990s, computer software has come to be recognized as a practical as well as legitimate ingredient of qualitative research (Fielding and Lee, 1998). This followed a surprisingly long period during which such resources were commonly considered alien – and alienating – in relation to the qualitative enterprise, as if binary numbers at the machine level entailed quantitative procedures at the methodological level. A variety of software packages for the administration and analysis of qualitative data have been developed, including modules for the examination of sound, still, and moving images (for an overview, see Lewins and Silver, 2007). Furthermore, their potentials (and problems) for both research design and theory development have been explored (Fielding and Lee, 1998; Kelle, 1995), including the uses of hypertext◀ in the case of digital media studies (Dicks, *et al.*, 2005).

Probably the main practical relevance so far has been qualitative software as a means of heuristic coding.◀ This is in addition to the basic, but essential function of documenting and retrieving large and heterogeneous data sets. Moreover, software facilitates the analysis as well as the presentation of materials in graphic, tabular, and other nonverbal formats. In a wider perspective, networked media can support several stages of the research process as a whole – from theoretical exploration, literature review, and project organization, through data collection, annotation, and analysis, to publication, debate, and collaboration with the various constituencies applying research findings. Not least, networked media allow for more extensive data sharing and collaborative qualitative projects, which have been quite rare in the past, compared to quantitative studies. In a longer perspective, the sharing of evidence and findings can involve not just colleagues, but respondents as well as policy circles and the general public. Computer-supported research facilitates member checks (Lindlof and Taylor, 2011: 278–280) – conferring with respondents about the interpretation of data (even while conclusions remain the researcher's right and responsibility). Networked media also provide another link from qualitative research to public and policy debates, which traditionally have been a domain dominated by quantitative research and arguments.

data sharing

member checks

One final perspective has to do with the publication of qualitative research projects, which frequently require so much space that they may not make it into some of the print journals that still define a field. For qualitative research in particular, but for media and communication studies at large, a growing number of differentiated publication formats can serve both as 'mass communication,' disseminating complementary evidence and background information, and as interactive fora for theoretical, methodological, and policy discussion. At the same time, networked media may provide a concrete interface between qualitative and quantitative research traditions, addressing coding, analysis, and other shared categories, and enabling interaction in the spirit of what, sixty years ago, Lazarsfeld and Barton (1951: 155) described as a logic of complementarity: "There is a direct line of logical continuity from qualitative classification to the most rigorous form of measurement." It is this logic that the next chapter revisits and updates.

▶ hypertext – Chapter 9, p. 184
▶ heuristic coding, p. 278

ANALYSIS BOX 15.1: THE 'SIGNS' OF SCIENCE

Media and communication researchers rely on diverse means ('signs') of representation and expression – in order to arrive at an understanding of the empirical field of inquiry, to share findings with colleagues, and to present the implications of studies to funders, stakeholders, and the general public. As recognized since classical rhetoric,◀ neither words nor numbers are neutral or innocent. A case in point are the models of communication that inform and frame undergraduate textbooks as well as international journal articles (McQuail and Windahl, 1993).

Whereas tables and figures are associated especially with quantitative research traditions, Chapter 14 noted how coding, modeling, and visual display are integral to qualitative studies, as well. Throughout this volume, a number of verbal, mathematical, and graphic forms are used to communicate different points. In review, some of main types can be described as follows:

- literature reviews and theoretical arguments in all chapters in *verbal discourse;*
- conceptual models of a portion of the field, as represented in either *graphic displays* (e.g., Figure 5.1) or *matrices* (e.g., Figure 6.3);
- analytical examples (e.g., the Analyses Boxes), employing both *verbal language*, *numbers*, and *images* to represent the object of analysis and aspects of the analytical process (e.g., Chapter 8 on *The Big Sleep* and Chapter 16 on reality television);
- tables summarizing findings in terms of a *numerical distribution* (e.g., Table 13.1);
- *scattergram*, indicating correlations between data elements concerning, for instance, opinions and media preferences (Figure 8.4);
- *time line*, locating shifting technologies and institutions of communication in historical perspective (Figure 2.1).

(Other common formats of presentation include bar charts, histograms, line graphs, and pie charts. See further Deacon, *et al.*, 2007: 96–100.)

but equal. They are complementary, not reducible to each other. They may be unified, not in the first instance – at the level of minimal measurements – but in the final instance – in concluding a process of inquiry, in a context, and for a purpose.

Departing from the received conceptual dichotomies that continue to inform the field, the chapter first notes the different and distinctive strengths of qualitative and quantitative methodologies. To begin a more detailed comparison, the chapter distinguishes several levels of analysis, emphasizing the distinction between *methods* – the concrete instruments for collecting and analyzing empirical data – and *methodologies* – the theoretically grounded research designs that motivate the selection of specific methods, and through which inferences can be made about the implications of findings. In the middle section, I return to the classic forms of inference – induction and deduction – and argue that a third form – abduction – though widely neglected in methods textbooks, has a special place in the process of research. In the last part of the chapter, I outline a realist position in the theory of science. The signs of science are all partial and preliminary. As communicated within scientific and other communities, however, they enable individuals, institutions, and societies to deliberate before committing themselves to conclusions and acting accordingly.

▶ rhetoric – Chapter 2, p. 27

CONFLICT AND COMPLEMENTARITY

Two paradigms

Figure 15.1 displays a list of familiar conceptual dichotomies. The two columns qualify as

15 The complementarity of qualitative and quantitative methodologies in media and communication research

Klaus Bruhn Jensen

- an overview of *two research paradigms* that have informed media and communication studies
- a presentation of *six levels of analysis*, which are shared across different research traditions
- a comparison, with examples, of *three forms of inference* from evidence to conclusions
- an account of the concepts of *reliability, validity, generalization*, and *probability* as they relate to qualitative as well as quantitative media studies
- a discussion of scientific *realism* as a framework for methodological complementarity

SIGNS OF SCIENCE

It is a basic insight of communication studies since classical rhetoric that language and other signs and symbols lend shape to human knowledge. The form is (part of) the message of science, bearing witness to distinctive procedures and purposes of inquiry. The prototypical social-scientific journal article, for example, implies that research questions, their operationalization in empirical research designs, the resulting findings, and the subsequent interpretive discussion can and should be separated into stages of inquiry and sections of reporting. In comparison, the equivalent humanistic essay typically moves more freely across the various stages of collecting, analyzing, interpreting, and presenting evidence and arguments. The two publication formats can be seen to mimic two classic communication models:◄ social scientists 'transmit' their findings to the audience; humanistic scholars invite their readers into a 'ritual' of communal deliberation.

The activity of research is itself a communicative practice that is conducted and concluded through distinctive 'signs' – verbal language, mathematical notations, graphical representations, and other meaningful units and processes (see Analysis Box 15.1). Scientific communication also articulates purposes or knowledge interests◄ (Habermas, 1971[1968]), whether administrative or critical (Lazarsfeld, 1941). The signs of science bear witness to their social origins, contexts, and objectives.

research as a communicative practice

At the intersection of arts and sciences, the field of media and communication research has inherited several different conceptions of evidence, inference, and interpretation. Its conflict of the faculties◄ is especially noticeable when it comes to the choice of analytical categories and procedures. This chapter suggests that the methodologies that constitute the field are different,

► transmission and ritual models of communication, Chapter 1, p. 12

► knowledge interests, Chapter 19, p. 358

► the conflict of the faculties, Chapter 1, p. 1

Methodology	
recurrence	occurrence
experiment	experience
measurement	exegesis
product	process
Theory of science	
Gesetzeswissenschaften (sciences about 'laws')	*Ereigniswissenschaften* (sciences about 'events')
Naturwissenschaften (sciences about nature)	*Geisteswissenschaften* (sciences about the human spirit)
nomothetic	idiographic
erklären (explain)	*verstehen* (understand)
external	internal
information	meaning
Epistemology	
nature	history
causes	intentions
objects	subjects

Figure 15.1 Two paradigms of research

contrasting paradigms (Kuhn, 1970), defined as particular configurations of ontological, epistemological, and methodological assumptions about reality and how to study it (Lincoln and Guba, 1985: 108).

paradigms

methodology

At the concrete level of methodology, quantitative research instruments are considered especially suited to establish the *recurrence* of events or objects (e.g., a specific feature of media content or a particular cognitive response). Qualitative approaches, in comparison, explore the singular *occurrence* of meaningful phenomena, with reference to their full context (e.g., a film narrative or everyday media uses in a household). Defined as an indivisible whole, human *experience* calls for an *exegesis* – an iterative interpretation of various elements whose meaning and context may be redefined as the interpretation proceeds. In contrast, the whole of human experience can also be understood as the sum of its parts, divisible at least in operational terms and, hence, manipulable in *experiments*, whose findings are expressed in *measurements*. In this last regard, the quantitative perspective can be seen to approach meaning as a delimited vehicle or *product*. Qualitative methodologies, in turn, emphasize meaning as a *process* unfolding in contexts. (For a discussion of 'quantity' and 'quality' in social research, see Bryman, 1988.)

The historical background to these different methodological perspectives was attempts within theory of science to arrive at procedures for studying society and culture, following the development of modern social sciences from the late 1800s. One famous statement of purpose was Max Weber's (1964: 88) definition of sociology as "a science which attempts the interpretive understanding of social action in order thereby to arrive at causal explanation of its course and effects," referring to *both* interpretations *and* causes. Interpretations may become causes. Many current debates were anticipated in the *Methodenstreit* (struggle over methods) of

theory of science

Methodenstreit

that early period, centered in German thought, which confronted historicist and naturalist notions of what are the 'facts' of social life (for an overview, see Hammersley, 1995). On the one hand, one may search for one or more laws (*Gesetz*), as previously established in sciences of nature (*Naturwissenschaften*). One thus takes a generalizing or *nomothetic* attitude and tries to explain (*erklären*) society.

On the other hand, one may study one or more singular events (*Ereignis*), as associated with philosophy, aesthetics, and other disciplines of the 'human spirit' (*Geist*). Here, one takes an individualizing or *idiographic* attitude with the aim of understanding (*verstehen*) society. In information and communication theory, several related distinctions emerged. Media and communication studies have tended to take either an *external* perspective on *information* as a technical, neutral carrier of insight, or an *internal* perspective on *meaning* as an always already interpreted construct.

These positions in the theory of science occupy a middle ground between concrete methodological choices and larger epistemological issues that seem 'eternal,' in the sense that they have refused to go away for millennia of documented inquiry. As such, they have returned, sometimes with a vengeance, in new fields of research.

epistemology

The media field has faced general questions of whether technologies and other aspects of matter or *nature* may be said to have determined particular forms of communication in specific societies throughout *history*. A recurring issue has been whether explanatory models from the natural sciences might be transferred, more or less directly, to the study of society and culture. Media practitioners, legislators, as well as ordinary users all bring *intentions* into their communications. Hence, it becomes necessary to ask specifically how – through which social structures and cultural processes – their motivated actions are coordinated, and become *causes*.

In the end, media and communication research is faced with the fundamental dichotomy of *subject* and *object*. This relationship is both a constitutive feature of communication and a condition of all research. In communicative interaction, perhaps the key 'object' of interest is other subjects, as suggested by George Herbert Mead's (1934) concept of the significant other. In empirical studies, the purpose is to describe, interpret, and explain such interaction, as seen inevitably from the researcher's perspective, even while recognizing the categories of understanding that the participating subjects rely on.

Code-based and case-based analysis

Most contemporary researchers will recognize – at least in principle – that their choice of methods depends on which aspects of communication are to be examined, and on the purpose of study – the 'how' of research depends on its 'what' and its 'why' (Kvale, 1987). Clearly, different approaches are required to account for editorial decision-making practices as opposed to gender-specific employment patterns in news media; the structure of metaphors in newspaper headlinese in contrast to the coverage of a particular event in different media; and audiences' decodings of, versus their basic exposure to, particular items of information.

The two paradigms can be characterized, at the level of concrete analytical procedures, by their reliance on either code-based or case-based operations (Fielding and Lee, 1998: 27). On the one hand, *code-based* analysis assumes that, for instance, a survey response can be assigned unequivocally to one category for analytical purposes. A classic example is the opinion polls leading up to a general election. The polls owe much of their predictive value to their clearly defined categories, not only because the options are mutually exclusive (one designated party, abstention, or undecided), but also because the act of voting (and of responding to a poll) is a familiar practice and a cultural convention.

On the other hand, *case-based* analysis seeks, at least initially, to minimize reduction of the data being generated, for instance, in a depth interview. Instead, the process of interacting with respondents can be seen to carry over into the process of analysis. The categories of understanding and meaning are identified, redefined, and clarified throughout the research process as a whole. To exemplify, a case-based analysis might explore conceptions of what is a 'political' issue, in the media and other contexts, and how, according to respondents, this relates to institutionalized political activities such as polls and elections.

In procedural terms, then, a code-based analysis relies on predefined categories which both disambiguate and decontextualize the units of meaning. A case-based analysis allows its categories to be informed and modified by their contexts – of data collection as well as of analysis – in an iterative fashion.

One particular issue that has continued to occupy, and divide, the paradigms is whether code-based analysis could, and should, gradually replace case-based analysis. This is the working strategy of a good number of projects and research programs; more controversially, it might apply as an ideal to entire disciplines as they mature. The qualitative, case-oriented emphasis of early social science has been explained, in part, by its preliminary search for "global, overall perspectives" (Jankowski and Wester, 1991: 46).

In the post-1945 period, code-based analysis became established as the norm in the social sciences. By the same token, qualitative research was commonly assigned the role of performing 'pilot studies'◄ that would pretest codes and, to a degree, develop theory. One question that has remained controversial, then, is whether case-based, qualitative research can be said to have an independent explanatory value. To clarify the nature of the disagreements, and to assess the prospects for convergence, it is helpful, first of all, to differentiate the several stages and levels of analysis which qualitative and quantitative studies share.

METHODS AND METHODOLOGIES

Six levels of analysis

Figure 15.2 distinguishes six levels of research, as associated with different stages of planning, conducting, documenting, and interpreting empirical studies. The levels are described here in

► pilot studies, p. 300

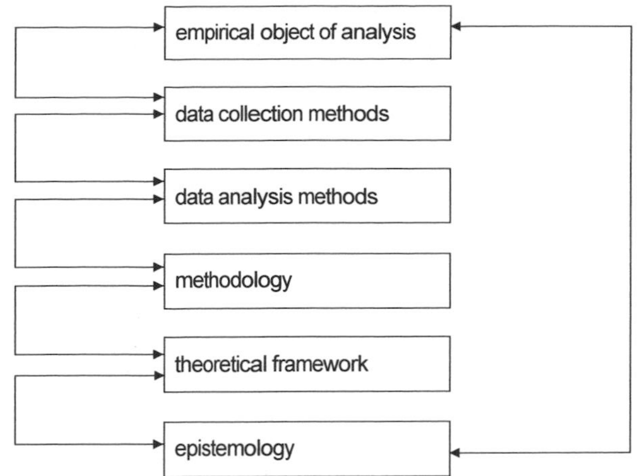

Figure 15.2 Six levels of empirical research

terms of their discourses or symbolic instruments – the varied social uses of language, mathematical symbols, graphical representations, and other media and modalities of research:

- The empirical *object of analysis* will be everyday as well as institutional discourses that arise from social interaction in and around media. The relevant materials range widely, from organizational memoranda and policy documents, to newspapers and web sites, to readership figures and user test responses. While some materials are 'found' (e.g., radio programs in a sound archive), and others 'made' (e.g., observations in a radio studio), each constitutes a possible source of evidence, depending on the purpose of inquiry.
- In the case of evidence that is 'found,' the second level of *data collection methods* – from content sampling frames to interview guides – also serves to demarcate and document a particular portion of reality for closer scrutiny. To a degree, the same methods of data collection may support both qualitative and quantitative research designs and analyses. (I return to the distinction between 'found' and 'made' data, which has taken on new salience for digital media.)◄

► data – found and made, p. 288

- *Data analysis methods* cover diverse operations of categorizing, segmenting, and interpreting evidence or data sets. In addition, empirical studies typically include 'quality control': a meta-analytical component in the form of statistical tests for significance or an 'audit trail' documenting the steps of a qualitative analysis.◀

meta-analytical quality control

- *Methodology* can be defined as a theoretically informed plan of action in relation to a particular empirical domain. It is at this level that the distinction between qualitative and quantitative research belongs; it is here that the status of the data that *methods* produce is explicated and justified. If methods are techniques, methodologies are technologies of research. As elaborated below, methodologies map theoretical 'macrocosms' onto necessarily selective empirical 'microcosms.'◀

methodology – a theoretically informed plan of action

- *Theoretical frameworks* of conjoined concepts lend meaning and relevance to a particular configuration of empirical findings. Theories can be thought of as frames,◀ broadly speaking (Goffman, 1974; Lakoff and Johnson, 1980), which enable – afford◀ (Gibson, 1979) – certain interpretations, while discouraging others. Crucially, quantitative and qualitative evidence may be subsumed under the same theoretical framework: it is methodology, not theory, that distinguishes qualitative and quantitative research.

methodology, not theory, distinguishes qualitative and quantitative research

- Theoretical frameworks are 'substantive,' in the sense that they account for a particular domain of reality, here media and communication. Theoretical choices, further, are supported by meta-theoretical or *epistemological* arguments and assumptions. The epistemological level of analysis provides preliminary definitions of the 'object' of study, as well as justifications concerning the nature of the 'analysis.'

As suggested at the opening of this chapter, noting the characteristic formats of humanistic and social-scientific publications, qualitative and quantitative methodologies are distinguished, not least, by their ways on joining – and separating – these levels of analysis. Quantitative research tends to prefer a separation of the moments of conceptualization, design, data collection, data analysis, and interpretation. This premise goes back to the distinction between 'the context of discovery' and 'the context of justification,' as originally associated with logical positivism (Glymour and Eberhardt, 2008). The argument has been that scientific research stands out by its procedures for justifying or testing beliefs, and that the process of discovering or hypothesizing beliefs is not part of science proper. Qualitative research, in its turn, holds that certain phenomena call for a research process that moves liberally between all the analytical levels in order to develop adequate analytical categories.

contexts of discovery and justification

Remediated methods

The six levels of analysis apply to both qualitative and quantitative research, and across different media and communicative practices. At the same time, it should be noted that digital media present new challenges – and opportunities – for empirical research, specifically regarding the methods of data collection and analysis. When the objects of analysis change, so does some of the relevant evidence; networked communications across the online-offline divide also invite more multimethod methodologies.

Digital media highlight a common distinction between research evidence that is either 'found' or 'made' (see further Jensen, in press-a). In one sense, all the evidence that is needed for studies of the internet and mobile media is already there, documented in and of servers and clients, with a little help from network administrators, service providers, and user panels. In this sense, the system *is* the method. In another sense, hardly anything is documented in advance, given the radically dispersed and locally embedded nature of networked communications. Joining the two extremes of auto-generated and contextualized evidence poses one of the main methodological challenges for current media studies.

data as found or made

Returning to the six prototypical methods of Figure III.1, the two lower cells – content analysis

▶ audit trails – Chapter 14, p. 276
▶ empirical microcosm, theoretical macrocosm, p. 300
▶ frames, Chapter 8, p. 164
▶ affordances, Chapter 1, p. 175

and discourse studies – have been coming back in style. A wealth of information lends itself to study as texts and documents. For example, subscribing to an RSS feed, forwarding a news story from a website, or meta-tagging a blog entry, first, produces an additional communicative event and, next, perhaps proliferating communicative sequences. Additional meta-information or metadata◀ situate this information in relation to diverse contexts of communication: the origins of the information, its interrelations with other items, their interdependent trajectories, the users accessing the information and, perhaps, adding meta-information themselves, etc. Not just the content, but the forms and some of the contexts of communication, thus, become available and accessible for analysis, depending on formal conditions of access, ethical considerations, as well as the sociological imagination (Mills, 1959a) of researchers anticipating information of interest to be auto-generated.

For other prototypical methods, as well, the line between what is made and what is found has been shifting. The most obvious case is digital or virtual ethnographies (Hine, 2000), in which the archives of social network sites and virtual worlds present themselves as 'contents' and 'discourses' for analysis. In comparison with the written and, later, electronic records of anthropological fieldwork, such archives provide a measure of real-time details, still to be complemented by other sources of evidence. Digital media, further, may give rise to natural or field experiments,◀ akin to earlier studies of how, for instance, the introduction of television affected the lives of communities. For surveys as well as qualitative interviews (Mann and Stewart, 2000), digital media provide a research tool that complements, for instance, the (still common) telephone interview – and a sprawling repository of data on the public's lifestyle preferences and everyday activities. Amid legal and ethical concerns, data mining◀ (Han and Kamber, 2006) has become another standard approach to examining what people say, think, and do in and around digital media.

digital ethnography

▶ metadata – Chapter 10, p. 194
▶ natural and field experiments – Chapter 13, p. 254
▶ data mining – Chapter 13, p. 262

The challenge of how to apply remediated methods to digital media is matched, or trumped, by the challenge of how to document the interplay of online and offline interactions in three-step flows – one-to-one, one-to-many, and many-to-many.◀ To what extent do digital media either replace or complement other media for diverse purposes? How do digital media users communicate within and across public and private contexts? And, in what ways do all these communicative practices serve to reproduce or reconfigure existing political, economic, and cultural institutions? Auto-generated evidence in computer systems is an instance of what Webb, *et al.* (2000) had referred to, in 1966, as 'unobtrusive measures,' which avoid the direct elicitation of input from research subjects. Since then, the resurgence of qualitative approaches in social and cultural research (Denzin and Lincoln, 2005) has brought new attention to the merits of unobtrusive and naturalistic data. The practical question is how to balance what evidence can be found, with what must be made. The next and more difficult question is how to proceed to inferences about the place of media – new and old – in human communication.

THREE FORMS OF INFERENCE

Induction, deduction, and abduction

Standard accounts of the theory of science still tend to assume that research infers either from a general principle or law to individual instances (deduction), or from the examination of several instances to a law (induction). The relevance of each for the humanities and the social sciences as well as for interdisciplinary fields has been debated fiercely since the *Methodenstreit*◀ of the late nineteenth century (for an overview, see Pitt, 1988). A third form of inference – abduction – has rarely been considered as an explicit model of scientific reasoning. While Aristotle had identified abduction as one type of inference (Blaikie, 2007; Hanson, 1958), it was reintroduced to modern philosophy by Charles Sanders Peirce

▶ three-step flows of communication – Chapter 10
▶ *Methodenstreit* – p. 285

in an 1878 article that related it to the other two types. His basic idea was that there are three components to an inference – a rule which, when applied to a single case, produces a conclusion or result. These components yield three possible combinations:

> DEDUCTION
> *Rule.* All the beans from this bag are white.
> *Case.* These beans are from this bag.
> *Result.* These beans are white.
>
> INDUCTION
> *Case.* These beans are from this bag.
> *Result.* These beans are white.
> *Rule.* All the beans from this bag are white.
>
> [ABDUCTION
> *Result.* These beans are white.
> *Rule.* All the beans from this bag are white.]
> *Case.* These beans are from this bag.
> (Peirce, 1986: 325–326)

Formally, only the deduction is a valid inference. Here, given the meaning of the constituent terms, the rule can be applied without any uncertainty to the case, so that the result follows as a matter of course. In the induction, the implication is that, if one examines a sufficient number of beans (cases), one may be willing to conclude that they are all white. Such reasoning appears commonsensical, and enters into both everyday life and research practice. The point of the abduction, finally, is that it introduces a rule that may explain why one encounters specific (more or less surprising) facts, such as white beans, in a particular context.

The bean example is, of course, trivial. In other cases, the newly devised rule represents an exceptionally bright idea, as in Sherlock Holmes' solution of crime mysteries, which are feats of abduction (Sebeok and Umiker-Sebeok, 1983). Also, theory development depends crucially on abduction.

In practice, the three forms of inference are rarely found in any pure form in empirical studies. In fact, it can be argued that an aspect of each type is required to produce new knowledge. Take the prototypical social-scientific study of a particular attitude or behavior. Such studies depart from a relatively specific hypothesis that has been derived from more general premises of a sociological or psychological nature (deduction), and which can be tested against a large number of concrete instances – responses or observations (induction). The outcome of the data analysis is a pattern of findings that may be only partly in accordance with the hypothesis, likely giving rise to the formulation of a new rule (abduction) to be investigated in further research. The original premise of the study, equally, might have been the outcome of a (more or less) bright idea – abduction.

One advantage of such a combinatorial understanding of scientific inferences is that it leaves open the question of whether, or to what extent, research projects in fact conform to the received models of either logic or methods textbooks. Studies of scientific practice suggest that they do not (e.g., Hacking, 1983; Latour, 1987). Another advantage is that this understanding of inference invites an open-ended consideration of which combinations may best account for specific domains and issues of research. All three forms of inference are part of the heritage of media and communication studies.

An inductive heritage

induction in research and human evolution

Induction is a heritage both of the history of science and of human evolution. The human capacity for abstracting and generalizing from single events has been a key factor in natural selection and social formations and, hence, an instrument of adaptation and survival (Megarry, 1995). The lay theories◀ (Furnham, 1988) that guide us all through the day hold important ingredients of induction. In scholarship, induction has represented a central problem for philosophers and empirical researchers alike since the Enlightenment. Whereas David Hume had noted, in the mid-1700s, that an induction from 'some' to 'all' can never, strictly speaking, be logically valid (Hume, 2006[1748]), the inductive approach remained attractive throughout the nineteenth century, as elaborated, for example, in John Stuart Mill's influential *A System of Logic* (Mill, 1973–74[1843]). In the twentieth century, an inductive ideal of science rose to new

▶ lay theories, Chapter 19, p. 352

prominence, and then fell definitively, in the shape of logical positivism.

logical positivism

Taking its cue from Mill's contemporary, Auguste Comte, and his call for a 'positive philosophy' that would be non-speculative and applicable to real human concerns, logical positivism developed into an influential school of thought between the two world wars of the twentieth century. A key inspiration was the linguistic, formal turn of philosophy,◀ assuming a correspondence between the structure of propositions and the structure of facts in reality. An additional premise of logical positivism was an absolute distinction not only between facts and values, but between empirical observations and theoretical conceptions of reality. Any meaningful statement about the world would be either elementary in itself (reducible to sense impressions in a given space and time), or decomposable into such elementary propositions. Within such a reductionist understanding of human knowledge, most topics of social-scientific and humanistic research would fall outside the realm of science.

As explicit epistemological programs, both positivism and inductivism generally are positions of the past. (Grounded theory still operates on inductive principles.◀) In the practice of research, however, induction still plays a central and frequently unacknowledged role. Most important, this applies to the mass of descriptive, applied, and administrative studies that inform and support the daily operation of the media sector – which is probably the majority of all studies in the area, published and unpublished. Among the main examples are continuous market research on digital, broadcast, and print audiences, and evaluation research (Patton, 2002) informing the financing of media and supporting government policy decisions. Whereas the aim normally is not to develop or test particular theories, the findings are commonly taken to offer dependable accounts of the infrastructures and uses of media, and are widely reported and debated as such in both specialized and mass media. Commercial companies and state agencies act on – base significant investments and legislation on – the resulting inferences and recommendations.

▶ the linguistic turn, Chapter 2, p. 34
▶ grounded theory – Chapter 14, p. 278

A deductive mainstream

The quantitative mainstream of international communication research, as applied for half a century to different media, is normally described as 'hypothetico-deductive.' Studies propose to test hypotheses that have been deduced from some general 'law.' In a first step, deduction ensures that a hypothesis is neither logically inconsistent nor tautological – which would make it irrelevant for empirical inquiry. If, next, a hypothesis can be seen to contradict or, more likely, specify an accepted law, it calls for further inquiry. It is deduction (from 'all' to 'some') that serves to predict what a study will find under specified circumstances. If, finally, the findings correspond to the predictions, the hypothesis is confirmed, and may be admitted into a body of accepted and cumulated theories in the field in question.

hypothetico-deductive research

Importantly, confirmation does not equal 'verification' in the stronger sense associated, not least, with logical positivism. The hypothetico-deductive position, as associated above all with the work of Karl Popper (1972a[1934]), instead assumes that scientists must seek to falsify their hypotheses. Only if falsification fails, is one justified in still holding the hypothesis, and only preliminarily. Further studies, by oneself or by the research community, may end up falsifying it after all (which, in effect, admits inductivism through the backdoor in a multistep process). What might appear as philosophical hair-splitting, nevertheless, has important consequences for what constitutes an accepted body of knowledge and for the research procedures supporting it. Most media and communication studies cannot unequivocally falsify or verify a given hypothesis. Instead, hypothetico-deductive research in this (and many other) fields is backed by measures of statistical probability: the 'laws' in question are ascertained in a stochastic rather than a determinist sense (Hempel and Oppenheim, 1988[1948]: 13–18).◀

falsification vs. verification

probabilism

▶ stochastic and other models of meaning – Chapter 1, p. 11

But, where do hypotheses come from? Popper (1963) himself suggested that they constitute bold conjectures, offering little systematic or historical specification of how they emerge. At least in the social sciences and humanities, hypotheses are, in part, a product of their times. In a negative aspect, this may result in what Marshall McLuhan dubbed 'rearview-mirrorism': the tendency to define new media and communicative practices in terms of the old, thus cutting short their potentials and perspectives (McLuhan, 1964; Theall, 1971). In a positive aspect, focused comparisons of present, delimited issues, as practiced by hypothetico-deductive research, is one necessary ingredient of theory development for the future, as exemplified by one of the classics of audience research.

Media as agenda-setters

One early insight of the field – that the media do not tell people *what* to think, but may nevertheless suggest to them what to think *about* (Cohen, 1963; Trenaman and McQuail, 1961) – was given conceptual and empirical substance by McCombs and Shaw (1972: 176) in a study of political communication:◄ "although the evidence that mass media deeply change attitudes in a campaign is far from conclusive, the evidence is much stronger that voters learn from the immense quantity of information available during each campaign." The authors, first, deduced a conceptual distinction between 'attitudes' and 'agendas,' and, next, operationalized this distinction in a comparison of news contents and voter statements. Their hypothesis stated that, "the mass media set the agenda for each political campaign, influencing the salience of attitudes toward the political issues."

To test this hypothesis, the study matched "what ... voters *said* were key issues of the campaign with the *actual content* of the mass media used by them during the campaign" (p. 177, emphasis in the original). To specify the test conditions, only voters who were undecided on who to vote for in the 1968 US presidential campaign, and hence might be more open to campaign information, were recruited as interviewees. In addition, these respondents were sampled randomly from lists of registered voters in a particular local community in North Carolina so as to limit other sources of variation, for example, regional differences in media coverage. (Following a pretest, major national sources such as television network news, *The New York Times, Time,* and *Newsweek* were also included in the content sample.)

The concrete empirical evidence consisted in respondents' answers regarding "major problems as they saw them" (p. 178) and news as well as editorial comments during a specified period, overlapping with the interview period. Each of these data sets was coded into predefined categories concerning political issues and other aspects of an electoral campaign. In sum, the analytical categories amounted to a mapping of conceptually deduced distinctions onto instances of political information, as offered by media and taken by some voters, to some extent.

Two findings, in particular, illustrate the hypothetico-deductive logic. First, the design aimed to establish causality, and found that the media had "exerted a considerable impact" (p. 180) on the respondents' perceptions of the political issues presented by the media. The coding of content had distinguished between 'major' and 'minor' coverage of topics and, in both instances, the analysis found strong correlations between media emphases and voters' judgments (+0.967 and +0.979).

Second, in order to determine whether voters might be attending to, and reproducing, the agenda that their preferred candidates advanced in the media, a further analysis was made of those respondents who had a preference for one candidate (without being finally committed). Both for major and minor issues, the findings suggested that "the voters attend reasonably well to *all* the news, *regardless* of which candidate or party issue is stressed" (p. 182, emphasis in the original). The fact that "the judgments of voters seem to reflect the *composite* of the mass media coverage" (p. 181, emphasis in the original), again lent support to the hypothesis that agenda-setting may be a general consequence of media use, at least in the political domain.

► agenda-setting research – Chapter 8, p. 161

In their discussion of findings, McCombs and Shaw (1972) were careful, again, to qualify their conclusions regarding the original hypothesis, acknowledging that the correlations did not *prove* the hypothesis. However, "the evidence is in line with the conditions that must exist if agenda-setting by the mass media does occur" (p. 184). Put differently, their carefully deduced design failed to falsify the hypothesis. The agenda-setting hypothesis, then, presents itself as a more justified alternative than, for example, theories concerning selective perception (Festinger, 1957; Klapper, 1960), which would have been supported if voters had been found to attend especially to their preferred candidates.

A more general lesson is that the weighing of competing hypotheses takes place at the theoretical level (Figure 15.2), not at the level of measurements, correlations, or other analytical procedures. Whereas the correlations between media coverage and voter judgments were indicative of interdependence or causality, the specific nature of this causation must be accounted for within a conceptual framework. Compared to the relatively familiar terrain of national political issues, and to the delimited set of print and broadcast media that McCombs and Shaw (1972) selected from, other media and genres, for instance, reality television,◀ complicate the question of how public agendas are to be defined and understood, and how they may be set. It is the nature of such communicative practices and consequences that the third form of inference – abduction – may help to capture.

An abductive substream

abduction – in theory development and in qualitative methodology

Abduction is at once a general aspect of theory development and a specific ingredient of qualitative methodologies. Since Peirce's original statement, the relevance of abduction has occasionally been considered in both philosophy and other disciplines, including mainstream sociology (Merton, 1968: 158). It was reintroduced to interdisciplinary theory of science by, among others, Hanson (1958) as part of the post-1945 questioning of inductive as well as hypothetico-deductive prototypes of research. In direct opposition to Hempel and Oppenheim's (1988[1948]) "covering-law model," Dray (1957) specified how historical events cannot be examined as a variant of natural events (which may all be 'covered' by one law), but require various other types of "rational explanation." In another influential contribution, Danto (1965) suggested that narratives provide a model for understanding, and for empirically studying, historical events and human actions. Ginzburg (1989) identified an "evidential paradigm" in which, for example, Sigmund Freud and Sherlock Holmes were able to identify underlying or deep structures,◀ respectively in crimes and dreams. More recently, abduction has been characterized in research methodology as a strategy of interpretive social science (Alvesson and Sköldberg, 2009); as one characteristic of qualitative media research (Jensen, 1995); and as a tool in software and other IT development (Ross, 2010).

covering-law model

narrative as research model

evidential paradigm

(Some work (e.g., Blaikie, 2007) further differentiates between abduction and 'retroduction.'◀ Following Peirce's position, this chapter treats abduction as a general type of inference that may include aspects of retroduction, which 'works back' from empirical phenomena to theoretical explanations.)

Reading as communicative practice

Why do people use various media and genres in the first place? What, for instance, does it mean to read popular fiction, as far as the readers are concerned? And, how can the act of reading be conceptualized and studied? The distinction between the native's internal perspective and the analyst's external perspective, and the effort of research at bridging the two – what anthropology and communication studies have referred as a balance between 'emic' and 'etic' approaches to culture and communication◀ – was illustrated in Janice Radway's (1984) classic study of women's romance reading.

▶ reality television – Chapter 16

▶ deep structures – Chapter 1, p. 12

▶ retroduction as research strategy – Chapter 18, p. 339

▶ emic and etic approaches to communication – Chapter 14, p. 267

Appearing at a time when popular culture was being revaluated in empirical reception studies for its significance and use value,◀ the study probed the motivations of romance readers or users. Through audience ethnography as well as in-depth textual analysis, it served, for instance, to differentiate a blanket term such as 'escape' into additional categories of relaxation and time for self-indulgence. Radway (1984) summed up one attraction of romance reading in her conclusion that "it creates a time or space within which a woman can be entirely on her own, preoccupied with her personal needs, desires, and pleasure" (p. 61). A central implication was a shift of emphasis from romances as texts that offer a more or less escapist universe for the reader's identification and gratification, toward an understanding of the very activity of reading as a social practice that enables readers to position themselves within, but also outside everyday life. Media discourses are not only representations of alternative possible worlds, but resources in a world of practice.

reading as social practice

Radway's research strategy might be taken as induction: the categories emerged from – were 'found' – in the field. It is more appropriate, however, to describe them as the outcome of communication: an interactive sequence aligning the informants' and the researcher's perspectives. By introducing concepts or rules that would make the informants' statements meaningful, the researcher was able to account for their experience, not just of the romantic narratives, but of the social practice of reading. Here, first, is Radway's recapitulation of this main finding:

> In summary, when the act of romance reading is viewed as it is by the readers themselves, from within a belief system that accepts as given the institutions of heterosexuality and monogamous marriage, it can be conceived as an activity of mild protest and longing for reform necessitated by those institutions' failure to satisfy the emotional needs of women. Reading therefore functions for them as an act of recognition and contestation whereby that failure is first admitted and then partially reversed. Hence, the Smithton readers' claim that romance reading is a "declaration of independence" and a way to say to others, "This is my time, my space. Now leave me alone."
>
> (Radway, 1984: 213)

Next, the central and somewhat surprising notion, that romance reading is a "declaration of independence," can be explicated in the form of an abduction:

> Romance reading is a declaration of independence.
>
> All uses of texts by readers to claim their own time are declarations of independence.
>
> Conclusion: Romance reading is a use of texts by readers for claiming their own time.

Whereas the first premise registers a puzzling fact from within the universe of romance readers (puzzling to the extent that the romance genre tends to represent women in dependent roles), the second premise introduces the conception or rule that texts are resources in the readers' everyday lives. At the same time, the second premise can be seen to sum up a research process that had gradually articulated – abduced – a conception of the romance genre and of the act of reading in an iterative process.

Radway's (1984) informants produced new insight, not only for research, but presumably also for themselves as they verbalized their conceptions, perhaps for the first time. Abduction (like induction, unlike deduction) is a common aspect of both everyday and scientific reasoning.

abduction in everyday reasoning

Umberto Eco (1984), accordingly, has suggested a wider typology of abduction:

- *Overcoded* abduction is a basic form of comprehension that works semi-automatically. "When someone utters /man/, I must first assume that this utterance is the token of a type of English word" (Eco, 1984: 41). No complex inference is needed to establish the fact that people speak different languages, and that English is the appropriate choice in context.

▶ revaluation of popular culture, Chapter 11, p. 207

- In performing an *undercoded* abduction, however, one must choose between several possible interpretations of a word or statement. In Eco's words, "when one utters /this is a man/, we have to decide whether one says that this is a rational animal, a mortal creature, or a good example of virility, and so on" (p. 42).
- *Creative* abduction, finally, occurs when the very rule of interpretation has to be invented for the specific purpose, for example, in the case of poetic language, as found in poetry, jokes, and advertising. In science, Darwin's interpretation of humans as one animal within the evolutionary chain was an (unusually) creative abduction.

By recognizing abduction as an innovative component of diverse traditions of inquiry, and by relating it to deduction and induction, research is in a better position to consider the potential combination of various forms of inference for different purposes of communication study. The hypotheses of quantitative projects can be understood as the outcome of undercoded abductions that articulate new configurations of explanatory concepts from earlier studies. Qualitative projects, in comparison, perform sequences or, perhaps, networks of undercoded abductions which, ideally, accumulate as a consolidated interpretive framework. In qualitative as well as quantitative methodologies, overcoded abduction enters into the administration of already familiar analytical categories and procedures. Creative abduction, last, is the kind of unusual event and scarce resource that all traditions might hope to produce at least once in a while: the operationalization of an innovative hypothesis (agenda-setting) and the explorative establishment of an unrecognized meaning of media use (reading the romance).

Media and communication research needs all the inferences it can devise in order to understand a complex media environment. The inductive monitoring of technologies, institutions, and users by commercial as well as public agencies provides indispensable baseline information. Hypothetico-deductive studies contribute focused comparisons of established and emerging media. Abductive research probes definitions and delimitations of what constitutes new and old media, genres, communicative practices, and contexts of use, simultaneously from the perspective of native users and researchers. In each case, studies seek to arrive at conclusions that will be accepted – in some sense, by some audience, and for some purpose – as valid, reliable, and general.

UNIFICATION IN THE FINAL INSTANCE

Validity and reliability reconsidered

A final stage of most research projects – supporting their primary analytical operations and inferences – is to perform and present various types of 'quality control.' The purpose is to assess analyses and conclusions according to the standards invoked by the study itself and, in a next step, to make both the standards and the findings accessible for collegial, public scrutiny.

Through categories of validity and reliability, quantitative research has provided an elaborate set of measures and procedures for evaluating empirical findings and inferences (Blaikie, 2003). At the same time, the specific techniques have been perceived as less relevant to the concerns of qualitative research (Kirk and Miller, 1986). In some cases, qualitative researchers have proposed new terminologies which would recognize the processual and contextual nature of qualitative research, for instance, trustworthiness, credibility, dependability, transferability, and confirmability (Lincoln and Guba, 1985). Such alternative terminologies have not taken hold, however, certainly in media studies. Instead, the conceptual and operational definitions of 'validity' and 'reliability' may be reconsidered and extended.

In brief, reliability addresses the consistency of descriptions and interpretations over time, typically in the form of repeated measurements. In the example from agenda-setting research above (McCombs and Shaw, 1972), the intersubjective agreement of coders was expressed in a measure of intercoder reliability (in this case above 0.90, indicating a high reliability of the coding procedures). Validity, in turn, addresses the extent to which a research 'instrument'

reliability

measures what it was intended or is claimed to measure – all research aims for truth in some such sense. A further distinction is made between *internal* validity (evaluating the consistency of the concepts and procedures being applied) and *external* validity (assessing whether the findings from one context generalize to other contexts or populations). In the agenda-setting example, both the conception of 'agenda' and the relationship between the community studied and the larger electorate were considered.

validity – internal and external

Validity and reliability have traditionally been expressed as summary measures in mathematical notations. In comparison, qualitative researchers have called for a more continuous and contextual assessment both of the research process and of its outcome – validation rather than, or in addition to, measures of validity (e.g., Kvale and Brinkmann, 2009). Figure 15.3 outlines a model in which to address this balance.

validation and/ vs. validity measures

Reliability, first of all, can be said to concern the intersubjective component of research generally. Intersubjectivity is established not only by comparing minimal measurements in the early stages of a study, but also by examining emerging findings, forms of documentation, and issues of interpretation. To exemplify, whereas two independent coders categorizing the same data set is standard procedure in quantitative research, intercoder reliability can also be ensured, for example, by consensual coding in a research group (e.g., Neuman, *et al.*, 1992). Moreover, informants contribute to reliability, through several waves of interviewing, and by 'member checks,' as employed in Radway's (1984) study of romance reading. Also, after the conclusion of the research process proper, reliability remains an issue. The collegial discussion of findings, the reanalysis of data, and the social uses of both single studies and research programs all converge on very practical questions such as, 'how certain can we be – in order to do what?'

member checks

Validity, equally, opens onto wider scientific as well as social issues. Compared to quantitative measures of validity, qualitative studies typically emphasize the internal validity of their categories in context, whereas an assessment of external validity must refer to additional cases, larger samples, or multimethod designs. This raises the larger issue of generalization. Is there one or several kinds of generalization – how does one generalize about generalization?

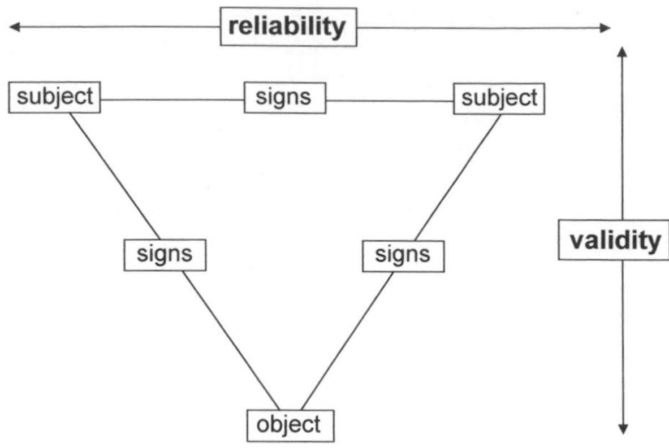

Figure 15.3 Dimensions of validity and reliability

Generalizing about generalization

Whereas it is common to suggest that only the findings of quantitative research can be generalized, the literature on methodology and theory of science recognizes two different conceptions of 'generalization' (e.g., Yin, 2003: 32). *Empirical* or statistical generalization refers to the capacity of quantitative methodologies to apply predefined (hypothetically deduced) categories to a representative set of empirical instances, thus supporting external validity. *Theoretical* or analytical generalization refers to the articulation (abduction) of new concepts or categories, typically in qualitative inquiry, that conceive empirical instances in a more consistent or insightful manner, thus giving priority to internal validity. While the two forms of generalization might be taken as instances of a division of labor between qualitative and quantitative methodologies, both perspectives are relevant for an assessment of the findings and insights of both qualitative and quantitative studies.

empirical and/ vs. theoretical generalization

The complexity of distinguishing between the two aspects of generalization has been reflected in debates over the concept of probability. More or less probable claims can be considered more or less general. In a historical analysis, the philosopher, Ian Hacking (1975), concluded that 'probability' gradually acquired an ambiguous meaning in modern philosophy and empirical sciences. Two distinct meanings were conflated:

stochastic and/vs. epistemological probability

- *Stochastic* probability has to do with stable relative frequencies, as established by statistical procedures. Here, the purpose is to rule out, beyond a reasonable doubt, that the particular configuration of empirical findings could have occurred by chance fluctuations or random error (the so-called null hypothesis).
- *Epistemological* probability, in comparison, concerns "the degree of belief warranted by evidence" (Hacking, 1975: 1). Here, the concept of probability refers to human knowledge of events and to underlying mechanisms to which measures and frequencies bear witness.

The implication of the distinction is sometimes summed up in the dictum that, 'correlation does not equal causation.' In other words, statistical measurements of correlation do not in themselves warrant conclusions about causality and other types of interdependence.

Relating Hacking's (1975) historical analysis to contemporary communication studies, Ritchie (1999) suggested that much empirical media research has failed on this crucial point. The slippage occurs when "the statistical probabilities associated with the null hypothesis are ... used to support inferences about the epistemological probabilities of a preferred interpretation" (p. 7). Put differently, the fact that the null hypothesis, which assumes random findings, is sufficiently improbable (statistically) is mistaken for evidence that a specific alternative hypothesis, namely, the one deduced at the outset of a study, is (more) probable (epistemologically). The logic of hypothesis testing, thus, may invite a confounding of two separate levels of scientific analysis and argument.

null hypothesis

In sum, Figure 15.3 conceives research as a communicative practice that depends on 'signs' – research instruments, analytical procedures, means of documentation – which enable researchers as 'subjects' to engage their 'objects' of analysis according to specified procedures and explicated purposes. Such diverse signs make reality researchable and communicable. In media and communication studies, the objects of analysis include subjects who contribute interpretations of themselves, their media, and their communicative practices.

signs make reality researchable and communicable

General findings constitute information that, having been communicated about, individuals, institutions, and entire societies may be prepared to act on. In pragmatist terminology (Thomas and Thomas, 1928: 572), general findings are real in their consequences.

Realism reasserted

Realism has become increasingly influential as a position in recent theory of science. Pavitt (1999), for one, suggested, not only that it is the dominant position, but also that it informs the practice of much current media and communication research. As noted in his overview, two prototypical positions of 'logical empiricism' (from logical positivism through Karl Popper) and constructivist 'perspectivism' (from Thomas Kuhn's (1970) account of conflicting paradigms, to poststructuralism and beyond) have sometimes been perceived as absolute opposites, or as the two legs of an unresolvable dilemma. Kuhn himself was less categorical about the incommensurability of paradigms than sometimes appears from textbooks; in his later work, he examined the potentials for translating between and learning several 'languages' of research (Conant and Haugeland, 2000). Realism presents itself as a third framework accommodating multiple types of evidence and inference, interpretation and explanation, as suggested also by other recent reference works in the media and communication field (Deacon, *et al.*, 2007; Schrøder, *et al.*, 2003).

Whereas different variants of realism have developed (see further Archer, *et al.*, 1998), the implications for media and communication research can be laid out with reference especially to the early work of Roy Bhaskar (1979) (who later turned to metaphysical and political concerns). His critical realism departs from three main premises:

critical realism

- *Ontological realism*. Rejecting skepticist and nominalist positions, which have held, variously, that no certain human knowledge of reality is possible, or that reality is nothing but the sum of our descriptions of it, realism reverses the burden of proof. Doubts about any and all aspects of reality must be justified. Realism approaches reality as a limit condition or regulatory ideal – what we must assume in order to account for the diverse natural and cultural phenomena that manifest themselves to the individual, and which we share in communication, in science as well as in everyday interaction. The proof of reality is in our interactions with and interventions into it (Hacking, 1983).

- *Epistemological relativism.* From a moderately constructivist position, realism assumes that knowledge of nature, culture, as well as other minds depends on sequences of perceptions, cognitions, and inferences, all of which may be questioned, rejected, or revised – communicated about – for any number of reasons. Relativism does not entail that "anything goes" (Feyerabend, 1975), but rather that several things may go together in unexpected ways according to informed and reflected judgments.
- *Judgmental rationality.* Like other social practices, science depends on the exercise of rationality which, at some point, must end in (fallible) judgments and conclusions about what to do next. In the meantime, the business of individual scholars and scientific communities is to compare and contrast alternative accounts of reality with reference to as wide a range of means of representing, interpreting, and intervening into it as theoretically and practically possible.

Considering the classic issue of how human subjects relate to their objects of inquiry, Bhaskar questioned a certain persistent and presumptuous 'anthropocentrism' in philosophy and theory of science: "Copernicus argued that the universe does not revolve around man. And yet in philosophy we still represent things as if it did" (cited in Archer, *et al.*, 1998: 45). Logical positivism,◄ for one, proposed to reduce reality – the reality that can be legitimately studied by science – to what is immediately accessible to the human senses. Realism, instead, allows for a diversified reality of entities, events, and emergents – which may, or may not, prove accessible to humans through information and inference, immediately or by media still to be imagined or invented. With one of Bhaskar's key terms, reality is, in grammatical terms, 'intransitive': it does not take – does not need – an object (that is, paradoxically, a human subject). Material reality, such as optical fibers, does not communicate to or with us, but is made transitive by humans in and for communication. Reality, further, is 'transfactual': facts of several kinds exist – fiber optics, private email exchanges, and the internet as a global institution. And, reality is 'stratified': fibers, emails, and the internet are not reducible to each other, nor do they constitute separate realities. A differentiated and distributed reality calls for an appropriately diversified set of methodologies.

intransitive, transfactual, and stratified reality

In methodological terms, critical realism involves a distinction between three domains of reality (Bhaskar (1979) and Figure 15.4):

- The *empirical* domain is the source of concrete evidence – *experience* of the world. By describing and documenting, for example, the concrete verbal expressions and images by which Facebook users present themselves to family, friends, acquaintances, and anonymous visitors, media studies procure a necessary, though far from sufficient, condition for interpreting and explaining many-to-many communications.
- The *actual* status of this information is matter of inference. It is by characterizing and conceptualizing empirical materials as evidence of particular *events* (e.g., formal birthday greetings or flirting via Facebook) that one may infer their status as instances of particular social practices.
- The domain of the *real*, importantly, is more inclusive than either the empirical or the actual. Research seeks to establish, for example, psychological and sociological *mechanisms* of a 'general' nature – in some sense of the word◄ – that may account for the events in question (e.g., social and cultural

► logical positivism, p. 291

► generalization, p. 296

	the real	the actual	the empirical
experiences	x	x	x
events	x	x	
mechanisms	x		

Figure 15.4 Three domains of reality

conventions, as compared to new technological potentials, as shapers of specific communicative practices on Facebook).

Experiences, events, and mechanisms are all real. Experiences may seem to 'push' themselves upon researchers as evidence of events. One task of scholarship is to mount a countervailing 'pull' – to infer underlying mechanisms through a great deal of methodological and theoretical labor.

The realist framework is of particular interest in the perspective of methodological convergence. It suggests that while different empirical procedures (e.g., experiments or depth interviews) focus on and, in a sense, privilege specific kinds of *events* (e.g., either the recall or the decoding of media content), they nevertheless may bear witness to the same, similar, or related *mechanisms*. Instead of engaging in paradigmatic conflicts over a singular definition of the empirical domain of inquiry, a realist strategy, thus, proposes to tap the full range of *experiences* of reality, and to take advantage of several methodologies in order to examine different aspects of media and communication.

All empirical research necessarily examines an empirical 'microcosm' with reference to a theoretical 'macrocosm' (for a history of these concepts in social research, see Alexander and Giesen, 1987). Qualitative and quantitative methodologies are defined, in part, by their conceptions of and approaches to empirical microcosms. Figure 15.5 indicates (top right corner) how the populations and samples of the prototypical quantitative project make up two levels of an empirical universe, whereas qualitative studies will emphasize the sampling and analysis of empirical cases in their contexts.

To sum up, the various qualitative and quantitative modes of data collection and analysis represent different ways of gaining *experience* of certain aspects of media and communicative practices – and not others. Quantitative and qualitative methodologies are suited for studying specific kinds of social and cultural *events* – and not others. What unites the two mainstreams of media and communication studies is that they address a middle range of social and cultural phenomena – media production, discourses, uses, and contexts – which call, at once, for detailed documentation (empirical experience) and grand theorizing (theoretical *mechanisms*).

Articulated since Aristotle as a differentiated and distributed conception of what exists (Jensen, 2010: Ch. 2), realism accommodates diverse levels at which media and communicative practices take shape. Chapter 1 of this Handbook introduced a premise of determination in the first instance.◄ In an ontological sense, communication is enabled and constrained by several types of conditions – material, discursive, and institutional – that determine what *cannot* be the case, but which, equally, cannot predict specifically what *will* be the case. In an epistemological sense, this chapter has outlined a principle of unification in the final instance: different methodologies pose and answer different questions, sometimes for a common purpose.

unification in the final instance

Realism is an epistemology without guarantees. At the same time, it avoids the sort of skeptical perspectives on reality that have been implied by both of the other two prototypical positions that Pavitt (1999) identified: logical empiricism and constructivist perspectivism. On the one hand, logical positivism depicted a reality which, tragically, is forever out of human reach. On the other hand, not least poststructuralist versions of constructivism have celebrated a comic view of the absence of any foundations of human knowledge (Baudrillard, 1988).◄ What communication research in a realist vein can offer are explanatory concepts, analytical procedures, and preliminary conclusions as one basis of public deliberation about media, old and new. Among the questions legitimately raised by research are what media do to people, and what people do with media (Katz, 1959), but also how people may change media in order to do something different with them – which is the topic of the final chapter of the Handbook.

► determination in the first instance, Chapter 1, p. 2
► poststructuralism – Chapter 2, p. 42

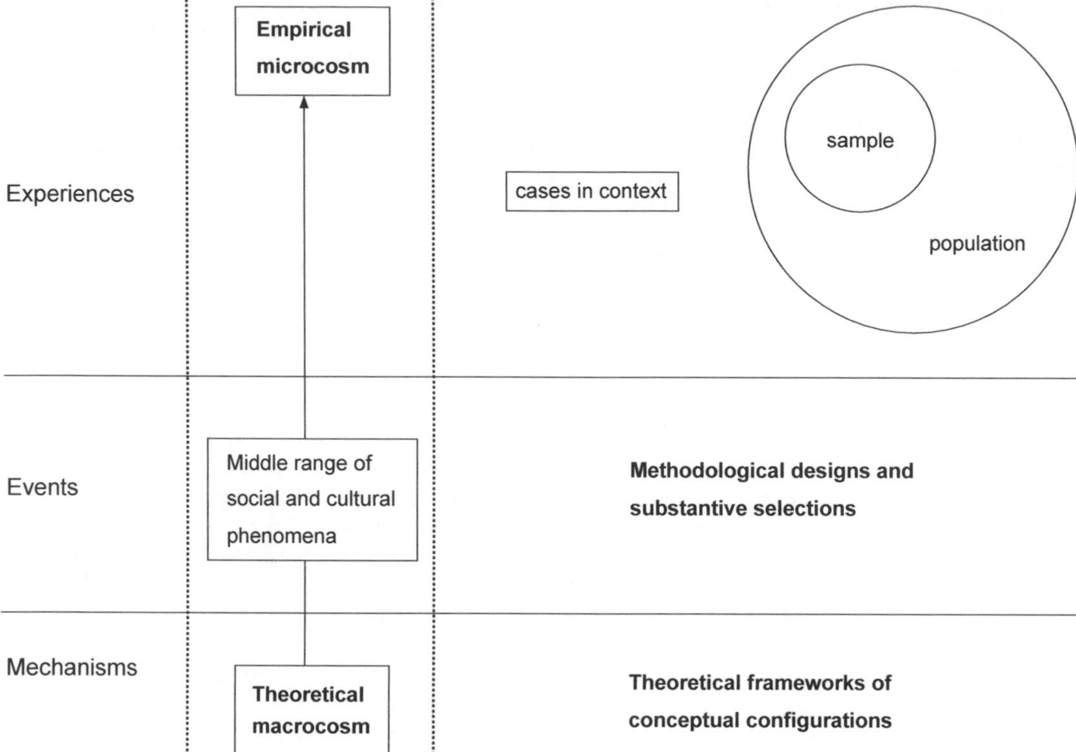

Figure 15.5 Empirical microcosms, theoretical macrocosms

CONVERGENCE IN PRACTICE: THREE APPROACHES

In a future perspective, much work is still required to integrate and consolidate elements from theory of science, communication theory, and diverse social-scientific and humanistic disciplines for a robust multimethod and multidisciplinary field of media and communication research. Methodologies constitute a strategic area of dialogue and collaboration, because they join abstract theoretical concerns with the practical requirements of empirical work. Flyvbjerg (2006), for example, has noted that case studies,◀ while normally associated with qualitative inquiry, can test general propositions by uncovering evidence that may not be compatible with findings from quantitative studies.

▶ case studies, Chapter 14, p. 270

In recent decades, a growing number of interdisciplinary publications, some of them in several editions, have outlined ways of 'mixing' or combining qualitative and quantitative methodologies (Bernard, 2006; Blaikie, 2009; Creswell, 2009; Tashakkori and Teddlie, 2010). In research so far, it is possible to single out three principal forms of combining qualitative and quantitative methodologies (Hammersley, 1996: 167–168):

- *Facilitation.* The most common practice traditionally has been to treat qualitative and quantitative approaches as relatively separate steps in a research sequence. In survey research, for example, on media consumption, it is standard procedure to conduct qualitative 'pilot' studies. The aim is to arrive at analytical categories and verbal formulations that are, at once, conceptually

pilot studies

precise and meaningful to respondents. While equally relevant, quantitative pilots, for instance, a mapping of a social or lifestyle segment that may facilitate subsequent in-depth analyses of members' interpretive categories, have been less widespread.

- *Triangulation.* As elaborated especially by Norman Denzin (1970), triangulation is a general strategy for gaining several perspectives on the same phenomenon. Triangulation may be performed through several data sets, several investigators, and several methodologies, in the last case combining, for instance, experimental and observational approaches to the use and interpretation of media contents. (Denzin's additional suggestion – that also theories might be triangulated – seems problematic, since theoretical interpretation involves commitment to and closure around a specific perspective or position, however preliminary. Also methodological triangulation leads up to a weighing of several sets of evidence from one interpretive position.)
- *Complementarity.* The most challenging, and so far the least common, approach is complementarity – in a methodological as well as epistemological respect. Different analytical categories and procedures may be appropriate for capturing particular aspects of the same empirical domain, or for addressing two different domains with a bearing on the same research question. In the final instance, two categorically different sets of findings can be joined with reference to a common theoretical framework. The existence of methodological 'camps' in this and other fields remains an obstacle. Nevertheless, the record – from classic studies such as Cantril's (1940) volume on *The Invasion from Mars,*◄ to more recent developments as reviewed in this chapter, to other reflections on the status of that knowledge which different methodologies produce (e.g., Potter, 1996) – suggests the relevance and value of continuing to explore the potential of complementarity in the practice of media and communication research.

► *The Invasion from Mars* – Chapter 9, p. 173

Audiences in the round

Multi-method research in factual and reality television

Annette Hill

- an exemplification of *large-scale multi-method* media and communication research
- illustrations of how to combine, on the one hand, *audience surveys, focus groups, and in-depth interviews* and, on the other hand, *industry and ratings analysis*
- comparisons of the development of *factual and reality television*, over time and across cultures
- reflections on both *media use and research as performative social practices*

INTRODUCTION

Imagine a world where celebrity chefs campaign for better children's school meals, or a politician stars in a ballroom dance competition. This is the mixed-up world of factual and reality television. News struggles to exist in a commercial marketplace; celebrities back political campaigns; and politicians become celebrities writing autobiographies and Twitter feeds. It is a story of the survival of the fittest. The traditional public service◀ genres of news, current affairs and documentary fight for survival as novel forms of popular factual genres like lifestyle and reality TV take over. These trends in factuality highlight a drive to hybridise content, mixing reality TV with current affairs, or politics with light entertainment. Hybridisation is good news for reality TV. This is a feral genre that is aggressive in the marketplace, crosses boundaries between the public and popular, and is resistant to re-containment. But, such a trend is bad news for journalism or documentary. These traditional genres are like endangered species, needing regulation and public support for continued development in the competitive media environment of today.

hybridisation

► public service media – Chapter 19, p. 354

Now imagine researching this world of factuality from the point of view of audiences. People's experiences of news, documentary or reality TV are not formed in isolation. Audiences experience factuality 'in the round'. This theatrical metaphor is useful for constructing research methods that capture a wide range of media experiences. If we watch a play in the round, then this drama has been designed and performed with the intention of an immersive experience for theatre goers. Similarly, if we see audiences in the round, then a research project should be designed and implemented with the intention of understanding the diversity of media experiences. Such an approach to audiences requires multiple methods that give researchers a wide perspective on media, culture and society. Drawn from quantitative and qualitative research in the social sciences and humanities, these methods help the researcher to gain insights into the complexity of cultural practices today.

RESEARCHING IN THE ROUND

The theatrical metaphor of audiences in the round is one way of understanding media experiences. For too long now, we have seen the outdated metaphor of viewers as couch potatoes in public debates about the media. This negative image of a sad, passive person implies that the media turns us bad, like rotting vegetables. This metaphor carries a message that when people watch television, or play a computer game, they become isolated from themselves and each other. It suggests an anxiety about the power of the media to make us somehow less than human, to become disembodied, losing our sense of self as we sit in front of a screen. Such an anxiety about media technologies as a form of disembodiment has been around since the early days of electronic communication (see Sconce 2000).◀ People do not lose themselves in a television or computer screen, but rather they immerse themselves in communication with friends, family or strangers, across various kinds of media technologies.

To see audiences in the round is to recognise the sociality of media experiences. When someone watches the news on TV, they may also have read a newspaper that day, listened to radio news, accessed news podcasts, and talked about the news with other people. Indeed, they may be watching the news whilst also simultaneously cross-referencing other news from mobile media, or through speaking with a friend.◀ Alongside these multiple forms, viewers draw on a variety of attitudes towards news and current affairs. This may include attitudes towards the quality of news reporting on public service or commercial channels. It may refer to genre knowledge of how news is put together, such as an assessment of professional values of impartiality and fairness. These complex cultural practices for news help to explain how press reports of recent wars in the Middle East can be described by audiences as unreal or 'reality infected'. People may switch off the news because they do not perceive it to be impartial or trustworthy, turning to other sources across multimedia environments. In short, people do not just watch or read the news; they engage with it as part of a wider horizon of understanding◀ of news as a profession and genre, a set of facts, a source of public opinion, and as a topic of debate for political, social, moral and ethical issues.

'Audiences in the round' is suggestive of how personal responses to TV, radio, print media or the web can also be collective media experiences. When people watch a play, they may be sitting or standing in their own space, but they are also aware of other spectators and their reactions at the same time. There may be quiet moments, or one theatregoer may laugh and everyone else follows suit. There can be times when one person's rapt attention to a drama is disturbed by their neighbour fidgeting in the seat next to them. In this way, people's responses to the media are connected to their awareness of themselves and their relations with others. Indeed, to experience in the round is to see and feel the sociality and spatiality of the media. It is that multidimensional perspective you get when attending a theatre in the round, seeing the actors on stage, other members of the audience, and yourself at the same time. People have multiple perspectives from which to participate in, observe, respond to or ignore the media.

If we wish to understand audiences in the round, then we can adopt a similarly multidimensional perspective of the research process. Researching in the round can involve different methods drawn from qualitative and quantitative traditions. The use of multi-method research offers different types of data for you to compare and contrast as you construct a picture of a problem or phenomenon. It can also involve flexibility in the research design and its implementation, adjusting your perspective of audiences as you look at a research question both close up and from a wider point of view in relation to other data or theories. There are different questions you can ask, open and closed questions, inviting written, verbal, physical and visual responses. The key aspect of the 'in the round' metaphor is to create a multidimensionality to your research project. The following sections present two multi-method studies of

▶ moral panics – Chapter 3, p. 55
▶ humans as media – Chapter 1, p. 5
▶ horizon of expectations – Chapter 9, p. 183

factual and reality television audiences, with reflections on how to research in the round.

RESEARCHING REALITY TV

If ever there was a genre on the move, it has to be reality TV. Throughout the 1990s this hybrid genre, also called infotainment or factual entertainment, dominated peak-time schedules in Britain and America. There were emergency services programmes where cameras followed crime and health professionals on the job. There were docusoaps where cameras followed ordinary people on the job at airports or hotels. Both of these types of reality TV popularised news (on the scene as it happens) and documentary (fly on the wall) though mixing factual genres with other more dramatic or entertaining ones like soap opera or lifestyle programmes.

infotainment

emergency services programmes

docusoaps

These shows were very popular, attracting at their peak up to half of the audience share at the time of transmission. Then in 2000 along came a new hybrid format: the reality gameshow. This format did not follow people around but instead created a scenario for the cameras. Reality gameshows mixed news, documentary, soap opera, gameshows, to create a successful format that could be sold around the world. This period was also the time when reality TV crossed the borders between television, radio, newspapers, magazines, mobiles and the web, with content on all platforms. It was truly a new phenomenon in the business of making media.

reality gameshows

format television

My project of researching reality TV in Britain began life before *Big Brother* (Endemol), *Pop Idol* (19 and Fremantle Media) and other reality formats took off. It was designed as a multi-method study into audiences of factual entertainment, such as emergency services programmes like *999* (BBC) or docusoaps like *Airline* (ITV). But it quickly became a year in the life of reality TV, a genre on the move. As such, it became a project that was researching a moving target. The target included a rapidly evolving genre as well as people's experiences of changes within popular factual television and multimedia environments. There were lots of assumptions about audiences at the time, for example, it was commonly assumed that viewers could not tell the difference between entertainment and information, or fiction and reality. The project set out to find what audiences had to say about their experiences. The objective was to provide information and analysis for understanding the transitional terrain of the reality genre, and to enhance critical understanding of contemporary audiences.

Without a range of methods that allowed for flexibility in design and data collection, this project would have been dead in the water. The main methods used were a scheduling and ratings analysis, genre analysis, a quantitative survey, semi-structured focus groups and in-depth interviews in households. Research assistant Caroline Dover had invaluable experience at production analysis and ethnographic methods that helped in the design of the industry research and in-depth interviews with families. The data collection period covered a year (2000–2001), the data analysis took another year, and the book *Reality TV* came out in 2005. The duration of the project overall from start to finish signals how rigorous media and communication search does not lend itself to rapid response. Whilst it is important to be flexible and fast on your feet with the design and data collection, the analysis requires you to take the long road to get a detailed and rich picture of the topic at hand. This does not rule out short reports along the way, or speculative articles that signal key issues to be addressed, but this kind of multi-method research into a complex phenomenon improves with time.◀

The first stage of this research relied on industry and genre analysis. There was an analysis of the scheduling of a range of reality TV across days, weeks, months and seasons; there was an analysis of the form and content of selected programmes and consultation with companies on programmes in production, specifically *Big Brother*. This data provided a comprehensive account of the range and type of programmes available to viewers at particular times, and which categories viewers would be familiar with during the main data collection period. It was the first, time-consuming, but necessary step in seeing reality TV from the point of view of audiences. What emerged was

industry analysis

genre analysis

▶ time frames of research projects – Chapter 19, p. 361

a picture of audiences navigating their way through a busy media environment jammed with reality TV.

Reality TV was the motor of peak time throughout the 1990s. This hybrid genre came at a time when networks were looking for a quick-fix solution to economic problems within media industries, such as increased costs in the production of drama, sitcom and comedy. The deregulation and marketisation of media industries, especially in the US and Western Europe, also contributed to its success as it performed well in a competitive, multichannel environment. The main types of programmes – infotainment, docusoaps, lifestyle programmes and reality gameshows – focused on telling stories about real people and real events in an entertaining style, usually foregrounding visuals, characterisation and narrative. This was a 'see it happen' style of reality TV.

Ratings◀ data told a story of the survival of the fittest within factuality as a whole. In 1984, the top rated factual programmes were natural history specials such as *Survival* (ITV/Anglia, 11.3 million) and *The Living Planet* (BBC, 9.9 million). There was the observational documentary *28 Up* (ITV/Granada, 9.4 million) and the infotainment series *Crimewatch UK* (BBC, 9.1 million). Ten years later, in 1994, the top rated factual programmes were dominated by infotainment series such as *Police Stop!* (ITV/Carlton, 13.4 million), *Police, Camera, Action!* (ITV/Carlton, 13.2 million), *999 Lifesavers* (BBC1, 10.2 million) and *Crimewatch* (9.7 million). In 1984 there was only one factual series in the top 20 about emergency services (*Crimewatch*); by 1994 there were 12. (Source for ratings, BARB, compiled by *Broadcast* 3 December 1994: 22.) Phillips (2000: 42) commented on the number of tabloid style series on offer from ITV during a period of decline in factual output:

> ITV transmitted 71 peaktime documentaries in 1996–1999, fewer than one a fortnight. On average they were seen by 7.19 million viewers, an audience share of 32 per cent, which is six percentage points below ITV's overall share on the nights they appeared [...] in reality most of the more successful programmes are not Prix Italia candidates. Nine of the Top 20 are in the *From Hell* occasional series: catalogues of conduct-unbecoming from different sources, which sometimes offered advice to victims but more often merely wallowed in the awfulness.

With market shares of up to 50 per cent for the *From Hell* series (neighbours, holidays, nannies, builders, drivers, traffic jams, garages and toilets), reality TV was a firm favourite of channel controllers and schedulers. Such industry and genre analysis highlighted television's ability to cannibalise itself in order to survive in a commercially uncertain media environment. The price of survival was a decrease in the commissioning of more traditional public-service categories such as news, current affairs and documentary.

The second stage of research involved a national survey◀ which contained a series of closed questions relating to audience preferences for form, content, subgenres, use of multimedia, and attitudes towards issues of privacy, information and entertainment. The survey was a self-completion questionnaire, distributed by the Broadcasters' Audience Research Board (BARB) to a representative sample of 8216 adults (16–65+) and 937 children (4–15) during August 2000. The data was analysed using descriptive statistics,◀ looking at programme types and content, and audience attitudes, cross-referencing this data with key demographic information relating to age, gender, class, education, and households with and without children.

Earlier research that I conducted for the British Film Institute Audience Tracking Study helped in the construction of the survey questions and provided a useful context to the analysis of the statistics. This was a longitudinal mass observation study◀ containing around 500 respondents who kept diaries for five years. Together with David Gauntlett, the data was

▶ ratings analysis – Chapter 8, p. 159

▶ surveys – Chapter 13, p. 242

▶ descriptive statistics – Chapter 13, p. 258

▶ mass observation studies – Chapter 9, p. 173

analysed in relation to television and everyday life (Gauntlett and Hill 1999). Two articles that I wrote from that data set were based on questions given to the respondents during the mid-1990s on infotainment and docusoaps. Those articles focused on how the genre of reality TV dramatised crisis, and how audiences reacted to the combination of information and entertainment within these programmes (see Hill 2000a, 2000b).

This early work proved helpful in designing survey questions about attitudes towards the hybridity of the genre. For example, one question asked respondents, 'here are some things people have said about entertainment programmes about real people. How much do you agree or disagree with what they said?' Respondents were given a five-point scale.◀ The statements were drawn from common responses by audiences that I had observed in my previous work on the genre. They included a range of positive and negative statements: 'real life stories are more entertaining than fiction'; 'I think these programmes are really useful as they give you all sorts of information about life'; 'these programmes give real people a chance to speak on TV about what matters to them'; 'I think true-life TV takes advantage of people who are in the programmes'; 'programmes about real people are boring because they are all the same'; 'I don't like watching TV programmes where real people face difficult emotional situations'. Even the use of different definitions of reality TV as 'entertainment programmes about real people' or 'true-life TV' was deliberate as I had found that audiences did not have one but several ways of defining this new hybrid genre.

Indeed, one of the ways of defining this new genre was in relation to scheduling. Respondents in the survey were most likely to watch popular factual programming after the six o'clock news, in between soap operas, drama and occasional light entertainment, and before the ten o'clock news on the UK terrestrial channels. The genre and industry analysis indicated that popular factual programming was so successful in the ratings because it offered a pick and mix of programming. Regular viewers of reality TV were in the minority. Overall, however, we could say that reality TV was watched occasionally by 70 per cent of the population. If we consider the statistics according to regular and occasional viewers, police/crime programmes were watched regularly by 24 per cent of adults, and occasionally by 48 per cent of adults; docusoaps about places such as airports or hospitals by 31 per cent (regular) and 40 per cent (occasional) of adults; home/garden shows by 26 per cent (regular) and 41 per cent (occasional) of adults. The picture was the same for children, except regarding programmes about pets, and home/garden shows, which attracted an even mix of regular and occasional young viewers – home/garden shows were watched by 44 per cent (regular) and 40 per cent (occasional) of young viewers.

▶ scales of measurement – Chapter 13, p. 241

In the focus groups, some answers emerged to explain why popular factual programming attracted so many occasional viewers. These 12–13 year old boys commented on scheduling in relation to their viewing habits:

> Michael: Yeah, *Changing Rooms* is after *EastEnders*.
> Garry: Which is probably why I watch it …
> Ed: I can find better things to watch cos I don't really like watching about normal life stuff.
> Michael: Yeah but we're talking about that here.
> Ed: Yeah, I know, I'm just saying I can find better things to watch but I have watched quite a lot of them.

There is something about many popular factual programmes that caused younger viewers to categorise them as "boring programmes on about eight o'clock when there's nothing else to do" (14-year-old schoolgirl).

Before *Big Brother* took off, what people liked most about reality TV were people's stories caught on camera. Of all the respondents, 75 per cent claimed to like informative elements, and 68 per cent liked observational elements. Their tastes matched viewing preferences, with observation- and information-style programmes more popular (around 65 per cent) than the (at the time) new reality gameshows (35 per cent)

(Hill 2005). Performance and authenticity were some of the criteria by which people evaluated the reality of these shows. Over 70 per cent of adults in the survey thought that stories about ordinary people in reality TV were made up or exaggerated. This was mainly because of the perception of people overacting for the cameras (70 per cent of adult respondents) rather than an understanding of editing techniques, or digital manipulation. Even though audiences were aware of the performative and entertaining aspects of the genre, at that time what people valued most was the ability to represent the public in a popular way. Of the adult respondents, 55 per cent claimed that reality TV 'gives you all sorts of information about life', and 48 per cent thought these shows 'give people a chance to speak on TV about what matters to them' (Hill 2005).

These kinds of evaluations of reality TV ensured that a line was already being drawn between what audiences expected of reality TV as infotainment, and what they saw as the next trend in reality TV as entertainment. The 'see it happen' style of the reality genre of the 1990s was beginning to be modified with reality gameshows. The following comment by a viewer was typical of the way people assessed the reality claims of this evolving genre:

> Well, like *Children's Hospital* is factual isn't it? It's not, it's not glossing over anything, you're seeing what is actually happening so that's the good point of it. If you're into real TV, you can't get more real than that … I mean, that's a real factual programme and 999 reconstructions, they're not made up are they, they're actual accidents … I find a lot of these so-called documentaries are not true to life and that's annoying cos I think people are easily taken in, you know. I just think it's a set-up … d'you know what I mean? I just can't hack it, it's so false to me and they play up, I'm sure they play up to the camera and it's nothing like real-life documentaries and that.
>
> (39-year-old groundsman)

This viewer had an instinctive sense that the reality claims of "these so-called documentaries" should be treated with scepticism. It would not take long before formats like *Big Brother* would be called reality TV, creating an even bigger divide between this hybrid genre and its factual and evidentiary roots.

The third stage of the research project overall involved semi-structured focus groups,◀ where the results of the survey were used to design focus group interviews with children (aged 11–14), young adults (aged 15–18) and adults (aged 18–44) who defined themselves as regular viewers of popular factual television, and were in the C1C2DE social categories (lower middle class and working class). The recruitment of participants involved the use of a professional qualitative recruitment agency and quota sampling◀ in a variety of suburban locations. I selected these participants because the results of the survey indicated that regular viewers of popular factual television were primarily in the above categories. Twelve focus groups were conducted in London, each group containing seven to eight participants, and were divided according to age, gender and access to terrestrial or satellite/cable/digital television. I selected these groups because the data from the survey indicated that age and gender were key variables relating to audience attraction to reality TV, and because it was necessary to consider a range of programming available across television platforms. Following an initial coding of the transcripts, I conducted a qualitative data analysis that considered group dynamics as well as substantive judgements.

The primary aim of these focus groups was to explore audience attraction to different types of programming, and to understand what strategies they used to watch hybrid formats within the genre. The focus groups contained a series of open questions relating to viewer responses to subgenres, use of non-professional actors and issues relating to information and entertainment in hybrid subgenres. For example, one of the focus group questions was designed to explore the extent to which the 'see it happen' style of early reality TV was understood by viewers as a construction and,

▶ focus groups – Chapter 14, p. 271
▶ quota sampling – Chapter 13, p. 245

perhaps at the same time, a representation of real life:

> A lot of these programmes are about real people and their everyday stories. What do you like or dislike about this?
> *Probe* whether you/anyone would agree to have their story retold or captured on TV
> *Probe* if you have personal experience of a certain job or situation, are you more or less likely to watch a programme about this?
> Look for specific examples
> SHOW CLIP FROM OBSERVATION PROGRAMME
> For young adults and sat/cable viewers use *Ibiza Uncovered II*
> For other groups use clip from *Airline*

The open nature of a semi-structured focus group ensured that participants could use the clip as resource for debate about both the staged elements of reality TV and the glimpses of reality that could be found within these docusoaps. Asking participants if they would agree to be filmed opened a discursive door to the issue of performance and authenticity.

Such a question offered a different perspective on the survey results which indicated that audiences valued stories caught on camera and at the same time expected people to act up in these docusoaps. From the perspective of the focus groups, it appeared that the very fact that most people watched reality TV in Britain made it a popular topic of debate and gossip. There was a high degree of genre knowledge. For example, "Well, *Big Brother* is entertainment ... you'd just watch it like you'd watch *EastEnders* or *Coronation Street*, really ... sort of along that line more than watching *Airport* or *Animal Hospital*" (40-year-old female part-time secretary). This finding fitted with Richard Kilborn's study *Staging the Real* (2003), which examined the close association between reality TV and soap opera. The sociability of the genre was perhaps more important to audiences than the content itself.◄ Many participants in the focus groups were critical of reality TV, saying it was just entertainment. And yet, they had much to say about topics that arose during and after watching reality TV, such as authenticity, emotions and ethics. If in the survey respondents said they liked reality TV because it gave ordinary people a chance to speak about what mattered to them, then in the focus groups it became clear that reality TV also gave audiences an opportunity for social interaction and debate about a range of issues that mattered to them.

For example, in relation to the issue of authenticity there was a general understanding that this was an illusive ideal for television. Most viewers argued that the only way ordinary people would be themselves on television was if they did not know they were on TV in the first place: "I wouldn't be who I really am ... trying to talk differently, talk posh and everything! [laughs] You know, I just wouldn't be myself" (40-year-old female part-time secretary). There was also a general assumption that if people could 'be themselves' 24 hours a day on TV, then this would not make for very exciting television: "They could follow me all day but it would be boring [laughs]. They could follow me all day and night, somebody might jump in front of me, other than that totally boring" (38-year-old underground train driver). The repetition of the word 'boring' to describe this train driver's typical day illuminated the way many viewers assumed stories in reality programmes were exaggerated or made up in order to make entertainment. Such analysis suggested that the reality status of many programmes in this hybrid genre was treated with a degree of scepticism.

The final stage of the research involved in-depth interviews◄ with ten families, with children of varying ages, over a six-month period (recruited from the focus groups). People were invited to participate if they were living in a family unit with at least one child over the age of 11 years. All of the families lived in the Greater London area and were, again, in the C1C2DE social categories. For example, one family included an Italian father and English mother with two children (aged 14 and 12). They had a combined yearly household income of around £40,000, and both parents had jobs, as a restaurant manager and part-time

► media use in everyday contexts – Chapter 9, p. 179

► in-depth interviews – Chapter 14, p. 271

administrative assistant. This was a media-rich household with five TVs, one VCR, one DVD player, digital TV access and one PC with internet. The family had a lot of knowledge of the media, including the variety of hybrid content that contributed to the broad genre of reality TV.

In the selection of interview subjects, the types of questions asked during the visits, and the timing of the visits, I was guided by a desire to follow new developments within the genre, and to further understand how family viewers responded to these developments in the home environment. Interviews were logged, and partially transcribed,◄ and field notes◄ written up during and after the period of data collection. Four visits were made to each family home. Combinations of methods were used – open discussions, observation of families and participation in watching programmes. For example, the first session involved a discussion of the family's viewing habits, the types of programmes regularly watched by different members and what ones they watched together as a family, their everyday work and home life, and other leisure activities. The third session contained more specific questions on the issue of 'information', exploring this in relation to the household space and family dynamics, and observing how the family watched certain shows, chatting along the way. The flexibility of these in-depth interviews provided a wealth of rich data and thick description.◄

What emerged from the home visits was an understanding of how reality TV was embedded in cultural practices. This was a hybrid genre that had overrun the schedules, had become a topic for social interaction, and was a feature of family relations. For example, one couple chatted about lifestyle makeover shows:

> Alison: When it's on, they'll sit and watch it even if I'm not. They'll sometimes have re-runs and they'll sit and watch it … I don't know if they watch it because I tend to watch those things, whether they watch it with me because they know I do the decorating and the gardening … they know I have more aesthetic sense and I will change things.
>
> Brian: This room's been decorated about six times!

Or, in another example, a girl played *Popstars* (ITV) in the garden with her friends, alternating roles of nice and nasty judges for singing auditions. The sociality of watching and engaging with reality TV that we saw in other discussions was amplified when observing families in their homes. Reality TV offered a space for performance, especially for younger audiences. A new generation of reality TV audiences had been born.

RESEARCHING FACTUALITY

At the end the reality TV project, it became urgent business to keep track of the phenomenon of hybridisation. Reality TV was mutating as part of the international trade in formats, and crossing over into other areas of factual production, such as news and light entertainment. The next project started in 2003 and the book *Restyling Factual TV* was published in 2007. The project took as a starting point the idea that factual television was being restyled, and that various kinds of news, current affairs, documentary and popular factual genres were part of a turbulent time in broadcasting. Whereas hybridisation was an emergent theme in the reality TV project, in the mid-2000s hybridity was now the distinctive feature of factuality. The boundaries between fact and fiction had been pushed to the limits in various popular factual formats that mixed non-fiction and fiction genres. The cross-pollination of styles increased the pace of change in news, current affairs or documentary. There was a very real sense that factuality was in crisis. As one viewer explained:

> the last couple of years or so, you know, Reality TV is going towards a documentary kind of thing, and documentary is moving down to Reality TV, and the news is just somewhere in between, so, none of them is actually factual?
>
> (Hill 2007: 2)

► transcription – Chapter 14, p. 276
► field notes – Chapter 14, p. 274
► thick description – Chapter 14, p. 273

My approach to researching audiences in the round was to design a comparative multi-method study of the hybridisation of different factual genres. Flexibility in the design of the data collection is crucial to researching in the round. At first, the research was designed for British audiences, but an opportunity to open up the project to an international perspective added one further comparative dimension to the approach.◀ The project evolved into a comparative study of audiences in two similar media environments (the UK and Sweden), but with quite different size populations and media industries. Early results from the data indicated that audience responses in both countries were remarkably similar, suggesting that the trend of hybridisation was well advanced in these two northern European countries. This is a good example of how important piloting◀ can be in the approach you take to research design. The driving force of the research after the pilot studies became an examination of how audiences in different national contexts responded to an international cultural trend of hybridisation.

There were four themes addressed in the design of the surveys and focus groups. These themes helped support the comparative approach as the same points of reference were used in the two countries. The first theme was the *viewers' evaluation of a changing environment of media genres* and involved questions about the categorisation of content and genre knowledge relating to news, documentary and reality TV. The next theme addressed the issue of *truth claims* and the representation of reality in and across these genres, with questions about the 'true to life' elements of a specific content, and the levels of performance or artifice within particular programmes. Another theme was that of *information*, including questions about the accuracy of information, and the use of information to form opinions about things. The final theme was related to *participation*, with questions about the fair treatment of different social groups within news and current affairs, documentary and reality TV.

The research methods in this second project included an analysis of the content of a range of programmes over a six-month period, and a scheduling and ratings analysis during the same time frame. Interviews were also conducted with media professionals working within the television industry. Next, this industry data was analysed in relation to genre as a cultural category. Factuality was broken down according to the common characteristics of four core genres: news, current affairs and investigations, documentary and popular factual. News has long-standing traditions and dominant practices that can be traced across other factual genres. Current affairs and investigations, in particular, are closely related to news and journalistic traditions. Documentary is made up of an additional variety of factual genres. And, the popular factual genre is the result of a marriage between factual and other genres, such as drama, or light entertainment. What emerged from the genre analysis was an understanding of factuality as resistant to simple categorisation.

Following this genre analysis, multiple categories were chosen to represent the broadest range of programmes available to viewers during peak-time weekday television schedules for the main public service and commercial channels. Minor adjustments were made to fit the categories to the two production contexts, so in Britain, fourteen categories were used, and in Sweden eleven. The categories that did not work in both countries revealed minor differences in production contexts. In the British survey, more subcategories of documentary were used, for example, specialist documentaries such as history, or observational documentary, which reflected the tradition of documentary television and its place in UK peak-time schedules, whereas in Sweden documentary series was the only category used, reflecting a smaller documentary production sector and an absence of different kinds of documentary in peak-time schedules here.

In Britain a quantitative survey was conducted with a representative sample of 4516 people aged 16–65+. The response rate in Britain was as high as 95 per cent, as this was an existing sample for the Broadcasters Audience Research Board carried out by Ipsos RSL. The sample included variables such as life stage, socio-educational factors, regions,

▶ culturally comparative research – Chapter 11
▶ pilot studies – Chapter 15, p. 300

age, sex, working status, ethnicity, marital status, children in the home, household size, newspaper readership and internet access. The survey contained one open question and seventeen closed questions. In Sweden a quantitative survey was conducted with a random sample of 2000 people. The sample included people aged 16–80 living in Sweden, including foreign citizens. The survey was conducted in co-operation with the SOM Institute, Gothenberg University, and carried out by Kinnmark Information AB. The net sample was 1854 people, with 944 respondents and a net response rate of 51 per cent. The distribution amongst responses compared with the Swedish population as a whole, and also compared with another representative survey (National SOM study 2004). Detailed analyses of comparable questions in both surveys show a very high similarity. In the survey for this project, questions contained fixed response alternatives, requiring a single mark, alongside two open-ended questions. Some questions were the same across the two countries, whilst others were specific to each country. The SPSS data was analysed using descriptive statistics, multivariate analysis and factor analysis. The quantitative research was conducted in association with Professor Lennart Weibull and Åsa Nilsson at the Department of Journalism and Mass Communication and the SOM Institute in Sweden (see Hill *et al.* 2007 for further details).

The genre analysis and industry data helped in the design of the questions in the survey and analysis of the results. The research highlighted how notions of traditional public-service and popular genres are connected to the shared tradition of factual television in Britain and Sweden. In the survey a question was designed to assess how respondents valued different types of factual content: 'How important do you think it is that these types of programmes are shown on television?' (very important, fairly important, not very important, not important at all). Figure 16.1 summarises the value of factual and reality genres (the indicators of 'fairly' and 'very' important are combined together). Two generic groups emerged in both countries. The first consisted of news, current affairs, investigative journalism, political and consumer programmes, nature and documentary series, which between 63 and 99 per cent of all respondents regarded as important. The second group, which only one-third or less regarded as important, consisted of lifestyle programmes, reality gameshows and life experiments. Together, the multiple perspectives on factuality from the survey and the genre and industry analysis suggested that, rather than resist or subvert the distinctions between traditional public-service and popular factual genres, audiences turned to these pre-existing categories as a starting point for understanding change.

An open question in the surveys asked respondents, 'what would you personally consider to be a factual television programme?' Patterns of viewers emerged – idealists, traditionalists, reality refuseniks, and cosmopolitans.◀ *Idealists* were typified by this quote: 'If it's not true it's not factual' (male, aged 65+, Socio Economic Status C2). The apparent simplicity of the statement barely masked a complex set of philosophical questions. What is truth and what is fact? And yet, there was something powerful and attractive to viewers in this kind of simple statement where the ideal concept of truth was used to answer the question. A *traditionalist* would typically respond with the answer 'News'. Older respondents in general were most likely to use traditional factual genres as examples for what factual TV meant to them. For example: "1) News 2) Investigations of *real* events (no added features)" (female, aged 65+, SES AB). Factuality was understood as traditional public-service content. Related to this position was *reality refusenik*. News, current affairs, documentary (all with some exceptions), were used as concrete examples of 'quality' factual content which respondents would also characterise as truthful and informative, objective and real. But, they found, this content was becoming increasingly vulnerable to other kinds of popular factual, or non-fiction, content. For idealists and traditionalists, news and current affairs and documentary were threatened species of factual television, and needed to be protected at all costs. The reality

▶ lifestyle research – Chapter 8, p. 168

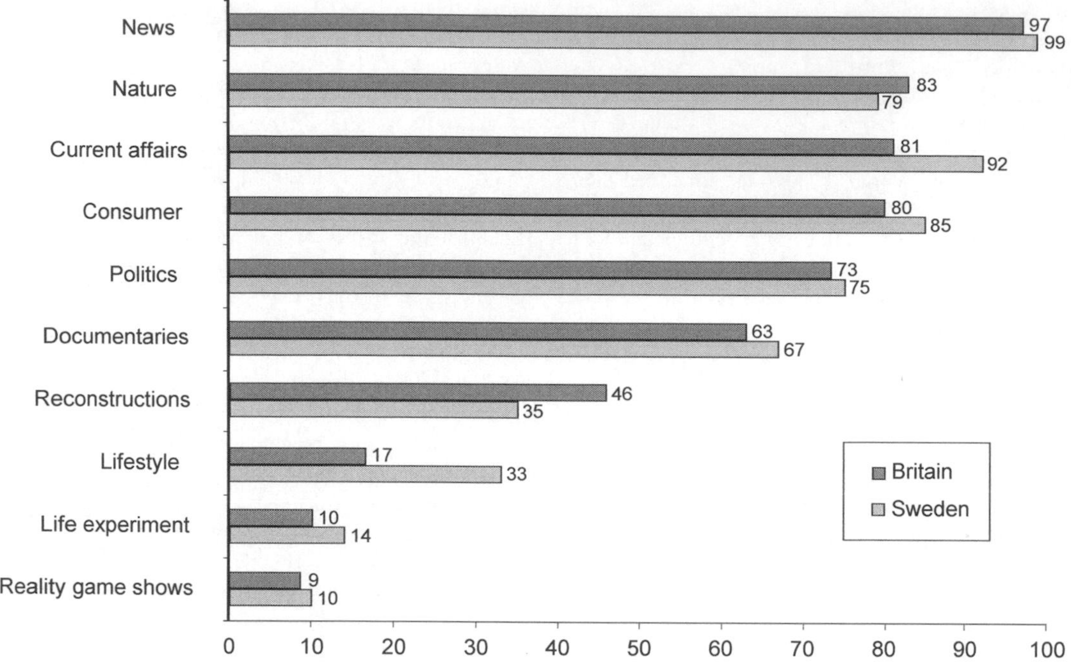

Figure 16.1 Public value of factual and reality TV in Britain and Sweden (per cent 'very important' and 'fairly important')

Note: British survey unweighted sample: 4516 respondents. Swedish survey unweighted sample: 944 respondents.

refusenik was the conservationist of the factual broadcasting environment: "Thousands of so-called reality programmes. These are devastating television programmes to the detriment of viewing. It is a descent into the pit" (Male, aged 65+, SES AB). Repetitive use of negatives such as 'drivel', 'rubbish' and the emphasis on traditional factual as the opposite of reality TV made the reality refusenik's position loud and clear. It was the most common position the public took towards reality TV in the earlier study, where even reality TV viewers tended to agree with this description of it as rubbish (Hill 2005).

Cosmopolitan viewers had diverse tastes. Most of these respondents echoed points made by traditionalists. But, what made them different was their reference to a wide range of genres as members of the whole factual family:

> Documentaries – *The Abyss*, *Life of Mammals*, Fly on the Wall – *The Salon*, Police Programmes – *Crimewatch*, Reality – *Big Brother*, *I'm a Celebrity Get Me Out of Here*, Makeovers/Home Programmes – *Changing Rooms*/*Property Ladder*, News and Features – *Sky News*/*Countryfile*.
>
> (female, aged 16–24, SES AB)

A minority of viewers, especially younger in age, referred to a narrow range: "I think the following are factual programmes, *Big Brother*, *Wife Swap*, *Airline* – all news programmes" (male, aged 25–34, SES C2), or "Programmes like *Big Brother*, *Pop Idol*, *I'm a Celebrity…*, *Fame Academy*" (female, aged 25–34, SES DE). Such viewers represented the 'neighbours from hell' for reality refuseniks.

A series of semi-structured focus groups was conducted in both Sweden and Britain. There were 24 groups,12 in each country, with a total of 129 respondents aged 18–60. The recruitment method used was quota sampling and snowball sampling.◀ The sample was based on the criteria of age (roughly split into two groups of 20–30 year olds, and 40–60 year olds), gender (even mix of male and female) and socio-economic status (working and middle class, and educational levels from primary school to university). In Sweden there were 56 respondents, 34 female, 22 male; in Britain there were 73 respondents, 31 male and 42 female. Occupations ranged from unemployed, students, administrators, teachers, sales assistants, technicians, office workers, carers, artists and retired people. In Sweden there were no ethnic minorities present in the focus group sample, although recruitment was conducted in and around Stockholm. In Britain there were people from White, Indian Bangladeshi, Black African, Black Caribbean ethnic groups and foreign nationals (German, Greek, Norwegian, Polish), which was not by design but reflected the diversity of the population of London where recruitment took place.

The focus groups were held in both professional market research settings (4), an educational setting (11), and informal household settings (9). Television clips from current affairs, documentary and reality programmes were used as visual prompts. The focus groups were audio recorded, and in addition notes were taken on general group behaviour and body language. The audio recordings were fully translated (in the case of Sweden), transcribed and coded using the qualitative software◀ package NVivo. In this part of the research three assistants helped with the recruitment and data collection and transcription, two of whom were native Swedish speakers.

The focus group questions were designed around the main themes of the project. For example, on the theme of participation, a question was designed to encourage discussion about fair treatment in factual programmes. This question, 'Are there right and wrong ways to treat people who take part in factual programmes?' was accompanied by a series of prompts from the moderator as necessary. These included prompts on different social groups, men, women, children, celebrities, or perceptions of participants in reality TV compared with documentary or news. There was a short clip from a reality TV show to aid discussion on this genre and the issues it raised for ethical treatment of different social groups. Such a question was based on previous knowledge of audience criticisms of ordinary people in reality TV from the earlier project. If those criticisms were beginning to be voiced in responses to the first reality gameshows, how would audiences perceive the issue of participation after these formats had flooded the market?

What emerged from the focus groups was that viewers differentiated between people participating in news or documentary and in reality TV, respectively. Many focus group members would acknowledge that, ideally, all people should be treated fairly, but the group discussions suggested that, in practice, reality TV was another ethical terrain. The majority of viewers felt the contract between the programme makers and the people in the show was evidence that these had given their informed consent, and therefore were themselves mainly responsible for anything that happened to them during filming. One viewer joked that if people were unhappy with their treatment, they should go to the reality TV union, implying both a professionalisation of reality participants and their lack of rights as non-professionals:

> There is a difference between somebody who has signed a contract and somebody who didn't. If you sign a contract, if you're stupid enough to sign it, you have to live with it.
>
> (21-year-old male artist)

> I think that they sort of know what they let themselves in for when they sign up for the shows, whilst I don't think it's wholly fair to really, really destroy someone and I don't like watching it.
>
> (25-year-old female illustrator)

The idea of 'the contract' became a get-out clause, not only for programme makers, but also for audiences, who perceived reality participants as resources for entertainment. Indeed, the term 'humiliation TV' was used so often in

▶ snowball sampling – Chapter 14, p. 270
▶ qualitative analysis software – Chapter 14, p. 282

the focus groups that, apparently, definitions of this hybrid genre had come to include a sense of shame as a natural development of these formats as popular entertainment.

The multidimensionality of researching in the round offers a rich site for data analysis from multiple vantage points. This wide perspective comes from the original design of the methods so that by the time the data collection is complete, you have several sets of different data that invite depth of analysis. For example, take the matter of genre classification. In the survey, there was an open question about how respondents defined factual programmes, and then closed questions about what specific types of programmes could be defined as informative, informative and entertaining, or entertaining. For both open and closed questions, a picture emerged of respondents categorising genres according to axes of information and entertainment. This categorisation of factual genres further mapped onto the value or importance accorded to these genres. Thus, news was categorised as important and informative, and reality gameshows were categorised as not important and entertaining. Some genres, such as nature or lifestyle series, were located somewhere in between in terms of both importance and categorisation (see Figure 16.2).

The open question in the survey added to what Waterton calls the construction sites for classification. These sites can reveal "tacit understandings, conceptual frameworks, and inclusions and exclusions that underpin a classificatory scheme" (2003: 113–114). Most respondents approached questions with an abstract concept of factual television as a public-service genre. Therefore the common way of defining factual television was to consider what factual ought to be, and to reflect on particular programmes that met one's personal criteria.

These findings were then incorporated into the focus groups, where participants were given lots of slips of paper with the names of different programmes written on them, and were asked to put the programmes into some kind of order, discussing this process with the group. At this stage in the research, we could observe the construction site in operation: understanding the process of categorisation was as, if not more, important than the actual definition. As one participant explained (Hill 2007: 101):

> I keep changing them around (laughter) while I hear the others talking about them. Erm, for me, *Sky News*, *Panorama*, *ITV News*, *Tonight With Trevor McDonald*, *BBC 24* are all sort of about what's going on in the world. So, they belong to one category for me. And *Channel Four News*. I have difficulty with *Jamie's School Dinners* and *Horizon*, because I think they're also about what's going on in the world, but they kind of blur into documentary.
>
> (60-year-old male design consultant)

Thus, the process of categorisation illuminated the various strategies viewers used for evaluating and critically responding to the restyling of factuality.

The multidimensional perspectives on factual and reality audiences also helped to explain a phenomenon such as hybridity. Peter Lunt has noted how reality TV has been dominated by a theme of social interaction where the ways individuals react to a problem or event is a means of reflecting on reality (2009: 141). We can see how the way audiences responded to the restyling of factuality during this period was a means of reflecting on reality claims. Over a relatively short period of time, people started to see many kinds of representations of reality as fake. It was as if reality TV had been genetically modified to fit commercial considerations.

A quick reference to the matter of authenticity within both projects highlights a change in viewers' perceptions of the reality claims within the genre. Respondents in the first study (2000–2001) thought there were authentic moments with reality TV. But the second panel of viewers (2003–2004) treated the reality genre as entertainment. Reconstruction shows that actually contained actors were thought to be more real than reality TV. A third of respondents (31 per cent) thought people acted up for the cameras in reconstruction shows compared to nearly the entire sample for reality gameshows (88 per cent). What is more, people stopped caring about whether reality TV represented the public in an authentic way. Less than 40 per cent

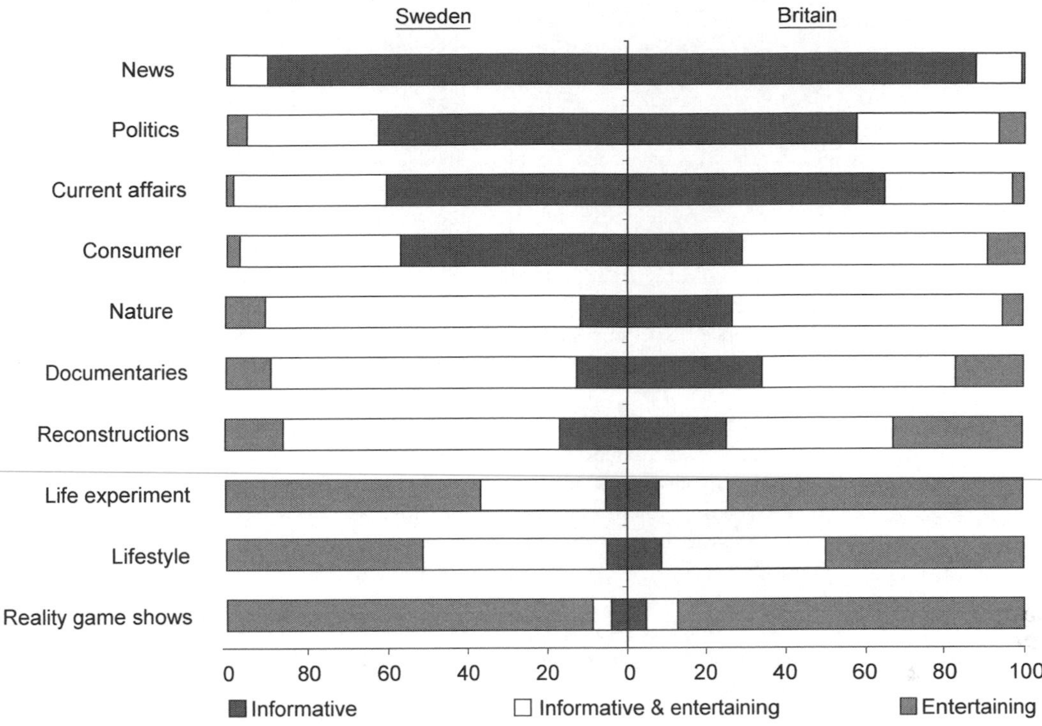

Figure 16.2 Categorisation of factual and reality TV as informative and entertaining in Britain and Sweden (per cent 'informative', 'informative and entertaining', 'entertaining')

Note: British survey unweighted sample: 4516 respondents. Swedish survey unweighted sample: 944 respondents.

claimed it was important that ordinary people did not act up for the cameras (Hill 2007: 125).

Audiences stopped caring about the authenticity of people and their experiences because of their increasing cynicism that these were ordinary people at all: reality TV participants were wannabes, hungry for celebrity status. The perception of reality TV as offering members of the public a chance to tell their story, and for audiences to learn a little something about life, gave the genre some public value in 2000. But, three years later, this style of factuality was to become known as humiliation TV, with little public value beyond that of entertainment. The hybridising tendencies so crucial to reality TV's success in the marketplace had also repositioned the genre as light entertainment, making audiences sceptical and cynical of its reality claims. Such a shift in the categorisation of the genre is part of the reason why reality TV producers moved on to entertainment formats that mixed the variety show with reality TV. The most popular shows around the world for 2010 were about singing and dancing competitions. The early generation of reality TV viewers who played *Popstars* in their gardens were now at the right age to compete in the shows themselves.

REFLECTIONS

The theatrical metaphor of 'in the round' is suggestive of how we become part of performances in the round. In audience research much has been made of identity as performative. Our subjective experiences involve a 'performance of the self' (Goffman 1959). Our political experiences involve a performance of citizenship (Dahlgren 2009). Our sense of belonging in popular cultural experiences is based on collective performances (Hermes 2005). My understanding of the roles we play in performances in the round is one where people are engaged in dynamic cultural practices. These cultural practices – watching, listening, laughing, crying, talking, interacting – help to create experiences. In turn, these cultural experiences do not happen in isolation but are connected to other people's experiences as part of an organic environment.

Research within a sociology of nature suggests that our experience of the world is connected to the natural environment and our relations with non-human species. Social practices, therefore, are not only about communicating and interacting with other people but also about our relationships with animals, or our attitudes and values towards the environment. One theory within this research is that nature is performed. Drawing on ideas from the Victorian naturalist Charles Darwin and the theory of evolution, nature as performance is a way of understanding how the human, non-human and natural environment are part of an organic, ever-changing process of life itself. This idea of performance is understood as several distinct, yet related processes. The act of performance can sometimes be associated with giving life to something through performance, so a person, object or experience would not exist outside the performative act. Performance also means repetitive practices. It is something we do on a daily basis, and yet something that slightly varies each time we perform so "variation and difference emerge in the spontaneous creative moments between iterations" (Szerszynski *et al.* 2003: 2–3). If we borrow ideas from nature as performance, then we can picture audiences in a mutual performance where their cultural practices are co-produced in an evolving environment. Human experience involves "a co-performance of a number of different, interactive and evolving individuals, species and processes" (p. 3).

The 'in the round' metaphor contains distinct, yet related processes. It is suggestive of the different perspectives we can have of a problem or phenomenon. But it is also suggestive of the immersive experiences we can have when engaged in performances in the round. In this way, the multidimensionality that is so crucial to understanding research in the round is also applicable to understanding identity and experience. If we imagine human experience as a theatrical performance in the round, then we can see ourselves and other actors improvising the drama of life. This is an immersive theatre where the audience becomes participants in an interactive performance that never ends. The film *Synecdoche New York* (director Phillip Kaufman, 2009) captures this sense of human experience as an evolving participatory play. The main character in the film is directing a play of the various stages of his life. He is both performer and producer of his own and other people's experiences of love, work, parenthood, sorrow and death.

In recent research on novel cultural formations such as ghost walks or magical entertainment I have come to perceive experience as multimodal (Hill 2011). When you walk into a house, you draw on various senses at the same time: sight, smell, sound, touch and taste. When you engage with the media you draw on multiple modalities at the same time: thinking, sensing, feeling. In classical literature the senses were perceived as media of communication, rather than as passive recipients of data: "the eyes for example, were believed to perceive by issuing rays which touched and mingled with the objects of which they were directed" (Classen 1993: 2). Although we know the senses work in ways directly related to the brain, the classical meaning of the senses as media of communication is suggestive of the complex ways we interact with our environment. We do not just watch television, we touch and are touched by it; we do not just sit in front of our laptops, we mingle with each other on the web.

The idea of audiences in the round is not about individual identities and experiences, although that is a necessary part of a performative act. This is not a play being performed for one person alone. Other prevalent metaphors of identity and experience overemphasise individualisation as a feature of late modern society and culture. Bowling alone (Putnam 2000).

Cloakroom communities (Bauman 2000). Here, the media are villains in this lonely drama of human experience. The 'in the round' metaphor comes as a direct response to these dominant negative associations of audiences as disembodied from themselves, as disconnected from society. In this metaphor people are seated together in places designed for interaction, in spaces for social relations. If we are in the round, then our performative acts give life to shared experiences.

CONCLUSION

The idea of audiences in the round is a metaphor that resonates with our understanding both of the research process and of the process of being an audience. In terms of the research process, 'in the round' suggests a multidimensional approach to audience research. This can mean multiple methods, drawn from the social sciences and humanities. It can mean various types of questions and approaches used within a specific method and across methods. Comparative research of different social groups, countries or contexts also offers multiple perspectives of a problem or phenomenon. Inductive and deductive approaches to the design, collection and analysis of data can generate various insights into the breadth and depth of audience research. The research process should generate multidimensional perspectives of audiences, as if the researcher is seated in the round and can observe and participate in a project. Above all the researcher should avoid a restricted view of audiences.

In terms of the process of being an audience, 'in the round' suggests a multidimensional approach to identity and experience. The two studies of news, documentary and reality TV have been used to illustrate how audiences experience factuality in the round. They are also seated so they can observe and participate in the media as an immersive experience. Reality TV is not watched in isolation but perceived and understood as part of wider issues concerning the hybridisation of information, entertainment, traditional public service and popular genres. It is because audiences experience factuality in the round that they are concerned about a hybrid genre that has run wild in a changing media environment. Such an understanding of audiences of factuality would be difficult without seeing things from their varied perspectives of the media today. Indeed, what audience research can show us is the performative and multidimensional nature of identity and experience. We perform our experiences in the round. One metaphor does not do justice to the complexity of audiences, but it is an idea that captures the creativity at play in the research process. Whilst some critics might say we perform alone in front of the mirror, and imagine an audience, the idea of 'in the round' suggests that we perform our identities and experiences in spaces specifically designed for social and cultural interaction.

NOTE

The research for the *Reality TV* book was funded by the public organisation the Economic and Social Research Council, the regulatory body The Independent Television Commission (now Ofcom) and the television company Channel 4. The research also received support from the Broadcasting Standards Commission (now Ofcom), the BBC and Channel Five (now Five). The research for the *Restyling Factual TV* book came from the former regulatory bodies the Broadcasting Standards Commission and Independent Television Commission; Jonköping International Business School; and the Society, Opinion and Media Institute, Gothenberg University. The University of Westminster funded sabbaticals that enabled both books to be written.

17 A multi-grounded theory of parental mediation

Exploring the complementarity of qualitative and quantitative communication research

Lynn Schofield Clark

- a meta-analysis of the relationship between *social-psychological and socio-cultural approaches* to communication studies
- a review of the *quantitative literature on parents' regulation* of children's and young people's media use
- a presentation of a *long-term qualitative study of parental mediation* in the U.S.
- a discussion of the specific *complementarity of qualitative and quantitative* approaches
- an outline of a *theory of parental mediation*, grounded in multiple methodologies

INTRODUCTION

My career as a qualitative researcher began with every graduate student's nightmare. After I had attempted to utilize the methodology of grounded theory◄ to present my findings on how the lower income U.S. teens that I had interviewed were employing discussions about television to talk about their own practices of identification, a senior researcher in the field stood up in the question and answer session. He authoritatively informed me that a number of scholars had already demonstrated television's role in identity-formation, and then asked: "so from your research, can you tell us something that is actually new?" I can no longer remember exactly how I answered his challenge, but as I had been well socialized into the historically rooted tradition of critical/cultural studies research, even in my shame I do remember thinking that his was the 'wrong' question.

I recall that moment now because whereas there is and can be complementarity between the qualitative and quantitative approaches to communication research, we need to recognize and address upfront the fact that researchers harbor differing expectations of what research is and what it is to do. Researchers interested in complementarity need to be articulate not only in their own methodological and theoretical traditions, but in the traditions of those with whom they would converse; in other words, with those who share some common questions, but perhaps not common theoretical ground. This kind of conversation is not easy to pursue, for as Craig has observed, scholars in the field of communication have "radically different conceptions of 'theory' " and "distinct ways of conceptualizing and discussing communication problems and practices" (Craig, 1999: 120). In his influential article on the metadiscourse of communication theory,◄ which captured the opening story exactly, Craig argued:

► grounded theory – Chapter 14, p. 278

► meta-levels of analysis – Chapter 15, p. 287

> Rather than addressing a field of theory, we appear to be operating privately in separate domains. Books and articles on communication theory seldom mention other works on communication theory except within narrow (inter)disciplinary specialities and schools of thought. Except within these little groups, communication theorists apparently neither agree nor disagree about much of anything. There is no canon of general theory to which they all refer. There are no common goals that unite them, no contentious issues that divide them. For the most part, they simply ignore each other.
>
> (Craig, 1999: 119–120)

Like many qualitative researchers, I had believed for a long time that quantitative researchers dismissed qualitative research as 'anecdotal' and 'descriptive,' a position occasionally reinforced in laments about "epistemological erosion" (Donsbach, 2006: 44) and calls for greater rigor in the development of communication theory. Yet another part of the reason for this mutual ignoring between the social-psychological and socio-cultural/critical traditions that I draw on is that ethnographically oriented constructivist and feminist communication researchers tend to dismiss 'theory' as a colonialist inheritance. We have preferred a humanistic stance toward research and toward our research participants, recognizing that we construct theory as a form of discourse and, in so doing, exercise a certain form of power (Ang, 1996; Mayer, 2005; Parameswaran, 2001). As a result, qualitative researchers in communication have been interested in the position of the researcher relative to the knowledge produced, calling for greater reflexivity and struggling over how to present research in the form of stories and narratives rather than 'findings' (see, e.g., Acosta-Alzuru, 2005; Clark, 2011; Hills, 2002; Markham, 2009; Murphy, 2008).

At the same time, as evidenced in this and in other volumes, researchers working on the development of communication theory have become more reflexive about the process of theory development, the intersubjective nature of knowledge, and the questionable assertion of a values-neutral science.◀ As a result, interest in research that results in general laws and predictions has generally fallen out of favor, and social psychological researchers have widened their own definitions of empirical research so as to embrace multi-methodological approaches that sometimes include interviewing and observation in an effort to better understand issues of context and other 'unconscious factors' that influence behavior. Rather than being accepted unproblematically as predictive truth claims, therefore, communication theories are now widely viewed as "organizing frameworks that allow situations to be 'meaningful' rather than chaotic; they provide an initial foundation of understanding but are subject to change and elaboration as we encounter inconsistencies and new information" (Baldwin, *et al.*, 2003: 3). Thinking of communication theory as a provisional and explanatory 'roadmap' is not very different from considering ethnography as a project of 'translation' that seeks to demonstrate how social action from one point of view makes sense from another (Heath and Bryant, 2000; Agar, 1995). That common epistemological ground suggests that this may be an appropriate moment to revisit the possibilities of dialogue between differing research traditions within communication studies.

Interestingly, Craig (1999, 2007) provided a framework for bringing differing traditions into dialogue by articulating a discursive understanding of theory.◀ He argued that we can move forward as a field as we embrace what he terms a "constitutive model of communication" or a "communicational perspective" that would distinguish communication theories from other disciplinary perspectives, foregrounding our common concerns with "who participates in what ways in the social processes that construct personal identities, the social order, and codes of communication" (Craig, 1999: 126). In order for us to make headway in finding complementarities within our own field relative to similar questions, we must understand and address ourselves to how we embrace differing conceptions of communicative practice, rather than attending only to our different epistemological commitments.

▶ values and knowledge interests – Chapter 19, p. 358
▶ theory as discourse – Chapter 15, p. 287

I begin this chapter with a description of my recent study, *Parenting in the Digital Age*, which explored how parents and their children made decisions about digital and mobile media use and its regulation as the children moved through the childhood, tween, and teen years. Although I did not initially set out to do so, I found that my analysis shed light on gaps within what has been known as the parental mediation literature,◀ a growing body of research that has largely embraced survey methodologies to explore how parents utilize differing strategies of interpersonal communication to mitigate the negative effects they presume the media have on their children. My basic argument, as I will present it here, is that a multi-grounded parental mediation theory can account for both the intentional and the non-intentional communicative actions of parents that shape the ways in which parents come to mediate young people's experiences with the media. In a sense, then, my work with multi-grounded theory embraces the complementarity of qualitative and quantitative research on communication by attending to the questions that differing scholars seek to address, and by foregrounding what we might want to address both together and separately in the future.

Before I introduce my own research, however, I want to answer the charge that the senior researcher gave me long ago, and which I felt ill-prepared to address at the time. I had felt that he had asked a question that was 'wrong' because, following symbolic interactionism's orientation, I had been seeking to understand communicational processes of interaction among teens in their discussions of television, and I was not testing which television programs were utilized by which groups for which purposes under which conditions. The problem with my research actually was not that I did not have anything 'new' to add to the existing theories within the social-psychological literature. The problem was that what was 'new' was that I was discovering a blind spot in existing approaches to the study of young people, media, and identity, which had been based on the experiences of middle class rather than less advantaged young people in the U.S. This was only a problem because, as a graduate student early in my career, I was not confident that I had indeed identified a blind spot, nor was I confident that I could make my case in a way that could convince this person who was so much more knowledgeable and senior to me in the field. Fortunately, others in the field were working on similar problems at the time, and soon a great deal of evidence would surface that suggested that the communication processes related to working class young people's media practices differed from those of the middle class young people who more frequently participated in survey and experimental research (see, e.g., Akindes, 2003; Fisherkeller, 2002). That experience convinces me that qualitative research can be beneficial in speaking not only with scholars within my socio-cultural and critical communities, but also with those engaged in researching other facets of communication in the lives of young people and families. Together we can contribute to richer understandings of how people participate in social processes that construct personal identities, the social order, and codes of communication, to use Craig's (1999) terminology.

▶ parental mediation research, p. 321

THE TEENS & THE NEW MEDIA @ HOME PROJECT

The study I conducted between 2001–2010, which I now refer to as Parenting in the Digital Age, focused on how parents and children made decisions about digital and mobile media use and its regulation as the children moved through the childhood, tween, and teen years. I wanted to know more about the process of the decision-making that involved both parents and young people within families. My interest came about as a result of an earlier study on parents, children, and media rules, in which my colleagues and I had found that even though parents articulated the belief that they should make and enforce household media rules, they did not always make their rules explicit; they did not enforce the rules consistently when they did have them; and their intentions were not always understood by their children in any event (Hoover, *et al.*, 2004).

In this follow-up study, it was not my aim to explore how a certain variable influenced or had an effect upon another variable, such as whether parents of younger children were more likely to make and enforce household media rules than were parents of older children, or whether more educated parents were more likely to have such rules than less educated parents (see Eastin, *et al.*, 2006, as their research has found evidence to support both of these hypotheses). It was also not my goal (at least initially) to find evidence for, or to contribute to, the research literature on parental mediation, which proposes that parents tend to employ some combination of three possible strategies of media regulation: restrictive mediation (rule-making), active mediation (discussion), or coviewing (watching together) (Nathanson, 1999; Valkenburg, *et al.*, 1999; for a review of parental mediation research, see Clark, in press). Rather, this study aimed to describe the process of how parents and their children negotiated over digital and mobile media in their lives together, so as to better understand why parents engaged in the regulatory practices that they did (or did not), and how their children played a role in shaping these household-level regulatory practices.

parental mediation research

I wanted to describe that process of negotiation rigorously, which meant carefully analyzing patterns in how parents addressed themselves to what they took to be the problems the media presented in the lives of their children. I also wanted to remain open to listening for the rationales parents gave regarding when and why they did *not* regulate media use for their children. I categorized the data so as to identify more clearly how various aspects that I was studying fit together. I found that I could identify four concerns that guided parental strategies of media regulation, but I also found that only two of these four concerns were accounted for in the existing theories of parental mediation, as I will discuss. Reflecting on existing theories and on my empirically grounded qualitative data, I then employed a multi-grounded theory approach to advance the emerging theory of parental mediation (on multi-grounded theory,◄ see Goldkuhl and Cronholm, 2010, discussed below). This chapter thus illustrates the way in which, rather than *testing* theories, reflexive qualitative research can provide a means by which to *think with* communication theories. It argues that through reflexive analysis of qualitative data, researchers can come to consider the assumptions that underlie studies, so as to broaden and enhance emerging communication theories.

The next section of this chapter offers a review of the research literature regarding parental mediation, which has largely developed out of the social-psychological approaches rooted in studies of media effects. The chapter then describes how the literature of parental mediation was not 'tested': the present study did find support for some of its claims, but the same literature also left unexplained some of the lived experiences of families regarding their practices of regulating media. The chapter concludes by discussing multi-grounded theory and considering the implications of such complementary reflections for the relevance of communication research in the public realm.

THE RESEARCH LITERATURE ON PARENTAL MEDIATION

Since the earliest days of communication research, scholars have been interested in parental efforts to mitigate negative media effects on children◄ (see, e.g., Barcus, 1969; Brown and Linné, 1976; Schramm, *et al.*, 1961; McLeod, *et al.*, 1982). Researchers recommended limiting television viewing time (Maccoby, 1954), cautioned that television informs children's desires for commercial products (Burr and Burr, 1976; Caron and Ward, 1974), and noted that parental role modeling was an important aspect of a child's socialization into media use (Banks and Gupta, 1980; Webster, *et al.*, 1986). Scholars began employing the term *parental mediation* as a way of recognizing that parents take an active role in managing and regulating their children's experiences with television (Dorr, *et al.*, 1989; Kaye, 1979; Lin and Atkin, 1989; Logan and Moody, 1979; Nathanson, 1999; Valkenburg, *et al.*, 1999). Parental mediation research

► multi-grounded theory, p. 332

► media effects on children – Chapter 8, p. 167

literature, therefore, has long been rooted in the assumption that restricting or regulating media influences is an important aspect of good parenting in contemporary culture (see, e.g., Lemish, 2006).

In several influential studies, Nathanson and Valkenburg and her colleagues developed a scale◀ to assess how parents engaged in each of three different strategies of mediation: *active* mediation, or talking with young people about the content they saw on television; *restrictive* mediation, or setting rules and regulations about children's television viewing; and *coviewing* (simply watching television with children) (Nathanson, 1998, 1999; Valkenburg, *et al.*, 1999; note that Eastin and colleagues (2006) prefer the term *evaluative* rather than active mediation; Valkenburg and colleagues (1999) prefer *instructive* mediation and *social* coviewing). Whereas active mediation assigns an importance to dialogue between parents and their children and coviewing involves primarily nonverbal communication and copresence, restrictive mediation tends to involve parent-to-child communication in the form of rule-making, rule-stating, and following through with consequences when rules are not followed.

active mediation, restrictive mediation, coviewing

Researchers following in the tradition of parental mediation have found that *active mediation*, or parent/child discussions about the television that young people view, can mitigate possible negative outcomes such as aggressive behavior or the cultivation of a skewed worldview (Nathanson, 2001; Austin, *et al.*, 1990; Desmond, *et al.* 1990).

Parental mediation researchers have also found that children whose parents engage in *restrictive mediation* experience more positive outcomes than those who engage with their parents in *coviewing* (Nathanson, 1999). This finding echoes scholarship that has found that firm behavioral control correlates with socializing children to social competence. However, very low and very high levels of restriction of media were associated with more aggression, suggesting that parents who create either no strategies or highly restrictive strategies may create hostilities in their children, a finding that echoes studies concluding that adolescents resist overly strict parental rules (Nathanson, 1999; Peterson and Hann, 1999; see also Hoffman, 1970). Parental mediation researchers further have found that, among adolescents, restrictive mediation was related to less positive attitudes toward parents, more positive attitudes toward the forbidden content, and a greater likelihood that the adolescents experiencing restrictive mediation would view the content with their peers (Nathanson, 2002). Children need to accept and internalize media rules in order to abide by them willingly, as previous research has suggested with regard to rules restricting risky behavior (Baxter, *et al.*, 2009). The cases that will be reviewed here from my own research address the strategy of restrictive mediation, as they highlight how two families adopt very different approaches to restrictive mediation, embracing differing rationales and experiencing very different outcomes.

Previous research into parental mediation offers several clues as to why parents may not be as engaged in parental mediation practices as researchers might expect or desire. Consistent with the notion of third-person effects, parents often underestimate the influence of media on their children when compared with how they estimate the influence of the media on other people's children (Davison, 1983; Hoffner and Buchanan, 2002; Krcmar, 1998; Meirick, *et al.*, 2009; Nathanson, *et al.*, 2002; Tsfati, *et al.*, 2005). A parent may view her own child as more mature than most, and thus may be overconfident in that child's ability to discern for herself either television's or the internet's nefarious messages (Livingstone and Helsper, 2008). Family interactions and family environment offer another explanation for lower levels of parental mediation, as the amount of time young people spend alone with media increases as parents' availability decreases, suggesting that parents with heavier work schedules may be less available for discussions and less capable of enforcing restrictions (Austin and Freeman, 1997; Brown, *et al.*, 1990; Warren, *et al.*, 2002). To explore when parental mediation fails, or when parents are unable to engage in parental mediation to the extent that either the parents or researchers would like, there is a need to

third-person effects

▶ scales of analysis – Chapter 13, p. 241

attend to the contexts in which parental mediation occurs.

At this point, therefore, it is helpful to introduce two extended case studies drawn from my research that illustrate how parents approached the felt need to regulate media practices on behalf of their children.

THE DOMENTARY FAMILY

Norma Domentary placed a high priority on her parental role as the person who needed to teach her 16-year-old daughter right from wrong. As an unemployed single parent, Norma encountered many problems in her daily life, and she desired her daughter Veronica's respect and appreciation for her efforts. Like many parents, Norma wanted her daughter to both know, and to agree with, her own way of seeing the world. In large part, she agreed with the assumptions behind the need for restrictive parental mediation as outlined earlier in this chapter, expressing concern about how television's portrayals were at odds with her lived experiences of economic instability and disadvantage.

Norma believed that, as a parent, it was her responsibility to counter what Veronica saw in the media and to inculcate in Veronica the views that she herself embraced: that no one was entitled to anything, and that you needed to work hard for what you got out of life. Yet she also believed that, at 16, Veronica was old enough to be trusted to make her own decisions regarding media use. Rather than actually imposing restrictions on digital and mobile media use, or reading the text messages on her daughter's phone as some other parents in this study had done, Norma preferred to offer criticism regarding the media behaviors of which she did not approve. She used the instance of the interviews about family media use as an occasion to convey her views to her daughter, thus providing opportunities to analyze the interactions between mother and daughter regarding media uses.

Veronica, who identified herself as biracial and Asian American, was a well-liked student whose friends were similarly high achievers at her diverse urban high school on the U.S. west coast. Although Veronica, like many young people, used her cell phone constantly, she also spoke of television as a primary source of leisure-time activity.

Veronica agreed with many of her mothers' views, noting that she thought that there was "too much" sexuality on MTV and VH1 (a music and reality cable channel) and that she, like her mother, believed that such representations could influence the ways that teens felt about and engaged in sexual activity. But, she also implicitly disagreed with her mother's views that such negative assessments should result in diminished viewing. "We don't have cable and we don't get good reception," Norma explained proudly when asked about how much television they watched together as a family. As a result, said Veronica, "There's nothing TO watch, so I don't spend my time with television." At least, Veronica meant, she did not spend her time with television at her own home. "I probably would be home more if there were things to watch. But instead I try to go out," she said, noting that she watched television at her friends' houses instead. She then added thoughtfully, "It's kind of weird 'cuz like every day after school I go to my friend's house. We go over there and hang out and watch BET [Black Entertainment Television], MTV, you know." When the interviewer, seeing the surprised look on Norma's face, asked her about this, Norma replied, "I didn't know that until just now!" and laughed uncomfortably. "You know that I go to friends' houses," Veronica countered. "Well, I know you go to friends' houses but I didn't think you'd be sitting there in front of the TV!" Norma replied. Interrupting the last part of Norma's statement, Veronica asked incredulously, "What do you think we do there?!" to which her mother replied defensively, "Well, you say sometimes you go to play tennis. You say you go sometimes to get something to eat. You just say you hang out." "Hang out IS watching TV," Veronica said. "Not talking?" asked her mother imperiously. "I don't know! I guess," Veronica said with increasing frustration. "We eat, we talk, and we watch TV!"

At this point the interviewer, sensing the rising tension, asked Veronica's mother to share her concerns about television viewing. Norma seemed to relish the opportunity to discuss this topic:

> Oh, my goodness, I can tell you why [she didn't like Veronica to view too much television]. Because every time you turn it on you see something that grieves your spirit. I mean –. Half the shows –. Everything that is not normal is made to look normal. I mean it is so distorted on TV that it is not real life. There are a few good shows on. I like news shows. *60 Minutes*, *20/20*, you know, informative shows. *Animal Planet*. There is some good quality TV. But these sitcoms when everyone is putting each other down and it's funny and the alternative lifestyles that are made normal and cool and funny, that's not how the real world is. No one has any money problems. I mean the *Real World*. I watched an episode of the *Real World* one time and the whole episode was about this one girl borrowing this other girl's shirt but not asking, or she stole it and –. That is NOT the real world, when your biggest problem in life is someone wearing your shirt without asking. I mean, they are living in this Las Vegas casino with these clothes. That's not the real world. That is distortion.

After this diatribe against television, Veronica, ignoring her mother's comments about young people's sense of entitlement and the concern that on television "no one has any money problems," responded animatedly that she did not believe that television programs depicting homosexuality were offensive:

> Because I mean we do have to be accepting to everybody else's lifestyles and not be stuck up to the fact that other people live differently. You know? So, it's just like you are seeing a different view. There are a lot of different things going on.

Television content, just like whether or not Veronica chose to watch it, became one more stage in which Veronica and Norma dueled over whose views of people and their actions were 'right.'

Veronica was also conscious of her mother's disapproval of her participation in the online spaces of social network sites.◄ Veronica liked to post information about herself on her online social networking profile, and when online, she had sought out forums that had enabled her to make connections with the Asian part of her identity. But she expected her mother to disagree with her online communication, as is evident in the aside to her mom in her telling of this story:

> We were online and said, "What are you doing tonight?" And we were both doing the same thing (going to the same club) and it was, "Cool. I'll see you there." And then there is this other –. (to her mom) You are not freaking out, are you? (returning to the interviewer's question about whether or not she interacts online with people she did not know beforehand) But there is this other thing, my friend, his sister is doing this modeling thing. He wants to do a photo shoot of me. So I have connections through that with other people, too.

The positive possibilities growing out of making connections to acquaintances was a major theme in the discussion that the interviewer had with Veronica and, later, with her friends. Veronica's mother, in contrast, expressed little interest in the online realm or the mobile phone. She said that she believed that if she improved her computer skills, it might be beneficial for her professionally. Yet, she said, she would rather read books or speak to someone in person than be online or on a mobile. She did wish that Veronica was more forthcoming about what she did online, however, complaining that whenever she walked into Veronica's room, Veronica quickly exited the screen on which any conversation was taking place.

What started as an expression of differing views on social networks seemed to escalate into yet another disagreement in their joint interview. This was their exchange:

> Norma: I would rather see people, see their facial expressions, do an activity together, not sitting there talking online or on the phone.
>
> Veronica: I would too, but it's just like when they are online you can talk to 20

► social network sites – Chapter 10, p. 199

people at one time. I don't like to talk on the phone either but it is just more convenient. You can talk to all these people at one time. So, that is kind of beneficial.

Norma: But sometimes you are talking to people, if you are in a group of 20 people, it would be so much more interesting to see their faces, to feel their spirits, to see if they were real because sometimes people are just fake on these things.

Veronica: At 10 o'clock at night??

Norma: I don't know! Does time make a difference??

Veronica: Yes! I'm at home at 8 PM talking to people, that is my hobby. I'd rather go out and talk to them but if it's 10 PM and I'm getting ready to go to bed, then it is just convenient to talk to them there, you know?

Norma: I personally feel like I am tired of talking to people and by 10 at night I'd rather be in my room or –

Veronica: It is just like "hey what did you do today" or "what's new," you know?

In this exchange, Norma made several statements expressing her belief that face-to-face communication was preferable to conversations that took place online, perhaps in an attempt to help Veronica to know and appreciate her views. Veronica, who did not challenge her mother's requirement that she needed to be in the house at 8 PM (with, perhaps, time in her room after 10 PM), argued for the benefits of being able to continue communication when within the confines of her house. This was a way for Veronica to maintain her ties with her peers even while she was under her mother's supervision. Norma might prefer not to communicate with people later in the evening, but it was clear that Veronica felt differently. Unfortunately, Norma seemed to be so interested in expressing her preferred way of doing things that she was unable to hear, or even express interest in, Veronica's friendships, her day-to-day practices, or her desire to follow her mother's household rules, much to the detriment of their own relationship.

The interviewer returned to Veronica and Norma's modest home for a follow-up interview about three months later. Veronica, who had recently graduated from high school, had moved out of her mother's house and into an apartment with a relatively new boyfriend. Veronica and Norma were not speaking to one another as a result of the move. Veronica explained the move in relation to the fact that her mother did not trust her. Her mother, on the other hand, attributed her move to outside influences such as the media, which, Norma felt, had given Veronica a set of unrealistic aspirations and a sense of entitlement.

Her mother, somewhat surprisingly, was especially indignant about the fact that when Veronica moved out of the house, she took their computer with her. Veronica's secretive removal of the computer from Norma's house was, to Norma, one more sign of Veronica's sense of entitlement. This made Norma angry, and perhaps this is why she insisted again – in the individual follow-up interview – on the benefits of face-to-face communication over computer- or phone-mediated conversation. The computer's removal was not the reason that Norma had chosen not to speak with Veronica after the move, however; in keeping with her approach to socialization, she wanted Veronica to get the message that she disapproved of her choice to move in with her boyfriend, and was therefore withholding contact as a way of voicing her objection. It was another way in which she was attempting to express 'strict' expectations of appropriate behavior.

The research literature on parental mediation has little to say about a case like Norma and Veronica's. That literature offers suggestions as to why a self-described 'strict' parent like Norma might engage in restricting media – but she does not. And although the literature suggests that the most effective means of mediating media is often active mediation, Norma's parental efforts at talking with Veronica about her media choices demonstrates that such talk is not always well-received by children, nor is it effective in achieving parental intentions regarding the mediation of media use.

The story of Norma and Veronica fleshes out previous findings regarding parental mediation, such as the fact that restrictive and active mediation can be less effective as children age. Yet it also suggests that the theory behind parental mediation – the belief that it is the parent's responsibility to provide judgment about the media that are presumed to be largely negative influences in the lives of young people – can provide justification for ineffective parental mediation strategies, such as those embraced by Norma in her relationship with Veronica. Unfortunately, Norma did not listen to Veronica's experiences in order to understand them on Veronica's terms. She felt justified in her inflexible responses to Veronica because she viewed media as a source of disruption to be mediated through argumentation. She thought she was helping Veronica to attain a more realistic sense of what to expect from life, whereas Veronica thought her mother was not able to appreciate her own relationships and aspirations. In this sense, then, the theories of parental mediation may be less helpful when put into practice, particularly among families whose older and increasingly independent children are managing a host of other difficulties, sometimes complicated by financial disadvantage.

THE BLAYNE-GALLAGHER FAMILY

The Blayne-Gallagher family took an entirely different approach, and one that similarly confounded the literature on parental mediation. Whereas many parents in the larger study were concerned about the possible dangers of television, and especially of the internet, the members of the Blayne-Gallagher family at first seemed to embrace a completely different approach. "The more you expose them to stuff, the better," said Gwen, mother of 16-year-old Maria and 11-year-old Nigel Blayne-Gallagher.

The Blayne-Gallaghers lived in a large city in the northeastern part of the U.S., where Maria and Nigel's father was in city government and their mother was a student in medical school. Maria, who preferred to identify herself as biracial, noted with an ironic smile that despite the fact that her biracial father identified himself as black, she did not like to claim that she was black, in part, because her father was West Indian rather than African American and, in part, as she said, because "You have to be Ghetto Fabulous and I'm not that." (On biracial identity in the U.S., see Foner, 2001; Foner and Frederickson, 2004; Vickerman, 1999.)

A straight-A student, Maria was active in her mostly black urban high school's after-school activities, and regularly spent time reading weekly newsmagazines and watching news programs on television with her parents. The Blayne-Gallagher house was a favorite hangout place for her high school friends, she noted, because in the living room there were many instruments that beckoned interaction (digeridoo, guitars, mariachis, tambourines, piano, drums). There was also a large screen TV and a PlayStation in the room.

Maria's parents had purchased a cell phone for her at the end of her ninth grade year. Nigel got one at the same time (at the end of his fifth grade year), so that she and Nigel could work out arrangements about getting home when both of their parents were busy. She had gotten an iPod earlier in the year as a gift, and her family had also given her several iTunes gift certificates so that she could download music without the threat of viruses. Maria did not mention that another benefit of having access to iTunes is legal downloading, which may have been more of a concern for her parents than for her (on how young people and parents negotiate the purchase and regulation of various technological gifts, see Pugh, 2009). Like many other young people her age, Maria spent a fair amount of time texting, instant-messaging, and communicating with her friends through social network sites.

At 16 and 11, Maria and Nigel recognized that their family did things somewhat differently from the families of their peers. As Maria noted, "My friends all think my family is pretty weird, in a really cool way ... like all my friends who went to my junior high, all their parents are so friggin' uptight." Maria and her parents talked together about the media rules and guidelines that they felt were appropriate, and both their mother and father shared in the responsibility of working with Maria and Nigel to maintain those guidelines and to set up consequences for when those guidelines were not met. Maria described these practices in terms of permissiveness, and not surprisingly, she was highly supportive of her parents' approach: "So we are not as strict. I think I am growing up so much happier. Thank you so much, mom."

In a separate interview, Maria's mother, Gwen, placed their practices of parental authority in a framework that might better be described as flexible and responsive rather than permissive, emphasizing the importance of warmth and caring: "I think being a parent is all about letting them know you are there, that you love them, you care, you will help them out," she said. "You want them to know that whatever they do is okay, that they can come to you. You give them the rules and guidelines and you expect them to follow that. But you know, you have to go day by day."

In the Blayne-Gallagher family, the emphasis was on respecting others and thinking through how your own actions affected the lives and choices of those around you as well as how they affected your own life. It was not so much that whatever they did was "okay" as Maria had said, but rather that the parents wanted their young people to trust them enough to admit when they had made mistakes, so that the parents could act as consultants as the children worked out solutions or next steps – and those next steps would differ depending on the circumstances. "You try to tell your kids 'use your brain,'" Gwen said. "Question these things. What do you think is right? How would you judge these people and what do you base that on?" Gwen said that she believed it was important to respect the dignity of all people. Then, with a note of irony, Gwen said, "I think my kids would agree with me and they're right!" (laughs).

Maria and Nigel's father, Stan, stated that the family had "no rules" regarding digital and mobile media use: "I look at this differently. It's not about what they can't do, but about what they can get out of it, the media. Another way of looking at this policy question is that we want the kids getting more information, not to limit their information." Gwen and Stan wanted Nigel and Maria to have regular access to magazines and newspapers as well as to what is online, because they felt that they would then be more likely to open something out of a slight interest and become more intrigued, and informed, about things they did not know that they were interested in. In the Blayne-Gallagher family, learning about different cultures was a highly valued part of their family life, and thus encouraging and sharing curiosity was a part of their individual and collective media experiences, as well.

Somewhat like Norma Domentary, the Blayne-Gallagher parents had a clear sense of 'right' and 'wrong' that they wanted to communicate with their children. In this regard, they agreed with the basic assumption that good parenting includes parental mediation of the media. In a separate interview, Maria's mother, Gwen, noted that when she saw Maria or Nigel watching something on television that she felt was insulting to women or to certain racial/ethnic groups, she would insist that they turn it off, exercising restrictive mediation. Gwen also did not hesitate to criticize Maria's favorite syndicated program, *Friends*, calling it, "stupid ... they are all white, rich, beautiful people," to which Stan added, "That is the bad thing about *Friends*. The black person that shows up will be the one that busses the table." Maria contradicted this, noting that Ross, a central character on *Friends*, had dated a black woman, and that the program had portrayed biracial relationships. Gwen then recognized Maria's observation and said, "Okay, well that's good," demonstrating to Maria that her views were heard and valued while also reaffirming her own perspective that inclusive representations of racial/ethnic diversity and biracial couples were desirable. In this sense, the family engaged in active mediation, not only to give voice to the parents' views, but also to hear the young person's responses to the media and to parental views.

The Blayne-Gallaghers appreciated it when they found in popular media a range of voices and representations of people who were often underrepresented or disadvantaged. For example, Gwen explained that Maria's music choices were "fine," offering an implicit critique of some kinds of lyrics when she described the music Maria preferred as, "It's not violence against women. It is just rock. We may not like the music but it's not offensive." This was a comment to which Maria added, "It's offensive if you're a corporate type of person," indicating her preference for music that sought to challenge the authority of the large-scale music industries through its distribution as well as its lyrics. Maria was not interested in 'testing' her parents' limits by trying to download or buy music that they might find offensive, but in turn, her parents were more willing than many to engage in active mediation about Maria's choices of entertainment. "Eminem, when he first came out, his lyrics were pretty out there and he said every word you can imagine and I used to think he is so disgusting, don't you be listening to that crap," said Gwen. "And then I started listening to his lyrics and even though he said the F word, he is brilliant. I just think he is totally brilliant." Maria appreciated this assessment, placing it in the framework of her parents' interest in giving things a chance before passing judgment: "That's the thing. Most adults don't ever give it a chance. If you listen to it, it's really pretty good," she noted.

Maria's mother, Gwen, similarly noted that while they did not have specific rules about computer use, "we have an understanding that there is some stuff that is not appropriate for you." Yet, when Gwen said that she did not monitor what her son or daughter was doing on the computer, Maria contradicted this information with an emphatic, "You do!" Gwen then nodded, noting, "Sometimes when she is IMing [instant-messaging] with her friends, I'll stand there and watch because it's fascinating just to see the kind of conversations." Maria indicated her displeasure with this practice, commenting, "It IS private." "Well," her mother said to her, "you could be on the phone and I'd be in the same room, standing next to you and hearing you talk. It would be the same thing. But this way you can see the back and forth and it is like, wow, that is fantastic." Gwen noted later in the interview that the family also employed a filtering system on the family computer, so that Maria and Nigel were automatically blocked from certain sites.

In this exchange, we see that perhaps Maria and Nigel's parents were more involved in the oversight and restriction of their children's digital media use than they cared to admit (or recognize). In contrast to the term "permissive" that Maria had used to express their distance from parents who took a more restrictive stance toward media, the Blayne-Gallagher parents engaged in differing parental mediation strategies as the circumstances changed, sometimes engaging in restriction, sometimes in active discussion about their children's media choices, and sometimes sharing in media consumption so as to better understand their children's experiences and tastes. They took an interest in their children's media practices, keeping the computer in a public space in the home and subtly indicating through their occasional observations that they expected their children's online interactions to be in line with what the family espoused as its values.

Respect and concern for the family also came up when Gwen voiced what she said were her only regrets regarding digital media:

> Sometimes I feel that we really need to stop being so separate, Nigel is doing a game, Maria is doing her thing on the computer, and I'm watching something. We all need to come into the same room and play Scrabble. Do something together. And, not every family occurrence can be about going to a movie. So that does come up for me a lot ... It takes more energy to NOT do something related to media. It really does. You gotta create it. Think about what you are going to do and get everybody in the same room. It takes a lot more energy.

In this statement, Maria's mother expressed a value in being 'unplugged' from media culture, and acknowledged that being unplugged today takes a new kind of emotional work in family life. Yet, unlike 'strict' parents who were concerned about avoiding the negatives of popular culture, the Blayne-Gallaghers' desire to unplug grew out of the desire for a home environment in which an ethic of mutual connection could be more wholeheartedly embraced. Such idealism about non-mediated 'family time' is common among U.S. families, who often find in the entertainment media an inexpensive option that requires less energy and less forethought than other forms of leisure (Borba, 2011; Sasha, 2010). Nevertheless, as is clear from Gwen's comment, the family's 'movie night' was the default family leisure activity that they had to work hard to replace. Coviewing in this family was perhaps a passive parental activity, as suggested in the parental mediation literature, but it also provided an avenue for family connection and common experience, an important goal espoused within this, as well as in other, families.

A GROUNDED THEORY OF PARENTAL MEDIATION

Throughout interviews with parents in the project as a whole, four concerns emerged that guided parental actions regarding the mediation of media use: concerns about the future of their children, concerns about family connectedness, concerns about balancing work and family time, and concerns regarding parental self-preservation and self-development. Parents discussed each of these concerns in relation to certain parental mediation *strategies*, and they relied upon sometimes differing and sometimes overlapping *terms* and *rationales* for why they engaged in the parental mediation strategies that they did (summarized in Figure 17.1).

future of children

First, parents were concerned about the future of their children, and this was often discussed in terms familiar to those concerned about the potentially negative effects of the media on children's cognitive processes. When parents spoke about limiting gaming, phone, texting, and television time, they noted that they wished to do so for the sake of attention to homework, concerns about their children's physical health, and concerns about the bad influences that stereotypes and violence might have on their children's development of what they considered to be an appropriate and desirable worldview. When parents like Norma Domentary and Gwen and Stan Blayne-Gallagher spoke of restrictions, they did so with a rationale that assumed, 'It's good parenting to restrict media influences.' As noted earlier, this approach to parental mediation is well addressed in existing literature.

family connectedness

Second, parents were concerned about family connectedness. When parents spoke about this concern, they sometimes mentioned the frequency of phone calls and text messages exchanged between family members throughout the day, and about movie nights they enjoyed together, sometimes simply coviewing, and sometimes referring to discussions that are described in earlier research in relation to the parental mediation strategy of active mediation. Some families took these practices further than the passive coviewing and even active discussion suggested in parental mediation literature, embracing what I have elsewhere termed *participatory learning*, in which both parents and children interact with one another and learn together through activities such as Wii Bowling, Guitar Hero, or Dance Dance Revolution (Clark, in press). Some parents even engaged in less commercially supported mediated activities such as creating and posting videos online for friends and family members, thus entering into a form of positive parental mediation that moves well beyond discussions of cognitive effects into active joint participation. Like the Blayne-Gallaghers, many families also spoke about the importance of developing trust between parents and teens that would enhance their relationships. Parents and young people offered two potentially competing rationales when they described why they embraced the parental mediation strategies related to these concerns, paraphrased here as the parental rationale of 'Media are acceptable when they are directed toward meeting familial goals,' and the young person's rationale: 'It's good parenting to trust in a teen's good judgment.'

participatory learning

The third concern of parents that guided parental mediation strategies was often not articulated, but provided an important lens through which these strategies were viewed: this was the concern of balancing work and family time. Parents and young people spoke indirectly of these concerns and their strategies regarding them, referring to the many after-school activities in which young people engaged, often while parents worked, and discussing the phone calls and text messages that allowed parents to stay in touch while meeting the demands of the workforce. The strategy of utilizing media to keep young people busy, and to keep them in contact with parents, were two important ways in which parents engaged in parental mediation strategies that had less to do with cognitive

balancing work and family time

Parental concerns	Strategies	Discussed in terms of	Rationales
Future of kids	• Restrictive mediation • Active mediation	• Homework, health, peers, bad influences • Cognitive development (stereotypes)	'It's good parenting to restrict.'
Family connectedness	• Active mediation • Coviewing • Calls, texts • Participatory learning	• Trust • Togetherness • Fun • Interaction, closeness	'Media are OK when meeting familial goals.' 'It's good parenting to trust.'
Work/family time	• Keep busy • Keep in touch	• Demands (school, sports, homework) • Checking in when not together	'Media are OK when meeting familial goals.' 'It's good parenting to trust.'
Self	• Keep busy	• Growing independence • Differing tastes	'It's good parenting to trust.'

Figure 17.1 Dimensions of parental mediation

awareness of media and more to do with demands on parents' time. Interestingly, parents often used the same kinds of rationales both for discussing the strategies of utilizing media to keep kids busy and for keeping kids in touch. Parents noted that they provided cell phones so that their children could keep in contact with them when they were apart, drawing upon the rationale that 'Media are acceptable when they are directed toward meeting familial goals.' They also accepted the fact that their children would sometimes utilize media in an unsupervised setting while the parents were otherwise engaged, drawing upon the rationale that 'It's good parenting to trust in a teen's good judgment.' Remaining unarticulated was the view that by allowing their young people to engage in unsupervised media time, media were being utilized to meet other familial goals, such as allowing a parent to go to work while the young person was at the home, or providing a young person with an in-home activity while the parent engaged in preparing meals, paying bills, cleaning, or otherwise maintaining the household.

The final concern of parents that guided parental mediation strategies, similarly, was not articulated explicitly, but also provided an important justification for parental mediation strategies. This was the concern for parental self-preservation and self-development. Often, discussions of strategies that addressed this concern surfaced in relation to the need to keep children busy while parents pursued their own interests or needs, and was also discussed in relation to the differing tastes in how parents and young people choose to spend their leisure time. The rationale that guided the strategy of keeping children busy (or allowing them to pursue their own separate interests) echoed earlier rationales: 'It's good parenting to trust in a teen's good judgment.'

parental self-preservation and self-development

More generally, the process through which parents make decisions about which course of action to take at any time can be termed the *emotional work of communication technologies*. Parents must take into consideration various aspects, including the emotional responses that they themselves will experience, and that they

emotional work of communication technologies

will encounter with their children, as they make their decisions. In the case of Norma Domentary, her concerns about Veronica's future development seemed to provide reinforcement for Norma's emphasis on 'strictness,' and provided her with a rationale for expressing her disapproving views about Veronica's media practices. But Norma, who had been through two divorces, had significant financial and health problems, and was currently unemployed, had a great number of stressors that demanded her attention. Veronica's separate activities, which included watching television at a friend's and being engaged in online and texting conversations while in their shared home, seemed to allow Norma to focus on her own concerns, even if, unfortunately, often at the expense of family connectedness. The conversations that they had about media and communication illustrated a dilemma: Veronica attempted to gain her mother's understanding, while her mother attempted to share her own views, but neither appeared to listen to and engage with one another in a process that would construct their family as one, and which might balance family and individual needs. In the end, Norma Domentary's emotional work of communication technologies seemed to further undermine their family's connectedness – Norma expressed a lack of trust in Veronica's media choices – and Veronica, in turn, experienced that lack of trust, and eventually moved out of the home.

The Blayne-Gallagher parents, Gwen and Stan, equally expressed concerns about their children's futures. This led them to engage in both active and restrictive forms of parental mediation. They put limitations on the websites that the children could visit, discussed the use of social network sites and other websites, and talked about stereotypes they encountered in the children's favorite media content. But, interestingly, the family viewed themselves as not 'restrictive' or 'strict,' but rather 'permissive' in relation to media. The family had a great deal of media available in their home, including not only magazines, computers, newspapers, music, and television, but additional electronic media and musical instruments in the home's 'public' spaces to encourage play and interaction. The parents utilized media as a means of inviting young people – both their own and their children's friends – into relationships, thereby addressing their family's concern with connectedness. They also used communication technologies such as the mobile phone as a means of keeping connected with one another, and of balancing work and family life. Gwen and Stan's lives were quite busy with the demands of work, but because their children would participate in individual media-related activities, they were able to pursue their own interests, which included reading and yoga.

In sum, the emotional work of communication technologies by the Blayne-Gallaghers seemed to enhance their family's connectedness, their parental ability to communicate their own values and to learn about the values of their children in turn, as well as their ability to balance needs of work, family, and self. There is no question that the Blayne-Gallaghers were a well-resourced family when compared to the Domentarys, and that their resources made it much easier for their family, among other things, to participate in parental mediation processes that constructed their individual and familial identities on the basis of mutual respect and connection.

By collectively assigning meaning to various strategies and rules, both children and parents in both families were participants in what Roger Silverstone has termed the "moral economy of the household" (Silverstone and Hirsch, 1992). Whereas Norma Domentary viewed the media as a problem that she as a parent needed to counteract, the Blayne-Gallaghers viewed media as a potential resource to be utilized in relation to parental and familial goals. Because their approach was echoed in other families, the study provided support for the development of a new category regarding parental mediation, namely, a strategy of *participatory learning* in which parents and young people strive to learn together through joint interactions with media.

moral economy of the household

The limitation of qualitative studies, of course, is that they cannot 'prove' that such a strategy is widespread, nor that such an approach is correlated with the factors that constitute the Blayne-Gallagher family: upper income, well educated, intact marriage, biracial, politically progressive. Each of these correlations must be tested in future research. Yet, the two case studies bring out at least two important facets of parental mediation theory. First, existing theories, generated and tested within quantitative research, proved useful in explaining several aspects of these cases. At the same time, the case studies identified one additional strategy (participatory learning), significant contextual variations of how each strategy is performed, as well as two additional concerns not accounted for in existing theories of parental mediation (balancing work and family time; parental self-preservation and self-development). Second, the cases shed light on the way in which communication research itself can be mobilized by parents in everyday life.◀ Like the Domentary family, the Blayne-Gallagher family articulated an awareness of the public discourse that advocates restrictive parental mediation, even while recasting this discourse in their own practices. Researchers need not take full responsibility for the uses of their research, for better or worse, but they should be mindful that the design of studies may result in arguments that variously reinforce, or challenge, the status quo.

GROUNDED – AND MULTI-GROUNDED – THEORY TRADITIONS

This chapter suggests that grounded theory◀ provides a useful way to think about complementary research traditions within the field of media and communication research. The tradition of grounded theory is one that has been examined extensively since its introduction in the late 1960s (Glaser and Strauss, 1967). Within communication studies, grounded theory has been employed in research that is rooted in symbolic interactionism and phenomenology◀ (see Arceneaux and Weiss, 2010; Dougherty, *et al.*, 2009; Hoffman and Cowan, 2010; Taxen, 2007; Thompson, 2008). The grounded theory approach is less prevalent, and thus perhaps less familiar, than are other forms of qualitative research within media scholarship (but see Livingstone, 2002, 2009a). Grounded theory, in brief, encourages researchers to gain an in-depth familiarity with the people and processes that shape a particular social group, organization, or institution, usually through in-depth interviewing and observation.

In recent years, scholars interested in grounded theory have reexamined what some have termed its 'pure inductivism,' or the idea that theories 'emerge' from data with little reference to prior knowledge (Bryant, 2002; Charmaz, 2000). In fact, many have argued for more attention to existing theories within the field that is being studied (Bruce, 2007; Kelle, 2005; Seaman, 2008). Goldkuhl and Cronholm (2010) have pointed out that the act of generating theory is separate from the act of grounding it, and that scholars need existing theory by which to ground their own work.

Goldkuhl and Cronholm have proposed 'multi-grounded theory' as a means by which to retain the creative aspects of data collection and data analysis that have been the hallmarks of the grounded theory tradition. They have advocated a three-pronged approach that includes:

multi-grounded theory

1 constructing theories that are grounded in empirical data (mainly obtained through an inductive approach);
2 exploring one's data in relation to preexisting theories that are selected with reference to the theorized phenomena; and
3 ensuring that emergent theory has what they term 'internal grounding,' or internal coherence and consistency across the analyst's own data, the existing theories reviewed, and the theory that the analyst ultimately develops.

Goldkuhl and Cronholm further argue that a multi-grounded theory can lead to three types of results: findings can help the analyst to comment on or criticize existing theories; they can provide a more explicit theoretical grounding of earlier research; or they can lead to an adaptation of an evolving theory.

In this chapter, I have suggested an adaptation of the evolving field of parental mediation research. Rather than concluding a study with a list of findings, a multi-grounded theory provides a conceptual account of how the participants in a study resolve their main concern, as Glaser

▶ double hermeneutics – Chapter 19, p. 351
▶ grounded theory – Chapter 14, p. 278
▶ phenomenology – Chapter 2, p. 30

(2001) argued (Giske and Artinian, 2007). In this way, grounded theory is a practice of *naming*: specifically, naming the process that has been observed, but also naming the main concerns of the study's participants, and naming the core categories that explain how participants resolve those concerns. In the present study, I identified four main concerns that surfaced in conversations with parents: the children's future, family connectedness, balancing work and family time, and parental self-preservation and self-development. I then outlined how these concerns related to parental mediation strategies, as established in previous quantitative research and complemented here by a qualitative approach. Specifically, I analyzed the terms in which parents and young people discussed both the concerns and the strategies, while also developing categories to account for the rationales that they used to describe the overall process. I summed up these practices in a reference to the emotional work that is involved in using and regulating communication technologies in family contexts.

CONCLUSION

In this chapter, I have suggested that multi-grounded theory provides a model within which researchers with differing epistemological commitments can work together in the development of communication theories. I have argued that 'thinking with,' rather than testing theories of communication is one of the ways in which qualitative researchers can advance the complementarity of different approaches within the field of media and communication research.

thinking with vs. testing theories

Because qualitative researchers work with small samples, their studies cannot 'disprove' a theory. However, qualitative researchers who are attentive to a potential disconnect between what a theory presumes and what is experienced and observable in actual social settings, can contribute to a grounded understanding of the limits of the theory, thereby developing the theory. In this chapter, I have shown how parental mediation theories need to look beyond the explicit intentions that are rooted in parents' concerns for the future of their children, taking into account, as well, those contextual actions that are rooted in additional concerns relating to family connectedness, the balancing of work and family demands, and the parent's own self-preservation and development. Parental mediation, thus, requires a theory of how parents and children participate in everyday communicative processes that serve to construct both personal and familial identities as part of a larger social order.

Because qualitative research, among other things, foregrounds issues concerning the researcher's own reflexivity, it lends itself to a questioning of the very forms of communication that researchers themselves participate in constructing. Different methodologies result in different deliverables, not just as coins of exchange or as representations of reality, but as forms of communication with diverse constituencies: colleagues, policy-makers, parents, and, importantly, research participants themselves. Qualitative research can enable researchers to consider their work from the standpoint of wider contemporary discussions, including the possibility that research may be used differently from that which we, as researchers, intended. This, in turn, suggests the very real possibility that our theories need to be revisited – not just for the sake of theory development, but as part of our responsibilities as researchers interacting with the public realm.

18 Personal media in everyday life

A baseline study

Rasmus Helles

- a study of the place of personal media – from *mobile phones to social network sites* – in everyday life
- an exploration of the relationship between *life phases* and the uses of personal media
- an illustration of the application of *multiple methodologies to new, digital media*
- a discussion of how to utilize *log data* of media use in communication research
- reflections on the translation of *epistemological premises into methodological practices*

INTRODUCTION

The study reported here began its life in a series of conversations during the fall of 2004, as I was finishing my master's thesis, and looking around for an interesting and fundable PhD project. I had given a presentation of my MA thesis work (a study of an online community) at a company that I was secretly hoping to convince to fund part of my PhD project. After the presentation, I was talking to a senior manager from the company, explaining my interest in new media and interpersonal communication when she interrupted me. She had just thought of something that would interest me: the mobile phone had ruined the equality of her marriage.

Both she and her husband held demanding, management-level career positions in large companies, and had done so since the beginning of their relationship some 15 years earlier. When they moved in together, they had made a clear agreement that traditional gender roles should have no place in their shared life. They had managed this through a strict division of domestic labor, and an equally strong separation of work and leisure time: no calling each other at work unless it was a matter of life and death. About a year prior to our conversation, their daughter, who was now ten years old, had begun using her mobile phone to call her parents at work, after school. The couple had explained their agreement about work and leisure to the daughter, who had been instructed to call only about really important things. But since children's interpretation of 'importance' differs from that of adults, the result had been a call or two per day. The man had upheld family policy, and would tell the daughter he had very little time to talk. The woman, however, had found that she actually liked those few minutes on the phone, and had come to think of the small chats about the daughter's day at school as small breaks in her busy schedule. The formal division of domestic labor in the home had continued, she told me, but because of her more or less daily chats with the daughter, a number of obligations had somehow shifted from being shared, to being hers. Both she and the daughter had come to see her as the obvious parent to handle requests concerning school and other activities because she was already involved.

The story made a deep impression on me as an illustration of the complex social effects of technologically mediated communication. Eventually, the conversation led to a research project that was designed as a baseline study of personal media in Denmark in a theoretical framework emphasizing the relationship between interpersonal communication and everyday life. After all, mobile phones follow their owner through all the different social contexts that make up everyday life. Also, mobile communication is largely trivial. Leaving aside those rare occasions when the content of the communication is of vital importance to those involved, such as the death of a loved one or a phone call to end an intimate relationship, mobile communication belongs in the realm of the quotidian, the repetitive—the everyday.

MASS MEDIA AND PERSONAL MEDIA

Interpersonal communicative practices

During most of the twentieth century, the number of media for interpersonal communication in the Western world remained relatively constant. Letters and the landline telephone were the primary media used to communicate over long distances and, for letters, with a time shift.◄

From the late 1980s, a number of new media technologies began to emerge. Fax machines challenged the position of ordinary letters, and during the first half of the 1990s, the mobile telephone began to be commercially available at prices that made it a potential consumer good, even if it took close to ten years before half the Danish population owned a mobile phone. With the arrival of the internet, also during the first half of the 1990s, people gained access to several new media for interpersonal communication. Some were variations on one-on-one-communication, such as chat, instant messaging, and, in particular, e-mail, which many met through professional use at work, but quickly appropriated for private purposes. Other new media afforded entirely new forms of technologically mediated communication, most notably chat rooms and online fora, allowing groups of people to interact, both in real-time and with a time delay. Some years later, the ill-defined and much hyped technologies of 'Web 2.0' essentially re-launched a number of these 'old' (in terms of internet history)◄ communication media, fitted for use with a standard web browser, and often with more user-friendly interfaces. Not all these media are used by everyone, as elaborated below, but with the internet reaching nine out of ten Danish households, and more than 90 percent of the population owning mobile phones (The National IT and Telecom Agency, 2011: 34), it is clear that the landscape of personal media has been profoundly changed by the arrival of the internet and the diffusion of the mobile phone.

The parallel existence of several different media technologies, which offer a host of different variations on the fundamental theme of interpersonal communication, calls for an integrated view of those media. Accordingly, the project broadened its original focus on mobile phones and mobile communication, to include all media that afford interpersonal communication, and adopted the term *personal media* for them.

In Table 18.1 (Jensen and Helles, 2011), some of the most common media are listed according to their central affordances◄ for communication. The model uses two dimensions of communication as organizing principles: the number of participants involved in the communication process, and the temporal dimension of communication, whether it is asynchronous or synchronous.

One way of defining personal media is to include all technological media that allow some form of turn-taking◄ among those involved. This definition effectively excludes mass media, which do not allow members of the audience to participate, at least not *en masse*, but at the same time broadens the field of interpersonal communication from one-to-one-communication to also include group communication (or many-to-many communication). (For an alternative definition of personal media, see Lüders, 2008.)

► timeline of communication technologies – Chapter 2, p. 26

► internet history – Chapter 12, p. 233
► affordances – Chapter 1, p. 5
► turn-taking – Chapter 6, p. 119

Table 18.1: A typology of communicative practices (personal media indicated with gray)

	Asynchronous	*Synchronous*
One-to-one	E-mail SMS, MMS Letters	Telephony (fixed-line and mobile) Instant messaging
One-to-many	Newspapers, books CDs 'Web 1.0'	Television Radio
Many-to-many	Social network services Online fora 'Web 2.0'	Online chatrooms Online multiplayer games

The other major distinction in Table 18.1 is between synchronous and asynchronous communication, depending on the users' ability to insert time delays in the flow of communication. Taken as a whole, the model also suggests the importance of considering the intermediality◀ (Jensen, 2008a) of the various forms of personal communication: The possibility of substituting one medium for another (using text messages (SMS) instead of telephony), obviously introduces a whole range of social and interactional potentials, which only become apparent once the various media are understood as a system of alternatives.

Trans-situational agency

In theoretical terms, the technological mediation of interpersonal communication allows human agents to exercise *trans-situational agency*. The term, which was coined for this study, indicates that, in contrast to face-to-face-communication, technologically mediated communication allows users to act across physical and, in some respects, temporal distances. We can reach people in other countries in a matter of seconds, and a text message may linger in an inbox for hours or months before it is read. The capacity of media to have communication transcend physical and temporal boundaries, and to influence activities in distant contexts, is a longstanding theme of medium theory.◀ However, compared to the texts of mass communication, which have been the focus of attention in medium theory, the transactions taking place in interpersonal communication are typically much more directly and immediately oriented towards ongoing activities that involve those communicating (Hutchby, 2001). The diffusion of personal media enables the ongoing flows of communication to cut across situational boundaries, and they allow individuals new degrees of freedom in choosing how to handle both their involvement with other people and the demands and opportunities that otherwise arise from the various contexts of everyday life.

Most previous work on media and everyday life concerns the mass media, especially television. Within the framework of domestication theory,◀ some work has been done on media for interpersonal communication (for references on early work see Haddon, 1998), but with a somewhat limited scope. Since its initial formulation (Silverstone and Hirsch, 1992), domestication theory has primarily focused on the dynamics of information and communication technologies in the home, as families negotiate a place for those media in their daily lives – a focus inherited from earlier studies of families' collective reception of television (Lull, 1980; Morley, 1986).◀ While several studies have been done on personal media (for an overview of recent developments see Bakardjieva, 2006;

▶ intermediality – Chapter 10, p. 188
▶ medium theory – Chapter 2, p. 24
▶ domestication theory – Chapter 9, p. 184
▶ contexts of media use – Chapter 9, p. 176

Hartmann, 2006), the theoretical tenets of domestication theory do not incorporate trans-situational agency. The tradition still conceives of media as technologies 'with texts inside,' which families and other users collectively make sense of, not as vehicles of communication across contexts.

In the case of personal media, this focus on processes of social interaction in contexts of copresence represents a shortcoming. Personal media are exactly – personal. This is true in a discursive sense, since these media typically address individuals: you have your own mobile phone, your own profile on Facebook, and you enter discussions in online fora as an individually addressable entity. It is also true in a physical sense: personal media may be carried around or, as with most e-mail accounts, the person may access them from computers anywhere in the world

The ubiquitous access◀ to personal media makes it possible to act in one social context, while being physically present in another. Whereas all technologically mediated communication is obviously contextualized (in the sense that, when placing a call, communicators are already present in some situation with a social logic of its own (see, e.g., Humphreys, 2005; Ling, 2008)), mobile phones and other new media of interpersonal communication introduce a second contextual layer. Arising from technologically mediated interaction at a distance, this layer may well be governed by completely different norms, which will somehow have to be balanced with those of the first context.

It can, in fact, be argued that trans-situational agency involves a third contextual layer, namely, the context in which the person in question negotiates his or her exercise of agency across two situations at once. Not only do personal media allow us to act across contexts; they demand that we decide whether and how we actually want to do so. My choice of whether or not to distract myself from my chores at work by calling a friend for a chat depends on several considerations: the culture and etiquette of my workplace, the willingness of my friend to chat, but also on my perception that this is a relevant activity in the first place. Perhaps I have not had a minute to myself for days, and so decide that I deserve the break, even if I suspect that my call may inconvenience both my friend and my coworkers; or I decide that although I would like the break, I cannot run the risk of my friend going into another one of his long monologues about his troublesome boss. In this perspective, the use of personal media should be understood not only with reference to newly developed cultures of communication in specific contexts such as work or home, but also in terms of the trans-situational agency that individuals exercise as part of their entire portfolio of everyday activities.

▶ ubiquitous communication – Chapter 1, p. 9

THE CONDUCT OF EVERYDAY LIFE

Trans-situational agency involves new degrees of freedom in the management of everyday communication, which requires a nuanced understanding of how people balance the different social contexts against each other. Such an understanding is provided by the sociological theory of the conduct of everyday life, developed by Gerd-Günter Voss (1991) (an English résumé of central points may be found in Dreier, 1999). The conduct of everyday life is defined as follows: "The conduct of everyday life is … the system a person has built to combine his or her activities in the various social spheres that he/she is part of in their current life phase" (Voss, 2001: 203ff., my translation RH).

The conduct of everyday life can be understood as a logic that we apply in order to make the various parts of our everyday life fit together. Although we all take part in many types of social activities which are prototypical (e.g., having a job which demands the same kinds of things of us as it does from thousands of others), the entire portfolio of elements in our lives is, in principle, unique: I am the only one to experience having *this* job, and *that* partner, live in *this* neighborhood, with relatives who have *these* needs, etc. The only one to experience the *totality* of demands, constraints, and possibilities offered to me by this particular constellation of elements is – me. So, even though many of the elements are relatively prototypical, in the

logic of everyday life

sense that there are many who face the same elements that I do (jobs, living arrangements, etc.), I am the only person to experience them in my *context*.

A simple example is that I may have a job that demands me to be somewhere at a particular time. Depending on where I choose to live (or can afford to live), that particular demand on my time will have different consequences. If I live close to work, I can fulfill that demand and still have time for a hobby that requires a lot of effort; but if I have a two-hour commute every day, this may be impossible, or it may require me to give up something else. Although such demands are prototypical, my everyday life is a unique totality woven out of a combination of these prototypes.

An important aspect of the conduct of everyday life is that it is not entirely up to me how to organize things; it rather constitutes a compromise between my obligations and the degrees of freedom which are afforded by the various social institutions that enter into my life. If I am married and live in a nuclear family, this places certain kinds of demands on my life; if I live alone, I have different degrees of freedom, but also different constraints.

degrees of freedom

The conduct of everyday life is the manner in which I accomplish all this – it is the overall logic that I rely on to make things come together. I may choose to do as little as possible, and take things as they come; or I may try to maximize control over all the elements of my life. Over time, we each develop a certain style of handling the different elements of our everyday lives. Like the account of trans-situational agency above, the theory thus emphasizes the individual component of human agency. Although interactional contexts have specific, local sets of norms and routines, the people interacting in them bring their own agendas, preferences, and resources, which contribute to the outcome of their interactions, on a par with the norms and values that are specific to the situation.

The theory of the conduct of everyday life, presented here only in a skeletal form, speaks directly to the location of personal media in everyday life, particularly in its emphasis on trans-situational agency. Personal media in everyday life are intimately connected to both the general logic and the specific balancing acts of everyday life, as we try to forge a vast number of heterogeneous elements into a coherent and meaningful whole.

Describing and understanding how people integrate the affordances of personal media into their conduct of everyday life was the fundamental aim guiding the design of the research project. Since the theory states that the conduct of everyday life is shaped in an interplay between individual and institutional factors, a mix of qualitative and quantitative methods appeared useful. This multi-method approach, together with the premises of the theoretical framework, also invited an assessment of the complementary forms of evidence within a realist framework, as presented in Analysis Box 18.1.

THE BIG PICTURE: QUANTITATIVE ANALYSIS

Secondary analysis◀ of available statistics

When the project was first begun, little data was available on the diffusion and use of various personal media in Denmark. Statistics Denmark, the national statistical authority, did not yet include them in their annual survey, and nobody had tried to collect and consolidate what data there was. In order to create an overview, all available representative surveys of the use of personal media were collected. It turned out that relatively comparable data existed, as most of the major personal media had been subject to individual studies within the same one-year period. Also, most of these studies satisfied the other minimum criterion for inclusion in a diffusion analysis,◀ namely, they had been based on a random sample with at least N = 1,200 respondents, ensuring a reasonable level of statistical representativity and accuracy of measurements. Also, studies had to focus on the use of the various media for private communication only.

The most difficult part of this exercise was not finding the actual numbers, but to secure sufficient documentation of the research behind

▶ secondary data analysis – Chapter 13, p. 247
▶ diffusion research – Chapter 8, p. 155

ANALYSIS BOX 18.1: REALISM AND RETRODUCTION

The theory of the conduct of everyday life lends itself to a realistic◄ interpretation of the relationship between social structure and human agency.◄ In a realist perspective, social structures have properties of their own which cannot be explained with reference to social agents alone (Archer, 1995; Elder-Vass, 2010). Social structures are held to exist in their own right, even if their functioning only manifests itself in human activities. Compared to mainstream sociological structuration theory (Giddens, 1984), which takes structure and agency as two aspects of the same process, a realist interpretation allows for two ontological domains, which are only united through practice. In the present case, the conduct of everyday life has an existence of its own, independent of the individual social actor who relies on it to manage the various elements of his/her life.

A realist ontology entails an epistemological and methodological stance. Social structures have qualities which can be expected, to some extent, to function independently of the perspectives placed on them by social scientists. Social regularities, moreover, are not *only* the product of interactions between individuals, but crucially *also* a product of certain mechanisms, of which the interactions are a part. Whereas a social constructivist◄ would expect surface interaction to be all there is to know about, a realist takes interaction as indicative of underlying social structures or mechanisms.

Realism, accordingly, favors a retroductive research strategy – the aim is to 'work back' from observable phenomena to uncover the mechanisms of the underlying social structures (see Blaikie, 2009: 87ff.).◄ The starting point of a retroductive strategy is the construction of a theoretical model of the social structure to be studied—in this case, a model of the interplay of the general conduct of everyday life, both with large-scale social institutions such as families and labor markets, and with the specific trans-situational affordances of personal media. The premise of the project was that particular models or types of the conduct of everyday life would shape people's use of personal media, which might in turn reshape that conduct to some extent. In order to address both structures and degrees of freedom, the project combined quantitative and qualitative approaches – both of which document real aspects of everyday life.

the numbers. About a third of the studies grew out of marketing efforts (when the buzz about 'social media' marketing was just beginning to gain momentum), and the results were often published at commercial websites or in newspapers, without links to documentation about sample sizes, sampling process, etc. Through repeated requests to people at various newspapers and marketing bureaus, documentation was eventually secured for a sufficient number of studies (five in total).

Ironically, and perhaps indicative of the 'presentism' of much work on new media (Wellman, 2004), the only two personal media that had to be left out of the comparison were landline phones and letters. It simply was not possible to determine how many people still use letters as part of their private communication. And although the numbers for landline phones were available, the unit of analysis◄ was the household, not the individual, so that it was not possible to compare these numbers to those for e-mail, chat, and mobile phones.

presentism

The results of the secondary analysis are shown in Figure 18.1. Perhaps the most notable finding was that the only new, personal media to have achieved full diffusion (at or above 84 percent) (Rogers, 2003) at the time were mobile telephony and SMS (text messages). E-mail was the only other new medium used by more than half the population. Although Facebook's

► realism – Chapter 15, p. 297
► structure and agency – Chapter 10, p. 200
► constructivism – Chapter 3, p. 51
► retroduction and abduction – Chapter 15, p. 293
► unit of analysis – Chapter 13, p. 249

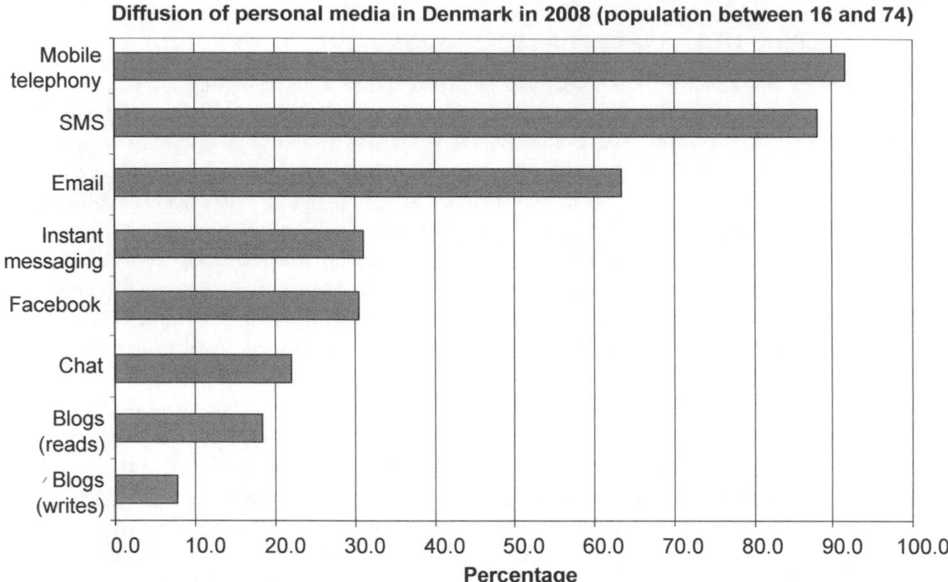

Figure 18.1 Diffusion of personal media

user base has grown substantially since the survey data used in the figure were collected, the numbers for Danish Facebook users still suggest a diffusion level of 'only' 51 percent of the population between 16 and 74 years of age (The National IT and Telecom Agency, 2011: 44). The numbers are noteworthy because they indicate that the diffusion process is both slower and more complex than often assumed in hype about new media in advertising and parts of academic research.

(Since the data available for landline phones were not directly comparable to other data (because of a different unit of analysis), they were not included in the figure. The numbers for landline phones, however, indicated that a minimum of 76 percent of the population had access to these at home, which suggests that landline phones at the time were actually the third largest medium for interpersonal communication, at least in terms of the percentage of the population who were potential users.)

The findings on diffusion were interesting for the wider project because they shed light on general changes in the media landscape of interpersonal communication. They clearly demonstrated that at least some new, personal media were now routinely used by the majority of the population. What these first findings did not address was the level at which these different media were used, and which social groups might be using them most. Specifically regarding the conduct of everyday life, the numbers had nothing to say about the way in which, and the extent to which these new media were being integrated into everyday life.

Mobile telephones and life phases

The second part of the empirical analysis took the form of a detailed study of mobile phones, conducted in cooperation with a major telecom provider in Denmark. The provider had a very large panel of customers, who had all agreed that their call logs could be used in analysis and development projects. The company agreed to make an anonymized sample (N = 10,000) of parts of the panelists' call logs for 2007–8 available for detailed study.◀

▶ research ethics – Chapter 19, p. 366

ANALYSIS BOX 18.2: SAMPLING AND REPRESENTATIVITY

The sample was drawn from the panel of the telecom provider, and was balanced in two ways. First, the age, gender, and regional variables were weighed, so that the sample would resemble the composition of the total population according to official demographic statistics. Second, the size of the sample was calculated so that it could be broken down into age and gender segments of five years, and still be used for statistical analyses and comparisons of sufficiently large groups. This led to a sample size of N=8,531.

It should be emphasized that the sample used, no matter how large, was not a random sample.◀ The participants in the panel had volunteered, which may introduce a bias, since not everybody is likely to agree to have their call logs analyzed. In addition, the sample was drawn from the customer base of one particular mobile phone company; although it is one of the three largest in the country, and probably the one with the most diverse customer base, its customers are not likely to be representative of the entire population. Although the sample was large (and could have been two or three times larger if desired), the *only* way to ensure that measurements of a sample yield results which are statistically representative of the population, is to draw the sample at random, that is, all individuals in the population must have an equal chance of being included in the sample (Blaikie, 2003). The non-representative sample had ramifications for the presentation of results: no confidence intervals for findings are given here (i.e. no mean values were presented as 'average number of SMS messages per day was 15(±3)'), since the calculation of confidence intervals requires a representative sample (but see Analysis Box 18.3 about the use of means in the analysis).

The data comprised a week-by-week summary of phone call and SMS activity over a period of 12 months, and a call-by-call log of one week of activity. In addition, the gender, age, and home municipality of the participants were included. No details that could identify the panelists were given and, importantly, no information at all was provided about the other people with whom the panelists had communicated. In other words, both samples contained only information of traffic generated by the panelists, not about calls or messages received. The one-year-sample contained week-by-week aggregated data on the number of phone calls, total number of minutes spoken, and total number of SMS messages sent. The week sample included information about the date and time of all SMS messages and phone calls, in addition to the duration of all phone calls. The week in question was the third week in March, which had been identified as the most normal (or least extreme) by comparing the total number of minutes spoken and SMS messages sent during all weeks of the year. (On sampling and representativity, see Analysis Box 18.2.)

▶ random sampling – Chapter 13, p. 245

The clearest finding, if not the most surprising one, was that age is extremely important in explaining both phone calls and SMS messages. Figure 18.2 shows the median value of weekly SMS and call volumes, distributed on age groups. It shows that almost 180 messages are sent every week by the group under 18. This is nearly double the volume of the 18–23 year-olds, who 'only' send 87 – two numbers that may seem impressive. However, since the analysis only documents outgoing traffic, the total number of SMS messages handled by members of each of the two age groups is probably twice as large: messages are, most likely, reciprocated. It is also clear that while the youngest respondents use SMS a lot, they do not make voice calls nearly as much: the number of weekly calls is at the same level as in the 30–39 group. It is further apparent that although both media are in use in all age groups, the appetite for either one appears to be inversely related to age after the mid-twenties: the volume of both SMS and voice calls is lower in the older age groups. (These apparently clear findings, however, present classic issues of reliability and validity.◀ See Analysis Box 18.3.)

▶ reliability and validity – Chapter 13, p. 240

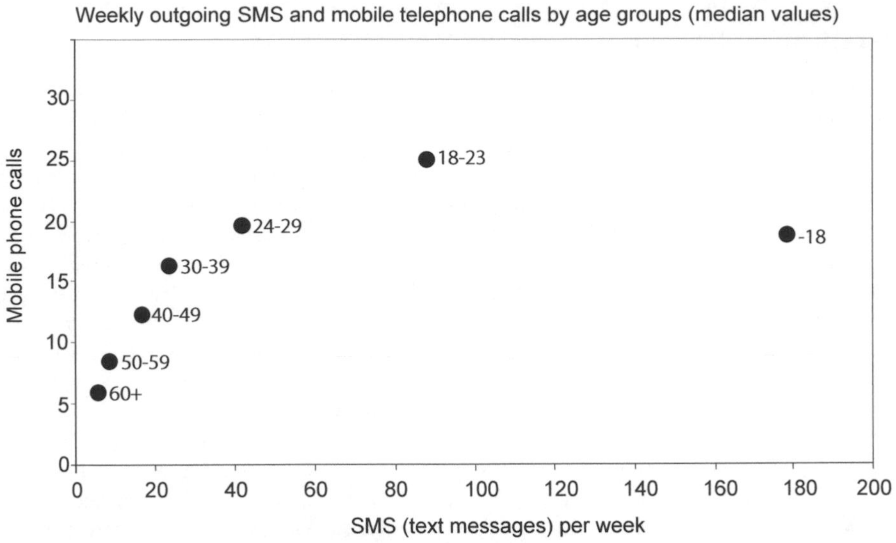

Weekly outgoing SMS and mobile telephone calls by age groups (median values)

Mobile phone calls

SMS (text messages) per week

-18 · 18-23 · 24-29 · 30-39 · 40-49 · 50-59 · 60+

Figure 18.2 Mobile media use and age

Note: Age groups do not span equal numbers of years.

ANALYSIS BOX 18.3: RELIABILITY AND VALIDITY

Quantitative analysis is, most fundamentally, about the quantification of some property of reality, and the subsequent analysis of data. Whereas elaborate statistical procedures are available, the analysis can sometimes be done simply by producing and inspecting a graphical representation of the data collected. Irrespective of the type of analysis, however, questions of reliability and validity must be addressed.A statistical procedure comes with a number of assumptions that the data must meet; otherwise the procedure is inappropriate, and is likely to produce misleading results.

The data behind Figure 18.2 provide an example of this consideration. The figure shows the median value of the weekly SMS and call frequencies of the different age groups, instead of the more commonly used mean or average value.◄ Because there are extreme differences in people's use of these media, reporting average values becomes problematic. This is because averages are often taken to say something central about a given phenomenon – and often does, as with people's heights: we know that some people are taller than others, but we also know that most people have roughly the same height, with men tending to be somewhat taller than women. By saying that Danish women have an average height of about 168 cm, we assume a number of things, above all that most women's height will be close to this average, say, within 10 cm to either side. Only about 4 percent of all Danish women deviate more than 30 cm from the average. Women's heights, then, are symmetrically distributed around the average: 50 percent of women below, 50 percent above the average height. This is because human heights follow the normal distribution, illustrated by the dotted line in Figure 18.3. The average height is located at the peak of the line, and the figure shows both that the average height is the most common, and that there are many people close to the average height.

► mean and median values – Chapter 13, p. 259

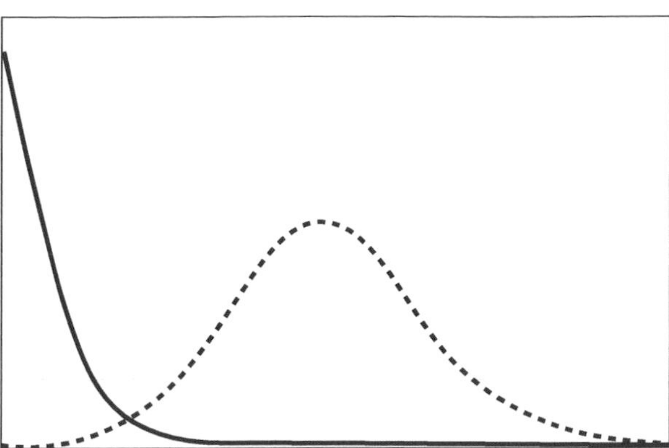

Figure 18.3 Normal (dotted) and log-normal (solid) distributions

SMS use patterns, in contrast, do not follow a normal distribution, but rather follow the solid line in Figure 18.3, a so-called lognormal distribution. Most people send a relatively small number of SMS messages, while a small number send many. Some of the top SMS users in the sample sent more than 1,000 SMS messages every week, while some of the least active users sent only one or two messages per month. Put differently, high-activity users send between 2,000 and 4,000 times as many messages as low-activity users. Compared to women's heights, someone tall (198 cm) is only about 1.4 times taller than someone short (138 cm). If, then, the average level of SMS activity (in the present sample it was 69 messages per week) is reported without reservations, readers might assume that this is a good approximation of what 'normal' SMS use is. But, in fact, almost 75 percent of the sample had an SMS use below the average. In a normal distribution, it would be 50 percent.

Reporting the median value (which in this sample was 26 messages per week) gives a very different impression of SMS use patterns. The median is the 'middle value' of a sample: lining up all users from high to low according to their SMS use volume, the median value is the SMS usage of the person in the middle of that line. The median value, thus, separates the top half from the bottom half of the sample values. On the one hand, using the median to represent the central tendency of a sample does not explain as much about the sample as the average value does about a normally distributed sample; the values are more extreme, and no single number can communicate this. On the other hand, this does place the given number closer to the SMS use patterns of most people in the sample, limiting the risk of misunderstandings. Moreover, the median is more robust in terms of fluctuations in the data, and tended to be constant from week to week in the present one-year sample, whereas the average value shifted on the order of almost 10 percent from week to week. In sum, even for such seemingly simple calculations as central tendency, issues arise both of their reliability (because the average value is vulnerable to small fluctuations) and of their validity (in the sense that an 'average' value may not correspond to what the term commonly suggests). Such difficulties help to explain why log data as used here are seldom encountered in media studies (but see Leskovec and Horvitz, 2007), which, in turn, may limit the use of a valuable type of data in this field.

One observation from Figure 18.2 sparked a more specific hypothesis. The figure indicates a remarkable difference between the 18–23 and the 24–29 groups. The activity on both media is quite a bit lower in the older group, yet the age difference is only a few years. This prompted an investigation of whether the differences between the two groups should be considered a cohort or dynamic phenomenon. If a cohort phenomenon, the use pattern for both media would be established at some point in life, and would later stay more or less the same. If dynamic, media use would be tied to external changes, such as the introduction of new media or other events in the users' lives. A review of the literature on digital media and age showed that the cohort hypothesis has been the dominant notion. A widely used concept is that of the 'digital native' (Prensky, 2001) – somebody who has grown up with digital media, and therefore has an intimate understanding of them, compared to others who have taken them up later in life. The notion that media habits are the outcome of socialization during childhood and in the teenage years seemed in conflict with the present finding of significant differences between the 18–23 and the 24–29 groups.

cohort and dynamic phenomena

In order to address the issue, data for the panel members' SMS use in November 2007 and 2008 were compared. (Together with March, November is the month when SMS and call activities are closest to the annual average.) The results showed a clear and statistically significant drop in activity in all age groups from one year to the next (Figure 18.4). The only exception was the 60+ group, in which no significant drop was found.

These results, next, were compared with data from the National IT and Telecom Agency, which showed that the total use of SMS in Denmark did not drop between 2007 and 2008, but had in fact grown by 6 percent per active subscription. The sample exhibited a drop in activity, then, whereas SMS use in Denmark as a whole did not. Together, the numbers strongly suggested that as members of the sample grew older, they reduced their level of SMS usage – indeed, quite a rapid change of media habits. As a way of further controlling the results, the level of activity for users who were 18 in November 2007 was compared to that of users who were 18 in November 2008, and this analysis showed no significant difference.

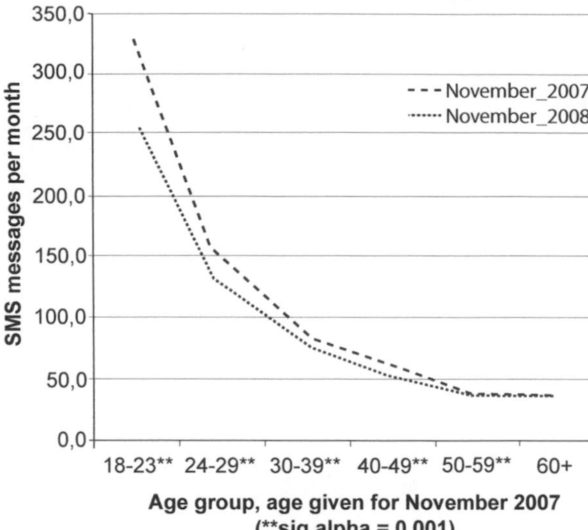

Figure 18.4 Age and text messaging

In other words, the activity level of 18-year-olds was constant between 2007 and 2008, but the panelists who were 18 years old in 2007 changed their use pattern during the following year. Research done by Rich Ling (2010), based on Norwegian survey data, found a similar pattern.

In sum, SMS patterns appear to change dynamically with age, and quite fast, not according to cohorts. This central finding is consistent with the view that technologically mediated communication is embedded in, and contextualized by, the rest of people's everyday lives. Whereas different theoretical frameworks might fit the data, the theory of the conduct of everyday life would suggest, as a preliminary explanation, that the changes in media use coincide with typical shifts in young people's life situations: leaving the social life of high school, including a large peer group with intense SMS communication, and replacing it with a smaller circle of close friends and a daily life balancing the demands of workplace and home. To further explore the implications – the concrete interplay between personal media use and the conduct of everyday life – the project also relied on qualitative analysis and on mixing methods (Analysis Box 18.4).

ANALYSIS BOX 18.4: MIXING METHODS

The project combined quantitative and qualitative methods in order to answer its research questions – despite the fact that qualitative and quantitative methods are still widely held to be incommensurable (Blaikie, 2009: 218ff.). Qualitative methods deal with the subjective experience of situated individuals; quantitative methods deal with patterns and regularities as discovered in data that are decontextualized and generalized via a process of quantification, such as the fixing of subjective experience to a limited choice of answers to a survey question.

This balkanization of qualitative and quantitative methods can be seen to rest upon a conflation of method and ontology.◀ While the data of qualitative methods normally do consist of accounts of subjective experience, such as interview discourses, the methodological constraints and affordances of these data depend on particular theoretical conceptions of 'subjectivity.' To a social constructionist, questions about the structural 'realities' that are reflected in subjective accounts make no sense, since there is no social realm beyond subjective experience (Collin, 1997). Under a realistic ontology, the notion of everyday life as an individual project of balancing the demands of various social structures and institutions against each other highlights the layered nature of both society and subjectivity. Social structures are open *to some degree* of interpretation and manipulation by the individual subject. But social structures are never merely optional objects of subjective experience.

THE DEEP PICTURE: QUALITATIVE ANALYSIS

A typology of everyday life with personal media

The qualitative dimension of the project sought to incorporate findings from the quantitative analyses, specifically via its sampling strategy. The quantitative findings indicated that people between 18 and 35 years of age are commonly engaged in an ongoing reorientation of their personal media use. In the theoretical perspective of the conduct of everyday life, these shifts could be addressed in qualitative analyses through two different considerations.

First, people who are in the process of changing their personal media habits as part of a (hypothesized) change of their conduct of everyday life are likely to have reflected, to a degree, on the potential benefits and drawbacks of these media. Respondents were chosen not because they would use such media more than others – people with low or no use of personal media might be just as interesting interview subjects – but because they would be in a position to recall and reflect on these in everyday contexts.

Second, sampling people in one age bracket – their twenties – would likely give access to, or insight into, other age groups, namely, friends and family members, who would be affected by their changing habits. At the same time, qualitative interviewing could provide additional perspectives on other personal media. The quantitative findings indicated that *something* is positively going on with the personal media use of people in their twenties, *at least* changes in their SMS and telephony patterns. Other things might be going on – with other media and in other age groups.

The qualitative design combined maximum variation sampling◀ and snowball sampling.◀ First of all, two women in their twenties were identified by way of the author asking friends for the names of people unknown to him, but which his friends knew and could characterize in terms of age (in their twenties) as well as social background. This resulted in contact with two young middle-class women who each, during the first part of an interview, were asked to fill in a 'network map' – a basic form with fields for entering the age and gender of a maximum of 20 network map

▶ levels of scientific analysis – Chapter 15, p. 287

▶ maximum variation sampling – Chapter 14, p. 269

▶ snowball sampling – Chapter 14, p. 270

friends and family members, and for indicating the nature of their relationship. For each person they also ticked a battery of boxes noting which personal media they used to communicate with that person, and how often. After the interview, the author selected two people on the map who were of different gender and different age from the respondent, and asked her to help establish contact with them. In this way, a total of 13 respondents, from 24-year-olds to 85-year-olds, and spanning the lower to the higher middle class, were identified. People between the ages of 18 and 35 were deliberately over-represented (6 of the 13) in view of the quantitative findings. All respondents, then, originated from one of the two social networks around the two initial respondents.◀

The qualitative analyses had a dual aim: to describe the everyday logic of the respondents, and to establish the specific ways in which they had incorporated personal media into this general logic. A special point of attention in the interviews was any dynamic change in habits, whether drastic (young people cutting the number of SMSs sent per month by several hundred within a couple of years) or minor (a middle-aged person perhaps sending five to ten messages less per month over the same time span). The theory of the conduct of everyday life proposes a typology of prototypical ways of handling the everyday. Although everyday logics are, in principle, individual, they draw on social templates. Individuals will pick up techniques for handling daily life from others, not least their parents, and they will refer to the wider culture. The theoretical tradition and many of the original studies into the conduct of everyday life came out of Germany, and while culturally close,◀ Danish everyday life differs, not least, when it comes to gender relations. The proportion of women in full-time jobs is higher than in Germany, and has been for many years, which is clearly reflected in the empirical findings. However, the general typology of three main categories – traditional, situational, and strategic everyday practices – proved highly applicable also to the Danish data.

▶ social network analysis – Chapter 10, p. 190
▶ cross-cultural research – Chapter 11, p. 212

The situational type

Popular reports about the influence of mobile phones on everyday life are often caricatures of the situational type: people who cannot plan ahead, with an attention span barely bridging the gap from one SMS to the next. The situational respondents, while certainly not planning ahead as people might do 'in the old days,' in fact do a lot of planning. They live life in an ad hoc fashion, making many plans, and nearly as many revisions, often at the very last minute. Life often appears hectic (not least to themselves), and the respondents made frequent reference to the problems (and disappointments) that their behavior would cause other people. When asked if they would be able to write down a list of events for the coming week which, importantly, they would expect to follow, the answer was typically a resounding 'no.'

The situational types are the *gourmands* of personal media. Available for contact on several platforms simultaneously, they make ample use of the potential of personal media for trans-situational agency, organizing their everyday life through a permanent flow of mediated conversations, messages, and e-mails. One example is Morten (27), who balances life as a medical student with two different part-time study jobs, a small company he runs with a couple of friends, and home life with his girlfriend. He uses media to engage in social interaction during short intervals when he can find the time:

> I find that I often use those five-minute breaks [between activities]. I don't know ... others may see it as a bad thing, but ... I think it is really useful. I mean, if I'm on my way to the supermarket, then I might as well use those five minutes to call a friend. [my translation, RH]

As mentioned, people living by the situational logic often find themselves in conflict with other people's values and expectations. In the quotation above, Morten hints that 'others' may see his constant re-mixing of social situations as 'bad.' In context, it is clear that this refers both to those who happen to be around him in the street or the supermarket, and to whoever he is talking to. Respondents note that people

ANALYSIS BOX 18.5: REDUCTION IN QUALITATIVE DATA ANALYSIS

Quantitative data analysis involves reduction in several obvious ways, such as the expression of the central tendency of thousands of data points in a single measurement. Qualitative data analysis, equally, involves reduction in important, if sometimes unrecognized ways. Interviews that are conducted face to face are usually analyzed in transcribed form; findings are aggregated and reported in (more or less dense) academic discourse, far from the social realities being reported. Whereas qualitative analysis is sometimes held to be holistic and 'thick',◀ it invariably involves a number of operations that recall the selective and sequential nature of quantitative data production (Blaikie, 2009: 208ff.).◀

In the present qualitative analysis, a number of characteristics that were shared across the everyday logics of the respondents were aggregated into a typology – which reduced the data in several important ways. Thirteen concrete presentations of everyday life with personal media were the foundation of three types, illustrating how contextualized and individual narratives can be abstracted in more general use patterns. None of the 13 respondents matched just one of the derived types exactly, but were assigned to the type with which they had the strongest affinity. The three types are just that – idealized and simplified analytical constructs, not likely to be found in identical form in reality.

resent being transformed into an audience by a stranger having a personal conversation right next to them, as well as receiving a call from a friend who has only five minutes in the supermarket for them.

Nevertheless, the media stereotype of heavy users of personal media with short attention spans did not apply to the four respondents in this study. On the contrary, they appeared extremely adept at multi-tasking: juggling many different situations at the same time, and keeping in mind the procedural hierarchies of each, more or less all the time. If they come across as sloppy, it may have more to do with the degrees of freedom they experience across various situations. Morten, quoted above, frequently shifts between physical locations (he works in three different offices), and often does not know exactly how long he will spend at his different jobs during a week. Stating very clearly that this makes planning difficult, he is looking forward to a phase of his life when things will be more stable. Indeed, the situational logic may not fit his personality.

multi-tasking

The same is true of Birgit (50), who also makes heavy use of personal media in a complex daily life. She has retired from the labor market due to a complicated illness that, in some periods, makes her so tired she is unable to do anything; these periods come without warning, and often last for several days. She lives alone, but has an active social life involving her two grown-up daughters and a number of friends. And, like the other three situational respondents, she is almost always available on several different media platforms. Messenger programs open automatically when she logs into her computer, and Facebook is the default home page in her browser:

> I don't go on Messenger because I want to contact anyone in particular. But when I open my computer there's always someone online, and often somebody writes 'hey you're online' or I write that to somebody, so ... To me, Messenger is about having fun and writing things like that.

It is clear from the interview that Birgit cultivates several different sets of friends on different media platforms. By mobile phone, she will arrange to meet a couple of friends at the café of the local mall; on Messenger and other chat sites, she sometimes spends hours writing with various friends, many of whom

▶ thick description – Chapter 14, p. 273
▶ qualitative data analysis – Chapter 14, p. 275

she has only met a few times face to face. The qualitative interview uncovers how the logic behind these elaborate media habits is closely linked to her illness, in particular the fact that sudden tiredness makes her unable to make and keep appointments. By maintaining different contacts on different media platforms and with different levels of involvement, she can participate in social circles that match her abilities at any given time.

It should be added that before she became ill, Birgit worked as a secretary at the senior management level in a large corporation, and led her life according to a very different logic, with a tightly controlled calendar and a strict set of priorities that she would never change with short notice. Like Morten, she makes it very clear that she would prefer to do things differently if she could. The situational logic of everyday life, then – the heavy use of personal media, and the juggling of many simultaneous social relations – is a way of managing very different contexts with very different types of demands, over which the individual has little or no control. Other people may find this social type disorganized and forgetful; they themselves experience a somewhat chaotic daily life. But, the alternative would be for them to reduce their involvement in these various contexts, at the risk of having nothing to do or nobody to talk to.

The traditional type

The traditional type is the direct opposite of the situational type. People living their everyday lives according to this logic follow a cyclical model in which social events are typically repeated on particular days and at set times. They maintain a clear division between work and leisure, and tend to follow traditional gender roles regarding the division of domestic labor. This repetitive character of everyday life makes the use of calendars almost superfluous. Several respondents in this category can recite long lists of who they are going to see, when and where, and what they will be doing together, as they have done so often before with those same people in exactly the same way. One person tells of recurrent dinner dates with two other couples, always on the second Friday of the month. In this group, spontaneous actions amount to what one of the respondents referred to as 'planned spontaneity': non-repetitive events, but planned well in advance. She and her husband would typically plan 'to do something' on a particular evening, and then decide 'what to do' on that day.

planned spontaneity

Respondents in the traditional group indicated that they would use personal media almost entirely for 'ritual' forms of communication: calling their spouse at work to make small talk or calling friends to confirm plans. Although they appear to use personal media less intensively than the situational type, the traditional respondents do make frequent use of them, also as a way of crossing the line between work and leisure, which otherwise is the central divide of their everyday logic. Compared to the other types, however, the traditional type has clear and firm rules guiding what kinds of contact can be initiated where and when. If they make private calls during the day, these only go to members of their household and very close friends, whereas they will contact other friends and acquaintances during the evening. This strict segregation of time zones follows largely from the orderly and repetitive organization of their everyday life, with little ad hoc coordination through communication. One respondent was not entirely comfortable with the way her everyday life came across in the interview (she thought she made her life sound boring and petit bourgeois) when she described how her husband would pick her up on their way home from work. This is organized on a day-to-day basis, but the 'spontaneity' only relates to the exact timing of the event within the same 30-minute window of every afternoon.

time zones

The ritual aspect of personal media use in this group also manifests itself as a preference for telephony over other personal media. The ritualized form and content of the telephone call fit the predictable timing of the call itself. Several in the traditional group emphasize that they like calling others and cherish the opportunity to go through the motions of a well-executed phone call with a friend. While they use other personal media, the synchronous and reciprocal nature of the phone call is presented as something special.

Not surprisingly, people operating by a traditional logic have a particularly hard time when they enter into social relations with situational types, who invariably break up an orderly everyday. When discussing the resulting conflicts, the traditional group of respondents in many ways mirrors, but inverts the arguments that were offered in the situational group. Both groups seem to acknowledge that the values underlying the traditional logic is the default social norm, so that other logics could be considered violations of a dominant norm. The traditionalists do what everybody says one ought to do; situationalists say what they might like to do in a different kind of everyday.

Age, again, matters: the traditional logic may seem more attractive to older people than to the young. Still, two of the five people in the traditional group were under 30, and described preferences very similar to the three older respondents – a clear and cyclical everyday logic – despite a more intensive social schedule.

The strategic type

The final type of everyday logic, while equally concerned with the stability of life, pursues a dynamic equilibrium, rather than a cyclical model. Like the traditional, unlike the situational group, on any given Monday morning these respondents know what their week will be like – but, in contrast to the traditional type, their weeks may differ. They allow the line between work and leisure to shift, but make sure that, if work predominates for a while, there will be additional leisure time at a later point. They also have clear principles regulating the division of domestic labor in the household but, in contrast to the traditional group, gender does not necessarily represent a principle guiding who will perform which tasks: the point is the total workload and its division among family members.

dynamic equilibrium

The strategic group accomplishes a dynamic balance of different obligations by being calendar enthusiasts (Nippert-Eng, 1996). They have strict principles about separating different spheres of their lives, even if they sometimes allow work to flow into their spare time. When they work at home, they do not want to be disturbed, just as they do not like family and friends calling them on the mobile phone at different times of the workday.

calendar enthusiasts

In terms of different personal communication practices (Table 18.1), they are strong believers in asynchronous communication. They switch off mobile phones and instant messenger programs when they know they do not have the time to communicate. In contrast, they like SMS and e-mail, precisely because it allows them to control the separation of different kinds of social activities. Anne (26) expressed this succinctly:

> I think it's because ... you give more of yourself in a phone call ... talking on the phone is kind of a social situation, and you don't control how things develop in quite the same way [as you do with e-mail] ... e-mail and SMS is more of a one-way situation, isn't it?

The ritual nature of phone calls makes them difficult to escape, and may tie you up in conversations that do not fit into the situation where you find yourself. The interviews in the strategic group returned several times to the issue of selectivity, specifically how to use personal media to control one's availability for communication. Unlike the traditional type, the strategic type has no problem sending people on to their voicemail if they do not have the time to talk. But, they emphasize that they always make sure to call the person back.

The strategic separation of different everyday activities is explained, in part, by a desire to do many things, and to do them all well. All respondents in the strategic group made explicit reference to career goals as a priority in their everyday lives. Another important point seemed to be securing uninterrupted time for other things. Like the situational type, they involve themselves in many different kinds of things, but they keep a clear focus on separating them from each other, so as to perform all activities to the best of their ability. Facilitated by the affordances of personal media for trans-situational agency, these separate spheres of action become a series of 'aquaria' in which to immerse oneself. The strategic type, thus, appears adept at creating the conditions for attaining a state of flow (Csikszentmihalyi,

1997), undisturbed by other people or by switches between different frames of mind.

CONCLUSION

The sampling strategy for the qualitative part of this project on personal media in everyday life was based on insights from its quantitative component. The profound changes in this regard among people in their twenties that were suggested by the quantitative analyses were articulated in distinctive ways in the interviews. Both the respondents in that age bracket and their networks of family and friends recognized that the communication patterns of the 20-somethings were changing – importantly, however, they did not conceive of these as 'communication' changes, but as changes in their entire way of life that 'necessitated' such changes. While all three logics – situational, traditional, and strategic – were in evidence among respondents between 20 and 30 years of age, the younger respondents evidently led a social life that involved a more intensive use of personal media. The transition to adult life, with new types of responsibility, was described as inevitably affecting one's conduct of everyday life in general, and one's personal media use in specific ways:

> [Why do you feel you're wasting your time on SMS?]
>
> It's because the exchanges grow so long. When many friends have to meet up, 1,700 SMS messages that are sent back and forth, or people call each other, instead of making an appointment for the next time you'll meet when you are actually together [...] I think that when people grow up and have full-time jobs and children, then [communication] becomes something that you can do only when you have time. (Mette, 25)

This quote by Mette, who follows a traditional logic, reflects an awareness of the way things will have to be once she has other obligations in life, including what may already be her preferences: fixed appointments and using media only when the time is right. The quote also suggests the dramatic changes of everyday life that people in their twenties experience. Two women in their twenties, who had given birth in the last couple of years, recognized, for one thing, that they spent more time talking on the phone to their mothers and close friends. For another thing, they noted that being a parent influenced the topics of these conversations. Across the life span, longer conversations with people who are intimately aware of one's life situation may be required. For this purpose, a new kind of personal media is now available.

The project documented a number of ways in which the social uptake of personal media is circumscribed by everyday life. The quantitative analyses demonstrated how changes in the patterns of media use among young adults coincide with changes in their life phases. The qualitative analyses detailed how the affordances of personal media are integrated into the conduct of everyday life by different age groups and social types in distinctive ways. Another theme emerging from this research was personal media as a system of communicative alternatives, rather than as separate media. Both of these perspectives – communication across the life span and intermediality – lend themselves to quantitative, qualitative and, as suggested by the present study, multiple methodologies.

19 The social origins and uses of media and communication research

Klaus Bruhn Jensen

- a presentation of several *types of 'theory'* that link research to social practice
- a review of the *normative theories* of media
- an account of media and communication *research as a social institution*
- a description of the main applications of media research in *policy* and *politics*
- a discussion of *ethics* and *logistics* as aspects of the interchange between *researchers*, the rest of the *academic community*, *respondents*, and *the public* at large

THEORIES IN PRACTICE

Making public

This final chapter returns to some of the 'big' issues that motivate both individual media researchers and the commercial and public organizations housing and funding them. Why study the media? (Silverstone, 1999). Media are sources of both meaning and power. Like their objects of analysis, media studies originate from particular historical, cultural, and institutional circumstances; they contribute to shaping the conditions under which communication will take place in the future. If media are institutions-to-think-with,◄ university departments and other research units constitute second-order institutions-to-think-with, describing, criticizing, and reflecting on the role of media in society – past, present, and future.

double hermeneutics

Media and communication research participates in a double hermeneutics (Giddens, 1979) by interpreting media – their institutions, discourses, and users – and feeding those interpretations back into society at large. One implication of hermeneutics is that all human and social practice is informed by 'theories' – generalized conceptions of what the world is like, and how we may engage it, individually and collectively (Lobkowicz, 1967). Whereas researchers are often, sometimes deservedly, perceived as too theoretical – detached from the world of practical affairs – "nothing is as practical as a good theory," as suggested by one of the founders of media studies, Kurt Lewin (1945: 129). By examining the different types of theory that media professionals, legislators, and ordinary users hold and act on, communication theory can make a practical difference.

Researchers publish. Publication in journals and at conferences, however, is only one way of presenting findings and insights. To make research public is to make it available and accessible for social use. The audiences of research can be large or small, specialized or general, representing consensual or oppositional views of society, and assessing its relevance in either

publication: research into social practice

► media as institutions-to-think-with – Chapter 1, p. 16

the short or the long term. Among the key audiences are media businesses that pay, not only to have studies conducted, but to make sure, for competitive reasons, that findings are *not* published. The further effects of media research, like those of media, are diverse and difficult to predict; they include unanticipated – and unrecognized – consequences for the media, their users, and for researchers themselves.

Following a brief account of five different kinds of theory, this chapter first reviews the so-called normative theories of media. Those theories have fueled the rise and subsequent transformations of the modern mass media, and they still motivate much contemporary research. The next section traces the development of media and communication research. The intellectual cultures driving its academic and commercial variants have emphasized, to varying degrees, either 'policy' or 'politics' – concrete collaborations with the end users of research, or long-term contributions to understanding, and perhaps changing, the role of media in society. Qualitative as well as quantitative approaches enter into studies from both policy and political perspectives – methodological boundaries, to a degree, dissolve when it comes to the social uses of research. In conclusion, the chapter reviews a number of political, ethical, and practical issues that arise in planning and conducting media studies – from student projects to national and international research programs.

Five types of theory

In his classic textbook, Denis McQuail (2010) has laid out five types of theory addressing media and communication:

- *Scientific* theory is the most common understanding of 'theory.' It refers to general explanatory concepts and models that apply to a specified set of empirical instances. Historically, it has been associated particularly with natural sciences, and with social-scientific research traditions that rely on surveys, experiments, and other quantitative methodologies.
- *Cultural* theory is the legacy of arts and humanities. It covers textual, historical, and other qualitative approaches to the interpretation and social uses of media.
- *Normative* theories address the legitimate ends and means of organizing media as a public infrastructure of communication. As such, they occupy a middle ground between scholarship and public debate and policy.
- *Operational* theory is made up of rules of thumb and sometimes tacit knowledge that (media) practitioners hold, including professional and ethical standards (Schön, 1983).
- *Everyday* theory, finally, underlies the common human practice of communication – our interaction with media institutions and with each other as citizens, consumers, and sources of information in our own right. While it often remains an implicit, practical consciousness,◄ everyday theory may be articulated through research.

Academic communication theories are, in one sense, much less important than other types of theory – neither media professionals nor media users need explicit or abstract theories in order to communicate. McQuail's typology itself illustrates the grounding of theories in practice. It emerged ad hoc, not as "a systematic, empirically grounded typology … It developed gradually as a way of describing what I was doing and accounting for different ways of thinking about mass media" (personal email communication, March 20, 2007). In preparing the first edition (McQuail, 1983), he was especially concerned that everyday or commonsense notions of media and communication be included as a kind of theory. Lay theories (Furnham, 1988) are indispensable guides to everyday life. The academic definitions of what counts as (scientific) theories themselves change over time. In the fifth edition of the textbook (McQuail, 2005), the original four types of theory had become five: cultural theory now appeared in parallel with (social) scientific theory. While rooted in the social sciences, McQuail recognized the two "as having more or less equal weight. I suppose this does reflect an obvious development and greater integration of the 'field.' "

lay theories

► practical consciousness – Chapter 8, p. 161

A common denominator for the five types of theory is that they enable action – in media research, production, policy, education, and public debate. The interrelations between the five types are of special interest in a field that has developed, in important ways, as a practical discipline that understands itself as solving communication problems.◀ As such, communication research has the opportunity to affect journalism and other media production (operational theory) as well as educational programs advancing media literacy (lay theory).

Normative conceptions of communication occupy a special place at the juncture of theory and practice. Like academic theories, they are general. They assess the pros and cons of different ways of organizing media and communicative practices on a macro-social scale. Unlike academic theories, normative theories of media involve the general public in assessments and deliberations. In addition to classic discussions concerning a commercial free press, a publicly funded broadcasting system, or an open-architecture internet, normative considerations bring up the ideological and existential implications of communication: the meaning of communication, as in "the meaning of life" (Jensen, 2008b: 2803). Political and existential aspects of communication are the questions that most people care most deeply about.

communication as a political and existential issue

NORMATIVE THEORIES

Normative theories illustrate how ideas with a long history can be mobilized for contemporary purposes. Some of their constituents date from the Renaissance and the Enlightenment, even from the Socratic dialogue as an avenue toward truth, and doing what is morally good. As currently defined, the normative theories of media and communication were formulated in the shadow of the Cold War. Also in the present field, that period pitted different models of society against each other. The classic publication (Siebert, *et al.*, 1956) identified four theories, with special reference to the printed press:

the Cold War

- *Authoritarian theory*. The medieval understanding of public communication took for granted a cosmology – at once social and religious – in which everything had its rightful place, and where information flowed top-down from the monarch, the representative of divine authority on earth. This so-called Great Chain of Being◀ – or pyramid – could be understood as enabling individuals to flourish en route toward their destiny. Only especially reliable individuals were allowed to disseminate information on any social scale, still subject to censorship. Audiences were just that – recipients of messages from political and religious authorities who knew better. While rarely advocated as such, authoritarian media theory provided a point of departure from which the other theories would distance themselves in distinctive ways.
- *Libertarian theory*. It was liberal theories of politics and communication that first came to challenge authoritarian models. Liberalism informed the larger shift from traditional to modern social structures, as articulated in and symbolized by the public sphere.◀ Not only were humans redefined as ends in themselves, with certain inalienable political, economic, and cultural rights; humans were also conceived as rational animals with the capacity to collectively define and administer such rights. One unifying metaphor became the 'marketplace of ideas' (Peters, 2005), suggesting both that ideas might be advertised, bought, or declined in a market of sorts, and that the economic market for goods and services could advance this cultural and political process. Free enterprise and the competition of ideas, arguably, would benefit the public interest and the common good.
- *Totalitarian theory*. The occasion for formulating the normative theories, as noted, was the Cold War, specifically the implementation of a totalitarian or communist theory of the press in a number of countries following World War II. The distinction between totalitarian and

▶ communication as a practical discipline, Chapter 1, p. 2

▶ the Great Chain of Being – Chapter 2, p. 29

▶ the public sphere – Chapter 1, p. 17

authoritarian theory (and their relationship to 1930s fascism) has been debated. A central characteristic of totalitarian theory, however, was the understanding of central control over the media as a means of fundamentally restructuring society, rather than preserving an existing social pyramid. Centralized state control, moreover, applied to all means of production, whether it was meaning or material goods being produced. Whereas the communist press systems in Europe broke
1989 down after 1989, in the People's Republic of China the Party-state remains in control of the main media.◀

- *Social responsibility theory*. After 1945, a growing concentration and conglomeration of media called into question the classic liberal notion of a 'free press.' In the case of radio and television, the number of channels was further limited, at least for a period, by the available bandwidth. More generally, because their operation requires significant economic resources and professional skills, mass media have tended to be few and large. In response, normative theory witnessed a shift of emphasis, from liberal and free-market ideals toward an understanding of the press and other media as trustees, or representatives of the general public, that ought to exercise social responsibility. European public service broadcasting represents a particular type of media that embody social responsibility theory. Other instances include quality newspapers that could be said to deliver "public service for private money" (Lund, 2001: 41).

public service broadcasting

Formulated in the 1950s, the four types of normative theory seemed less applicable to some later media developments. Specifically, media systems in the developing world, and media that facilitate public participation – from community radio to the internet – prompted the formulation of two additional positions (McQuail, 1983):

- *Development theory*. In the wake of decolonization, the 1960s witnessed renewed debates about media in the 'Third World' (while the other two 'worlds' were confronting each other in the Cold War). As addressed also in theories of intercultural communication, cultural imperialism, and postcolonialism,◀ the issues included structural inequalities as well as imbalances in the flow of news and entertainment in the world. Interests in the area were complex and often conflicting: the generally desirable 'free' flow of information in the world must be weighed against the rights of states and nations to shape their own media systems, and to gain a hearing in world media. At the same time, references to 'free flow' and 'self-determination' could be used as fronts for either economic expansionism or the silencing of critical voices locally. While difficult to articulate as one normative position or theory, development communication has continued to generate both research and public debate, including the existence of digital divides (Compaine, 2001), both between and within countries. digital divides
- *Democratic-participant theory*. Particularly in the Western world, the 1960s witnessed a second type of social upheaval, centered in anti-authoritarian movements that engaged in social and cultural criticism as well as political mobilization.◀ On the one hand, the quality and diversity of the mass media was again being questioned. On the other hand, new information and communication technologies offered cheaper and more accessible means of political and cultural expression (Enzensberger, 1972[1970]). Just as social-responsibility theory had identified the limitations of liberal press theory, democratic-participant theory pointed to a lack of social responsibility in practice in mainstream media. The participatory ambition fueled various print and electronic 'grassroots' media (Downing, 2000; Glessing, 1970), and it gained new momentum with reference to the interactive potentials of the internet (Jenkins, 2006; Rheingold, 1994).

▶ Chinese media system – Chapter 11, p. 208

▶ intercultural communication, cultural imperialism, and postcolonialism – Chapter 11, p. 212

▶ anti-authoritarian movements – Chapter 3, p. 65

Research has continued to develop and debate normative media theory (Christians, *et al.*, 2009; McQuail, 1992; Nerone, 1995), with implications for national, international, as well as intercultural communication. One difficulty of assessing the relative merits of the various positions has been the vagueness of some of the key concepts that they share, specifically the 'freedom' of media in relation to both state and market, and the 'rights' of individuals, groups, and private and public organizations to communicate. As noted by Jürgen Habermas (1989[1962]: 226) in his classic treatise on the public sphere,◄ rights come in two main variants – positive and negative. Whereas some political theorists and practitioners have advanced a negative definition (freedom *from* state interference into the affairs of individual citizens), others have emphasized a positive definition (freedom *to* require certain provisions and services from the collective). A negative definition marked the transition to the modern period when, from the eighteenth century, the new middle classes asserted their rights in opposition to the authority of the state. A positive redefinition, involving more substantial economic regulation and social services along Keynesian principles, was the outcome of world economic crises in the late nineteenth century and during the 1930s. Recently, a positive conception of rights reappeared on the agenda of international politics and communication, following the financial and economic crises that generated massive state support of markets from 2008.

from negative to positive definitions of freedoms and rights

When considering positive and negative rights of communication (and of other social interaction), one should keep in mind that current research, policy, and public debate address highly regulated societies and media. The relevant question is not so much the presence, absence, or *degree* of regulation – 'less state interference, more freedom of expression' – but the *kinds* of regulation that apply to different types of media at various levels of social organization – from legislation supporting national film production to international agreements governing the assignment of internet domain names. Also in the future, media and communication researchers will be asked to assess who benefits most from specific conceptions of the general right to communicate – which was included in the 1948 Universal Declaration of Human Rights (United Nations, 1948: Art. 19). The 'four-plus-two' normative theories continue to provide useful reference points for clarifying some of the abstract political, economic, and cultural ideals that inform public and policy debates.

► the public sphere – Chapter 1, p. 17

The normative theories represent, in pragmatist terminology (Perry, 2001), beliefs that individual communicators, media corporations, and entire societies are prepared to act on. Roughly since the 1956 formulation of the normative theories, the field of media and communication research has established itself as a social institution with diverse instrumental as well as reflective uses. The field emerged at several crossroads of theory and practice, state and market, and conflicting intellectual currents.

MEDIA AND COMMUNICATION RESEARCH AS A SOCIAL INSTITUTION

Intellectual cultures

In a classic statement on theory and practice, Karl Marx noted, in his *Theses on Feuerbach* (1845), that "The philosophers have only interpreted the world, in various ways; the point, however, is to change it." While individual researchers may see themselves as administrators, reformers or, occasionally, revolutionaries, research as an institution necessarily participates in shaping and maintaining modern society. Over time, a great deal of basic research comes to be applied. Compared, however, to a widespread nineteenth-century notion of science as a means of both material and cultural progress, much twentieth-century research found itself struggling with its sense of a mission. For one thing, the complicity of research in world wars, colonialism, and debatable forms of social engineering raised profound doubts about the traditional legitimacy of institutions of learning. For another thing, the growing availability and accessibility of information through mass media meant that the status and social uses of research lent themselves to increased and intense public scrutiny.

basic and applied research

Media and communication research took shape after 1945 at the juncture of several intellectual and disciplinary cultures. The history of the modern university (Fallon, 1980; Rudy, 1984), in one aspect, is the history of reality being partitioned into manageable domains, to be studied through increasingly specialized theory and methods, and to be managed in practical affairs by specialist graduates from these domains. Following the founding of the modern research university in the early 1800s,◀ the late nineteenth and early twentieth centuries had witnessed the establishment of social sciences as a separate faculty alongside the humanities.◀ A recognizable specialty of (mass) media research emerged from the 1930s, as witnessed by the early 'milestone' studies that are laid out Figure 9.1.

It was not until the 1950s, however, that an institutionalization of the field occurred, centered internationally in the social sciences, but in diverse national configurations (Resource Box 19.1). Studies began to accumulate a distinctive body of findings, theory, and methodology. During the same period, humanities departments, including film, literature, linguistics, and history, similarly prepared important contributions to the field. They did so, both by extending their domain of interest beyond high arts and histories emphasizing the classic institutions of political and economic power, and by revising their analytical procedures and theoretical frameworks. Following the anti-authoritarian upheavals of the 1960s, which questioned both establishment uses and disciplinary boundaries of research, a process of interdisciplinary convergence across social-scientific and humanistic traditions gained momentum from the 1980s, while collaborations with partners in public administration, private business, and civil society, were consolidated and diversified.

One continuing debate has considered whether media and communication research constitutes an established (or emerging) discipline, or a more loosely configured interdisciplinary field (for an overview, see Levy and Gurevitch, 1994). Regardless of nomenclature, there is no doubt that the field has a permanent presence in academia, in the media themselves, and in other social institutions; the indicators include university departments, scholarly journals, conferences, consultancies, and participation in public debate. At the same time, it should be recognized that the field has remained heterogeneous. First, summative studies have suggested the existence of three relatively self-contained literatures, representing social sciences, interpretive studies, and critical analysis (Fink and Gantz, 1996). Second, other analyses have found that, at least in journal publications, quantitative studies outnumber qualitative ones, and that combinations of the two are still comparatively rare (Kamhavi and Weaver, 2003; Trumbo, 2004). Third, until quite recently, communication study has consisted of two separate subspecialties, focusing on interpersonal and mass communication, respectively (Rogers, 1999). Last but not least, digital media have recently produced increased interest in research across the mass and interpersonal prototypes, both in existing flagship journals and in new journals (Tomasello, *et al.*, 2010); digital media also provide specific opportunities for research across traditional qualitative-quantitative and online-offline divides (Jensen, 2011).

field or discipline?

interpersonal vs. mass communication

In his frequently cited account of divisions within academia, C. P. Snow (1964) identified two separate, even opposed cultures, represented by "the literary intellectuals" and "the physical scientists" (p. 4). The social sciences occupy a third position, sometimes a middle ground. Humanistic, natural-scientific, and social-scientific◀ research traditions generate specific forms of knowledge about different reality domains, each with characteristic social uses. Furthermore, the three faculties have been associated with distinctive conceptions of epistemology and politics – how human knowledge of reality is possible in the first place, and why new knowledge should be produced. All scientific knowledge is interested in the sense that it serves (more or less controversial) human and social interests.

arts and sciences

▶ the modern research university – Chapter 2, p. 23
▶ social sciences as a separate faculty – Chapter 3
▶ humanistic, natural-scientific, and social-scientific models of communication – Chapter 1, p. 10

RESOURCE BOX 19.1: HISTORIES OF MEDIA AND COMMUNICATION RESEARCH AS A FIELD

In recent decades, more historical accounts of the development of the field have begun to appear (for overview, see Park and Pooley, 2008). While such publications bear witness to the fact that media and communication research has been consolidated, both as an academic discipline and as a social institution, its origins and implications have remained contested. In overview, two main tendencies internationally have been the centrality of US social science in setting research agendas around the world since the 1950s, and a more recent move, since the 1980s, toward a convergence of social-scientific and humanistic traditions.

Debates reflect the various administrative and critical, functionalist and emancipatory positions that have informed the field from the outset, theoretically and politically; history is being claimed and written by several self-defined victors. In addition, different national and regional research traditions have developed. The following sources offer a variety of accounts and reflections on the development of the field:

- *The International Encyclopedia of Communication*. This milestone reference work (Donsbach, 2008) includes overviews of developments in different regions of the world, under the common heading of 'Communication as an Academic Field.'
- *North America*. As a prime mover of international communication studies, North American research has produced some of the most comprehensive – and contested – accounts of itself. Following an early contribution by Delia (1987), the 1990s witnessed a number of interventions in the genre of 'remembered history,' as told by key figures in the field. Wilbur Schramm, widely considered the central figure shaping and institutionalizing communication studies in the US, published a personal memoir, supported by perspectives from Steven M. Chaffee and Everett M. Rogers (Schramm, 1997). Dennis and Wartella (1996) presented an edited collection with contributions from several central US figures, including accounts of the roots of the field in Europe and in Chicago School sociology. In a review of that volume, Hanno Hardt (1999) suggested that this 'remembered history' by key individuals served more as professional position statements than as an analytical historiography. In a monograph, Hardt (1992), in contrast, emphasized critical and interpretive aspects of US communication studies, linking these to philosophical pragmatism and the wider intellectual history of the United States. Recently, more researchers have revisited and, in part, rewritten the North American history of the field, as exemplified by contributions in Park and Pooley (2008) and an article by Karin Wahl-Jørgensen (2004), who documented important interdisciplinary sources and tendencies before – and in contrast to – 'the founding of the field' by Schramm.
- *Europe*. Compared to North America, media and communication research in Europe has been shaped, to a degree, by differences between countries – in their media systems, academic traditions, and national cultures (McQuail, 2008). Vroons (2005) offered an overview of the different starting points in the mid-1950s. Nevertheless, European research can be characterized as a crossroads between significant US influences and a variety of humanistic sources and critical perspectives. Together, current European and North American communication research can be taken as an international ecosystem in which studies are characterized more by theoretical and methodological traditions that span the continents than by their origins in national academic cultures.
- *Asia*. The field of communication naturally gives rise to considerations about national, regional, and cultural specificities,◄ first, of the media and, second, of research *about* media and the

► intercultural communication and cultural imperialism research – Chapter 11, p. 212

communicative practices they afford – its methodologies, epistemologies, and ontologies. While such considerations are ongoing, to varying degrees, in different regions of the world, research in east and south Asia, traditionally dominated by US approaches, has recently advanced debates about whether and how to 'de-westernize' communication research. A collection edited by Georgette Wang (2011) includes a range of perspectives from Asia, Europe, and North America on culture-specific and universal aspects of human communication, and on the complementarity of different regional research traditions.

Knowledge interests

The concept of knowledge interests implies that purposes – sometimes implicit or unrecognized – are fundamental to any scientific inquiry. Importantly, knowledge interests are not merely reflections of the personal convictions of researchers or of the institutional agendas of their commercial or public funders. Knowledge interests are constitutive of methodology and epistemology – the principles and procedures that guide different research practices.

While the notion is familiar from classic debates about human and social values in science and scholarship, the concept of knowledge interests was formulated as such by Jürgen Habermas (1971[1968]). He distinguished three types, each relating to a particular reality domain and university faculty:

- *Control through prediction*. In natural sciences, a central purpose of inquiry is to be able to plan activities in the material world. Predictions and hypotheses that can be tested under controlled circumstances enable human intervention into and, to a degree, control over nature. Modern experimental sciences have mastered the natural environment to an unprecedented degree by developing, refining, and accumulating criteria that describe and anticipate physical, chemical, and biological processes. As such, science has facilitated the management of natural resources, time, and space in social planning on a grand scale, notably in agriculture and industrial production. (*Media example*: Quantitative surveys predicting the preferences of media audiences.)
- *Contemplative understanding*. In the humanities, scholarship has traditionally centered on cultural forms of expression that are examined by contemplation – interpretation through introspection. Artworks, for one, can be understood as ends in themselves that are analyzed for their immanent meaning and value. Historical events, for another, might bear witness to universal, even eternal aspects of the human condition, even if the religious overtones of contemplating mundane events have gradually been downplayed. By disseminating their interpretations of cultural artifacts and historical events to the general public, humanistic scholars have served as the professional keepers of cultural tradition. (*Media example*: Qualitative studies interpreting media representations of social reality.)
- *Emancipation through critique*. The modern social sciences came to occupy a middle ground between natural and human sciences, addressing both material and experiential, collective and individual perspectives on social life. Because it is in a position to imagine unrealized potentials, Habermas suggested, the distinctive knowledge interest of social-scientific inquiry is one of human emancipation. By performing a critique of prevailing forms of social organization, and identifying alternatives, the social sciences can promote the emancipation of humans from the conditions in which they find themselves. (*Media example*: Democratic-participant models of communication.)

The three forms of knowledge interest are, of course, ideal types, subject to a great deal of variation and combination in scientific practice. (Habermas later changed his position (Wessler, 2008), but his original account still offers a helpful comparative framework.) Habermas (1971[1968]), further, argued that the different knowledge interests do not transfer well from one reality domain to another. In particular, he noted that if the more technical knowledge interest of the natural sciences is pursued within the social sciences, their emancipatory potential may be lost. The argument is familiar from media studies that consider, for instance, television audience meters and the online tracking of internet users as means of social control (e.g., Ang, 1991).

It should be added that a critical knowledge interest does not equal, and does not necessarily entail, a specific ideological criticism of the social status quo. If criticism involves a rejection of what is, and the identification of a preferred alternative, critique amounts to asking, what if? Like communication as such, research draws on the human capacity to consider how things might be different (Jensen, 2010). Also critical research is concerned with researchable, rather than merely debatable issues, with a view to action. The relationship between knowledge and action has been approached in distinctive ways in different social sectors.

critique and/vs. criticism

Sectors of research

The intellectual currents and knowledge interests of the field have fed variously into companies, organizations, and agencies that depend on research findings and insights as part of their operations. Early on, Lazarsfeld (1941) pointed to two main purposes of media and communication studies:

- *Administrative research* refers to goal-oriented and instrumental studies that resolve specific issues for the purpose of developing, planning, or maintaining some communication activity, typically in the commercial sector. Studies in this vein "solve little problems, generally of a business character" (p. 8).
- *Critical research* addresses the wider social, cultural, and historical issues that technologically mediated communication raises, often in a user perspective and with reference to the public interest. Here, studies take up "the general role of our media of communication in the present social system" (p. 9).

When describing the critical variety of communication research, Lazarsfeld (1941) did so, in part, under the influence of the first generation of Frankfurt School scholars, who had fled Nazi Germany and continued their work in the US. While fundamentally suspicious of "the culture industry" (Adorno and Horkheimer, 1977[1944]) that they encountered there, the Frankfurt scholars did not simply reject US popular culture on ideological grounds. As suggested by the distinction between critique and criticism, one purpose of critical research is to identify the material as well as immaterial conditions of people's beliefs about self and society, which, in turn, condition the status quo (Hammersley, 1995: 30). By reflecting on media as they currently exist, critical studies outline *what might be*. Lazarsfeld also noted this potential of critical research. And, it was this quality that Habermas, who is commonly considered the central representative of a second generation of the Frankfurt School, specified as the characteristic knowledge interest of social science.

the Frankfurt School

Lazarsfeld (1941) found that critical and administrative research could and should cross-fertilize as basic and applied forms of inquiry. His own accomplishments, centered in the Bureau of Applied Social Research at Columbia University, suggested the potential of that strategy. In addition to some of the early 'milestones' in media studies,◀ he and his collaborators pioneered several methodological approaches, from panel studies◀ to focus groups.◀ Critical researchers, however, including European expatriates who, like Theodor Adorno, found a temporary home in Bureau projects, were mostly quite unsympathetic to administrative research (Delia, 1987: 52). Commercial and other instrumental interests, arguably, would narrow the theoretical scope of studies, limit their later social uses, and, in the longer term, undermine the

▶ milestone studies – Chapter 9, p. 173
▶ panel studies – Chapter 13, p. 247
▶ focus groups – Chapter 14, p. 271

intellectual freedom of researchers to choose both their research questions and their methods. Readers of the very last sentence of Lazarsfeld's original article may have felt confirmed in the view that critical research was assigned the role of generating bright ideas to be exploited (financially and ideologically) in the administrative mainstream of research:

> there is here a type of approach which, if it were included in the general stream of communications research, could contribute much in terms of challenging problems and new concepts useful in the interpretation of known, and in the search for new, data.
>
> (Lazarsfeld, 1941: 16)

On closer examination, the two approaches to communication research exhibit a number of similarities, and are often combined in practice. For one thing, both types rely on qualitative as well as quantitative methodologies – a fact that is sometimes missed in accounts associating administrative with quantitative, and critical with qualitative, approaches. In commercial settings, qualitative studies provide evidence that decision makers are willing act on to a significant extent. For another thing, both critical and administrative studies may be either reactive or proactive, evaluating what already is, or shaping what is not yet. Critical projects, in some cases, are the most instrumental of all, developing research designs to address inequalities of access to communication resources, or in order to develop such resources. In cultural studies,◄ some researchers have advocated more focused social uses of this tradition in policy contexts (Bennett, 1992), while others have called for a greater reliance on quantitative evidence to support the critical points of cultural studies (Lewis, 1997).

reactive and proactive research

Figure 19.1 displays some main types of media research organizations, with national and cultural variations. The nature and output of research projects is explained, in large part, by the infrastructures embedding and enabling them – funding, organizations, time frames, and anticipated uses. Together, these infrastructures entail more or less administrative or critical practices, and different forms of reflexivity on behalf of research communities, commercial clients, political agencies, and the public at large.

As in other contemporary social life, a central divide exists between private enterprise and public service – commercial research entities and university departments. Even though the relative size of each of these main sectors of research is difficult to calculate, it is safe to say that commercial projects outdistance academic ones in terms of both financial resources and the number of studies undertaken. At the same time, commercial media and universities, in many countries, increasingly enter into collaboration: universities fund (part of) their research through commercial sponsorship, and media can base business development on research evidence, with an added bonus of legitimacy deriving from such collaboration. The research entities of public-service media occupy an additional middle ground.

The third type – independent research institutes – has been a staple of media and communication research since Lazarsfeld's Bureau, avoiding some of the negative connotations of both 'state' and 'market,' and attracting clients from both sides of the divide. The fourth type – documentation centers – has more commonly been associated with historical, arts, and other humanistic archives than with empirical research on contemporary culture and society (although some film institutes have filled this role). At present, such entities are gaining importance, both as strategic resources in media production and planning, and as a support function for their affiliated research activities.◄

It should be added that the internet and other digital media have raised additional issues concerning the social production, organization, and dissemination of knowledge in society, including the relationship between proprietary and public-domain research (for overviews, see Benkler, 2006; Lessig, 2006). Such issues have gained new centrality and urgency in view of the collaborative, storage, and distribution capacities of digital media, as exemplified by open-source initiatives, file sharing, and peer

► cultural studies – Chapter 2, p. 46

► museums and archives – p. 363

	Commercial company	University department	Independent research institute	Documentation center
Funding	Income from clients	Public funding	Commercial income and/or public funding	Commercial income and/or public funding
Organization of research activity	Management hierarchy	Autonomous researchers within (degree of) collegial government	Board of trustees and management hierarchy	Board of trustees and management hierarchy
Time frames	Days to years	Years to decades	Days to decades	Years to centuries
Anticipated uses of results	Strategic planning and product development	Description and critique of past and present media forms	Descriptive as well as proactive analyses	Description and documentation of media content and uses
Examples	Marketing sections; Advertising agencies; Consultancies	Media studies departments; Schools of communication	Research bureaus and ad hoc centers; Thinktanks	Archives with proprietary and/or public (museum) access

Figure 19.1 Types of media research organizations

production. One classic debate, familiar from public-service broadcasting, concerns the extent to which certain forms of knowledge should be understood as public goods (Samuelson, 1954), like water and electricity – from updated and reliable information about political issues and events, to diverse analyses and reviews of the state of the economy. At stake, once again, are the interrelations and relative powers of different social agents and institutions representing market, state, and civil society.

public goods

The production and application of knowledge takes time. A distinctive feature of each of the four types of research organization is its time frame. Whereas commercial projects typically are scheduled for short-term instrumental purposes, academic studies suggest courses of action in the (very) long term. Research can be defined summarily as the collective representation of reality for a common purpose; the practical question is when, where, and how this purpose is to be enacted. Short-term and long-term purposes of research translate into three categories of social uses: policy, politics, and a third, more indirect and diverse set of 'standpoint' interventions into social practice.

POLITICS AND/VERSUS POLICY

Policy contexts

Policies are codified plans of action. The importance of policy in both public administration and commercial enterprise is a structural consequence of the increased complexity of modern societies, in material production, in organizational bureaucracies, and in politics from the local to the global level (Beniger, 1986). Collective and coordinated action depends on deliberation and planning through explicit policies; because of their scale and cost, policies, further, require evaluation and adjustment. Both the nature of such deliberations and the criteria of evaluation follow largely from predefined goals. Policies focus on specific contexts of action, and on agendas set by existing social institutions. The area of policy research has expanded since 1945, one key figure being the communication scholar, Harold D. Lasswell (Lerner and Lasswell, 1951).◀ The field of evaluation research (Patton, 2002), which examines organizational ends, means, and outcomes across the private and public sectors, can be seen as a variant of policy studies.

evaluation research

Media studies have contributed, from their inception, to planning and evaluating media and their performance. Three main policy contexts can be identified:

- *Business administration.* Within private enterprise, media employ in-house as well as commissioned research to support their business. In addition to audiences or customers, studies address the development of content, the internal work practices, and the strategic placement of the given organization in relation to competitors, regulators, and the general public (Jablin and Putnam, 2001).
- *Public planning.* Compared to the more ad hoc policies of media businesses, public policy delineates the general frameworks in which media operate. A central area of influence for researchers is commission work leading into legislative and executive decisions, sometimes supported by specially funded studies. To exemplify, most European countries during the 1980 and 1990s witnessed a great deal of commission work and research regarding satellite and cable technologies and their implications for public-service broadcasting (Blumler and Gurevitch, 1995).
- *Non-governmental organizations.* Beyond and between state and market, citizens' groups, think tanks, and other organizations regularly develop and advocate particular policies. They do so with a view to a variety of stakeholders in politics, business, as well as the educational system. One example of civil-society involvement in international media policy is the Internet Governance Forum (n.d.) that followed the World Summit on the Information Society (2003–05)

organizational communication

state or government commissions

The three policy contexts – business, state, and civil society – correspond to the three columns of the public-sphere model of modern society.◀ It is by engaging organizations and agencies in each of these domains – as collaborators or adversaries – that researchers may, most directly, affect the future infrastructures and conditions of communication in society at large.

Political processes

Compared to the relatively delimited *contexts* of policy, a second set of strategies shifts the emphasis toward certain less well-defined, but potentially more far-reaching *processes* of change. Here, studies typically question or bracket current institutional agendas. (As in the case of policy contexts, both qualitative and quantitative approaches to media and communication research lend themselves to such political processes.) By critiquing and sometimes criticizing institutional logics, much academic research adopts a long-term strategy of change, seeking to identify the unacknowledged and sometimes covert interests driving either commercial or government policies. In this regard, academic media and communication researchers carry on aspects of the classic role of the intelligentsia that Karl Mannheim described as relatively autonomous or 'free-floating' (Mannheim, 1976[1922]: 136–146).

critical role of the intelligentsia

Corner (1991) identified two different political projects, originally within reception studies, but with wider implications for media and communication research as such. On the one hand, the field has been broadly committed to Enlightenment ideals concerning the democratic accessibility of *public knowledge*, as typified by factual genres. From propaganda research to decoding studies of news to research on politics online, an important research question has been how well media users are able to process

public knowledge project

▶ Lasswell's communication model – Chapter 1, p. 12

▶ the public-sphere model – Chapter 1, p. 17

the information on offer, and to apply it in political and other forms of participation. On the other hand, recent decades, particularly, have witnessed much textual and audience research seeking to rehabilitate *popular culture*, especially fiction genres, as relevant and valuable resources of cultural participation and personal identity.

popular culture project

The central arenas of political influence for media studies range from various public-sector institutions to the public sphere as a general forum of social and cultural reflexivity:

- *Public debate.* Media and communication research regularly contributes to (and occasionally initiates) debates in the public sphere, its political as well as cultural domains (Figure 1.3). The interventions range from popular publications and interviews at the conclusion of projects to syndicated commentaries. In the process, researchers also feed the self-reflexivity of media, as they address contemporary issues such as political 'spin doctors' and lifestyle advertising. Through online media such as blogging (Rettberg, 2008; Schmidt, 2007),◀ researchers are in a position to participate more directly in public debates concerning the media field.
- *Media education.* Beyond their own graduate and undergraduate students, media and communication researchers have contributed to a democratization (or relativization) of the cultural heritage – canonic texts and other standards that inform curricula at various educational levels. In addition, the field has been successful, in a number of countries, in advancing a component of media literacy in general education (Masterman, 1985; Messaris, 1994; Potter, 2011). This is in spite of the fact that the exact purpose and placement of media education (separately or within other subjects) has remained debated. The ubiquity of digital media, along with more computer-supported learning, pose additional questions concerning the definition of literacy and its implications for political and cultural participation.

media literacy

- *Museums and archives.* As suggested in Figure 19.1, documentation centers constitute a strategic resource for media research as well as media production. Also in a longer historical perspective, the preservation of contemporary media, their software and hardware, poses important public issues (Jensen, 1993b). One key question is whether and how the breadth and depth of modern media, including their everyday uses, will remain available and accessible alongside the high cultural forms that still reign supreme in museums and archives (and among employed archivists). If not, future scholars may not be able to (re)write the history of contemporary media, or to reassess our theories and findings. The Payne Fund (Jowett, *et al.*, 1996) and Mass Observation (Richards and Sheridan, 1987) studies of the 1930s, along with more recent work (Day-Lewis, 1989; Gauntlett and Hill, 1999), suggest the value of such evidence for an understanding of media in their social and historical contexts.

▶ blogging – Chapter 10, p. 199

Standpoint interventions

A third and more heterogeneous group of strategies share an explicit commitment to social and cultural change – in and through the practice of research, through alliances with particular constituencies or stakeholders, and in the (very) long term. Emphasizing political and epistemological alternatives to mainstream social uses of research, studies in this vein mostly rely on qualitative forms of analysis and argument.

Several of the strategies in question can be considered revolutionary rather than reformist, at least in their own understanding. They are not only anti-establishment but, sometimes, anti-institutions, opposing the constitutive operations of, for instance, markets and families as they currently exist, even the very institutionalization of society. Some of them, further, advocate a radical break with the methodological and epistemological premises of other research traditions, which might be said to reproduce knowledge in the service of power. A common figure of thought is that alternative social arrangements are to be identified through alternative epistemologies. As theorized most influentially by Michel Foucault (1972), this argument shades into a position questioning the legitimacy of any and all forms of knowledge, a fundamental distrust of "power/knowledge" (Foucault, 1980).

power/ knowledge

Within media and communication research, it is particularly the cultural-studies tradition,◄ broadly speaking, that has considered these strategies, generating debate with other research traditions (e.g., Ferguson and Golding, 1997). Since the 1970s, a great deal of work has taken other social and cultural research to task for articulating and promoting interests associated with the Western world, the economic middle-class, the political mainstream, and a patriarchal mode of social interaction. One counter-strategy has been to treat knowledge in the plural, also terminologically, exploring alternative 'knowledges' in the interest of the disempowered. In response, other participants in these debates have argued that attempts by research to make up for past and present silences and injustices in society may result in political correctness (for overview, see Levy, 1992): studies can be seen to shy away from certain controversial questions and hypotheses and may, as a result, produce less than robust empirical findings and theoretical frameworks. Unless scholars are allowed to make claims to knowledge, however debatable and fallible, and regardless of their immediate legitimacy and relevance, the critical potential of research – for or against change – might be lost.

political correctness

At least three kinds of standpoint interventions can be identified.

Feminist methodology

The term 'standpoint' derives from methodology and theory of science in the feminist tradition, as elaborated especially by Sandra Harding (1986). The premise is that all knowledge is produced from a socially situated standpoint, and that the life experiences of women – silenced in much of the history of ideas – provide a necessary corrective to other standpoints, also in scholarship. Accordingly, feminist research might enable an enhanced or 'strong' objectivity by allowing women (and men) to transcend classic canons of objectivism and to take up (more) reflexive positions within the research process (see also Alcoff and Potter, 1993; Harding, 2004).

standpoint epistemology

Compared to the biological essentialism that has characterized some other feminist work,◄ standpoint feminism represents an attempt to historicize the nexus between knowledge and power. In practice, however, the position easily slides into another extreme of sociological essentialism, suggesting that feminism and cognate critical traditions offer more insightful theories, and better empirical bases of change, not because of the quality of the scholarship, but because they tap the experience of – stand on the shoulders of – the disempowered. In media studies, a related tendency can be found in work asserting that studies of women's culture, of ethnic minorities, and of marginalized youth subcultures are the unrecognized origins of key ideas regarding the place of media in everyday life (Drotner, 1996: 41).

Feminist methodology and epistemology orient themselves toward change in the long term. By reshaping the research institution, feminist studies may, in turn, help to reshape other social institutions. In doing so, feminist standpoint research can be understood as a socially situated practice within wider feminist movements.◄

Textual deconstructionism

A second, related position – deconstructionism – joins feminism in challenging unified conceptions of knowledge. Compared to feminism, however, deconstructionism focuses more narrowly on texts, not only as a source of social dominance, but also as the site of critique and change. Departing from poststructuralist theories of discourse and postmodernist conceptions of culture,◄ textual studies in this tradition seek to expose misrepresentations, or reified representations, of social reality by media.

Deconstructionism dissolves boundaries, not only between text and reality, but between the text being analyzed and the text performing and presenting the analysis. Like criticism in

► cultural studies – Chapter 2, p. 46

► essentialist feminism – Chapter 2, p. 44

► feminism as theory and practice – Chapter 2, p. 43

► poststructuralism and postmodernism – Chapter 2, p. 41

the arts, media criticism in this vein could be understood as an artwork in its own right. The work of the philosopher, Richard Rorty, has been influential in promoting a definition of research as one kind of story-telling (e.g., Rorty, 1979, 1991). Science and scholarship might be taken as one contribution to 'the conversation of humankind,' on a par with literature or journalism, and without epistemological privileges. This view has had some influence in the literature on qualitative methodology, which, among other things, has proposed to expand the range of genres in which researchers tell their stories (Denzin and Lincoln, 2005).

research as story-telling

It is characteristic of deconstructionist media and communication studies that they rarely address empirical audiences or the social contexts in which texts are used, interpreted, and take effect. Instead, deconstructionist studies perform an interpretive reworking of media texts, and offer their own preferred reinterpretations. While key publications have expressed revolutionary aims (e.g., Kristeva, 1984[1974]), the likely agents of revolutionary or other social action have mostly been unclear. In practice, there appears to be an inverse relationship between the political ambitions and the methodological details of deconstructionism.

Given its comparative isolation from other social institutions, textual deconstructionism might have an impact in and through the educational system, which may trickle down to other social sectors. One specific area of impact is the media themselves, where notions of postmodernism have been widespread, and where program developers have taken inspiration from deconstructionism (e.g., Caldwell, 1995).

Action research

A third type of standpoint intervention is action research, including several participatory and applied variants (for overviews, see Greenwood and Levin, 2007; Reason and Bradbury, 2008). Like the other two types, action studies challenge established institutions and practices, sometimes in fundamental ways. Unlike the other types, action research emphasizes concrete and operational strategies for social change, in cooperation with, or initiated by, stakeholders within the organizations in question, for example, for community development or workplace democracy. (Action research also incorporates quantitative approaches.) By involving everyday theorists◀ as partners in the formulation of research questions, as well as in the research procedures, studies become collaborative ventures of generating new and applicable knowledge.

In media and communication studies, action research has apparently been less widespread than in community and workplace studies, education, and some other fields. Development communication programs included some involvement by the cultures and communities that were the end users of the technologies being diffused.◀ Studies of community media◀ and of human-computer interaction (HCI) (Sears and Jacko, 2008) have also relied on strategies involving end users. Given their participatory and broadly interactive features, digital media lend themselves to, and may stimulate, additional forms of action research (Hearn, *et al.*, 2009).

Like political and policy approaches to research, standpoint interventions return the field to the 'big' ideological and epistemological questions: why study the media – with or on behalf of whom? In practice, in student projects as well as in comprehensive research programs, researchers face these questions as logistical as well as ethical considerations – which are addressed in the final section.

THE SOCIAL TRIAD OF RESEARCH PRACTICE

Research practice can be understood as a specific kind of social interaction, involving three key agents:

- the *researcher*
- his/her *respondents* (and other sources of evidence)
- the community of *peers* or colleagues who assess the quality both of findings and insights, and of the researcher's professional conduct.

▶ everyday theory – p. 352
▶ development communication – Chapter 11, p. 212
▶ community media – Chapter 11, p. 210

The social triad applies to studies across the various sectors and intellectual cultures of media studies. It is through innumerable concrete interchanges within the triad that the field accumulates and adjusts a body of theory and evidence, simultaneously reproducing itself as a social institution on a daily basis.

Researchers' relations with respondents and colleagues are examined in research ethics (for an overview, see Israel and Hay, 2006). Ethics, to one side, blends into *politics*. Politics articulates and enforces rules of conduct at a collective or structural level, whereas ethics addresses standards of conduct in the perspective of the individual social agent. To the other side, ethics, as it applies to particular domains of social activity such as research, overlaps with *morality* – general standards of conduct that are prevalent in a historical period and cultural setting.

research ethics

Certain aspects of research ethics are stated in legislation and codes of conduct, and are subject to enforcement by national authorities and institutional boards. Whereas the legal and ethical frameworks of media and communication research vary between countries, some of the main issues can be laid out with reference, first, to research subjects and, next, to the research community (see also Deacon, *et al.*, 2007: 357–378).

Research subjects

Research subjects are just that – subjects. Unlike rocks and books, subjects can be harmed, socially and emotionally, by empirical studies. It is the responsibility of researchers to anticipate and prevent such harm. Research competence requires not only theoretical and methodological skills, but also an awareness of ethical pitfalls, as established in previous work, and a general capacity for empathy and respect in encounters with others. It is worth noting that organizations such as the International Communication Association and the International Association for Media and Communication Research have not developed codes of research ethics; other fields such as psychology and sociology offer codes that can provide guidance for media researchers, as well.

The requirements of ethical research can be summarized as practical rules of thumb: "Do as you would be done by" and "Leave things as you find them" (Deacon, *et al.*, 2007: 377). The first principle is a variation on Immanuel Kant's (2004b[1785]: n.p.) categorical imperative: "Act always on such a maxim as thou canst at the same time will to be a universal law." The second principle emphasizes the right of human subjects to self-determination. A researcher should not intervene proactively in a domain of study unless this is part of an explicit agreement, for instance, in action research.

the categorical imperative

Depending on their research questions and concrete fields of analysis, empirical studies face various dilemmas. First, harm can take many different forms, and may only manifest itself in the longer term. Although empirical media studies rarely pose issues of life and death, as in medical research, the disclosure of, for instance, documents concerning product development can result in significant losses, financially and in terms of the legitimacy of people within the media organization in question. Equally, the publication of politically controversial viewpoints from focus groups without sufficient anonymization may cause participants to lose social status or 'face' in their community.

Second, these examples further suggest that research subjects are vulnerable in different respects and to different degrees. In their reception study of women viewing mediated violence, Schlesinger, *et al.* (1992) exercised special care in screening and debriefing their respondents, some of whom had been physically abused in their own lives. By comparison, in production and other organizational studies, informants are normally approached as representatives of a company or profession, who are aware of this relationship and, to a degree, of the nature of academic research. Nevertheless, also in professional settings, ethical dilemmas arise when considering the appropriate means of serving the ends of research. A case in point is the undercover work of the Glasgow University Media Group (1976) in documenting and criticizing practices of news production within British television.

The standard procedure is informed consent. Its purpose is to enable subjects to agree or decline to participate in a specific study. The

informed consent

decision should be based on information about the elements of the study, its potential consequences for themselves, and its anticipated social uses. Informed consent is one key element of the Nuremberg Code (1949), a set of protocols for research on human subjects that was established during the Nuremberg Trials on Nazi war crimes, which had included cruel scientific experimentation. While debated in terms of both its sufficiency and its practicability, informed consent represents a central operational principle in determining what (not) to do with research subjects. In medical and natural-scientific research, a standard procedure of double-blind experiments is observed (neither patient nor therapist knows who gets the active drug being tested, and who gets the placebo). In comparison, informed consent aims for a standard of double insight that, ideally, involves also the objects of research as subjects.

double-blind and double-insight procedures

When next reporting findings and conclusions, researchers face additional issues of confidentiality in general, and anonymity in particular – issues that can be stated in terms of information and communication theory. In most instances, it is an ethical requirement that researchers preserve the anonymity of respondents by not communicating or *withholding* information. In quantitative research, abuses may follow from a recycling and recombination of data sets, for instance, so that particular individuals are targeted in subsequent marketing campaigns. In qualitative research, harm is more likely to result when the readers of a report are able to identify a given individual through a rich contextual description. In both cases, the problem is not so much that the information in itself is publicized. (Such problems arise when the information is proprietary, typically for commercial reasons, and, hence, confidential.) The problem arises if the communication by a researcher links the information to its original source. In most cases, neither qualitative nor quantitative methodologies depend for their explanatory value on such links. From the researcher's perspective, media practitioners and media users are of interest, not as unique entities with biographical, demographic, and biological characteristics, but as prototypes, and as representative or illustrative instances of a social category.

confidentiality and anonymity

From the sources' perspective, they have a right *not* to be associated with the information that they offer in the context of research. This right can be understood as a reverse copyright: most media studies imply a social contract according to which subjects speak as types, not tokens – as an Anybody, not a Somebody. The principles of reverse copyright and double insight respond to the position of media and communication studies – and of social sciences generally – somewhere on a continuum between nomothetic and idiographic research – between studies of laws and of cases.◄

reverse copyright

Figure 19.2 outlines a set of guidelines for the conduct of empirical studies, with implications for student projects as well as research programs.

The research community

A second set of issues within the triad of research concerns the relationship between researchers and their professional peers. As an ideal community, scholarship calls for the complete dissemination of all potentially relevant information as far as possible in global media of presentation. As an interested social practice, research requires individual scholars to weigh this ideal against anonymity and confidentiality requirements, but also against material considerations such as intellectual property rights and their own careers. The research community is itself a social system of checks and balances, privileges and sanctions. The chief issues can be reviewed with reference to the different stages of the research process.

Especially in academic research, an early and decisive juncture is the approval of an empirical project by a national or institutional review board (IRB). In some countries, such approval is required before any study can be undertaken with human subjects, and officially on behalf of a university. While debated along similar lines as the informed consent procedure, an initial review process provides some assurance that gross ethical misconduct will not occur. Next, the basic criteria of ethical research include intellectual honesty in the presentation of the

Institutional Review Boards

► idiographic and nomothetic research – Chapter 15, p. 285

- 1. First make sure to ascertain the rules and procedures in your social and cultural context and academic institution regarding *review* of research involving human subjects.
- 2. Always treat the people under study as *people*. They are neither things nor texts. A standard procedure for ensuring their rights and preventing harm is 'informed consent.'
- 3. Exercise *caution* and *concretion*. Be prepared to give up a question (or an entire study) if, in context, it violates the ethical, cultural, or personal limits of the people involved. Be prepared to explain concretely the relevance of any question to informants and others.
- 4. Practice *reflexivity*. The analysis of (cautiously collected and concrete) data begins in the empirical field. In qualitative as well as quantitative projects, supplementary evidence and notes will support both the respectful use of respondents' contributions and the explanatory value of later interpretations.
- 5. Safeguard the *anonymity* of people and the *confidentiality* of information throughout the research process.
- 6. Be honest about the *sources of ideas* informing a study and the *contributions of peers* in developing and conducting it.
- 7. A research report includes accounts both of *process and outcome*, and of *successes and failures* in each respect.
- 8. Two key requirements of a research report are a systematic *documentation* of evidence and an explication of the bases of theoretical *inference.*
- 9. Explore several different *publication formats,* including a means of *feedback* to the people contributing to a study.
- 10. Consider *what's next* – further research, the social relevance of findings, and the possible unanticipated consequences of the research.

Figure 19.2 Ten rules for the conduct of empirical studies

sources of ideas, a complete accounting of successes and failures in data collection and analysis, and a systematic documentation of evidence and the bases of theoretical inference.

At their conclusion, research projects normally face a second review, typically in the form of a peer review – an anonymous (double-blind) evaluation by experienced researchers. This has been standard procedure in many fields since the mid-twentieth century, and determines whether a study will be published in major journals. Once again, peer review has been the object of criticism, for example, for favoring entrenched traditions. Still, the procedure presents itself as perhaps the least worst alternative in the inevitably controversial enterprise of evaluating the quality of new contributions to research. In a further step, access to the original data sets of other researchers is a way of keeping the research community critically reflective and in dialogue. An example of debates arising from such a secondary data analysis was Hirsch's (1980, 1981) questioning of Gerbner and colleagues' cultivation hypothesis.◀

peer review

The wider intellectual backdrop of media and communication research, during recent decades, has been intense conflicts – 'wars' – over the status and social uses of scientific knowledge. Within the research community, science wars flared up following Alan Sokal's hoax in a 1996 article (reprinted in Sokal and Bricmont, 1998) – a deliberately nonsensical publication that invoked the vocabulary of atomic physics, and which was submitted to a major journal in order

science wars

▶ cultivation research – Chapter 8, p. 166

to expose the lack of scientific rigor in postmodern cultural studies and related traditions. Beyond the confrontations, this provocation also helped to generate insightful debates about epistemology and politics across theoretical and disciplinary boundaries (Ashman and Baringer, 2001; Labinger and Collins, 2001).

culture wars

In the wider public sphere, two types of culture wars have been ongoing. First, especially in US public debate, orthodox (religious) and progressivist (modern) conceptions of humanity – what we can know, and how we should act as individuals and societies – have been pitted against each other (Hunter, 1991). A second conflict continues to revolve around the relative aesthetic value and social relevance of high arts and popular culture, occupying and occasionally dividing media and communication researchers.

Intellectual conflicts with social implications are inherent in the study of media and communication, both in a contemporary and in a historical perspective. A particularly bitter controversy that brought history into the present centered on the work of Elisabeth Noelle-Neumann (1984) on the spiral of silence. The theory suggests that if people perceive their views to be in the minority, as represented, not least, in the media, they are less likely to express these views. As a result, they come to participate in a circle or spiral of silence that is potentially vicious for democracy. One of Noelle-Neumann's specific arguments was that a predominance of leftwing views among German journalists and media helped to silence rightwing political views in that country.

Noelle-Neumann herself was quite explicit regarding her rightwing political sympathies and her work as a strategy adviser for the German Christian Democratic Party. However, following up on previous public criticism, Simpson (1996), in a *Journal of Communication* article, drew attention to her apparent sympathies with the Nazi party during World War II. Most important, Simpson linked the conclusions about a spiral of silence in the present with a set of theoretical assumptions and methodologies that had originally been developed for Noelle-Neumann's research in Germany during the war. In a fierce response, Kepplinger (1997) suggested that the critique was *ad hominem*. His counterargument, in essence, was that the quality of research methodologies as well as of the findings they produce can be judged independent of their origins and applications, past and present.

Whereas this particular debate was especially vehement and painful against the background of world-war atrocities, the issue it raised is general: what is, and what ought to be, the relationship between scientific knowledge and social action? Like other forms of communication, researchers' deliberations about evidence, inferences, and potential courses of action necessarily come to an end.

THE END OF COMMUNICATION

In an imagined dialogue between two central twentieth-century American social scientists – C. Wright Mills and Paul F. Lazarsfeld – Stein (1964) pinpointed two approaches to social and cultural research. Mills reads aloud the first sentence of *The Sociological Imagination* (Mills, 1959a): "Nowadays men often feel that their private lives are a series of traps." The fantasy imagines Lazarsfeld replying: "How many men, which men, how long have they felt this way, which aspects of their private lives bother them, do their public lives bother them, when do they feel free rather than trapped, what kinds of traps do they experience, etc., etc., etc." (Stein, 1964: 215) (discussed in Gitlin, 1978: 223).

The field of media and communication research continues to engage in such dialogue and debate concerning the comparative relevance and legitimacy of qualitative and quantitative methodologies. This can be considered part of the self-reflective business of any field; sometimes, self-reflection takes the form of self-criticism. While rooted in cultural studies,◀ Morris (1990), for one, put this tradition on trial for banality, a solemn textual paraphrasing of the fact that cultures and societies are complex and contradictory phenomena. Ritchie (1999), for another, questioned the validity of much survey and other quantitative research because of its ambiguous conception of probability.◀

▶ cultural studies – Chapter 2, p. 46
▶ probability – Chapter 15, p. 296

What different traditions and temperaments typically share is the ambition of having research respond to real-life problems and concerns. Both Mills' sweeping generalizations and Lazarsfeld's mundane operationalizations assumed that, by describing and interpreting contemporary social and cultural conditions, research may make a practical difference. The orientation toward social action is a common denominator for research and (other) communication. Both media studies and communicative practices have ends – and they end.

the end of communication is to end

The end of communication is to end: ideally, having been enlightened and empowered through communication, individuals, groups, institutions, as well as entire societies and cultures go on to act. Political democracy is a case in point.

> Michael Schudson (1997: 307), for one, has critiqued a [...] 'romance of conversation' that confuses ordinary sociable conversation with problem-solving conversation, which is of a formal, rule-governed, and public nature. It is counterproductive, to the point of undermining political democracy itself, to think of public debate among citizens as just another conversation among either intimates or strangers. [...] At least as far as democracy is concerned, the response to the familiar rhetorical question, 'Can't we just talk about it?' must be: No.
>
> (Jensen, 2010: 5)

It is the conclusion of communication and its transformation into concerted social action that is a hallmark of democracy.

Research, equally, comes to an end. The end of the research process is the beginning of other social practices. By reflecting on its origins, uses, and potential consequences, media and communication research can stake a claim to being both a scientifically mature and a socially relevant field of study.

References

Note: Original publication dates are given in square brackets, where relevant.

Aarseth, E. J. (1997). *Cybertext: Perspectives on Ergodic Literature*. Baltimore, MD: Johns Hopkins University Press.

Aarseth, E. (2003). We All Want to Change the World: The Ideology of Innovation in Digital Media. In G. Liestøl, A. Morrison, and T. Rasmussen (eds.), *Digital Media Revisited*. Cambridge, MA: MIT Press.

Aarseth, E. (2004). Genre Trouble: Narrativism and the Art of Simulation. In N. Wardrip-Fruin and P. Harrigan (eds.), *First Person: New Media as Story, Performance, and Game*. Cambridge: The MIT Press.

Aarseth, E., Smedstad, S. M., and Sunnana, L. (2003). What's in a Game? A Multi-Dimensional Typology of Games. In M. Copier and J. Raessens (eds.), *Level Up. Digital Games Research Conference*. Utrecht: Universiteit Utrecht University Press.

Abbate, J. (1999). *Inventing the Internet*. Cambridge, MA: MIT Press.

Abell, J. and Myers, G. (2008). Analyzing Research Interviews. In R. Wodak and M. Krzyzanowski (eds.), *Qualitative Discourse Analysis in the Social Sciences*. Basingstoke: Palgrave Macmillan.

Abrams, M. H. (gen. ed.) (1962). *The Norton Anthology of English Literature Vol. 2*. New York: Norton.

Abt, V. and Seesholtz, M. (1994). The Shameless World of Phil, Sally and Oprah: Television Talk Shows and the Deconstruction of Society. *Journal of Popular Culture*, 28(1): 171–191.

Ackland, R. (2005). Mapping the U.S. Political Blogosphere: Are Conservative Bloggers More Prominent? Paper presented to BlogTalk Downunder, May 19–22, 2005, Sydney. Online, available at: http://voson.anu.edu.au/papers/polblogs.pdf.

Ackland, R. and Gibson, R. (2004). Mapping Political Party Networks on the WWW. Paper presented at the Australian Electronic Governance Conference, April 14–15 2004, University of Melbourne. Online, available at: http://voson.anu.edu.au/papers/political_networks.pdf.

Ackland, R., O'Neil M., Standish, R., and Buchhorn, M. (2006). VOSON: A Web Services Approach for Facilitating Research into Online Networks. Paper presented at the Second International Conference on e-Social Science, June 28–30, 2006, University of Manchester. Online, available at: http://voson.anu.edu.au/papers/ncess-conf06-full-paper-final.pdf.

Acosta-Alzuru, C. (2005). Home Is Where My Heart Is: Reflections on Doing Research in My Native Country. *Popular Communication*, 3(3): 181–193.

Adorno, T. and Horkheimer, M. (1977[1944]). The Culture Industry: Enlightenment as Mass Deception. In J. Curran, M. Gurevitch, and J. Woollacott (eds.), *Mass Communication and Society*. London: Edward Arnold.

Agar, M. (1995). *The Professional Stranger: An Informal Introduction to Ethnography*. New York: Academic press.

Akindes, F. (2003). Methodology as Lived Experience: Rhizomatic Ethnography in Hawai'i. In P. Murphy and M. Kraidy (eds.), *Global Media Studies: Ethnographic Perspectives*. London: Routledge, pp. 147–164.

Alasuutari, P. (ed.) (1999). *Rethinking the Media Audience: The New Agenda*. London: Sage.

Alcoff, L. and Potter, E. (eds.) (1993). *Feminist Epistemologies*. New York: Routledge.

Alexander, A., Owers, J., Carveth, R., Hollifield, C. A., and Greco, A. N. (2003). *Media Economics: Theory and Practice* (3rd ed.). New York: Routledge.

Alexander, J. and Giesen, B. (1987). From Reduction to Linkage: The Long View of the Micro-Macro Link. In J. Alexander, B. Giesen, R. Münch, and N. Smelser (eds.), *The Micro-Macro Link*. Berkeley, CA: University of California Press.

Alexander, J., Boudon, R., and Cherkaoui, M. (eds.) (1997). *The Classical Tradition in Sociology: The American Tradition*. London: Sage.

Allen, J., Livingstone, S., and Reiner, R. (1997). The Changing Generic Locations of Crime in Film: A Content Analysis of Film Synopses, 1845–1991. *Journal of Communication*, 47(4): 89–101.

Allern, S. (2002). Journalistic and Commercial News Values: News Organizations as Patrons of an Institution and Market Actors. *Nordicom Review*, 23(1–2): 137–152.

Altenloh, E. (1913). *Zur Soziologie des Kino* [The Sociology of the Cinema]. Leipzig: Spamersche Buchdruckerei.

Altheide, D. L. and Snow, R. P. (1979). *Media Logic*. Beverly Hills, CA: Sage.

Altheide, D. L. and Snow, R. P. (1991). *Media Worlds in the Postjournalism Era*. New York: Walter de Gruyter.

Althusser, L. (1977[1965]). *For Marx*. London: Verso.

Altman, R. (1986). Television/Sound. In Tania Modleski (ed.), *Studies in Entertainment*. Bloomington, IN: Indiana University Press.

Altman, R. (1999). *Film/Genre*. London: British Film Institute.

Altman, R. (ed.) (1980). Cinema/Sound. *Yale French Studies*, 60 (special issue).

Altman, R. (ed.) (1992). *Sound Theory/Sound Practice*. New York: Routledge.

Alvesson, M. and Sköldberg, K. (2009). *Reflexive Methodology: New Vistas for Qualitative Research* (2nd ed.). London: Sage.

Ancu, M. and Cozma, R. (2009). MySpace Politics: Uses and Gratifications of Befriending Candidates. *Journal of Broadcasting and Electronic Media*, 53(4): 567–583.

Anderson, B. (1991). *Imagined Communities: Reflections on the Origin and Spread of Nationalism* (2nd ed.). London: Verso.

Anderson, D. R. and Burns, J. (1991). Paying Attention to Television. In J. Bryant and D. Zillmann (eds.), *Responding to the Screen: Reception and Reaction Processes*. Hillsdale, NJ: Lawrence Erlbaum Associates.

Anderson, J. (1996). *Communication Theory: Epistemological Foundations*. New York: The Guilford Press.

Andrén, G., Ericsson, L. O., Ohlsson, R., and T. Tännsjö (1978). *Rhetoric and Ideology in Advertising*. Stockholm: Liber Förlag.

Andrew, J. D. (1976). *The Major Film Theories: An Introduction*. New York: Oxford University Press.

Ang, I. (1985). *Watching Dallas*. London: Methuen.

Ang, I. (1991). *Desperately Seeking the Audience*. London: Routledge.

Ang, I. (1996). Ethnography and Radical Contextualism in Audience Studies. In J. Hay, L. Grossberg, and E. Wartella (eds.), *The Audience and Its Landscape*. Boulder: Westview Press, pp. 247–262.

Anon (1935–58). *The History of the Times Vols 1–5*. London: The Times.

Appadurai, A. (1996). *Modernity at Large: Cultural Dimensions of Globalization*. Minneapolis, MN: University of Minnesota Press.

Arceneaux, N. and Weiss, A. S. (2010). Seems Stupid Until You Try It: Press Coverage of Twitter, 2006–2009. *New Media & Society*,12(8): 1262–1279.

Archer, M. (1995). *Realist Social Theory: The Morphogenetic Approach*. Cambridge: Cambridge University Press.

Archer, M., Bhaskar, R., Collier, A., Lawson, T., and Norrie, A. (eds.). (1998). *Critical Realism: Essential Readings*. London: Routledge.

Aristotle. (2007). *On Interpretation*. Online, available at: http://etext.library.adelaide.edu.au/a/aristotle/interpretation/complete.html [accessed August 15, 2007].

Arnheim, R. (1974). *Art and Visual Perception*. Berkeley, CA: University of California Press.

Arnold, M. (2003[1869]). *Culture and Anarchy*. Online, available at: www.gutenberg.org/etext/4212 [accessed March 15, 2009].

Ashcroft, B., Griffiths, G., and Tiffin, H. (eds.) (2006). *The Post-Colonial Studies Reader* (2nd ed.). London: Routledge.

Ashman, K. M. and Baringer, P. S. (eds.) (2001). *After the Science Wars*. London: Routledge.

Austin, E. W. and Freeman, C. (1997). Effects of Media, Parents and Peers on African-American Adolescents' Efficacy Toward Media Celebrities. *Howard Journal of Communication*, 8: 275–290.

Austin, E.W., Roberts, D., and Nass, C. (1990). Influences of Family Communication on Children's Television-interpretation Process. *Communication Research*, 17(4): 545–564.

Austin, J. L. (1962). *How to Do Things with Words*. Oxford: Oxford University Press.

Avilés, J. A. G., Leon, B., Harrison, J., and Sanders, K. (2004). Journalists at Digital Television Newsrooms in Britain and Spain: Workflow and Multiskilling in a Competitive Environment. *Journalism Studies*, 5(1): 87–100.

Babbie, E. (1990). *Survey Research Methods* (2nd ed.). Belmont, CA: Wadsworth Publishing Company.

Bagdikian, B. H. (2004). *The New Media Monopoly*. Boston, MA: Beacon.

Bailey, K. D. (1994). *Methods of Social Research* (4th ed.). New York: The Free Press.

Bakardjieva, M. (2006). Domestication Running Wild. From the Moral Economy of the Household to the Mores of a Culture. In T. Berker, M. Hartmann,

Y. Punie, and K. J. Ward (eds.), *Domestication of Media and Technology*. Glasgow: Open University Press, pp. 62–79.

Bakhtin, M. M. (1981). *The Dialogic Imagination*. Austin, TX: University of Texas Press.

Bal, M. (1977). *Narratologie. Essais sur la signification narrative dans quatre romans modernes*. Paris: Klincksieck. [English translation: *Narratology. Introduction to the Theory of Narrative*. Toronto: University of Toronto Press, 1985.]

Baldwin, J. R., Perry, S. D., and Moffitt, M. A. (2003). *Communication Theories for Everyday Life*. Boston, MA: Allyn & Bacon.

Ball-Rokeach, S. and Jung, J.-Y. (2009). The Evolution of Media System Dependency Theory. In R. L. Nabi and M. B. Oliver (eds.), *Media Processes and Effects*. Los Angeles, CA: Sage, pp. 531–544.

Bambach, C. R. (1995). *Heidegger, Dilthey and the Crisis of Historicism*. Ithaca, NY/London: Cornell University Press.

Bandura, A. and Walters, R. (1963). *Social Learning and Personality Development*. New York: Holt, Rinehart & Winston.

Banks, S. and Gupta, R. (1980). Television as a Dependent Variable, for a Change. *Journal of Consumer Research*, 7(3): 327–330.

Barbour, R. S. (2007). *Doing Focus Groups*. London: Sage.

Barbour, R. S. and Kitzinger, J. (eds.) (1999). *Developing Focus Group Research: Politics, Theory, and Practice*. London: Sage.

Barcus, F. E. (1969). Parental Influence on Children's Television Viewing. *Television Quarterly*, 8(3): 63–73.

Barker, M. and Brooks, K. (1998). *Knowing Audiences: Judge Dredd, Its Friends, Fans, and Foes*. Luton: University of Luton Press.

Barkho, L. (2010). *News from the BBC, CNN, and Al-Jazeera. How the Three Broadcasters Cover the Middle East*. Cresskill, NJ: Hampton Press.

Barnes, S. H. (1988). *Muzak. The Hidden Messages in Music: A Social Psychology of Culture*. Lewiston, NY: The Edwin Mellen Press.

Barnhurst, K. G. and Nerone, J. (2001). *The Form of News, a History*. New York: Guilford Press.

Barnhurst, K. G. and Wartella, E. (1998). Young Citizens, American TV Newscasts, and the Collective Memory. *Critical Studies in Mass Communication*, 15(3), 279–305.

Barnouw, E. (1966–1970). *A History of Broadcasting in the United States. Vols. 1–3*. New York: Oxford University Press.

Baron, N. S. (2008). *Always On: Language in an Online and Mobile World*. New York: Oxford University Press.

Barthes, R. (1966). Introduction à l'analyse structurale des récits. *Communications*, 8: 1–27. [English translation: Introduction to the Structural Analysis of Narratives. In S. Sontag (ed.), *A Barthes Reader*. London: Jonathan Cape, 1982.]

Barthes, R. (1967[1964]). *Elements of Semiology*. New York: Hill & Wang. [Originally published as Éléments de sémiologie. *Communications*, 4: 91–135.]

Barthes, R. (1970). *S/Z*. Paris: Seuil.

Barthes, R. (1973[1957]). *Mythologies*. London: Paladin.

Barthes, R. (1977[1964]). Rhetoric of the Image. In R. Barthes, *Image Music Text*. London: Fontana Press. [Originally published as Rhétorique de l'image. *Communications*, 4: 40–51.]

Barthes, R. (1980). *La chambre claire: note sur la photographie*. Paris: Gallimard. [English translation: *Camera Lucida: Reflections on Photography*. New York: Hill & Wang, 1981].

Bateson, G. (1972). *Steps to an Ecology of Mind*. London: Granada (a collection of essays across several decades).

Baudrillard, J. (1988). *Selected Writings*. Cambridge: Polity Press.

Bauer, M. W. and Gaskell, G. (eds.) (2000). *Qualitative Researching with Text, Image, and Sound: A Practical Handbook*. London: Sage.

Bauman, Z. (2000). *Liquid Modernity*. Cambridge: Polity Press.

Bawarshi, A. (2000). The Genre Function. *College English*, 62(3): 335–356.

Baxter, L., Bylund, C., Imes, R., and Routsong, T. (2009). Parent-child Perceptions of Parental Behavioral Control through Rule-setting for Risky Health Choices during Adolescence. *Journal of Family Communication*, 9(4): 251–271.

Baym, N. K. (2000). *Tune In, Log On: Soaps, Fandom, and Online Community*. Thousand Oaks, CA: Sage.

Bazin, A. (1967–71). *What Is Cinema?* Berkeley, CA: University of California Press.

Bechtel, R. B., Achelpohl, C., and Akers, R. (1972). Correlates between Observed Behavior and Questionnaire Responses on Television Viewing. In E. A. Rubinstein, G. A. Comstock, and J. P. Murray (eds.), *Television in Day-to-Day Life: Patterns of Use* (Vol. 4). Washington, DC: Government Printing Office.

BBC (2005). Indian Tax Drummers to get Encore. Online, available at: http://news.bbc.co.uk/1/hi/world/south_asia/4397907.stm [accessed July 4, 2005].

Beck, U. (1994). The Reinvention of Politics: Towards a Theory of Reflexive Modernization. In U. Beck, A. Giddens, and S. Lash. *Reflexive Modernization: Politics, Tradition, and Aesthetics in the Modern Social Order*. Cambridge: Polity Press.

Beck, U., Giddens, A., and Lash, S. (1994). *Reflexive Modernization: Politics, Tradition, and Aesthetics in the Modern Social Order*. Cambridge: Polity.

Behlmer, R. (ed.) (1981[1972]). *Memo From David O. Selznick*. New York: Viking.

Bell, A. (1991). *The Language of News Media*, Oxford: Blackwell.

Bell, A. (1994). Climate of Opinion: Public and Media Discourse on the Global Environment. *Discourse & Society*, 5 (1): 33–64.

Bell, D. (1973). *The Coming of Post-Industrial Society*. New York: Basic Books.

Bell, D. and Kennedy, B. M. (eds.) (2000). *The Cybercultures Reader*. London: Routledge.

Bellour, R. (1973). L'Évidence et le code. In Dominique Noguez (ed.), *Cinéma: théorie, lectures*. Paris: Ed. Klincksieck. [English translation: The Obvious and the Code. In P. Rosen (ed.), *Narrative, Apparatus, Ideology: A Film Theory Reader*. New York: Columbia University Press, 1986].

Bellour, R. (1979). *L'analyse du film* [Film analysis]. Paris: Albatros.

Belson, W. A. (1967). *The Impact of Television*. London: Crosby Lockwood & Son.

Benedikt, M. (ed.) (1991). *Cyberspace: First Steps*. Cambridge, MA: MIT Press.

Beniger, J. R. (1978). Media Content as Social Indicators: The Greenfield Index on Agenda-setting. *Communication Research*, 5(4): 437–453.

Beniger, J. R. (1986). *The Control Revolution*. Cambridge, MA: Harvard University Press.

Beniger, J. R. (1992). Comparison, Yes, But – The Case of Technological and Cultural Change. In J. G. Blumler, J. M. McLeod, and K. E. Rosengren (eds.), *Comparatively Speaking: Communication and Culture across Space and Time*. Newbury Park, CA: Sage.

Benjamin, W. (1977[1936]). The Work of Art in the Age of Mechanical Reproduction. In J. Curran, M. Gurevitch, and J. Woollacott (eds.), *Mass Communication and Society*. London: Edward Arnold.

Benkler, Y. (2006). *The Wealth of Networks: How Social Production Transforms Markets and Freedom*. New Haven, CT: Yale University Press.

Bennett, T. (1992). Putting Policy into Cultural Studies. In L. Grossberg, C. Nelson, and P. Treichler (eds.), *Cultural Studies*. New York: Routledge.

Bennett, T. (1995). *The Birth of the Museum*. London: Routledge.

Bennett, T. and Woollacott, J. (1987). *Bond and Beyond*. London: Methuen.

Bennett, W. L. and Paletz, D. L. (eds.) (1994). *Taken by Storm: The Media, Public Opinion, and U.S. Foreign Policy in the Gulf War*. Chicago, IL: University of Chicago Press.

Benson, R. and Neveu, E. (eds.) (2005). *Bourdieu and the Journalistic Field*. Cambridge: Polity Press.

Benveniste, É. (1985[1969]). The Semiology of Language. In R. E. Innis (ed.), *Semiotics: An Introductory Anthology*. Bloomington, IN: Indiana University Press, pp. 228–246.

Berelson, B. (1949). What "Missing the Newspaper" Means. In P. F. Lazarsfeld and F. M. Stanton (eds.), *Communications Research 1948–9*. New York: Duell, Sloan, and Pearce.

Berelson, B. (1952). *Content Analysis in Communication Research*. Glencoe, IL: The Free Press.

Bergen, L. A. and Weaver, D. (1988). Job Satisfaction of Daily Newspaper Journalists and Organization Size. *Newspaper Research Journal*, 9(2): 1–14.

Berger, C. R., Roloff, M. E., and Roskos-Ewoldsen, D. E. (eds.) (2009). *The Handbook of Communication Science* (2nd ed.). Los Angeles, CA: Sage.

Berger, J. (1972). *Ways of Seeing*. Harmondsworth: Penguin.

Berger, P. L. and Luckmann, T. (1966). *The Social Construction of Reality*. London: Allen Lane.

Berkowitz, L. (1964). The Effects of Observing Violence. *Scientific American*, 210: 35–41.

Berkowitz, L. and Geen, R. G. (1966). Film Violence and the Cue Properties of Available Targets. *Journal of Personality and Social Psychology*, 3(5): 525–530.

Berman, M. (1982). *All That Is Solid Melts into Air: The Experience of Modernity*. London: Verso.

Bernard, H. R. (2006). *Research Methods in Anthropology: Qualitative and Quantitative Approaches* (4th ed.). Walnut Creek, CA: Alta Mira Press.

Bertaux, D. (ed.) (1981). *Biography and Society*. Beverly Hills, CA: Sage.

Bhabha, H. K. (1994). *The Location of Culture*. London: Routledge.

Bhaskar, R. (1979). *The Possibility of Naturalism*. Brighton: Harvester Press.

Bignell, J. (2000). *Postmodern Media Culture*. Edinburgh: Edinburgh University Press.

Billig, M. (1995). *Banal Nationalism*. London: Sage.

Biltereyst, D. (1991). Resisting American Hegemony: A Comparative Analysis of the Reception of Domestic and US Fiction. *European Journal of Communication*, 6(4), 469–497.

Biocca, F., Harms, C., and Burgoon, J. K. (2003). Toward a More Robust Theory and Measure of Social Presence: Review and Suggested Criteria. *Presence*, 12(5), 456–480.

Bird, S. E. (ed.) (2010). *The Anthropology of News & Journalism: Global Perspectives*. Bloomington, IN: Indiana University Press.

Blaikie, N. (2003). *Analyzing Quantitative Data: From Description to Explanation*. London: Sage.

Blaikie, N. (2007). *Approaches to Social Enquiry: Advancing Knowledge* (2nd ed.). Cambridge: Polity Press.

Blaikie, N. (2009). *Designing Social Research: The Logic of Anticipation* (2nd ed.). Cambridge: Polity Press.

Blum, R. (2005). Bausteinen zu einer Theorie der Mediensysteme [Constituents of a Theory of Media Systems]. *Medienwissenschaft Schweiz*, 2: 5–11.

Blumer, H. and Hauser, P. H. (1933). *Movies, Delinquency, and Crime*. New York: The Macmillan Company.

Blumler, J. G. (1979). The Role of Theory in Uses and Gratifications Studies. *Communication Research*, 6(1): 9–36.

Blumler, J. G. (ed.) (1992). *Television and the Public Interest: Vulnerable Values in Western European Broadcasting*. Newbury Park, CA: Sage.

Blumler, J. G. and Gurevitch, M. (1977). Linkages Between the Mass Media System and Politics: A Model for the Analysis of Political Communication Systems. In J. Curran, M. Gurevitch, and J. Woollacott (eds.), *Mass Communication and Society*. London: Edward Arnold.

Blumler, J. G. and Gurevitch, M. (1981). Politicians and the Press: An Essay on Role Relationships. In D. D. Nimmo and K. R. Sanders (eds.), *Handbook of Political Communication*. Beverly Hills, CA: Sage.

Blumler, J. G. and Gurevitch, M. (1995). *The Crisis of Public Communication*. London: Routledge.

Blumler, J. G. and Katz, E. (eds.) (1974). *The Uses of Mass Communications*. Beverly Hills, CA: Sage.

Blumler, J. G., McLeod, J., and Rosengren, K. E. (eds.) (1992). *Comparatively Speaking: Communication and Culture across Space and Time*. Newbury Park, CA: Sage.

Boddy, W. (1990). *Fifties Television: The Industry and Its Critics*. Urbana, IL: University of Illinois Press.

Boden, D. (1994). *The Business of Talk: Organizations in Action*. Cambridge: Polity Press.

Boden, M. (ed.) (1996). *Artificial Intelligence*. San Diego, CA: Academic Press.

Bogdanovich, P. (1967). *John Ford*. Berkeley, CA: University of California Press.

Bolter, J. D. (1991). *Writing Space: The Computer, Hypertext, and the History of Writing*. Hillsdale, NJ: Lawrence Erlbaum.

Bolter, J. D. and Grusin, R. (1999). *Remediation: Understanding New Media*. Cambridge, MA: MIT Press.

Boorstin, D. (1961). *The Image: A Guide to Pseudo-Events in America*. New York: Atheneum.

Booth, W. (1961). *The Rhetoric of Fiction*. Chicago, IL: University of Chicago Press.

Borba, M. (2011, February 4). *Plugged-in Reduces Family Time: Parenting in a digital world*. Online, available at: http:///www.thefutureoffriendship.org/?p=175.

Borde, R. and Chaumeton, E. (1955). *Panorame du film noir americain* [Outline of the American 'Black' Film]. Paris: Les Éditions de Minuit.

Bordwell, D. (1985a). *Narration in the Fiction Film*. London: Methuen.

Bordwell, D. (1985b). The Classical Hollywood style, 1917–60. In D. Bordwell, J. Staiger, and K. Thompson, *The Classical Hollywood Cinema: Film Style and Mode of Production to 1960*. New York: Columbia University Press.

Bordwell, D. (1989). Historical Poetics of Cinema. In R. Barton Palmer (ed.), *The Cinematic Text: Methods and Approaches*. New York: AMS Press.

Bordwell, D. and Carroll, N. (eds.) (1996). *Post-Theory: Reconstructing Film Studies*. Madison, WI: University of Wisconsin Press.

Bordwell, D. and Thompson, K. (2009). *Film Art: An Introduction* (9th ed.). New York: McGraw-Hill.

Bordwell, D., Staiger, J., and Thompson, K. (1985). *The Classical Hollywood Cinema: Film Style and Mode of Production to 1960*. New York: Columbia University Press.

Born, G. (2005). *Uncertain Vision: Birt, Dyke and the Reinvention of the BBC*. London: Random House.

Borzekowski, D. L. G. and Robinson, T. N. (1999). Viewing the Viewers: Ten Video Cases of Children's Television Viewing Behaviors. *Journal of Broadcasting and Electronic Media*, 43(4), 506–528.

Boudon, R., Cherkaoui, M., and Alexander, J. (eds.) (1997). *The Classical Tradition in Sociology: The European Tradition*. London: Sage.

Bourdieu, P. (1977). *Outline of a Theory of Practice*. Cambridge: Cambridge University Press.

Bourdieu, P. (1984[1979]). *Distinction: A Social Critique of the Judgement of Taste*. London: Routledge & Kegan Paul.

Bourdieu, P. (1988). *Homo Academicus*. Cambridge: Polity Press.

Bower, G. H. and Cirilo, R. K. (1985). Cognitive Psychology and Text Processing. In T. A. Van Dijk (ed.), *Handbook of Discourse Analysis, Vol. 1: Disciplines of Discourse*. New York: Academic Press.

Bower, R. T. (1973). *Television and the Public*. New York: Holt, Rinehart & Winston.

Bowrey, K. and Rimmer, M. (2002). *Rip, Mix, Burn: The Politics of Peer to Peer and Copyright Law*. Online, available at: www.firstmonday.org/issues/issue7_8/bowrey [accessed July 25, 2007].

Boyarin, J. (ed.) (1992). *The Ethnography of Reading*. Berkeley, CA: University of California Press.

Boyd-Barrett, O. and Thussu, D. (1992). *Contra-Flow in Global News*. London: John Libbey.

Boyd, D. M. and Ellison, N. B. (2007). Social Network Sites: Definition, History, and Scholarship. *Journal of Computer-Mediated Communication*, 13(1): 210–230.

Boyle, R. (2006). *Sports Journalism: Context and Issues*. London: Sage.

Braman, S. (2006). *Change of State: Information, Policy, and Power*. Cambridge, MA: MIT Press.

Branigan, E. (1992). *Narrative Comprehension and Film*. London: Routledge.

Braudel, F. (1972, 1974). *The Mediterranean and the Mediterranean World in the Age of Philip II. Vols. 1 and 2*. New York: Harper and Row.

Braudel, F. (1980). *On History*. London: Weidenfeld & Nicolson.

Braudy, L. and Cohen, M. (eds.) (2004). *Film Theory and Criticism: Introductory Readings* (6th ed.). New York: Oxford University Press.

Brecht, B. (1993[1932]). The Radio as an Apparatus of Communication. In N. Strauss and D. Mandl (eds.), *Radiotext(e)*. New York: Columbia University Press.

Bremond, C. (1966). La logique des possibles narratifs, *Communications*, 8: 60–76. [English translation: The Logic of Narrative Possibilities. *New Literary History* 11(3): 387–411, 1980].

Briggs, A. (1961–95). *The History of Broadcasting in the United Kingdom. Vols. 1–5*. Oxford: Oxford University Press.

Briggs, A. (1980). Problems and Possibilities in the Writing of Broadcasting History. *Media, Culture & Society*, 2(1): 5–13.

Briggs, A. and Burke, P. (2010). *A Social History of the Media: From Gutenberg to the Internet* (3rd ed.). Cambridge: Polity Press.

Brockman, J. (ed.) (1995). *The Third Culture*. New York: Simon & Schuster.

Brosius, H.-B. and Weimann, G. (1996). Who Sets the Agenda? Agenda-Setting as a Two-Step Flow. *Communication Research*, 23(5), 561–580.

Brown, J. R. and Linné, O. (1976). The Family as Mediator of Television's Effects. In R. Brown (ed.), *Children and Television*. Beverly Hills, CA: Sage, pp. 184–198.

Brown, J. R., Childers, K. W., Bauman, K. E., and Koch, G. (1990). The Influence of New Media and Family Structure on Young Adolescents' Television and Radio Use. *Communication Research*, 17(1): 65–82.

Bruce, C. D. (2007). Questions Arising about Emergence, Data Collection, and its Interaction with Analysis in a Grounded Theory Study. *International Journal of Qualitative Methods*, 6(1): 1–12.

Bruner, J. (1986). *Actual Minds, Possible Worlds*. Cambridge, MA: Harvard University Press.

Bruner, J. (1994). The Narrative Construction of 'Reality.' In M. Ammaniti and D. N. Stern (eds.), *Psychoanalysis and Development*. New York: New York University Press.

Bruns, A. (2005a). 'Anyone Can Edit': Understanding the Produser. Guest Lecture at SUNY, Buffalo/New School, New York City/Brown University/Temple University. Online, available at: http://snurb.info/index.php?q=node/286 [accessed April 15, 2011].

Bruns, A. (2005b). *Gatewatching: Collaborative Online News Production*. New York: Peter Lang.

Bruns, A. (2008a). *Blogs, Wikipedia, Second Life, and Beyond: From Production to Produsage*. New York: Peter Lang.

Bruns, A. (2008b). The Active Audience: Transforming Journalism. In C. Paterson and D. Domingo (eds.), *Making Online News: The Ethnography of New Media Production*. New York: Peter Lang.

Brunsdon, C. (1989). Text and Audience. In E. Seiter, H. Borchers, G. Kreutzner, and E.-M. Warth (eds.), *Remote Control: Television, Audiences, and Cultural Power*. London: Routledge.

Brunsdon, C. and Morley, D. (1978). *Everyday Television: 'Nationwide'*. London: British Film Institute.

Bryant, A. (2002). Re-grounding Grounded Theory. *Journal of Information Technology Theory and Application*, 4(1): 25–42.

Bryant, J. and Oliver, M. B. (eds.) (2009). *Media Effects: Advances in Theory and Research* (3rd ed.). New York: Routledge.

Bryant, J., Carveth, R. A., and Brown, D. (1981). Television Viewing and Anxiety: An Experimental Examination. *Journal of Communication*, 31(1): 106–119.

Bryman, A. (1988). *Quantity and Quality in Social Research*. London: Unwin Hyman.

Bryman, A. (2008). *Social Research Methods* (3rd ed.). Oxford: Oxford University Press.

Bryman, A. and Burgess, R. G. (eds.) (1999). *Qualitative Research*. London: Sage.

Bryman, A. and Cramer, D. (2008). *Quantitative Data Analysis with SPSS 14, 15 and 16: A Guide for Social Scientists*. London: Routledge.

Bryson, N. (1991). Semiology and Visual Interpretation. In N. Bryson, M. A. Holly, and K. Moxey (eds.), *Visual Theory. Painting and Interpretation*. Cambridge: Polity Press.

Buckingham, D. (2003). *Media Education: Literacy, Learning and Contemporary Culture*. Cambridge: Polity Press.

Buckingham, D. (2009). 'Creative' Visual Methods in Media Research: Possibilities, Problems, and Proposals. *Media, Culture & Society*, 31(4): 633–652.

Buckingham, D. (ed.) (1993). *Reading Audiences: Young People and the Media*. Manchester: Manchester University Press.

Buckland, W. (2000). *The Cognitive Semiotics of Film*. Cambridge: Cambridge University Press.

Bull, M. and Back, L. (eds.) (2003). *The Auditory Culture Reader*. Oxford: Berg.

Burgess, J. and Green, J. (2009). *YouTube: Online Video and Participatory Culture*. London: Polity Press.

Burgess, R. G. (1982). Keeping Field Notes. In R. G. Burgess (ed.), *Field Research: A Sourcebook and Field Manual*. London: Unwin Hyman.

Burke, K. (1950). *A Rhetoric of Motives*. New York: Prentice-Hall.

Burke, K. (1957). *The Philosophy of Literary Form*. New York: Vintage.

Burke, P. (1992). *History and Social Theory*. Cambridge: Polity Press.

Burke, P. (ed.) (1991). *New Perspectives on Historical Writing*. Cambridge: Polity Press.

Burr, P. and Burr, R. (1976). Television Advertising to Children: What Parents Are Saying about Government Control. *Journal of Advertising*, 5(4): 37–41.

Butterworth, H. (1965). *The Whig Interpretation of History*. New York/London: W. W. Norton and Co.

Caldwell, J. T. (1995). *Televisuality: Style, Crisis, and Authority in American Television*. New Brunswick, NJ: Rutgers University Press.

Caldwell, J. T. (2006). Cultural Studies in Media Production: Critical Industrial Practices. In M. White and J. Schwoch (eds.), *Questions of Method in Cultural Studies*. Malden, MA: Blackwell.

Calhoun, C. (ed.) (1992). *Habermas and the Public Sphere*. Cambridge, MA: MIT Press.

Campbell, W. J. (2001). *Yellow Journalism: Puncturing the Myths, Defining the Legacies*. Westport, CT: Praeger.

Cantor, J. (1994). Fright Reactions to Mass Media. In J. Bryant and D. Zillmann (eds.), *Media Effects: Advances in Theory and Research*. Hillsdale, NJ: Lawrence Erlbaum Associates.

Cantor, M. (1988 [1971]). *The Hollywood Television Producer: His Work and His Audience* (revised ed.). New Brunswick, NJ: Transaction Books.

Cantril, H. (1940). *The Invasion from Mars*. Princeton, NJ: Princeton University Press.

Cappella, J. N. (1996). Symposium: Biology and Communication. *Journal of Communication*, 46(3), 4–84.

Carey, J. W. (1989a). *Communication as Culture*. Boston, MA: Unwin Hyman.

Carey, J. W. (1989b[1975]). A Cultural Approach to Communication. *Communication as Culture*. Boston, MA: Unwin Hyman, pp. 13–36.

Carey, J. W. and Kreiling, A. W. (1974). Popular Culture and Uses and Gratifications: Notes toward an Accommodation. In J. G. Blumler and E. Katz (eds.), *The Uses of Mass Communications*. Beverly Hills, CA: Sage.

Caron, A. and Ward, S. (1974). Gift Decisions by Kids and Parents. *Journal of Advertising Research*, 15(4): 15–20.

Carragee, K. M. and Roefs, W. (2004). The Neglect of Power in Recent Framing Research. *Journal of Communication*, 54(2), 214–233.

Carringer, R. (1996). *The Making of Citizen Kane*. Berkeley, CA: University of California Press.

Carter, C. and Steiner, L. (eds.) (2004). *Critical Readings: Media and Gender*. Maidenhead: Open University Press.

Carvalho, A. (2005). Representing the Politics of the Greenhouse Effect: Discursive Strategies in the British Media. *Critical Discourse Studies*, 2(1):1–29.

Carvalho, A. (2008). Mediated Discourse and Society. Rethinking the Framework of Critical Discourse Analysis. *Journalism Studies*, 9(2): 161–177.

Castells, M. (1996). *The Rise of the Network Society*. Oxford: Blackwell.

Castells, M. (2009). *Communication Power*. New York: Oxford University Press.

Castells, M. (ed.) (2004). *The Network Society: A Cross-Cultural Perspective*. Cheltenham: Edward Elgar.

Castells, M., Fernández-Ardèval, M., Qiu, J. L., and Sey, A. (2007). *Mobile Communication and Society*. Cambridge, MA: MIT Press.

Cater, D. (1959). *The Fourth Branch of Government*. Boston, MA: Houghton-Mifflin.

Centerwall, B. S. (1989). Exposure to Television as a Cause of Violence. *Public Communication and Behavior*, 2: 1–58.

Cerquiglini, B. (1999). *In Praise of the Variant: A Critical History of Philology*. London: Johns Hopkins University Press.

Chaffee, S. H. and Hochheimer, J. (1985). The Beginnings of Political Communication Research in the United States: Origins of the 'Limited Effects' Model. In E. M. Rogers and F. Balle (eds.), *The Media Revolution in America and Western Europe*. Norwood, NJ: Ablex.

Chamberlayne, P., Bornat, J., and Wengraf, T. (eds.) (2000). *The Turn to Biographical Methods in Social Science*. London: Routledge.

Charlton, T. (1997). The Inception of Broadcast Television: A Naturalistic Study of Television's Effects. In T. Charlton and K. David (eds.), *Elusive Links: Television, Video Games and Children's Behaviour*. Tewkesbury: Park Published Papers.

Charmaz, K. (2000). Grounded Theory: Objectivist and Constructivist Methods. In N. K. Denzin and Y. S. Lincoln (eds.), *Handbook of Qualitative Research* (2nd ed.). Thousand Oaks, CA: Sage, pp. 509–536.

Charmaz, K. (2006). *Constructing Grounded Theory: A Practical Guide through Qualitative Analysis*. London: Sage.

Chatman, S. (1989[1978]). *Story and Discourse. Narrative Structure in Fiction and Film* (5th paperback ed.). Ithaca, NY: Cornell University Press.

Chatman, S. (1990). *Coming to Terms. The Rhetoric of Narrative in Fiction and Film*. Ithaca, NY: Cornell University Press.

Chion, M. (1982). *La voix au cinéma*. Paris: Éditions de l'Étoile. [English translation: *The Voice in Cinema*. New York: Columbia University Press, 1999.]

Chion, M. (1985). *Le son au cinéma* [*Sound in Cinema*]. Paris: Éditions de l'Étoile.

Chion, M. (1988). *La toile trouée* [*The Perforated Screen*]. Paris: Seuil.

Chion, M. (1990). *L'audio-vision*. Paris: Nathan. [English translation: *Audio-vision. Sound on Screen*. New York: Columbia University Press, 1994.]

Chion, M. (1995). *La musique au cinéma* [Music in cinema]. Paris: Fayard.

Chion, M. (1998). *Le son* [Sound]. Paris: Nathan.

Chomsky, N. (1965). *Aspects of the Theory of Syntax*. Cambridge, MA: MIT Press.

Christians, C. G. and Traber, M. (eds.) (1997). *Communication Ethics and Universal Values*. Thousand Oaks, CA: Sage.

Christians, C. G., Glasser, T. L., McQuail, D., Nordenstreng, K., and White, R. A. (2009). *Normative Theories of the Media: Journalism in Democratic Societies*. Urbana, IL: University of Illinois Press.

Clark, L. S. (2011). Reflexivity in Data Analysis: Constructing Narratives of Family Digital Media Use In, Through, and For Public Engagement. In R. Parameswaran (ed.), *Handbook for Audience Studies*. London/New York: Blackwell.

Clark, L. S. (in press). Toward the Development of a Theory of Parental Mediation: Exploring Emotions, Child Agency, and Participatory Learning in the Digital Era. *Communication Theory*.

Clarke, D. S. (1990). *Sources of Semiotic*. Carbondale, IL: Southern Illinois University Press.

Classen, C. (1993). *Worlds of Sense: Exploring the Senses in History and Across Cultures*. London: Routledge.

Clifford, J. and Marcus, G. E. (eds.) (1986). *Writing Culture: The Poetics and Politics of Ethnography*. Berkeley, CA: University of California Press.

Coakley, J. (ed.) (2000). *Handbook of Sports Studies*. London: Sage.

Cohen, A., Levy, M., Roeh, I., and Gurevitch, M. (1996). *Global Newsrooms, Local Audiences: A Study of the Eurovision News Exchange*. London: John Libbey.

Cohen, B. (1963). *The Press and Foreign Policy*. Princeton, NJ: Princeton University Press.

Cohen, E. L. and Willis, C. (2004). One Nation under Radio: Digital and Public Memory after September 11. *New Media & Society*, 6(5), 591–610.

Collin, F. (1997). *Social Reality*. London: Routledge.

Collingwood, A., Cheshire, H. *et al.*, (2010). *A Review of the Longitudinal Study of Young People in England (LSYPE): Recommendations for a second cohort*. London: Department for Education. Online, available at: www.education.gov.uk/publications/eOrderingDownload/DFE-RR048.pdf [accessed June 26, 2011].

Collins, C. (1997). Viewer Letters as Audience Research: The Case of *Murphy Brown*. *Journal of Broadcasting and Electronic Media*, 41(1), 109–131.

Compaine, B. M. (ed.) (2001). *The Digital Divide: Facing a Crisis or Creating a Myth?* Cambridge, MA: MIT Press.

Comscore (2008). Press Release: Baidu Ranked Third Largest Worldwide Search Property by comScore in December 2007. Online, available at: www.comscore.com/press/release.asp?press=2018 [accessed April 15, 2011].

Comstock, G. (1998). Television Research: Past Problems and Present Issues. In J. K. Asamen and G. L. Berry (eds.), *Research Paradigms, Television and Social Behavior*. Thousand Oaks, CA: Sage.

Comstock, G. A., Murray, J. P., and Rubinstein, E. A. (eds.) (1971). *Television and Social Behavior*. Washington, DC: Government Printing Office.

Conant, J. and Haugeland, J. (eds.) (2000). *Thomas S. Kuhn: The Road since Structure*. New York: Basic Books.

Converse, J. M. (1987). *Survey Research in the United States: Roots and Emergence, 1890–1960*. Berkeley, CA: University of California Press.

Conway, J. C. and Rubin, A. M. (1991). Psychological Predictors of Television Viewing Motivation. *Communication Research*, 18(4), 443–463.

Cook N. (1998). *Analysing Musical Multimedia*. Oxford: Oxford University Press.

Cook, P. (ed.) (1999). *The Cinema Book*. London: British Film Institute.

Cook, T. D., Kendziersky, D. A., and Thomas, S. A. (1983). The Implicit Assumptions of Television Research: An Analysis of the 1982 NIMH Report on Television and Behavior. *Public Opinion Quarterly*, 47(2): 161–201.

Cook, T. E. (1998). *Governing With the News: The News Media as a Political Institution*. Chicago, IL: University of Chicago Press.

Cooley, C. H. (1894). The Theory of Transportation. *Publications of the American Economic Association*, 9(3): 221–370.

Cooper, B. (1999). The Relevancy and Gender Identity in Spectators' Interpretations of *Thelma and Louise*. *Critical Studies in Mass Communication*, 16(1), 20–41.

Corley, K. M. and Kaufer, D. S. (1993). Semantic Connectivity: An Approach for Analyzing Symbols in Semantic Networks. *Communication Theory*, 3(3), 183–213.

Corner, J. (1991). Meaning, Genre, and Context: The Problematics of 'Public Knowledge' in the New Audience Studies. In J. Curran and M. Gurevitch (eds.), *Mass Media and Society*. London: Edward Arnold.

Cottle, S. (1999). From BBC Newsroom to BBC News Centre: On Changing Technology and Journalist Practices. *Convergence: Journal of New Information and Communication Technologies*, 5(3): 22–43.

Cottle, S. (2000). New(s) Times: Towards a 'Second Wave' of News Ethnography, *Communications. The European Journal of Communication Research*, 25(1): 19–41.

Couldry, N. (2003). *Media Rituals: A Critical Approach*. London: Routledge.

Cowan, G. (1979). *See No Evil: The Backstage Battle Over Sex and Violence on Television*. New York: Simon and Schuster.

Coward, R. and Ellis, J. (1977). *Language and Materialism*. London: Routledge Kegan Paul.

Craig, R. T. (1999). Communication Theory as a Field. *Communication Theory*, 9: 119–161.

Craig, R. T. (2007). Pragmatism in the Field of Communication Theory. *Communication Theory*, 17: 125–145.

Creswell, J. W. (2009). *Research Design: Qualitative, Quantitative, and Mixed Methods Approaches* (3rd ed.). Thousand Oaks, CA: Sage.

Crisell, A. (ed.) (2008). *Radio*. London/New York: Routledge.

Csikszentmihalyi, M. (1975). *Beyond Boredom and Anxiety*. San Francisco, CA: Jossey-Bass.

Csikszentmihalyi, M. (1997). *Finding Flow. The Psychology of Engagement with Everyday Life*. New York: Basic Books.

Cunningham, S. (1988). Kennedy-Miller: 'House Style' in Australian Television. In S. Dermody and E. Jacka (eds.), *The Imaginary Industry: Australian Film in the late '80s*. North Ryde: Australian Film Television and Radio School.

Curran, J. (2002). *Media and Power*. London: Routledge.

Curran, J. and Seaton, J. (2009). *Power Without Responsibility* (7th ed.). London: Routledge.

Curran, J., Iyengar, S., Lund, A. B., and Salovaara-Moring, I. (2009). Media System, Public Knowledge and Democracy: A Comparative Study. *European Journal of Communication*, 24(1): 5–26.

Cushion, S. and Lewis, J. (eds.) (2010). *The Rise of 24-Hour News Television. Global Perspectives*. New York: Peter Lang.

D'Acci, J. (1994). *Defining Women: The Case of Cagney and Lacey*. Chapel Hill, NC: University of North Carolina Press.

Dahl, H. F. (1976). The Art of Writing Broadcasting History. *Gazette: International Journal for Mass Communication Studies*, 3: 130–137.

Dahl. H. F. (1994). The Pursuit of Media History. *Media, Culture & Society*, 16(4): 551–564.

Dahlgren, P. (2006). Doing Citizenship: The Cultural Origins of Civic Agency in the Public Sphere. *European Journal of Cultural Studies*, 9(3): 267–286.

Dahlgren, P. (2009). *Media and Political Engagement: Citizens, Communication and Democracy*. Cambridge: Cambridge University Press.

Danet, B. and Herring, S. (eds.) (2007). *The Multilingual Internet: Language, Culture, and Communication Online*. New York: Oxford University Press.

Danto, A. C. (1965). *Analytical Philosophy of History*. Cambridge: Cambridge University Press.

Davis, A. (2003). Public Relations and News Sources. In S. Cottle (ed.), *News, Public Relations and Power*. London: Sage.

Davis, A. (2010). *Political Communication and Social Theory*. London: Routledge.

Davison, W. P. (1983). The Third-person Effect in Communication. *Public Opinion Quarterly*, 47(1): 1–15.

Day-Lewis, S. (1989). *One Day in the Life of Television*. London: Grafton.

Dayan, D. and E. Katz (1992). *Media Events*. Cambridge, MA: Harvard University Press.

Deacon, D., Fenton, N., and Bryman, A. (1999). From Inception to Reception: The Natural History of a News Item. *Media, Culture & Society*, 21(1): 5–31.

Deacon, D., Pickering, M., Golding, P., and Murdock, G. (2007). *Researching Communications: A Practical Guide to Methods in Media and Cultural Analysis* (2nd ed.). London: Hodder Arnold.

Dearing, J. and Rogers, E. M. (1996). *Agenda-Setting*. Thousand Oaks, CA: Sage.

DeFleur, M. L. (1964). Occupational Roles as Portrayed on Television. *Public Opinion Quarterly*, 28(1): 57–74.

DeFleur, M. L. and Larsen, O. N. (1987). *The Flow of Information*. New Brunswick, NJ: Transaction Press.

Dekimpe, M. and Hanssens, D. M. (2007). Advertising Response Models. In G. J. Tellis and T. Ambler (eds.), *The Sage Handbook of Advertising*. London: Sage, pp. 247–263.

Deleuze, G. (1986). *Cinema 1: The Movement-Image*. London: Athlone Press.

Deleuze, G. (1989). *Cinema 2: The Time-Image*. London: Athlone Press.

Delia, J. (1987). Communication Research: A History. In C. R. Berger and S. H. Chaffee (eds.), *Handbook of Communication Science*. Newbury Park, CA: Sage.

Demers, D. P. and Wackman, D. B. (1988). Effect of Chain Ownership on Newspaper Management Goals. *Newspaper Research Journal*, 9(2): 59–68.

Dennis, E. E. and Wartella, E. (eds.) (1996). *American Communication Research: The Remembered History*. Mahwah, NJ: Lawrence Erlbaum.

Denzin, N. (1970). *The Research Act: A Theoretical Introduction to Sociological Methods*. Englewood Cliffs, NJ: Prentice-Hall.

Denzin, N. K. and Lincoln, Y. S. (eds.) (2005). *The Sage Handbook of Qualitative Research* (3rd ed.). Thousand Oaks, CA: Sage.

Derrida, J. (1976[1967]). *Of Grammatology*. Baltimore, MD: Johns Hopkins University Press.

Desmond, R. J., Singer, J. L., and Singer, D. G. (1990). Family Mediation: Parental Communication Patterns and the Influence of Television on Children. In J. Bryant (ed.), *Television and the American Family*. Hillsdale, NJ: Erlbaum, pp. 293–310.

Deuze, M. (2007). *Media Work*. Cambridge: Polity Press.

Dewey, J. (1926). *The Public and its Problems*. London: George Allen & Unwin.

Dichter, E. (1947). Psychology in Market Research. *Harvard Business Review*, 25(4): 432–443.

Dicks, B., Mason, B., Coffey, A., and Atkinson, P. (2005). *Qualitative Research and Hypermedia: Ethnography for the Digital Age*. London: Sage.

Dissanayake, W. (1988a). The Need for Asian Approaches to Communication. In W. Dissanayake (ed.), *Communication Theory: The Asian Perspective*. Singapore: Asian Mass Communication Research and Information Center.

Dissanayake, W. (ed.) (1988b). *Communication Theory: The Asian Perspective*. Singapore: Asian Mass Communication Research and Information Center.

Divers, J. (2002). *Possible Worlds*. London: Routledge.

Doherty, T. (1999). *Pre-Code Hollywood: Sex, Immorality, and Insurrection in American Cinema*. New York: Columbia University Press.

Domingo, D. (2008). When Immediacy Rules: Online Journalism Models in Four Catalan Online Newsrooms. In C. Paterson and D. Domingo (eds.), *Making Online News: The Ethnography of New Media Production*. New York: Peter Lang.

Donnerstein, E. and Berkowitz, L. (1981). Victim Reactions in Aggressive Erotic Films as a Factor in Violence against Women. *Journal of Personality and Social Psychology*, 41(4): 710–724.

Donohue, G., Olien, C., and Tichenor, P. (1987). Media Access and Knowledge Gaps. *Critical Studies in Mass Communication*, 4(1), 87–92.

Donohue, G., Tichenor, P., and Olien, C. (1975). Mass Media and the Knowledge Gap. *Communication Research*, 2(1): 3–23.

Donsbach, W. (2006). The Identity of Communication Research. *Journal of Communication*, 56(3): 437–448.

Donsbach, W. (ed.) (2008). *International Encyclopedia of Communication*. Malden, MA: Wiley-Blackwell.

Dorfman, A. and Mattelart, A. (1975[1971]). *How to Read Donald Duck: Imperialist Ideology in the Disney Comic*. New York: International General.

Dorr, A., Kovaric, P., and Doubleday, C. (1989). Parent-child Coviewing of Television. *Journal of Broadcasting & Electronic Media*, 33(1): 35–51.

Dougherty, D. S., Kramer, M. W., Klatzke, S. R., and Rogers, K. K. (2009). Language Convergence and Meaning Divergence: A Meaning Centered Communication Theory. *Communication Monographs*, 76(1): 20–46.

Douglas, M. (1987). *How Institutions Think*. London: Routledge Kegan Paul.

Douglas, M. (1997). The Depoliticization of Risk. In R. Ellis and M. Thompson (eds.), *Culture Matters: Essays in Honour of Aaron Wildavsky*. Boulder, CO: Westview Press.

Downing, J. D. H. (2000). *Radical Media: Rebellious Communication and Social Movements*. Thousand Oaks, CA: Sage.

Doyle, B. (1989). *English and Englishness*. London: Routledge.

Dray, W. (1957). *Laws and Explanation in History*. London: Oxford University Press.

Dreier, O. (1999). Personal Trajectories of Participation across Contexts of Social Practice. *Outlines* 1(1): 1–52.

Drew, P. and Heritage, J. (1992). Analyzing Talk at Work: An Introduction. In P. Drew and J. Heritage (eds.), *Talk at Work: Interaction in Institutional Settings*. Cambridge: Cambridge University Press.

Drotner, K. (1994). Ethnographic Enigmas: 'The Everyday' in Recent Media Studies. *Cultural Studies*, 8(2), 341–357.

Drotner, K. (1996). Less Is More: Media Ethnography and Its Limits. In P. I. Crawford and S. B. Hafsteinsson (eds.), *The Construction of the Viewer*. Højbjerg: Intervention Press.

Drotner, K. and Schrøder, K. C. (2010). *Digital Content Creation. Perceptions, Practices, and Perspectives*. New York: Peter Lang.

Drotner, K., Jensen, K. B., Poulsen, I., and Schrøder, K. C. (1996). *Medier og kultur [Media and Culture]*. Copenhagen: Borgen.

Dublin Core (n.d.). Online, available at: www.dublincore.org [accessed April 15, 2011].

Duke, L. (2000). Black in a Blonde World: Race and Girls' Interpretations of the Feminine Ideal in Teen Magazines. *Journalism and Mass Communication Quarterly*, 77(2), 367–392.

Dunaway, D. K. and Baum, W. K. (eds.) (1996). *Oral History: An Interdisciplinary Anthology* (2nd ed.). Walnut Creek, CA: Alta Mira Press.

Duncan, H. D. (1968). *Symbols in Society*. New York: Oxford University Press.

During, S. (ed.) (2007). *The Cultural Studies Reader* (3rd ed.). London: Routledge.

Eagleton, T. (1983). *Literary Theory: An Introduction*. Minneapolis, MN: Minnesota University Press.

Eastin, M. S., Greenberg, B., and Hofshire, L. (2006). Parenting the Internet. *Journal of Communication*, 56(3): 486–504.

Eco, U. (1968). *La struttura assente. Introduzione alla ricerca semiologica* [The Absent Structure. Introduction to Semiological Research]. Milano: Bompiani.

Eco, U. (1975). *Trattato di semiotica generale*. Milano: Bompiani. [Revised version of Eco (1968). English translation: *A Theory of Semiotics*. Bloomington, IN: Indiana University Press, 1976.]

Eco, U. (1976). *A Theory of Semiotics*. Bloomington, IN: Indiana University Press.

Eco, U. (1979). *The Role of the Reader. Explorations in the Semiotics of Texts*. Bloomington, IN/London: Indiana University Press.

Eco, U. (1984). *Semiotics and the Philosophy of Language*. London: Macmillan.

Eco, U. (1987a[1965]). Narrative Structures in Fleming. In U. Eco (ed.), *The Role of the Reader*. London: Hutchinson.

Eco, U. (1987b). *The Role of the Reader*. London: Hutchinson.

Edelman, M. (1971). *Politics as Symbolic Action*. Chicago, IL: Markham.

Edwards, M. (2004). *Civil Society*. Cambridge: Polity Press.

Eide, M. (2010). Dialogical Ambiguities: Journalism, Professionalism, and Flattery. *Northern Lights: Film and Media Studies Yearbook 2010*, 8(1): 9–23.

Eide, M. and Knight, G. (1999). Public/Private Service: Service Journalism and the Problems of Everyday Life. *European Journal of Communication*, 14(4): 525–547.

Eilders, C. (2006). News Factors and News Decisions: Theoretical and Methodological Advances in Germany. *Communications*, 31(1): 5–24.

Eisenstein, E. L. (1979). *The Printing Press as an Agent of Change: Communication and Cultural Transformation in Early Modern Europe. Vols. 1–2*. Cambridge: Cambridge University Press.

Eisler, H. and Adorno, T. W. (1947). *Composing for the Films*. Dobson: London

Eksterowicz, A. J. and Roberts, R. N. (2000). *Public Journalism and Political Knowledge*. Lanham, MD: Rowman & Littlefield Publishers.

Ekström. M., Kroon, Å., and Nylund, M. (eds.) (2006). *News from the Interview Society*. Gothenburg: Nordicom.

Elder-Vass, D. (2010). *The Causal Powers of Social Structures. Emergence, Structure and Agency*. Cambridge: Cambridge University Press.

Ellen, R. F. (ed.) (1984). *Ethnographic Research: A Guide to General Conduct*. London: Academic Press.

Elliott, P. (1974). Uses and Gratifications Research: A Critique and a Sociological Alternative. In J. G. Blumler and E. Katz (eds.), *The Uses of Mass Communications*. Beverly Hills, CA: Sage.

Ellis, J. (1975). Made at Ealing. *Screen*, 16:(1): 78–127.

Ellis, J. (1982). *Visible Fictions*. London: Routledge Kegan Paul.

Emmison, M. and Smith, P. (2000). *Researching the Visual: Images, Objects, Contexts, and Interactions in Social and Cultural Inquiry*. London: Sage.

Entman, R. M. (1993): Framing: Toward Clarification of a Fractured Paradigm. *Journal of Communication*, 43 (4): 51–58.

Enzensberger, H. M. (1972[1970]). Constituents of a Theory of the Media. In D. McQuail (ed.), *Sociology of Mass Communications*. Harmondsworth: Penguin.

Ericson, R. V., Baranak, P. M., and Chan, J. B. L. (1987). *Visualizing Deviance: A Study of News Organization*. Toronto: University of Toronto Press.

Ericson, R. V., Baranek, P. M., and Chan, J. B. L. (1989). *Negotiating Control. A Study of News Sources*. Milton Keynes: Open University Press.

Ericson, R. V., Baranek, P. M., and Chan, J. B. L. (1991). *Representing Order: Crime, Law and Justice in the News Media*. Milton Keynes: Open University Press.

Erlich, V. (1955). *Russian Formalism: History, Doctrine*. The Hague: Mouton.

Eskelinen, M. (2001). The Gaming Situation. *Game Studies*, 2(1). Online, available at: www.gamestudies.org/0101/eskelinen [accessed April 15, 2011].

Ettema, J. S. and Whitney, D. C. (eds.) (1994). *Audiencemaking: How the Media Create the Audience*. Thousand Oaks, CA: Sage.

Evetts, J. (2006). The Sociology of Professional Groups: New Directions. *Current Sociology*, 54(1): 133–143.

Fairclough, N. (1992). *Discourse and Social Change*. Cambridge: Polity Press.

Fairclough, N. (1993). Critical Discourse Analysis and the Marketization of Public Discourse: The Universities. *Discourse & Society*, 4(2):133–168.

Fairclough, N. (1995). *Media Discourse*. London: Edward Arnold.

Fairclough, N. (2009). A Dialectical-Relational Approach to Critical Discourse Analysis in Social Research. In R. Wodak and M. Meyer (eds.), *Methods of Critical Discourse Analysis*. London: Sage.

Fairclough, N. and Wodak, R. (1997). Critical Discourse Analysis. In T. A. Van Dijk (ed.), *Discourse as Social Interaction*. London: Sage.

Fallon, D. (1980). *The German University: A Heroic Ideal in Conflict with the Modern World*. Boulder, CO: Colorado Associated University Press.

Farrell, T. B. (1987). Beyond Science: Humanistic Contributions to Communication Theory. In C. R. Berger and S. H. Chaffee (eds.), *Handbook of Communication Science*. Newbury Park, CA: Sage.

Feldman, L. (2007). The News about Comedy: Young Audiences, The Daily Show, and Evolving Notions of Journalism. *Journalism: Theory, Practice & Criticism*, 8(4), 406–427.

Ferguson, M. and Golding, P. (eds.) (1997). *Cultural Studies in Question*. London: Sage.

Feshbach, S. (1961). The Stimulating vs. Cathartic Effects of a Vicarious Aggressive Experience. *Journal of Abnormal and Social Psychology*, 63(2): 381–385.

Festinger, L. (1957). *A Theory of Cognitive Dissonance*. Evanston, IL: Row.

Feuer, J., Kerr, P., and Vahamagi, T. (eds.) (1984). *MTM: 'Quality Television.'* London: British Film Institute.

Feyerabend, P. (1975). *Against Method: Outline of an Anarchistic Theory of Knowledge*. London: New Left Books.

Fielding, N. G. and Lee, R. M. (1998). *Computer Analysis and Qualitative Research*. London: Sage.

Filmer P., Philipson, M., Silverman, D., and Walsh, D. (1972). *New Directions in Sociological Theory.* London: Collier-Macmillan.

Findahl, O. (1985). Some Characteristics of News Memory and Comprehension. *Journal of Broadcasting and Electronic Media*, 29(4): 379–396.

Fink, A. (1995a). *The Survey Handbook*. Thousand Oaks, CA: Sage.

Fink, A. (1995b). *How To Ask Survey Questions*. Thousand Oaks, CA: Sage.

Fink, E. J., and Gantz, W. (1996). A Content Analysis of Three Mass Communication Research Traditions: Social Science, Interpretive Studies, and Critical Analysis. *Journalism and Mass Communication Quarterly*, 73(1), 114–134.

Fish, S. (1979). *Is There a Text in This Class? The Authority of Interpretive Communities*. Cambridge, MA: Harvard University Press.

Fisher, W. A. and Grenier, G. (1994). Violent Pornography, Antiwomen Thoughts, and Antiwomen Acts: In Search of Reliable Effects. *Journal of Sex Research*, 31(1): 23–38.

Fisherkeller, J. (2002). *Growing Up with Television: Everyday Learning Among Young Adolescents*. Philadelphia, PA: Temple University Press.

Fiske, J. (1987). *Television Culture*. London: Methuen.

Fiske, J. (1990). *Introduction to Communication Studies*. London: Routledge.

Flick, U. (ed.) (2007). *The Sage Qualitative Research Kit*. London: Sage.

Flitterman-Lewis, S. (1983). The Real Soap Operas. In E. A. Kaplan (ed.), *Regarding Television: Critical Approaches – An Anthology*. Frederick, MD: University Publications of America.

Florida, R. (2002). *The Rise of the Creative Class, and How It's Transforming Work, Leisure, Community, and Everyday Life*. New York: Basic Books.

Flyvbjerg, B. (2006). Five Misunderstandings About Case-Study Research. *Qualitative Inquiry*, 12(2), 219–245.

Foner, N. (2001). *Islands in the City: West Indian Immigration to New York*. Berkeley, CA: University of California Press.

Foner, N. and Fredrickson, G. (eds.) (2004). *Not Just Black and White: Historical and Contemporary Perspectives on Immigration, Race, and Ethnicity in the United States*. New York: Russell Sage Foundation.

Forster, M. (2008). *Johann Gottfried von Herder*. Online, available at: http://plato.stanford.edu/archives/fall2008/entries/herder/ [accessed August 10, 2010].

Foster, H. (ed.) (1985). *Postmodern Culture*. London: Pluto Press.

Foucault, M. (1972[1969]). *The Archaeology of Knowledge*. London: Tavistock.

Foucault, M. (1980). *Power/Knowledge: Selected Interviews and Other Writings, 1972–1977*. New York: Vintage.

Fowler, R. (1985). Power. In T. A. Van Dijk (ed.), *Handbook of Discourse Analysis, Vol. 4*. London: Academic Press.

Fowler, R., Hodge, B., Kress G., and Trew, T. (1979). *Language and Control*. London: Routledge & Kegan Paul.

Fox, J. R., Koloen, G., and Sahin, V. (2007). No Joke: A Comparison of Substance in *The Daily Show with Jon Stewart* and Broadcast Network Television Coverage of the 2004 Presidential Election Campaign. *Journal of Broadcasting and Electronic Media*, 51(2): 213–227.

Frasca, G. (1999). Ludology Meets Narratology: Similitude and Differences Between (Video)Games and Narrative. *Ludology.org: video game theory*. Online, available at: www.ludology.org/articles/ludology.htm.

Fraser, N. (1992). Rethinking the Public Sphere: A Contribution to the Critique of Actually Existing Democracy. In C. Calhoun (ed.), *Habermas and the Public Sphere*. Cambridge, MA: MIT Press, pp. 109–142.

Fraser, N. (2007). Transnationalizing the Public Sphere: On the Legitimacy and Efficacy of Public Opinion in a Post-Westphalian World. *Theory, Culture, & Society*, 24(4), 7–30.

Fredin, E. S., Monnett, T. H., and Kosicki, G. M. (1994). Knowledge Gaps, Social Locators, and

Media Schemata: Gaps, Reverse Gaps, and Gaps of Disaffection. *Journalism and Mass Communication Quarterly*, 71(1), 176–190.

Freud, S. (1911[1899]). *The Interpretation of Dreams*. Online, available at: www.psywww.com/books/interp/toc.htm [accessed July 15, 2009].

Friedman, T. (1995). Making Sense of Software: Computer Games as Interactive Textuality. In S. Jones (ed.), *Cybersociety: Computer-Mediated Communication and Community*. Thousand Oaks, CA: Sage.

Fuller, M. and Jenkins, H. (1995). Nintendo and New World Travel Writing: A Dialogue. In S. Jones (ed.), *Cybersociety: Computer-Mediated Communication and Community*. Thousand Oaks, CA: Sage.

Furnham, A. F. (1988). *Lay Theories: Everyday Understanding of Problems in the Social Sciences*. Oxford: Pergamon Press.

Furnham, A. and Schofield, I. (1986). Sex-role Stereotyping in British Radio Advertisements. *British Journal of Social Psychology*, 25(2): 165–171.

Furnham, A. and Skae, E. (1997). Changes in the Stereotypical Portrayal of Men and Women in British Television Advertisements. *European Psychologist*, 2(1): 44–51.

Furnham, A., Abramsky, S., and Gunter, B. (1997). A Cross-cultural Content Analysis of Children's Television Advertisements. *Sex Roles*, 37(1/2): 91–99.

Gadamer, H.-G. (1975[1960]). *Truth and Method*. New York: The Seabury Press.

Gallie, W. B. (1956). Essentially Contested Concepts. *Proceedings of the Aristotelian Society*, 56 (New Series): 167–198.

Galtung, J. and Ruge, M. H. (1965). The Structure of Foreign News: The Presentation of the Congo, Cuba and Cyprus Crises in Four Norwegian Newspapers. *Journal of Peace Research*, 2(1): 64–90.

Gamson, W. A. (1992). *Talking Politics*. New York: Cambridge University Press.

Gans, H. J. (1957). The Creator-Audience Relationship in the Mass Media: An Analysis of Movie Making. In B. Rosenberg and D. White (eds.), *Mass Culture: The Popular Arts in America*. New York: The Free Press.

Gans, H. J. (1970). Broadcaster and Audience Values in Mass Media. *Transactions of the Sixth World Congress of Sociology*, Evian.

Gans, H. J. (1979). *Deciding What's News: A Study of CBS Evening News, NBC Nightly News, Newsweek, and Time*. New York: Pantheon.

Gardner, G. (1987). *The Censorship Papers: Movie Censorship Letters From the Hays Office: 1934–1968*. New York: Dodd Mead.

Gardner, H. (1985). *The Mind's New Science: A History of the Cognitive Revolution*. New York: Basic Books.

Garfinkel, H. (1967). *Studies in Ethnomethodology*. Englewood Cliffs, NJ: Prentice-Hall.

Gauntlett, D. and Hill, A. (1999). *TV Living: Television Audiences and Everyday Life*. London: Routledge.

Gaziano, C. (1997). Forecast 2000: Widening Knowledge Gaps. *Journalism and Mass Communication Quarterly*, 74(2): 237–264.

Gee, J. P., Michaels, S., and O'Connor, M. C. (1992). Discourse Analysis. In M. D. LeCompte, W. L. Millroy, and J. Preissle (eds.), *The Handbook of Qualitative Research in Education*. San Diego, CA: Academic Press.

Geertz, C. (1973). Thick Description. *The Interpretation of Cultures*. New York: Basic Books.

Gelder, K. (ed.) (2005). *The Subcultures Reader* (2nd ed.). London: Routledge.

Genette, G. (1972). *Figures III*, Paris: Seuil. [English translation: *Narrative Discourse*, Oxford: Basil Blackwell, 1980.]

Genette, G. (1997[1982]). *Palimpsests: Literature in the Second Degree*. Lincoln, NE: University of Nebraska Press.

Genova, B. K. L. and Greenberg, B. S. (1979). Interests in News and the Knowledge Gap. *Public Opinion Quarterly*, 43(1): 79–91.

Gerbner, G. (1972). Violence in Television Drama: Trends and Symbolic Functions. In G. A. Comstock & E. A. Rubinstein (eds.), *Television and Social Behavior, Vol.1: Media Content and Control*. Washington, DC: US Government Printing Office.

Gerbner, G. and Gross, L. (1976). Living With Television: The Violence Profile. *Journal of Communication*, 26(2): 173–194.

Gerbner, G., Gross, L., Eleey, M. F., Jackson-Beeck, M., Jeffries-Fox, S., and Signorielli, N. (1977). Television Violence Profile No. 8: The Highlights. *Journal of Communication*, 27(2): 171–180.

Gerbner, G., Gross, L., Morgan, M., and Signorielli, N. (1986). Living with Television: The Dynamics of the Cultivation Process. In J. Bryant and D. Zillmann (eds.), *Perspectives on Media Effects*. Hillsdale, NJ: Lawrence Erlbaum Associates.

Gerbner, G., Gross, L., Morgan, M., Signorielli, N., and Jackson-Beeck, M. (1979). The Demonstration of Power: Violence Profile No.10. *Journal of Communication*, 29(3): 177–196.

Gerth, H. and Mills, C. W. (1954). *Character and Social Structure: The Psychology of Social Institutions*. London: Routledge & Kegan Paul.

Gibson, J. J. (1979). *The Ecological Approach to Visual Perception*. Boston, MA: Houghton-Mifflin.

Giddens, A. (1979). *Central Problems in Social Theory*. London: Macmillan.

Giddens, A. (1984). *The Constitution of Society*. Berkeley, CA: University of California Press.

Giddens, A. (1990). *The Consequences of Modernity*. Cambridge: Polity Press.

Giddens, A. (1991). *Modernity and Self-Identity*. Cambridge: Polity Press.

Giddens, A. (1994). Living in a Post-traditional Society. In U. Beck, A. Giddens, and S. Lash, *Reflexive Modernization: Politics, Tradition, and Aesthetics in the Modern Social Order*. Cambridge: Polity Press.

Giles, H. and Watson, B. (2008). Intercultural and Intergroup Communication. In W. Donsbach (ed.), *International Encyclopedia of Communication, Vol. 6*. Malden, MA: Wiley-Blackwell, pp. 2337–2348.

Giles, H., Reid, S., and Harwood, J. (eds.) (2010). *The Dynamics of Intergroup Communication*. New York: Peter Lang.

Gillespie, M. (1995). *Television, Ethnicity, and Cultural Change*. London: Routledge.

Gilligan, C. (1982). *In A Different Voice*. Cambridge, MA: Harvard University Press.

Gillis, S., Howie, G., and Munford, R. (eds.) (2005). *Third Wave Feminism: A Critical Exploration*. Basingstoke: Palgrave Macmillan.

Ginzburg, C. (1989). Clues: Roots for an Evidential Paradigm. In C. Ginzburg (ed.), *Clues, Myths, and the Historical Method*. Baltimore, MD: Johns Hopkins University Press.

Giske, T. and Artinian, B. (2007). A Personal Experience of Working with Classical Grounded Theory: From Beginner to Experienced Theorist. *International Journal of Qualitative Methods*, 6(4): 67–80.

Gitlin, T. (1978). Media Sociology: The Dominant Paradigm. *Theory and Society*, 6(2): 205–253.

Gitlin, T. (1994[1983]). *Inside Prime Time*. New York: Pantheon.

Gitlin, T. (1997). The Anti-Political Populism of Cultural Studies. In M. Ferguson and P. Golding (eds.), *Cultural Studies in Question*. London: Sage.

Glaser, B. G. (1992). *Basics of Grounded Theory Analysis: Emergence vs. Forcing*. Mill Valley, CA: Sociology Press.

Glaser, B. G. (2001). *The Grounded Theory Perspective: Conceptualization Contrasted with Description*. Mill Valley, CA: Sociology Press.

Glaser, B. G. and Strauss, A. L. (1967). *The Discovery of Grounded Theory: Strategies for Qualitative Research*. Chicago, IL: Aldine.

Glasgow University Media Group (1976). *Bad News*. London: Routledge.

Glasgow University Media Group (1980). *More Bad News*. London: Routledge.

Glasser, T. L (ed.) (1999). *The Idea of Public Journalism*. New York: The Guilford Press.

Glessing, R. J. (1970). *The Underground Press in America*. Bloomington, IN: Indiana University Press.

Glymour, C. and Eberhardt, F. (eds.) (2008). *Stanford Encyclopedia of Philosophy*. Online, available at: http://plato.stanford.edu/ [accessed June 26, 2011].

Glynos, J., Howarth, D., Norval, A., and Speed, E. (2009). Discourse Analysis: Varieties and Methods. ESRC National Centre for Research Methods, University of Essex. Online, available at: http://eprints.ncrm.ac.uk/796/1/discourse_analysis_NCRM_014.pdf [accessed January 20, 2011].

Goffman, E. (1959). *The Presentation of Self in Everyday Life*. London: Pelican Books [reprinted 1969].

Goffman, E. (1974). *Frame Analysis*. Cambridge, MA: Harvard University Press.

Goffman, E. (1976). Gender Advertisements. *Studies in the Anthropology of Visual Communication*, 3(2): 69–154.

Goggin, G. and McLelland, M. (eds.) (2009). *Internationalizing Internet Studies: Beyond Anglophone Paradigms*. New York: Routledge.

Golding, P. and Elliott, P. (1979). *Making the News*. London: Longman.

Golding, P. and Harris, P. (eds.) (1997). *Beyond Cultural Imperialism*. London: Sage.

Goldkuhl, G. and Cronholm, S. (2010). Adding Theoretical Grounding to Grounded Theory: Toward Multi-grounded Theory. *International Journal of Qualitative Methods*, 9(2): 187–205.

Gombrich, E. H. (1960). *Art and Illusion*. Princeton, NJ: Princeton University Press.

Gomery, D. (1992). *Shared Pleasures: A History of Movie Presentation in the United States*. Madison, WI: University of Wisconsin Press.

Gomm, R., Hammersley, M., and Foster, P. (eds.) (2000). *Case Study Method: Key Issues, Key Texts*. London: Sage.

Goode, W. J. and Hatt, P. K. (1952). *Methods in Social Research*. New York: McGraw-Hill.

Goody, J. (1987). *The Interface between the Written and the Oral*. Cambridge: Cambridge University Press.

Goody, J. (2000). *The Power of the Written Tradition*. Washington, DC: Smithsonian Institution Press.

Goody, J. (ed.) (1968). *Literacy in Traditional Societies*. Cambridge: Cambridge University Press.

Goody, J. and Watt, I. (1963). The Consequences of Literacy. *Comparative Studies in Society and History*, 5(3): 304–345.

Gorbman, C. (1987). *Unheard Melodies: Narrative Film Music*. Bloomington and Indianapolis, IN: Indiana University Press.

Gorden, R. L. (1969). *Interviewing: Strategy, Techniques, and Tactics*. Homewood, IL: The Dorsey Press.

Gorney, R., Loye, D., and Steele, G. (1977). Impact of Dramatised Television Entertainment on Adult Males. *American Journal of Psychiatry*, 134(2): 170–174.

Gottlieb, S. (ed.) (1995). *Hitchcock on Hitchcock: Selected Writings and Interviews*. Berkeley, CA: University of California Press.

Grabe, M. E., Lang, A., Zhou, S., and Bolls, P. D. (2000). Cognitive Access to Negatively Arousing News: An

Experimental Investigation of the Knowledge Gap. *Communication Research*, 27(1), 3–26.

Graber, D. (1984). *Processing the News: How People Tame the Information Tide*. New York: Longman.

Gramsci, A. (1971). *Selections from the Prison Notebooks*. New York: International Publishers.

Grant, B. K. (1986). *Film Genre Reader*. Austin, TX: University of Texas Press.

Grant, B. K. (1995). *Film Genre Reader II*. Austin, TX: University of Texas Press.

Gray, A. (1992). *Video Playtime: The Gendering of a Leisure Technology*. London: Routledge.

Greatbatch, D. (1998). Conversation Analysis: Neutralism in British News Interviews. In A. Bell and P. Garrett (eds.), *Approaches to Media Discourse*. Oxford: Blackwell.

Greenacre, M. J. (2007). *Correspondence Analysis in Practice* (2nd ed.). London: Chapman & Hall.

Greenberg, B. S. (1964). Person-to-Person Communication in the Diffusion of a News Event. *Journalism Quarterly*, 41: 489–494.

Greenberg, B. S. (1975). British Children and Televised Violence. *Public Opinion Quarterly*, 38(4): 531–547.

Greene, R. (2003). *Internet Art*. London: Thames & Hudson.

Greenfield, A. (2006). *Everyware: The Dawning Age of Ubiquitous Computing*. Indianapolis, IN: New Riders.

Greenwood, D. J. and Levin, M. (2007). *Introduction to Action Research: Social Research for Social Change* (2nd ed.). Thousand Oaks, CA: Sage.

Greimas, A. J. (1966). *Sémantique structurale. Recherche de methode*. Paris: Larousse. [English translation: *Structural Semantics. An Attempt at a Method*, Lincoln, NE: University of Nebraska Press, 1983.]

Gripsrud, J. (1995). *The Dynasty Years: Hollywood Television and Critical Media Studies*. London: Routledge.

Grodal, T. K. (1997). *Moving Pictures: A New Theory of Film Genres, Feelings, and Cognition*. New York: Oxford University Press.

Grodal, T. K. (2009). *Embodied Visions: Evolution, Emotion, Culture, and Film*. Oxford: Oxford University Press.

Grossberg, L., Nelson, C., and Treichler, P. (eds.) (1992). *Cultural Studies*. London: Routledge.

Gruber, H. (2008). Analyzing Communication in the New Media. In R. Wodak and M. Krzyzanowski (eds.), *Qualitative Discourse Analysis in the Social Sciences*. Basingstoke: Palgrave Macmillan.

Gubrium, J. F. and Holstein, J. A. (2009). *Analyzing Narrative Reality*. Los Angeles, CA: Sage.

Gudykunst, W. B. and Kim, Y. Y. (1992). *Communicating with Strangers: An Approach to Intercultural Communication* (2nd ed.). New York: McGraw-Hill.

Gudykunst, W. B. and Mody, B. (eds.) (2002). *Handbook of International and Intercultural Communication*. Thousand Oaks, CA: Sage.

Gulati, G. J., Just, M. R., and Crigler, A. N. (2004). News Coverage of Political Campaigns. In L. L. Kaid (ed.), *Handbook of Political Communication Research*. Mahwah, NJ: Lawrence Erlbaum Associates.

Gulich, E. and Quasthoff, U. M. (1985). Narrative Analysis. In T. A. Van Dijk (ed.), *Handbook of Discourse Analysis, Vol. 2: Dimensions of Discourse*. New York: Academic Press.

Gumpert, G. and Cathcart, R. (eds.) (1986). *Inter/Media: Interpersonal Communication in a Media World*. New York: Oxford University Press.

Gunter, B. (1979). Recall of Television News Items: Effects of Presentation Mode, Picture Content and Serial Position. *Journal of Educational Television*, 5(2): 57–61.

Gunter, B. (1985). News Sources and News Awareness: A British Survey. *Journal of Broadcasting*, 29(4): 397–406.

Gunter, B. (1987a). *Television and the Fear of Crime*. London: John Libbey.

Gunter, B. (1987b). *Poor Reception: Misunderstanding and Forgetting Broadcast News*. Hillsdale, NJ: Lawrence Erlbaum Associates.

Gunter, B. (2000). *Media Research Methods: Measuring Audiences, Reactions, and Impact*. London: Sage.

Gunter, B. and Harrison, J. (1998). *Violence on Television: An Analysis of Amount, Nature, Location and Origin of Violence in British Programmes*. London: Routledge.

Gunter, B. and Machin, D. (eds.) (2009). *Media Audiences: Measurement of Audiences, Vol. 2*. London: Sage.

Gunter, B. and Wober, J. (1982). Television Viewing and Public Trust. *British Journal of Social Psychology*, 22(2): 174–176.

Gunter, B., Furnham, A., and Lineton, Z. (1995). Watching People Watching Television: What Goes on in Front of the TV Set? *Journal of Educational Television*, 21(3): 165–191.

Gunter, B., Gibson, R., Campbell, V., Touri M., and Ackland, R. (2008). *Blogging and the Impact of Citizen Journalism*. Report for the Nuffield Foundation.

Gunter, B., Harrison, J., Arundel, J., and Osborn, R. (1999). Female Victimisation on Television: Extent, Nature and Context of On-screen Portrayals. *Communications*, 24(4): 387–405.

Gunter, B., Harrison, J., Arundel, J., Osborn, R., and Crawford, M. (1996). *Violence on Television in Britain: A Content Analysis*. Report to the BBC, BSC, BSkyB, Channel 4, ITC, and ITV. Sheffield, UK: University of Sheffield, Department of Journalism Studies.

Gunter, B., Harrison, J., and Wykes, M. (2003). *Violence on Television: Distribution, Form, Context and Themes*. Hillsdale, NJ: Lawrence Erlbaum Associates.

Habermas, J. (1971[1968]). *Knowledge and Human Interests*. Boston, MA: Beacon Press.

Habermas, J. (1989[1962]). *The Structural Transformation of the Public Sphere*. Cambridge, MA: MIT Press.

Hacker, K. L., Coste, T. G., Kamm, D. F., and Bybee, C. R. (1991). Oppositional Readings of Network Television News: Viewer Deconstruction. *Discourse and Society*, 2(2), 183–202.

Hacking, I. (1975). *The Emergence of Probability*. London: Cambridge University Press.

Hacking, I. (1983). *Representing and Intervening: Introductory Topics in the Philosophy of Natural Science*. Cambridge: Cambridge University Press.

Hacking, I. (1999). *The Social Construction of What?* Cambridge, MA: Harvard University Press.

Haddon, L. (1998). *The Experience of the Mobile Phone*. Paper presented to the XIV World Congress of Sociology, 'Social Knowledge: Heritage, Challenges, Prospects,' Montreal, July 26–August 1.

Halavais, A. (2000). National Borders on the World Wide Web. *New Media & Society*, 2(1), 7–28.

Halavais, A. (2009). *Search Engine Society*. Cambridge: Polity Press.

Hall, E. T. (1959). *The Silent Language*. New York: Doubleday.

Hall, S. (1973). *Encoding and Decoding in the Television Discourse* (Stencilled Occasional Paper No. 7). Birmingham: Centre for Contemporary Cultural Studies.

Hall, S. (1980). Cultural Studies: Two Paradigms. *Media, Culture & Society*, 2(1): 57–72.

Hall, S. (1983). The Problem of Ideology: Marxism without Guarantees. In B. Matthews (ed.), *Marx: A Hundred Years On*. London: Lawrence & Wishart, pp. 57–85.

Hall, S. and Jefferson, T. (eds.) (1975). *Resistance through Rituals*. London: Hutchinson.

Hall, S., Connell, I., and Curti, L. (1976). *The Unity of Current Affairs Television*. Working Papers in Cultural Studies, No. 9, Center for Contemporary Cultural Studies, University of Birmingham, pp. 51–94.

Hall, S., Critcher, C., Jefferson, T., Clarke, J., and Roberts, B. (1978). *Policing the Crisis: Mugging, the State, and Law and Order*. Basingstoke: Macmillan.

Hall, S., Hobson, D., Lowe, A., and Willis, P. (eds.) (1980). *Culture, Media, Language*. London: Hutchinson.

Halliday, M. A. K. (1973). *Explorations in the Functions of Language*. London: Edward Arnold.

Halliday, M. A. K. (1978). *Language as Social Semiotic*. London: Longman.

Hallin, D. C. and Mancini, P. (2004). *Comparing Media Systems: Three Models of Media and Politics*. Cambridge: Cambridge University Press.

Halloran, J., Elliott, P., and Murdock, G. (1970). *Communications and Demonstrations. A Case Study*. Harmondsworth: Penguin.

Hammersley, M. (1995). *The Politics of Social Research*. London: Sage.

Hammersley, M. (1996). The Relationship between Qualitative and Quantitative Research: Paradigm Loyalty versus Methodological Eclecticism. In J. T. E. Richardson (ed.), *Handbook of Qualitative Research Methods for Psychology and the Social Sciences*. Leicester: British Psychological Society.

Hammersley, M. (2003). Conversation Analysis and Discourse Analysis: Methods or Paradigms? *Discourse & Society*, 14 (6):751–781.

Hammersley, M. and Atkinson, P. (2007). *Ethnography: Principles in Practice* (3rd ed.). London: Routledge.

Han, J. and Kamber, M. (2006). *Data Mining: Concepts and Techniques* (2nd ed.). Boston, MA: Elsevier.

Hannerz, U. (1996). *Transnational Connections: Culture, People, Places*. London: Routledge.

Hannington, W. (1977). *Unemployed Struggles, 1919–1936*. London: Lawrence and Wishart.

Hansen, M. (1990). Early Cinema: Whose Public Sphere? In T. Elsaesser (ed.), *Early Cinema: Space, Frame, Narrative*. London: British Film Institute.

Hanson, N. R. (1958). *Patterns of Discovery: An Inquiry into the Conceptual Foundations of Science*. Cambridge: Cambridge University Press.

Haraway, D. J. (1991). *Simians, Cyborgs, and Women: The Reinvention of Nature*. New York: Routledge.

Harcup, T. and O'Neill, D. (2001). What Is News? Galtung and Ruge Revisited. *Journalism Studies*, 2(2): 261–280.

Harding, S. (1986). *The Science Question in Feminism*. Ithaca, NY: Cornell University Press.

Harding, S. (ed.) (2004). *The Feminist Standpoint Theory Reader: Intellectual and Political Controversies*. New York: Routledge.

Hardt, H. (1979). *Social Theories of the Press: Early German and American Perspectives*. London: Sage.

Hardt, H. (1992). *Critical Communication Studies: Communication, History, and Theory*. London: Routledge.

Hardt, H. (1999). Review of Dennis and Wartella. *Communications: The European Journal of Communication Research*, 24(2), 239–240.

Hargittai, E. (2007). Special Theme I: The Social, Political, Economic, and Cultural Dimensions of Search Engines. *Journal of Computer-Mediated Communication*, 12(3): art.1.

Harrison, C. and Wood, P. (eds.) (1992). *Art in Theory 1900–1990: An Anthology of Changing Ideas*. Oxford: Blackwell.

Hartley, J. (1982). *Understanding News*. London: Methuen.

Hartley, J. (2009). Journalism and Popular Culture. In K. Wahl-Jorgensen and T. Hanitzsch (eds.), *The Handbook of Journalism Studies*, London: Routledge, pp. 310–324.

Hartley, J. and Pearson, R. (eds.) (2000). *American Cultural Studies: A Reader*. Oxford: Oxford University Press.

Hartmann, M. (2006). The Triple Articulation of ICTs. Media as Technological Objects, Symbolic Environments and Individual Texts. In T. Berker, M. Hartmann, Y. Punie, and K. J. Ward (eds.), *Domestication of Media and Technology*. Glasgow: Open University Press, pp. 80–102.

Hartnagel, T. F., Teevan Jr., J. J., and McIntyre, J. J. (1975). Television Violence and Violent Behaviour. *Social Forces*, 54(2): 341–351.

Harvey, D. (1989). *The Condition of Postmodernity*. Oxford: Blackwell.

Hauser, A. (1951). *The Social History of Art*. New York: Vintage.

Have, P. T. (1999). *Doing Conversation Analysis: A Practical Guide*. London: Sage.

Havelock, E. A. (1963). *Preface to Plato*. Oxford: Blackwell.

Havens, T. (2008). *Global Television Marketplace*. London: British Film Institute.

Havens, T., Lotz, A. D., and Tinic, S. (2009). Critical Media Industry Studies: A Research Approach. *Communication, Culture and Critique*, 2(2): 234–253.

Hawthorn, G. (1991). *Plausible Worlds: Possibility and Understanding in History and the Social Sciences*. Cambridge: Cambridge University Press.

Hayles, N. K. (1999). *How We Became Posthuman: Virtual Bodies in Cybernetics, Literature, and Informatics*. Chicago, IL: University of Chicago Press.

Hays, W. L. (1973). *Statistics for the Social Sciences*. New York: Holt, Rinehart & Winston.

Headland, T., Pike, K., and Harris, M. (eds.) (1990). *Emics and Etics: The Insider/Outsider Debate*. Newbury Park, CA: Sage.

Hearn, G., Tacchi, J., Foth, M., and Lennie, J. (2009). *Action Research and New Media: Concepts, Methods, and Cases*. Creskill, NJ: Hampton Press.

Heath, C. and vom Lehn, D. (2004). Configuring Reception: (Dis-)Regarding the 'Spectator' in Museums and Galleries. *Theory, Culture, & Society*, 21(6), 43–65.

Heath, R. L. and Bryant, J. (2000). *Human Communication Theory and Research: Concepts, Contexts, and Challenges*. New York: Routledge.

Heath, S. (1975). Films and System: Terms of Analysis. Part I, *Screen*, 16(1): 7–77; Part II, *Screen* 16(2): 91–113.

Hebdige, D. (1979). *Subculture: The Meaning of Style*. London: Methuen.

Heider, F. (1958). *The Psychology of Interpersonal Relations*. New York: Wiley.

Heim, M. (1987). *Electric Language*. New Haven, CT: Yale University Press.

Hektner, J. M., Schmidt, J. A., and Csikszentmihalyi, M. (eds.) (2007). *Experience Sampling Method: Measuring the Quality of Everyday Life*. Thousand Oaks, CA: Sage.

Held, D., McGrew, A., Goldblatt, D., and Perraton, J. (2000). *Global Transformations: Politics, Economics, and Culture*. Cambridge: Polity Press.

Hempel, C. G. and Oppenheim, P. (1988[1948]). Studies in the Logic of Explanation. In J. Pitt (ed.), *Theories of Explanation*. New York: Oxford University Press.

Hennigan, K. M., Del Rosario, M. L., Heath, L., Cook, T. D., Wharton, J. D., and Calder, B. J. (1982). Impact of the Introduction of Television on Crime in the United States: Empirical Findings and Theoretical Implications. *Journal of Personality and Social Psychology*, 42(3): 461–477.

Heritage, J. (1985). Analyzing News Interviews: Aspects of the Production of Talk for an Overhearing Audience. In T. A. Van Dijk (ed.), *Handbook of Discourse Analysis, Vol. 3*, London: Academic Press.

Heritage, J. and Greatbatch, D. L. (1991). On the Institutional Character of Institutional Talk: The Case of News Interviews. In D. Boden and D. H. Zimmerman (eds.), *Talk and Social Structure: Studies in Ethnomethodology and Conversation Analysis*. Oxford: Polity.

Herman, E. S. and Chomsky, N. (1988). *Manufacturing Consent*. New York: Pantheon.

Hermes, J. (1995). *Reading Women's Magazines: An Analysis of Everyday Media Use*. Oxford: Polity Press.

Hermes, J. (2005). *Re-reading Popular Culture*. Oxford: Blackwell.

Herring, S. (1999[1996]). Posting in a Different Voice: Gender and Ethics in Computer-Mediated Communication. In P. A. Mayer (ed.), *Computer Media and Communication: A Reader*. Oxford: Oxford University Press.

Herring, S. (2004). Slouching toward the Ordinary: Current Trends in Computer-Mediated Communication. *New Media & Society*, 6(1), 26–36.

Herring, S. (2007). A Faceted Classification Scheme for Computer-Mediated Discourse. *Language@Internet*, 4: art. 1. Online, available at: www.languageatinternet.de/articles/2007 [accessed January 20, 2011].

Herzog, H. (1941). On Borrowed Experience: An Analysis of Listening to Daytime Sketches. *Studies in Philosophy and Social Science*, 9(1): 65–95.

Herzog, H. (1944). What Do We Really Know about Daytime Serial Listeners? In P. F. Lazarsfeld (ed.), *Radio Research 1942–3*. New York: Duell, Sloan, and Pearce.

Hesmondhalgh, D. (2007). *The Cultural Industries* (2nd ed.). London: Sage.

Hesmondhalgh, D. (2010). Media Industry Studies, Media Production Studies. In J. Curran (ed.), *Media and Society* (5th ed.). London: Bloomsbury.

Hill, A. (2000a). Crime and Crisis: British Reality TV in Action. In E. Buscombe (ed.), *British Television: A Reader*. Oxford: Oxford University Press.

Hill, A. (2000b). Fearful and Safe: Audience Response to British Reality Programming. *Television and New Media*, 1(2): 193–214.

Hill, A. (2005). *Reality TV: Audiences and Popular Factual Television*. London: Routledge.

Hill, A. (2007). *Restyling Factual TV: Audiences of News, Documentary and Reality Genres*. London: Routledge.

Hill, A. (2011). *Paranormal Media: Audiences, Spirits and Magic in Popular Culture*. London: Routledge.

Hill, A., Weibull, L., and Nilsson, Å. (2007). Public and Popular: British and Swedish Audience Trends in Factual and Reality Television. *Cultural Trends*, 16(1): 17–41.

Hills, M. (2002). *Fan Cultures*. London: Routledge.

Hilmes, M. (1990). *Hollywood and Broadcasting: From Radio to Cable*. Urbana, IL: University of Illinois Press.

Himelboim, I. (2010). The International Network Structure of New Media: An Analysis of Hyperlinks Usage in News Web Sites. *Journal of Broadcasting and Electronic Media*, 54(3), 373–390.

Himelboim, I., Gleave, E., and Smith, M. (2009). Discussion Catalysts in Online Political Discussions: Content Importers and Conversation Starters. *Journal of Computer-Mediated Communication*, 14: 771–789.

Himmelweit, H. T., Vince, P., and Oppenheim, A. N. (1958). *Television and the Child*. London: Oxford University Press.

Hine, C. (2000). *Virtual Ethnography*. London: Sage.

Hirsch, P. M. (1980). The 'Scary World' of the Non-Viewer and other Anomalies – A Reanalysis of Gerbner *et al.*'s Findings in Cultivation Analysis. *Communication Research*, 7(4): 403–456.

Hirsch, P. (1981). On Not Learning from One's Mistakes, Part II. *Communication Research*, 8(1), 3–38.

Hjarvard, S. (1992). 'Live': On Time and Space in Television News. *Nordicom Review*, 13(2): 111–126.

Hjarvard, S. (2008a). On the Mediatization of Religion: A Theory of the Media as Agents of Religious Change. *Northern Lights*, 6(1): 9–26.

Hjarvard, S. (2008b). The Mediatization of Society: A Theory of the Media as Agents of Social and Cultural Change. *Nordicom Review*, 29(2): 105–134.

Hjarvard, S. (2010a). Introduction: Newspapers and Journalism in Transition. *Northern Lights. Film and Media Studies Yearbook 2010*, 8(1): 3–7.

Hjarvard, S. (2010b). The Views of the News: The Role of Political Newspapers in a Changing Media Landscape. *Northern Lights. Film and Media Studies Yearbook 2010*, 8(1): 25–48.

Hjelmslev, L. (1963[1943]). *Prolegomena to a Theory of Language*. Madison, WI: University of Wisconsin Press.

Hobson, D. (1980). Housewives and the Mass Media. In S. Hall, D. Hobson, A. Lowe, and P. Willis (eds.), *Culture, Media, Language*. London: Hutchinson.

Hockings, P. (ed.) (1995). *Principles of Visual Anthropology* (2nd ed.). Berlin: Mouton de Gruyter.

Hodge, B. and Kress, G. (1988). *Social Semiotics*. Cambridge: Polity Press.

Hoffman, M. F. and Cowan, R. L. (2010). Be Careful What You Ask For: Structuration Theory and Work/Life Accommodation. *Communication Studies*, 61(2): 205–213.

Hoffman, M. L. (1970). Conscience, Personality, and Socialization Techniques. *Human Development*, 13(2): 90–126.

Hoffner, C. and Buchanan, M. (2002). Parents' Responses to Television Violence: The Third Person Perception, Parental Mediation, and Support for Censorship. *Media Psychology*, 4(3): 231–252.

Hoffner, C. and Cantor, J. (1985). Developmental Differences in Responses to a Television Character's Appearance and Behavior. *Developmental Psychology*, 21(6): 1065–1074.

Hoggart, R. (1957). *The Uses of Literacy*. Harmondsworth: Penguin.

Hollstein, B. and Straus, F. (eds.) (2006). *Qualitative Netzwerkanalyse. Konzepte, Methoden, Anwendungen*. Wiesbaden: VS-Verlag.

Holsti, O. R. (1969). *Content Analysis for the Social Sciences and Humanities*. Reading, MA: Addison-Wesley.

Holt, J. (2003). Vertical Vision: Deregulation, Industrial Economy and Prime-time Design. In M. Jancovich and J. Lyons (eds.), *Quality Popular Television: Cult TV, the Industry and Fans*. London: British Film Institute.

Holt, J. and Perren, A. (eds.) (2009). *Media Industries: History, Theory, and Method*. Malden, MA: Wiley-Blackwell.

Holtzhausen, D. (2008). Strategic Communication. In W. Donsbach (ed.), *International Encyclopedia of Communication*. Malden, MA: Blackwell.

Holub, R. C. (1984). *Reception Theory: A Critical Introduction*. London: Methuen.

Hoover, S. M., Clark, L. S., and Alters, D. A. (2004). *Media, Home, and Family*. New York: Routledge.

Horton, D. and Wohl, R. (1956). Mass Communication and Parasocial Interaction: Observations on Intimacy at a Distance. *Psychiatry*, 19(3), 215–229.

Hoskins, C., McFadyen, S., and Finn, A. (1997). *Global Television and Film: An Introduction to the Economics of the Business*. Oxford: Clarendon and New York: Oxford University Press.

Hovland, C. I., Janis, I. L., and Kelley, H. H. (1953). *Communication and Persuasion*. New Haven, CT: Yale University Press.

Hovland, C. I., Lumsdaine, A. A., and Sheffield, F. D. (1949). *Experiments on Mass Communication*. Princeton, NJ: Princeton University Press.

Høyer, S., Lauk, E., and Vihalemm, P. (eds.) (1993). *Towards a Civic Society: The Baltic Media's Long Road to Freedom*. Tartu: Nota Baltica.

Huberman, A. M. and Miles, M. B. (eds.) (2002). *The Qualitative Researcher's Companion*. Thousand Oaks, CA: Sage.

Huesmann, L. R., Eron, L. D., Lefkowitz, M. M., and Walder, L. O. (1984). Stability of Aggression over Time and Generations. *Developmental Psychology*, 20(6): 1120–1134.

Hughes, H. M. (1937). Human Interest Stories and Democracy. *Public Opinion Quarterly*, 1(2): 73–87.

Hujanen, J. (2008). RISC Monitor Audience Rating and Its Implications for Journalistic Practice. *Journalism*, 9(2), 182–199.

Hume, D. (2006[1748]). *An Enquiry Concerning Human Understanding*. Online, available at: www.gutenberg.org/etext/9662 [accessed April 7, 2009].

Humphreys, L. (2005). Cell Phones in Public: Social Interactions in a Wireless Era. *New Media & Society*, 7(6), 810–833.

Hunter, J. D. (1991). *Culture Wars: The Struggle to Define America*. New York: Basic Books.

Hur, K. K. (1984). A Critical Analysis of International News Flow Research. *Critical Studies in Mass Communication*, 1(4): 365–378.

Hutchby, I. (2001). *Conversation and Technology: From the Telephone to the Internet*. Cambridge: Polity.

Hutchby, I. (2006). *Media Talk: Conversation Analysis and the Study of Broadcasting*. Maidenhead: Open University Press.

Huyssen, A. (1986). *After the Great Divide: Modernism, Mass Culture, and Postmodernism*. London: Macmillan.

Hwang, Y. and Jeong, S.-H. (2009). Revisiting the Knowledge Gap Hypothesis: A Meta-Analysis of Thirty-Five Years of Research. *Journalism and Mass Communication Quarterly*, 86(3), 513–532.

Inglehart, R. (1990). *Culture Shift in Advanced Industrial Society*. Princeton, NJ: Princeton University Press.

Inglehart, R. (2008). Changing Values among Western Publics from 1970 to 2006. *West European Politics*, 31(1/2): 130–146.

Inglehart, R., Basanez, M., and Moreno, A. (1998). *Human Values and Beliefs: A Cross-Cultural Sourcebook*. Ann Arbor, MI: University of Michigan Press.

Innis, H. A. (1951). *The Bias of Communication*. Toronto: University of Toronto Press.

Innis, H. A. (1956[1930]). *The Fur Trade in Canada: An Introduction to Canadian Economic History* (2nd ed.). Toronto: Toronto University Press.

Innis, H. A. (1972[1950]). *Empire and Communications*. Toronto: University of Toronto Press.

Internet Governance Forum (n.d.). Online, available at: www.intgovforum.org/cms [accessed April 15, 2011].

International Motion Picture Almanac (annual publication). New York: Quigley Publishing Co.

International Television and Video Almanac (annual publication). New York: Quigley Publishing Co.

Introna, L. D. and Nissenbaum, H. (2000). Shaping the Web: Why the Politics of Search Engines Matters. *The Information Society*, 16(3), 169–185.

Irigaray, L. (1997[1977]). This Sex Which Is Not One. In L. Nicholson (ed.), *The Second Wave: A Reader in Feminist Theory*. London: Routledge.

Irwin, R. (2006). *For Lust of Knowing: The Orientalists and their Enemies*. London: Allen Lane.

Irwin, W. (1969[1911]). The American Newspaper: A Study of Journalism in its Relation to the Public, *Colliers*, January-June. Reprinted with comments by Clifford F. Weigle and David G. Clark. Ames, IA: Iowa State University Press.

Iser, W. (1972). *Der implizite Leser. Kommunikationsformen des Romans von Bunyan bis Beckett*. München: Wilhelm Fink. [English translation: *The Implied Reader. Patterns of Communication in Prose Fiction from Bunyan to Beckett*. Baltimore, MD: Johns Hopkins University Press, 1974.]

Iser, W.(1978[1976]): *The Act of Reading. A Theory of Aesthetic Response*. London: Routledge & Kegan Paul. Originally published as *Der Akt des Lesens: Theorie ästhetischer Wirkung*. München: Wilhelm Fink.

Israel, M. and Hay, I. (2006). *Research Ethics for Social Scientists: Between Ethical Conduct and Regulatory Compliance*. London: Sage.

ITU (2005). The Internet of Things: Executive Summary. Online, available at: www.itu.int/dms_pub/itu-s/opb/pol/S-POL-IR.IT-2005-SUM-PDF-E.pdf [accessed March 28, 2008].

ITU (2010). *Measuring the Information Society*. Geneva: International Telecommunication Union.

Iyengar, S. and Kinder, D. R. (1987). *News that Matters*. Chicago, IL: University of Chicago Press.

Jablin, F. M. and Putnam, L. L. (eds.) (2001). *The New Handbook of Organizational Communication*. Thousand Oaks, CA: Sage.

Jackson, H.-J. (2001). *Marginalia: Readers Writing in Books*. New Haven, CT: Yale University Press.

Jakobson, R. (1960). Closing Statement: Linguistics and Poetics. In T. A. Sebeok (ed.), *Style in Language*. Cambridge, MA: MIT Press.

Jakubowicz, K. (2007). The Eastern European/Post-Communist Media Model Countries. In G. Terzis (ed.), *European Media Governance*. Bristol: Intellect (pp. 301–314 in electronic edition).

James, J. (1995). *The Music of the Spheres: Music, Science, and the Natural Order of the Universe*. London: Abacus.

Jameson, F. (1991). *Postmodernism, Or, The Cultural Logic of Late Capitalism*. London: Verso.

Jankowski, N. W. and Wester, F. (1991). The Qualitative Tradition in Social Science Inquiry: Contributions to Mass Communication Research. In K. B. Jensen and N. W. Jankowski (eds.), *A Handbook of Qualitative Methodologies for Mass Communication Research*. London: Routledge.

Janowitz, M. (ed.) (1966). *W. I. Thomas on Social Organization and Social Personality: Selected Papers*. Chicago, IL: University of Chicago Press.

Janson, H. W. and Janson, A. F. (2001). *History of Art* (6th ed.). Upper Saddle River, NJ: Prentice-Hall.

Jauss, H. R. (1982). *Toward an Aesthetic of Reception*. Brighton: Harvester Press.

Jenkins, H. (1992). *Textual Poachers: Television Fans and Participatory Culture*. New York: Routledge.

Jenkins, H. (2006). *Convergence Culture: Where Old and New Media Collide*. New York: New York University Press.

Jenkins, H. (2007). Transmedia Storytelling 101. *Confessions of an Aca/Fan*. Online, available at: www.henryjenkins.org/2007/03/transmedia_storytelling_101.html [accessed November 11, 2010].

Jensen, J. F. (1999). Interactivity: Tracking a New Concept in Media and Communication Studies. In P. A. Mayer (ed.), *Computer Media and Communication: A Reader*. Oxford: Oxford University Press.

Jensen, K. B. (1986). *Making Sense of the News: Towards a Theory and an Empirical Model of Reception for the Study of Mass Communication*. Aarhus: University of Aarhus Press.

Jensen, K. B. (1988a). Answering the Question: What Is Reception Analysis? *Nordicom Review*, 9(1): 2–5.

Jensen, K. B. (1988b). News as Social Resource. *European Journal of Communication*, 3(3): 275–301.

Jensen, K. B. (1990a). The Politics of Polysemy: Television News, Everyday Consciousness, and Political Action. *Media, Culture & Society*, 12(1): 57–77.

Jensen, K. B. (1990b). Television Futures: A Social Action Methodology for Studying Interpretive Communities. *Critical Studies in Mass Communication*, 7(2): 129–146.

Jensen, K. B. (1991). When Is Meaning? Communication Theory, Pragmatism, and Mass Media Reception. In J. Anderson (ed.), *Communication Yearbook, Vol. 14*. Newbury Park, CA: Sage.

Jensen, K. B. (1993a). One Person, One Computer: The Social Construction of the Personal Computer. In P. B. Andersen, B. Holmqvist, and J. F. Jensen (eds.), *The Computer as Medium*. Cambridge: Cambridge University Press.

Jensen, K. B. (1993b). The Past in the Future: Problems and Potentials of Historical Reception Studies. *Journal of Communication*, 43(4): 20–28.

Jensen, K. B. (1994). Reception as Flow: The 'New Television Viewer' Revisited. *Cultural Studies*, 8(2), 293–305.

Jensen, K. B. (1995). *The Social Semiotics of Mass Communication*. London: Sage.

Jensen, K. B. (1999). Local Empiricism, Global Theory: Problems and Potentials of Comparative Research on News Reception. *Communications: The European Journal of Communication Research*, 23(4): 427–445.

Jensen, K. B. (2006). Sounding the Media: An Interdisciplinary Review and a Research Agenda for Digital Sound Studies. *Nordicom Review*, 27(2): 7–33.

Jensen, K. B. (2008a). Intermediality. In W. Donsbach (ed.), *International Encyclopedia of Communication*. Malden, MA: Blackwell.

Jensen, K. B. (2008b). Meaning. In W. Donsbach (ed.), *International Encyclopedia of Communication, Vol. 6*. Malden, MA: Blackwell.

Jensen, K. B. (2009). Three-step Flow. *Journalism: Theory, Practice & Criticism*, 10(3): 335–337.

Jensen, K. B. (2010). *Media Convergence: The Three Degrees of Network, Mass, and Interpersonal Communication*. London, New York: Routledge.

Jensen, K. B. (2011). New Media, Old Methods: Internet Methodologies and the Online/Offline Divide. In M. Consalvo and C. Ess (eds.), *The Blackwell Companion to Internet Studies*. Malden, MA: Wiley-Blackwell.

Jensen, K. B. (ed.) (1998). *News of the World: World Cultures Look at Television News*. London, New York: Routledge.

Jensen, K. B. (in press-a). Lost, Found, and Made: Qualitative Data in the Study of Three-Step Flows of Communication. In I. Volkmer (ed.), *Handbook of Global Media Research*. Malden, MA: Wiley-Blackwell.

Jensen, K. B. (in press-b). Meta-media and Meta-communication: Revisiting the Concept of Genre in the Digital Media Environment. *MedieKultur, Journal of Media and Communication Research*.

Jensen, K. B. and Helles, R. (2011). The Internet as a Cultural Forum. Implications for Research. *New Media & Society*, 13(4): 517–533.

Jensen, K. B. and Jankowski, N. W. (eds.). (1991). *A Handbook of Qualitative Methodologies for Mass Communication Research*. London: Routledge.

Jensen, K. B. and Larsen, P. (2010). The Sounds of Change: Representations of Music in European Newspapers 1960–2000. In J. Gripsrud and L. Weibull (eds.), *Media, Markets, Public Spheres*. Bristol: Intellect Press.

Jensen, K. B., Schrøder, K. C., Stampe, T., Søndergaard, H., and Topsøe-Jensen, J. (1994). Super Flow, Channel Flows, and Audience Flows: A Study of Viewers' Reception of Television as Flow. *Nordicom Review*, 2: 1–13.

Jewitt, C. (ed.) (2009). *Handbook of Multimodal Analysis*. London: Routledge.

Johansen. J. D. (1993). *Dialogic Semiosis*. Bloomington, IN: Indiana University Press.

Johnson, A., del Rio, E., and Kemmitt, A. (2010). Missing the Joke: A Reception Analysis of Satirical Texts. *Communication, Culture & Critique*, 3(3), 396–415.

Johnson, D. (2011). *Creative License: Media Franchising, Shared Content, and the Collaborative Production of Culture*. New York: New York University Press.

Johnson, J. H. (1995). *Listening in Paris: A Cultural History*. Berkeley, CA: University of California Press.

Johnson, L. (1988). *The Unseen Voice: A Cultural History of Early Australian Radio*. London: Routledge.

Johnson, M. (1987). *The Body in the Mind*. Chicago, IL: University of Chicago Press.

Jones, S. G. (ed.) (1998). *Cybersociety 2.0*. Thousand Oaks, CA: Sage.

Jordan, A. (1992). Social Class, Temporal Orientation, and Mass Media Use within the Family System. *Critical Studies in Mass Communication*, 9(4): 374–386.

Jørgensen, K. (2009). *A Comprehensive Study of Sound in Computer Games: How Audio Affects Player Action*. Lewiston, NY: Edwin Mellen Press.

Jørgensen, M. W. and Phillips, L. (2002). *Discourse Analysis as Theory and Method*. London: Sage.

Jowett, G., Jarvie, I. C., and Fuller, K. H. (1996). *Children and the Movies: Media Influence and the Payne Fund Controversy*. Cambridge: Cambridge University Press.

Jungk, R. and Müllert, N. (1981). *Zukunftwerkstätten [Workshops on the Future]*. Hamburg: Hoffmann und Campe.

Juul, J. (2001). Games Telling Stories – A Brief Note on Games and Narratives. *Game Studies*, 1(1). Online, available at: www.gamestudies.org/0101/juul-gts/ [accessed April 15, 2011].

Kakihara, M. and Sørensen, C. (2002). *Mobility: An Extended Perspective*. Paper presented at the Hawai'i International Conference on System Sciences, Big Island, Hawai'i, January 7–10.

Kalinak, K. (1992). *Settling the Score: Music and the Classical Hollywood Film*. Madison, WI: University of Wisconsin Press.

Kamhavi, R. and Weaver, D. (2003). Mass Communication Research Trends from 1980 to 1999. *Journalism and Mass Communication Quarterly*, 80(1): 7–27.

Kaminsky, S. M. and Mahan, J. H. (1985). *American Television Genres*. Chicago, IL: Nelson-Hall.

Kant, I. (1992[1798]). *The Conflict of the Faculties* (M. J. Gregor, trans.). Lincoln, NE: University of Nebraska Press.

Kant, I. (2004a[1790]). *The Critique of Judgment*. Online, available at: http://etext.library.adelaide.edu.au/k/kant/immanuel/k16j/ [accessed January 15, 2009].

Kant, I. (2004b[1785]). *Fundamental Principles of the Metaphysic of Morals*. Online, available at: www.gutenberg.org/etext/5682 [accessed May 15, 2009].

Kaplan, E. A. (1988). *Rocking Around the Clock: Music Television, Postmodernism, and Consumer Culture*. New York: Routledge.

Katz, E. (1959). Mass Communication Research and the Study of Popular Culture: An Editorial Note on a Possible Future for this Journal. *Studies in Public Communication*, 1(2): 1–6.

Katz, E. and Lazarsfeld, P. F. (1955). *Personal Influence*. Glencoe, IL: Free Press.

Katz, E. and Liebes, T. (2007). 'No More Peace!' How Disaster, Terror, and War Have Upstaged Media Events. *International Journal of Communication*, 1: 157–166.

Katz, E. and Wedell, G. (1977). *Broadcasting in the Third World: Promise and Performance*. Cambridge, MA: Harvard University Press.

Katz, E., Blumler, J. G., and Gurevitch, M. (1974). Utilization of Mass Communication by the Individual. In J. G. Blumler and E. Katz (eds.), *The Uses of Mass Communications*. Beverly Hills, CA: Sage.

Katz, E., Gurevitch, M., and Haas, H. (1973). On the Use of Mass Media for Important Things. *American Sociological Review*, 38(2): 164–181.

Katz, E., Peters, J. D., Liebes, T., and Orloff, A. (eds.) (2003). *Canonic Texts in Media Research: Are There Any? Should There Be? How About These?* Cambridge: Polity Press.

Kay, A. and Goldberg, A. (1999[1977]). Personal Dynamic Media. In P. A. Mayer (ed.), *Computer Media and Communication: A Reader*. Oxford: Oxford University Press, pp. 111–119.

Kaye, E. (1979). *The ACT Guide to Television or… How to Treat TV with TLC*. Boston, MA: Beacon.

Kearney, M. C. (ed.) (2010). *The Gender and Media Reader*. London: Routledge.

Kelle, U. (2005). 'Emergence' vs. 'Forcing' of Empirical Data? A Crucial Problem of 'Grounded Theory' Reconsidered. *Forum: Qualitative Social Research*, 6(2): art. 27. Online, available at: www.qualitative-research.net/index.php/fqs/index.

Kelle, U. (ed.) (1995). *Computer-Aided Qualitative Data Analysis: Theory, Methods, and Practice*. London: Sage.

Kenix, L. J. (2009). Blogs as Alternative. *Journal of Computer-Mediated Communication*, 14(4): 790–822.

Kennedy, G. A. (1980). *Classical Rhetoric and Its Christian and Secular Tradition from Ancient to Modern Times*. Chapel Hill, NC: University of North Carolina Press.

Kepplinger, H.-M. (1997). Political Correctness and Academic Principles: A Reply to Simpson. *Journal of Communication*, 47(4), 102–117.

Kerlinger, F. N. (1986). *Foundations of Behavioral Research* (3rd ed.). New York: Holt, Rinehart & Winston.

Kern, S. (1983). *The Culture of Time and Space, 1880–1918*. Cambridge, MA: Harvard University Press.

Kilborn, R. (2003). *Staging the Real: Factual TV Programming in the Age of Big Brother*. Manchester: Manchester University Press.

Kim, M.-S. (2002). *Non-Western Perspectives on Human Communication: Implications for Theory and Practice*. Thousand Oaks, CA: Sage.

Kim, S. (2004). Rereading David Morley's "The Nationwide Audience." *Cultural Studies*, 18(1): 84–108.

Kim, S.-H. and Scheufele, D. A. (2002). 'Think About It This Way': Attribute Agenda-Setting Function of the Press and the Public's Evaluation of a Local Issue. *Journalism and Mass Communication Quarterly*, 79(1): 7–25.

Kincaid, D. L. (ed.) (1987). *Communication Theory: Eastern and Western Perspectives*. San Diego, CA: Academic Press.

Kinder, M. (1984). Music Video and the Spectator: Television, Ideology, and Dream. *Film Quarterly*, 38(1): 2–15.

Kingsford, P. (1982). *The Hunger Marchers in Britain, 1920–1940*. London: Lawrence and Wishart.

Kiousis, S. (2002). Interactivity: A Concept Explication. *New Media & Society*, 4(3): 355–383.

Kirk, J. and Miller, M. (1986). *Reliability and Validity in Qualitative Research*. Beverly Hills, CA: Sage.

Kittler, F. A. (1999[1986]). *Gramophone, Film, Typewriter*. Stanford, CA: Stanford University Press.

Kjørup, S. (2001). *Humanities, Geisteswissenschaften, Sciences humaines: Eine Einführung [The Human Sciences: An Introduction]*. Stuttgart: J. B. Metzler.

Klapper, J. (1960). *The Effects of Mass Communication*. Glencoe, IL: The Free Press.

Klevjer, R. (2008). Dataspillanalyse: reisen og kartet [Game Analysis: The Journey and the Map]. In P. Larsen and L. Hausken (eds.), *Medievitenskap [Media Studies]*, Vol 2. Bergen: Fagbokforlaget.

Klingender, F. D. and Legg, S. (1937). *Money Behind the Screen*. London: Lawrence and Wishart.

Klinger, B. (2006). *Beyond the Multiplex: Cinema, New Technologies, and the Home*. Berkeley, CA: University of California Press.

Koss, S. (1981, 1984). *The Rise and Fall of the Political Press in Britain, Vols 1 and 2*. London: Hamish Hamilton.

Kozloff, S. (1988). *Invisible Storytellers: Voice-over Narration in American Fiction Film*. Berkeley, CA: University of California Press.

Kozloff, S. (2000). *Overhearing Film Dialogue*. Berkeley, CA: University of California Press.

Kracauer, S. (1953). The Challenge of Qualitative Content Analysis. *Public Opinion Quarterly*, 16(2): 631–642.

Kracauer, S. (1960). *Theory of Film: The Redemption of Physical Reality*. London: Oxford University Press.

Kracauer, S. (1995[1963]). *The Mass Ornament: Weimar Essays*. Cambridge, MA: Harvard University Press.

Krcmar, M. (1998). The Contribution of Family Communication Patterns to Children's Interpretations of Television Violence. *Journal of Broadcasting & Electronic Media*, 42(2): 250–265.

Kress, G. (2010). *Multimodality: A Social Semiotic Approach to Contemporary Communication*. London : Routledge.

Kress, G. and van Leeuwen, T. (1996). *Reading Images: The Grammar of Visual Design*. London: Routledge.

Kress, G. and van Leuwen, T. (2001). *Multimodal Discourse: The Modes and Media of Contemporary Communication*. London: Edward Arnold.

Kripke, S. A. (1980). *Naming and Necessity*. Oxford: Blackwell.

Krippendorff, K. (1980). *Content Analysis. An Introduction to Its Methodology*. Newbury Park, CA: Sage.

Krippendorff, K. (2004). *Content Analysis: An Introduction to Its Methodology* (2nd ed.). Thousand Oaks, CA: Sage.

Krippendorff, K. (2008a). Cybernetics. In W. Donsbach (ed.), *International Encyclopedia of Communication, Vol. 3*. Malden, MA: Blackwell, pp. 1152–1159.

Krippendorff, K. (2008b). Information. In W. Donsbach (ed.), *International Encyclopedia of Communication, Vol. 5*. Malden, MA: Blackwell, pp. 2213–2221.

Kristeller, P. O. (1961). *Renaissance Thought: The Classic, Scholastic, and Humanist Strains*. New York: Harper.

Kristensen, N. N. (2010). The Historical Transformation of Cultural Journalism. *Northern Lights: Film and Media Studies Yearbook 2010*, 8(1): 69–92.

Kristensen, N. N. and Ørsten, M. (2007). Danish Media at War: The Danish Media Coverage of the Invasion of Iraq 2003. *Journalism: Theory, Practice & Criticism*, 8(3): 323–344.

Kristeva, J. (1984[1974]). *Revolution in Poetic Language*. New York: Columbia University Press.

Kroeber, A. L. and Kluckhohn. (1952). *Culture: A Critical Review of Concepts and Definitions*. Cambridge, MA: Peabody Museum of American Archaeology and Ethnology.

Krzyzanowski, M. (2008). Analyzing Focus Group Discussions. In R. Wodak and M. Krzyzanowski (eds.), *Qualitative Discourse Analysis in the Social Sciences*. Basingstoke: Palgrave Macmillan.

Kubey, R. and Csikszentmihalyi, M. (1990). *Television and the Quality of Life: How Viewing Shapes Everyday Experience*. Hillsdale, NJ: Lawrence Erlbaum.

Kuhn, A. (2002). *An Everyday Magic: Cinema and Cultural Memory*. London: I. B. Tauris.

Kuhn, T. S. (1970). *The Structure of Scientific Revolutions* (revised ed.). Chicago, IL: University of Chicago Press.

Kvale, S. (1987). Validity in the Qualitative Research Interview. *Methods*, 1(2): 37–72.

Kvale, S. and Brinkmann, S. (2009). *InterViews: Learning the Craft of Qualitative Research Interviewing* (2nd ed.). London: Sage.

Labinger, J. A. and Collins, H. (eds.) (2001). *The One Culture? A Conversation about Science*. Chicago, IL: University of Chicago Press.

Labov, W. and Waletzky, J. (1967). Narrative Analysis. In J. Helm (ed.), *Essays on the Verbal and Visual Arts*. Seattle, WA: University of Washington Press, pp. 12–44.

Lacan, J. (1977). *The Four Fundamental Concepts of Psychoanalysis*. Harmondsworth: Penguin.

Lacey, K. (1994). From *Plauderei* to Propaganda: On Women's Radio in Germany, 1924–35. *Media, Culture & Society*, 16(4): 589–608.

Lakoff, G. and Johnson, M. (1980). *Metaphors We Live By*. Chicago, IL: University of Chicago Press.

Lakoff, G. and Johnson, M. (1999). *Philosophy in the Flesh: The Embodied Mind and Its Challenge to Western Thought*. New York: Basic Books.

Landow, G. P. (1997). *Hypertext 2.0: The Convergence of Contemporary Critical Theory and Technology* (2nd ed.). Baltimore, MD: Johns Hopkins University Press.

Lang, G. E. and Lang, K. (1981). Watergate: An Exploration of the Agenda-Building Process. In G. C. Wilhoit and H. de Bock (eds.), *Mass Communication Review Yearbook, Vol. 2*. Beverly Hills, CA: Sage.

Lang, K. and Lang, G. E. (1953). The Unique Perspective of Television and Its Effects: A Pilot Study. *American Sociological Review*, 18(1): 3–12.

Lang, K. and Lang, G. E. (1991). Studying Events in Their Natural Settings. In K. B. Jensen and N. W. Jankowski (eds.), *A Handbook of Qualitative Methodologies for Mass Communication Research*. London: Routledge.

Lange, D. L., Baker, R. K., and Ball, S. J. (1969). *Mass Media and Violence*. Washington, DC: Government Printing Office.

Langer, J. (1998). *Tabloid Television. Popular Journalism and the 'Other News'*. London: Routledge.

Lanza, J. (1994). *Elevator Music: A Surreal History of Muzak, Easy-Listening, and Other Mood-Song*. New York: Picador.

Larsen, P. (1974). Analyse af TV-avisen [Analysis of Television News]. In M. B. Andersen and J. Poulsen (eds.), *Mediesociologi. Introduktion til massekommunikationsforskning [Media Sociology: An Introduction to Mass Communication Research]*. Copenhagen: Rhodos,

Larsen, P. (1989). Beyond the Narrative. Rock Videos and Modern Visual Fictions: Readings, Experiences. In M. Skovmand (ed.), *Media Fictions*. Aarhus: Aarhus University Press.

Larsen, P. (2007). *Film Music*. London: Reaktion Books.

Larsson, A. O. and Hrastinski, S. (2011). Blogs and Blogging: Current Trends and Future Directions. *First Monday*, 16(3). Online, available at: http://firstmonday.org/htbin/cgiwrap/bin/ojs/index.php/fm/rt/printerFriendly/3101/2836.

Lashley, K. S. and Watson, J. B. (1922). *A Psychological Study of Motion Pictures in Relation to Venereal Disease Campaigns*. Washington, DC: Interdepartmental Social Hygiene Board.

Lasorsa, D. and Reese, S. (1990). News Source Use in the Crash of 1987: A Study of Four National Media. *Journalism Quarterly*, 67(1): 60–71.

Lasswell, H. D. (1938). *Propaganda Technique in the World War*. New York: Alfred Knopf.

Lasswell, H. D. (1948). The Structure and Function of Communication in Society. In L. Bryson (ed.), *The Communication of Ideas*. New York: Harper, pp. 32–51.

Latour, B. (1987). *Science in Action*. Milton Keynes: Open University Press.

Lazarsfeld, P. F. (1934). The Psychological Aspect of Market Research. *Harvard Business Review*, 13(1): 54–71.

Lazarsfeld, P. F. (1941). Remarks on Administrative and Critical Communications Research. *Studies in Philosophy and Social Science*, 9(1): 2–16.

Lazarsfeld, P. F. and Barton, A. H. (1951). Qualitative Measurement in the Social Sciences: Classification,

Typologies, and Indices. In D. Lerner and H. D. Lasswell (eds.), *The Policy Sciences: Recent Developments in Scope and Method*. Stanford, CA: Stanford University Press.

Lazarsfeld, P. F. and Merton, R. K. (1960[1948]). Mass Communication, Popular Taste, and Organized Social Action. In W. Schramm (ed.). *Mass Communications*. Urbana, IL: University of Illinois Press.

Lazarsfeld, P. F., Berelson, B., and Gaudet, H. (1944). *The People's Choice*. New York: Duell, Sloan, and Pearce.

Lefkowitz, M., Eron, L. D., Walder, L. O., and Huesmann, L. R. (1972). Television Violence and Child Aggression. In E. Rubinstein, G. Comstock, and J. Murray (eds.), *Television and Adolescent Aggressiveness*. Washington, DC: US Government Printing Office.

Leiss, W., Kline, S., and Jhally, S. (1986). *Social Communication in Advertising. Persons, Products and Images of Well-Being*. London: Methuen.

Leiss, W., Kline, S., and Jhally, S. (2005). *Social Communication in Advertising. Consumption in the Mediated Marketplace*. New York: Routledge.

Lemish, D. (1982). The Rules of Viewing Television in Public Places. *Journal of Broadcasting and Electronic Media*, 26(4): 757–791.

Lemish, D. (2006). *Children and Television: A Global Perspective*. London: Wiley-Blackwell.

Lemke, J. L. (2002). Travels in Hypermodality. *Visual Communication*, 1(3): 299–325.

Lerner, D. (1958). *The Passing of Traditional Society*. New York: Free Press.

Lerner, D. and Lasswell, H. D. (eds.) (1951). *The Policy Sciences: Recent Developments in Scope and Method*. Stanford, CA: Stanford University Press.

Leskovec, J. and Horvitz, E. (2007). *Planetary-Scale Views on an Instant-Messaging Network*. Redmond, WA: Microsoft.

Lessig, L. (2006). *Code Version 2.0*. New York: Basic Books.

Lévi-Strauss, C. (1963[1958]). *Structural Anthropology*. New York: Penguin.

Lévi-Strauss, C. (1991[1962]). *Totemism*. London: Merlin Press.

Levine, E. (2001). Toward a Paradigm for Media Production Research: Behind the Scenes at *General Hospital*. *Critical Studies in Media Communication*. 18(1): 66–82.

Levine, L. W. (1988). *Highbrow/Lowbrow: The Emergence of Cultural Hierarchy in America*. Cambridge, MA: Harvard University Press.

Levy, M. (1993). Symposium: Virtual Reality: A Communication Perspective. *Journal of Communication*, 43(4): 4.

Levy, M. (ed.) (1992). Symposium: Communication Scholarship and Political Correctness. *Journal of Communication*, 42(2): 3–4.

Levy, M. and Gurevitch, M. (eds.) (1994). *Defining Media Studies: Reflections on the Future of the Field*. Oxford: Oxford University Press.

Levy, M. and Windahl, S. (1985). The Concept of Audience Activity. In K. E. Rosengren, P. Palmgreen, and L. Wenner (eds.), *Media Gratifications Research: Current Perspectives*. Beverly Hills, CA: Sage.

Lewin, K. (1945). The Research Center for Group Dynamics at Massachusetts Institute of Technology. *Sociometry*, 8(2): 126–136.

Lewin, K. (1947). Frontiers in Group Dynamics II. Channels of Group Life; Social Planning and Action Research. *Human Relations*, 1(2): 143–153.

Lewins, A. and Silver, C. (2007). *Using Software in Qualitative Research: A Step-by-Step Guide*. Los Angeles, CA: Sage.

Lewis, J. (1983). The Encoding/Decoding Model: Criticisms and Redevelopments for Research on Decoding. *Media, Culture & Society*, 5(2): 179–197.

Lewis, J. (1985). Decoding Television News. In P. Drummond and R. Paterson (eds.), *Television in Transition*. London: British Film Institute.

Lewis, J. (1991). *The Ideological Octopus: An Exploration of Television and Its Audience*. New York: Routledge.

Lewis, J. (1997). What Counts in Cultural Studies. *Media, Culture & Society*, 19(1): 83–97.

Lewis, J., Williams, A., and Franklin, B. (2008). A Compromised Fourth Estate? UK News Journalism, Public Relations and News Sources. *Journalism Studies*, 9(1): 1–20.

Lewis, L. (ed.) (1991). *The Adoring Audience*. London: Routledge.

Lichtenstein, A. and Rosenfeld, L. B. (1983). Uses and Misuses of Gratifications. *Communication Research*, 10(1): 97–109.

Licklider, J. C. R. and Taylor, R. W. (1999[1968]). The Computer as a Communication Device. In P. A. Mayer (ed.), *Computer Media and Communication: A Reader*. Oxford: Oxford University Press.

Liebes, T. and Katz, E. (1990). *The Export of Meaning*. New York: Oxford University Press.

Lievrouw, L. and Livingstone, S. (eds.) (2009). *New Media*. Los Angeles, CA: Sage.

Lin, C. A. and Atkin, D. J. (1989). Parental Mediation and Rulemaking for Adolescent Use of Television and VCRs. *Journal of Broadcasting and Electronic Media*, 33(1): 53–67.

Lincoln, Y. S. and Guba, E. G. (1985). *Naturalistic Inquiry*. London: Sage.

Lindlof, T. R. (1987). Ideology and Pragmatics of Media Access in Prison. In T. R. Lindlof (ed.), *Natural Audiences: Qualitative Research of Media Uses and Effects*. Norwood, NJ: Ablex.

Lindlof, T. R. and Taylor, B. C. (2011). *Qualitative Communication Research Methods* (3rd ed.). Los Angeles, CA: Sage.

Ling, R. (2008). *New Tech, New Ties. How Mobile Communication is Reshaping Social Cohesion*. Cambridge, MA: MIT Press.

Ling, R. (2010). Texting as a Life Phase Medium. *Journal of Computer-Mediated Communication*, 15(2): 277–292.

Ling, R. and Donner, J. (2009). *Mobile Communication*. Cambridge: Polity Press.

Ling, R. and Yttri, B. (2002). Hyper-coordination via Mobile Phones in Norway. In J. E. Katz and M. Aakhus (eds.), *Perpetual Contact: Mobile Communication, Private Talk, Public Performance*. Cambridge: Cambridge University Press, pp. 139–169.

Lippmann, W. and Merz, C. (1920). A Test of the News: An Examination of the News Reports in the *New York Times* on Aspects of the Russian Revolution of Special Importance to Americans March 1917–March 1920. *The New Republic [Special Supplement]*, Vol. XXIII, Part II, No. 296, August 4.

Livingstone, S. (1998). *Making Sense of Television: The Psychology of Audience Interpretation* (2nd ed.). London: Routledge.

Livingstone, S. (2002). *Young People and New Media*. Routledge, London.

Livingstone, S. (2009a). *Children and the Internet: Great Expectations, Challenging Realities*. Oxford: Polity Press.

Livingstone, S. (2009b). On the Mediation of Everything. *Journal of Communication*, 59(1): 1–18.

Livingstone, S. and Bovill, M. (eds.) (2001). *Children and their Changing Media Environment: A European Comparative Study*. Hillsdale, NJ: Lawrence Erlbaum.

Livingstone, S. and Haddon, L. (2009). *EU Kids Online: Final report*. LSE, London: EU Kids Online.

Livingstone, S. and Helsper, E. J. (2008). Parental Mediation of Children's Internet Use. *Journal of Broadcasting and Electronic Media*, 52(4): 581–599.

Livingstone, S. and Lunt, P. (1994). *Talk on Television: Audience Participation and Public Debate*. London: Routledge.

Lobkowicz, N. (1967). *Theory and Practice: History of a Concept from Aristotle to Marx*. Notre Dame: University of Notre Dame Press.

Logan, B. and Moody, K. (eds.) (1979).*Television Awareness Training: The Viewer's Guide for Family and Community*. Nashville, TN: Abingdon Press.

Lothe, J. (2000). *Narrative in Fiction and Film. An Introduction*. Oxford: Oxford University Press.

Lotz, A. D. (2004). Textual (Im)Possibilities in the U.S. Post-Network Era: Negotiating Production and Promotion Processes on Lifetime's *Any Day Now*. *Critical Studies in Media Communication*, 21(1): 22–43.

Lotz, A. D. (2005). Seventeen Days In July at Hollywood and Highland: Examining the Television Critics Association Tour. *Journal of Popular Film and Television*, 33(1): 22–28.

Lotz, A. D. (2007). The Promotional Role of the Network Upfront Presentations in the Production of Culture. *Television & New Media*, 8(1): 3–24.

Lovejoy, A. O. (1936). *The Great Chain of Being*. Cambridge, MA: Harvard University Press.

Lowenthal, L. (1961[1941]). The Triumph of Mass Idols. In Lowenthal, L. *Literature, Popular Culture, and Society*. Englewood Cliffs, NJ: Prentice-Hall.

Lowery, S. A. and DeFleur, M. L. (1983). *Milestones in Mass Communication Research: Media Effects*. New York: Longman.

Lowery, S. A. and DeFleur, M. L. (1988). *Milestones in Mass Communication Research: Media Effects* (2nd ed.). New York: Longman.

Lowery, S. A. and DeFleur, M. L. (1995). *Milestones in Mass Communication Research: Media Effects* (3rd ed.). New York: Longman.

Lowrey, W. and Latta, J. (2008). The Routines of Blogging. In C. Paterson and D. Domingo (eds.), *Making Online News: The Ethnography of New Media Production*. New York: Peter Lang.

Lüders, M. (2008). Conceptualizing Personal Media. *New Media & Society*, 10(5): 683–702.

Lukacs, G. (1989[1916]). *The Historical Novel*. London: Merlin Press.

Lull, J. (1980). The Social Uses of Television. *Human Communication Research*, 6(3): 197–209.

Lull, J. (1988a). Critical Response: The Audience as Nuisance. *Critical Studies in Mass Communication*, 5(3): 239–243.

Lull, J. (1991). *China Turned On: Television, Reform, and Resistance*. London: Routledge.

Lull, J. (ed.) (1988b). *World Families Watch Television*. Newbury Park, CA: Sage.

Lund, A. B. (2001). The Genealogy of News: Researching Journalistic Food-Chains. *Nordicom Review*, 22(1): 37–42.

Lundby, K. (ed.) (2009). *Mediatization: Concept, Changes, Consequences*. New York: Peter Lang.

Lunt, P. (2009). *Stanley Milgram: Understanding Obedience and its Implications*. London: Palgrave Macmillan.

Lutz, C. A. and Collins, J. L. (1993). *Reading National Geographic*. Chicago, IL: University of Chicago Press.

Lynd, R. S. and Lynd, H. M. (1929). *Middletown: A Study in American Culture*. London: Constable.

Lyotard, J.-F. (1984[1979]). *The Postmodern Condition*. Minneapolis, MN: University of Minnesota Press.

Lyytinen, K. and Yoo, Y. (2002). Issues and Challenges in Ubiquitous Computing. *Communications of the ACM*, 45(12): 63–65.

Macaulay, M. (in press). Father Knows Best: Therapy as Entertainment. *Pragmatics and Society*.

MacBeth, T. M. (1998). Quasi-experimental Research on Television and Behavior: Natural and Field Experiments. In J. K. Asamen and G. L. Berry (eds.), *Research Paradigms, Television and Social Behavior*. Thousand Oaks, CA: Sage.

MacBride, S. (ed.) (1980). *Many Voices, One World*. Paris: UNESCO.

MacCabe, C. (ed.) (1986). *High Theory/Low Culture: Analysing Popular Television and Film*. Manchester: Manchester University Press.

Maccoby, E. (1954). Why Do Children Watch Television? *Public Opinion Quarterly*, 18(3): 239–244.

Machill, M., Beiler, M., and Zenker, M. (2008). Search-engine Research: a European-American Overview and Systematization of an Interdisciplinary and International Research Field. *Media, Culture & Society*, 30(5): 591–608.

Machill, M., Neuberger, C., Schweiger, W., and Wirth, W. (2004). Navigating the Internet: A Study of German-Language Search Engines. *European Journal of Communication*, 19(3): 321–347.

Malinowski, B. (1922). *Argonauts of the Western Pacific*. London: Routledge.

Malinowski, B. (1967). *A Diary in the Strict Sense of the Term*. London: Routledge Kegan Paul.

Mankekar, P. (1999). *Screening Culture, Viewing Politics: An Ethnography of Television, Womanhood, and Nation in Postcolonial India*. Durham, NC: Duke University Press.

Mann, C. and Stewart, F. (2000). *Internet Communication and Qualitative Research: A Handbook for Researching Online*. London: Sage.

Mannheim, K. (1976[1922]). *Ideology and Utopia*. London: Routledge Kegan Paul.

Marcus, G. E. and Fischer, M. M. J. (1999). *Anthropology as Cultural Critique* (2nd ed.). Chicago, IL: University of Chicago Press.

Markham, A. (2009). Response to Nancy Baym, What Constitutes Quality in Qualitative Internet Research. In A. Markham and N. Baym (eds.), *Internet Inquiry: Conversations About Method*. Los Angeles, CA: Sage, pp. 190–197.

Marks, E. and de Courtivron, I. (eds.) (1981). *New French Feminisms*. Brighton: Harvester.

Marshall, C. and Rossman, G. B. (2006). *Designing Qualitative Research* (4th ed.). Thousand Oaks, CA: Sage.

Masterman, L. (1985). *Teaching the Media*. London: Comedia.

Mathieson, M. (1975). *The Preachers of Culture: A Study of English and its Teachers*. London: George Allen & Unwin Ltd.

Mautner, G. (2009). Checks and Balances: How Corpus Linguistics Can Contribute to CDA. In R. Wodak and M. Meyer (eds.), *Methods of Critical Discourse Analysis*. London: Sage.

Mayer, J. P. (1948). *British Cinemas and Their Audiences: Sociological Studies*. London: Denis Dobson Ltd.

Mayer, V. (2003). Living Telenovelas/Telenovelizing Life: Mexican-American Girls' Identities and Transnational Telenovelas. *Journal of Communication*, 53(3): 479–495.

Mayer, V. (2005). Research Beyond the Pale: Whiteness in Audience Studies and Media Ethnography. *Communication Theory*,15(2): 148–167.

Mayer, V., Banks, M., and Caldwell, J. T. (eds.) (2009). *Production Studies: Cultural Studies of Media Industries*. New York: Routledge.

McAdams, D. (1999). Opportunity of a Lifetime. *Broadcasting and Cable*, October 18: 23–28.

McCarthy, E. D., Langner, T. S., Gerstein, J. C., Eisenberg, V. G., and Orzeck, L. (1975). Violence and Behavior Disorders. *Journal of Communication*, 25(4): 71–85.

McChesney, R. (1999). *Rich Media, Poor Democracy: Communication Politics in Dubious Times*. Urbana, IL: University of Illinois Press.

McChesney, R. and Nichols, J. (2010). *The Death and Life of American Journalism: The Media Revolution that Will Begin the World Again*. Philadelphia, PA: First Nation Books.

McCombs, M. (2004). *Setting the Agenda. The Mass Media and Public Opinion*. Cambridge: Polity Press.

McCombs, M. E. and Shaw, D. L. (1972). The Agenda-Setting Function of Mass Media. *Public Opinion Quarterly*, 36(2): 176–187.

McCombs, M. E., Lopez-Escobar, E., and Llamas, J. P. (2000). Setting the Agenda of Attributes in the 1996 Spanish General Election. *Journal of Communication*, 50(2): 77–92.

McGuire, W. J. (1973). Persuasion, Resistance, and Attitude Change. In I. de Sola Pool (ed.), *Handbook of Communication*. Chicago, IL: Rand McNally.

McLeod, J. M., Atkin, C. K., and Chaffee, S. H. (1972). Adolescents, Parents, and Television Use: Adolescent Self-report Measures from Maryland and Wisconsin Samples. In G. A. Comstock and E. A. Rubinstein (eds.), *Television and Social Behaviour, Vol. 3, Television and Adolescent Aggressiveness*. Washington, DC: US Government Printing Office.

McLeod, J. M., Fitzpatrick, M. A., Glynn, C. J., and Fallis, S. F. (1982). Television and Social Relations: Family Influences and Consequences for Interpersonal Behavior. In D. Pearl, L. Bouthillet, and J. Lazar (eds.), *Television and Behavior: Ten Years of Scientific Progress and Implications for the Eighties* (HHS Publication No. ADM 82-1196, Vol. 2). Washington, DC: U.S. Government Printing Office, pp. 272–286.

McLuhan, M. (1962). *The Gutenberg Galaxy*. Toronto: Toronto University Press.

McLuhan, M. (1964). *Understanding Media: The Extensions of Man*. New York: McGraw-Hill.

McManus, J. (1994). *Market-driven Journalism. Let the Citizens Beware?* Thousand Oaks, CA: Sage.

McMillan, S. J. (2002). Exploring Models of Interactivity from Multiple Research Traditions: Users, Documents, and Systems. In L. Lievrouw and S. Livingstone (eds.), *Handbook of New Media: Social Shaping and Consequences of ICTs*. London: Sage, pp. 163–182.

McMurria, J. (2003). Long-format TV: Globalisation and Network Branding in a Multi-Channel Era. In M. Jancovich and J. Lyons (eds.), *Quality Popular Television: Cult TV, the Industry and Fans*. London: British Film Institute.

McNair, B. (2000). *Journalism and Democracy*. London: Routledge.

McNelly, J. T. (1959). Intermediary Communicators in the International Flow of News. *Journalism Quarterly*, 36(1): 23–26.

McQuail, D. (1983). *Mass Communication Theory: An Introduction*. London: Sage.

McQuail, D. (1992). *Media Performance: Mass Communication and the Public Interest*. London: Sage.

McQuail, D. (2000). *McQuail's Mass Communication Theory* (4th ed.). London: Sage.

McQuail, D. (2005). *McQuail's Mass Communication Theory* (5th ed.). London: Sage.

McQuail, D. (2008). Communication as an Academic Field: Western Europe. In W. Donsbach (ed.), *International Encyclopedia of Communication*. Malden, MA: Wiley-Blackwell.

McQuail, D. (2010). *McQuail's Mass Communication Theory* (6th ed.). London: Sage.

McQuail, D. and Windahl, S. (1993). *Communication Models for the Study of Mass Communication*. London: Longman.

McQuail, D., Blumler, J. G., and Brown, J. R. (1972). The Television Audience: A Revised Perspective. In D. McQuail (ed.), *Sociology of Mass Communications*. Harmondsworth: Penguin.

McRobbie, A. (1991). *Feminism and Youth Culture: From "Jackie" to "Just Seventeen."* Basingstoke: Macmillan.

Mead, G. H. (1934). *Mind, Self, and Society*. Chicago, IL: University of Chicago Press.

Meadel, C. (1994). *Histoire de la radio dans les années trente [History of Radio During the 1930s]*. Paris: Anthropos/INA.

Meehan, E. (1991). 'Holy Commodity Fetish, Batman!': The Political Economy of a Commercial Intertext. In R. E. Pearson and W. Uricchio (eds.), *The Many Lives of the Batman: Critical Approaches to a Superhero and his Media*. New York: Routledge.

Megarry, T. (1995). *Society in Prehistory: The Origins of Human Culture*. London: Macmillan.

Meirick, P. C., Sims, J., Gilchrist, E., and Croucher, S. (2009). All the Children Are Above Average: Parents' Perceptions of Education and Materialism as Media Effects on Their Own and Other Children. *Mass Communication & Society*, 12(2): 217–237.

Meraz, S. (2009). Is There an Elite Hold? Traditional Media to Social Media Agenda Setting Influence in Blog Networks. *Journal of Computer-Mediated Communication*, 14(3): 682–707.

Merleau-Ponty, M. (1962[1945]). *Phenomenology of Perception*. London: Routledge Kegan Paul.

Merolla, A. J. (2010). Relational Maintenance and Noncopresence Reconsidered: Conceptualizing Geographic Separation in Close Relationships. *Communication Theory*, 20(2): 169–193.

Merten, K. (1996). Reactivity in Content Analysis. *Communications*, 21(1): 65–76.

Merton, R. K. (1949). Patterns of Influence: A Study of Interpersonal Influence and Communications Behavior in a Local Community. In P. F. Lazarsfeld and F. Stanton (eds.), *Communications Research, 1948–49*. New York: Harper Brothers.

Merton, R. K. (1968). *Social Theory and Social Structure* (enlarged ed.). New York: The Free Press.

Merton, R. K. (1987). The Focussed Interview and Focus Groups: Continuities and Discontinuities. *Public Opinion Quarterly*, 51(4), 550–566.

Merton, R. K. and Kendall, P. L. (1946). The Focused Interview. *American Journal of Sociology*, 51: 541–557.

Merton, R. K. and Kendall, P. L. (1955). The Focused Interview. In P. F. Lazarsfeld and B. Rosenberg (eds.), *The Language of Social Research*. Glencoe, IL: The Free Press.

Merz, C. (1926). When American Movies Go Abroad. *Harpers*, January: 159–165.

Messaris, P. (1994). *Visual 'Literacy': Image, Mind, and Reality*. Boulder, CO: Westview Press.

Messaris, P. (1997). *Visual Persuasion*. Thousand Oaks, CA: Sage.

Metz, C. (1968). *Essais sur la signification au cinéma*. Paris: Klincksieck. [English translation: *Film Language: A Semiotics of the Cinema*. New York: Oxford University Press, 1974].

Metz, C. (1974). *Language and Cinema*. The Hague: Mouton.

Metz, C. (1982). *The Imaginary Signifier: Psychoanalysis and the Cinema*. Bloomington, IN: Indiana University Press.

Meyrowitz, J. (1985). *No Sense of Place: The Impact of Electronic Media on Social Behavior*. New York: Oxford University Press.

Meyrowitz, J. (1994). Medium Theory. In D. Crowley and D. Mitchell (eds.), *Communication Theory Today*. Cambridge: Polity Press.

Mick, D. G. and Buhl, C. (1992). A Meaning-Based Model of Advertising Experience. *Journal of Consumer Research*, 19(3): 317–338.

Middleton, R. (1990). *Studying Popular Music*. Milton Keynes: Open University Press.

Milavsky, J. R., Kessler, R., Stipp, H., and Rubens, W. S. (1982). *Television and Aggression: Results of a Panel Study*. New York: Academic Press.

Miles, M. B. and Huberman, A. M. (1994). *Qualitative Data Analysis: An Expanded Sourcebook* (2nd ed.). Thousand Oaks, CA: Sage.

Mill, J. S. (1973–74[1843]). *Collected Works of John Stuart Mill, Vol. 7 and 8*. Toronto: University of Toronto Press.

Millard, A. (1995). *America on Record: A History of Recorded Sound*. Cambridge: Cambridge University Press.

Miller, C. R. (1984). Genre as Social Action. *Quarterly Journal of Speech*, 70(2): 151–167.

Miller, C. R. (1994). Rhetorical Community: The Cultural Basis of Genre. In A. Freedman and P. Medway (eds.), *Genre and the New Rhetoric*. London: Taylor & Francis, pp. 67–78.

Mills, C. W. (1959a). *The Sociological Imagination*. London: Oxford University Press.

Mills, C. W. (1959b). *The Power Elite*. Oxford: Oxford University Press.

Mills, C. W. (1970[1959]). *The Sociological Imagination* (3rd printing). London: Oxford University Press.

Millum, T. (1975). *Images of Woman: Advertising in Women's Magazines*. London: Chatto & Windus.

Moi, T. (2002). *Sexual/Textual Politics: Feminist Literary Theory* (2nd ed.). London: Routledge.

Monge, P. and Contractor, N. S. (2003). *Theories of Communication Networks*. New York: Oxford University Press.

Montgomery, K. (1989). *Target: Prime Time: Advocacy Groups and the Struggle Over Entertainment Television*. New York: Oxford University Press.

Montgomery, M. (2008). The Discourse of the Broadcast News Interview. *Journalism Studies*, 9(2): 260–277.

Moores, S. (1988). 'The Box on the Dresser': Memories of Radio and Everyday Life. *Media, Culture & Society*, 10(1): 23–40.

Moran, A. (ed.) (1996). *Film Policy: International, National, and Regional Perspectives*. London, New York: Routledge.

Morgan, M. (2008). Cultivation Theory. In W. Donsbach (ed.), *International Encyclopedia of Communication, Vol. 3*. Malden, MA: Blackwell, pp. 1091–1095.

Morley, D. (1980). *The 'Nationwide' Audience*. London: British Film Institute.

Morley, D. (1981). "The 'Nationwide' Audience": A Critical Postscript. *Screen Education*, 39: 3–14.

Morley, D. (1986). *Family Television: Cultural Power and Domestic Leisure*. London: Comedia.

Morley, D. (2000). *Home Territories: Media, Mobility, and Identity*. London: Routledge.

Morley, D. and Chen, K.-H. (eds.) (1996). *Stuart Hall: Critical Dialogues in Cultural Studies*. London: Routledge.

Morris, M. (1990). Banality in Cultural Studies. In P. Mellencamp (ed.), *Logics of Television*. Bloomington, IN: Indiana University Press.

Morrison, D. E. (1992). *Television and the Gulf War*. London: John Libbey.

Morrison, D. E. (1998). *The Search for a Method: Focus Groups and the Development of Mass Communication Research*. Luton: University of Luton Press.

Morrison, D. E. and Tumber, H. (1988). *Journalists at War*. London: Sage.

Mortensen, F. (1977). The Bourgeois Public Sphere: A Danish Mass Communications Research Project. In M. Berg, P. Hemanus, and J. Ekecrantz (eds.), *Current Theories in Scandinavian Mass Communication*. Grenaa: GMT.

Moser, C. A. and Kalton, G. (1971). *Survey Methods in Social Investigation*. Aldershot: Gower.

Mowlana, H. (1993). The New Global Order and Cultural Ecology. *Media, Culture & Society*, 15(1): 9–27.

Mulvey, L. (1992[1975]). Visual Pleasure and Narrative Cinema. In G. Mast, M. Cohen, and L. Braudy (eds.), *Film Theory and Criticism: Introductory Readings* (4th ed.). New York: Oxford University Press.

Munakata, T. (ed.) (2007). Beyond Silicon: New Computing Paradigms. *Communications of the ACM*, 50(9): 30–72.

Münsterberg, H. (1970[1916]). *The Film: A Psychological Study*. New York: Dover Publications Inc. (Orig. publ. 1916 with the title *The Photoplay*).

Muntigl, P., Weiss, G., and Wodak, R. (2000). *European Union Discourses of Unemployment: An Interdisciplinary Approach to Employment Policy-making and Organizational Change*. Amsterdam: Benjamins.

Murdock, G. (1997). Thin Descriptions: Questions of Method in Cultural Analysis. In J. McGuigan (ed.), *Cultural Methodologies*. London: Sage.

Murdock, G. (2000). Talk Shows: Democratic Debates and Tabloid Tales. In J. Wieten, G. Murdock, and P. Dahlgren (eds.), *Television Across Europe: A Comparative Introduction*. London: Sage.

Murdock, G. and Golding, P. (1977). Capitalism, Communication, and Class Relations. In J. Curran, M. Gurevitch, and J. Woollacott (eds.), *Mass Communication and Society*. London: Edward Arnold.

Murphy, P. (2008). Writing Media Culture: Representation and Experience in Media Ethnography. *Communication, Culture, & Critique*, 1(3): 268–286.

Myers, G. (1994). *Words in Ads*. London: Edward Arnold.

Myers, G. (2008). Analyzing Interaction in Broadcast Debates. In R. Wodak and M. Krzyzanowski (eds.), *Qualitative Discourse Analysis in the Social Sciences*. Basingstoke: Palgrave Macmillan.

Nabi, R. L. and Oliver, M. B. (eds.) (2009). *The SAGE Handbook of Media Processes and Effects*. Los Angeles, CA: Sage.

Napoli, P. M. (2003). *Audience Economics: Media Institutions and the Audience Marketplace*. New York: Columbia University Press.

Nathanson, A. (1998). *The Immediate and Cumulative Effects of Television Mediation on Children's Aggression*. Unpublished doctoral dissertation, University of Wisconsin-Madison.

Nathanson, A. (1999). Identifying and Explaining the Relationship between Parental Mediation and Children's Aggression. *Communication Research*, 26(6): 124–143.

Nathanson, A. (2001). Parent and Child Perspectives on the Presence and Meaning of Parental Television Mediation. *Journal of Broadcasting & Electronic Media*, 45(2): 210–220.

Nathanson, A. (2002). The Unintended Effects of Parental Mediation of Television on Adolescents. *Mediapsychology*, 4(3): 207–230.

Nathanson, A., Eveland, W. P., Park, H. S, and Paul, B. (2002). Perceived Media Influence and Efficacy as Predictors of Caregivers' Protective Behaviors. *Journal of Broadcasting and Electronic Media*, 46(3): 385–411.

National Television Violence Study Vol.1 (1997). Thousand Oaks, CA: Sage.

Neale, S. (1980). *Genre*. London: British Film Institute.

Neale, S. (2000). *Genre and Hollywood*. New York: Routledge.

Negrine, R. (2008). *The Transformation of Political Communication: Continuities and Changes in Media and Politics*. Basingstoke: Palgrave Macmillan.

Negt, O. (ed.) (1973). *Kritische Kommunikationsforschung [Critical Communication Research]*. Munich: Carl Hanser Verlag.

Negt, O. and Kluge, A. (1993[1972]). *Public Sphere and Experience*. Minneapolis, MN: University of Minnesota Press.

Nelson, T. H. (1965). *Complex Information Processing: A File Structure for the Complex, the Changing, and the Indeterminate*. Paper presented at the 20th National ACM Conference, Cleveland, Ohio.

Nerone, J. C. (ed.) (1995). *Last Rights: Revisiting Four Theories of the Press*. Urbana, IL: University of Illinois Press.

Neuman, W. L. (2005). *Social Research Methods: Qualitative and Quantitative Approaches* (6th ed.). Boston, MA: Allyn and Bacon.

Neuman, W. R. (1976). Patterns of Recall among Television News Viewers. *Public Opinion Quarterly*, 40(1): 115–123.

Neuman, W. R. (1989). Parallel Content Analysis: Old Paradigms and New Proposals. In G. A. Comstock (ed.), *Public Communication and Behavior, Vol. 2*. Orlando, FL: Academic Press.

Neuman, W. R., Just, M., and Crigler, A. N. (1992). *Common Knowledge: News and the Construction of Political Meaning*. Chicago, IL: University of Chicago Press.

Newcomb, H. (1974). *Television. The Most Popular Art*. Garden City, NY: Anchor Press.

Newcomb, H. (1978). Assessing the Violence Profile of Gerbner and Gross: A Humanistic Critique and Suggestion. *Communication Research*, 5(3), 264–282.

Newcomb, H. (ed.) (2004). *Encyclopedia of Television*. London, New York: Routledge.

Newcomb, H. and Alley, R. (1983). *The Producer's Medium: Conversations with Creators of American TV*. New York: Oxford University Press.

Newcomb, H. and Hirsch, P. (1983). Television as a Cultural Forum: Implications for Research. *Quarterly Review of Film Studies*, 8(3): 45–55.

Newman, N. (2009). *The Rise of Social Media and its Impact on Mainstream Journalism*. Working Paper, Reuters Institute for the Study of Journalism, University of Oxford. Online, available at: http://reutersinstitute.politics.ox.ac.uk/fileadmin/documents/Publications/The_rise_of_social_media_and_its_impact_on_mainstream_journalism.pdf [accessed February 24, 2011].

Nicholson, L. (ed.) (1997). *The Second Wave: A Reader in Feminist Theory*. London: Routledge.

Nippert-Eng, C. E. (1996). Calendars and Keys: The Classification of 'Home' and 'Work.' *Sociological Forum*, 11(3): 563–582.

Noelle-Neumann, E. (1984). *The Spiral of Silence*. Chicago, IL: University of Chicago Press.

Nofsinger, R. E. (1991). *Everyday Conversation*. Newbury Park, CA : Sage.

Nordenstreng, K. (1972). Policy for News Transmission. In D. McQuail (ed.), *Sociology of Mass Communications*. Harmondsworth: Penguin.

Nordenstreng, K. and Schiller, H. I. (eds.) (1979). *National Sovereignty and International Communication*. Norwood, NJ: Ablex.

O'Donnell, H. (1999). *Good Times, Bad Times: Soap Operas and Society in Western Europe*. London: Leicester University Press.

O'Halloran, K. L. (2011). Multimodal Discourse Analysis. In K. Hyland and B. Paltridge (eds.), *Continuum Companion to Discourse*. London and New York: Continuum.

O'Neil, M. and R. Ackland (2006). The Structural Role of Nanotechnology-Opposition in Online

Environmental-Activist Networks. Paper presented to 26th International Sunbelt Social Network Conference, April 24–30, Vancouver. Online, available at: http://voson.anu.edu.au/papers/environmental_activists_structural_role.pdf.

O'Sullivan, T. (1991). Television, Memories and the Culture of Viewing. In J. Corner (ed.), *Popular Television in Britain*. London: British Film Institute.

O'Sullivan, T., Hartley, J., Saunders, D., Montgomery, M., and Fiske, J. (1993). *Key Concepts in Communication and Cultural Studies* (2nd ed.). London: Routledge.

Oberhuber, F. and Krzyzanowski, M. (2008). Discourse Analysis and Ethnography. In R. Wodak and M. Krzyzanowski (eds.), *Qualitative Discourse Analysis in the Social Sciences*. Basingstoke: Palgrave Macmillan.

Ong, W. (1982). *Orality and Literacy: The Technologizing of the Word*. New York: Cornell University Press.

Oppenheim, A. N. (1992). *Questionnaire Design, Interviewing and Attitude Measurement*. London: Pinter Publishers.

Örnebring, H. (2008). The Consumer as Producer – Of What? User-Generated Tabloid Content in *The Sun* (UK) and *Aftonbladet* (Sweden). *Journalism Studies*, 9(5): 771–785.

Örnebring, H. (2009). *The Two Professionalisms of Journalism: Journalism and the Changing Context of Work*. Working Paper, Reuters Institute for the Study of Journalism, University of Oxford. Online, available at: http://reutersinstitute.politics.ox.ac.uk/fileadmin/documents/Publications/The_Two_Professionalisms_of_Journalism_Working_Paper.pdf [accessed February 24, 2011].

Outhwaite, W. (1975). *Understanding Social Life: The Method Called Verstehen*. London: George Allen & Unwin Ltd.

Palmer, J. (2000). *Spinning Into Control: News Values and Source Strategies*. London: Leicester University Press.

Palmgreen, P. and Rayburn, J. D. III. (1985). An Expectancy-Value Approach to Media Gratifications. In K. E. Rosengren, L. Wenner, and P. Palmgreen (eds.), *Media Gratifications Research: Current Perspectives*. Beverly Hills, CA: Sage.

Palmgreen, P., Wenner, L., and Rayburn, J. D., III. (1980). Relations between Gratifications Sought and Obtained: A Study of Television News. *Communication Research*, 7(2): 161–192.

Parameswaran, R. (1999). Western Romance Fiction as English-Language Media in Postcolonial India. *Journal of Communication*, 49(3): 84–105.

Parameswaran, R. (2001). Feminist Media Ethnography in India: Exploring Power, Gender, and Culture in the Field. *Qualitative Inquiry*, 7(1): 69–103.

Park, D. W. and Pooley, J. (eds.) (2008). *The History of Media and Communication Research: Contested Memories*. New York: Peter Lang.

Park, J. H., Gabbadon, N. G., and Chernin, A. R. (2006). Naturalizing Racial Differences through Comedy: Asian, Black, and White Views on Racial Stereotypes in *Rush Hour 2*. *Journal of Communication*, 56(1): 157–177.

Park, R. E. (1922). *The Immigrant Press and Its Control*. New York: Harper.

Park, R. E. (1940). News as a Form of Knowledge: A Chapter in the Sociology of Knowledge. *American Journal of Sociology*, 45(5): 669–686.

Parkin, F. (1971). *Class Inequality and Political Order*. London: MacGibbon and Kee.

Parsons, T. (1951). *The Social System*. Glencoe, IL: The Free Press.

Partridge, D. (1991). *A New Guide to Artificial Intelligence*. Norwood, NJ: Ablex.

Patterson, T. E. (1998). Political Roles of the Journalist. In D. Graber, D. McQuail, and P. Norris (eds.), *The Politics of News. The News of Politics*. Washington, DC: CQ Press.

Patton, M. Q. (2002). *Qualitative Research and Evaluation Methods* (3rd ed.). Thousand Oaks, CA: Sage.

Paul, C. (2008) *Digital Art* (Revised and expanded ed.). London: Thames & Hudson.

Pavitt, C. (1999). The Third Way: Scientific Realism and Communication Theory. *Communication Theory*, 9(2): 162–188.

Pearl, D., Bouthilet, L., and Lazar, J. (eds.). (1982). *Television and Behavior: Ten Years of Scientific Progress and Implications for the Eighties*. Washington, DC: US Government Printing Office.

Pearson, R. and Uricchio, W. (eds.) (1990). *The Many Lives of the Batman*. New York: Routledge.

Peirce, C. S. (1931–58). *Collected Papers*. Cambridge, MA: Harvard University Press.

Peirce, C. S. (1985). Logic as Semiotic: The Theory of Signs. In R. Innis (ed.), *Semiotics: An Introductory Anthology*. London: Hutchinson.

Peirce, C. S. (1986). *Writings of Charles S. Peirce: A Chronological Edition, Vol. 3*. Bloomington, IN: Indiana University Press.

Peirce, C. S. (1992–98). *The Essential Peirce, Vols 1-2*. Bloomington, IN: Indiana University Press.

Pelfrey, R. (1985). *Art and Mass Media*. New York: Harper & Row.

Perelman, C. (1979). *The New Rhetoric and the Humanities*. Dordrecht: Reidel.

Perks, R. and Thomson, A. (eds.) (1998). *The Oral History Reader*. London: Routledge.

Perren, A. (2001–02). Sex, Lies and Marketing: Miramax and the Development of the 'Quality Indie' Blockbuster. *Film Quarterly*, 55(2): 30–39.

Perron, B. and Wolf, M. J. P. (eds.) (2008). *The Video Game Theory Reader 2*. London, New York: Routledge.

Perry, D. K. (ed.) (2001). *American Pragmatism and Communication Research*. Mahwah, NJ: Lawrence Erlbaum.

Peters, J. D. (1999). *Speaking into the Air: A History of the Idea of Communication*. Chicago, IL: University of Chicago Press.

Peters, J. D. (2005). *Courting the Abyss: Free Speech and the Liberal Tradition*. Chicago, IL: University of Chicago Press.

Peters, J. D. (2008). Communication, History of the Idea. In W. Donsbach (ed.), *International Encyclopedia of Communication, Vol. 2*. Malden, MA: Blackwell, pp. 689–693.

Pettegree, A. (2005). *Reformation and the Culture of Persuasion*. Cambridge: Cambridge University Press.

Pew (2010). *New Media, Old Media. How Blogs and Social Media Agendas Relate and Differ from the Traditional Press*. Report from The Pew Research Center's Project for Excellence in Journalism, May 23. Online, available at: www.journalism.org/analysis_report/blogosphere [accessed March 2, 2011].

Phillips, L. and Winther Jørgensen, M. (2002). *Discourse Analysis as Theory and Method*. London: Sage.

Phillips, W. (2000). Real Life Ratings. *Royal Television Society Journal*, January: 42–43.

Philo, G. (1990). *Seeing and Believing: The Influence of Television*. London: Routledge.

Philo, G. (2007). Can Discourse Analysis Successfully Explain the Content of Media and Journalistic Practice? *Journalism Studies*, 8(2): 175–196.

Pike, K. L. (1967). *Language in Relation to a Unified Theory of the Structure of Human Behavior* (2nd ed.). The Hague: Mouton.

Pitt, J. (ed.) (1988). *Theories of Explanation*. New York: Oxford University Press.

Plantinga, C. R. (1997). *Rhetoric and Representation in Nonfiction Film*. New York: Cambridge University Press.

Popper, K. R. (1963). *Conjectures and Refutations: The Growth of Scientific Knowledge*. London: Routledge & Kegan Paul.

Popper, K. R. (1972a[1934]). *The Logic of Scientific Discovery*. London: Hutchinson.

Popper, K. R. (1972b). *Objective Knowledge: An Evolutionary Approach*. London: Oxford University Press.

Porat, M. (1977). *The Information Economy: Definition and Measurement*. Washington, DC: Government Printing Office.

Porter, R. (1991). The History of the Body. In P. Burke (ed.), *New Perspectives on Historical Writing*. Cambridge: Polity Press.

Posner, R., Robering, K., and Sebeok, T. A. (eds.) (1997–98). *Semiotics: A Handbook of the Sign-Theoretic Foundations of Nature and Culture*. Berlin: Walter de Gruyter.

Potter, J. (1996). *Representing Reality. Discourse, Rhetoric and Social Construction*. London: Sage.

Potter, J. and Wetherell, W. (1987). *Discourse and Social Psychology: Beyond Attitudes and Behaviour*. London: Sage.

Potter, J. and Wetherell, M. (1996). Discourse Analysis. In J. A. Smith, R. Harré, and L. Van Langenhove (eds.), *Rethinking Methods in Psychology*. London: Sage.

Potter, W. J. (1996). *An Analysis of Thinking and Research about Qualitative Methods*. Mahwah, NJ: Lawrence Erlbaum.

Potter, W. J. (2011). *Media Literacy* (5th ed.). Los Angeles, CA: Sage.

Potter, W. J. and Smith, S. (1999). Consistency of Contextual Cues about Violence across Narrative Levels. *Journal of Communication*, 49(4): 121–133.

Pound, R. and Frankfurter, F. (eds.) (1922). *Criminal Justice in Cleveland*. Cleveland, OH: The Cleveland Foundation.

Prabowo, R. and Thelwall, M. (2010). Sentiment Analysis: A Combined Approach. *Journal of Informatics*, 3(1): 143–157.

Prensky, M. (2001). Digital Natives, Digital Immigrants: I. *On the Horizon*, 9(5): 1–6.

Press, A. (1991). *Women Watching Television: Gender, Class, and Generation in the American Television Experience*. Philadelphia, PA: University of Pennsylvania Press.

Preston, P. (2009). *Making the News: Journalism and News Cultures in Europe*. London: Routledge,

Pritchard, D. and Hughes, K. D. (1997). Patterns of Deviance in Crime News. *Journal of Communication*, 47(3): 49–67.

Propp, V. (1958[1928]). *Morphology of the Folktale*. Bloomington, IN: Indiana University Press.

Prosser, J. (ed.) (1998). *Image-Based Research: A Sourcebook for Qualitative Researchers*. London: Routledge.

Puchta, C. and Potter, J. (2004). *Focus Group Practice*. London: Sage.

Pugh, A. (2009). *Longing and Belonging: Parents, Children, and Consumer Culture*. Berkeley, CA: University of California Press.

Punch, K. F. (2005). *Introduction to Social Research: Quantitative and Qualitative Approaches* (2nd ed.). London: Sage.

Putnam, R. (2000). *Bowling Alone: The Collapse and Revival of American Community*. New York: Simon and Schuster.

Quaero (n.d.). Online, available at: www.quaero.org/modules/movie/scenes/home [accessed April 15, 2011].

Quandt, T. (2008). News Tuning and Content Management: An Observation Study of Old and New Routines in German Online Newsrooms. In C. Paterson and D. Domingo (eds.), *Making Online News: The Ethnography of New Media Production*. New York: Peter Lang.

Qiu, J. L. (2009). *Working-Class Network Society: Communication Technology and the Information Have-Less in Urban China*. Cambridge, MA: MIT Press.

Radway, J. (1984). *Reading the Romance: Women, Patriarchy, and Popular Literature*. Chapel Hill, NC: University of North Carolina Press.

Radway, J. (1988). Reception Study: Ethnography and the Problem of Dispersed Audiences and Nomadic Subjects. *Cultural Studies*, 2(3): 359–376.

Ragin, C. C. (1987). *The Comparative Method: Moving Beyond Qualitative and Quantitative Strategies*. Berkeley, CA: University of California Press.

Ragin, C. C. (1994). *Constructing Social Research: The Unity and Diversity of Method*. Thousand Oaks, CA: Pine Forge Press.

Ray, L. and Sayer, A. (eds.) (1999). *Culture and Economy after the Cultural Turn*. London: Sage.

Reason, P. and Bradbury, H. (eds.) (2008). *The SAGE Handbook of Action Research: Participative Inquiry and Practice* (2nd ed.). London: Sage.

Reese, S. D., Grant, A., and Danielian, L. H. (1994). The Structure of News Sources on Television: A Network Analysis of *CBS News*, *Nightline*, *McNeil/Lehrer*, and *This Week With David Brinkley*. *Journal of Communication*, 44(2): 64–83.

Reeves, B. and Nass, C. (1996). *The Media Equation: How People Treat Computers, Television, and New Media Like Real People and Places*. New York: Cambridge University Press.

Reich, Z. (2008). How Citizens Create News Stories: The 'News Access' Problem Reversed. *Journalism Studies*, 9(5): 739–758.

Reinharz, S. (1992). *Feminist Methods in Social Research*. New York: Oxford University Press.

Reisigl, M. and Wodak, R. (2009). The Discourse-Historical Approach. In R. Wodak and M. Meyer (eds.), *Methods of Critical Discourse Analysis*. London: Sage.

Rekimoto, J. (2008). Organic Interaction Technologies: From Stone to Skin. *Communications of the ACM*, 51(6): 38–44.

Renn, O. (1991). Risk Communication and the Social Amplification of Risk. In R. Kasperson and P. Stallen (eds.), *Communicating Risks to the Public: International Perspectives*. Dordrecht: Kluwer Academic Publishers.

Rennie, E. (2006). *Community Media: A Global Introduction*. Lanham, MD: Rowman & Littlefield.

Rentz, J., Reynolds, F., and Stout, R. (1983). Analyzing Changing Consumption Patterns with Cohort Analysis. *Journal of Marketing Research*, 20(1): 12–20.

Rettberg, J. W. (2008). *Blogging*. Cambridge: Polity.

Rheingold, H. (1994). *The Virtual Community*. London: Minerva.

Rheingold, H. (2002). *Smart Mobs: The Next Social Revolution*. New York: Perseus.

Rice, R. E. and Atkin, C. K. (eds.) (2001). *Public Communication Campaigns* (3rd ed.). Thousand Oaks, CA: Sage.

Richards, J. and Sheridan, D. (eds.) (1987). *Mass Observation at the Movies*. London: Routledge Kegan Paul.

Richardson, K. and Meinhof, U. H. (1999). *Worlds in Common? Television Discourse in a Changing Europe*. London: Routledge.

Ricoeur, P. (1981). *Hermeneutics and the Human Sciences: Essays on Language, Action and Interpretation*. Cambridge: Cambridge University Press.

Ricouer, P. (1983). *Time and Narrative, Vol. 1*. Chicago, IL, London: University of Chicago Press.

Riesman, D. (1950). *The Lonely Crowd: A Study of the Changing American Character*. New York: Doubleday.

Riessman, C. K. (2008). *Narrative Methods for the Human Sciences*. Los Angeles, CA: Sage.

Rimmon-Kenan, S. (1983). *Narrative Fiction: Contemporary Poetics*. London: Methuen.

Ritchie, D. (1999). *Probably, Probably Not: Rhetoric and Interpretation in Communication Research*. Paper presented at the International Communication Association Conference, San Francisco, CA.

Roach, C. (1997). The Western World and the NWICO: United They Stand? In P. Golding and P. Harris (eds.), *Beyond Cultural Imperialism: Globalization, Communication, and the New International Order*. London: Sage.

Robertson, R. (1992). *Globalization: Social Theory and Global Culture*. London: Sage.

Robertson, R. (1995). Glocalization: Time-Space and Homogeneity-Heterogeneity. In M. Featherstone, S. Lash, and R. Robertson (eds.), *Global Modernities*. London: Sage.

Robinson, J. P. and Converse, P. (1972). The Impact of Television on Mass Media Usage. In A. Szalai (ed.), *The Use of Time*. The Hague: Mouton.

Robinson, J. and Bachman, J. (1972). Television Viewing Habits and Aggression. In G. A. Comstock and E. A. Rubinstein (eds.), *Television and Social Behavior, Vol.3. Television and Adolescent Aggressiveness*. Washington, DC: US Government Printing Office.

Roe, K. and De Meyer, G. (2000). Music Television: MTV-Europe. In J. Wieten, G. Murdock, and P. Dahlgren (eds.), *Television Across Europe: A Comparative Introduction*. London: Sage.

Rogers, E. M. (1962). *The Diffusion of Innovations*. Glencoe, IL: Free Press.

Rogers, E. M. (1976). Communication and Development: The Passing of the Dominant Paradigm. *Communication Research*, 3(2): 213–240.

Rogers, E. M. (1986). *Communication Technology*. New York: Free Press.

Rogers, E. M. (1999). Anatomy of Two Subdisciplines of Communication Study. *Human Communication Research*, 25(4): 618–631.

Rogers, E. M. (2003). *Diffusion of Innovations* (5th ed.). New York: Free Press.

Rogers, E. M. and Storey, J. D. (1987). Communication Campaigns. In C. R. Berger and S. H. Chaffee (eds.), *Handbook of Communication Science*. Newbury Park, CA: Sage.

Rorty, R. (1979). *Philosophy and the Mirror of Nature*. Princeton, NJ: Princeton University Press.

Rorty, R. (1989). *Contingency, Irony, and Solidarity*. Cambridge: Cambridge University Press.

Rorty, R. (1991). Feminism and Pragmatism. *Michigan Quarterly Review*, 30(2): 231–258.

Rorty, R. (ed.) (1967). *The Linguistic Turn*. Chicago, IL: University of Chicago Press.

Rose, B. G. (1985). *TV Genres: A Handbook and Reference Guide*. Westport, CT: Greenwood Press.

Rose, G. (2007). *Visual Methodologies: An Introduction to the Interpretation of Visual Materials* (2nd ed.). London: Sage.

Rosenberg, B. and White, D. M. (eds.) (1957). *Mass Culture: The Popular Arts in America*. Glencoe, IL: Free Press.

Rosenberg, B. and White, D. M. (eds.) (1971). *Mass Culture Revisited*. New York: Van Nostrand Reinhold.

Rosengren, K. E. and Windahl, S. (1972). Mass Communication as a Functional Alternative. In D. McQuail (ed.), *Sociology of Mass Communications*. Harmondsworth: Penguin, pp. 166–194.

Rosengren, K. E. and Windahl, S. (1989). *Media Matter: TV Use in Childhood and Adolescence*. Norwood, NJ: Ablex.

Rosengren, K. E., Arvidson, P., and Sturesson, D. (1978). The Barsebäck Panic. In C. Winick (ed.), *Deviance and Mass Media*. Beverly Hills, CA: Sage.

Rosengren, K. E., Wenner, L., and Palmgreen, P. (eds.). (1985). *Media Gratifications Research: Current Perspectives*. Beverly Hills, CA: Sage.

Ross, E. A. (1910). The Suppression of Important News. *Atlantic Monthly*, 60: 303–311.

Ross, J. M. (2010). Informatics Creativity: A Role for Abductive Reasoning? *Communications of the ACM*, 53(2): 144–148.

Ross, K. and Nightingale, V. (2003). *Media and Audiences: New Perspectives*. Maidenhead: Open University Press.

Ross, S. S. (1998). Journalists' Use of On-line Technology and Sources. In D. L. Borden and K. Harvey (eds.), *The Electronic Grapevine: Rumor, Reputation and Reporting in the New On-Line Environment*. Mahwah, NJ: Lawrence Erlbaum Associates.

Rothenbuhler, E. W. and Coman, M. (eds.) (2005). *Media Anthropology*. Thousand Oaks, CA: Sage.

Rowbottom, S. (1974). *Hidden From History*. Harmondsworth: Pelican Books.

Rudy, W. (1984). *The Universities of Europe 1100–1914: A History*. London: Associated University Presses.

Ruesch, J. and Bateson, G. (1987[1951]). *Communication: The Social Matrix of Psychiatry*. New York: Norton.

Rush, M. (2005). *New Media in Art* (2nd ed.). London: Thames & Hudson.

Ryan, M.-L. (1991). *Possible Worlds, Artificial Intelligence, and Narrative Theory*. Bloomington, IN: Indiana University Press.

Ryle, G. (1971). *Collected Papers, Vol. 2*. London: Hutchinson.

Sacks, H., Schegloff, E. A., and Jefferson, G. (1974). A Simplest Systematics for the Organisation of Turn-Taking in Conversation. *Language*, 50(4): 696–735.

Saïd, E. (1978). *Orientalism*. New York: Random House.

Salen, K. and Zimmerman, E. (2004). *Rules of Play: Game Design Fundamentals*. Cambridge, MA: MIT Press.

Samuelson, P. A. (1954). The Pure Theory of Public Expenditure. *The Review of Economics and Statistics*, 36(4): 387–389.

Sarris, A. (1968). *The American Cinema: Directors and Directions, 1929–1968*. New York: Dutton.

Sasha. (2010). *It's National TV Turn-off Week*. Online, available at: www.parenting.com/blogs/show-and-tell/it-s-national-tv-turn-week.

Saussure, F. de (1959[1916]). *Course in General Linguistics*. London: Peter Owen.

Sayer, A. (2000). *Realism and Social Science*, London: Sage.

Scannell, P. (1986). 'The Stuff of Radio': Developments in Radio Features and Documentaries before the War. In J. Corner (ed.), *Documentary and the Mass Media*. London: Edward Arnold.

Scannell, P. (1988). Radio Times: The Temporal Arrangements of Broadcasting in the Modern World. In P. Drummond and R. Paterson (eds.), *Television and Its Audience*. London: British Film Institute.

Scannell, P. (1990). Public Service Broadcasting: The History of a Concept. In A. Goodwin and G. Whannel (eds.), *Understanding Television.* London: Routledge.

Scannell, P. (1996a). Public Service Broadcasting: From National Culture to Multiculturalism 1923–1995. In M. Raboy (ed.), *Public Broadcasting for the Twenty-First Century*. London: John Libbey.

Scannell, P. (1996b). *Radio, Television, and Modern Life*. Oxford: Blackwell.

Scannell, P. (2000). For-Anyone-as-Someone Structures. *Media, Culture & Society*, 22(1): 5–24.

Scannell, P. (2007). *Media and Communication.* London: Sage.

Scannell, P. (2008). The Question of Technology. In M. Bailey (ed.), *Narrating Media History.* London: Routledge.

Scannell, P. (ed.) (1991). *Broadcast Talk*. London: Sage.

Scannell, P. and Cardiff, D. (1991). *A Social History of British Broadcasting: 1922–1939 Serving the Nation, Vol. 1*. Oxford: Blackwell.

Schafer, R. M. (1977). *The Tuning of the World.* New York: Alfred A. Knopf.

Schaffer, J. (2007). *Citizen Media: Fad or the Future of News? The Rise and Prospects of Hyperlocal Journalism.* Online, available at: www.kcnn.org/research/citizen_media_report [accessed June 21, 2011].

Schatz, T. (1988). *The Genius of the System.* New York: Pantheon.

Schensul, J. J., LeCompte, M. D., Nasasti, B. K., and Borgatti, S. P. (1999). *Enhanced Ethnographic Methods: Audiovisual Techniques, Focused Group Interviews, and Elicitation Techniques, Vol. 3.* Walnut Creek, CA: Alta Mira Press.

Schensul, S. L., Schensul, J. J., and LeCompte, M. D (1999). *Essential Ethnographic Methods: Observations, Interviews, and Questionnaires, Vol. 2.* Walnut Creek, CA: Alta Mira Press.

Scheufele, D. (1999). *Agenda-Setting, Priming, and Framing Revisited: Another Look at Cognitive Effects of Political Communication.* Paper presented at the International Communication Association, San Francisco, CA.

Schiller, H. (1969). *Mass Communications and American Empire*. Boston, MA: Beacon Press.

Schlesinger, P. (1978). *Putting 'Reality' Together*. London: Constable.

Schlesinger, P. (1987). *Putting 'Reality' Together* (2nd ed.). London Methuen.

Schlesinger, P. (1990). Rethinking the Sociology of Journalism. In M. Ferguson (ed.), *Public Communication: The New Imperatives*. London: Sage.

Schlesinger, P., Dobash, R. E., Dobash, R. P., and Weaver, C. (1992). *Women Viewing Violence*. London: British Film Institute.

Schmidt, J. (2007). Blogging Practices: An Analytical Framework. *Journal of Computer-Mediated Communication*, 12(4): art. 13.

Schmitt, K. L., Woolf, K. D., and Anderson, D. R. (2003). Viewing the Viewers: Viewing Behaviors by Children and Adults During Television Programs and Commercials. *Journal of Communication*, 53(2): 265–281.

Schön, D. A. (1983). *The Reflective Practitioner: How Professionals Think in Action*. New York: Basic Books.

Schramm, W. (1964). *Mass Media and National Development*. Stanford, CA: Stanford University Press.

Schramm, W. (1997). *The Beginnings of Communication Study in America: A Personal Memoir*. Thousand Oaks, CA: Sage.

Schramm, W. and Lerner, D. (eds.) (1976). *Communication and Change: The Last Ten Years – and the Next*. Honolulu: University Press of Hawaii.

Schramm, W., Lyle, J., and Parker, E. (1961). *Television in the Lives of Our Children*. Palo Alto, CA: Stanford University Press.

Schrøder, K. C. (1997). Cynicism and Ambiguity: British Corporate Responsibility Advertisements and their Readers in the 1990s. In M. Nava, A. Blake, I. MacRury and B. Richards (eds.), *Buy This Book: Studies in Advertising and Consumption since the 1950s*. London: Routledge.

Schrøder, K. C. (1999). The Best of Both Worlds? Media Audience Research Between Rival Paradigms. In P. Alasuutari (ed.), *Rethinking the Media Audience: The New Agenda*. London: Sage.

Schrøder, K. C. (2007). Media Discourse Analysis: Researching Cultural Meanings from Inception to Reception. *Textual Cultures*, 2 (2): 77–99.

Schrøder, K. C. and Phillips, L. (2007). Complexifying Media Power: A Study of the Interplay between Media and Audience Discourses on Politics. *Media, Culture & Society*, 29 (6): 890–915.

Schrøder, K. C., Drotner, K., Kline, S., and Murray, C. (2003). *Researching Audiences: A Practical Guide to Methods in Media Audience Analysis*. London: Hodder Arnold.

Schudson, M. (1978). *Discovering the News*. New York: Basic Books.

Schudson, M. (1984). *Advertising, the Uneasy Persuasion*. New York: Basic Books.

Schudson, M. (1997). Why Conversation Is Not the Soul of Democracy. *Critical Studies in Mass Communication*, 14(4): 297–309.

Schudson, M. (2008). *Why Democracies Need an Unlovable Press*. Cambridge: Polity Press.

Schulz, W. (1976). *Die Konstruktion von Realität in den Nachrichtenmedien, Analyse der aktuellen Berichterstattung [The Construction of Reality in the News Media: Analysis of Current Reporting]*. Freiburg: Karl Alber.

Schütz, A. (1956[1932]). *The Phenomenology of the Social World*. London: Heinemann.

Scollon, R. (2002). Action and Text: Toward an Integrated Understanding of the Place of Text in Social (Inter)action, Mediated Discourse Analysis and the Problem of Social Action. In R. Wodak and M. Meyer (eds.), *Methods in Critical Discourse Analysis*. London: Sage.

Scollon, R. and Scollon, S. W. (2004). *Nexus Analysis. Discourse and the Emerging Internet*. London: Routledge.

Sconce, J. (2000). *Haunted Media*. Durham, NC: Duke University Press.

Scott, J. (1991). Women's History. In P. Burke (ed.), *New Perspectives on Historical Writing*. Cambridge: Polity Press.

Scribner, S. and Cole, M. (1981). *The Psychology of Literacy*. Cambridge, MA: Harvard University Press.

Seaman, J. (2008). Adopting a Grounded Theory Approach to Cultural-historical Research: Conflicting Methodologies or Complementary Methods? *International Journal of Qualitative Methods*, 7(1). Online, available at: http://ejournals.library.ualberta.ca/index.php/IJQM/index

Searle, J. R. (1969). *Speech Acts*. London: Cambridge University Press.

Sears, A. and Jacko, J. A. (eds.) (2008). *The Human-Computer Interaction Handbook: Fundamentals, Evolving Technologies, and Emerging Applications* (2nd ed.). New York: Lawrence Erlbaum.

Sebeok, T. A. (ed.) (1986). *Encyclopedic Dictionary of Semiotics* (2nd ed.). Berlin: Mouton de Gruyter.

Sebeok, T. A. and Umiker-Sebeok, J. (1983). "You Know My Method": A Juxtaposition of Charles S. Peirce and Sherlock Holmes. In U. Eco and T. A. Sebeok (eds.), *The Sign of Three*. Bloomington, IN: Indiana University Press.

Sellitz, C., Jahoda, M., Deutsch, M., and Cook, S. (1976). *Research Methods in Social Relations*. New York: Holt, Rinehart & Winston.

Sennett, R. (1998). *The Corrosion of Character: The Personal Consequences of Work in the New Capitalism*. New York: Norton.

Sepstrup, P. (1989). Research into International TV Flows. *European Journal of Communication*, 4(4): 393–408.

Shanahan, J. and Morgan, M. (1999). *Television and Its Viewers: Cultivation Theory and Research*. Cambridge: Cambridge University Press.

Shannon, C. E. (1948). A Mathematical Theory of Communication. *The Bell System Technical Journal*, 27(July): 379–423; 27(October): 623–656.

Shannon, C. E. and Weaver, W. (1949). *The Mathematical Theory of Communication*. Urbana, IL: University of Illinois Press.

Shapiro, M. A. (2008). Memory, Message. In W. Donsbach (ed.), *International Encyclopedia of Communication*. Malden, MA: Blackwell.

Sharpe, J. (1991). History from Below. In P. Burke (ed.), *New Perspectives on Historical Writing*. Cambridge: Polity Press.

Sharrock, W. and Anderson, B. (1986). *The Ethnomethodologists*. London: Tavistock.

Shi, Y. (2010). Product Placement and Digital Piracy: How Young Chinese Viewers React to the Unconventional Method of Corporate Cultural Globalization. *Communication, Culture & Critique*, 3(3): 435–463.

Shoemaker, P. J. (1991). *Gatekeeping*. Newbury Park, CA: Sage.

Shoemaker, P. J. and Reese, S. D. (1996). *Mediating the Message*. London: Longman.

Shoemaker, P. J., Vos, T. P., and Reese, S. D. (2009). Journalists as Gatekeepers. In K. Wahl-Jorgensen and T. Hanitzsch (eds.), *The Handbook of Journalism Studies*. London: Routledge.

Shrum, L. J. (1996). Psychological Processes Underlying Cultivation Effects: Further Tests of Construct Accessibility. *Human Communication Research*, 22(4): 482–509.

Siebert, F., Peterson, T., and Schramm, W. (1956). *Four Theories of the Press*. Urbana, IL: University of Illinois Press.

Siegel, P. M. and Hodge, R. W. (1968). A Causal Approach to the Study of Measurement Error. In H. M. Blalock, Jr. and A. B. Blalock (eds.), *Methodology in Social Research*. New York: McGraw-Hill.

Siegel, S. (1956). *Nonparametric Statistics for the Behavioral Sciences*. Tokyo: McGraw-Hill.

Silj, A. (1988). *East of Dallas: The European Challenge to American Television*. London: British Film Institute.

Silverman, D. (2006). *Interpreting Qualitative Data: Methods for Analyzing Talk, Text, and Interaction* (3rd ed.). London: Sage.

Silverman, D. (2010). *Doing Qualitative Research: A Practical Handbook* (3rd ed.). London: Sage.

Silverstone, R. (1999). *Why Study the Media?* London: Sage.

Silverstone, R. (2006). Domesticating Domestication: Reflections on the Life of a Concept. In T. Berker, M. Hartmann, Y. Punie, and K. J. Ward (eds.), *Domestication of Media and Technology*. Maidenhead: Open University Press, pp. 229–248.

Silverstone, R. and Hirsch, E. (eds.) (1992). *Consuming Technologies: Media and Information in Domestic Spaces*. London: Routledge.

Simon, N. (1966). *The Odd Couple*. New York: Random House.

Simons, J. (2007). Narrative, Games, and Theory. *Game Studies*, 7(1). Online, available at: http://gamestudies.org/0701/articles/simons, [accessed April 15, 2011].

Simonson, P. and Peters, J. D. (2008). Communication and Media Studies, History to 1968. In W. Donsbach (ed.), *International Encyclopedia of Communication*. Malden, MA: Blackwell.

Simpson, C. (1996). Elisabeth Noelle-Neumann's 'Spiral of Silence' and the Historical Context of Communication Theory. *Journal of Communication*, 46(3): 149–173.

Sinclair, J., Jacka, E., and Cunningham, S. (1996). *New Patterns in Global Television: Peripheral Vision*. New York: Oxford University Press.

Sinclair, U. (1920). *The Brass Check: A Study of American Journalism*. Long Beach, CA: Published by the author.

Singer, J. B. (2004). Strange Bedfellows? The Diffusion of Convergence in Four News Organizations. *Journalism Studies*, 5(1): 3–18.

Singer, J. B. (2006). Stepping Back from the Gate: Online Newspaper Editors and the Co-Production of Content in Campaign 2004. *Journalism and Mass Communication Quarterly*, 83(2): 265–280.

Singer, J. B. and Ashman, I. (2009). User-Generated Content and Journalistic Values. In S. Allan and E. Thorsen (eds.), *Citizen Journalism: Global Perspectives*. New York: Peter Lang.

Singhal, A., Cody, M. J., Rogers, E. M., and Sabido, M. (eds.) (2004). *Entertainment-Education and Social Change: History, Research, and Practice*. Mahwah, NJ: Lawrence Erlbaum.

Slemon, S. (2006). The Scramble for Post-Colonialism. In B. Ashcroft, G. Griffiths, and H. Tiffin (eds.), *The Post-Colonial Studies Reader* (2nd ed.). London: Routledge, pp. 51–56.

Smith, D. W. (2009). *Phenomenology*. Online, available at: http://plato.stanford.edu/archives/sum2009/entries/phenomenology/ [accessed July 5, 2010].

Smith, N. C. (1990). *Morality and the Market. Consumer Pressure for Corporate Accountability*. London: Routledge.

Smulyan, S. (1994). *Selling Radio: The Commercialization of American Broadcasting, 1920–1934*. Washington, DC: Smithsonian Institute Press.

Smythe, D. W. (1977). Communications: Blindspot of Western Marxism. *Canadian Journal of Political and Social Theory*, 1(3): 1–27.

Snow, C. P. (1964). *The Two Cultures and a Second Look*. Cambridge: Cambridge University Press.

Sokal, A. and Bricmont, J. (1998). *Fashionable Nonsense: Postmodern Intellectuals' Abuse of Science*. New York: Picador.

Solso, R. L. (1994). *Cognition and the Visual Arts*. Cambridge, MA: MIT Press.

Sonesson, G. (1989). *Pictorial Concepts: Inquiries into the Semiotic Heritage and its Relevance to the Interpretation of the Visual World*. Lund: Lund University Press.

Sonic Memorial Project (2002–2006). Online, available at: www.sonicmemorial.org [accessed April 15, 2011].

Sparks, C. and Tulloch, J. (2000). *Tabloid Tales: Global Debates over Media Standards*. Boulder, CO: Rowman & Littlefield.

Sparks, G. G. and Cantor, J. (1986). Developmental Differences in Fright Responses to a Television Programme Depicting a Character Transformation. *Journal of Broadcasting and Electronic Media*, 30(3): 309–323.

Spigel, L. (1992). *Make Room for TV: Television and the Family Ideal in Postwar America*. Chicago, IL: University of Chicago Press.

Spigel, L. and Jenkins, H. (1990). Same Bat Channel, Different Bat Times: Mass Culture and Popular Memory. In R. Pearson and W. Uricchio (eds.), *The Many Lives of the Batman: Critical Approaches to a Superhero and His Media*. London: British Film Institute.

Spivak, G. C. (1988). Can the Subaltern Speak? In C. Nelson and L. Grossberg (eds.), *Marxism and the Interpretation of Culture*. London: Macmillan.

Spradley, J. P. (1979). *The Ethnographic Interview*. Fort Worth, TX: Harcourt Brace Jovanovich.

Sreberny, A., Nordenstreng, K., Stevenson, R., and Ugboajah, F. (eds.). (1985). *Foreign News in the Media: International Reporting in 29 Countries*. Paris: UNESCO.

Stacey, J. (1994). *Star Gazing: Hollywood Cinema and Female Spectatorship*. London: Routledge.

Stahl, G., Koschmann, T., and Suthers, D. (2006). Computer-Supported Collaborative Learning: An Historical Perspective. In R. K. Sawyer (ed.), *Cambridge Handbook of the Learning Sciences*. Cambridge: Cambridge University Press, pp. 409–426.

Stam, R., Burgoyne, R., and Flitterman-Lewis, S. (1992). *New Vocabularies in Film Semiotics: Structuralism, Post-Structuralism and Beyond*. London: Routledge.

Standage, T. (1998). *The Victorian Internet*. London: Weidenfeld and Nicholson.

Stein, M. (1964). The Eclipse of Community: Some Glances at the Education of a Sociologist. In A. Vidich, J. Bensman, and M. Stein (eds.), *Reflections of Community Power*. New York: Wiley.

Stempel, G. H. (1952). Sample Size for Classifying Subject Matter in Dailies. *Journalism Quarterly*, 29(June): 333–334.

Stevenson, R. L. and Shaw, D. L. (eds.) (1984). *Foreign News and the New World Information Order*. Ames, IA: Iowa State University.

Stipp, H. and Milavsky, R. (1988). US Television Programming Effects on Aggressive Behavior of Children and Adolescents. *Current Psychology: Research and Reviews*, 7: 76–92.

Stokes, M. and Maltby, R. (eds.) (1999). *American Movie Audiences: From the Turn of the Century to the Early Sound Era*. London: British Film Institute.

Stokes, M. and Maltby, R. (eds.) (2004). *Hollywood Abroad: Audiences and Cultural Exchange*. London: British Film Institute.

Stone, L. (1979). *The Family, Sex and Marriage, 1500–1800*. Harmondsworth: Penguin.

Stone, L. (1987). *The Past and the Present Revisited*. London, New York: Routledge & Kegan Paul.

Straubhaar, J. D. (2007). *World Television: From Global to Local*. Los Angeles, CA: Sage.

Strauss, A. L. (1987). *Qualitative Analysis for Social Scientists*. Cambridge: Cambridge University Press.

Strauss, A. L. and Corbin, J. (1990). *Basics of Qualitative Research*. Newbury Park, CA: Sage.

Street, A. T. (1909). The Truth about Newspapers. *Chicago Tribune*, July 25.

Strömbäck, J. (2008). Four Phases of Mediatization: An Analysis of the Mediatization of Politics. *International Journal of Press/Politics*, 13(3): 228–246.

Strömbäck, J. and Kiousis, S. (2010). A New Look at Agenda-Setting Effects: Comparing the Predictive Power of Overall Political News Consumption and Specific News Media Consumption Across Different Media Channels and Media Types. *Journal of Communication*, 60(2): 271–292.

Strömbäck, J. and Nord, L. W. (2006). Do Politicians Lead the Tango? A Study of the Relationships between Swedish Journalists and their Political Sources in the Context of Election Campaigns. *European Journal of Communication*, 21(2): 147–164.

Summers, D. (2003). *Real Spaces: World Art History and the Rise of Western Modernism*. London: Phaidon.

Surgeon-General's Scientific Advisory Committee on Television and Social Behavior (1972). *Volumes I-VI*. Washington, DC: US Government Printing Office.

Szalai, A. (ed.) (1972). *The Use of Time*. The Hague: Mouton.

Szerszynski, B., Heim, W., and Waterton, C. (eds.) (2003). *Nature Performed: Environment, Culture and Performance*. Oxford: Blackwell.

Tamborini, R., Zillmann, D., and Bryant, J. (1984). Fear and Victimization: Exposure to Television and Perceptions of Crime and Fear. In R. N. Bostrum (ed.), *Communication Yearbook, Vol. 8*. Beverly Hills, CA: Sage.

Tan, Y. and Weaver, D. H. (2007). Agenda-Setting Effects, the Public, and Congress, 1946–2004. *Journalism and Mass Communication Quarterly*, 84(4): 729–744.

Tannenbaum, P. H. (1954). Effect of Serial Position on Recall of Radio News Stories. *Journalism Quarterly*, 31: 319–323.

Tannenbaum, P. H. and Kernick, J. (1954). Effects of Newscast Item Leads upon Listener Interpretation. *Journalism Quarterly*, 31: 33–37.

Tashakkori, A. and Teddlie, C. (eds.) (2010). *The Sage Handbook of Mixed Methods in Social and Behavioral Research* (2nd ed.). Thousand Oaks, CA: Sage.

Taxen, L. (2007). Activity Modalities: A Multidimensional Perspective on Coordination, Business Processes and Communication. *Systems, Signs & Actions*, 3(1): 93–133

The National IT and Telecom Agency (2011). *Det Digitale Samfund 2010 [The Digital Society 2010]*. Copenhagen.

The Daily Show with Jon Stewart, (1995–2011). Available on television, and online www.thedailyshow.com [accessed April 15, 2011].

Theall, D. F. (1971). *The Medium Is the Rear View Mirror: Understanding McLuhan*. Montreal: McGill-Queen's University Press.

Thelwall, M. (2008a). How Are Social Network Sites Embedded in the Web: An Exploratory Link Analysis. *Cybermetrics*, 12(1): Paper 1.

Thelwall, M. (2008b). Social Networks, Gender and Friending: An Analysis of MySpace Member Profiles. *Journal of the American Society for Information Science and Technology*, 59(8): 1321–1330.

Thomas, W. I. and Thomas, D. S. (1928). *The Child in America: Behavior Problems and Programs*. New York: Alfred A. Knopf.

Thomas, W. I. and Znaniecki, F. (1927). *The Polish Peasant in Europe and America*. New York: Knopf.

Thompson, B. (2008). How College Freshmen Communicate Support: A Grounded Theory Study. *Communication Education*, 57(1): 123–144.

Thompson, E. P. (1963). *The Making of the English Working Class*. London: Gollancz.

Thompson, E. P. (1991). *Customs in Common*. London: Merlin.

Thompson, J. B. (1995). *The Media and Modernity*. Cambridge: Polity Press.

Thompson, J. B. (2000). *Political Scandal: Power and Visibility in the Media Age*. Cambridge: Polity Press.

Thompson, K. (1998). *Moral Panics*. London: Routledge.

Thompson, K. and Bordwell, D. (2010). *Film History: An Introduction* (3rd ed.). New York: McGraw-Hill.

Thorlacius, L. (2010). Visual Communication in Web Design. In J. Hunsinger, L. Klastrup, and M. Allen (eds.), *International Handbook of Internet Research*. Dordrecht: Springer.

Thrasher, F. M. (1927). *The Gang*. Chicago, IL: University of Chicago Press.

Thussu, D. K. (2007a). *News as Entertainment: The Rise of Global Infotainment*. London, Sage.

Thussu, D. K. (ed.) (2007b). *Media on the Move: Global Flow and Contra-Flow*. London: Routledge.

Thussu, D. K. (ed.) (2009). *Internationalizing Media Studies*. London: Routledge.

Tichenor, P., Olien, C., and Donohue, G. (1970). Mass Media Flow and Differential Growth in Knowledge. *Public Opinion Quarterly*, 34(2): 159–170.

Todorov, T. (1971). The Two Principles of Narrative. *Diacritics*, 1(1): 37–44.

Todorov, T. (1978). *Les genres du discours*. Paris: Seuil. [English translation: *Genres in Discourse*. Cambridge: Cambridge University Press, 1990.]

Toffler, A. (1980). *The Third Wave*. New York: William Morrow.

Tolson, A. (2001). *Television Talk Shows: Discourse, Performance, Spectacle*. Mahwah, NJ: Lawrence Erlbaum.

Tolson, A. (2006). *Media Talk: Spoken Discourse on TV and Radio*. Edinburgh: Edinburgh University Press.

Tomasello, T. K., Lee, Y., and Baer, A. P. (2010). 'New Media' Research Publication Trends and Outlets in Communication, 1990–2006. *New Media & Society*, 12(4): 531–548.

Tomlinson, J. (1999). *Globalization and Culture*. Cambridge: Polity Press.

Tönnies, F. (1974[1887]). *Community and Association*. London: Routledge Kegan Paul.

Toulmin, S. (2003[1958]). *The Uses of Argument* (updated ed.). Cambridge: Cambridge University Press.

Trenaman, J. (1967). *Communication and Comprehension*. London: Longman.

Trenaman, J. S. M. and McQuail, D. (1961). *Television and the Political Image*. London: Methuen.

Trumbo, C. (2004). Research Methods in Mass Communication Research: A Census of Eight Journals 1990–2000. *Journalism and Mass Communication Quarterly*, 81(2): 417–436.

Tsfati, Y., Ribak, R., and Cohen, J. (2005). Rebelde Way in Israel: Parental Perceptions of Television Influence and Monitoring of Children's Social and Media Activities. *Mass Communication & Society*, 8(1): 3–22.

Tuchman, G. (1972). Objectivity as Strategic Ritual: An Examination of Newsmen's Notions of Objectivity. *American Journal of Sociology*, 77(4): 660–679.

Tuchman, G. (1973). Making News by Doing Work: Routinizing the Unexpected. *American Journal of Sociology*, 79(1): 110–131.

Tuchman, G. (1978). *Making News. A Study in the Construction of Reality*. New York: The Free Press.

Tuchman, G., Daniels, A. K., and Benet, J. (eds.). (1978). *Hearth and Home: Images of Women in Mass Media*. New York: Oxford University Press.

Tulloch, J. (1989). Approaching the Audience: The Elderly. In E. Seiter, H. Borchers, G. Kreutzner, and E.-M. Warth (eds.), *Remote Control: Television, Audiences, and Cultural Power*. London: Routledge.

Tunstall, J. (1977). *The Media Are American*. London: Constable.

Tunstall, J. (2007). *The Media Were American: US Mass Media in Decline*. New York: Oxford University Press.

Turner, F. (2006). *From Counterculture to Cyberculture: Stewart Brand, the Whole Earth Network, and the Rise of Digital Utopianism*. Chicago, IL: University of Chicago Press.

Turner, G. (2006). *Film as Social Practice* (4th ed.). London: Routledge.

Umiker-Sebeok, J. (ed.) (1987). *Marketing and Semiotics*. Berlin: Mouton de Gruyter.

UNESCO (1985). *Foreign News in the Media: International Reporting in 29 Countries*. Reports and Papers on Mass Communication, No. 93. Paris: UNESCO.

United Nations (1945). *Charter of the United Nations*. Online, available at: www.un.org/en/documents/charter/chapter2.shtml [accessed April 15, 2011].

United Nations (1948). *The Universal Declaration of Human Rights*. Online, available at: www.un.org/en/documents/udhr/index.shtml [accessed April 15, 2011].

Urry, J. (2000). *Sociology Beyond Societies: Mobilities for the Twenty-First Century*. London: Routledge.

Valkenburg, P. M., Krcmar, M., Peeters, A. L., and Marseille, N. M. (1999). Developing a Scale to Assess Three Styles of Television Mediation: Instructive Mediation, Restrictive Mediation, and Social Coviewing. *Journal of Broadcasting and Electronic Media*, 43(1): 52–67.

van Dijk, T. A. (2009). Critical Discourse Studies: A Sociocognitive Approach. In R. Wodak and M. Meyer (eds.), *Methods of Critical Discourse Analysis*. London: Sage.

van Dijk T. A. and Kintsch W. (1983). *Strategies of Discourse Comprehension*. New York: Academic Press.

Van Maanen, J. (1988). *Tales of the Field*. Chicago, IL: University of Chicago Press.

van Zoonen, L. (1992). *Feminist Media Studies*. London: Sage.

van Zoonen, L. and Wieten, J. (1994). "It Wasn't Exactly a Miracle": The Arrival of Television in Dutch Family Life. *Media, Culture & Society*, 16(4): 641–660.

Venturi, R., Brown, D. S., and Izenour, S. (1972). *Learning from Las Vegas*. Cambridge, MA: MIT Press.

Vertegaal, R. and Poupyrev, I. (2008). Organic User Interfaces. *Communications of the ACM*, 51(6): 26–30.

Vestergaard, A. (2008). Humanitarian Branding and the Media: The Case of Amnesty International. *Journal of Language and Politics*, 7(3): 471–493.

Vestergaard, T. and Schrøder, K. C. (1985). *The Language of Advertising*. Oxford: Basil Blackwell.

Vettehen, P. G. H., Schaap, G., and Schlösser, S. (2004). What Men and Women Think While Watching the News: An Exploration. *Communications: The European Journal of Communication Research*, 29(2): 235–251.

Vickerman, M. (1999). *Cross Currents: West Indian Immigrants and Race*. New York: Oxford University Press.

Viehöfer, W. (2003). Die Wissenschaft und die Wiederverzauberung des sublunaren Raumes. Der Klimadiskurs im Licht der narrativen Diskursanalyse. In R. Keller, A. Hirseland, W. Schneider, and W. Viehöfer (eds.), *Handbuch Sozialwissenschaftliche Diskursanalyse*. Opladen: Leske and Budrich.

Vigsø, O. (2010). Naming Is Framing: Swine Flu, New Flu, and A(H1N1). *Observatorio*, 4(3): 229–241.

Vihalemm, P. (ed.) (2002). *Baltic Media in Transition*. Tartu: Tartu University Press.

Vincent, D. (2000). *The Rise of Mass Literacy: Reading and Writing in Modern Europe*. Cambridge: Polity Press.

Viswanath, K. and Finnegan, J. R. (1996). The Knowledge Gap Hypothesis 25 Years Later. *Communication Yearbook*, 19: 187–227.

Volkmer, I. (1999). *CNN – News in the Global Sphere: A Study of CNN and Its Impact on Global Communication*. Luton: University of Luton Press.

Volosinov, V. N. (1973[1929]). *Marxism and the Philosophy of Language*. New York: Seminar Press.

von Clausewitz, C. (2006[1832]). *On War*. Online, available at: www.gutenberg.org/etext/1946 [accessed August 5, 2010].

Von Hippel, E. (2005). *Democratizing Innovation*. Cambridge, MA: MIT Press.

Voss, G. G. (1991). *Lebensführung als Arbeit: Über die Autonomie der Person im Alltag der Gesellschaft [Conduct of Life as Labor: About the Autonomy of the Individual in Everyday Social Life]*. Stuttgart: Ferdinand Enke.

Voss, G. G. (2001). Der eigene und der fremde Alltag. [The personal and the alien everyday]. In G. G. Voss and M. Weihrich (eds.), *Tagaus, tagein: neue Beiträge zur Soziologie alltäglicher Lebensführung*. München: R. Hampp Verlag, pp. 203–219.

Vroons, E. (2005). Communication Studies in Europe: A Sketch of the Situation around 1955. *Gazette*, 67(6): 495–522.

Vu, H. N. N. and Gehrau, V. (2010). Agenda Diffusion: An Integrated Model of Agenda Setting and Interpersonal Communication. *Journalism and Mass Communication Quarterly*, 87(1): 100–116.

Wahl-Jørgensen, K. (2004). How Not to Found a Field: New Evidence on the Origins of Mass Communication Research. *Journal of Communication*, 54(3): 547–564.

Wahl-Jorgensen, K., Williams, A., and Wardle, C. (2010). Audience Views on User-Generated Content: Exploring the Value of News from the Bottom Up. *Northern Lights: Film and Media Studies Yearbook 2010*, 8(1): 177–194.

Walker, J. A. (2001). *Art in the Age of Mass Media* (3rd ed.). London: Pluto Press.

Wallerstein, I. (1974). *The Modern World-System, Vol. 1*. New York: Academic Press.

Wallerstein, I. (1980). *The Modern World-System, Vol. 2*. London: Academic Press.

Wallerstein, I. (1989). *The Modern World-System, Vol. 3*. London: Academic Press.

Wanamaker, J. (n.d.). Online, available at: www.en.wikipedia.org/wiki/John_Wanamaker [accessed April 15, 2011].

Wang, G. (ed.) (2011). *De-Westernizing Communication Research: Altering Questions and Changing Frameworks*. London: Routledge.

Warren, R., Gerke, P., and Kelly, M. A. (2002). Is There Enough Time on the Clock? Parental Involvement and Mediation of Children's Television Viewing. *Journal of Broadcasting and Electronic Media*, 46(1): 87–112.

Wasserman, S. and Faust, K. (1994). *Social Network Analysis: Methods and Applications*. Cambridge: Cambridge University Press.

Waterton, C. (2003). Performing the Classification of Nature. In B. Szerszynski, W. Heim, and C. Waterton (eds.), *Nature Performed: Environment, Culture and Performance*. Oxford: Blackwell.

Watson, J. B. (1924). *Psychology from the Standpoint of a Behaviorist*. Philadelphia, PA: J. B. Lippincott Company.

Watson, J. B. (1930). *Behaviorism*. Chicago, IL: University of Chicago Press.

Watzlawick, P., Beavin, J. H., and Jackson, D. D. (1967). *Pragmatics of Human Communication: A Study of Interactional Patterns, Pathologies, and Paradoxes*. New York: Norton.

Weaver, D. H. and Wilhoit, G. C. (1986). *The American Journalist. A Portrait of U.S. News People and Their Work*. Bloomington, IN: Indiana University Press.

Webb, E. J., Campbell, D. T., Schwartz, R. D., and Sechrest, L. (2000[1966]). *Unobtrusive Measures* (revised ed.). Thousand Oaks, CA: Sage.

Weber, M. (1964). *The Theory of Social and Economic Organization*. New York: The Free Press.

Webster, D. (1988). *Looka Yonder! The Imaginary America of Populist Culture*. London: Routledge.

Webster, F. and Dimitriou, B. (eds.) (2004). *Manuel Castells*. London: Sage.

Webster, J. G. and Phalen, P. F. (1997). *The Mass Audience: Rediscovering the Dominant Model*. Mahwah, NJ: Lawrence Erlbaum.

Webster, J. G., Pearson, J., and Webster, D. (1986). Children's Television Viewing as Affected by Contextual Variables in the Home. *Communication Research Reports*, 3: 1–8.

Weiser, M. (1991). The Computer for the Twenty-First Century. *Scientific American*, 265(3): 94–104.

Wellman, B. (2004). The Three Ages of Internet Research: Ten, Five, and Zero Years Ago. *New Media and Society*, 6(1): 123–129.

Wessler, H. (2008). Knowledge Interests. In W. Donsbach (ed.), *International Encyclopedia of Communication, Vol. 6*. Malden, MA: Blackwell, pp. 2617–2618.

Wetherell, M. and Potter, J. (1992). *Mapping the Language of Racism: Discourse and the Legitimation of Exploitation*. London: Harvester Wheatsheaf.

Wetherell, M., Taylor, S., and Yates, S. (eds.) (2001). *Discourse Theory and Practice: A Reader*. London: Sage.

White, D. M. (1950). The 'Gate Keeper': A Case Study in the Selection of News. *Journalism Quarterly*, 27: 383–390.

Whittle, M. (1996–2000). Online, available at: www.astro.virginia.edu/~dmw8f/index.php [accessed April 15, 2011].

Wieten, J., Murdock, G., and Dahlgren, P. (eds.) (2000). *Television Across Europe: A Comparative Introduction*. London: Sage.

Wilcox, D. F. (1900). The American Newspaper: A Study in Social Psychology. *Annals of the American Academy of Political and Social Science*, 16: 56–92.

Wilke, J. (1984). *Nachrichtenauswahl und Medienrealität in vier Jahrhunderten [News Selection and Media Reality in Four Centuries]*. Berlin: Walter de Gruyter.

Williams, D. (2006). Virtual Cultivation: Online Worlds, Offline Perceptions. *Journal of Communication*, 56(1): 69–87.

Williams, D. (2010). The Mapping Principle, and a Research Framework for Virtual Worlds. *Communication Theory*, 20(4): 451–470.

Williams, D., Caplan, S., and Xiong, L. (2007). Can You Hear Me Now? The Impact of Voice in Online Communities. *Human Communication Research*, 33(4): 427–449.

Williams, R. (1974). *Television: Technology and Cultural Form*. London: Fontana.

Williams, R. (1975[1958]). *Culture and Society 1780–1950*. Harmondsworth: Penguin.

Williams, R. (1977). *Marxism and Literature*. London: Oxford University Press.

Williams, R. (1983). *Keywords*. London: Fontana.

Williams, T. M. (ed.) (1986). *The Impact of Television: A Natural Experiment in Three Communities*. New York: Academic Press.

Williamson, J. (1978). *Decoding Advertisements. Ideology and Meaning in Advertising*. London: Marion Boyars.

Willig, I. (2010). Constructing the Audience: A Study of the Segmentation of the Danish Press. *Northern Lights: Film and Media Studies Yearbook*, 8(1): 93–114.

Wilson, T. (1993). *Watching Television: Hermeneutics, Reception, and Popular Culture*. Cambridge: Polity Press.

Wimmer, R. D. and Dominick, J. R. (2011). *Mass Media Research: An Introduction*. (9th ed.). Belmont, CA: Wadsworth Publishing Company.

Wimsatt, W. (ed.) (1954). *The Verbal Icon*. London: Methuen.

Wimsatt, W. and Brooks, C. (1957). *Literary Criticism: A Short History*. New York: Alfred A. Knopf.

Windahl, S., Signitzer, B., and Olson, J. (2009). *Using Communication Theory* (2nd ed.). Los Angeles, CA: Sage.

Winston, B. (1998). *Media, Technology, and Society – A History: From the Telegraph to the Internet*. London: Routledge.

Winthrop-Young, W. and Wutz, M. (1999). Translators' Introduction. In F. A. Kittler, *Gramophone, Film, Typewriter*. Stanford, CA: Stanford University Press.

Witschge, T. and Nygren, G. (2009). Journalism: A Profession under Pressure? *Journal of Media Business Studies*, 6(1): 37–59.

Wittgenstein, L. (1953). *Philosophical Investigations*. Oxford: Basil Blackwell.

Wittgenstein, L. (1972[1921]). *Tractatus Logico-Philosophicus*. London: Routledge & Kegan Paul.

Wober, M. and Gunter, B. (1988). *Television and Social Control*. Aldershot: Avebury.

Wodak, R. (2000). Recontextualization and Transformation of Meanings: A Critical Discourse Analysis of Decision-Making in EU Meetings about Employment Policies. In S. Sarangi and M. Coulthard (eds.), *Discourse and Social Life*. London: Longman.

Wodak, R. and Meyer, M. (2009). Critical Discourse Analysis: History, Agenda, Theory and Methodology. In R. Wodak and M. Meyer (eds.), *Methods of Critical Discourse Analysis*. London: Sage.

Wodak, R., Nowak, P., Pelikan, J., Gruber, H., de Cilia, R., and Mitten, R. (1990). *Wir sind alle unschuldige Täter!: Diskurshistorische Studien zum Nachkriegsantisemitismus*. Frankfurt: Suhrkamp.

Wood, H. (2007). The Mediated Conversational Floor: An Interactive Approach to Audience Reception Analysis. *Media, Culture & Society*, 29(1): 75–103.

Wood, R. (1965). *Hitchcock's Films*. London: Zvemmer Limited.

Wood, R. (1968). *Howard Hawks*. London: Secker & Warburg.

Wright, C. R. (1959). *Mass Communication: A Sociological Perspective*. New York: Random House.

Yates, J. and Orlikowski, W. (1992). Genres of Organizational Communication: A Structurational Approach to Studying Communication and Media. *Academy of Management Review*, 17(2): 299–326.

Yin, R. K. (2003). *Case Study Research: Design and Methods* (3rd ed.). Thousand Oaks, CA: Sage.

Zelizer, B. (2004). *Taking Journalism Seriously, News and the Academy*, Thousand Oaks: Sage.

Zhao, Y. (2008). *Communication in China: Political Economy, Power, and Conflict*. Lanham, MD: Rowman & Littlefield.

Zillmann, D. and Vorderer, P. (eds.) (2000). *Media Entertainment: The Psychology of Its Appeal*. Mahwah, NJ: Lawrence Erlbaum.

Znaniecki, F. (1934). *The Method of Sociology*. New York: Farrar and Rinehart.

Zuckerman, M. (1994). *Behavioural Expressions and Biosocial Bases of Sensation Seeking*. Cambridge: Cambridge University Press.

Index